THE BASEBALL
ROOKIES
ENCYCLOPEDIA

ALSO FROM BRASSEY'S SPORTS

Wrigley Field: The Unauthorized Biography
by Stuart Shea

The Conscience of the Game: Baseball's Commissioners from Landis to Selig
by Larry Moffi

Chasing Steinbrenner: Pursuing the Pennant in Boston and Toronto
by Rob Bradford

Gehrig and the Babe: The Friendship, the Feud
by Tony Castro

Baseball Prospectus: 2004 Edition
by Gary Huckabay, et al

Deadball Era Stars Volume 1: The National League
by the Society for American Baseball Research

*The World Series' Most Wanted: The Top 10 Book of
Championship Teams, Broken Dreams, and October Oddities*
by John Snyder

Getting in the Game: Inside Baseball's Winter Meetings
by Josh Lewin

ALSO BY DAVID NEMEC

Great Baseball Feats, Facts, and Firsts

The Great Encyclopedia of 19th Century Major League Baseball

The Great Book of Baseball Knowledge: The Ultimate Test for the Ultimate Fan

The Rules of Baseball

The Absolutely Most Challenging Baseball Quiz Book, Ever

The Even More Challenging Baseball Quiz Book

*The Beer and Whisky League: The Illustrated History of the
American Association—Baseball's Renegade Major League*

THE BASEBALL
ROOKIES
ENCYCLOPEDIA

DAVID NEMEC and DAVE ZEMAN

Brassey's, Inc.
Washington, D.C.

Text design and composition by Susan Mark
Coghill Composition Company
Richmond, Virginia

Library of Congress Cataloging-in-Publication Data

Nemec, David.
　　The baseball rookies encyclopedia / David Nemec and Dave Zeman.—1st ed.
　　　　p.　cm.
　　Includes index.
　　ISBN 1-57488-670-3 (pbk. : alk. paper)
　　1. Baseball—United States—History.　2. Baseball—United States—Encyclopedias.
　3. Baseball players—United States—Registers.　I. Zeman, Dave, 1967–　II. Title.

　GV863.A1N4663　2004
　796.357'03—dc22

2004011632

Printed in Canada on acid-free paper that meets the American National Standards Institute Z39-48 Standard.

Brassey's, Inc.
22841 Quicksilver Drive
Dulles, Virginia 20166

First Edition

10　9　8　7　6　5　4　3　2　1

To Marilyn.

—David Nemec

To my parents—my mother, Donna, and my late father, Frank—
both of whom always believed in me.

—Dave Zeman

Dear John:
7/8/06

Hope you enjoy
this book. Happy
Birthday — Love
Lydia

Contents

Photographs

Foreword

Talk about a labor of love. Authors David Nemec and Dave Zeman, devoted researchers, have produced a baseball encyclopedia unlike any other. *The Baseball Rookies Encyclopedia* tracks the rookie seasons of more than 2,000 major league players. It was thirteen years in the making, a massive achievement and triumph of perseverance.

Every player had a rookie season, but those listed had distinguished themselves, good or bad. Or were of special interest, such as Maurice Archdeacon of the 1923 Chicago White Sox: in 22 games he batted .402, with two five-hit games; and Bob Hazle of more recent times, who helped the Milwaukee Braves win the 1957 National League pennant.

A late-season call-up, he hit .403 in 41 games and was known as "Hurricane Hazle." After hitting a home run in Philadelphia, lightning struck above the mound; a hurricane followed. I knew him fairly well. I remember sitting next to him on the Milwaukee team bus and hearing him complain that he had received so much publicity that too much was expected of him. He flopped the next season and soon thereafter disappeared from view.

Shoeless Joe Jackson and Ted Williams, both left-handed hitting outfielders, had outstanding rookie seasons. Jackson, with Cleveland in 1911, batted .408: 233 hits, including 45 doubles and 19 triples. Williams made his bow a quarter of a century later, in 1939, and topped the American League in RBI with 145.

Joe DiMaggio, in his first big league season, led the Yankees to the pennant, his first of nine, and batted .323. The Great DiMag had 88 extra base hits and drove in 125 runs. Willie Mays also broke in with a bang: .274, 20 home runs, and 68 driven in. He would have had better numbers if he hadn't been brought up until late May.

Mark McGwire set the rookie home run record, 49, with Oakland in 1987. Ichiro Suzuki, Seattle 2001, batted .350 and was the sixth and last freshman to lead a league in hitting. Oppositely, John Gochnauer, 1902 Cleveland, a shortstop, hit .185 with no home runs in 459 at-bats, the weakest rookie season by a position-player. Gochnauer was consistent. He hit .185 again the next season.

Thirty-two rookies have pitched no-hitters, two of them perfect games, by Lee Richmond, with the 1880 National League Worcester club, and Charlie Robertson, 1922 White Sox. Grover Cleveland Alexander, in 1911 with the Phillies, had 31 completions and won the most games, 28, the modern rookie record. Reliever Mark Eichhorn, Toronto 1986, also had a big rookie season, 14–6 with ten saves. More significantly, he worked 157 innings and is among the few pitchers to give up fewer hits and walks, combined, than innings pitched.

This is merely a sampling. Nemec and Zeman have provided a dazzling array of stats accompanied by accumulative sidebars. Except for the Turkin-Thompson Encyclopedia and the original Macmillan, the so-called Big-Mac, I can't think of a more challenging research project. The most knowledgeable fans will have enough to chew on for a lifetime.

Jerome Holtzman
Offcial MLB Historian

Acknowledgments

The authors would like to give their heartfelt thanks to the following people who helped us in making this book a reality. In alphabetical order, Al Blumkin and Scott Flatow, two of the most preeminent baseball historians, loaned their sharp eyes in reviewing our final manuscript. Jerome Holtzman, the official historian of baseball, graciously wrote the foreword. Brassey's Chris Kahrl shepherded our project in its early and middle stages. Mark Rucker of Transcendental Graphics provided precious material from his extraordinary collection of the game's photographic history. Richard Topp generously offered his computer expertise and skills, helping create the database upon which the authors have heavily relied. And last, but certainly not least, Walt Wilson—a dedicated and resourceful baseball researcher—who has unearthed innumerable hidden treasures from the game's wonderful past.

Introduction

If ten baseball historians were asked what player had the greatest rookie season ever, we might expect to get ten different opinions ranging from Candy Cummings way back in 1872 to Ichiro in 2001—and all ten opinions would probably be equally valid. But if the question were refined so that it asked what player had the greatest rookie season for a particular team, a consensus in all probability would begin to occur . . . unless, of course, the team were, say, the predecessor of the present-day Baltimore Orioles, the St. Louis Browns. There, even our most prominent baseball historians are likely to flounder a bit. Part of the reason is that in their entire 52-year history (1902–53) the Browns never had a single rookie pitcher who won 20 games whereas most other long-term franchises have had half a dozen or more. Another part of the reason is that Roy Sievers, the Brownies' lone Rookie of the Year honoree, won out over a relatively mediocre field. Furthermore, while the Browns had several Hall of Famers wear their orange, brown, and white colors, none of them had particularly good rookie seasons, at least not any of those who debuted with the Browns.

Though we're not really in the business of settling who was the all-time best rookie or even who was the best on a particular team, we are ready to provide the tools for each reader to form his or her own judgment. Among the many unique features offered here are yearly summaries of each major league rookie crop from 1872 through the present and complete lists of rookie batting and pitching leaders in each major league season, followed by a roundup of other significant rookie highlights in that particular season. These features we hope will combine to fulfill what we think is our most important service, which is to explore a part of baseball that other researchers have never given its due attention and end by providing the first historical overview of major league rookies.

As to what constitutes a rookie, our task has been complicated by the fact that for nearly a century after the first major league season there was never a consensus of what rules, if any, should be applied to determine rookie status. Many players, including several potential rookie record setters, were not viewed as being rookies when they had their first full seasons. Among them were Shoeless Joe Jackson, who had a total of 115 at bats prior to 1911 when he hit .408 in what many authorities now consider his official rookie season, and Russ Ford, whose 26 wins in 1910 are still not deemed the American League rookie record by most sources even though his prior big league experience consisted of just three innings. At the other end of the spectrum are cases like Billy Hamilton, whose 1888 debut campaign would not disqualify him from rookie status under current rules if only because it is impossible now to determine how many days he was actually on a major league roster that year. An even more befuddling example is Pete Reiser, the 1941 NL batting champion at the age of only 22. Most of the media at that time regarded Reiser as a rookie despite the fact that he had compiled 225 at bats in big league garb the previous year. What adds still more grease to the slide through rookie lore is that the definition of what should qualify a player as a rookie has changed three times just since the inception of the first official Rookie of the Year Award in 1947.

Since no definition of what constitutes a rookie holds true across the entire span of major league history, we have applied the current rules regarding rookie status, plus several of our own refinements, to all major league seasons. For seasons in the nineteenth century, the same standards apply, with numerical adjustments made for shorter schedules. However, in nineteenth century leagues where a number of teams failed to fulfill their required slate of games, we took the average number of games played by a team in a particular league to determine the plate appearance and innings pitched totals needed to terminate rookie status. For example, if teams played an average of 53 games in 1875, once a batter reached a total of 53 at bats and bases on balls combined he could not have rookie status in any future year. We selected 1875 to illustrate our methodology for a reason beyond the fact that schedules at the time were considerably shorter and teams were in such a state of flux that only a handful would usually complete the full season. The 1875 campaign was in addition the National Association's final breath, and we recognize the National Association here and in all of our other work as having been the first major league. Hence any performer who cut his teeth in the National Association in so doing lost his rookie status as far as our record-keeping is concerned even though Major League Baseball, which stubbornly refuses to acquaint itself with the NA, continues to regard several of its performers, with George Bradley perhaps being the most prominent example, as all-time rookie record holders for their first-year accomplishments in subsequent leagues.

Finally, our rules with respect to rookie status for all seasons since 1872 are that a player shall be considered a rookie unless, during a previous season or seasons, he has (a) played either a total of 50 games or (b) accumulated a combination of one AB or BB for each game scheduled; or, if a pitcher, either 50 innings or 25 games pitched. In all, we feel that our criteria are both flexible (adjusting to scheduled length) and fair.

Enough about rules and the like. Let's cut to the chase. We hope that each and every reader has as much fun with our book as we did in putting it together.

David Nemec, San Francisco, California
Dave Zeman, Addison, Illinois

1870s

1872

On St. Patrick's Day in 1871, the first professional base-ball league was born in a Manhattan bar on the corner of Broadway and Thirteenth Street. Since the moving forces behind the new league were many of the most prominent professional players of their day, it was fittingly called the National Association of Professional Base-Ball Players. Today most scholars of the game consider the National Association to be the first major league and the first major league season, therefore, to have been 1871. In a sense then, in 1871 every player in the fledgling league was a rookie in that he was participating in his initial major league season, but in reality the vast majority were seasoned professionals who were long experienced in playing for pay.

Among them were men like the Wright brothers, George and Harry, who had been members of the legendary Cincinnati Red Stockings, which went undefeated for the entire 1869 season, as well as Joe Start, the 28-year-old first baseman on the 1870 Brooklyn team that ended Cincinnati's record winning streak. To be sure, there were also a fair number of novice players in

the newly formed league, several of them still in their teens. Fort Wayne's pitcher when it faced Cleveland on May 4, 1871, in what is generally viewed by historians to have been the first major league game, was 19-year-old Bobby Mathews, who would go on to win nearly 300 games in major league competition; the Rockford, Illinois, team employed at third base 19-year-old Adrian Anson, destined to become the first player to collect over 3,000 hits; and the Washington Olympics, in late June, received two wins from 18-year-old Bill Stearns, fated in his remaining four seasons to win only 11 of 75 decisions. But it is significant that in 1871 the teams like Fort Wayne, Rockford, and the Olympics that relied to a large extent on novice players, or recruits as they were then known, all had losing records, and the same pattern held true in 1872 and, indeed, throughout most of the first decade of major league play.

In 1872, for instance, five new teams joined the National Association. Of the five only one, the Baltimore Canaries, filled its roster exclusively with veterans of the 1871 NA campaign. As a consequence, Baltimore's reward was a strong second-place finish while the other four newcomers, all of which were loaded with rookie or

1872 ROOKIE LEADERS

Batting	Pitching
G—56, Nat Hicks, MUT*	W—33, Candy Cummings, MUT
B—268, Nat Hicks, MUT	**L—28, Jim Britt, ATL**
H—82, Nat Hicks, MUT	PCT—.623, Candy Cummings, MUT
2B—12, Nat Hicks, MUT	**GP—55, Candy Cummings, MUT**
3B—5, Jack Remsen, ATL	**GS—55, Candy Cummings, MUT**
HR—3, Count Gedney, TRO/ECK	**CG—53, Candy Cummings, MUT**
R—55, Nat Hicks, MUT	**IP—497.0, Candy Cummings, MUT**
RBI—33, Nat Hicks, MUT	**H—605, Candy Cummings, MUT**
WK—6, Bill Boyd, MUT	BB—30, Candy Cummings, MUT
SO—14, Candy Cummings, MUT	K—43, Candy Cummings, MUT
SB—7, Tom Barlow, ATL	ERA—2.97, Candy Cummings, MUT
BA—.359, Tim Murnane, MAN	**SHO—3, Candy Cummings, MUT**
SLG—.390, Count Gedney, TRO/ECK	SV—No Qualifiers
OBP—.359, Tim Murnane, MAN	

*Data in bold denotes not only the rookie leader that year but also the league leader. The guidelines for determining rookie leaders are the same as those used by Major League Baseball to determine league leaders. Our sole refinement is that ERA qualifiers also qualify for the winning percentage (PCT) leadership regardless of their number of decisions. "NA" denotes that the needed information is not available.

The New York Mutuals were not the only team to introduce an illustrious all-rookie battery in 1872. Veteran third baseman Bob Ferguson, who had been with the Mutuals in 1871, opted to help organize the Brooklyn Atlantics as a new entry for the 1872 season and serve as the team's playing captain. Ferguson was free to do as he wished because as yet there was no reserve clause in player contracts to restrict performers from changing teams at will after each season, but he was unable to convince any other veteran players to join his virgin enterprise. Hence the Atlantics opened their season on May 2, 1872, against the Middletown Mansfields with a lineup of Ferguson and eight rookies. For his catcher, Ferguson had young Tom Barlow, but precisely how young Barlow was in 1872 remains a mystery as both his birth and death dates are still unknown. But if Barlow's relatively tender age is only speculative, that of his battery mate, Brooklyn native Jim Britt, has been ascertained through research. On May 2, 1872, in the Atlantics' inaugural game, Britt set a record that will almost certainly never be surpassed for being the youngest Opening Day starting hurler in major league history. When he threw his first pitch in what would become an 8–2 loss to the Mansfields' Frank Buttery, Britt, who was born on February 25, 1856, was just 16 years old.

recruit performers, proved to be so hopelessly uncompetitive that they compiled a composite winning percentage of .168. The defending champion Philadelphia Athletics meanwhile went through the entire 1872 season without using a single rookie player, and Boston, the coming champion, introduced only one newcomer, rightfielder Fraley Rogers. Yet it was not as though there was no room in the NA for fresh blood. The New York Mutuals in 1872 unveiled an all-rookie pairing in catcher Nat Hicks and pitcher Candy Cummings that not only quickly established itself as one of the best batteries in the game but also blended so well with the team's veteran corps that the Mutuals finished just a game out of second place. One of the five new teams, the Mansfields, which represented Middletown, Connecticut, on April 26, 1872, became the first nine in history to field a lineup composed solely of men who were making their major league debuts. Though the Mansfields' all-rookie crew lost 10–0 to Troy and was able to win just five of 24 games before disbanding in August, it featured no fewer than three recruits who would go on to distinguish themselves in baseball annals. The three were first baseman Tim Murnane, later to become one of Boston's most prominent sportswriters;

Candy Cummings (left) poses with a teammate on the Star club of Brooklyn in the late 1860s. As a rookie in 1872, Cummings paced the National Association in five major pitching departments. Whether or not Cummings was the first pitcher to feature a curveball will probably always be a matter of dispute, but he is incontrovertibly the first hurler to win both ends of a major league doubleheader. On September 9, 1876, Cummings, then with Hartford of the National League, beat Cincinnati rookie Dale Williams 14–4 in the AM game and then in the PM contest topped another Queen City rookie, Dory Dean, 8–4. *Transcendental Graphics*

ironman catcher John Clapp, who at one point held the major league record for consecutive games played; and shortstop Jim O'Rourke, only 21 when he appeared in his first major league game that April but 54 in 1904 when he played in the 1999th and last game of a long career that would lead him to the Hall of Fame in 1945.

Other Highlights

April 22—Candy Cummings of the New York Mutuals is the first rookie pitcher to start his team's opening game of the season when he loses 14–8 to Cherokee Fisher of Baltimore.

May 6—Troy's recruit leftfielder Count Gedney slugs two home runs in a 17–1 rout over Brooklyn and finishes the day as the loop leader in four-baggers with three, only to go homerless for the rest of the season.

May 22—Cy Bentley of the Middletown Mansfields beats Cleveland 10–5 for his first ML win after losing his initial four starts by a combined score of 67–20.

July 2—After beginning his ML career with nine straight losses, Jim Britt of the Brooklyn Atlantics bags his first win, topping fellow rookie Candy Cummings of New York, 11–10.

September 1—Rookie outfielder Al Thake of the Brooklyn Atlantics is the first major league player to die in the course of a season when he falls out of a fishing boat and drowns.

1873

The 1873 season again brought several new teams to the National Association. The honor of hosting the first game of the campaign fell to one of the fledglings, a patchwork nine that called itself the Marylands and used Madison Avenue Grounds in Baltimore as its home field. On Monday, April 14, around 500 fans were on hand at the Madison Avenue facility to watch another NA parvenu, the Washington Blue Legs, trounce the hosts 24–3. Pitching for the Marylands was a rookie named McDoolan, first name unknown, and the rest of the new entry's starting cast consisted for the most part of equally obscure recruits. Only one team member, shortstop Lou Say, went on to play more than a handful of games at the major league level. So inept was the Maryland entry that in the six championship games it played before folding on July 15 it not only lost all six but also surrendered a whopping total of 152 runs while scoring just 26.

A second new team, the Resolutes, representing Elizabeth, New Jersey, fared only slightly better, winning just twice in 23 outings. Like the Marylands, the Resolutes banked heavily on inexperienced rookies, centered around the team's captain, Doug Allison, who had served as the catcher on the 1869 Cincinnati Red Stockings, and Allison's brother Art, a veteran outfielder. But a third new entry in the NA, the Philadelphia White Stockings, followed the example the Baltimore Canaries had set in 1872 by filling its ranks with veteran players and was likewise rewarded with a second-place finish, just four games back of the defending titlist Boston Red Stockings. The fact is that 1873 was one of the leanest years in history for rookies. Of all the players on the five teams that finished above .500—Boston, the White Stockings, Baltimore, the New York

In addition to the Allisons, the Elizabeth Resolutes in 1873 featured a second pair of brothers, Hugh and Mike Campbell. Little is known about the Campbells beyond the fact that they were born in Ireland, but they nonetheless are now recognized to have been the first sibling rookie duo in history to play on the same team. Mike exhibited little batting skill, especially for a first baseman, collecting just 12 singles in the 21 games he played to give him both a .145 batting and slugging average, but Hugh, while only marginally better as a hitter (.149 BA and .172 SA), had a fair amount of pitching talent. In his 18 starts he logged the only two Resolutes' victories, including a stunning 11–2 verdict over the champion Boston team in the first game of a July 4 doubleheader at Boston's South End Grounds. The win proved to be the Resolutes' last as well as Hugh Campbell's last; neither he nor his brother Mike ever again played a major league game after the Elizabeth club folded in mid-August.

The 1873 season was the first that failed to introduce a single newcomer who later made the Hall of Fame at least in part on the basis of his accomplishments as a player. There have been relatively few such seasons throughout the game's long history, but significantly more than half come from the nineteenth century. Baseball scholars have long been aware that nineteenth-century players are vastly underrepresented in Cooperstown. Here is a complete list of the seasons that are still without a Hall of Famer: 1873, 1874, 1876, 1877, 1878, 1883, 1886 (Connie Mack debuted late in 1886 but hardly can be said to be in the Hall of Fame for his playing ability), 1887 (Mack's true rookie year came in 1887; no other 1887 rookies are in the Hall of Fame), 1889 (Billy Hamilton, while considered a rookie in 1889 under modern guidelines, was not viewed as a rookie at that time), 1906, 1934, 1935, 1943, and 1953 (though both Ernie Banks and Al Kaline played a bit in 1953, the official rookie season for both was 1954).

Mutuals, and the Philadelphia Athletics—only Boston's Jack Manning and Jim Devlin of the White Stockings appeared in enough games in their rookie seasons to qualify as more than token subs.

Manning and Devlin would both become outstanding players, Devlin in particular before his career was marred in 1877 when he was implicated in the Louisville Scandal and barred from further play for his complicity in dumping games. However, the two rookies in 1873 who would have the most enduring impact both

belonged to the weakling Washington Blue Legs, dead last among the seven NA teams that finished the season. One of the pair, Pop Snyder, joined the club in early June and, after quickly taking over the regular catching duties, remained on the major league scene until 1891. The other, Joe Gerhardt, did not make his Washington debut until September 1 in a 14–7 loss to the White Stockings at Philadelphia when he first filled what had been a gaping hole all season at shortstop. In the 13 games he played as a rookie, Gerhardt hit just

1873 ROOKIE LEADERS

Batting	Pitching
G—32, Jack Manning, BOS	W—2, Hugh Campbell, RES
AB—159, Jack Manning, BOS	L—16, Hugh Campbell, RES
H—43, Jack Manning, BOS	PCT—.143, John Greason, WAS
2B—6, Jack Manning, BOS	GP—19, Hugh Campbell, RES
3B—4, Jim Devlin, PHI	GS—18, Hugh Campbell, RES
HR—No Qualifiers	CG—18, Hugh Campbell, RES
R—29, Jack Manning, BOS	IP—165.0, Hugh Campbell, RES
RBI—22, Jack Manning, BOS	H—250, Hugh Campbell, RES
WK—3, Pop Snyder, WAS	BB—7, Hugh Campbell, RES
SO—11, Jack Manning, BOS	John Greason, WAS
SB—1, Hugh Campbell, RES	K—5, Hugh Campbell, RES
Mike Campbell, RES	ERA—2.84, Hugh Campbell, RES
John Greason, WAS	SHO—No Qualifiers
Jack Manning, BOS	SV—No Qualifiers
BA—.270, Jack Manning, BOS	
SLG—.321, Jack Manning, BOS	
OBP—.275, Jack Manning, BOS	

.214, a harbinger of the failing that would haunt him his entire career. Considered by some analysts to be the best defensive performer at second base in the nineteenth century, Gerhardt managed to achieve only a meager .227 career batting average over 15 seasons.

Other Highlights

June 4—The Elizabeth Resolutes earn their first win after a 0–6 start when rookie Hugh Campbell tops Brooklyn 12–9.

June 6—Pop Snyder, whose nickname deliberately belies his years as he will not celebrate his 19th birthday until October 6, 1873, debuts for Washington and proceeds to catch 28 of his team's 39 games to become the first teenager to serve as an ML club's regular catcher.

August 27—Washington's John Greason launches his ML career by beating Brooklyn 9–7 and then proceeds to lose his six remaining starts to finish with a .143 winning percentage.

October 2—Rookie Jim Devlin of the Philadelphia Whites makes the first pinch-hitting appearance in ML history when he bats for an injured teammate and singles in an 18–7 loss to Boston.

1874

Rookies of consequence continued to be scarce in 1874. Only five recruit position players emerged as regulars: shortstop John Peters of a new entry from Chicago, second baseman Joe Battin of the Philadelphia Athletics, rightfielder Harry Deane of Baltimore, catcher-outfielder Billy Barnie of a new team representing Hartford, and rightfielder Jack Chapman of the Brooklyn Atlantics. Deane disappeared from the major league scene after the 1874 season, and both Barnie and Chapman (who made his NA debut at the advanced age of 31 after playing professionally for many years with independent teams in the New York area) achieved much greater distinction in years to come as managers than they ever did as players, but Peters matured into one of the better middle infielders of his era, peaking in 1876 when he hit .346 and led all shortstops in fielding average, and Battin, like another

slick-fielding Joe—Gerhardt, who had debuted the previous year—survived grave deficiencies as a hitter to linger for well over a decade mainly on his defensive proficiency.

Furthermore, Battin was the sole rookie of consequence on any of the four first-division finishers—Boston, New York, and the two Philadelphia entries, the Athletics and the White Stockings (which were now more commonly called the Pearls). Because the NA in 1874 shrank to only eight teams in the most stable season of its brief five-year sojourn, there was little call for newcomers even on the weaker clubs. So dominant was the influence of veteran performers that only two rookies logged decisions as pitchers. One, Dan Collins of Chicago, split his only two starts and never again pitched in the majors. The second rookie tosser, however, was Tommy Bond of the Brooklyn Atlantics. Though just a month past his 18th birthday when he made his first appearance in the Atlantics' opener on May 5, Bond almost immediately established himself as the best all-around performer on his team. Starting all but one of Brooklyn's 56 games, Bond, as would be expected since his was a weak team, led the NA in losses with 32, but he also finished third in pitching strikeouts, fifth in ERA, and second only to the Athletics' Dick McBride in lowest opponents' on-base percentage (OOBP).

With the reserve clause still not in effect, Bond was free to move to greener pastures the following season, and move he did. He joined with 1872 New York Mutuals rookie star Candy Cummings to give the Hartford club the first outstanding pitching tandem in history, as the pair each toiled over 350 innings and, led by Bond, finished first and third among all full-time NA pitchers in lowest OOBP and first and fourth in ERA.

Other Highlights

May 5—Tommy Bond of Brooklyn is the first rookie to win his team's opening game of the season when he drubs Asa Brainard of Baltimore 24–3.

May 30—Orator Shaffer of Hartford is the first rookie to homer in 1874 when he hits a ball that skids under the rightfield fence in a 14–8 loss to Chicago.

July 9—Tommy Bond coughs up an NA single-game record four home runs in a 14–0 loss to Boston.

As a rookie in 1874, Tommy Bond posted a glittering 2.03 ERA, allowing just 112 earned runs in 497 innings. In his sophomore season with Hartford the following year, his ERA shrank to a minuscule 1.41 as he was charged with only 55 earned runs in 352 innings. Given that he finished in 1884 with a career 2.10 ERA, it would seem that Bond must have worked in hordes of low-scoring games, but that impression is deceptive. In Bond's time, when few fielders as yet wore even rudimentary gloves and scorers were nonetheless conservative in crediting batters with hits, it was not uncommon for teams to post double-digit error totals in a game. The 1874 season was typical of the NA years. On the average, 15 runs were scored per game, but more than two-thirds of them—10.6 to be exact—were unearned. As can be seen from the chart below, Bond's percentage of unearned runs in 1874 was considerably above average, nearly 75 percent, reflecting the poor defensive quality of the team behind him. Also below are Bond's complete career totals. They show that while he allowed an average of only 2.14 earned runs per game, opponents actually scored 4.79 runs per game against him. Imagine what the average score would be today if pitchers customarily gave up more than double the number of earned runs that were charged against them.

EARNED RUNS AS A PERCENTAGE OF TOTAL RUNS, 1874–84

Year	IP	ERA	Total Runs	Earned Runs	Pct Earned Runs
1874	497	2.03	440	112	25.5
1875	352	1.41	152	55	36.2
1876	408	1.68	164	76	46.3
1877	521	2.11	248	122	49.2
1878	532.2	2.06	222	122	55
1879	555.1	1.96	206	121	58.7
1880	493	2.67	298	146	49
1881	25.1	4.26	17	12	70.6
1882	12.1	4.38	13	6	46.2
1884	232	3.49	171	90	52.6
Total	3628.2	2.10	1931	862	44.6

1874 ROOKIE LEADERS

Batting

G—55, Tommy Bond, ATL
  John Peters, CHI
AB—245, Tommy Bond, ATL
H—69, John Peters, CHI
2B—10, Tommy Bond, ATL
  Jack Chapman, ATL
  John Peters, CHI
3B—2, Billy Barnie, HAR
  Jack Chapman, ATL
HR—1, John Peters, CHI
  Orator Shaffer, HAR/MUT
R—39, John Peters, CHI
RBI—25, Jack Chapman, ATL
  John Peters, CHI
WK—5, Johnny Ryan, BAL
SO—**13, Billy Barnie, HAR**
  Johnny Ryan, BAL
SB—3, Johnny Ryan, BAL
BA—.289, John Peters, CHI
SLG—.343, John Peters, CHI
OBP—.295, John Peters, CHI

Pitching

W—22, Tommy Bond, ATL
L—**32, Tommy Bond, ATL**
PCT—.407, Tommy Bond, ATL
GP—55, Tommy Bond, ATL
GS—55, Tommy Bond, ATL
CG—55, Tommy Bond, ATL
IP—497.0, Tommy Bond, ATL
H—606, Tommy Bond, ATL
BB—8, Tommy Bond, ATL
K—39, Tommy Bond, ATL
ERA—2.03, Tommy Bond, ATL
SHO—1, Tommy Bond, ATL
SV—No Qualifiers

September 30—Tommy Bond surrenders his 15th home run of the season (easily an ML record to that point) when George Wright goes yard against him, but Bond nonetheless hangs on to beat the champion Boston team, 9–8.

1875

To the horror of Henry Chadwick, the game's leading observer in its early years, the National Association swelled to 13 teams in 1875. In Chadwick's opinion, the unwarranted expansion would create insurmountable scheduling and travel problems and destroy all semblance of competitive balance. Unhappily for the NA, Chadwick's prognostications all came true, as the Boston Red Stockings, in the process of romping to their fourth straight pennant, finished a record 240 percentage points ahead of runner-up Hartford. When four of the new entrants disbanded after completing less than a third of their schedule and two other teams—New Haven and Brooklyn—had their games thrown out in mid-September after it became obvious that they too would be unable to fulfill their schedules, it left the NA ripe barely halfway through the 1875 season for William Hulbert clandestinely to sign several of Boston's stars to play for his Chicago team in 1876. Hulbert's piracy effectively killed the NA and opened the door for him to form a new circuit the following year in its stead that would forever remove control of the game from the players and place it in the hands of team owners and officials.

But if the players were doomed to suffer in the long run for the tactical mistakes they made in 1875, their choice to expand had one important short-term benefit. The addition of five new teams, including two in St. Louis—the Reds and the Browns—brought a plethora of fresh talent into the NA. For the first time every club, even the top contenders, introduced at least one rookie performer who saw a significant amount of playing time. The two Mound City entries were an especially fertile source of future stars. Though the Reds lasted a scant two months, playing their first game on May 4 and breathing their last in a 12–5 loss to Washington on July 4, their catcher, Silver Flint, would become the backstopping linchpin for five Chicago pennant winners in the 1880s. The Browns supplemented a veteran cast of position players with not one but two rookie pitchers whose names would soon grace record books. The first, George Bradley, won 33 games in 1875 to tie Candy Cummings's then-existing rookie record. That mark has since been eclipsed, but the following year Bradley bagged 16 shutouts to set a new season standard that he still shares with Pete Alexander. To spell Bradley on occasion, the Browns deployed an 18-year-old local amateur named Jim "Pud" Galvin. In his eight appearances in 1875, Galvin collected the first four wins in a career that in 1888 would see him become the first 300-game winner in major league history.

After a 9–3 win in Brooklyn on July 22, Philadelphia Pearls pitcher Cherokee Fisher clashed with team captain Mike McGeary and was booted from the Pearls for the rest of the season, ostensibly for excessive drinking. To replace Fisher, the Pearls landed George Zettlein of the Chicago club, but Zettlein took his time reporting. Forced to find an emergency fill-in, the Pearls hired a Philadelphia amateur named Joe Borden, who agreed to an interim contract only on the condition that he be listed as "Josephs" in game accounts and box scores so that his father would not find out that he was playing ball for pay. In his first start, on July 24, Josephs lost inauspiciously 11–4 to Dick McBride of the Philadelphia Athletics. But four days later, pitching in front of a home crowd against Mike Golden, Zettlein's replacement in Chicago, Josephs stunned the entire baseball world by fashioning the first no-hit game in professional history. Josephs then proceeded to lose his next three decisions before blanking fellow rookie Pud Galvin 16–0 on August 9 at St. Louis. Ten days later, when the Pearls played their next championship game, Zettlein was in the box and the mysterious Josephs temporarily disappeared.

So heady had his initial taste of professional ball been, however, that after the 1875 season Josephs signed with Boston to replace Chicago-bound Al Spalding and reverted to using his real name of Borden. Hence it was that on April 22, 1876, some nine months after notching the first professional no-hitter as Joe Josephs, Joe Borden beat Philadelphia to win the first game in the history of the National League. Less than three months later Borden was permanently gone from the major league arena after suffering an ignominious 15–0 loss on July 15 to Spalding at Chicago.

Batting	Pitching
G—62, Bill Hague, STL	W—33, George Bradley, STL
AB—260, Bill Hague, STL	L—29, Tricky Nichols, NH
H—62, George Bradley, STL	PCT—.559, George Bradley, STL
2B—10, Henry Luff, NH	GP—60, George Bradley, STL
Charlie Waitt, STL	GS—60, George Bradley, STL
3B—4, John Dailey, WAS/ATL	CG—57, George Bradley, STL
Charley Jones, WES/HAR	IP—535.2, George Bradley, STL
HR—2, Henry Luff, NH	H—540, George Bradley, STL
R—32, Bill Harbidge, HAR	**BB—20, Mike Golden, WES/CHI**
RBI—26, Bill Harbidge, HAR	K—60, George Bradley, STL
WK—9, Bill Harbidge, HAR	**ERA—1.16, Pud Galvin, STL**
SO—19, George Bradley, STL	SHO—5, George Bradley, STL
SB—6, Juice Latham, BOS/NH	SV—1, Pud Galvin, STL
BA—.244, George Bradley, STL	Frank Heifer, BOS
SLG—.295, George Bradley, STL	
OBP—.272, Bill Harbidge, HAR	

But while the Browns may have introduced the most immediately productive rookie in Bradley and the most enduringly productive one in Galvin, the novitiate New Haven team launched by far the most interesting crop of rookies. Foremost among them was shortstop Sam Wright, who joined with older brothers George and Harry to make the Wrights the first sibling trio in major league history. Also of import were 17-year-old Jim Keenan, the youngest man to catch a major league game to that point; fancy-fielding first baseman Juice Latham, a midseason gift from Boston; pitcher Tricky Nichols, so nicknamed because he was an early master at changing the speeds of his deliveries; Fred Goldsmith, who went unnoticed in his debut at second base on October 23 in an 8–3 loss to Hartford, but five years later would team with Larry Corcoran to form one of the finest pitching tandems ever; ex-Yale star George Knight, the lone NA performer to register a complete-game win in his one and only pitching appearance; Tim McGinley, to whom would come the honor of scoring the first run in National League history the following April; and the nefarious Billy Geer and Henry Luff, road roommates who were arrested midseason while the team was on a trip to Philadelphia and charged with a string of hotel burglaries.

Other Highlights

May 6—George Bradley of the St. Louis Browns notches the first of what will be a rookie-high five shutouts when he blanks Chicago 10–0 in the second game of the season.

August 9—Pud Galvin of the St. Louis Browns is blasted 16–0 by the Philadelphia Whites but nevertheless ends the season leading all NA hurlers with a 1.16 ERA, as almost all of the Whites' 16 runs are unearned.

September 11—New Haven's Henry Luff, the rookie home run leader with two, hits his second and final dinger of the season in a 13–6 win over Brooklyn.

September 28—Future physician George Knight is the first player to achieve a complete-game win in his one and only big league appearance as a pitcher when he edges New York 8–6.

1876

The National League began its inaugural season with eight teams but finished in October with only six when the New York and Philadelphia clubs both refused to embark on their final western road trips of the season after dropping out of contention. The two largest cities in the United States at that time were summarily ejected from the new league and would not be allowed to return until seven years later, in 1883, as replacements for bankrupt franchises in Troy and Worcester. Meanwhile NL founder and president William Hulbert was unable to find replacements for the two ousted teams the following year, forcing the new loop to struggle along with just six entries. The reduction in teams naturally led to a corresponding reduction in jobs at the major league level. As expected, the main casualties were the 1876 crop of fledgling players. Gone after only one season were numerous novices of varying promise, ranging from sub outfielder Fred Andrus of the pennant-winning Chicago White Stockings, the lone rookie to crack the roster of any of the top three clubs—Chicago, St. Louis, and Hartford—to leftfielder Redleg Snyder of last-place Cincinnati, the embarrassed owner of a .150 BA, the lowest of any NL regular in 1876.

Boston was the lone team in 1876 to generate more than one rookie of lasting substance. In addition to 18-year-old Lew Brown, the youngest man ever to serve as his team's regular catcher, team manager Harry Wright gave a uniform to John Morrill, who not only was Brown's backup receiver but also served as the first-string second baseman. So versatile was Morrill that by the time he left Boston in 1888 after 13 seasons he had been a regular at each of the four infield spots and also had played every other position on the diamond. Yet a third Boston rookie of some note was pitcher Foghorn Bradley who began the season with the Live Oak club of Lynn, Massachusetts, and was not acquired by Wright until late August. Despite his belated arrival, Bradley instantly became Wright's pet hurler, starting 21 of Boston's final 22 games and easily leading all rookies in wins with nine. When Wright lured Tommy Bond away from Hartford prior to the 1877 season, Bradley, realizing that Bond would usurp his role as Boston's ace and render him a sub, elected to sell his services for 1877 to the powerhouse minor league Tecumseh team, based in London, Ontario.

But while Boston led the league in notable rookies, the Cincinnati club led in the sheer number of players it gave their first major league exposure. No fewer than

Charley Jones holds a multitude of distinctions. Probably the one for which he is best remembered is that in 1879 he became the first man in major league history to slam two home runs in an inning. That same year Jones established a new season four-bagger record with nine and in the process assumed the lead in career circuit clouts. All of Jones's season and career slugging marks have long since been eclipsed, but there is one distinction that almost certainly will always remain his.

Although Jones's official rookie season was 1876, his actual unveiling came a year earlier with the Keokuk Westerns, one of the four short-lived entries in the NA's final season. Jones played just 12 games with Keokuk, not enough to lose his rookie status, but in his first game he achieved something that has been done by no one else. When Jones played left field in Keokuk's opening contest, at its Perry Park home ground on May 4, 1875, in a 15–1 loss to Chicago, he became the only future home run king ever to make his major league debut in the state of Iowa.

five regulars and two of the cellar-dwelling team's three main pitchers—Dory Dean and Dale Williams—were rookies. In addition to the aforementioned Redleg Snyder were catcher-shortstop Amos Booth, third baseman Will Foley, catcher-outfielder Dave Pierson, and centerfielder Charley Jones. Dean, Williams, Snyder, Booth, Foley, and Pierson were no more than marginal major leaguers and as such are mere footnotes in a history of rookie performers, but Jones was quite another matter. Time would demonstrate that he was the game's greatest slugger in its early years, and some historians would even argue that he was the finest all-around rookie to emerge during the entire decade of the 1870s.

Other Highlights

April 22—In the first game in the history of the newly formed National League, catcher Bill Coon of Philadelphia is the first rookie both to collect a hit and score a run in an NL game when he singles and then registers Philadelphia's first tally in a 6–5 loss to Boston.

May 2—Charley Jones, the game's first great slugger, hits his initial ML home run off Al Spalding in a 15–9 loss to Spalding's Chicago White Stockings.

Batting	Pitching
G—66, John Morrill, BOS	W—9, Foghorn Bradley, BOS
AB—278, John Morrill, BOS	L—26, Dory Dean, CIN
H—79, Charley Jones, CIN	PCT—.474, Foghorn Bradley, BOS
2B—17, Charley Jones, CIN	GP—30, Dory Dean, CIN
3B—6, Lew Brown, BOS	GS—30, Dory Dean, CIN
HR—4, Charley Jones, CIN	CG—26, Dory Dean, CIN
R—40, Charley Jones, CIN	IP—262.2, Dory Dean, CIN
RBI—38, Charley Jones, CIN	H—397, Dory Dean, CIN
WK—9, Amos Booth, CIN	BB—24, Dory Dean, CIN
SO—22, Lew Brown, BOS	K—22, Dory Dean, CIN
SB—NA	ERA—2.49, Foghorn Bradley, BOS
BA—.286, Charley Jones, CIN	SHO—1, Foghorn Bradley, BOS
SLG—.420, Charley Jones, CIN	SV—1, Foghorn Bradley, BOS
OBP—.304, Charley Jones, CIN	

May 20—Novice hurler Terry Larkin prevents veteran Bobby Mathews from starting all of New York's 57 games when he suffers a complete-game 7–4 loss to Boston in his only appearance of the season.

October 9—Dory Dean, in later life a noted tennis player still good enough to play tournaments when he was in his 80s, makes his tenth straight start for Cincinnati and suffers his fifth straight loss, an 11–0 shellacking at the hands of Hartford, in both the closing game of Cincinnati's season and the final appearance of Dean's brief ML career.

1877

July 20, 1877, was a drizzly day in Cincinnati, disinclining locals from attending that afternoon's game with Boston at Avenue Grounds, especially since theirs was once again a sorry last-place team, but those hardy souls who braved the elements saw not one but *two* famous firsts in major league history. In the box for Boston that day, making his initial appearance, was Will White. Though White lost 15–11 to Candy Cummings, few who saw the contest remembered the result. What was most remarkable about the event is that White's catcher in his debut was his brother Deacon, making the pair the game's first sibling battery. Those Queen City fans paying close attention to the

action on the diamond quickly noticed something else that was unique about Will White: The myopic pitcher was the first performer to take the field wearing spectacles.

For all that, White was not the most influential new face to surface in 1877, as he hurled only three games for Boston and, significantly, as it turned out, thereby retained his rookie status for the following season. Had there been a frosh award in 1877, the honor undoubtedly would have gone to one of these three yearlings: Terry Larkin, Mike Dorgan, or Bill Crowley. The three were the only newcomers to gain posts as regulars after the National League shrank to just six teams. Crowley grabbed the centerfield job on the ill-fated Louisville club that lost what seemed a sure pennant when four of its members conspired to throw enough games down the stretch to hand the flag to Boston. The multitalented Dorgan played every position except first base and pitcher while leading St. Louis in total bases and slugging average. Hartford was able to survive the defection of both of its pitchers, Tommy Bond and Candy Cummings, to other teams after the 1876 season when Larkin emerged to win 29 games and finish second only to Bond in ERA and lowest OOBP.

Yet, while Crowley, Dorgan, and Larkin unquestionably achieved the best full-season rookie performances, in the final month of the campaign a frosh hurler on by far the worst team in the league garnered all the attention. On September 6, deep in last place, Cincinnati captain Jack Manning, with nothing to lose, put the team's newest acquisition, 21-year-old Bobby Mitchell (formerly of the Champion Citys team of Springfield, Ohio) in the box at Louisville against Jim Devlin. Mitchell proceeded to beat the Falls City ace 1–0, allowing just seven hits. After a 3–2 loss to Louisville the following day, Mitchell then topped Devlin again, 6–2, on September 8. Over the next four weeks Mitchell made 11 starts and won six of them. His victory total, accomplished in less than a month, represented 40 percent of Cincinnati's 15 wins for the entire season. These statistics were of secondary importance to observers at the time. What got everyone's attention was that Mitchell was the first southpaw hurler in National League history and, as such, helped to demolish a long-standing myth that the pitcher's box was the only position on the diamond that a left-handed player could not occupy successfully.

After his spectacular showing in the final month of the 1877 season, Mitchell never again approached stardom, but he did take part in a significant first on July 19, 1879, at Cleveland. When Mitchell beat Boston rookie Curry Foley, 8–2, it marked the first occasion that southpaws occupied the pitcher's box for both teams in a major league game.

By late September of 1877, the vaunted Chicago White Stockings, runaway winners of the first National League pennant in 1876, had tumbled all the way to fifth place in the six-team circuit. Perhaps impressed by the astonishing success that lowly Cincinnati was enjoying after installing Bobby Mitchell as its new pitching ace, White Stockings manager Al Spalding invited Laurie Reis, a former Windy City amateur who had spent most of the 1877 season with the Valley City, Iowa, club, to try his luck with Chicago. Joining the White Stockings on October 1, Reis immediately sent all other pitchers on the club to the bench, as he hurled five games in the final six days of the season, including an exhibition win against St. Louis on October 4, and posted three official League victories against just one loss. Furthermore, in the 36 innings he tossed, Reis allowed just three earned runs, giving him an eye-popping 0.75 ERA.

On the basis of those meteoric six days, Chicago signed Reis for 1878. But after two poor starts in May, he was consigned to the bench for most of the remainder of the season before being granted one last chance. The ephemeral Reis concluded his major league career on September 3 at Chicago with an 8–0 drubbing at the hands of Providence's rookie star, John Ward.

Other Highlights

May 8—St. Louis leftfielder Mike Dorgan is the first rookie in National League history to serve as his team's

1877 ROOKIE LEADERS

Batting	Pitching
G—61, Bill Crowley, LOU	W—29, Terry Larkin, HAR
AB—266, Mike Dorgan, STL	**L—25, Terry Larkin, HAR**
H—82, Mike Dorgan, STL	PCT—.537, Terry Larkin, HAR
2B—9, Bill Crowley, LOU	GP—56, Terry Larkin, HAR
Mike Dorgan, STL	GS—56, Terry Larkin, HAR
3B—7, Mike Dorgan, STL	CG—55, Terry Larkin, HAR
HR—1, Bill Crowley, LOU	IP—501.0, Terry Larkin, HAR
Terry Larkin, HAR	H—510, Terry Larkin, HAR
R—45, Mike Dorgan, STL	**BB—53, Terry Larkin, HAR**
RBI—23, Bill Crowley, LOU	K—96, Terry Larkin, HAR
Mike Dorgan, STL	ERA—2.14, Terry Larkin, HAR
WK—9, Mike Dorgan, STL	SHO—4, Terry Larkin, HAR
SO—23, Terry Larkin, HAR	SV—No Qualifiers
SB—NA	
BA—.308, Mike Dorgan, STL	
SLG—.395, Mike Dorgan, STL	
OBP—.331, Mike Dorgan, STL	

leadoff hitter in the opening game of the season when he goes hitless in the Browns' 3–2 win over Boston's Tommy Bond.

June 12—Terry Larkin of Hartford blanks Boston 7–0 in back-to-back starts, the first whitewash coming three days earlier on June 9.

July 7—Terry Larkin, the rookie leader in every pitching department, also is the first frosh in the 1877 season to homer when he goes deep against Jim Devlin of Louisville; Devlin's teammate Bill Crowley is the only other freshman to notch a dinger, on August 4 off George Bradley of St. Louis.

September 20—After debuting on September 6 with a 1–0 win over Louisville in ten innings, lefty Bobby Mitchell starts his tenth game in a 15-day period for Cincinnati, all ten games coming against the Falls City club, including five exhibition contests.

1878

In the winter of 1877–78 the National League appeared to be on its last legs. At one point the loop was shaved to just three teams after St. Louis and Hartford followed Louisville's lead and surrendered their franchises on the heels of the game-dumping scandal in Falls City. To restore his circuit to six entries, Hulbert spirited Providence away from the International Association, a strong minor league that was threatening to replace the NL as the game's foremost enterprise, and then enticed two independent teams from Milwaukee and Indianapolis to board his leaky vessel.

Even after losing Providence, IA moguls gleefully rubbed their hands together in wait for what seemed the NL's certain collapse, but it never happened. To the astonishment of all observers, the 1878 season, instead of spelling the demise of the NL, firmly entrenched the three-year-old circuit as a permanent fixture on the national scene. There were a number of reasons for the NL's abrupt shift in fortune, not the least of which was the complete reversal of form shown by the Cincinnati club. After finishing a dreadful last in both 1876 and 1877, and even dropping out of the league for a brief while in the latter season, Cincinnati leaped all the way to second place in 1878. The Queen City club's renaissance was

traceable in large part to an infusion of outstanding veteran players from disbanded clubs, plus the free-agent addition of Deacon White from Boston's 1877 flag winner. But there was another equally important factor. When White insisted that his brother Will accompany him to Cincinnati as a condition of his signing for the 1878 season, it provided the crown jewel in the most glittering array of rookie talent found on any one team to that point in time. Along with Will White, a 30-game winner in his first full season, Cincinnati showcased three other frosh regulars, first baseman Chub Sullivan; centerfielder Buttercup Dickerson, a midseason replacement for Lip Pike; and most importantly, a 20-year-old phenom named Mike Kelly, who in short order would become better known as "King" Kelly.

But if Cincinnati could boast of having the finest rookie crop in 1878, several of the other clubs were not far behind. Ironically, one of them was the last-place Milwaukee Cream Citys, winners in only 15 of their 60 games. Managed by former NA outfielder Jack Chapman, the Wisconsin entry actually introduced nearly as many estimable recruits as all the rest of the clubs combined. In the long view the best of the lot was Charlie Bennett, ranked by historians among the elite catchers in the nineteenth century, but Bennett hit only .245 in his first season. At the other end of the spectrum was leftfielder Abner Dalrymple, who sported a .354 BA at the close of the 1878 campaign and became the first rookie in major league history to be awarded a league batting crown. Dalrymple's title is a matter of dispute, depending on whether or not hits made in tie games are factored into computations. In 1878 all such hits were dismissed to the distress of Providence outfielder Paul Hines, who otherwise would have hit .358 to Dalrymple's .354, but today many researchers consider Hines to have been the true batting leader. Not in dispute, however, is that in 1878 yet another Milwaukee rookie, Sam Weaver, was the most difficult pitcher against whom to reach base safely. Weaver's .247 mark, even though it enabled him to collect only 12 wins in 43 decisions, made him irrefutably the first rookie to top his loop in lowest opponents' on-base percentage.

Just four points behind Weaver, with a .251 OOBP, was a fellow yearling pitcher with Providence who achieved a rookie first of his own when he paced the NL with a 1.51 ERA. In the years to follow, his influence on the game would exceed even that of the legendary King Kelly. His full name was John Montgomery Ward.

Other Highlights

May 1—In the first Opening Day in history to feature matchups between two rookie hurlers, Cincinnati's Will White tops Sam Weaver of Milwaukee 6–4.

May 1—Fred Corey of Providence and "The Only" Nolan of Indianapolis join with White and Weaver, as four of the six NL teams in 1878 are represented by rookie starters in their season openers.

Of the 56 players who notched at least 100 at bats in 1878, 16—or a remarkable 29 percent—were rookies. Few other seasons, let alone in a six-team league, have witnessed anywhere near such a profusion of neophyte regulars. Should there be any lingering doubt that 1878, for a variety of reasons, was one of the greatest years ever for rookies, we offer a second statistic. In 1878 a total of 180 games were played to a decision in the National League, resulting in a corresponding total of 180 pitching wins. Astoundingly, of those 180 wins, rookies logged a record 53 percent of them. Here, by team, is a complete rundown of the 96 rookie wins in 1878:

Boston	0
Cincinnati	30
Will White	30
Providence	29
John Ward	22
Harry Wheeler	6
Fred Corey	1
Chicago	1
Laurie Reis	1
Indianapolis	24
The Only Nolan	13
Tom Healey	6
Jim McCormick	5
Milwaukee	12
Sam Weaver	12

Abner Dalrymple continues to be recognized by Major League Baseball as the first rookie to win a batting crown even though most historians consider his title to be specious. In any event, Dalrymple started a trend among outstanding rookie batsmen that would be repeated many times when his first ML season proved to be far and away his best. Following his .354 debut in 1878, Dalrymple's career BA declined every year thereafter with the sole exception of his final season in 1891 when he hit .311 albeit in just 32 games. *Transcendental Graphics*

Batting	Pitching
G—63, Russ McKelvy, IND	W—30, Will White, CIN
Ned Williamson, IND	**L—31, Sam Weaver, MIL**
AB—271, Abner Dalrymple, MIL	PCT—.629, John Ward, PRO
H—96, Abner Dalrymple, MIL	GP—52, Will White, CIN
2B—10, Abner Dalrymple, MIL	GS—52, Will White, CIN
Ned Williamson, IND	CG—52, Will White, CIN
3B—4, Abner Dalrymple, MIL	IP—468.0, Will White, CIN
John Ward, PRO	H—477, Will White, CIN
HR—2, Russ McKelvy, IND	**BB—56, The Only Nolan, IND**
R—52, Abner Dalrymple, MIL	K—169, Will White, CIN
RBI—36, Russ McKelvy, IND	**ERA—1.51, John Ward, PRO**
WK—11, Sam Weaver, MIL	SHO—6, John Ward, PRO
SO—41, Will White, CIN	**SV—1, Tom Healey, PRO/IND**
SB—NA	
BA—.354, Abner Dalrymple, MIL	
SLG—.421, Abner Dalrymple, MIL	
OBP—.368, Abner Dalrymple, MIL	

May 4—Indianapolis is the first team in NL history to field a lineup with eight rookies as the Hoosiers' lone veteran starter in a 4–1 loss to Chicago is second baseman John Peters.

May 9—Sam Weaver of Milwaukee tops Indianapolis 2–1 in a game that is now officially considered a one-hitter but that some papers at the time listed as a no-hitter.

September 7—Ned Williamson of Indianapolis hits his first career homer in a game against Milwaukee; six years later Williamson will hit 27 homers to set a season record that will last until 1919.

September 14—Sam Weaver beats John Ward of Providence 4–3 in Milwaukee's season finale; the September 14 closing date is the earliest in history for a ML team that played a complete schedule.

1879

Taught by bitter experience that few western cities were ready as yet to support a major league franchise, NL president William Hulbert jettisoned Milwaukee and Indianapolis after the 1878 season and inveigled the two strongest members of the rival International Association, Syracuse and Buffalo, to take their place. When Hulbert was also able to add Troy, the top club in the New York State Association, and a new entry from Cleveland, the League was assured of fielding eight teams in 1879 for the first time since its maiden season of 1876.

As always when a sizable expansion occurs, many new faces were needed to fill the ranks. All four of the novice clubs, as one would expect, were studded with players new to the League. Buffalo, the best of the four, brought several key members of its 1878 IA pennant winner including leftfielder Joe Hornung, pitcher-outfielder Bill McGunnigle, and 1875 St. Louis Browns rookie right-hander Pud Galvin. Syracuse, the 1878 IA runner-up, re-signed its pitching ace Harry Mc-Cormick, plus third baseman Hick Carpenter, second baseman Jack Farrell, and leftfielder Mike Mansell. The Troy team featured Mansell's brother Tom, centerfielder Al Hall, rightfielder Jake Evans, and a young pitcher–first baseman named Dan Brouthers, who would forewarn the nation that the top hitter in the nineteenth century had arrived by leading his team in both batting and slugging and being responsible for all four of the club's home runs in 1879. The Cleveland Blues were paced in batting by rookie rightfielder Charlie Eden but proved the poorest-hitting team in the league when three other freshman regulars—Jack Glasscock, George Strief, and catcher Barney Gilligan—batted .209, .174, and .171, respectively. A fifth Cleveland recruit, first sacker Bill Phillips, who led the club in runs by a wide margin (58 to runner-up Eden's 40), in addition became the first Canadian-born major leaguer when he went 0-for-4 on May 1, Opening Day in 1879, in a 15–4 Blues loss to Providence's John Ward.

Each of the four veteran teams also presented its followers with at least one prominent rookie. On Opening Day against Troy, in center field and batting leadoff for Cincinnati was Pete Hotaling. Chicago handed its centerfield slot on Opening Day to future batting champ George Gore. At shortstop for the Boston Red Caps on Opening Day when they squared off against the neophyte Buffalo team was newcomer Sadie Houck and in center field and batting second was John O'Rourke, brother of Hall of Famer Jim and destined in his frosh season to become the first rookie to lead his league in slugging average as well as tying for the lead in RBI, with teammate Charley Jones. Only the Providence Grays, the 1879 pennant winner, began the season without a rookie in their starting lineup. By the final month of the campaign, however, the Grays had two. Jack Farrell, after commencing the season with the Syracuse Stars, joined the Rhode Island club on September 12 when the Stars disbanded and took over from Mike McGeary at second base as McGeary moved to third, supplanting weak-hitting Bill Hague. A month earlier, fed up with the chronic misbehavior of catcher Lew Brown, player-manager George Wright had looted the Detroit minor league club of its first-string backstop, Emil Gross, and put him behind the plate for Providence. In the 30 games the Grays had left to play, Gross scored 31 runs, knocked home another 24, and hit .348. Between Gross's bat and Farrell's solid defense at second base, Providence put on a finishing kick that left second-place Boston five games in arrears at the final curtain and thereupon became the first team in major league history to feature rookies that played an all-important role in bringing home a pennant.

Among all the nineteenth-century players who caught a minimum of 200 games, *Total Baseball* credits only one with a career adjusted OPS of better than 140. Just once in the 30 seasons of major league play in the nineteenth century did a man catch every inning of every championship game that his team played that year. The same performer accomplished both feats, and until you encountered him in this chapter chances are that you never heard of him. Yes, it's Emil Gross. In his first game with Providence on August 13, 1879, Gross replaced Jim O'Rourke, who was idle that day, and for the sake of convenience, was assigned O'Rourke's cleanup spot in the batting order. O'Rourke never got his job back as Gross immediately went on a tear that made him the League's most feared batsman in the last month of the season.

The following year, Providence didn't even bother to sign a substitute catcher to spell Gross. Occasionally, when the Grays played an exhibition game, rightfielder Mike Dorgan would don the chest protector, but in every one of Providence's 87 championship contests it was worn by Gross. What happened to Gross after that is not entirely clear. In 1881 the Grays signed Barney Gilligan and let him share the catching duties with Gross. Following that season, rigid disciplinarian Harry Wright became the new Providence manager, and Gross was put on the League's blacklist, rendering him ineligible to play in 1882. Whether Wright was responsible for Gross's banishment has never been established, but when Gross was restored to eligibility in 1883, he seemed unaffected by his enforced absence as he led the new League entry in Philadelphia in both batting and slugging. Despite Gross's sensational comeback season, he apparently was again declared a persona non grata and began the 1884 season without a team. In June he joined the upstart Union Association to play for a club based in his hometown of Chicago, but then, barely five weeks later, while again leading his team in both batting and slugging, he jumped ship after going 1-for-3 in a 4–2 loss at Washington and never appeared in another major league game.

Other Highlights

May 1—Centerfielder John O'Rourke of Boston debuts with four total bases in five at bats for an .800 SA; in 1879, O'Rourke will become the first rookie to be a league leader in SA.

May 10—After dropping his first five starts, Syracuse's Harry McCormick breaks into the win column with a 7–6 victory over Cincinnati; in 1879, McCormick will lead all rookies in both wins and losses as well as every other department except ERA.

1879 ROOKIE LEADERS

Batting	Pitching
G—81, Charlie Eden, CLE	W—18, Harry McCormick, SYR
Pete Hotaling, CIN	L—33, Harry McCormick, SYR
Bill Phillips, CLE	PCT—.353, Harry McCormick, SYR
AB—369, Pete Hotaling, CIN	GP—54, Harry McCormick, SYR
H—108, John O'Rourke, BOS	GS—54, Harry McCormick, SYR
2B—**31, Charlie Eden, CLE**	CG—49, Harry McCormick, SYR
3B—11, John O'Rourke, BOS	IP—457.1, Harry McCormick, SYR
HR—6, John O'Rourke, BOS	H—517, Harry McCormick, SYR
R—69, Sadie Houck, BOS	BB—31, Harry McCormick, SYR
John O'Rourke, BOS	K—96, Harry McCormick, SYR
RBI—**62, John O'Rourke, BOS**	ERA—2.22, Harry Salisbury, TRO
WK—16, Hardy Richardson, BUF	SHO—5, Harry McCormick, SYR
SO—45, Mike Mansell, SYR	SV—No Qualifiers
SB—NA	
BA—.341, John O'Rourke, BOS	
SLG—**.521, John O'Rourke, BOS**	
OBP—.357, John O'Rourke, BOS	

September 23—In his ML debut Jim Tyng of Boston beats first-place Providence 7–3; replacing the injured Tommy Bond, Tyng will start three games in four days against Providence and then never make another starting appearance in the majors.

September 27—In his ML debut and only appearance in 1879, Brown college student Lee Richmond, the first great southpaw in big league history, tops league-leading Providence 12–6.

1880s

1880

Casual historians know the 1880 season best as the year that a rudimentary version of the modern reserve clause was first introduced to restrict players from "revolving" or jumping freely from one team to another depending on which club made the highest offer or promised the most playing time. Nineteenth-century authorities know it best for producing perhaps the most outstanding rookie crop ever. From top to bottom, the eight League teams furnished the baseball public with an unparalleled wave of performers who would leave an indelible mark on the game during the decade of the 1880s.

Chicago not only became the first pennant winner ever to employ a rookie (Tom Burns) at shortstop, but it also became the first to designate a rookie as its pitching ace. Player-manager Cap Anson's choice to restore the Windy City to prominence was 20-year-old Larry Corcoran, and for the icing on the cake Anson also pilfered Fred Goldsmith, Corcoran's pitching teammate on the Springfield, Massachusetts, team for part of the 1879 season, from Troy when the Trojans

failed to protect him under the new reserve rule. Between them the pair won 64 games, a rookie-record 43 of them belonging to Corcoran. Third-place Cleveland was topped in both batting and slugging by frosh second sacker Fred Dunlap, ranked by many analysts as the best middle infielder of the early 1880s, and the Blues in 1880 also launched Ned Hanlon, an outstanding young fly chaser and future Hall-of-Fame manager. Troy, a cellar dweller in 1879, climbed all the way to a first-division perch largely on the strength of the most dazzling assemblage of rookie talent ever to gather on one team in the same season. In addition to leftfielder Pete Gillespie, Trojans skipper Bob Ferguson unearthed no fewer than four future Hall of Famers during the course of the season. One, lefty third baseman Roger Connor, paced the team in all major batting and slugging departments; a second, Mickey Welch, would have shattered the rookie record for wins with 34 were it not for Corcoran appearing in the same year; a third, Buck Ewing, joined the team too late in the campaign to show more than a smattering of the skills that would gain him almost universal recognition as the best catcher in the nineteenth century; and the fourth, Tim Keefe, set an all-time record for the lowest ERA when he allowed just ten earned runs in the 105 innings he labored after being acquired from the Albany minor league club.

A length back of Troy, in fifth place, the new Worcester franchise, a replacement for Syracuse, claimed bragging rights to Harry Stovey, the first rookie home run king as well as the first to lead the League in triples. But Stovey, unbelievably, was only Worcester's third-best freshman. Ahead of him was 32-game-winner Lee Richmond, the author of the first perfect game in history when he blanked Cleveland 1–0 on June 12 without allowing a single enemy base runner. And even more highly regarded than Richmond was the first rookie ever to be accorded the ranking of the top position player in the game by *Total Baseball* with a 3.3 TPR, shortstop Arthur Irwin. A forgotten figure today, Irwin was one of the first fielders to recognize the value of wearing a glove and for a brief while reigned as "The King of Shortstops" before los-ing a substantial amount of his range and speed after breaking his leg sliding in a game against Providence in August 1881.

Other Highlights

May 1—Chicago's Larry Corcoran beats Cincinnati 4–3 on Opening Day for the first of what will be his league-leading 43 wins to set an all-time rookie record for victories.

May 1—Lefty third baseman Roger Connor of Troy goes just 1-for-4 in his ML debut but nonetheless will lead the richest rookie crop thus far in ML history in BA, SA, and OBP.

May 24—Roger Connor hits his first career home run off Boston's Tommy Bond; Connor will finish with 138 career home runs, a record that will last until Babe Ruth breaks it in 1921.

When Nolan Ryan could log only an 8–16 record for Houston in 1987 despite leading the National League in ERA and posting the loop's lowest opponents' batting average (OBA), it sent historians scurrying through encyclopedias in search of the most luckless ERA leader in history. High on every list must be Tim Keefe who won just six of his 12 decisions as a rookie in 1880 despite registering a microscopic 0.86 figure. Keefe did not make his major league debut with Troy until August 6 when he began sharing the pitching chores with fellow rookie Mickey Welch. Keefe's entrance also marked the first time in major league history that two future 300-game winners were teammates. His final appearance of the season came less than five weeks later on September 9 when he strained his arm in a 1–0 loss to Providence. A chronology of Keefe's 12 decisions in 1880 swiftly establishes why he could do no better than .500. In his six losses his Trojan teammates managed to score just ten runs in his support. Moreover, Keefe was not nearly as stingy as his ERA would make it seem. Although he allowed just ten earned runs in 1880—or less than one per game—errors by his Troy teammates caused him actually to be scored upon 27 times.

TIM KEEFE'S PITCHING LOG, 1880

Date	Opponent	Site	Score	W–L
August 6	Cincinnati	Troy	4–2	1–0
August 10	Buffalo	Buffalo	3–2	2–0
August 12	Buffalo	Buffalo	5–1	3–0
August 17	Cleveland	Cleveland	3–5	3–1
August 24	Cincinnati	Cincinnati	11–1	4–1
August 25	Cincinnati	Cincinnati	3–5	4–2
August 27	Cincinnati	Cincinnati	3–2	5–2
August 31	Chicago	Chicago	1–2	5–3
September 2*	Chicago	Chicago	0–1	5–4
September 2	Chicago	Chicago	5–1	6–4
September 4	Boston	Troy	3–4	6–5
September 9	Providence	Troy	0–1	6–6

*Doubleheader in which Keefe pitched both games

1880 ROOKIE LEADERS

Batting	Pitching
G—85, Tom Burns, CHI Fred Dunlap, CLE Arthur Irwin, WOR	W—43, Larry Corcoran, CHI
	L—32, Lee Richmond, WOR
	PCT—.754, Larry Corcoran, CHI
AB—373, Fred Dunlap, CLE	GP—**74, Lee Richmond, WOR**
H—113, Roger Connor, TRO	GS—66, Lee Richmond, WOR
2B—**27, Fred Dunlap, CLE**	CG—64, Mickey Welch, TRO
3B—**14, Harry Stovey, WOR**	IP—590.2, Lee Richmond, WOR
HR—**6, Harry Stovey, WOR**	H—575, Mickey Welch, TRO
R—76, Harry Stovey, WOR	BB—**99, Larry Corcoran, CHI**
RBI—47, Roger Connor, TRO	K—**268, Larry Corcoran, CHI**
WK—17, Pete Gillespie, TRO	ERA—**0.86, Tim Keefe, TRO**
SO—46, Harry Stovey, WOR	SHO—5, Lee Richmond, WOR
SB—NA	SV—**3, Lee Richmond, WOR**
BA—.332, Roger Connor, TRO	
SLG—.459, Roger Connor, TRO	
OBP—.357, Roger Connor, TRO	

June 12—Lee Richmond of Worchester hurls the first perfect game in ML history when he beats Cleveland 1–0; Richmond's gem will remain the only perfecto by a rookie until 1922.

July 10—Fred Dunlap's two-run homer in the bottom of the ninth gives Cleveland's Jim McCormick a 2–0 win over Chicago that ends the White Stockings' nineteenth-century NL record winning streak at 21.

July 13—Larry Corcoran blanks Cleveland 3–0 to log his 13th straight win and set a new rookie mark for consecutive victories that will last until 1886.

July 17—On his way to being the first rookie home run leader in ML history, Harry Stovey goes yard for the first of six times in 1880; his initial victim is Cleveland's Jim McCormick.

August 19—Larry Corcoran tosses the first of his nineteenth-century record three no-hitters, topping Boston 6–0.

September 30—Charlie Guth, a local Chicago amateur, is the first performer in National League history to hurl a complete-game win in his only big league appearance when his White Stockings stagger to a 10–8 verdict over Buffalo after leading 10–1 going into the eighth inning.

1881

At the conclusion of the 1880 season, the Cincinnati club was expelled from the League for selling beer at its home park and threatening to schedule games on Sundays, both of which were prohibited in the staid Victorian Age by the other League franchises. To replace Cincinnati, Detroit, at that time still only a modest-sized city, was granted its first major league opportunity. Nicknamed the Wolverines, the novice club blended veteran position players who were not reserved by their former teams with hard-hitting rookie first baseman Martin Powell and yearling pitcher George Derby to achieve a surprising first-division finish. Powell led the Wolves with a .338 BA, a heady mark that was second in the entire League only to the great Cap Anson, but Derby was an even greater prize as he topped the loop in both pitching strikeouts and shutouts with nine, a figure that still stands as the record for the most ever by a rookie.

On August 30, a miserably hot day in Detroit, Derby injured his shoulder in a 12–8 loss to Chicago and was useless the rest of the season. In retrospect, Derby's injury was probably a torn rotator, for he was never again the same pitcher, but in any case, it almost certainly prevented him from leading the League in wins as he finished with 29, just two behind the two co-leaders. Nonetheless, *Total Baseball* rates Derby the best pitcher in the loop in 1881 although many historians would argue that he was not even the best *rookie* pitcher that season. Providence followers favored a recruit who had played a spot of second base for Buffalo in 1880 and then was not reserved when he hit just .143 in his brief trial. Converted to a box man by the Rhode Islanders, Hoss Radbourn notched 25 wins and became the first rookie to lead his loop in winning percentage. Making his stats all the more arresting is the fact that Radbourn began the season as no better than Providence's third-string pitcher, behind John Ward and Bobby Mathews, but displaced both when they combined to finish a lackluster 22–26 to his 25–11.

But Radbourn's impressive rookie season, and even Derby's massive frosh achievements, paled in comparison to what Boston yearling Jim Whitney accomplished. When Tommy Bond, Boston's longtime ace, reported in the spring of 1881 with a lame arm, skipper Harry Wright gave the Opening Day starting assignment to Whitney, late of the San Francisco Knickerbockers. In his inaugural game on May 2 at Providence, Whitney topped John Ward 4–2 and went 3-for-4. He also got the starting nod the following day against Providence, and then again the day after that, a pattern that would persist for the entire season as he started 63 of Boston's 83 games and relieved in three others. So matchless is Whitney's rookie campaign that he attained a pinnacle that has been reached only once since (by Phil Niekro in 1979). In the process of topping all pitchers in games and innings worked, he also paced the League in *both* wins and losses. Moreover, Whitney attained a second pinnacle that has never been reached by anyone else. In 1881 he became the only man in history to lead his league in walks issued by a pitcher and lead his team in walks received by a batter.

Other Highlights

April 30—Future Hall-of-Fame catcher Buck Ewing hits the first of his rookie-high seven triples on Opening Day off Lee Richmond of Worcester; Ewing at this point in his career is so lightly regarded as a hitter that he bats last in the Troy order, behind even pitcher Tim Keefe.

Jim Whitney's sophomore season was equally as imposing as his rookie campaign. Nearly as gifted with a bat in his hand as he was with a ball, in 1882 he not only led Boston in wins again with 24 but also finished fifth in the League in batting and third in both SA and OBP. At the close of 1884, his fourth season in the majors, Whitney had collected 115 wins and 89 losses for a .564 winning percentage. After that his career spiraled rapidly downward, owing mostly to the abysmal quality of the teams for which he played. Over the remainder of his ten-year career, he garnered just 76 wins in 191 decisions to shave his overall winning percentage 80 points to .484.

The sharp reversal of fortune puts Whitney in very select company. Just five pitchers in all of major league history have been as many as 20 games above .500 at some point in their careers, only to finish with a losing record. None of the other four sank as far below .500 as Whitney did.

Name	Seasons	Pinnacle	G + .500	Career	G − .500
Jim Whitney	1881–90	115–89	26	191–204	13
Jack Powell	1897–1912	119–96	23	245–254	9
Sam Gray	1924–33	82–60	22	111–115	4
Frank Sullivan	1953–63	75–53	22	97–100	3
Larry Benton	1923–35	80–53	27	127–128	1

1881 ROOKIE LEADERS

Batting	Pitching
G—85, Jerry Denny, PRO	W—**31**, Jim Whitney, BOS
AB—320, Jerry Denny, PRO	L—**33**, Jim Whitney, BOS
H—77, Jerry Denny, PRO	PCT—.694, Hoss Radbourn, PRO
2B—17, Jim Whitney, BOS	GP—**66**, Jim Whitney, BOS
3B—7, Buck Ewing, TRO	GS—**63**, Jim Whitney, BOS
HR—1, Jerry Denny, PRO	CG—**57**, Jim Whitney, BOS
Martin Powell, DET	IP—**552.1**, Jim Whitney, BOS
R—47, Martin Powell, DET	H—**548**, Jim Whitney, BOS
RBI—38, Martin Powell, DET	BB—**90**, Jim Whitney, BOS
WK—19, Jim Whitney, BOS	K—**212**, George Derby, DET
SO—44, Jerry Denny, PRO	ERA—2.20, George Derby, DET
SB—NA	SHO—**9**, George Derby, DET
BA—.338, Martin Powell, DET	SV—No Qualifiers
SLG—.429, Martin Powell, DET	
OBP—.380, Martin Powell, DET	

May 5—Hoss Radbourn begins his conversion from a position player to a pitcher when he leads Providence to a 4–2 win over Boston in his first major league start.

May 17—Detroit's George Derby collects the first of his rookie-record nine shutouts when he blanks Troy 4–0.

August 25—Martin Powell of Detroit is the first rookie to homer in 1881 when he goes deep against Chicago's Larry Corcoran; two days later Providence third baseman Jerry Denny will land the only other home run hit by a rookie in 1881.

September 30—Jim Whitney of Boston beats Cleveland 8–3 on the closing day of the season to assure that he will become the first pitcher in history to pace his league in both wins and losses.

1882

Baseball enthusiasts in Cincinnati did not suffer lightly the ouster of their beloved Reds by the League after the 1880 season. Over the winter of 1881–82, Queen City newspaperman Opie Caylor orchestrated a clandestine campaign that resulted in the advent of a rival major league that would permit its teams to sell alcohol in their parks and play games on Sunday in cities where

the law allowed. Caylor and his fellow conspirators christened their rebel loop the American Association, but League loyalists jeeringly dubbed it "The Beer and Whisky League" and were given reason to gloat when the Association, on the eve of the 1882 season, found itself down to only five teams after the Brooklyn Atlantics, a charter member, were unable to secure a home field and had to withdraw. Since a minimum of six teams was necessary for scheduling purposes, in mid-March a franchise was reluctantly awarded to Baltimore. Though frantic efforts were undertaken by the other five clubs to help stock the dilatory entry with enough talent to make it competitive, by early April Baltimore still had only two players signed and was forced to embark on a mad scramble to fill its ranks.

Thus it was that when Baltimore played its opening Association game on Tuesday afternoon, May 2, against the Philadelphia Athletics, the lineup cards for both teams were dotted with 11 names that had never before appeared in a big league box score, a record number for one game with the sole exception of the inaugural contests in 1871 when every player was, in a loose sense, a rookie. Baltimore alone had six newcomers. That same afternoon in St. Louis, the Browns, the first Mound City major league entry since the scandal-ridden 1877 League season, entertained the Louisville Eclipse, the first Falls City major league entry since the last previous Louisville major league club that had perpetrated the infamous scandal. Like Milwaukee's lineup on May 1, 1878, the Eclipse batting order on May 2, 1882, contained seven names that were brand new to big league audiences and an eighth that was also technically a rookie. But while Baltimore's neophytes were for the most part a ragtag bunch, Louisville presented Association followers with the richest assortment of talent ever to make its debut in the same game. The seven complete newcomers included two future batting champions, Pete Browning and Jimmy Wolf, and the future Association season record holder for most wins, Guy Hecker. For good measure, the eighth rookie appearing with Louisville that day was Tony Mullane, destined to win more games than any other pitcher eligible for the Hall of Fame who has never been enshrined.

Browning dominated pitchers in the Association's first season as few hitters, let alone rookies, have ever done. His .378 BA not only earned him the first undisputed batting title by a rookie, but purists, who contend that only a player without any previous major league experience should be considered a rookie, view Browning's figure as the all-time frosh record. Second on the Eclipse in batting was Wolf, who would win the 1890 Association bat crown. With Mullane bagging 30 wins and leading the loop in starts and pitching strikeouts, it is something of a puzzle at first glance why Louisville finished only a few games above .500 in the struggling new circuit and was never even in mild contention. The answer lies in the way Hecker was used in 1882. His enormously talented right arm remained buried for too long as he began the season as strictly a first baseman and did not make his pitching debut until August 18, by which time Louisville was out of the race. Consequently Hecker's 1.30 ERA and .199 OOBP over the closing weeks were able to help the Eclipse secure no better than third place.

A step behind, in the fourth spot, was the Allegheny club, the first major league team to represent the Pittsburgh area, which likewise failed to come together until late in the campaign for lack of a decent second pitcher. Soon after rookie southpaw Denny Driscoll joined the club in that role on July 12, he actually became Allegheny's frontline pitcher owing to his loop-leading 1.21 ERA and a .218 OOBP that was

second only to Hecker's. In the closing week of the season the two rookie latecomers hooked up in a pair of memorable duels. Hecker won the first, on September 19 at Pittsburgh, by dint of a no-hitter, but

Denny Driscoll and Guy Hecker were both rather old for rookies, particularly in the nineteenth century, when it was not uncommon for players to step directly from a high-school diamond into a major league uniform. In April 1882, Hecker turned 26, and Driscoll celebrated his 27th birthday a few weeks after the season ended. Their antithesis that year was St. Louis's rookie ace Jumbo McGinnis, who bagged 69 percent of his team's pitching wins while sustaining only 42 percent of its losses. McGinnis's 25–18 record for an outfit that finished a mere one rung above last-place Baltimore gains even more stature in light of the fact that he was just 18 years old.

Born in February 1864, the Mound City boy wonder established a record in 1882 that almost certainly will never be surpassed (assuming his birth date is correct) by becoming the youngest 25-game winner ever. When good seasons followed in 1883 and again in 1884, McGinnis joined John Montgomery Ward as one of only two pitchers to post three 20-win seasons before their 21st birthdays. Soon after that McGinnis met with arm trouble, just as Ward had while still in his early twenties. But unlike Ward, a good hitter whose arm recovered sufficiently to enable him to play the infield for another decade, McGinnis had little aptitude for any position but pitcher. Just 23 years old, he was released in June 1887 by Cincinnati after being racked for 30 runs in his final two starts. Despite his relatively brief career, McGinnis is second in career wins among pitchers who never played in either the National or American leagues.

MOST WINS, CAREER, NEVER PITCHED IN EITHER NL OR AL

Rank	Name	Years	Leagues	W
1	Toad Ramsey	1885–90	AA	114
2	Jumbo McGinnis	1882–87	AA	102
3	Henry Porter	1884–89	UA & AA	96
4	Al Mays	1885–90	AA	53
5	Al Atkinson	1884–87	AA & UA	51
6	Nat Hudson	1886–89	AA	48
7	Bob Emslie	1883–85	AA	44
8	Billy Mountjoy	1883–85	AA	31
9	Steve Toole	1886–90	AA	27
10	George Pechiney	1885–87	AA	23

Driscoll gained revenge when he won the season finale four days later to allow Allegheny to finish respectably at an even .500.

In marked contrast to the Association also-rans was the pennant-winning Cincinnati team. The Reds opened their season on May 2 with only two rookies on their roster. One, first baseman Bill Tierney, was released after only one game, but the other, future Hall of Famer Bid McPhee, would be the club's Opening Day second baseman for the next 18 years despite his team-low .228 BA in 1882.

The vast majority of the 117 men who possessed rookie status at the beginning of the 1882 season were members of Association teams, and though the League was not without illustrious freshmen like Charlie Buffinton and Fred Pfeffer, none of them had much immediate impact. Indeed, the top three teams—Chicago, Providence and Boston—all fielded lineups comprised entirely of established veterans, and Chicago even went so far as to employ no rookies at all for the entire season until the very last day, on September 30, when Cap Anson, with the club's third straight pennant long since clinched, took a rare afternoon off and stationed at first base, in his stead, Milt Scott, a 16-year-old local amateur.

1882 ROOKIE LEADERS

Batting

G—AA 79, Bill Gleason, STL
   NL 85, Fred Pfeffer, TRO
AB—AA 347, Bill Gleason, STL
   NL 341, Mike Muldoon, CLE
H—AA 109, Pete Browning, LOU
   NL 88, Jackie Hayes, WOR
2B—AA 18, Ed Swartwood, PIT
   NL 22, Jackie Hayes, WOR
3B—AA 11, Ed Swartwood, PIT
   NL 6, Chief Roseman, TRO
HR—AA 5, Pete Browning, LOU
   NL 6, Mike Muldoon, CLE
R—AA 86, Ed Swartwood, PIT
   NL 50, Mike Muldoon, CLE
RBI—AA 45, Charlie Comiskey, STL*
   NL 54, Jackie Hayes, WOR
WK—AA 27, Jack Gleason, STL
   NL 19, Ed Rowen, BOS
SO—AA NA
   NL 45, Sam Wise, BOS
SB—AA NA
   NL NA
BA—AA .378, Pete Browning, LOU
   NL .270, Jackie Hayes, WOR
SLG—AA .510, Pete Browning, LOU
   NL .399, Jackie Hayes, WOR
OBP—AA .430, Pete Browning, LOU
   NL .289, Ed Rowen, BOS

Pitching

W—AA 30, Tony Mullane, LOU
   NL 15, Hugh Daily, BUF
L—AA 29, Doc Landis, PHI/BAL
   NL 14, Hugh Daily, BUF
PCT—AA .581, Jumbo McGinnis, STL
   NL .517, Hugh Daily, BUF
GP— AA 55, Tony Mullane, LOU
   NL 29, Hugh Daily, BUF
GS—AA 55, Tony Mullane, LOU
   NL 29, Hugh Daily, BUF
CG—AA 51, Tony Mullane, LOU
   NL 29, Hugh Daily, BUF
IP—AA 460.1, Tony Mullane, LOU
   NL 255.2, Hugh Daily, BUF
H—AA 432, Doc Landis, PHI/BAL
   NL 246, Hugh Daily, BUF
BB—AA 78, Tony Mullane, LOU
   NL 70, Hugh Daily, BUF
K—AA 170, Tony Mullane, LOU
   NL 116, Hugh Daily, BUF
ERA—AA 1.21, Denny Driscoll, PIT
   NL 2.99, Hugh Daily, BUF
SHO—AA 5, Tony Mullane, LOU
   NL 1, Charlie Buffinton, BOS
SV—AA 1, Ed Fusselbach, STL
   NL—No Qualifiers

*incomplete data for league.

Other Highlights

May 2—Jumbo McGinnis, St. Louis's 18-year-old rookie ace, becomes the youngest pitcher in ML history to post an Opening Day victory when he beats Louisville 9–7.

May 16—Pete Browning, the AA rookie home run leader with five, tags his first career round tripper off Sam Weaver of Philadelphia; all of Browning's home runs will come on the road as his Louisville team sets a new record for the most homers in a season (nine) without any of them coming in its home park.

June 15—Cleveland's Mike Muldoon, the 1882 ML frosh home run king with six, hits his first career dinger off John Ward of Providence; ironically, as with Browning, all of Muldoon's four-baggers will come on the road.

September 11—Louisville's Tony Mullane produces the first no-hitter in American Association history, beating Cincinnati 2–0.

September 11—In the eighth inning of Mullane's no-hit game, teammate Pete Browning loses credit for a base hit that would have swelled his final BA to .382 when he forgets that he has been granted a courtesy runner because he has a leg injury and is called out for being an illegal base runner after he mistakenly bolts out of the batter's box to first base in his excitement after singling sharply to right field.

September 19—Guy Hecker is the second Louisville rookie hurler in just an eight-day span to bag a no-hit game when he beats Pittsburgh 3–1.

October 1—On the closing day of the season, Baltimore's Doc Landis suffers his AA-high 29th loss, to Philadelphia 6–3, in what proves to be the final game of his brief ML career.

1883

When National League moguls took stock after the 1882 season, they grudgingly acknowledged that the American Association, in one short year, had established itself as a formidable rival. Final attendance figures revealed that the Association, despite having only six clubs to the League's eight, won the turnstiles battle by a sizable margin. Much of the Association's success could be traced to placing a franchise in Philadelphia, then the nation's second-largest city, and when the rebel loop annexed the New York Metropolitans, a strong independent team based in the nation's largest city, prior to the 1883 season, the League promptly forgave the two metropolises for their transgressions in 1876 and ceded them the vacancies that were created when the impoverished Troy and Worcester clubs were both dismissed.

Wiser observers, particularly in Boston, also recognized that the Association had stolen a march on the League in 1882 when its teams were permitted to corral the vast majority of the talented recruit players in the country. While Chicago and Providence, winners of the four most recent League pennants, stubbornly elected to stand pat with their veterans, the Beantown club opened the 1883 campaign with rookie Paul Radford in right field and two rookies, Mike Hines and Mert Hackett, sharing the catching duties. A month into the season, Boston added a fourth rookie, Edgar Smith, to its lineup as a temporary replacement in center field and an emergency third catcher. The number of teams to that point that had won a pennant with four rookies playing prominent roles was zero, and the number of teams in all of history that have won a pennant relying on a rookie catcher, let alone three, can be counted on one hand. Yet Boston terminated Chicago's three-year reign as League champion by a comfortable four-game margin as Hines, Hackett, and Smith caught every inning of every game.

Philadelphia, the Association winner, dethroned Cincinnati with veterans at every position. But a close examination of the Association season reveals that the Athletics received major rookie contributions at two separate junctures. Early in the campaign, while player-manager Lon Knight was casting about for a reliable second pitcher to support his ace, Bobby Mathews, Philadelphia amateur Jersey Bakely stepped forward to win several key games. In the late going, when Mathews tired, Knight turned to recent Yale graduate "Jumping" Jack Jones after Jones parted ways with the Detroit League club. Jones, whose nickname stemmed from a bizarre pitching delivery that reportedly caused him to resemble a jumping jack when he released the ball, made his initial appearance with the A's on September

After winning five of his seven starts for the A's in the closing days of the 1883 season, Jack Jones quit baseball and opened a dentistry practice. Departing the A's also was Jones's Eli teammate, Al Hubbard, who had linked up with him on September 15 at Cincinnati to form the first Ivy League battery to perform together in a major league game. Among the numerous other rookies who never again saw action in the majors after the 1883 season was Will Sawyer, a southpaw pitcher from Brimfield, Ohio, who was pressed into heavy service toward the end of the season by Cleveland when the Blues ace hurler, Jim McCormick, hurt his arm.

Since he won just four games and had an execrable .286 winning percentage, Sawyer seemingly was no great loss. However, he left the holder of a record that begs historians to give his work with Cleveland thorough scrutiny. Sawyer's .286 winning percentage is the lowest ever by a pitcher who topped his league in opponents' BA. What's more, the ephemeral lefty, who was only 19 when he threw his last major league pitch, also ranks as the youngest OBA king. Here is a chronology of Sawyer's 17 career pitching appearances that were compressed into just nine weeks and resulted in League batters hitting a mere .217 against him. Note that in addition to his four wins Sawyer also participated in two tie games, both coming in low-scoring battles with future Hall of Famer Mickey Welch. Sawyer's early exit is all the more mysterious in view of the fact that in 1884 the major league season commenced with 28 teams, 12 more than there had been the previous year, and yet he was not deemed good enough for any of them and toiled instead for a minor league entry in Grand Rapids.

WILL SAWYER'S 17 CAREER PITCHING APPEARANCES

Date	Location	Opp Team	Score	Opp Pitcher	Hits
July 21*	Cleveland	Providence	0–2	Ward	2
July 26	Cleveland	Providence	5–2	Radbourn	5
July 28	Cleveland	Providence	2–9	Radbourn	15
August 2	Cleveland	Boston	1–4	Whitney	4
August 4	Cleveland	Boston	3–7	Buffinton	8
August 9	Cleveland	Buffalo	14–5	Galvin–Brouthers	6
August 14	Cleveland	Detroit	0–5	Jones	7
August 30	Chicago	Chicago	1–9	Goldsmith	11
Sept. 4	Buffalo	Buffalo	3–9	Galvin	11
Sept. 14	Philadelphia	Philadelphia	5–2	Purcell	6
Sept. 15	New York	New York	1–1	Welch	2
Sept. 17	New York	New York	0–5	Welch	5
Sept. 19**	New York	New York	2–2	Welch	6
Sept. 21	Providence	Providence	3–6	Radbourn	11
Sept. 25	Providence	Providence	3–2	Radbourn–Sweeney	5
Sept. 27	Boston	Boston	1–4	Whitney	9
Sept. 29	Boston	Boston	4–6	Whitney	6

*Relieved Jim McCormick in seventh inning when McCormick tore a tendon in his pitching arm.
**Relieved McCormick in first inning after McCormick threw just two pitches, both balls, and again tore a tendon in his arm, finishing him for the season.

4 against the hard-rushing Browns and beat Tony Mullane in front of some 10,000 disappointed St. Louis denizens. The following afternoon, Jones again held off the Browns' charge by edging Jumbo McGinnis in a 5–4 thriller. On September 22, Jones allowed the Browns a final ray of hope when he lost to McGinnis 9–6, but then, exactly a week later, he yanked it all away from them when he beat Guy Hecker 7–6 at Louisville to wrap up the flag for the A's.

Other Highlights

May 4—In his first start of the season, Charlie Buffinton, the 1883 rookie leader in wins with 25, staggers to an 11–10 victory over Philadelphia; Buffinton's Boston teammates will present him with 16 runs in his next start on May 12 but then score just one run in his third start on May 17 when he loses 11–1 to Cleveland.

1883 ROOKIE LEADERS

Batting	Pitching
G—AA 98, Arlie Latham, STL	W—AA 10, Ren Deagle, CIN
NL 99, Sid Farrar, PHI	Hardie Henderson, BAL
AB—AA 406, Arlie Latham, STL	NL 25, Charlie Buffinton, BOS
NL 377, Sid Farrar, PHI	L—AA 32, Hardie Henderson, BAL
H—AA 102, Jerry McCormick, BAL	**NL 48, John Coleman, PHI**
NL 88, Sid Farrar, PHI	PCT—AA .556, Ren Deagle, CIN
2B—AA 16, Jerry McCormick, BAL	NL .641, Charlie Buffinton, BOS
NL 19, Sid Farrar, PHI	GP—AA 45, Hardie Henderson, BAL
3B—AA 14, Bill Kuehne, COL	NL 65, John Coleman, PHI
NL 8, John Coleman, PHI	GS—AA 42, Hardie Henderson, BAL
Sid Farrar, PHI	NL 61, John Coleman, PHI
HR—AA 2, Pop Corkhill, CIN	CG—AA 38, Hardie Henderson, BAL
Ed Kennedy, NY	NL 59, John Coleman, PHI
Dave Orr, NY	IP—AA 358.1, Hardie Henderson, BAL
NL 2, Mert Hackett, BOS	NL 538.1, John Coleman, PHI
R—AA 86, Arlie Latham, STL	H—AA 383, Hardie Henderson, BAL
NL 46, Paul Radford, BOS	**NL 772, John Coleman, PHI**
RBI—AA 46, Pop Corkhill, CIN*	BB—AA 87, Hardie Henderson, BAL**
NL 32, John Coleman, PHI	NL 64, Tip O'Neill, NY
WK—AA 18, Arlie Latham, STL	K—AA 145, Hardie Henderson, BAL
NL 15, John Coleman, PHI	NL 188, Charlie Buffinton, BOS
SO—AA NA	ERA—AA 2.31, Ren Deagle, CIN
NL 48, Mert Hackett, BOS	NL 2.36, Will Sawyer, CLE
SB—AA NA	SHO—AA 1, Ren Deagle, CIN
NL NA	Bob Emslie, BAL
BA—AA .262, Jerry McCormick, BAL	NL 4, Charlie Buffinton, BOS
NL .238, Charlie Buffinton, BOS	SV—**AA 1, Bob Barr, PIT**
SLG—AA .339, Jim Field, COL	NL 1, Charlie Buffinton, BOS
NL .326, Sid Farrar, PHI	
OBP—AA .272, Jim Field, COL	
NL .266, John Coleman, PHI	

*incomplete data for league.

**Henderson issued two walks for Philadelphia in the National League to bring his total to 89.

May 15—John Coleman of the NL Philadelphia Quakers collects his first win after seven straight losses when he squeaks by Detroit 4–3 in ten innings; Coleman will lose a record 48 games in 1883.

May 29—In his first AA start of the 1883 season, Baltimore's Hardie Henderson loses 11–3 to Louisville; despite not making his AA debut until the season is nearly a month old, Henderson will suffer a loop rookie-high 32 losses.

May 31—While his Yale team is in New York over the Memorial Day weekend, collegian Sam Childs plays first base for shorthanded Columbus in an Association game against the New York Mets; Childs's lone ML appearance is not discovered until 2002.

September 21—John Coleman suffers his 48th and final loss of the 1883 season, 9–8 to Detroit.

September 22—Burly first baseman Dave Orr of the New York Mets hammers two home runs and a triple in a 7–1 win over Columbus's deaf-mute rookie hurler Dummy Dundon; Orr's banner slugging day enables him to tie for the ML rookie lead in four-baggers in 1883 despite collecting just 53 at bats all year.

1884

Many players initially welcomed the introduction of a reserve clause in their contracts in 1880, or at least had neutral feelings about it, but by 1884 most had already begun to view it as at best a necessary evil. When Henry Lucas, the 26-year-old scion of a wealthy St. Louis banking family, proclaimed that the reserve clause was not only unnecessary but intolerable and formed a third major league committed to eliminating it from player contracts, he found plenty of supporters. In 1884, during the one season that Lucas's rebel loop, the Union Association, was alive, a record 34 teams saw action at one time or another at the major league level. As might be expected under the chaotic conditions, a record number of rookies also saw action at one time or another in 1884, but the total is nonetheless staggering. Ranging alphabetically from John Ake, a 13-gamer with the Baltimore

In brutal contrast to Bob Caruthers, Dave Foutz, John Clarkson, and Ed Morris—who posted a combined 66–24 won-lost total as rookies in 1884—were several dozen hurlers whose brief exposures to major league audiences would seemingly best be forgotten. Among them were the likes of Milo Lockwood (1–9), John Hamill (2–17), Alex Voss (5–20), Frank Brill (2–10), Ed Trumbull (1–9), and the lowest of the low in 1884, Jim McElroy (1–13). The standard explanation for any of them ever to have been issued a major league uniform is that the poorer teams among the 34 that tested the water that year desperately needed warm bodies, but in the case of McElroy at least there is more to the story. A fairly strong argument can even be mounted that McElroy, under more forgiving circumstances, might actually have had the makings of an outstanding pitcher.

We first encounter him in 1884 on May 2 pitching for the Baltimore Monumentals in the Eastern League, the victim of an 11–1 shellacking at the hands of the Wilmington Quicksteps in which he gave up eight walks, uncorked two wild pitches, and caused his catcher, Briel, to be charged with three passed balls. Later in the month, on May 26 at Philadelphia, McElroy made his big league entrance with the Philadelphia Phillies in a 10–4 loss to Boston's Charlie Buffinton in which he walked five, threw five wild pitches, and watched his catcher, Joe Kappel, who was also appearing in his first major league game, allow seven passed balls.

McElroy's second start with the Phils came in the afternoon game of a Memorial Day doubleheader at Providence. Though he lost 9–2 to Hoss Radbourn, he was "so wild and swift that there was only one base hit made in the first seven innings {off him}." Nevertheless, he trailed 3–2 at that point and then apparently fell apart. His catcher that day was Frank Ringo, a second-year man who also handled him in his next two starts—both losses—before sustaining a split hand in the second, on June 4 at Providence, and being replaced behind the plate by rookie John Crowley. Ringo's exit on June 4 signaled the last time in his major league career that McElroy would work with a veteran catcher (albeit of only one season). Indeed, in his ten remaining starts, McElroy was teamed with six different receivers, four of whom could later say that he was the first pitcher they ever caught in a major league game.

Probably no other pitcher has ever ushered in so many new catchers in one season, and it's also doubtful that any other major league pitcher had to work with as many as seven different catchers while making only 14 appearances. The reason McElroy had such a multitude of catchers and, in particular, so many who were raw recruits is obvious. In 1884 the protective gear catchers wore was still very meager, and injuries were rampant. Because McElroy threw hard and had poor control, no one wanted to catch him if it was humanly possible to avoid it.

Less obvious is the reason that McElroy lingered in the majors for nearly three full months despite ten straight losses, most by lopsided scores, before he earned his first and only win on July 22. Prior to the 1884 season, Harry Wright was hired to manage the Phillies, and Wright, if he knew nothing else about the game, knew a good young pitcher when he spotted one. One might imagine that in Jim McElroy, Wright saw something very similar to the raw but nonetheless extraordinary talent that baseball people in Brooklyn saw in Sandy Koufax in the mid-1950s. Only Wright never found a catcher ready, willing, and able to harness his young wild man and finally had to give up on him.

One last ironic note on the short, unhappy career of Jim McElroy: His lone win should by rights have been a loss, saddling him with an 0–14 career record, second-worst in history only to Terry Felton. The game McElroy won came at Providence on the notorious afternoon when the Grays hit the absolute low point in their season after Charlie Sweeney, with a commanding lead, was removed from the box by manager Frank Bancroft and ordered to change places with rightfielder Joe Miller so Miller could get a couple innings of experience. But Sweeney, in feigned anger, stalked off the field instead, having been given an excuse to jump his contract with Providence, and caught a train to St. Louis where he joined Lucas's Union Association team. Since the rules in 1884 did not allow substitutes except in the case of injuries, Sweeney's exodus forced Providence to finish the game with only eight men and turned a 6–2 Phillies deficit into a 10–6 McElroy victory when Philadelphia scored eight unearned runs in the ninth inning against Miller and the undermanned Grays.

Association club, to Chief Zimmer, a catcher with the Detroit League team who would not play his final big league innings until 1903, an incredible 417 participants in the 1884 season crowded under the rookie umbrella.

Also rather astonishing is that only two eventually made the Hall of Fame. Foremost is John Clarkson, who had flunked a short test with Worcester in 1882 and then had kicked around the minors for two years before joining the Chicago League team in August 1884. While Clarkson instantly showed himself a force to be reckoned with by winning ten of 13 starts in his rookie season, Tommy McCarthy, the second future Hall of Famer from the class of 1884 and the only Cooperstown member to make his debut in the Union Association, wound up back in the minors after hitting just .215 for the Boston Unions and losing all seven of his pitching appearances.

The better League teams in 1884 followed the same formula: an all-veteran lineup with rookies at most playing only bit roles. Providence, the League champion and an easy winner in the first ever World Series against the Association champion New York Mets, looked at several young arms hoping to find one that could spell Hoss Radbourn, who had to assume the club's entire pitching load when Charlie Sweeney defected to the Union Association, but the only newbie to show much promise was Ed Conley. After his first four starts, Conley was 4–0, only to be blasted in his next four outings and then released. The Mets had no need for additional pitching strength, as veterans Tim Keefe and Jack Lynch worked every game save one, but the first pennant winner in history that represented the nation's largest city did have a hole at first base after Steve Brady was moved to the outfield. To fill it, Mets skipper Jim Mutrie chose hefty Dave Orr, whose numbers made him easily the game's top freshman hitter in 1884 as well as the second recruit in three years to win the Association batting title.

Association runner-up Columbus was home to the game's best rookie pitcher in Ed Morris, but during the summer of 1884 the fourth-place Browns remarkably managed to acquire two hurlers from minor league teams less than six weeks apart who rank first and second in career winning percentage among all pitchers involved in a minimum of 150 decisions in the American Association. The leader, Bob Caruthers, finished at .732 (175–64) after beating Philadelphia 6–2 in his debut on September 7, 1884. Second to Caruthers at .701 (129–55) is Dave Foutz, who needed 13 innings to beat Cincinnati's Will White 6–5 in his career lid-lifter on July 29.

Other Highlights

May 6—Luckless Larry McKeon, who will lose an AA-record 41 games for Indianapolis, no-hits Cincinnati for six innings but earns only a 0–0 draw for his effort when heavy rain halts the game after his Indy teammates twice fail to score despite loading the bases with none out.

May 24—Philadelphia A's rookie Al Atkinson hurls a 10–1 no-hit win over Pittsburgh.

May 29—Columbus's Ed Morris, the leading rookie winner in 1884, fires a no-hitter at Pittsburgh, beating the Allegheny club 5–0.

July 31—White Stockings southpaw John Hibbard, the son of the Chicago Register in Bankruptcy, blanks Detroit 4–0 in his ML debut.

August 11—Charlie Geggus of the Washington Unions sets a pre-1954 rookie record when he fans 14 Boston Unions en route to a 5–3 win in his first ML game as a pitcher; Geggus had previously played shortstop in two games for Washington.

August 13—Just days after the Grand Rapids minor league team becomes defunct, all four members of Grand Rapids's top two batteries make their ML debuts in a sensational pitchers' duel as John Henry, caught by Jerrie Moore, allows just two hits to spearhead Cleveland to a 1–0 win over Charlie Getzein of Detroit, who is caught by Ed Gastfield.

September 4—Fleet Walker catches his final contest for Toledo of the American Association in a 5–2 win against Pittsburgh, marking the last time until 1947 that an African-American player will appear in a ML game.

October 1—Detroit's Charlie Getzein no-hits the Philadelphia Quakers and wins a 1–0 nail-biter that is shortened to six innings by rain.

October 4—Brooklyn frosh Sam Kimber becomes the first hurler in history to fail to win a full-length no-hit game when his gem against Toledo ends in a 0–0 10-inning tie.

1884 ROOKIE LEADERS

Batting

G—AA 110, Dave Orr, NY
  NL 116, Alex McKinnon, NY
  UA 111, Henry Moore, WAS
AB—AA 458, Dave Orr, NY
  NL 470, Alex McKinnon, NY
  UA 467, Emmett Seery, BAL/KC
H—**AA 162, Dave Orr, NY**
  NL 128, Alex McKinnon, NY
  UA 155, Henry Moore, WAS
2B—**AA 39, Sam Barkley, TOL**
  NL 21, Ed Andrews, PHI
    Alex McKinnon, NY
  UA 26, Emmett Seery, BAL/KC
3B—AA 17, John Peltz, IND
  NL 13, Alex McKinnon, NY
  UA 8, Buster Hoover, PHI
    Bill Kienzle, PHI
    Lou Sylvester, CIN
HR—AA 9, Dave Orr, NY
  NL 6, Frank Meinke, DET
  UA 12, Ed Crane, BOS
R—AA 94, Frank Fennelly, WAS/CIN
  NL 74, Ed Andrews, PHI
  UA 115, Emmett Seery, BAL/KC
RBI—AA 112, Dave Orr, NY*
  NL 73, Alex McKinnon, NY
  UA NA
WK—AA 31, Frank Fennelly, WAS/CIN
  NL 20, Jim Fogarty, PHI
  UA 37, Yank Robinson, BAL
SO—AA NA
  NL 89, Frank Meinke, DET
  UA NA
SB—AA NA
  NL NA
  UA NA
BA—**AA .354, Dave Orr, NY**
  NL .272, Alex McKinnon, NY
  UA .336, Henry Moore, WAS
SLG—AA .539, Dave Orr, NY
  NL .391, Alex McKinnon, NY
  UA .451, Ed Crane, BOS
OBP—AA .367, Frank Fennelly, WAS/CIN
  NL .285, Alex McKinnon, NY
  UA .363, Henry Moore, WAS

Pitching

W—AA 34, Ed Morris, COL
  NL 21, Charlie Ferguson, PHI
  UA 23, Bill Wise, WAS
L—**AA 41, Larry McKeon, IND**
  NL 32, John Harkins, CLE
  UA 20, Alex Voss, WAS/KC
PCT – **AA .723, Ed Morris, COL**
  NL .457, Charlie Ferguson, PHI
  UA .833, Henry Boyle, STL
GP—AA 61, Larry McKeon, IND
  NL 50, Charlie Ferguson, PHI
  UA 50, Bill Wise, WAS
GS—AA 60, Larry McKeon, IND
  NL 47, Charlie Ferguson, PHI
  UA 41, Bill Wise, WAS
CG—AA 59, Larry McKeon, IND
  NL 46, Charlie Ferguson, PHI
  UA 34, James Burke, BOS
    Bill Wise, WAS
IP—AA 512.0, Larry McKeon, IND
  NL 416.2, Charlie Ferguson, PHI
  UA 364.1, Bill Wise, WAS
H—AA 496, Fleury Sullivan, PIT
  NL 443, Charlie Ferguson, PHI
  UA 383, Bill Wise, WAS
BB—AA 96, Fleury Sullivan, PIT
  NL 111, Billy Serad, BUF
  UA 60, Bill Wise, WAS
K—AA 308, Larry McKeon, IND
  NL 194, Charlie Ferguson, PHI
  UA 268, Bill Wise, WAS
ERA—AA 2.18, Dave Foutz, STL**
  NL 1.95, Charlie Getzien, DET
  UA 1.74, Henry Boyle, STL
SHO—AA 4, Sam Kimber, BRO
  NL 3, John Harkins, CLE
  UA 4, Bill Wise, WAS
SV—**AA 1, Oyster Burns, BAL**
  Hank O'Day, TOL
  NL 1, Charlie Ferguson, PHI
  UA 1, Henry Boyle, STL
    Lou Sylvester, CIN

*incomplete data for league.
**Foutz's ERA of 2.177 edged Ed Morris's of 2.178.

When the Union Association collapsed after only one season and its champion St. Louis Maroons were absorbed by the National League in place of Cleveland, the number of major league slots was reduced abruptly by more than a third. Where there had been over 300 players on big league payrolls at the close of the 1884 season, there was now room for fewer than 200. The immediate result was that, with the sole exception of 1873, 1885 proved to be by far the leanest year for rookies in the nineteenth century. So few openings existed, particularly at the beginning of the campaign, that each of the six members of the 1885 rookie class who in the course of time would have the deepest impact on the game opened the season in the minors.

The six were Sam Thompson, Lady Baldwin, Jimmy Ryan, Denny Lyons, Toad Ramsey, and Jim McTamany; of them, only Baldwin, who arrived in Detroit in late June from Milwaukee after the Western League folded, got enough playing time to qualify for either a batting title or an ERA crown. Actually, Baldwin's frosh numbers for Detroit were strong enough to rank fourth in the League in ERA and first among all pitchers in the majors in OOBP at .228. But while there were several other frosh pitching qualifiers in addition to Baldwin who put up stats worthy of mention, there were precisely none on the hitting side of the ledger. While it is true that Thompson hit .303 for Detroit, his work came in only 62 games. With 80 games generally accepted as the minimum needed in 1885 to qualify as a batting leader, just three rookies in both major circuits met the standard, Al Myers, Charlie Bassett, and Charlie Bastian. All three were middle infielders who had played a bit in 1884 and signed with League teams for 1885. They had something else in common—they were rotten hitters. Bassett split the year between second base and short for Providence and hit all of .144. Bastian and Myers formed the Phillies' keystone combo and batted .167 and .204, respectively.

Consequently, among all rookie qualifiers, by default, the honor of being both the top batter and slugger in 1885 goes to Al Myers, with a .204 BA and .261 SA.

A notch below the six players with rookie status in 1885 who would construct the most substantial career achievements were pitchers Ed Daily and Ed Seward. Seward appeared in only one game and actually did not celebrate his true rookie year until 1887, but Daily's accomplishments in 1885 included 26 wins for the Phils, tying him with teammate Charlie Ferguson for the fifth highest total in the League.

In 1890, scarcely a year before he died of tuberculosis, Daily performed a feat that has never received its due. While serving as both a pitcher and an outfielder with three different teams, he became the only player in major league history to log as many as 500 plate appearances and 300 innings in the same season.

Another League rookie pitcher in 1885, Ted Kennedy of Chicago, performed a unique feat that has never before received so much as an iota of recognition. After beginning the year in the minors with Keokuk, Kennedy was brought to Chicago in early June when Larry Corcoran's arm failed, stripping the White Stockings of a reliable second pitcher behind John Clarkson. Kennedy won his first three starts before suffering his initial loss on June 26 to Ed Daily. Following two more wins, Kennedy lost for a second time to Providence's Hoss Radbourn. While Providence was in Chicago, White Stockings owner Al Spalding learned that the Grays' second pitcher, Jim McCormick, who had fallen into manager Frank Bancroft's doghouse, was available for a price and began successful negotiations to secure him. McCormick joined the Chicago team when it visited Providence on July 22, spelling Kennedy's return to the minors but not before the White Stockings pressed the rookie into service one final time. On July 16 in Buffalo, after Clarkson had won a tough 4–2 battle the day before, it was decided the teams would play a postponed game in addition to the regularly scheduled one. With Clarkson unavailable, Kennedy, perforce, had to pitch both games of the twin bill. He won the morning contest 9–3 against Billy Serad and then beat Pete Wood 13–9 in the afternoon affair although he had to be relieved by Ned Williamson after the seventh inning when his arm wearied.

Since Kennedy never threw another pitch for Chicago after that memorable day in Buffalo, he stands as the only pitcher in major league history to start and win both ends of a doubleheader in his final appearance with a team.

Other Highlights

April 12—Louisville's Norm Baker blanks Pittsburgh 11–0 in his first start of the season; Baker's effort is not only his first ML win but his lone ML shutout and ties him for the AA rookie lead in shutouts in 1885.

1885 ROOKIE LEADERS

Batting	Pitching
G—AA 56, Ed Greer, BAL	W—AA 13, Norm Baker, LOU
NL 103, Charlie Bastian, PHI	NL 26, Ed Daily, PHI
AB—AA 211, Ed Greer, BAL	L—AA 12, Norm Baker, LOU
NL 389, Charlie Bastian, PHI	NL 23, Ed Daily, PHI
H—AA 42, Ed Greer, BAL	PCT—AA .520, Norm Baker, LOU
NL 77, Sam Thompson, DET	NL .531, Ed Daily, PHI
2B—AA 7, Ed Greer, BAL	GP—AA 25, Norm Baker, LOU
Jim McTamany, BRO	NL 50, Ed Daily, PHI
NL 13, Al Myers, PHI	GS—AA 24, Norm Baker, LOU
3B—AA 2, Jim McTamany, BRO	NL 50, Ed Daily, PHI
NL 9, Sam Thompson, DET	CG—AA 24, Norm Baker, LOU
HR—AA 1, Jim McTamany, BRO	NL 49, Ed Daily, PHI
NL 7, Sam Thompson, DET	IP—AA 217.0, Norm Baker, LOU
R—AA 32, Ed Greer, BAL	NL 440.0, Ed Daily, PHI
NL 63, Charlie Bastian, PHI	H—AA 210, Norm Baker, LOU
RBI—AA 21, Ed Greer, BAL	NL 370, Ed Daily, PHI
NL 44, Sam Thompson, DET	BB—AA 69, Norm Baker, LOU
WK—AA 9, Jim McTamany, BRO	NL 90, Ed Daily, PHI
NL 35, Charlie Bastian, PHI	K—AA 83, Toad Ramsey, LOU
SO—AA NA	NL 140, Ed Daily, PHI
NL 82, Charlie Bastian, PHI	ERA—AA 2.76, Al Mays, LOU
SB—AA NA	NL 1.86, Lady Baldwin, DET
NL NA	SHO—AA 1, Norm Baker, LOU
BA—AA No Qualifiers	Dug Crothers, NY
NL .204, Al Myers, PHI	Tom Lovett, PHI
SLG—AA No Qualifiers	George Pechiney, CIN
NL .261, Al Myers, PHI	NL 4, Ed Daily, PHI
OBP—AA No Qualifiers	SV—AA No Qualifiers
NL .236, Charlie Bastian, PHI	NL 1, Lady Baldwin, DET

July 2—Sam Thompson is 1-for-2 in his ML debut with Detroit after replacing injured rightfielder Gene Moriarity in the fifth inning; Moriarity will never get his job back as Thompson goes on to lead all freshmen in home runs, triples, and RBI despite playing scarcely half the season.

July 3—Lady Baldwin marks his debut with Detroit by beating Boston 6–1; despite being with the Wolverines just half the season, Baldwin will lead all rookies in ERA.

August 15—Jim McTamany is 1-for-4 in his ML debut for Brooklyn and proceeds to lead all AA freshmen in several hitting departments despite his belated start, which permits him time to play in only 35 games.

September 3—Jim McTamany hits the lone home run by an AA rookie in 1885 when he goes deep against Dug Crothers of the New York Mets.

September 5—In his ML debut with Louisville, southpaw knuckleballer Toad Ramsey loses 4–3 to St. Louis; though he allows enemy hitters to bat just .150 against him in his rookie season and posts a 1.94 ERA, Ramsey receives so little offensive and defensive support from his Louisville mates that he drops his first five starts and finishes the season 3–6.

October 3—In a game shortened to six innings by darkness, Bill Stemmeyer of Boston blanks Buffalo 18–0 in his ML debut.

In almost every season during the 1880s, the pitching sides of the rookie leaders charts are sprinkled with names of freshmen who brilliantly lit up major league box scores in their debut campaigns, only to disappear after all too brief a stay. The 1886 season was no excep-

tion. Though the statistics in the hitting section of the rookie leaders chart for the most part are very unimposing, several of the men to whom they belong, especially Lou Bierbauer and Jimmy Ryan, enjoyed lengthy and illustrious careers. The same was not true for any of the pitchers.

There are a number of reasons why young hurlers in the 1880s often experienced swift and in many cases even overwhelming success against major league hitters and then fell into almost immediate decline. In 1886, as an example, the pitcher's box was lengthened and a rule that had been tried the previous year by the National League, requiring hurlers to keep both feet on the ground while delivering a pitch, was abolished. With a longer box and no more foot restrictions, a pitcher could now crank up by getting a running start or even, as had Jack Jones a few years earlier, leave his feet entirely when he released the ball. The result, in 1886, was an alarming profusion of strikeouts, up more than 25 percent from 1885. When the rules changed again in 1887, growing much more restrictive for pitchers in an effort to increase offensive production, and then continued to change almost yearly until 1893, when the present pitching distance was first instituted, the long-term result was that many young hurlers, after being deprived of pet quirks that had brought them early success, either could not adjust or else ruined their arms in an effort to alter their deliveries.

Severe overuse was another important reason that so few outstanding rookie pitchers had more than one or two fruitful seasons before vanishing. Matt Kilroy, the Baltimore southpaw who set not only a rookie record but also the all-time season record for strikeouts in 1886, was pretty well finished by the time he was 24 after hurling a mind-numbing total of 1172.1 innings in his first two seasons. Jocko Flynn, the foremost rookie sensation in 1886, was unable even to survive a full season with Chicago. With a revamped Detroit club hard on the heels of his defending-champion White Stockings, Chicago manager Cap Anson could not afford to rest Flynn when his arm began to ail. After hanging on to win the darkness-shortened final game of a crucial series with the Wolverines on September 22, Flynn was belted 11–4 in his next start three days later in Philadelphia. Anson got only one more pitching effort out of his rookie ace. On October 2, in Washington, Flynn edged

> In 1886, just two short years after winning the Association pennant, the New York Mets were spared an ignominious cellar finish only by the presence of the even more abysmal Baltimore Orioles and the late-season arrival of a pitcher whose fame was even more transient than that of Jocko Flynn or Matt Kilroy or Nat Hudson or, indeed, any of the multitude of short-lived young arms of the period. On September 13, when the loop-leading Browns arrived at the Mets' Staten Island home park, they were pleased to discover the New York starter that afternoon would be John Shaffer, fresh from the Southern League, where he had labored most of that summer for Atlanta. The Browns' pleasure turned to shock when Shaffer beat them 6–3 and then set down their vaunted bats again three days later 2–1.
>
> Shaffer won his first four games in the majors to secure seventh place for the Mets. The victory that put his career mark at 4–0 was his zenith, a 7–0 shutout on September 29 at Louisville that would have been a no-hitter save for Pete Browning, who collected all three of Louisville's safeties. Subsequently, Shaffer finished the year at 5–3, giving him the only winning record on the Mets staff. Moreover, his .164 OBA outstripped all pitchers in both major leagues though his 69 innings were not enough to qualify him as a loop leader. His final start of the season was his lone bad outing. On October 12, in what would be the Pittsburgh club's last game in the American Association before it defected to the National League, Shaffer led Pud Galvin 2–1, but then his control, which was normally one of his fortes, deserted him, and Pittsburgh scored six unanswered runs in the last three innings to saddle him with a 7–2 loss.
>
> Shaffer's momentary control failure grew into a chronic problem the following year when the pitching rules changed dramatically. Named the Mets' Opening Day starter in 1887, he swiftly lost his first eight decisions and was released soon thereafter. His finale came on June 30 at Staten Island. Returning to the box "after a long rest," he was thrashed 15–4 by Baltimore. Shaffer's meteoric ascension to stardom in the nation's media capital in the closing weeks of the 1886 season was so fleeting that he was gone before any of the local sportswriters thought to put on record with which arm he threw.

1886 ROOKIE LEADERS

Batting	Pitching
G—AA 137, Lou Bierbauer, PHI	W—AA 29, Matt Kilroy, BAL
Reddy Mack, LOU	NL 23, Jocko Flynn, CHI
NL 84, Jimmy Ryan, CHI	**L—AA 34, Matt Kilroy, BAL**
AB—AA 561, Joe Werrick, LOU	NL 18, Bill Stemmeyer, BOS
NL 327, Jimmy Ryan, CHI	PCT—AA .615, Nat Hudson, STL
H—AA 140, Joe Werrick, LOU	**NL .793, Jocko Flynn, CHI**
NL 100, Jimmy Ryan, CHI	GP—**AA 68, Matt Kilroy, BAL**
2B—AA 23, Reddy Mack, LOU	NL 41, Bill Stemmeyer, BOS
NL 17, Jimmy Ryan, CHI	GS—**AA 68, Matt Kilroy, BAL**
3B—AA 14, Joe Werrick, LOU	NL 41, Bill Stemmeyer, BOS
NL 6, Jimmy Ryan, CHI	CG—**AA 66, Matt Kilroy, BAL**
HR—AA 3, Joe Werrick, LOU	NL 41, Bill Stemmeyer, BOS
NL 4, Jocko Flynn, CHI	IP—AA 583.0, Matt Kilroy, BAL
Jimmy Ryan, CHI	NL 348.2, Bill Stemmeyer, BOS
R—AA 82, Reddy Mack, LOU	H—AA 476, Matt Kilroy, BAL
NL 58, Jimmy Ryan, CHI	NL 300, Bill Stemmeyer, BOS
RBI—AA 62, Joe Werrick, LOU	BB—AA 182, Matt Kilroy, BAL
NL 53, Jimmy Ryan, CHI	NL 144, Bill Stemmeyer, BOS
WK—AA 68, Reddy Mack, LOU	K—**AA 513, Matt Kilroy, BAL**
NL 18, Jocko Flynn, CHI	NL 239, Bill Stemmeyer, BOS
SO—AA NA	ERA—AA 3.03, Nat Hudson, STL
NL 48, Frank Graves, STL	NL 2.24, Jocko Flynn, CHI
SB—AA 33, Wilbert Robinson, PHI	SHO—AA 5, Matt Kilroy, BAL
NL 11, Frank Graves, STL	NL 2, Jocko Flynn, CHI
BA—AA .250, Joe Werrick, LOU	SV—**AA 1, Bones Ely, LOU**
NL No Qualifiers*	**Nat Hudson, STL**
SLG—AA .351, Joe Werrick, LOU	**Joe Strauss, LOU/BRO**
NL No Qualifiers*	NL 1, Jim Devlin, NY
OBP—AA .342, Reddy Mack, LOU	Jocko Flynn, CHI
NL No Qualifiers*	Jimmy Ryan, CHI

*Jimmy Ryan was easily the NL rookie leader in BA (.306), SLG (.431), and OBP (.330) but had only 339 plate appearances, 52 short of the minimum for qualification.

the Nationals' novice "Bones Battery" of Frank Gilmore and Connie Mack, 5–4. He was then useless for the World Series that fall against the Association champion Browns and made only one more appearance in the majors. Hoping to find a use for Flynn's bat even if his arm was gone, Anson started Flynn in right field the following spring on May 23 in Philadelphia, but the experiment failed when Flynn "split a finger on the first ball hit to right, and retired in favor of {Dell} Darling."

Other Highlights

May 17—Matt Kilroy sports a glittering 8–2 record after beating Cincinnati 6–4 to help Baltimore get off to a 10–8 start; Kilroy will go 21–32 the rest of the way while the rest of the Orioles staff goes 17–43 to insure the club's fourth last-place finish since 1882.

May 19—Chicago's all-around rookie sensation Jocko Flynn hits his first career home run when he connects off Dupee Shaw of Providence; Flynn will not only lead all rookie pitchers in many departments but will also tie teammate Jimmy Ryan for the overall frosh lead in dingers with four.

September 22—Jocko Flynn tops Detroit 6–3 for his 14th consecutive win to set a rookie record that will stand until 1890.

September 23—Shortstop Chippy McGarr of the Philadelphia A's is the first rookie ever to hit for the cycle when he goes 4-for-5 in a 15–6 win over Nat Hudson of the St. Louis Browns.

October 6—Matt Kilroy of Baltimore puts the icing on his phenomenal rookie season when he sets Pittsburgh down without a hit, 6–0, fans 11 batters, and goes 2-for-3.

October 9—On the closing day of the NL season Boston's Bill Stemmeyer unleashes four wild pitches in a 12–3 loss to Chicago to finish with an all-time season record of 64 errant tosses.

October 9—Louisville second baseman Reddy Mack is 2-for-3 and draws his 68th walk to establish a rookie record that will last until 1888 when Washington's Dummy Hoy breaks it.

October 10—In Louisville's final championship game of the season, third sacker Joe Werrick drives in five runs with a triple and a homer, but his three errors help the Philadelphia A's to tally seven unearned runs and win 8–6.

1887

Rules makers had a field day prior to the 1887 season when officials in both major leagues licensed them to make whatever changes they deemed necessary to promote a more equitable balance between hitters and pitchers. Along with inflicting harsh restrictions on pitching deliveries, the rules in 1887, for the one and only time in big league history, hiked the number of strikes required for a strikeout from three to four and then, to further insure that batting averages would increase, counted each walk received as a base hit. The changes had the desired effect in that 1.8 more runs were scored per game, but the four-strikes and walks-as-hits rules were both quickly scrapped when the average hitter in 1887 compiled a .326 BA following three consecutive years in which the composite BA for both leagues had been below .250.

Interestingly, despite the radical rule alterations in 1887, little changed with regard to the manner in which rookies impacted the game. As was true throughout the decade of the 1880s, the contributions crafted by yearling pitchers far exceeded those of yearling hitters. That was especially true in the Association, where St. Louis romped to its third straight pennant when 19-year-old Silver King joined with Bob Caruthers and Dave Foutz to make the Browns the first team ever to showcase three 25-game winners. Meanwhile the Philadelphia Athletics, after several of their veterans suffered early-season injuries, were compelled to place virtually their entire pitching load on the shoulders of two rookies, Ed Seward and Gus Weyhing, and consequently reaped the only pair of recruit 25-game-winning teammates in history. At the other end of the continuum, cellar-dwelling Cleveland, a replacement team in the Association for Pittsburgh, had the distasteful honor of introducing a pair of rookie 25-game losers in Billy Crowell and Mike Morrison.

But if rookie hitters were unable to match their pitching counterparts in putting up gaudy numbers across the board, they excelled in one department: home runs. Novice leftfielder Mike Tiernan, with ten

Billy O'Brien, the only future National League or American Association home run king to debut in the Union Association. In a 12-game baptism in 1884, O'Brien hit just .234 and then spent most of the next two seasons in the fledgling Southern League before joining Washington in 1887. His 19 homers broke the previous rookie record of 12 belonging to Ed "Cannonball" Crane of the 1884 Boston Unions. *Transcendental Graphics*

The Philadelphia Athletics actually had three yearling pitchers on their roster at the beginning of the 1887 season. Along with Ed Seward and Gus Weyhing, owner-manager Charlie Mason took a look at Cannonball Titcomb, who had been dumped the previous year by Philadelphia's League entry after he was shelled in five straight outings. Still regarded as a rookie in 1887, Titcomb began the season third on the A's pitching depth chart, behind Seward and Al Atkinson. He won his first start on April 30 at Brooklyn, outlasting Hardie Henderson 10–9, but when he was battered by Baltimore in his next two appearances, Mason gave him his walking papers and moved Weyhing into his spot in the rotation.

Titcomb was the type of pitcher who first gave life to the legend that left-handers are wildly unpredictable. After a stint in the minors with Jersey City, he was purchased in early September 1887 by the New York Giants and did so spectacularly well, at least initially, that manager Jim Mutrie appointed him New York's Opening Day starter in 1888, ahead of the Giants' two Hall of Famers, Tim Keefe and Mickey Welch. Titcomb's popularity in New York quickly waned. By the spring of 1889, he was back in the minors, but the addition of a third major league in 1890 gave him a final chance with Rochester, a one-year guest in the Association. His last major league win, on October 11, 1890, was significant in that it was also the last win ever achieved by a major league team representing Rochester.

Titcomb's first major league win, in 1887, was no less significant. When added to the 51 games won jointly by Seward and Weyhing, it provided the 1887 Athletics with a total of 52 victories achieved by rookie pitchers, a nineteenth-century record and just one short of the all-time mark. The A's might well be tied now for the record had the game started by 14-year-old rookie hurler Fred Chapman, on July 22 against Cleveland, been played to completion. Instead the lone contest worked by the youngest player in history is on the books as an A's win by forfeit because Cleveland protested an umpire's decision and refused to continue play.

NINETEENTH-CENTURY TEAMS RECEIVING MOST WINS, SEASON, FROM ROOKIES

Rank	Team	Year	Wins	Rookie Pitchers
1	Phi–AA	1887	52	Weyhing (26), Seward (25), Titcomb (1)
2	Chi–NL	1889	48	Hutchison (16), Gumbert (16), Dwyer (16)
3	Chi–NL	1880	46	Corcoran (43), Poorman (2), Guth (1)
4	StL–UA	1884	41	Boyle (15), Hodnett (12), Werden (12), Cattanach (1), Matterson (1)
5	Bal–NL	1899	41	McGinnity (28), Howell (13)

Like Cannonball Titcomb, Gus Weyhing won his first start for the Philadelphia Athletics in 1887. Ed Seward, the third member of the A's rookie record-setting trio, did not. His initial start for the A's on April 16, Opening Day, resulted not only in an 8–3 loss to Baltimore's Matt Kilroy but in his participation in a famous first. In the opening frame, Seward was tapped for four runs and served up a gopher ball to the Orioles' sixth hitter in the order, rookie centerfielder Mike Griffin, thereupon making Griffin the first man in history to homer in his first major league plate appearance.

Oddly, that same afternoon, in Cincinnati, another rookie center fielder, White Wings Tebeau of the hometown Reds, also homered in his first at bat. The evidence that Griffin's home run preceded Tebeau's is admittedly skimpy at best, based largely on the fact that Griffin hit sixth in the order and Tebeau seventh. Otherwise, both home runs occurred in the first inning, and Baltimore and Cincinnati both batted first even though each was the home team.

What is truly remarkable, in any case, is that these two home runs, occurring on the same day and probably just minutes apart, for years were considered to have been the only two first-plate-appearance home runs prior to 1898. However, not long ago two other such four-base blows were unearthed. Here are all the first-plate-appearance home runs struck in the nineteenth century.

Name	Team	Date	Opponent	Score	Pitcher	Inning
Mike Griffin	Baltimore–AA	4/16/87	Philadelphia	8–3	Seward	1st
White Wings Tebeau	Cincinnati–AA	4/16/87	Cleveland	16–6	Pechiney	1st
Billy Gumbert	Pittsburgh–NL	6/19/90	Cleveland	9–2	Wadsworth	2nd
Joe Harrington	Boston–NL	9/10/95	St. Louis	4–8	Kissinger	2nd
Bill Duggleby	Philadelphia–NL	4/21/98	New York	14–4	Seymour	2nd*

*Grand slam, the only one ever by a player in his first ML plate appearance

Batting	Pitching
G—AA 136, Mike Griffin, BAL	W—AA 32, Silver King, STL
Tommy Tucker, BAL	NL 21, Kid Madden, BOS
NL 115, Marty Sullivan CHI	L—AA 31, Billy Crowell, CLE
AB—AA 559, Hub Collins, LOU	NL 17, Mark Baldwin, CHI
NL 472, Marty Sullivan, CHI	PCT—AA .727, Silver King, STL
H—AA 162, Hub Collins, LOU	NL .600, Kid Madden, BOS
NL 134, Marty Sullivan, CHI	GP—AA 55, Ed Seward, PHI
2B—AA 32, Mike Griffin, BAL	Gus Weyhing, PHI
NL 16, Billy O'Brien, WAS	NL 40, Mark Baldwin, CHI
3B—AA 13, Mike Griffin, BAL	GS—AA 55, Gus Weyhing, PHI
Ed McKean, CLE	NL 39, Mark Baldwin, CHI
Darby O'Brien, NY	CG—AA 53, Gus Weyhing, PHI
NL 16, Marty Sullivan, CHI	NL 36, Kid Madden, BOS
HR—AA 6, Tommy Tucker, BAL	IP—AA 470.2, Ed Seward, PHI
NL 19, Billy O'Brien, WAS	NL 334.0, Mark Baldwin, CHI
R—AA 142, Mike Griffin, BAL	H—AA 541, Billy Crowell, CLE
NL 98, Marty Sullivan, CHI	NL 329, Mark Baldwin, CHI
RBI—AA 94, Mike Griffin, BAL	BB—**AA 205, Mike Morrison, CLE**
NL 77, Marty Sullivan, CHI	NL 122, Mark Baldwin, CHI
WK—AA 60, Ed McKean, CLE	Kid Madden, BOS
NL 36, Marty Sullivan, CHI	K—AA 193, Gus Weyhing, PHI
SO—AA NA	NL 164, Mark Baldwin, CHI
NL 53, Marty Sullivan, CHI	ERA—AA 3.78, Silver King, STL
SB—AA 94, Mike Griffin, BAL	NL 3.40, Mark Baldwin, CHI
NL 35, Marty Sullivan, CHI	SHO—AA 3, Ed Seward, PHI
BA—AA .301, Darby O'Brien, NY*	NL 3, Kid Madden, BOS
NL .287, Mike Tiernan, NY	SV—AA 1, Silver King, STL
SLG—AA .437, Darby O'Brien, NY	**NL 1, done by six pitchers**
NL .492, Billy O'Brien, WAS	
OBP—AA .375, Mike Griffin, BAL	
NL .344, Mike Tiernan, NY	

*O'Brien's average of .30077 nipped Mike Griffin's .30075.

dingers, was second on the New York Giants only to the nineteenth-century career home run leader, Roger Connor, who logged 17. Another recruit left fielder, Myron Allen, led the fledgling Cleveland team in four-baggers. Still a third frosh left fielder, Darby O'Brien, topped the New York Mets not only in homers but also in hits, doubles, RBI, and total bases. And a second O'Brien, first sacker Billy of Washington, was not content just to lead his team in homers. In 1887 Billy O'Brien became the first rookie since the inception of the American Association in 1882 to top both major leagues in circuit clouts when he went deep 19 times and in the process set a frosh record that endured until 1899. A free swinger who benefited greatly from the one-year experiment with the four-strike rule, O'Brien would be history in Washington after his BA shrank to .225 in 1888 and his strikeout total jumped from 17 to 70.

Other Highlights

May 8—Cleveland's Billy Crowell beats Cincinnati 7–6 for his first win after a 0–5 start; Crowell will lose a rookie-high 31 games in 1887.

August 20—In the second game of a doubleheader, Billy O'Brien hits a walk-off home run in the bottom of the ninth inning to give Washington a 4–3 victory over Boston.

September 13—Kid Madden stands at a glittering 21–7 after beating Detroit 2–0 for his NL rookie-high third shutout; Madden will lose his last seven starts to finish at 21–14

September 15—Silver King edges Baltimore 4–2 in the second game of a doubleheader for his 30th win; King will win a rookie-high 32 games in 1887.

October 5—Kid Madden gives up five home runs, just one short of the single-game record at that time, in a 12–9 Boston loss to Washington's Jim Whitney, who himself is tapped for three round trippers.

October 6—Billy O'Brien hits his 19th and final home run of the 1887 season off Hoss Radbourn in a 6–4 Washington loss to Boston.

➤ 1888 ➤

In many ways 1888 was the most stable season during the decade of the 1880s. There was only one franchise shift, that in the Association where the New York Mets were replaced by Kansas City, and the only significant revisions on the playing field restored the three-strikes rule and did away with counting bases on balls as both an at bat and a hit. Though seemingly minor, at least on the surface, these rule adjustments once again tilted the balance heavily toward the pitchers' side of the scale, as BAs tumbled an average of 31 points and the average ERA declined correspondingly by nearly 1.25 runs per pitcher.

Given those advantages, rookie pitchers again prevailed over their hitting counterparts, much as they had in almost every season to that point. And it was also once again true that all the novice names that appeared among the loop pitching leaders in 1888 were gone within a few years. The most salient example was Gus Krock. After pacing Chicago in every major pitching department, Krock followed his 25-win frosh season with just seven more career victories. Brooklyn's Mickey Hughes, likewise a 25-game winner and multiple team leader as a yearling, finished with just 39 career victories. Lee Viau posted 27 wins for Cincinnati in 1888, followed up with another 20-win season in 1889, and then collected only 34 more victories before departing in 1892. Of the frosh pitching leaders, only

the Phillies' Ben Sanders, second in the League with a 1.90 ERA and first in shutouts, remained a solid presence in the majors for longer than two seasons though he never again approached his accomplishments as a neophyte.

Conversely, not a single member of the freshman class of 1888 graced the hitting side of the leader board in either major league. Yet the 1888 season must be regarded as perhaps the most fertile producer of outstanding future batsmen in the nineteenth century. Foremost among them, based on his rookie achievements, was Jake Beckley. Installed at first base by Pittsburgh in mid-June after being purchased from a minor league club along with pitcher Harry Staley, Beckley hit a robust .343 in his first 71 games and was threatening to lead the League in batting when he sprained an ankle on September 19, finishing him for the season. A second June purchase from the minors was Hugh Duffy, who also played just 71 games in 1888 for Chicago but already began to demonstrate the bat work that would bring him many hitting accolades in the 1890s, including his all-time record .440 BA in 1894. The last-place Kansas City Association club also dipped into the minors in midsummer to acquire outfielder Billy Hamilton. Destined to win two batting crowns in the decade ahead, Hamilton promptly displayed an equally prominent offensive talent when he stole 19 bases in his first 35 games before being shelved by an injury.

Among the rookie hitters who spent the entire 1888 season in the majors, the best overall statistics belonged to Dummy Hoy, Washington's new center fielder. The only deaf mute ever to serve as a big league regular, Hoy batted second in the order on Opening Day in a 6–0 loss to Cannonball Titcomb of the Giants but soon was promoted to the leadoff spot and thereafter led Washington in runs, walks, steals, total bases, BA, SA, and OBP.

Beckley, Duffy, and Hamilton are in the Hall of Fame for their offensive achievements, and many observers believe that Hoy also should be enshrined. All four of them, in any case, gave clear signs as freshmen that they were offensive stars in the making. There was another member of the class of 1888 who made the Hall of Fame entirely on the basis of his offensive exploits—Ed Delahanty. In point of fact, Delahanty's career batting credentials are arguably the strongest of any nineteenth-century performer. Yet, in his rookie year, he was such a bust with the Phillies as both a hitter (.228 BA) and a second baseman (44 errors in 56 games) that he lost his job to lightweight Charlie Bastian (.193 BA).

As a sophomore in 1889, Delahanty improved marginally as a hitter but continued to exhibit little hint of the power that would terrorize pitchers throughout the remainder of his career. Indeed, after his first four full seasons in the majors, Delahanty still had just nine career home runs and a .360 SA before raising his SA 145 points in his 12 remaining seasons to finish at .505.

In all of major league history, there has never been a hitter of Hall-of-Fame caliber who exhibited less promise of future greatness during his novice phase than Ed Delahanty.

Other Highlights

April 20—Kid Gleason, later the manager of the infamous Chicago Black Sox, earns the Phillies' Opening Day starting assignment and loses a 4–3 squeaker to Boston's John Clarkson; Gleason, who will pitch in hard luck all year, would lose also his second start three days later, again to Clarkson, 3–1.

April 24—Dummy Hoy, the 1888 rookie leader in runs, scores his first ML tally in Washington's fourth game of the season as the Senators collect 15 runs off two New York Giants pitchers on just seven hits but still lose 19–15 when both teams combine to surrender a total of 28 unearned runs.

May 14—After beating New York 5–1, Chicago rookie Gus Krock is off to a 5–0 start en route to leading all NL frosh with 25 wins.

June 1—Cincinnati rookie Lee Viau suffers his first loss, a 3–1 heartbreaker at Brooklyn, to end the AA rookie record eight-game winning streak with which he began his career.

June 29—After losing his first two ML starts, Phillies rookie Ben Sanders notches his first win, beating Boston 3–2; Sanders will top all NL frosh in winning percentage.

On the afternoon of June 26, 1888, a Louisville amateur with the improbable name of Hercules Burnett played right field for the local Colonels against Brooklyn and "did well" according to *Sporting Life*. While it is true that Burnett collected a walk in one of his five plate appearances and then stole second base and later scored, he actually did anything but well, muffing one of the three fly balls hit his way and fanning in all four of his other plate appearances, making him one of only three men in the nineteenth century to go down on strikes four times in their first major league games.

Burnett had to wait seven years before Louisville gave him another opportunity, and he made the most of it. In five games in 1895, he hit .412 and enjoyed one of the most sensational codas ever. On September 29 that year, in his final major league contest, Burnett went 3-for-5, including a triple, scored three runs, and then hammered a home run in his last ML at bat off lefty Phil Knell.

The last four-strikeout victim in a nineteenth-century debut game did not fare quite as well. In the morning contest of a June 17, 1889, doubleheader at their home park, the Baltimore Orioles tried recruit George Goetz in the box. Goetz fanned in all four of his at bats and was racked for six runs by Louisville but managed to escape the ninth inning with the game tied 6–6. After Baltimore scored four runs in the top of the tenth, Goetz was relieved by Bert Cunningham and then told to turn in his uniform, never to pitch again in the majors.

Somewhat amusingly, the first documented four-strikeout victim in his initial big league appearance was future evangelist Billy Sunday. After riding the Chicago bench in the early weeks of the 1883 season, Sunday finally was privileged to see his name on a lineup card for the first time on May 22 as a replacement for leftfielder Abner Dalrymple. Put in the leadoff spot, Sunday whiffed in each of his four at bats against Boston's Jim Whitney and then, as punishment, was made to sit idle again until July 4 when he got into the first game of the holiday doubleheader as a late-inning injury replacement.

July 14—Ben Sanders allows just four hits in blanking Pittsburgh for the first of his NL-leading eight shutouts in 1888.

September 20—In his ML debut with Chicago, Frank Dwyer whitewashes Washington 11–0 and allows just three hits.

October 16—On the final day of the season, Baltimore third baseman Billy Shindle has his best outing in the majors thus far, scoring two runs and going 3-for-4

Batting		Pitching	
G—AA 135, Billy Shindle, BAL		**W**—AA 27, Lee Viau, CIN	
NL 136, Dummy Hoy, WAS		NL 25, Gus Krock, CHI	
AB—AA 514, Billy Shindle, BAL		**L**—AA 29, Bert Cunningham, BAL	
NL 503, Dummy Hoy, WAS		NL 16, Kid Gleason, PHI	
H—AA 107, Billy Shindle, BAL		**PCT**—AA .659, Lee Viau, CIN	
NL 138, Dummy Hoy, WAS		NL .655, Ben Sanders, PHI	
2B—AA 14, Billy Shindle, BAL		**GP**—AA 51, Bert Cunningham, BAL	
NL 16, Walt Wilmot, WAS		NL 39, Gus Krock, CHI	
3B—AA 8, Billy Shindle, BAL		**GS**—AA 51, Bert Cunningham, BAL	
NL 9, Walt Wilmot, WAS		NL 39, Gus Krock, CHI	
HR—AA 4, Harry Lyons, STL		**CG**—AA 50, Bert Cunningham, BAL	
NL 7, Hugh Duffy, CHI		NL 39, Gus Krock, CHI	
R—AA 66, Harry Lyons, STL		**IP**—AA 453.1, Bert Cunningham, BAL	
NL 77, Dummy Hoy, WAS		NL 339.2, Gus Krock, CHI	
RBI—AA 63, Harry Lyons, STL		**H**—AA 412, Bert Cunningham, BAL	
NL 43, Walt Wilmot, WAS		NL 295, Gus Krock, CHI	
WK—AA 41, Gus Alberts, CLE		**BB**—**AA 157, Bert Cunningham, BAL**	
NL 69, Dummy Hoy, WAS		NL 73, Bill Sowders, BOS	
SO—AA NA		**K**—AA 186, Bert Cunningham, BAL	
NL 55, Walt Wilmot, WAS		NL 161, Gus Krock, CHI	
SB—AA 52, Billy Shindle, BAL		**ERA**—AA 2.13, Mickey Hughes, BRO	
NL 82, Dummy Hoy, WAS		NL 1.90, Ben Sanders, PHI	
BA—AA .208, Billy Shindle, BAL		**SHO**—AA 2, John Ewing, LOU	
NL .274, Dummy Hoy, WAS		Mickey Hughes, BRO	
SLG—AA .272, Billy Shindle, BAL		Scott Stratton, LOU	
NL .338, Dummy Hoy, WAS		**NL 8, Ben Sanders, PHI**	
OBP—AA .299, Gus Alberts, CLE		**SV**—AA No Qualifiers	
NL .374, Dummy Hoy, WAS		NL 1, Jim Tyng, PHI	

to hike his BA four points to .208; despite his lowly BA, Shindle nonetheless will lead all AA rookies in batting, slugging, and stolen bases, as the only two other AA frosh qualifiers, Cleveland's Gus Alberts and St. Louis's Harry Lyons, hit just .206 and .194, respectively.

1889

Many analysts view the 1889 season as the true inception of the game as we know it today. Much of their logic can be attributed to two rule changes. The first pared the number of called balls needed for a walk from five to four, where the figure has remained ever since. A second rule change in 1889 permitted a team to substitute for one player per game for any reason at the end of a completed inning. Modifications to this rule over the next few years would create more openings on major league rosters by paving the way for the use of relief pitchers, pinch hitters, and pinch runners. In 1889 John Montgomery Ward established yet a third link to the modern game. That year Ward was the shortstop and field captain of the defending World Series champion New York Giants by day. By night, in his capacity as the president of an early forerunner of the current players union, the Brotherhood of Professional Base Ball Players, Ward served as the clandestine organizer of a rebel circuit that he named the Players League.

But most fans in 1889 were little concerned with posterity, not when there was so much excitement on the playing fields of almost every team. For the first time, the pennant races in both major leagues went down to the final day before they were resolved.

Equally important, the two teams that emerged as winners, the New York Giants and the Brooklyn Bridegrooms, created the first "Subway" World Series. Both clubs took the standard road to the pennant, assembling lineups comprised entirely of veterans. While Brooklyn was forced to turn to rookie Joe Visner in the late going after injuries depleted its regular catching corps, the Giants succeeded in becoming the first and only team ever to capture a championship without receiving a single inning of work from a recruit participant.

Another novelty about the 1889 season rested in the fact that frosh pitchers, with the exception of Cincinnati's Jesse Duryea and St. Louis's Jack Stivetts, failed to crack the loop leader boards whereas yearling hitters were heavily represented, particularly in the Association. The Cincinnati team was exceptionally blessed. In addition to Duryea's 32 frosh wins, the Reds received stellar work from Ollie Beard, who played every inning of all 141 of the club's games at shortstop, and a spectacular output from centerfielder Bug Holliday. Indeed, Holliday's achievements rank as quite possibly the most prolific by a rookie hitter in the Association's 10-year history. His final tally included second-place finishes in SA and total bases, fifth in BA, and a tie for the Association lead in home runs with 19, a figure that also tied him with Billy O'Brien of the 1887 Washington League team for the pre-1899 rookie record.

Only slightly less laden than Cincinnati with rookie talent were the second-year Kansas City Cowboys. Frosh hurler Park Swartzel, in his only big league season, paced the club in every major pitching department except ERA, and three rookies—centerfielder Jim Burns, shortstop Herman Long and rightfielder Billy Hamilton—combined to lead the Cowboys in every important batting department. Hamilton's status as a rookie in 1889 is a matter of debate in view of the fact that he was a member of the Cowboys for 35 games the previous year and was prevented only by an injury from exceeding the 45-day freshman limit in time spent on the active roster of his club. Purists are at liberty to reject Hamilton's all-time rookie runs and stolen base records and assign the former instead to Mike Griffin, with 142 tallies in 1887, and the latter to Vince Coleman, with 110 in 1985.

In his first six seasons (1889–94), Bug Holliday tabulated 63 home runs, only two less than Roger Connor, the ML leader during that span. The following year, however, Holliday barely survived an appendectomy and was never again more than a part-time player. He finished with just 65 career dingers and the distinction of being the only performer in ML history to play in a World Series game before he played in a regular-season contest. In the 1885 Series, Chicago manager Cap Anson pressed Holliday, a St. Louis native, into service when the White Stockings found themselves short an outfielder prior to Game Four in the Mound City. *Transcendental Graphics*

By dint of a controversial forfeit loss to Brooklyn on September 8, 1889, the St. Louis Browns were prevented from capturing their fifth straight Association pennant. If the game had been played as scheduled and the Browns been victorious, they would have won the flag by a margin of two percentage points. Had that occurred, St. Louis's triumph would have been of further significance in that player-manager Charlie Comiskey broke the mold that had worked so well for him prior to 1889 and went with novice players at two key positions: shortstop and center field. Though technically not a rookie, Shorty Fuller had played just barely enough at short for a poor Washington team the previous year to sacrifice his recruit status. Slugging centerfielder Charlie Duffee was a complete neophyte, however, as was yet a third important frosh contributor to the Browns' stab at a fifth straight pennant, pitcher Jack Stivetts.

In many ways, Stivetts played the most significant role of any rookie in the two 1889 major league pennant races even though he did not join the Browns until June 26 when they were about to play their 58th game of the season. After dropping his first two starts, he was relegated to serving as the club's sparingly used third pitcher, behind its twin aces Silver King and Icebox Chamberlain, until Game 119, the nightcap of a doubleheader against Baltimore. At that point Stivetts abruptly was moved to the head of the rotation and started ten of St. Louis's final 22 games. He finished with just 12 wins despite leading the Association in both ERA and OOBP, but with only slightly more luck he could have posted 16 victories and been renowned as the rookie that spurred the Browns to their fifth straight pennant.

Instead he is largely known for setting a very unenviable frosh record. In his 20 starts, Stivetts amazingly was embroiled in four tie games, the most ever by a hurler in his rookie season. The last of the four was particularly costly, coming in Game 128 at St. Louis against a dismal Louisville team that won only 27 times in 1889.

JACK STIVETTS'S FOUR TIE GAMES, 1889

Game	Date	Location	Opponent	Score	Opposing Pitcher	Notes
85	July 29	Baltimore	Baltimore	0–0	Kilroy	7-inning game
113	September 5	Baltimore	Baltimore	6–6	Foreman	
119	September 14	Philadelphia	Philadelphia	4–4	Bausewine	*see below
128	September 28	St. Louis	Louisville	2–2	Ewing	10 innings

*St. Louis scored two runs in the top of the tenth inning off Sadie McMahon in relief of Bausewine to go ahead 6–4 before the umpire overrode the heated protests of the Browns and declared it was too dark to continue; the score reverted to what it had been after the ninth inning, 4–4.

Other Highlights

April 14—Bill Hutchison loses to Pittsburgh 8–5 on Opening Day; Hutchison is just one of three rookies Chicago manager Cap Anson will employ in 1889 in the first-ever five-man pitching rotation.

April 17—Park Swartzel beats Louisville 7–4 on Opening Day in his ML debut; Swartzel will get off to a blazing 6–1 start for Kansas City, only to lead all rookies in losses with 27.

April 17—Also in Kansas City's Opening Day game, the Missouri club's new shortstop, Herman Long, makes the first of his all-time rookie-record 117 errors.

April 24—Cincinnati's Jesse Duryea wins his first career start, beating Kansas City 7–5; within a month Duryea will be the Reds' ace pitcher after beginning the season as no better than the team's fourth starter.

April 30—Bug Holliday, Cincinnati's recruit slugging sensation, hits the first of his rookie record-tying 19 home runs in 1889; his initial victim is Kansas City rookie John McCarty.

May 2—Ad Gumbert of Chicago hits his first career home run off Bill Burdick of Indianapolis; in 1889 Gumbert will hammer five home runs while serving as a pitcher (plus two more while playing the outfield) to set an NL record for hurlers that will last until 1934 when Hal Schumacher of the Giants bangs six dingers.

September 9—Bill Hutchison, the ML rookie leader in shutouts, hurls a 0–0 tie game against Boston ace John Clarkson that is halted by darkness after seven innings;

Batting		Pitching	
G—**AA 141, Ollie Beard, CIN**		W—AA 32, Jesse Duryea, CIN	
NL 136, Patsy Tebeau, CLE		NL 17, Alex Ferson, WAS	
AB—AA 579, Jim Burns, KC		L—AA 27, Park Swartzel, KC	
NL 521, Patsy Tebeau, CLE		NL 19, George Haddock, WAS	
H—AA 181, Bug Holliday, CIN		PCT—AA .627, Jesse Duryea, CIN	
NL 147, Patsy Tebeau, CLE		NL .552, Frank Dwyer, CHI	
2B—AA 32, Herman Long, KC		Ad Gumbert, CHI	
NL 21, Bill Hallman, PHI		GP—AA 53, Jesse Duryea, CIN	
3B—**AA 15, Lefty Marr, COL**		NL 37, Bill Hutchison, CHI	
NL 8, Bill Hallman, PHI		GS—AA 48, Jesse Duryea, CIN	
HR—**AA 19, Bug Holliday, CIN**		NL 36, Bill Hutchison, CHI	
NL 8, Patsy Tebeau, CLE		CG—AA 45, Park Swartzel, KC	
R—AA 144, Billy Hamilton, KC		NL 33, Bill Hutchison, CHI	
NL 72, Patsy Tebeau, CLE		IP—AA 410.1, Park Swartzel, KC	
RBI—AA 104, Bug Holliday, CIN		NL 318.0, Bill Hutchison, CHI	
NL 76, Patsy Tebeau, CLE		H—**AA 481, Park Swartzel, KC**	
WK—AA 87, Billy Hamilton, KC		NL 319, Alex Ferson, WAS	
Lefty Marr, COL		BB—AA 127, Jesse Duryea, CIN	
NL 37, Patsy Tebeau, CLE		NL 123, George Haddock, WAS	
SO—**AA 81, Charlie Duffee, STL**		K—AA 183, Jesse Duryea, CIN	
NL 54, Bill Hallman, PHI		NL 136, Bill Hutchison, CHI	
SB—**AA 111, Billy Hamilton, KC**		ERA—**AA 2.25, Jack Stivetts, STL**	
NL 37, Jimmy McAleer, CLE		NL 3.54, Bill Hutchison, CHI	
BA—AA .321, Bug Holliday, CIN		SHO—AA 2, Jesse Duryea, CIN	
NL .282, Patsy Tebeau, CLE		Sadie McMahon, PHI	
SLG—AA .497, Bug Holliday, CIN		Jack Stivetts, STL	
NL .390, Patsy Tebeau, CLE		NL 3, Bill Hutchison, CHI	
OBP—AA .413, Billy Hamilton, KC		SV—AA 1, done by six pitchers	
NL .332, Patsy Tebeau, CLE		NL 2, Bill Bishop, CHI	

Boston will later lose the NL pennant by the margin of a single game.

October 9—Third baseman Charlie Reilly is the first and only player prior to Bob Nieman in 1951 to hit two home runs in his first ML game as he debuts by going 3-for-3 for Columbus of the American Association in a 10–4 win over Philadelphia.

1890s

1890

On November 4, 1889, less than a week after he sparked the Giants to their second straight World Series triumph, John Montgomery Ward and his war party launched the Players League and announced that it would commence operation the following spring. Ward's enterprise differed from Henry Lucas's third major league in 1884 in that, whereas Lucas's Union Association was the weakest rebel loop in history, the Players League was not only the strongest but was also far superior in 1890 to the two established circuits. The source of its strength lay in the fact that National League and American Association moguls had so thoroughly antagonized most players with their draconian bargaining tactics that Ward was able to convince almost all of the leading luminaries in both circuits to join his cause. Nevertheless, each of the eight Players League teams, with the sole exception of New York, was forced to supplement its veteran cast with at least one rookie who saw considerable duty before the season was out. The four recruits who would leave the deepest imprint on the game during the 1890s were shortstop

Tommy Corcoran of Pittsburgh; pitcher George Hemming, who split the season between Cleveland and Brooklyn; 16-year-old southpaw Willie McGill, who followed upon his 11 wins with Cleveland in 1890 to become the youngest 20-game winner ever a year later; and Brooklyn third baseman Bill Joyce, the PL leader in walks with an all-time rookie record 123. However, the rookie who had the greatest impact on the 1890 PL season was southpaw Phil Knell, a marvelous 22–11 for a Philadelphia entry that received only a composite 46–52 figure from the rest of its pitching staff.

Control problems shortened Knell's career (his 226 walks for Columbus in 1891 remain the most ever by a lefthander), but his counterpart that year in the League as the top-winning rookie, Billy Rhines of Cincinnati, parlayed his 28 victories and glittering 6.5 *Total Baseball* TPR rating into a lengthy stay in the majors. Three other rookie League hurlers from the class of 1890 enjoyed even longer and more productive tours: Kid Nichols, Cy Young, and Jesse Burkett. That Burkett, a three-time batting titlist, originally was a pitcher is generally forgotten, and Burkett himself would have preferred to forget his first outing for the Giants on April

22, 1890, when he surrendered six walks and an equal number of hits in his first two innings.

Though the Association was the only one of the three loops in 1890 to generate no rookie 20-game winners, it hardly lacked for outstanding freshmen. Actually, *Total Baseball* deems its best position player that year to have been Syracuse's frosh second baseman Cupid Childs with a 6.6 TPR. Syracuse in a normal year would probably have had the most bountiful recruit crop in the majors with Tim O'Rourke, John Keefe, Rasty Wright, and Ed Mars complementing Childs, but 1890 was not a normal year. Owing largely to the decimation at the hands of the Players League that most of the better teams suffered, the Louisville Colonels, after posting the poorest record in the majors in 1889, became the only team prior to 1991 to go from worst to first when they bagged the Association pennant. While Louisville's worst-to-first leap has since been matched several times over, the team owns three other distinctions that have never been equaled. The Colonels' four rookie regulars—leftfielder Charlie Hamburg, second baseman Tim Shinnick, first baseman Harry Taylor, and catcher John Ryan—stand as the most ever on a pennant winner. Louisville manager Jack Chapman also had the highest percentage of rookie players on his complete season roster (52 per-

In addition to Phil Knell, Billy Rhines, and Kid Nichols, there was a fourth rookie 20-game winner in the majors in 1890, Jack Luby of Chicago. His name is on the rookie leader board for the best winning percentage, but as late as August 5, 1890, no one would have bet a cent that Luby would even be on the Chicago roster at the end of the season.

Luby came to Chicago in mid-June from the Galveston club after the Texas League folded, accompanied by his catcher, Jake Stenzel. After Luby lost five of his first six starts with Stenzel handling him, Chicago player-manager Cap Anson benched Stenzel in favor of another rookie backstopper, Mal Kittridge, but the move failed to halt Luby's slide. On July 24, after sustaining a 10–4 blasting at the hands of Brooklyn, Luby was 3–9 and in grave peril of being released. Were it not for his bat (his .440 SA led everyone on the Chicago team who had at least 125 plate appearances), he almost surely would have been. Instead, Anson decided to give Luby one final chance, against the seventh-place Cleveland Spiders in the afternoon game of an August 6 doubleheader. The rest is history as Luby proceeded to reel off a rookie-record 17 straight wins. In so doing, he also became the only pitcher prior to John Tudor in 1985 to win more than two-thirds of his decisions after being as many as six games under .500. Note that of the four catchers who handled Luby during his streak, three were rookies and the fourth was his 38-year-old manager, Anson.

JACK LUBY'S 17-GAME WIN STREAK, 1890

Date	Location	Opponent	Score	Catcher	L/ Pitcher
August 6 PM	Cleveland	Cleveland	7–1	Nagle	Garfield
August 9	Pittsburgh	Pittsburgh	6–4	Kittridge	B. Gumbert
August 13	Cincinnati	Cincinnati	6–4	Nagle	Mullane
August 19 AM	Chicago	Pittsburgh	7–4	Nagle	Osborne
August 25	New York	New York	6–5	Nagle	Rusie
August 28	Philadelphia	Philadelphia	13–3	Nagle	K. Gleason
September 1 AM	Boston	Boston	4–1	Nagle	Nichols
September 5	Chicago	Cincinnati	12–8	Nagle	Dolan
September 10	Chicago	Pittsburgh	8–1	Nagle	Hecker
September 12 AM	Chicago	Cleveland	17–2	Nagle	Beatin
September 15	Chicago	Cincinnati	6–3	Nagle	Rhines
September 18 AM	Chicago	Cincinnati	8–4	Kittridge	Mullane
September 19	Chicago	Brooklyn	10–5	Nagle	Terry
September 22	Chicago	Brooklyn	14–1	Anson	Lovett
September 27	Chicago	Boston	6–2	Nagle	Getzein
September 30	Chicago	Boston	6–4	Nagle	Clarkson
October 3	Chicago	New York	3–2	Honan	Rusie

cent) of any flag team. And third, whereas the 1883 Boston League champions employed three rookies to catch every inning of every game, they were gone one better when four freshmen did all the backstopping for the 1890 Colonels.

Let's hear it for this hitherto unrecognized quartet: John Ryan, Pete Weckbecker, Ned Bligh, and Harry Taylor.

In 1890, for the only time in history, a major league team had two teenage rookie regulars who each played at least 100 games. What makes the feat even more striking is that both men actually appeared in every one of the team's 136 contests. The team was Cleveland's National League entry and its two teenage iron men were centerfielder George Davis and third baseman Will Smalley. Following the 1890 season, the pair took very divergent career paths. Davis matured into a Hall-of-Fame shortstop and at one time held a multitude of batting records by a switch-hitter. After playing every inning of every game at third base as a rookie with Cleveland, Smalley was dead from a kidney ailment barely a year later.

The two rookie teammates are in very select company. To date, only 15 teenagers have played as many as 120 games in a season, and none have done it since 1989.

TEENAGE REGULARS, SEASON, MINIMUM 120 GAMES

Name	Team	Year	Age	Games
Bob Kennedy	Chi-AL	1940	19*	154
Rusty Staub	Hou-NL	1963	19	150
Robin Yount	Mil-AL	1975	19*	147
Phil Cavarretta	Chi-NL	1935	18	146
Buddy Lewis	Was-AL	1936	19*	143
Al Kaline	Det-AL	1954	19*	138
George Davis	Cle-NL	1890	19*	136
Will Smalley	Cle-NL	1890	19	136
Cass Michaels	Chi-AL	1945	19	129
Ken Griffey, Jr.	Sea-AL	1989	19*	127
Mel Ott	NY-NL	1928	19	124
Phil Cavarretta	Chi-NL	1936	19*	124
Sibby Sisti	Bos-NL	1940	19*	123
Les Mann	Bos-NL	1913	19*	120
Jose Oquendo	NY-NL	1983	19*	120

*Starred players celebrated their 20th birthdays during the season but not until after July 1.

Other Highlights

May 8—In his ML debut, 16-year-old southpaw Willie McGill of the Cleveland PL team beats Buffalo 4–1 and in the process becomes the youngest hurler in ML history to pitch a complete game; among the Buffalo players McGill faces is Deacon White, who was playing big league ball before McGill was even born.

May 21—Kid Nichols of the Boston Beaneaters lifts his record to 3–6 when he tosses his first career shutout, edging Cleveland 1–0 in ten innings; Nichols will finish with an ML-leading seven shutouts, plus 27 wins, just one short of the rookie high in 1890.

May 22—Errors by his Cincinnati teammates cause Billy Rhines to suffer his first loss—5–4 to Brooklyn—after beginning his career with five straight wins.

June 7—In his big league debut, 20-year-old Jack McFetridge beats Brooklyn 4–1, but *Sporting Life* comments that "for all practical purposes McFetridge's trial amounted to nothing, as his father has absolutely refused to permit the boy, who is a minor, to play professional ball." *Sporting Life* proves to be right, for McFetridge will not pitch in the majors again until 1903.

September 23—George Nicol of St. Louis survives nine walks and four errors by his teammates to become the first pitcher in history to hurl a no-hitter in his ML debut when he tops the Philadelphia Athletics 21–2; because darkness shortens the game to just seven innings, Nicols's no-no is not recognized as such by ML baseball.

October 4—Boston Reds rookie Bill Daley drops his final Players League start of the season 10–6 to Pittsburgh to reduce his record to 18–7 but nonetheless paces all rookies with a .720 winning percentage.

October 13—Mike Lehane completes his rookie season having played every inning of every game at first base for Columbus of the AA; by the end of the year Lehane has been dropped from fifth to eighth in the batting order after hitting just .211 and posting a .544 OPS, the lowest ever to that point by a first baseman with at least 500 at bats.

October 15—In a doubleheader against Baltimore that draws the curtain on the 1890 AA season, rookie right-

Batting

G—**AA 140, Mike Lehane, COL**
  NL 136, George Davis, CLE
       Will Smalley, CLE
  PL 133, Bill Joyce, BRO
AB—AA 553, Harry Taylor, LOU
  NL 574, Jimmy Cooney, CHI
  PL 503, Tommy Corcoran, PIT
H—AA 170, Cupid Childs, SYR
  NL 156, Jimmy Cooney, CHI
  PL 123, Bill Joyce, BRO
2B—**AA 33, Cupid Childs, SYR**
  NL 25, Ed Mayer, PHI
  PL 18, Bill Joyce, BRO
3B—AA 15, John Sneed, TOL/COL
  NL 13, Eddie Burke, PHI/PIT
       Jesse Burkett, NY
  PL 18, Bill Joyce, BRO
HR—AA 8, Ed Cartwright, STL
  NL 7, Howard Earl, CHI
  PL 4, Tom Kinslow, BRO
R—AA 117, John Sneed, TOL/COL
  NL 114, Jimmy Cooney, CHI
  PL 121, Bill Joyce, BRO
RBI—AA 89, Cupid Childs, SYR
  NL 73, George Davis, CLE
  PL 78, Bill Joyce, BRO
WK—AA 96, Jack Crooks, COL
  NL 87, Bob Allen, PHI
  PL 123, Bill Joyce, BRO
SO—AA NA
  NL 54, Bob Allen, PHI
  PL 77, Bill Joyce, BRO
SB—AA 77, Ted Scheffler, ROC
  NL 45, Jimmy Cooney, CHI
  PL 43, Tommy Corcoran, PIT
       Bill Joyce, BRO
BA—AA .345, Cupid Childs, SYR
  NL .309, Jesse Burkett, NY
  PL .252, Bill Joyce, BRO
SLG—AA .481, Cupid Childs, SYR
  NL .461, Jesse Burkett, NY
  PL .368, Bill Joyce, BRO
OBP—AA .434, Cupid Childs, SYR
  NL .387, Steve Brodie, BOS
  PL .413, Bill Joyce, BRO

Pitching

W—AA 19, Fred Smith, TOL
  NL 28, Billy Rhines, CIN
  PL 22, Phil Knell, PHI
L—**AA 24, John Keefe, SYR**
  NL 22, Tom Vickery, PHI
  PL 11, Phil Knell, PHI
PCT—AA .594, Fred Smith, TOL
  NL .690, Pat Luby, CHI
  PL .720, Bill Daley, BOS
GP—AA 43, John Keefe, SYR
  NL 48, Kid Nichols, BOS
  PL 35, Phil Knell, PHI
GS—AA 41, John Keefe, SYR
  NL 47, Kid Nichols, BOS
  PL 31, Phil Knell, PHI
CG—AA 36, John Keefe, SYR
  NL 47, Kid Nichols, BOS
  PL 30, Phil Knell, PHI
IP—AA 352.1, John Keefe, SYR
  NL 424.0, Kid Nichols, BOS
  PL 286.2, Phil Knell, PHI
H—AA 355, John Keefe, SYR
  NL 405, Tom Vickery, PHI
  PL 287, Phil Knell, PHI
BB—AA 148, John Keefe, SYR
  NL 184, Tom Vickery, PHI
  PL 167, Bill Daley, BOS
K—AA 148, Frank Knauss, COL
  NL 222, Kid Nichols, BOS
  PL 110, Bill Daley, BOS
ERA—AA 2.81, Frank Knauss, COL
  NL 1.95, Billy Rhines, CIN
  PL 3.60, Bill Daley, BOS
SHO—AA 3, Frank Knauss, COL
       George Meakim, LOU
  NL 7, Kid Nichols, BOS
  PL 2, Bill Daley, BOS
       Phil Knell, PHI
SV—**AA 4, Herb Goodall, LOU**
  NL 1, Pat Luby, CHI
       John Taber, BOS
  PL 3, George Hemming, CLE/BRO

fielder Ted Scheffler of Rochester goes 3-for-6 and scores three runs; the two games not only spell Rochester's coda in major league competition but also Scheffler's despite his having led Rochester in runs, walks, and stolen bases.

1891

Even though the Players League's attendance figures topped those of both the National League and the American Association in 1890, by the close of the campaign most of its teams were in deep financial trouble. By cleverly disseminating a jumble of misinformation, Al Spalding and other League owners disguised the fact that many of the established teams were in even worse shape and brought John Montgomery Ward's rebel organization to its knees. The immediate casualty of the Players League war was Ward's Brotherhood, which was declawed to the extent that players' salaries were slashed in 1891 by more than 50 percent in many cases and would not reach pre-1891 levels again for another decade.

A second and equally critical casualty was the American Association. After losing one political skirmish after another with Spalding and his fellow League moguls, Association moguls, headed by St. Louis Browns' owner Chris Von der Ahe, grudgingly agreed to a December 1891 meeting in Indianapolis that resulted in the demise of the Association and the absorption of its four strongest franchises by the League to form a new 12-team circuit. For several years afterward, as a sop to Von der Ahe and other Association magnates, the loop was officially called the National League and American Association of Base Ball Clubs and carried the label "League-Association" at the head of its weekly team standings in many publications. But for all intents and purposes, the Association was dead. It left a rich legacy, however. Along with introducing Sunday play, cheaper admission prices, and the sale of alcoholic beverages in its parks, its teams launched the majority of the outstanding rookie performers who appeared during its ten-year sojourn.

The Association's swan-song campaign was no exception. While the League provided fans with two of the most prominent figures in the 12-team loop who would reign throughout the 1890s in Bill Dahlen and Joe Kelley, the Association gave first exposure to three figures who would continue to be among the game's most pivotal personages deep into the twentieth century. Each of them is in very select company in that he was ultimately enshrined in the Hall of Fame almost equally for his playing and non-playing accomplishments. In order of their appearance, the trio consisted of Clark Griffith and the two most fabled members of the legendary Baltimore Orioles' powerhouse clubs of the mid-1890s, Hughie Jennings and John McGraw.

Griffith's pitching debut came in the Browns' third game of the season on April 11 when he bested Cincinnati's 17-year-old lefty sensation Willie McGill 13–5. Some six weeks later, on June 1, Jennings played his first game at short for Louisville in a 14–5 loss to Washington's Frank Foreman; after struggling early on to find his batting eye, he finished the year as the team leader in SA. Like Louisville, Baltimore had shortstop problems in 1891 and in the early part of the season filled the hole

Four days before John McGraw made his initial appearance with Baltimore, the Orioles acquired John O'Connell, an infielder of no particular distinction, from the New England League, and gave him a brief three-game whirl at shortstop. In his first taste of big-time competition, O'Connell batted third and went 0-for-5 in a 3–2 loss to Washington rookie Ed Eiteljorge in a contest that was otherwise memorable only for the fact that it proved to be Eiteljorge's lone major league victory. O'Connell continued to play short for the next two games, including the August 26 match against Columbus when McGraw debuted for the Orioles and occupied second base. The following afternoon the two swapped positions, and O'Connell never again performed at shortstop in the major leagues.

Indeed, he played only five more Association games with the Orioles and then drifted back to the minors where he remained for nearly 11 years before resurfacing just long enough to play eight American League games for the Detroit Tigers in 1902. Apart from having been the other half of the Orioles' keystone combination in John McGraw's first major league game, O'Connell seemingly had a thoroughly insignificant career. However, he achieved something that no other big league performer will ever match.

John O'Connell is the only man to appear in a major league game in both the nineteenth and the twentieth centuries without ever playing in the National League.

Batting		Pitching	
G—AA 139, Pete Gilbert, BAL		W—AA 14, Kid Carsey, WAS	
NL 135, Bill Dahlen, CHI		Warren Fitzgerald, LOU	
AB—AA 568, Jim Canavan, CIN/MIL		Clark Griffith, STL/BOS	
NL 549, Bill Dahlen, CHI		NL 15, John Thornton, PHI	
H—AA 135, Jim Canavan, CIN/MIL		**L—AA 37, Kid Carsey, WAS**	
NL 143, Bill Dahlen, CHI		NL 16, John Thornton, PHI	
2B—AA 18, Tom Cahill, LOU		PCT—AA .609, Clark Griffith, STL/BOS	
NL 19, Frank Shugart, PIT		NL .484, John Thornton, PHI	
3B—AA 18, Jim Canavan, CIN/MIL		GP—AA 54, Kid Carsey, WAS	
NL 13, Bill Dahlen, CHI		NL 37, John Thornton, PHI	
HR—AA 10, Jim Canavan, CIN/MIL		GS—AA 53, Kid Carsey, WAS	
NL 9, Bill Dahlen, CHI		NL 32, John Thornton, PHI	
R—AA 107, Jim Canavan, CIN/MIL		CG—AA 46, Kid Carsey, WAS	
NL 114, Bill Dahlen, CHI		NL 23, John Thornton, PHI	
RBI—AA 87, Jim Canavan, CIN/MIL		IP—AA 415.0, Kid Carsey, WAS	
NL 76, Bill Dahlen, CHI		NL 269.0, John Thornton, PHI	
WK—AA 63, Larry Murphy, WAS		**H—AA 513, Kid Carsey, WAS**	
NL 67, Bill Dahlen, CHI		NL 268, John Thornton, PHI	
SO—AA 77, Pete Gilbert, BAL		BB—AA 161, Kid Carsey, WAS	
NL 60, Bill Dahlen, CHI		NL 115, John Thornton, PHI	
SB—AA 39, Tom Cahill, LOU		K—AA 174, Kid Carsey, WAS	
Tommy Dowd, BOS/WAS		NL 52, John Thornton, PHI	
NL 21, Bill Dahlen, CHI		ERA—AA 3.07, Willard Mains, CIN/MIL	
Frank Shugart, PIT		NL 3.68, John Thornton, PHI	
BA—AA .265, Larry Murphy, WAS		SHO—AA 3, Warren Fitzgerald, LOU	
NL .260, Bill Dahlen, CHI		NL 1, Bert Inks, BRO	
SLG—AA .380, Jim Canavan, CIN/MIL		John Thornton, PHI	
NL .390, Bill Dahlen, CHI		SV—AA 1, done by five pitchers	
OBP—AA .372, Larry Murphy, WAS		NL 2, John Thornton, PHI	
NL .348, Bill Dahlen, CHI			

with former lefty pitcher George Van Haltren, who was more comfortable as an outfielder. After joining the Orioles on August 26 in Columbus and going 1-for-4 in a 5–1 win over Phil Knell, McGraw manned short most of the rest of the way and then split the following season between second base and the outfield before finding his niche as perhaps the game's finest all-around third baseman during the decade of the 1890s.

Other Highlights

April 13—Jim Canavan hits his first career home run off Joe Neale of St. Louis; Canavan will lead the Cincinnati team in homers before it disbands and then will join Milwaukee, which replaces Cincinnati in the AA, and also will lead the Wisconsin club in four-baggers.

April 23—After a four-game debut with the pennant-bound Boston Reds, Tommy Dowd joins last-place Washington as a replacement at second base for the injured Fred Dunlap; for the remainder of his ten-year career, Dowd will play on a long string of last-place teams (including the worst cellar-dweller ever, the 1899 Cleveland Spiders) and will never again perform for a pennant-winner.

April 24—Kid Carsey of Washington is off to a 3–2 start after beating Philadelphia 4–2; Carsey will finish with just 14 wins and a rookie-high 37 losses while giving up a staggering total of 513 hits.

May 30—In his big league debut with Washington, Larry Murphy is installed as leadoff hitter and goes 2-for-4 with two runs; Murphy will lead all AA rookies in batting in the loop's final season, only to drop from view and remain a ghostly figure in ML annals to this day.

August 18—In the Milwaukee Brewers' first game after they replace Cincinnati in the AA, rookie George Davies celebrates his ML debut by topping the St. Louis Browns 7–2.

September 10—In Milwaukee's first home game, rookie southpaw Frank Killen cruises to a complete-game 30–3 win over Washington and scores four runs.

September 19—John Thornton of the Phillies bags his 15th and final win of the 1891 campaign in the second game of a doubleheader against Cincinnati; Thornton's 15 victories will lead all rookies, as there are no recruit 20-game winners for the first time since 1879, when ML teams still played less than 100 games.

October 4—St. Louis Browns rookie southpaw Ted Breitenstein is the first pitcher to toss a no-hitter in his first big-top start that is officially recognized by ML baseball when he shuts down Louisville, 8–0, in the first game of a doubleheader.

October 6—When Pete Gilbert plays both games at third base for Baltimore in a season-ending double-header against Washington, he becomes the only rookie in 1891 to participate in all of his club's contests; ironically, Gilbert will never again play regularly in the majors.

1892

Where there had been 24 major league teams extant at the close of the 1890 season, when the reorganized National League opened play on April 12, 1892, that number was down to only 12. Even though the substitution rules were further liberalized in the early 1890s making it imperative for each team to increase its roster size by a man or two, jobs still had shrunk by nearly 50 percent since the collapse of the Players League. The contraction, as expected, was felt most deeply by aspiring rookies. Much as had happened in 1885 when jobs also had been cut drastically, in 1892 only one recruit position player—outfielder Sam Dungan of Chicago—participated in enough games to qualify for the batting title.

But if novice hitters were scarce in the first season

In July 1891, the Cleveland Spiders bought Nig Cuppy from the Meadville, Pennsylvania, team but were in no hurry to test their new pitching acquisition and so agreed to let him finish out the season with Meadville. Cuppy continued to be held in such light regard that when he finally arrived in Cleveland, he began the 1892 season fourth on the Spiders' pitching depth chart behind Cy Young, Lee Viau, and George Davies. But Cleveland player-manager Patsy Tebeau soured on Viau after only one bad start and replaced him in the rotation with Cuppy on April 23 against Cincinnati. Cuppy won 14–5 while striking out only two batters. It was the start of a pattern that would persist throughout his career—few walks, even fewer strikeouts, and a steady diet of wins.

Among pitchers with a minimum of 200 career decisions who finished with more walks than strikeouts, Cuppy has by far the highest winning percentage. He also owns both the fewest walks and the fewest strikeouts of anyone on the Top Ten list.

Rank	Name	Years	W–L	Ks	Walks	WP
1	Nig Cuppy	1892–1901	162–98	504	609	.623
2	Rip Sewell	1932–49	143–97	636	748	.596
3	General Crowder	1926–36	167–115	799	800	.592
4	Dutch Ruether	1917–27	137–95	708	739	.591
5	Eddie Rommel	1920–32	171–119	599	724	.590
6	Guy Bush	1923–45	176–136	850	859	.564
7	Eldon Auker	1933–42	130–101	594	706	.563
8	Harry Gumbert	1935–50	143–113	709	721	.559
9	Frank Killen	1891–1900	164–131	725	822	.556
10	Earl Whitehill	1923–39	218–185	1350	1431	.541

Like Cleveland, the Baltimore Orioles commenced the 1892 season with a four-man pitching rotation comprised of three veterans and one rookie, and also like Cleveland, which received disappointing work from two of its veterans, two of the hurlers the Orioles had counted on, Charlie Buffinton and Egyptian Healy, were no longer with the team by the Fourth of July. But there the similarity ended. As can be seen from the 1892 rookie leaders board, Nig Cuppy, Cleveland's frosh box man, headed the novice hurlers class while Baltimore rookie George Cobb brought up the rear.

Cobb's numbers, though bad (10–37 and a 4.86 ERA), are not really as awful as they appear. In 1892, Baltimore was an execrable team, last in fielding as well as in wins and losses. Still, when manager Ned Hanlon conducted a postseason evaluation of his players, he could find no compelling reason to retain Cobb. Hence the rookie departed with a record that will almost certainly never again be even remotely threatened. Cobb's 37 losses, in addition to tying him for third on the all-time rookie loser list, are the most ever by a pitcher that lasted only one season.

RANK	NAME	TEAM	YEAR	LOSSES
1.	John Coleman	Phi-NL	1883	48
2.	Larry McKeon	Ind-AA	1884	41
3.	Kid Carsey	Was-AA	1891	37
	George Cobb	Bal-NL	1892	37
5.	Fleury Sullivan	Pit-AA	1884	35
	Adonis Terry	Bro-AA	1884	35
7.	Matt Kilroy	Bal-AA	1886	34
8.	Hardie Henderson	Phi-NL/Bal-AA	1883	33
	Harry McCormick	Syr-NL	1879	33
	Jim Whitney	Bos-NL	1881	33

the major league arena had been pared to just one circuit, the freshman pitching class produced an abundance of new talent. Though only Nig Cuppy of Cleveland won as many as 20 games, in the years ahead Brickyard Kennedy, Ted Breitenstein, Pink Hawley, and Jack Taylor would also help demonstrate that the 1892 rookie crop, while short on quantity, suffered no lack of quality.

In addition to experiencing a rocky first full season, which saw him notch just nine wins in 28 decisions, Breitenstein also saw his hitherto unprecedented feat of the previous year gone one better on October 15, the final day of the 1892 season, by Cincinnati's Bumpus Jones, a recent purchase from the Southern League. Whereas Breitenstein had no-hit Louisville in his first major league start, earlier in the 1891 season he had worked several games in relief, even winning one. Jones, in contrast, was making his first major league appearance when he set down Pittsburgh without a hit. Further distinguishing his exploit was that October 15 marked not only the finish of the 1892 campaign but the last time a pitcher in a regular-season game would toil from a distance of only 50 feet from home plate.

Other Highlights

April 12—Sam Dungan, the lone rookie with enough playing time in 1892 to qualify for the batting title, debuts with three hits on Opening Day as his Chicago team beats St. Louis in a 14–10 slugfest.

April 20—Hoping for his first career victory, Baltimore rookie George Cobb sees a 6–5 lead over New York end in a forfeit loss for his team when the Orioles stop play in the sixth inning so they can rush to catch a train to Boston; Cobb will thus have to wait until May 7 for his first win.

September 8—St. Louis outfielder Gene Moriarity hits his first career home run in a 7–1 win over Boston's Jack Stivetts; despite not joining St. Louis until late in the season and batting just .175, Moriarity leads all rookies in homers with three.

September 23—Shooting for his 29th win, Cleveland's Nig Cuppy blows a 6–2 lead in the last of the ninth against Louisville and, to add insult, strains his arm and is unable to pitch in the final three weeks of the season, thus falling short of what had seemed certain to be a 30-win rookie season.

September 26—Louisville lefty Fritz Clausen white-washes Chicago 11–0 to make him the lone rookie in 1892 with as many as two shutouts; Clausen's first shutout was a 0–0 five-inning tie against St. Louis on August 10.

Batting	Pitching
G—113, Sam Dungan, CHI	W—28, Nig Cuppy, CLE
AB—433, Sam Dungan, CHI	**L—37, George Cobb, BAL**
H—123, Sam Dungan, CHI	PCT—.683, Nig Cuppy, CLE
2B—19, Sam Dungan, CHI	GP—53, George Cobb, BAL
3B—7, George Decker, CHI	GS—47, George Cobb, BAL
Sam Dungan, CHI	CG—42, George Cobb, BAL
Joe Kelley, PIT/BAL	IP—394.1, George Cobb, BAL
Jack McMahon, NY	H—495, George Cobb, BAL
HR—3, Gene Moriarity, STL	BB—148, Ted Breitenstein, STL
R—46, Sam Dungan, CHI	K—159, George Cobb, BAL
RBI—53, Sam Dungan, CHI	ERA—2.51, Nig Cuppy, CLE
WK—35, Sam Dungan, CHI	SHO—2, Fritz Clausen, LOU
SO—49, George Decker, CHI	SV—1, Bert Abbey, WAS
SB—15, Sam Dungan, CHI	Nig Cuppy, CLE
John McGraw, BAL	Brickyard Kennedy, BRO
BA—.284, Sam Dungan, CHI	Ben Stephens, BAL
SLG—.360, Sam Dungan, CHI	
OBP—.346, Sam Dungan, CHI	

◄— 1893 —►

Linking an alarming decline in attendance to low-scoring games, the League-Association rules committee enacted the last major change in the geometry of the playing field by lengthening the pitching distance to 60'6" prior to the 1893 season. To further ensure that there would be an increase in hitting and scoring, hurlers were compelled to deliver the ball with their rear foot anchored to a white rubber plate 12 inches long and their front foot in contact with the ground at the point of release. Not surprisingly, the sudden imposition of these handicaps spelled the ruin of many of the game's most lustrous veteran pitchers and put an enormous stumbling block in the career paths of aspiring rookie slingers. In 1893, for only the second time since 1879, the majors did not have a recruit 20-game winner.* What's more, only three freshmen posted double-figure win totals. In addition to the leader, John Clarkson's younger brother Dad, with a dozen victories, Jack Taylor won ten games for the Phillies and Tom Parrott a like number after coming to Cincinnati in a midsummer deal with Chicago.

The offensive half of the 1893 rookie leader board

would suggest that while several freshman hitters had solid entry seasons, none could be deemed spectacular. Missing from the board, however, is the man generally considered to be the retrospective 1893 Rookie of the Year, Pittsburgh outfielder Jake Stenzel, who failed to play in enough games to qualify as the rookie batting king. Missing too is the lone Hall of Famer that emerged from the 1893 frosh harvest, Wee Willie Keeler. Splitting the season between the Giants and Brooklyn, Keeler collected only 104 at bats, just enough, when added to the 53 at bats he accumulated toward the tail end of the 1892 season, to exceed the rookie limit and spoil his opportunity to dominate the 1894 rookie leader board, as he otherwise would have done.

Ironically, Keeler was traded by Brooklyn to Baltimore over the winter for a fellow rookie outfielder, George Treadway. It was the first major exchange involving two freshman performers, and it also swiftly proved to be among the most one-sided trades ever.

Other Highlights

April 27—Washington shortstop Joe Sullivan makes his first career error on Opening Day in a 7–5 win over Baltimore; Sullivan will finish the season with 102 miscues, a new record for an NL rookie.

---

*The other season was 1891, when rookies were scarce owing to the demise of the PL.

No nineteenth-century star of the first magnitude had a more difficult time establishing that he belonged in the majors than Jake Stenzel. Part of Stenzel's problem was that he began his career as a catcher but was not a particularly good one. Further compounding his lack of progress was that he also showed little evidence, at least initially, that he could hit big league pitching.

Stenzel first surfaced in 1890 when he got into a few games with Chicago after being acquired from the disbanded Texas League along with his battery mate, pitcher Pat Luby. He then bounced around the minors for two more years before he was purchased from the Portland, Oregon, team late in the summer of 1892 by Pittsburgh. Stenzel was already past 25 when he made his debut in a Pirates uniform on September 2, 1892. He played left field, went 0-for-3, and batted last. The following day he again played left field, batted last, and went 0-for-4. Stenzel got into one more game in 1892, this time as a catcher, and then rode the bench for the rest of the season after another 0-for. He began the 1893 campaign still on the bench but received an early opportunity when George Van Haltren, the regular center fielder, was idled for several games by an injury. After Van Haltren returned to action, Stenzel went back to the bench, where he remained for most of the next two months. Finally, on July 15, he got manager Al Buckenberger's attention when he went 5-for-6 with a grand-slam homer and a triple against Washington's Jesse Duryea while subbing for rightfielder Patsy Donovan.

From that point on, Buckenberger began contriving ways to squeeze Stenzel into the lineup on a daily basis, but it was a bit too late both for Stenzel and for Pittsburgh. A strong finishing kick elevated the Pirates to second place, their highest finish since joining the National League, but still left them five games back of first-place Boston. As for Stenzel, he played in just 60 games in 1893. Nevertheless, for years early encyclopedias credited him with having won the loop batting title by dint of his stupendous .409 BA.

Careful research has since reduced Stenzel's BA to .362. In 1969 a decision was formally made to deem his 224 at bats too few even to rank him among the leaders, but his long-deferred rookie season still rates among the best frosh hitting performances ever. Beginning in 1894, Stenzel assumed his place as the fulcrum of the Pittsburgh club and one of the most dominant hitters in the League-Association. For the next three seasons, he consistently headed the Pirates in just about every offensive department including stolen bases and ranked among the best center fielders in the game. Traded to Baltimore in 1897 for Steve Brodie, Stenzel had one last outstanding season and then began to decline precipitously. Only his relatively short reign among the elite players of his time keeps him from Hall-of-Fame recognition.

1893 NATIONAL LEAGUE ROOKIE LEADERS

Batting	Pitching
G—130, Heinie Reitz, BAL	W—12, Dad Clarkson, STL
AB—508, Joe Sullivan, WAS	L—12, Bill Rhodes, LOU
H—140, Heinie Reitz, BAL	PCT—.571, Dad Clarkson, STL
2B—17, Heinie Reitz, BAL	GP—26, Tom Parrott, CHI/CIN
3B—17, George Treadway, BAL	GS—21, Dad Clarkson, STL
HR—8, Bill Lange, CHI	CG—17, Dad Clarkson, STL
R—92, Bill Lange, CHI	Bill Rhodes, LOU
RBI—88, Bill Lange, CHI	IP—186.1, Dad Clarkson, STL
WK—65, Heinie Reitz, BAL	H—244, Bill Rhodes, LOU
SO—50, George Treadway, BAL	BB—87, Tom Parrott, CHI/CIN
SB—47, Bill Lange, CHI	K—41, Jack Taylor, PHI
BA—.286, Heinie Reitz, BAL	ERA—3.48, Dad Clarkson, STL
SLG—.380, Heinie Reitz, BAL*	SHO—1, done by six pitchers
OBP—.377, Heinie Reitz, BAL	SV—2, **Tom Colcolough, PIT**
	Frank Donnelly, CHI

*Reitz at .3796 edged Lange at .3795.

May 22—Rookie home run, RBI, and stolen base leader Bill Lange of Chicago hits his first career round tripper in a 10–5 loss to Cleveland's Cy Young.

August 15—Bill Rhodes of Louisville is released after dropping his final start to Chicago 11–6 and allowing 18 hits; Rhodes finishes with a 7.60 ERA, the highest in history by a rookie ERA qualifier who pitched in the majors only one season.

September 3—Former Northwestern star Frank Donnelly wins his third straight start for Chicago, beating Baltimore 9–8, but needs last-minute relief help from teammate Fritz Clausen when he is so winded after hitting a triple in the top of the ninth that he immediately gives up two runs in the bottom half of the inning.

September 8—Cleveland's Jack Scheible is the first hurler to toss a shutout at the new pitching distance in his big league debut when he blanks Washington 7–0 and scatters just six hits; the groundbreaking effort proves to be Scheible's lone win in majors.

◄ 1894 ►

In 1893 the three worst teams in the 12-club League-Association were St. Louis, Louisville, and Washington, in that order. St. Louis and Louisville then took turns finishing last for the next five years whereas the Washington Nationals began a slow but steady climb to semi-respectability that culminated in a tie for sixth place in 1897. Much of the reason for the Nationals' relative success in comparison to their two fellow bottom-feeders could be traced to their superiority in assessing rookie talent. As but one example, on June 15, 1893, in a game at Boston, the Browns mustered only six hits in a 5–1 loss to Harry Staley, but three of the safeties were notched by rightfielder Jimmy Bannon in his very first major league game. Despite his 3-for-3 debut, Bannon played only sparingly for the rest of the season and then was let go by St. Louis even though he finished with a .336 BA in 26 games. Unable to believe his luck, Boston manager Frank Selee snatched up Bannon as a replacement for fading veteran Cliff Carroll and merrily watched his new acquisition rule the hitting half of the rookie leader chart in 1894.

Meanwhile, late in the 1893 season, the Nationals hired leftfielder Charlie Abbey and remained calm when he got off to a horrendous start, going hitless in his first three games. Their patience was rewarded in 1894, as Abbey led the team in hits and joined with Win Mercer, Bill Hassamaer, and Kip Selbach to make the nation's capital home to the finest rookie yield of any team that season.

As for the Louisville Colonels, with one notable exception, in 1894 they continued to demonstrate that they were among the poorest organizations ever at judging players. The previous year Louisville's chief rookie contributor had been Bill Rhodes, a pitcher whose main distinction apart from his horrendous 7.60 ERA was that in his second appearance with the team, on June 18, he surrendered 14 runs in the first inning and 32 hits altogether in a 30–12 loss to Cincinnati. In 1894, the greatest offensive year ever, when the average player (pitchers included) batted a gaudy .310, Louisville skipper Billy Barnie chose as his regular at first base, a position usually reserved for one of the top hitters on the team, rookie Lute Lutenberg, who hit .192 and achieved a *Total Baseball* OPS+ rating of 34, the lowest ever by a first-string first sacker. In the same package with Lutenberg, who was acquired in late June from the Memphis club after the Southern League disbanded, came outfielder Ollie Smith. Smith got into just 39 games for Louisville even though he led the team with a .855 OPS. Then, at the end of the season, the Colonels tossed the baby out with the bathwater, releasing Smith as well as Lutenberg.

But while we will never know what kind of player Ollie Smith might have become if his skills had received a full test, we do know all that is necessary about the skills of another outfielder that Louisville picked up on the cheap when the Southern League collapsed. Making his first appearance on June 30 after traveling northward from the Savannah team, Fred Clarke promptly went 5-for-5 in a 13–6 loss to Gus Weyhing of the Phils. Although he hit just .262 the rest of the season, Clarke played while Smith for the most part sat. Since Clarke eventually put together a 21-year career that culminated in a plaque at Cooperstown, it would be unfair to say that Barnie and the entire Colonels' organization never got it right when it came to evaluating rookies. It was just that prior to 1897, when a second rookie that was destined to be a future Hall of Famer arrived in Louisville, one Honus Wagner, they almost always got it wrong.

Win Mercer is generally viewed to have been the retrospective 1894 Rookie of the Year. An excellent argument can even be mounted that he had one of the finest recruit seasons in the nineteenth century if not in all of history. What is so amazing is that such a strong case can be made for a pitcher who lost his first eight starts in the majors and was further involved in two other maulings as a reliever, putting him on the losing side in every one of his first ten hill appearances. To add insult, in those ten games Mercer was 0-for-27 at the plate. On May 29, at Washington, he finally got off the schneid in both columns when he earned both his first win and his first hits, going 2-for-4 in a 12–2 triumph over Louisville. The victory represented not only a twin first for Mercer but also broke a 17-game Washington losing streak that had buried the Nationals deep in the cellar with a 3–25 start.

From that point on, Washington played .404 ball to push Louisville into the basement, and Mercer went 17–13 to lead the team in every pitching department including saves. He also overcame his 0-for-27 start to finish at .291 by collecting 48 hits in his remaining 137 at bats for a torrid .350 pace. The remainder of Mercer's nine-year career was uneven and ended tragically when he committed suicide in January 1903, reportedly after an unhappy love affair. His career highlight came on August 31, 1896, when he beat Chicago's Danny Friend 1–0 in 11 innings for Washington's first shutout win since September 17, 1893. That year, Mercer was 25–18 and the rest of the Nationals' staff went 33–55.

Other Highlights

April 19—Boston's rookie batting sensation Jimmy Bannon garners two hits and three runs against Brooklyn on Opening Day "but showed that he had much to learn to cover right field . . . in the face of the sun" in his home park by making two errors.

May 22—Jimmy Bannon slugs the first of his rookie-leading 13 home runs; his victim is the NL's best pitcher in 1894, Amos Rusie.

June 22—Win Mercer is 2-for-5 and scores two runs before allowing Mike Sullivan to take his place in the box and finish Washington's 26–12 rout of Boston.

June 27—Huyler Westervelt of the Giants records the only shutout by a rookie in 1894 when he blanks St. Louis 11–0 at the Browns' Sportsman's Park home.

August 31—In his only ML game, Washington's Bill Wynne fans two batters before being relieved in the ninth inning of an 11–5 loss to Philadelphia after giving up ten hits, eight walks, and six earned runs; Wynne's performance, bad as it is, makes him the lone pitcher on the Washington staff to fan as many as two batters per game, as his team sets a post-1893 record low for pitcher strikeouts, with just 190 in 132 games, led by rookie Win Mercer with 72.

1894 NATIONAL LEAGUE ROOKIE LEADERS

Batting	Pitching
G—129, Charlie Abbey, WAS	W—17, Win Mercer, WAS
AB—523, Charlie Abbey, WAS	L—23, Win Mercer, WAS
H—166, Jimmy Bannon, BOS	PCT—.425, Win Mercer, WAS
2B—33, Bill Hassamaer, WAS	GP—50, Win Mercer, WAS
3B—18, Charlie Abbey, WAS	GS—39, Win Mercer, WAS
HR—13, Jimmy Bannon, BOS	CG—30, Win Mercer, WAS
R—130, Jimmy Bannon, BOS	IP—339.1, Win Mercer, WAS
RBI—114, Jimmy Bannon, BOS	H—445, Win Mercer, WAS
WK—63, Charlie Irwin, CHI	BB—126, Win Mercer, WAS
SO—42, Jimmy Bannon, BOS	K—72, Win Mercer, WAS
SB—47, Jimmy Bannon, BOS	ERA—3.85, Win Mercer, WAS
BA—.336, Jimmy Bannon, BOS	SH—1, Huyler Westervelt, NY
SLG—.514, Jimmy Bannon, BOS	SV—3, Win Mercer, WAS
OBA—.414, Jimmy Bannon, BOS	

September 29—Jimmy Bannon finishes the season as he began it, going 2-for-4 in Boston's 7–6 win over Pittsburgh in the closing game for both teams.

September 30—Late-season addition Jake Boyd ends Washington's 1894 campaign with his third straight double-digit defeat when he loses 10–4 to St. Louis; Boyd will finish two years later with a 7.02 career ERA and just three wins in 19 decisions.

— **1895** —

A cursory scan of the 1895 rookie roll generates an impression that it was an average year in that only two class members—Jimmy Collins and Bobby Wallace—are currently in the Hall of Fame. However, the leader board belies that notion. In reality, it can be argued that the 1895 season yielded the two most outstanding rookie achievements of the post-1893 era.

Bill Everitt, with his .358 mark with Chicago, for well over a century now has held the record for the highest BA since 1893 by a rookie with no previous major league experience. While Everitt's record may one day be broken, Baltimore's great yearling pitching star, Bill Hoffer, almost undoubtedly will always remain the post-1893 rookie record-holder for the most wins. In addition, Hoffer's percentage of .838, derived from a 31–6 won-lost total, will perhaps also always stand as the highest winning rate by a rookie pitcher involved in a minimum of 25 decisions.

Between them, Everitt and Hoffer shattered so many frosh records that they dwarfed the performances of all the other yearling hitters and pitchers in 1895, but interestingly each of them had a recruit teammate that also achieved some rather remarkable records. Part of Hoffer's supporting cast in Baltimore was fellow recruit Scoops Carey, a poor hitter, particularly for a first baseman, but an excellent fielder. The good-field no-hit combination manufactured a fielding title for Carey in his rookie season along with the record for the fewest runs (59) by a regular position player (100 games minimum) on a team that scored as many as 1,000 runs. Carey put in only one other season as a major league regular, in 1902 with Washington of the American League. When he again posted his loop's top fielding average, he emerged as the only man ever to lead two different major leagues in FA in the only two seasons he played enough to be eligible for a glove crown.

In 1895 Chicago unveiled two new infield regulars, Everitt at third base and Ace Stewart at second base. On Opening Day, at St. Louis, Stewart collected only one hit, but it was a home run. For the next four months, he continued to average around one hit a game, keeping his BA in the vicinity of .250 but all the while exhibiting exceptional power. In mid-August, even though Stewart was leading Chicago in both home runs and RBI, he was suddenly released, ostensibly because he clashed once too often with the club's prickly player-manager, Cap Anson. Stewart never played another game in the majors. For many years his eight home runs remained the most by anyone who played only one ML season, and his 76 RBI are still the most ever by a National League or American League One Year Wonder.

Save for their intriguing records, Carey and Stewart are otherwise unmemorable. Strangely, Hoffer and

A .377 season in 1894 with Detroit of the Western League earned Bill Everitt a shot at Chicago's third-base slot the following season. Everitt (who frequently appeared in box scores as "Everett") proceeded to set several rookie records when he hit .358 for the Colts. Three years later he replaced long-time fixture Cap Anson at first base in Chicago. *Transcendental Graphics*

After notching 31 wins as a rookie, Bill Hoffer netted just 61 more victories to finish with 92 total. Nonetheless, he ranks second in career wins among pitchers who celebrated their official rookie seasons in 1895. Solidly in first place, with 204, is Al Orth. Some early-day record books listed Orth, rather than Hoffer, as the loop winning-percentage champ in 1895 with .889, but Hoffer is now universally considered the leader because Orth was involved in only nine decisions. Just the same, Orth's 8–1 won-lost record stood alone among post-1893 rookie starting pitchers until Howie Krist bettered it in 1941 by going 10–0.

Two features of Orth's frosh season bear scrutiny. First off, Orth did not lose his first game until his final start of the season and actually, with just a tad more luck, could have been 9–0 prior to his initial loss. Secondly, in his first nine mound appearances, Orth had already had more luck than some pitchers have in an entire career.

As a teenager in Danville, Indiana, Orth got to know Danville's proudest son at the time, outfielder Sam Thompson of the Phillies. The friendship paid off for Orth when Thompson urged the Phils to purchase him from the Lynchburg minor-league team in the summer of 1895. Orth made his Phils' debut on August 15 at Philadelphia when he worked the last two innings in relief of a 23–9 blowout win over the New York Giants in which the Phils racked up 26 hits. It was but a small taste of the kind of offensive barrage Orth was to enjoy from that point on just about every time he stepped on the mound. Here, in detail, are his ten starts in his rookie season.

AL ORTH'S TEN STARTS IN ROOKIE SEASON, 1895

Date	Opponent	Score	Phillies Hits
August 17	Boston	17–7	21
August 23 PM	Louisville	12–3	15
August 28	Chicago	5–3	9
September 2	Pittsburgh	13–7	17
September 7	Louisville	9–2	15
September 10 AM	Louisville	11–5	24
September 14 AM	Washington	21–9	23
September 20	Washington	15–6	27
September 24	Baltimore	7–7	12
September 28 AM	Brooklyn	3–6	9

In just one of Orth's first nine starts did the Phils fail to support him with less than a dozen hits. His luck finally ran out at Baltimore on September 24. Leading Sadie McMahon 7–6 with two out in the ninth inning, Orth was on the verge of launching his career with nine straight wins, only to see victory suddenly slip away when Phils first sacker Jack Boyle dropped shortstop Joe Sullivan's throw to allow Willie Keeler to score the tying run. Minutes later the game was halted by darkness. The following Saturday, in the first game of a doubleheader, Orth not only sustained his first loss but received so little support that he would have been shut out 6–0 were it not for a pinch double in the ninth inning by fellow Danville native, Sam Thompson.

1895 NATIONAL LEAGUE ROOKIE LEADERS

Batting	Pitching
G—133, Bill Everitt, CHI	W—31, Bill Hoffer, BAL
AB—550, Bill Everitt, CHI	L—19, Mike McDermott, LOU
H—197, Bill Everitt, CHI	PCT—.838, Bill Hoffer, BAL
2B—21, Scoops Carey, BAL	GP—41, Bill Hoffer, BAL
3B—14, John Anderson, BRO	GS—38, Bill Hoffer, BAL
HR—9, John Anderson, BRO	CG—32, Bill Hoffer, BAL
R—129, Bill Everitt, CHI	IP—314.0, Bill Hoffer, BAL
RBI—88, Bill Everitt, CHI	H—296, Bill Hoffer, BAL
WK—41, Billy Clingman, PIT	BB—124, Bill Hoffer, BAL
SO—43, Billy Clingman, PIT	K—80, Bill Hoffer, BAL
SB—47, Bill Everitt, CHI	ERA—3.21, Bill Hoffer, BAL
BA—.358, Bill Everitt, CHI	SHO– 4, Bill Hoffer, BAL
SLG—.444, John Anderson, BRO	SV—3, Ernie Beam, PHI
OBA—.399, Bill Everitt, CHI	

Everitt never were able to build substantial careers out of their dazzling rookie exploits either. Both were only marginal big leaguers by the end of the nineteenth century and gone altogether by the close of the 1901 season.

Other Highlights

April 19—Jimmy Collins, the only third baseman who began his career prior to 1901 to make the Hall of Fame primarily for his playing accomplishments, plays his first major league game, collecting two doubles and two runs in the Boston Beaneaters' Opening Day victory over Washington; unable to dislodge incumbent Boston star Billy Nash at third base in 1895, Collins plays right field in his debut.

May 20—Ace Stewart hits a grand slam for the Chicago Colts in their 24–6 pasting of the Philadelphia Phillies; Stewart also nets a triple, single, and stolen base while his fellow rookie teammate Bill Everitt goes 4-for-6, scores five times, and steals a base.

May 22—Bobby Wallace, a future Hall-of-Fame shortstop but a pitcher as a rookie, tosses a three-hitter as the Cleveland bests Brooklyn 8–0.

July 1—Bill Hoffer goes 4-for-4 with a run as the Orioles, behind Hoffer, top the Washington Senators 13–3.

September 10—Joe Harrington homers in his first major league plate appearance but Boston loses to St. Louis 8–4; Harrington is 3-for-4 with two runs in his debut in the show.

September 18—Cozy Dolan throws his second shutout of the month for Boston; it is the first time the vaunted Orioles are held scoreless in 1895.

September 20—Doc Parker and the Chicago Colts top St. Louis 4–0; it is the fifth time the Browns have been blanked by a rookie pitcher in 1895.

September 21—Bill Hoffer tosses his rookie-leading fourth shutout of the year, blanking Brooklyn 4–0 on five hits.

September 27—John Anderson hits a grand slam for Brooklyn in the bottom of the ninth to tie the Bridegrooms' game with Philadelphia at 14–14; the game is then called at the end of the inning, meaning that if Anderson hadn't connected Brooklyn would have lost.

1896

By 1896 pitchers had begun to recover from the colossal handicaps that were imposed on their craft prior to the 1893 season. Their gains were reflected in a sharp reduction in the number of runs scored. Whereas nine of the 12 League-Association teams had tallied at least 900 runs in 1894 and a record five had scored over 1000, in 1896 only Baltimore, in the process of capturing its third straight pennant, notched as many as 900 runs. Yet pitchers for the most part were still a long way from catching up to hitters. As but one illustration of the difference between pre- and post-1893 conditions, prior to 1893 rookie 20-game winners were bountiful, but in the first four years after the pitching distance was lengthened, Bill Hoffer, Baltimore's record-setting 31-game winner in 1895, was the lone frosh to attain the charmed circle.

But if there were no yearling 20-game winners in 1896, there were a host of torrential losers. Red Donahue dropped 24 of 31 decisions with the 11th-place St. Louis Browns but was only the third heaviest rookie loser in the loop. Even more luckless than Donahue were two members of the last-place Louisville Colonels, Chick Fraser and Bill Hill. Between them, Fraser and Hill came out on the short end of the score 55 times in their 76 combined decisions. When their losses are added to the eight the club's four other freshman hurlers suffered, the resulting total of 63 confers upon the 1896 Louisville Colonels a post-1893 record for the most defeats sustained by rookie arms that lasted until 1902.

Somewhat ironically, one of those 63 defeats belonged to Tom McCreery, the only rookie to pace the League-Association in a major batting department in 1896. McCreery actually arrived in Louisville late in the 1895 season and took the town by storm when he won three of his first four decisions and served as a hard-hitting outfielder between pitching assignments. Perhaps more than any other player in history, McCreery points out the difficulty in applying rookie eligibility standards that were instituted fairly late in the twentieth century to nineteenth-century performers, who often doubled as both pitchers and position players, especially early in their careers. In 1895 McCreery logged 48.2 innings pitched and nearly 120 plate appearances, short of the allowable maximums on both counts and so leaving him technically still a rookie when the 1896 season commenced. In any event, in his official rookie season McCreery paced the entire loop as well as all other novice hitters in triples.

Vying with McCreery for honors as the leading luminary of the 1896 freshman class were two other members of second-division teams, shortstop Gene DeMontreville of Washington and Brooklyn gardener Fielder Jones. Like McCreery, both men stood tall not only among rookie hitters but also on their own teams. Each of the three topped his club in BA, and McCreery in addition finished third in the League-Association in SA with a sterling .546 figure.

Other Highlights

April 17—Doc McJames goes 4-for-5 in beating the New York Giants 14–6 while his rookie Washington battery mate, Pat McCauley, hits a three-run homer.

May 5—Herm McFarland of Louisville hits the only grand slam by a rookie in 1896; the shot comes in the second inning of the Colonels' 15–11 victory over the New York Giants' Dad Clarke.

July 2—Fielder Jones has his third four-hit game for Brooklyn in a three-week span, this time against Philadelphia, helping fellow rookie Harley Payne to beat the Phillies 4–3.

August 12—Brooklyn's Harley Payne pitches a two-hit shutout against pennant-bound Baltimore, winning 3–0.

August 22—Nap Lajoie has his first big day in the majors, going 4-for-5 with a double, triple, and two runs as Philadelphia rips hapless St. Louis 9–1.

September 5—Billy Hulen, the last lefty to serve as a regular ML shortstop, is 4-for-4 with a triple and three runs as Philadelphia topples Chicago 10–5.

October 8—Joe Corbett, brother of the heavyweight boxing champ at that time, Gentlemen Jim Corbett, becomes the first rookie to throw a postseason shutout at the 60'6" distance and gets three hits in his own cause as the Orioles win 5–0 to complete a sweep of Cleveland in the Temple Cup Series.

1896 NATIONAL LEAGUE ROOKIE LEADERS

Batting	Pitching
G—**133, Gene DeMontreville, WAS**	W—18, Danny Friend, CHI
AB—533, Gene DeMontreville, WAS	L—28, Bill Hill, LOU
H—183, Gene DeMontreville, WAS	PCT—.667, Arlie Pond, BAL
2B—24, Gene DeMontreville, WAS	GP—43, Chick Fraser, LOU
3B—**21, Tom McCreery, LOU**	Bill Hill, LOU
HR—8, Gene DeMonteville, WAS	GS—39, Bill Hill, LOU
R—94, Gene DeMontreville, WAS	CG—36, Chick Fraser, LOU
RBI—77, Gene DeMontreville, WAS	IP—349.1, Chick Fraser, LOU
WK—66, Billy Lush, WAS	H—396, Chick Fraser, LOU
SO—**58, Tom McCreery, LOU**	BB—**166, Chick Fraser, LOU**
SB—28 Gene DeMontreville WAS	K—104, Bill Hill, LOU
Billy Lush ,WAS	ERA—3.39, Harley Payne, BRO
BA—.354, Fielder Jones, BRO	SHO—2, Harley Payne, BRO
SLG—.546, Tom McCreery, LOU	Arlie Pond, BAL
OBP—.427, Fielder Jones, BRO	SV—2, Bill Hill, LOU

While it is certainly arguable whether or not Tom Mc-Creery's exceptional hitting achievements in 1896 should be treated as those of a rookie, there is no dispute as to what rookie, in the long view, was the best hitter to surface that season. On August 12, in a home game against Washington, Phillies player-manager Billy Nash, seeking a replacement at first base for ailing and aging Dan Brouthers, wrote the name Lajoie on a major league lineup card for the first time. After an inauspicious 1-for-5 debut, Nap Lajoie went on a hitting rampage for the remainder of the season that put him second in the final team statistics only to Ed Delahanty, the loop's top all-around batsman.

Owing to his late start, Lajoie fell short of the requisite number of plate appearances to qualify as a leader in any of the rookie batting departments, but he finished with well above the amount needed to rank at the head of the list seen below. Here are the top ten slugging averages among nineteenth-century rookies who collected at least 100 at bats but failed to have enough to qualify as a loop or rookie leader.

Name	Year	AB	BA	SA
Nap Lajoie	1896	175	.326	.543
Oyster Burns	1884	138	.290	.536
Buck Freeman	1898	107	.364	.523
Mike Grady	1894	190	.363	.516
Ducky Holmes	1895	161	.373	.516
Jake Stenzel	1893	224	.362	.509
Joe Sugden	1894	139	.331	.496
Emil Gross	1879	132	.348	.492
Dell Darling	1887	141	.319	.489
Jesse Hoffmeister	1897	188	.309	.484

◄ 1897 ►

The Baltimore Orioles opened the 1897 campaign as prohibitive favorites to win their fourth consecutive League-Association pennant, especially after manager Ned Hanlon bagged centerfielder Jake Stenzel in a trade with Pittsburgh and talked the Phillies out of Jerry Nops, a promising southpaw curveball artist, late in the 1896 season. But even though Stenzel slammed .353 and the rookie Nops teamed with Baltimore's 1895 frosh sensation Bill Hoffer, the Orioles' 1896 rookie whiz Arlie Pond, and Joe Corbett, a staff-leading 24-game winner in his first full big league season, to give Hanlon a four-man rotation that was a collective

None of the three future Hall of Famers that made their first big league appearances in 1897 can be found on the rookie leaders chart. In each case the reason is the same: a late arrival. Honus Wagner did not join Louisville until July 19 when the season was more than half over. In his first game he played center field, went 1-for-2, and became an almost immediate fixture in the Falls City but never, oddly, at shortstop. Some six weeks later, on September 8, Rube Waddell took the mound for the first time, also for Louisville, in a game at Baltimore and lost 5–1 to Jerry Nops. Significantly, Waddell's catcher that day was Ossee Schrecongost, who was also making his major league debut. The pair would not work together again until 1902 when Waddell was bought by the American League Philadelphia A's, at which point they swiftly formed one of the most famous batteries in history.

The third future Hall of Famer fared much better than Waddell in his hill debut with Washington. On August 27, freshly arrived in the nation's capital from the Lima, Ohio, club, he whitewashed St. Louis 3–0 while giving up just six hits. He then went on to win all the rest of his decisions to finish the season a perfect 4–0 and actually, by rights, ought to have been 5–0—or even 6–0, in the sense that his team won every one of the six games he started.

Forty-eight years later he was enshrined at Cooperstown even though he never won another game in the majors. His name was Roger Bresnahan.

Here is a log of Bresnahan's sizzling pitching performance in 1897. Note that although record books credit him with appearing in only six games that year, he actually pitched in seven.

ROGER BRESNAHAN'S PITCHING RECORD, 1897

Date	Opponent	Pitcher(s)	Score
August 27	St. Louis	Sudhoff	3–0
September 2	Pittsburgh	Tannehill–Hughey	5–6*
September 6	Louisville	Fraser	7–3**
September 8	Cleveland	Young	Forfeit***
September 11	Cincinnati	Dwyer	8–4
September 18	Brooklyn	Fisher–Payne	10–9
October 2	Baltimore	Amole	6–3****

*Relieved Win Mercer, who was ejected for abusive language; Mercer took the loss.
**7-inning game
***Led Cleveland 6–2 after four innings when umpire Carpenter forfeited the game to Washington after Cleveland manager Tebeau refused to continue following a dispute whether Ed McKean was hit by a pitch; all stats from the game, including what would have been Bresnahan's third major league start, were subsequently erased.
****Relieved by Cy Swaim after he gave up three runs in the second inning; Swaim got the win.

82–33, the League-Association produced a new champion in 1897 when the Boston Beaneaters edged out the Orioles at the wire by a two-game margin.

There are a number of reasons that Boston won, but one of the most salient is that while the Orioles received strong contributions from their new club members, the Beaneaters got even more extraordinary production out of their 1897 neophytes. Rookie rightfielder Chick Stahl led Boston in both BA and SA as he hit .354 to Stenzel's .353, and rookie right-hander Ted Lewis won 21 games to Nops's 20 while Fred Klobedanz, in his first full season with Boston, posted two more victories than his counterpart in Baltimore, Joe Corbett.

Nops and Lewis, as the first two 20-game-winning rookies at the new pitching distance apart from Hoffer in 1895, would herald a gradual return in the next few years to the pre-1893 climate when recruit mound sensations abounded. Stahl meanwhile would continue an odd tradition started by Jimmy Bannon in 1894 and furthered by both Bill Everitt in 1895 and Tom Mc-Creery in 1896. Each of the four, after emerging as the game's most outstanding frosh hitter in his rookie season, failed ever again to match his recruit stats.

Another rookie who would prove an even bigger disappointment after his splendid debut in 1897 was Cleveland outfielder Louis Sockalexis. Ten years earlier the Cleveland Association team had featured the first American Indian player in major league history, Jim Toy, but Toy had possessed limited talent whereas Sockalexis gave every appearance, at least initially, of curing a perennial ailment in Cleveland during the 1890s—the glaring lack of an outfielder who could hit with power. Problems with alcohol truncated Sockalexis's career, however, after a fine start. In contrast, a pair of Cleveland's rookie lesser lights, pitcher Jack Powell and catcher Lou Criger, would evolve into two of the most enduring members of the class of 1897.

Other Highlights

May 1—Louis Sockalexis collects four hits, including a bases-loaded triple, as Cleveland beats St. Louis 8–3.

May 17—Jerry Nops holds the Louisville Colonels scoreless while he singles, doubles, and scores a run in the Baltimore Orioles' 5–0 triumph.

June 29—Nixey Callahan goes 5-for-7 with two doubles and four runs and pitches Chicago to a 36–7 annihilation of the Colonels; rookie second baseman Jim Connor scores four times and has four hits for the Colts.

July 30—John Houseman goes 4-for-4 and participates in a triple play at second base for the Browns, which beat Louisville 7–6.

August 20—Jack Powell whitewashes mighty Baltimore 5–0 for Cleveland; the Orioles, who will lead the Na-

1897 NATIONAL LEAGUE ROOKIE LEADERS

Batting	Pitching
G—114, Chick Stahl, BOS	W—21, Ted Lewis, BOS
AB—469, Chick Stahl, BOS	L—18, Jack Fifield, PHI
H—166, Chick Stahl, BOS	PCT—.769, Jerry Nops, BAL
2B—30, Chick Stahl, BOS	GP—38, Ted Lewis, BOS
3B—13, Chick Stahl, BOS	GS—34, Ted Lewis, BOS
HR—4, Chick Stahl, BOS	CG—30, Ted Lewis, BOS
R—112, Chick Stahl, BOS	IP—290.0, Ted Lewis, BOS
RBI—97, Chick Stahl, BOS	H—316, Ted Lewis, BOS
WK—56, Phil Geier, PHI	BB—125, Ted Lewis, BOS
SO—NA	K—69, Jerry Nops, BAL
SB—23, Dick Harley, STL	ERA—2.81, Jerry Nops, BAL
BA—.354, Chick Stahl, BOS	SH—2, Ted Lewis, BOS
SLG—.499, Chick Stahl, BOS	Jack Powell, CLE
OBA—.406, Chick Stahl, BOS	SV—1, Charlie Hickman, BOS
	Ted Lewis, BOS
	Jesse Tannehill, PIT

tional League with a .325 team batting average, manage but five singles.

August 25—Bill Magee shuts out the pennant-bound Beaneaters in the second game of a doubleheader as Louisville wins 11–0; Honus Wagner doubles twice and scores once for the Colonels.

September 8—Rube Waddell goes the distance in his first big league game for Louisville but falls to the Orioles' Jerry Nops, 5–1.

September 11—Jake Gettman is 5-for-5 and scores three times, but Washington loses to Cincinnati 19–10 in the opener of a twin bill; Gettman then singles in his first at bat of the nightcap, extending his streak to ten straight ABs with a hit but is stopped his next time up; Gettman's skein is still tied for the National League record.

1898

The close of the 1897 season found two teams that had been among the League-Association's top clubs earlier in the decade lurking near the bottom. In Cap Anson's final season as Chicago's player-manager, the Windy City entry suffered its worst finish since 1877 when it plummeted to ninth place in the 12-team circuit. Meanwhile George Stallings, later to win acclaim as "The Miracle Man" for piloting the 1914 Boston Braves to a surprise pennant, could do no better than bring the Philadelphia Phillies home tenth in his final full season at their helm. Both clubs regained the first division in 1898 thanks largely to their successful commitment to a youth movement.

Chicago's rookie explosion occurred late in the campaign. On September 17, with the Cubs (then known as the Colts) locked in a four-way battle for fourth place, pitcher Bill Phyle arrived from St. Paul, which functioned unofficially as a Chicago farm team that year, and blanked Washington 9–0. Some three weeks later, on October 9, Phyle whitewashed St. Louis 2–0 while allowing just one hit. In the interim, between Phyle's two shutout gems, the Colts brought aboard a rookie trio comprised of third baseman Harry Wolverton, catcher Art Nichols, and a second novice pitching sensation, Jack Taylor, who all appeared together for the first time on September 25 in a

Wiley Piatt, the Phils 1898 mound sensation, had much in common with Elmer Flick, the team's newest hitting sensation. Both began the season at the bottom of manager George Stallings's depth chart and each made only a single appearance in a Phils' box score until May 13, when Flick permanently replaced Thompson in right field and Piatt sealed a regular spot in the pitching rotation by beating Baltimore 5–4.

Piatt's hill debut had come three full weeks earlier at Philadelphia and resulted in a return to the bench after he gave up eight walks and seven runs to the Giants. The previous day, April 21, had marked the debut of another Phils rookie hurler who at the time was more highly regarded than Piatt, right-hander Bill Duggleby. After surrendering three runs in the bottom of the first to the Giants, Duggleby faced his mound opponent that day, Cy Seymour, in the top of the second with the sacks jammed and sailed a pitch over the right field wall to give the Phils a 4–3 lead they never lost in what ultimately was a 13–4 victory.

Duggleby's grand slam was not only the first in major league history by a player in his initial plate appearance but it remains the only such feat to date. Ironically, later in the 1898 season, another Phils rookie pitcher achieved almost the exact opposite first. In the afternoon half of a doubleheader on September 16, Bill Shettsline, who had earlier replaced Stallings as the Phils manager, "experimented with {Bert} Conn, a semi-professional, and the result was a merited defeat," 10–5 to Chicago, in which Jimmy Ryan, the first batter Conn faced in the majors, took him deep.

It seems more than a bit incredible that no other rookie pitcher prior to 1898 had suffered Conn's fate, but such is the case. Here are the first ten pitchers to be dinged for a dong by the first batters they faced.

FIRST TEN PITCHERS TO SURRENDER HR TO FIRST BATTER FACED IN ML

Name	Team	Date
Bert Conn	Philadelphia-NL	9/16/98
Henry Schmidt	Brooklyn-NL	4/17/03
Ernie Baker	Cincinnati-NL	8/18/05
Harry Sullivan	St. Louis-NL	8/11/09
Clarence Mitchell	Detroit-AL	6/2/11
Joe Martina	Washington-AL	4/19/24
Spencer Pumpelly	Washington-AL	7/11/25
Charlie Biggs	Chicago-AL	9/3/32
Bobby Coombs	Philadelphia-AL	6/8/33
Bill Kerksieck	Philadelphia-NL	6/21/39

game against Pittsburgh. Wolverton and Nichols immediately locked up first-string jobs for the rest of the season, but Taylor was the real prize as he started five of Chicago's final 13 games and won all five. Among them, the four rookies helped immeasurably to seal Chicago's best finish since 1891.

The Phillies' recruit crop, though never as impressive as Chicago's in the short run, proved itself to be by far the richest in the majors over the course of the full season. While Baltimore for the fourth straight year uncovered a superb rookie pitcher in Jay Hughes and Boston for the second straight season produced the leading frosh winner in Vic Willis, Philadelphia portsider Wiley Piatt topped both in several key departments and also shared with Cleveland's Jack Powell the honor of establishing a new post-1893 record for shutouts. Piatt also led the Phils staff in everything except ERA.

In addition to Piatt, Philadelphia had no less than 11 rookies on its roster at one time or another during the 1898 campaign. Oddly, the lone neophyte to appear in the Phils' lineup on Opening Day was third sacker Ed Abbaticchio, who was not even on the team by the end of the season. One of the first major league players of Italian descent, Abbaticchio gave way to another rookie, Kid Elberfeld, who began the season on the DL after being hurt in a practice game. Expected to replace longtime stalwart Billy Nash at the hot corner, Elberfeld in turn gave way eventually to yet a third rookie third baseman, Billy Lauder, after demonstrating that he needed further seasoning.

Elmer Flick, the Phils top rookie position player in 1898, also appeared to be ticketed for a return trip to the minors at the beginning of the campaign. Save for a lone pinch-hitting appearance on May 2, Flick languished on the bench until May 13 when veteran right-fielder Sam Thompson suddenly decided to call it quits even though he was leading the team in hitting at the time. But once Flick stepped into the breach, Thompson was hardly missed as the rookie right gardener, notwithstanding his belated start, paced the Phils in walks, triples, and home runs.

Other Highlights

April 18—Jay Hughes of the Baltimore Orioles two hits the Washington Senators in his ML debut and wins 9–0.

April 22—Jay Hughes throws a no-hitter against the mighty Boston Beaneaters; the Orioles win 8–0 and Hughes becomes one of the few pitchers to toss shutouts in their first two major league starts.

June 20—Elmer Flick goes 4-for-5 with three triples and three runs in Philadelphia's 14–2 pasting of St. Louis.

1898 NATIONAL LEAGUE ROOKIE LEADERS

Batting	Pitching
G—134, Elmer Flick, PHI	W—25, Vic Willis, BOS
AB—486, Algie McBride, CIN	L—22, Joe Yeager, BRO
H—147, Algie McBride, CIN	PCT—.658, Vic Willis, BOS
2B—18, Harry Steinfeldt, CIN	GP—41, Vic Willis, BOS
3B—13, Elmer Flick, PHI	GS—38, Vic Willis, BOS
HR—8, Elmer Flick, PHI	CG—33, Wiley Piatt, PHI
R—94, Algie McBride, CIN	IP—311.0, Vic Willis, BOS
RBI—81, Elmer Flick, PHI	H—333, Joe Yeager, BRO
WK—86, Elmer Flick, PHI	BB—148, Vic Willis, BOS
SO—NA	K—160, Vic Willis, BOS
SB—23, Elmer Flick, PHI	ERA—2.84, Vic Willis, BOS
BA—.30247, Algie McBride, CIN*	SH—**6, Wiley Piatt, PHI**
SLG—.448, Elmer Flick, PHI	SV—2, Charlie Hickman, BOS
OBP—.430, Elmer Flick, PHI	

*Algie McBride's .30247 batting average edged Elmer Flick's .30243.

July 14—Wiley Piatt, who will tie for the NL lead in shutouts, four hits the Cleveland Spiders as the Philadelphia Phillies win 1–0; Cleveland rookie Cowboy Jones surrenders only three hits in eight innings but suffers the defeat.

September 13—Walt Woods tosses a two-hitter for the Colts, besting Pittsburgh 4–0.

September 19—Buck Freeman hits two home runs and a double in the Senators' 8–5 win over Chicago.

October 13—Late-season sensation Jack Taylor improves his record to 5–0 for Chicago by beating Pittsburgh 5–1.

1899

Two of the greatest mysteries in the nineteenth century still linger today and may always remain inexplicable. No one has ever offered an adequate reason why hitting and scoring rocketed to an all-time high in 1894, the second season after the pitching distance was lengthened, rather than a year earlier, in 1893, when pitchers first were forced to labor under vastly altered conditions. A no less intriguing mystery surrounds the 1899 season. No year in major league history bestowed a richer and deeper crop of rookies on the game than 1899, and we have yet to hear from anyone who has even a clue why that was so.

Just how rich and deep a crop was it? For one, Pittsburgh frosh Ginger Beaumont failed to win the rookie batting crown, let alone the league crown, even though he hit .352. What's more, he was not even the top rookie batsman on his own team. Then there was the case of Baltimore's recruit shortstop Bill Keister. In 1899 Keister hit .329 with 16 triples and 96 runs scored, numbers that in many seasons would have earned him top frosh honors in all three departments. But they earned Keister exactly nothing—his name is nowhere to be found on the rookie leader board.

And what about some of those stats on the leader board? Several are all-time records among either National League or American League rookies: Jimmy Williams, triples; Roy Thomas, both walks and runs; Sam

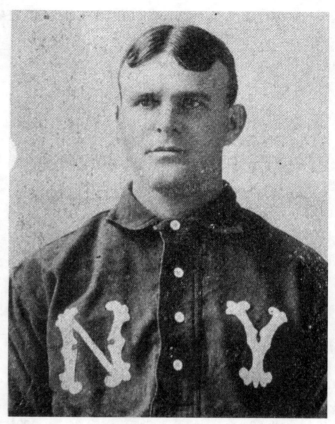

After hitting .354 as a rookie, Jimmy Williams finished the nineteenth century a year later with a .318 career BA as his average fell 90 points in 1900. He rebounded the following year, however, to lead the fledgling American League in triples after deserting Pittsburgh to sign with the new Baltimore entry under John McGraw. *Transcendental Graphics*

Leever, most innings since 1893. Plus Buck Freeman's 25 homers remained the frosh standard until 1930.

The competition for accolades was no less stiff for rookie pitchers. Three major loop hill departments were topped by frosh hurlers in 1899—wins, innings, and strikeouts. That in itself was extraordinary, but what made it utterly astounding was that each of the three departments was paced by a different freshman. Leever led in innings, Baltimore's Joe McGinnity tied 1898 yearling whiz Jay Hughes for the lead in wins, and Cincinnati's Noodles Hahn was the strikeout king.

Often lost in the proliferation of record-setting rookie hitting and pitching feats in 1899 is the work of Jimmy Slagle. The frosh gardener might be remembered for leading the last club to date that represented the nation's capital in the National League in at bats and walks. He might also be remembered for being

POS	Name	Team	G	AB	H	R	HR	RBI	BA	SA	OBP
1B*	Buck Freeman	Wash	155	588	187	107	25	122	.318	.563	.362
2B**	Tommy Leach	Lou	106	406	117	75	5	57	.288	.379	.349.
3B	Jimmy Williams	Pit	153	621	220	126	9	116	.354	.530	.416
SS	Bill Keister	Bal	136	523	172	96	3	73	.329	.449	.368
Inf	Harry Wolverton	Chi	99	389	111	50	1	49	.285	.386	.350
Inf	Doc Casey	Was/Bro	143	559	145	78	1	45	.259	.322	.304
RF	Emmet Heidrick	StL	146	591	194	109	2	82	.328	.421	.368
CF	Roy Thomas	Phil	150	547	178	137	0	47	.325	.362	.457
LF	Ginger Beaumont	Pit	111	437	154	90	3	38	.352	.444	.416
OF	Jimmy Slagle	Was	147	599	163	92	0	41	.272	.324	.338
OF	Mike Donlin	StL	66	266	86	49	6	27	.323	.470	.366
OF	Pop Foster	NY	84	301	89	48	3	57	.296	.402	.348
OF	Jack O'Brien	Was	127	468	132	68	6	51	.282	.365	.331
Util	Pearce Chiles	Phil	97	338	108	57	2	76	.320	.462	.352
C	Ossee Schrecongost	StL/Cle	115	427	124	57	2	47	.290	.375	.328
C	Bob Wood	Cin	63	195	61	34	0	24	.313	.441	.404

Th	Name	Team	G	IP	W	L	CG	K	BB	SHO	ERA
R	Joe McGinnity	Balt	48	366.1	28	16	38	74	93	4	2.68
R	Sam Leever	Pit	51	379	21	23	35	121	122	4	3.18
L	Noodles Hahn	Cin	38	309	23	8	32	145	68	4	2.68
R	Deacon Phillippe	Lou	42	321	21	17	33	68	64	2	3.17
R	Jack Taylor	Chi	41	354.2	18	21	39	67	84	1	3.76
R	Ned Garvin	Chi	24	199	9	13	22	69	42	4	2.85
R	Harry Howell	Balt	28	209.1	13	8	21	58	69	0	3.91
R	Bill Carrick	NY	44	361.2	16	27	40	60	122	3	4.65
P	Rube Waddell	Lou	10	79	7	2	9	44	14	1	3.08
P	Tully Sparks	Pit	28	170	8	6	8	53	82	0	3.86

*As was true of almost every season in the 1890s, quality rookie first basemen were scarce; Freeman is the choice here because he played first later in his career; backing him up is Pat Crisham, who hit .291 for Baltimore in 53 games.

**Leach played only two games at second base in 1899 but throughout his career played every position—and played them all well—except pitcher. The best pure second baseman in 1899 was Art Madison, who hit .271 for Pittsburgh in 42 games.

the center fielder in the first all-rookie outfield since 1893, with homer king Buck Freeman beside him in right and leftfielder Jack O'Brien on his other flank. But what he definitely must be remembered for are his 407 putouts, the most by any outfielder, rookie or otherwise, prior to 1914 when someone named Speaker notched 423.

The 1899 recruit harvest was enormous not only in the number of rookie records its graduates achieved but also in terms of career accomplishments. Four future Hall of Famers had recruit status that year: McGinnity, Rube Waddell, Jack Chesbro, and Sam Crawford. Among the many other performers whose names are missing from the 1899 leader board but

would grace future loop leader lists are Tommy Leach, Mike Donlin, Jack Taylor, Harry Howell, and Bill Bernhard.

Yet, for all that was unique and amazing about the 1899 rookie crop, it continued the puzzling trend that had begun in 1894 with Jimmy Bannon. Jimmy Williams, easily the most exciting newcomer in the final season of the League-Association's brief eight-year history, would become the sixth straight recruit batting leader who would never again equal his rookie performance.

Above, for the sake of any who might care to pick an argument with us as to whether 1899 truly had by far the most glittering array of rookie performances, is our

If space permitted, it would be fun to post a leader board for each season that featured not only the best rookie performances but also the worst. The 1899 campaign is particularly enlightening, thanks largely to the presence of the Cleveland Spiders, losers of a record 134 games after their once-strong roster was decimated by syndicate ownership. That year, the Spiders presented a lineup that contained four of the ten worst-hitting regulars in the loop, headed by rookie shortstop Harry Lochhead, who somehow contrived to collect only 141 total bases in 148 games.

But the Spiders' hitters were a Murderers' Row compared to the team's pitching staff. In 1899 Cleveland's three principal rookie hurlers—Charlie Knepper, Frank Bates, and Harry Colliflower—were an aggregate 6–51. Bates actually began the year with St. Louis, which was under the same ownership as Cleveland, and was shipped to the Spiders after two quality relief appearances. Since Bates had also done well in a late-season trial the previous year, his transfer was curious, as Cleveland from the very outset of the season was used as a dumping ground for St. Louis rejects. But we must assume, from Bates's subsequent performance with Cleveland, that St. Louis player-manager Patsy Tebeau spotted something about Bates that he didn't like. In 1899 Bates joined with veteran Jim Hughey to saddle Cleveland with two of the ten worst pitching seasons ever in terms of *Total Baseball's* TPI ratings.

Just a hair below the top ten and tied for the 11th spot, with a –5.1 rating, is a third member of the Spiders' 1899 staff, Bates's fellow rookie sufferer, Knepper.

THE TEN WORST PITCHING SEASONS IN HISTORY

Rank	Name	Team	Year	W/L	ERA	TPI
1	Jersey Bakely	Phi/Wil/KC-UA	1884	16–30	4.29	–9.1
2	John Coleman	Phi-NL	1883	12–48	4.87	–8.2
3	Steve Blass	Pit-NL	1973	3–9	9.85	–6.5
4	Pat Caraway	Chi-AL	1931	10–24	6.22	–6.2
5	Red Donahue	StL-NL	1897	10–35	6.13	–6.0
6	Jim Hughey	Cle-NL	1899	4–30	5.41	–5.9
7	Bill Greif	SD-NL	1972	5–16	5.60	–5.5
8	Frank Bates	Stl/Cle-NL	1899	1–18	6.90	–5.3
9	Lev Shreve	Ind-NL	1888	11–24	4.63	–5.2
	Kid Carsey	Was-AA	1891	14–37	4.99	–5.2

1899 rookie All-Star squad. We believe that the individual years that each of its members had would, if assembled on one team, have been good enough to win the pennant in any major league season in history.

Other Highlights

May 11—Noodles Hahn of the Cincinnati Reds tosses a three-hitter versus the Pittsburgh Pirates and beats fellow rookie Sam Leever, 1–0.

May 25—Deacon Phillippe of Louisville no-hits the New York Giants and wins 7–0.

June 20—Jack O'Brien goes 5-for-5 with a triple, homer, and two runs for Washington, as the visiting Senators beat the St. Louis Perfectos, 5–3.

July 22—Ginger Beaumont goes 6-for-6 with six runs in Pittsburgh's 18–4 rout of Philadelphia.

Sam Leever was not the only rookie pitcher in 1899 who was made into his team's workhorse. Two other frosh hurlers labored hard enough to rank in the top ten for the most innings toiled by a rookie since 1893. Note that 1896 was the only other year to produce more than one list member.

MOST INNINGS PITCHED, SEASON, ROOKIE, SINCE 1893

Rank	Name	Team	Year	W-L	IP
1	Sam Leever	Pit-NL	1899	21–23	379
2	Irv Young	Bos-NL	1905	20–21	378
3	Pete Alexander	Phi-NL	1911	28–13	367
4	Joe McGinnity	Bal-NL	1899	28–16	366.1
5	Bill Carrick	NY-NL	1899	16–27	361.2
6	George McQuillan	Phi-NL	1908	23–17	359.2
7	Jack Taylor	Chi-NL	1899	18–21	354.2
8	Stoney McGlynn	StL-NL	1907	14–25	352.1
8	Chick Fraser	Lou-NL	1896	12–27	349.1
10	Win Mercer	Was-NL	1894	17–23	339.1

1899 NATIONAL LEAGUE ROOKIE LEADERS

Batting	Pitching
G—**155, Buck Freeman, WAS**	W—28, Joe McGinnity, BAL
AB—621, Jimmy Williams, PIT	L—27, Bill Carrick, NY
H—220, Jimmy Williams, PIT	PCT—.742, Noodles Hahn, CIN
2B—28, Pearce Chiles, PHI	GP—**51, Sam Leever, PIT**
Jimmy Williams, PIT	GS—**43, Bill Carrick, NY**
3B—**27, Jimmy Williams, PIT**	CG—**40, Bill Carrick, NY**
HR—**25, Buck Freeman, WAS**	IP—**379.0, Sam Leever, PIT**
R—137, Roy Thomas, PHI	H—**485, Bill Carrick, NY**
RBI—122, Buck Freeman, WAS	BB—122, Bill Carrick, NY
WK—**115, Roy Thomas, PHI**	Sam Leever, PIT
SO—NA	K—**145, Noodles Hahn, CIN**
SB—55, Emmet Heidrick, STL	ERA—2.6779, Joe McGinnity, BAL*
BA—.354, Jimmy Williams, PIT	SH—4, Ned Garvin, CHI
SLG—.563, Buck Freeman, WAS	Noodles Hahn, CIN
OBA—.457, Roy Thomas, PHI	Sam Leever, PIT
	Joe McGinnity, BAL
	SV—**3, Sam Leever, PIT**

*McGinnity edged Noodles Hahn, 2.6779 to 2.6796

September 8—Jimmy Williams is held hitless in three at bats, snapping his nineteenth-century rookie-record 27-game hitting streak for Pittsburgh; Deacon Phillippe of Louisville, who terminated a Williams's 26-game skein earlier in the season, does so again while besting the Pirates 5–3.

September 20—Buck Freeman hits his 20th homer of the season, breaking the rookie record jointly held by Billy O'Brien (1887) and Bug Holliday (1889); Freeman's victim is Rube Waddell, who pitches Louisville to a 6–4 win over Washington in the second game of a doubleheader.

October 12—Buck Freeman hits a grand slam in the ninth inning of the first game of a doubleheader against New York, but the Giants hang on to beat the Senators 9–7. Freeman's shot is his 25th and final home run of the season, a rookie mark that will be tied twice in the late 1920s before being surpassed by Wally Berger in 1930.

1900s

1900

If the 1899 season was a rookie paradise, the 1900 campaign was among the cruelest ever for young players who harbored major league ambitions. In the winter of 1899–1900, the League-Association trimmed its four most financially troubled teams along with its name to become once again an eight-team loop labeled the National League. The cutback reduced jobs at the major league level by a third. As a result, openings for novice players in 1900 were so scarce that the leading frosh performer on any of the top three teams—Brooklyn, Pittsburgh, and Philadelphia—in terms of playing time was first baseman Pop Dillon, who got into all of five games for Pittsburgh and collected just 18 at bats. The Brooklyn Bridegrooms meanwhile threatened until nearly the very end of the season to join the 1889 New York Giants as the only pennant winner in history to go through an entire campaign without using a rookie player for even so much as a single inning. In 1900 the lone Bridegrooms performer with recruit status to appear in a box score was catcher Farmer Steelman. On October 11, three days before the season ended, Steel-man was behind the plate in a 7–4 loss to New York that was shortened by darkness to eight innings.

Only Cincinnati and Chicago, both of which lost key figures to retirement after the 1899 season, were accommodating to aspiring newcomers in 1900. Of the five rookie qualifiers in the revamped League for either the batting title or the ERA crown, four played for the Queen City entry—leftfielder Sam Crawford, center-fielder Jimmy Barrett, and two hurlers, Ed Scott and Doc Newton. The fifth rookie qualifier was Chicago third baseman Bill Bradley. The five qualifiers, predictably, ruled the 1900 frosh leaders chart, with Barrett the putative kingpin. Barrett in the fullness of time would also put an end to the disturbing six-year run of rookie batting leaders who were never again able to live up to their yearling achievements.

Indeed, all four of the names that appear on the batting side of the rookie leaders ledger would remain among the game's elite performers for the better part of the next decade and even, in Crawford's case, well beyond it. The same unfortunately was not true of any of the pitchers. Rome Chambers's save that tied him for the rookie lead in 1900 came in his lone major league

In January 1900, deep in the throes of a particularly harsh New England winter, Marty Bergen, Boston's regular catcher for the past four seasons, murdered his wife and two young sons with an axe and then took his own life by slitting his throat with a razor. The Bergen tragedy opened the door for Billy Sullivan, a 25-year-old rookie receiver who had joined the team near the tag end of the 1899 season. Sharing the Boston catching job in 1900 with veteran Boileryard Clarke, Sullivan collected just 238 at bats, far short of the number needed to qualify for the rookie batting title, but nevertheless led all freshmen in home runs with eight. More than that, Sullivan led all League hitters in home run percentage and in addition posted very respectable figures across the board with a .273 BA, .302 OBP, and .399 SA.

Following his stellar rookie season, Sullivan jumped to the Chicago entry in the rebel American League and played another 14 years in the majors. He never again even remotely approached any of his rookie batting figures. Worse, his BA during the remainder of his career was .207, he hit just 11 more home runs in 3335 at bats, and his SA was a paltry .270.

Did Sullivan's homer splurge in 1900 induce him to start swinging for the fences? Was he injured subsequent to the 1900 season? Did he have some egregious batting weakness that pitchers suddenly uncovered? No, no, and no again. The answer is that while Sullivan's offensive decline was extreme for that period, it was by no means atypical. Very soon after Sullivan's rookie season, the game began to change dramatically, so that by 1906 when he fashioned a seemingly execrable .559 OPS, it was only 28 points below his team's mark of .587. And his team that year happened to be the best in the majors, the celebrated Hitless Wonders, the prototypical creation of the heart of the Deadball Era when the *average* pitcher achieved an ERA (2.69) that was a half run better than Ted Breitenstein, the League-Association ERA leader, had posted 12 years earlier (3.18) in the first season the pitching distance was lengthened to its present location.

game, a four-inning stint on May 7 when he relieved Bill Dinneen after Boston went ahead 18–5 and then gave up six runs to make the final tally 18–11. After winning 26 games between them for the seventh-place Reds in 1900, Scott and Newton produced just 51 more career wins.

In contrast, the last-place New York Giants, after getting just four wins in 1900 from rookie pitchers, would watch Dummy Taylor (4–3) and Christy Mathewson (0–3) combine for 485 more victories.

Other Highlights

May 25—Ed Scott beats the Boston Beaneaters 2–1 in ten innings, allowing seven hits and no walks; Scott's double in the tenth drives in the winning run for Cincinnati.

June 5—Sam Crawford collects four hits, one a triple, and scores twice for Cincinnati as the Reds beat the hosting New York Giants 14–8.

1900 NATIONAL LEAGUE ROOKIE LEADERS

Batting	Pitching
G—137, Jimmy Barrett, CIN	W—17, Ed Scott, CIN
AB—545, Jimmy Barrett, CIN	L—20, Ed Scott, CIN
H—172, Jimmy Barrett, CIN	PCT—.459, Ed Scott, CIN
2B—21, Bill Bradley, CHI	GP—42, Ed Scott, CIN
3B—15, Sam Crawford, CIN	GS—35, Ed Scott, CIN
HR—8, Billy Sullivan, BOS	CG—31, Ed Scott, CIN
R—114, Jimmy Barrett, CIN	IP—315.0, Ed Scott, CIN
RBI—59, Sam Crawford, CIN	H—370, Ed Scott, CIN
WK—72, Jimmy Barrett, CIN	BB—100, Doc Newton, CIN
SO—NA	K—88, Doc Newton, CIN
SB—44, Jimmy Barrett, CIN	ERA—3.86, Ed Scott, CIN
BA—.316, Jimmy Barrett, CIN	SH—1, Doc Newton, CIN
SLG—.429, Sam Crawford, CIN	SV—1, Rome Chambers, BOS
OBA—.400, Jimmy Barrett ,CIN	Ed Scott, CIN

July 17—Christy Mathewson makes his ML debut in relief for New York but surrenders six Brooklyn runs; Mathewson, who will later be known for impeccable control, hits three batters and walks two and gets a no-decision in the Giants' 13–7 loss.

August 2—John Ganzel homers, doubles, hits two singles, and scores three times as his Chicago Colts nip New York 7–6.

August 18—Cincinnati's Doc Newton blanks Philadelphia on four hits and no walks in a 3–0 win that will be the only shutout by a rookie in the 1900 season.

September 12—Sammy Strang goes 7-for-8 in the Chicago Colts' doubleheader split with the Giants.

September 15—Jimmy Barrett goes 4-for-5 with a double and three runs, but Cincinnati loses to the Phillies 6–5 in 12 innings.

◄━━━ 1901 ━━►

May 1901 marked the beginning of Christy Mathewson's lengthy tenure as a dominant pitcher. The previous month the New York Giants 20-year-old right-hander had won both his starts, but in May he turned downright unbeatable. After nipping the Boston Beaneaters 2–1 on May 3, Mathewson threw three consecutive shutouts, permitting a combined 16 hits. His string was broken when he yielded a run to Pittsburgh in his May 21 victory, but three days later he limited Cincinnati to three safeties, notching his fourth blanking of the month. Mathewson was now a sizzling 8–0 but then dropped his final two games of May—one of them in relief—despite surrendering just two runs in 12 innings. For the month, Mathewson yielded a mere four tallies in 66 frames, and enemy batters were only just beginning to get a taste of his miserly ways. On July 15 at St. Louis, he held the Cardinals hitless, beating them 5–0.

In 1901 Mathewson went 20–17 altogether, with a 2.41 ERA for the seventh-place Giants. His 221 strikeouts ranked fourth in the NL while the .230 average batters attained against his "fadeaway" slants was the second lowest in the loop.

But Mathewson was only one of many rookie pitchers to shine in 1901. The American League, for the first time deemed to be a major circuit, provided ample opportunities for freshmen to show their wares. No fewer than 17 rookies won at least ten games in 1901, the most in any season that did not feature three major leagues. Of the 17, just five played in the NL, with Jack Harper the only big winner besides Mathewson. Harper won 23 games—one of the highest totals by a freshman from any St. Louis franchise—and dropped 13 for the Cardinals.

MOST WINS BY ST. LOUIS ROOKIE PITCHER

33, George Bradley, 1875 StL NA
32, Silver King, 1887 StL AA
25, Jumbo McGinnis, 1882 StL AA
23, Jack Harper, 1901 StL NL
21, Johnny Beazley, 1942 StL NL

Roscoe Miller of Detroit duplicated Harper's record. Miller made the top five in several categories and was joined on the Tigers staff by Ed Siever, who nabbed 18 victories for the Bengals. In the second game on August 17, Miller twirled a four-hit shutout at Washington, the Senators getting a nice effort from Case Patten, who also permitted but a quartet of hits.

Patten won 18 times and was tied for third in shutouts by fellow rookies Roy Patterson and Earl Moore. Patterson started Opening Day for the Chicago White Stockings on April 24, the first game in the AL's major league history, beating Cleveland 8–2. On May 5 he was thrashed by Milwaukee, allowing 25 hits, including five apiece to freshmen Billy Gilbert and Bill Hallman and four more to Irv Waldron. The Brewers won 21–7. Patterson had his own offensive highlight on June 13 when he connected for a three-run homer off Joe McGinnity while blanking Baltimore 12–0. A little more than a month earlier, on May 9, Cleveland's Moore held the White Stockings hitless for nine innings, but the game was deadlocked at 2–2. For nearly a century Moore's effort was considered the first no-hitter in AL history, but Major League Baseball no longer deems it a no-no because Chicago got a pair of hits and two runs in the tenth to win 4–2. Some 13 weeks later, however, Moore exacted his revenge, one-hitting the White Stockings on August 13, the first whitewashing Chicago suffered in the AL's fledgling season as a major loop.

Ed Siever combined with fellow rookie Roscoe Miller to win 41 games for the first Detroit AL entry. The following year the pair won just 14 games for the Tigers, but Siever nonetheless paced the AL in ERA despite a lackluster 8–11 record. In 1907 Siever matched his rookie win total when he bagged 18 victories for Detroit's first AL flag winner. *Transcendental Graphics*

Many of the American League's premier players in its initial season with major league status were carryovers from the days when the circuit was still known as the Western League. Among them was Irv Waldron, a 24-year-old outfielder who had begun his professional career in 1895 at age 19 with Pawtucket of the Northeastern League. Waldron subsequently moved on to the Western League and had been a member of the Milwaukee club ever since 1897. He opened the 1901 campaign as the Brewers center fielder and later was sent to Washington, where he finished the season.

After his rookie year, Waldron, for reasons of his own, opted to return to a new version of the Western League rather than stay with Washington. He remained a quality player in the high minors for another decade but never played another game at the major league level. Owing to his outstanding rookie performance, he currently holds the all-time records among one-year players for hits and runs and the AL marks for triples, stolen bases, and BA.

In his lone season, Waldron also led AL rookies in a number of departments and all junior loop players in games. Because of the way his move to Washington was timed, Waldron set a bizarre all-time record in that he participated in two more games (141) than any of the teams in his league played (139). Here are the 1901 AL leaders in games. Note that Hallman, Ferris, and Parent also were rookies and that Dungan, like Waldron, never played another major league game.

Rank	Name	Team	Games
1	Irv Waldron	Mil-Wash	141
2	Bill Hallman	Milwaukee	139
3	Sam Dungan	Washington	138
	Hobe Ferris	Boston	138
	Jimmy Collins	Boston	138
	John Anderson	Milwaukee	138
	Freddy Parent	Boston	138

Eddie Plank of the Philadelphia Athletics, who would become the first southpaw to win 300 games, earned the first 17 of his victories in 1901, including a two-hitter on June 13 against Milwaukee. Along with Earl Moore, three other AL freshmen picked up 16 wins—Watty Lee for Washington, the Brewers' Bill Reidy, and George Winter for the Boston Somersets. Winter started his career 7–0 before losing for the first time on July 15.

While the pennant-winning White Stockings got most of their rookie assistance from pitchers, the NL champion Pirates relied on freshman hitters. First baseman Kitty Bransfield hit .295 and drove in 91 runs, and outfielder Lefty Davis scored 87 times in 87 games after starting the season with Brooklyn. Including his stay with the Superbas, Davis tallied 98 times in 112 contests, making him the lone rookie since 1900 with as many as 90 runs in fewer than 115 games.

Socks Seybold hit .334 and slugged .503 for the Athletics, flashing the power that led to his AL home run title the following year. Two junior loop freshmen reached the century mark in runs, John Farrell of the Senators and Irv Waldron, who began his one ML season with Milwaukee before joining Farrell in the nation's capital. Twenty-three years would pass before the Senators again had two players who scored in triple digits.

1901 ROOKIE LEADERS

Batting	Pitching
G—AL 141, Irv Waldron, MIL/WAS	W—AL 23, Roscoe Miller, DET
NL 142, Otto Krueger, STL	NL 23, Jack Harper, STL
AB—AL 598, Irv Waldron, MIL/WAS	L—AL 20, Bill Reidy, MIL
NL 566, Kitty Bransfield, PIT	NL 23, Tom Hughes, CHI
H—AL 186, Irv Waldron, MIL/WAS	PCT—AL .643, Case Patten, WAS
NL 167, Kitty Bransfield, PIT	NL .639, Jack Harper, STL
2B—AL 32, John Farrell, WAS	GP—AL 41, Roy Patterson, CHI
NL 26, Kitty Bransfield, PIT	NL 40, Christy Mathewson, NY
3B—AL 15, Hobe Ferris, BOS	GS—AL 36, Roscoe Miller, DET
NL 16, Kitty Bransfield, PIT	NL 38, Christy Mathewson, NY
HR—AL 8, Socks Seybold, PHI	CG—AL 35, Roscoe Miller, DET
NL 2, done by five players	NL 36, Christy Mathewson, NY
R—AL 102, Irv Waldron, MIL/WAS	IP—AL 332.0, Roscoe Miller, DET
NL 98, Lefty Davis, BRO/PIT	NL 336.0, Christy Mathewson, NY
RBI—AL 90, Socks Seybold, PHI	H—AL 364, Bill Reidy, MIL
NL 91, Kitty Bransfield, PIT	NL 309, Tom Hughes, CHI
WK—AL 52, John Farrell, WAS	BB—AL 107, Earl Moore, CLE
NL 66, Lefty Davis, BRO/PIT	NL 115, Tom Hughes, CHI
SO—AL NA	K—AL 127, Roy Patterson, CHI
NL NA	NL 225, Tom Hughes, CHI
SB—AL 25, John Farrell, WAS	ERA—AL 2.80, George Winter, BOS
NL 26, Lefty Davis, BRO/PIT	NL 2.41, Christy Mathewson, NY
BA—AL .334, Socks Seybold, PHI	SHO—AL 4, Earl Moore, CLE
NL .295, Kitty Bransfield, PIT	Case Patten, WAS
SLG—AL .503, Socks Seybold, PHI	Roy Patterson, CHI
NL .398, Kitty Bransfield, PIT	NL 5, Christy Mathewson, NY
OBP—AL .397, Socks Seybold, PHI	SV—AL 1, Dale Gear, WAS
NL .389, Lefty Davis, BRO/PIT	Zaza Harvey, CHI
	Bert Husting, MIL
	Roscoe Miller, DET
	NL No Qualifier

Other Highlights

April 25—Detroit's rookie mound ace, Roscoe Miller, is blasted in his ML debut, and the Tigers trail Milwaukee 13–4 in last of ninth, only to rally and score ten runs for the greatest Opening Day comeback ever, with first sacker Pop Dillon hitting two doubles in the inning (and a record four in the game); Miller's early kayo in the Tigers' opener is only time all year that he fails to complete a game.

April 25—Cleveland second sacker Erve Beck connects for the first home run in junior circuit annals, but his Blues lose nonetheless to Chicago 7–3.

April 26—Christy Mathewson earns his first ML victory, hurling his New York Giants to a 5–2 win over Brooklyn.

April 26—Win Kellum starts and loses the first game in Boston's American League history as the Baltimore Orioles beat his Somersets 10–6.

May 15—In beating Boston 4–0, Watty Lee of Washington tosses the first shutout in American League history.

May 24—Christy Mathewson improves to 8–0 with his fourth shutout of the month, beating the Cincinnati Reds 1–0.

May 27—Jimmy Burke commits four errors at third base in the fourth inning for Milwaukee, becoming the only American League third sacker ever to be so clumsy in one frame; the Athletics and Eddie Plank top the Brewers 8–3.

June 13—Eddie Plank earns his first big league shutout, whitewashing the Brewers 6–0.

August 10—Snake Wiltse hits two doubles and two triples for the Philadelphia Athletics, becoming the only rookie pitcher in history with four extra-base hits in one game; Wiltse scores four times and beats the Washington Senators 13–0 in the second game of a doubleheader as Washington rookie Dale Gear surrenders 23 hits and a post-1900 record 41 total bases in a losing effort.

September 3—Bill Cristall breaks in with Cleveland in the second game of a doubleheader with Boston by shutting out the Somersets 4–0 in his first major league start.

September 15—Ed Siever blanks Cleveland 21–0 for Detroit; the contest, limited to eight innings so Cleveland can catch a train, is still tied for the most lopsided shutout in AL history.

September 21—Tom Hughes throws a 17-inning 1–0 shutout for the Colts against Boston, whiffing 13 Beaneaters and yielding only eight hits.

◄ 1902 ►

The first time AL batters encountered Addie Joss should have been a lesson to them that he would be one of the stingiest pitchers ever to trod the mound. Joss, whose 1.89 career ERA is the second lowest in history, debuted on April 26, 1902, for the Cleveland Blues and was unhittable—or at least he should have been. In the sixth inning future Hall of Famer Jesse Burkett of the St. Louis Browns was credited with a single after his short fly to right field was ruled to have been trapped. This dubious call was followed by another the next inning. Joss clubbed what appeared to many onlookers to have been a three-run homer but was credited only with a ground-rule double. Consequently, in beating the Browns 3–0, Joss was forced to settle for a one-hitter

and also denied the rare feat of both hitting a home run and pitching a shutout in his ML debut. The consolation was that it was the first of a league-best five shutouts the right-hander would twirl en route to a 17–13 record. Joss's 2.77 ERA was the highest he'd post in nine major league seasons before dying of tubercular meningitis on April 14, 1911, two days after his 31st birthday.

Joss's teammate, shortstop John Gochnauer, was at the other end of the baseball spectrum. Gochnauer hit .185, becoming one of only eight rookie qualifiers to fall short of the Mendoza line.

ROOKIE BAs BELOW .200 (MINIMUM 400 ABs)

Name	Team	Year	BA
Ben Conroy	Phi-AA	1890	.171
Ed Zimmerman	Bro-NL	1911	.1847
John Gochnauer	Cle-AL	1902	.1852
Henry Easterday	KC-AA	1888	.190
Dick Schofield	Cal-AL	1984	.192
Harry Lyons	StL-AA	1888	.194
Joe Dugan	Phi-AL	1918	.195
Gair Allie	Pit-NL	1954	.199

Garnering 65 more hits in 21 fewer at bats than Gochnauer was Patsy Dougherty, the left fielder of the Boston Red Sox. Dougherty batted .342, the apogee for a freshman in this pitcher-dominated decade.

HIGHEST ROOKIE BA, 1901–10 (MINIMUM 400 ABs)

.342, Patsy Dougherty, 1902 Bos AL
.334, Socks Seybold, 1901 Phi AL
.311, Irv Waldron, 1901 Mil/Was AL
.3108, Homer Smoot, 1902 StL NL
.309, Tris Speaker, 1909 Bos AL

Smoot, the lone senior circuit batsman on this list, and George Barclay gave the St. Louis Cardinals two batters in 1902 who exceeded 150 hits—the only such rookie duo any team featured from 1900 through 1913. Barclay collected 163 knocks while Smoot smote 161 hits. On April 25 Smoot, whose first name actually was Homer, hit his first two round trippers as he and Barclay combined on a 7-for-10 day in St. Louis's win over Cincinnati.

As these two Cardinal outfielders topped rookies in

hits in 1902, a pair of Redbird pitchers headed the freshman innings pitched list. The previous year, Mike O'Neill had pitched 41 innings, with a two-hit shutout contributing mightily to his stingy 1.32 ERA. In 1902, while unable to maintain that torrid pace, O'Neill was the ace for the sixth-place club, going 16–15 in 288⅓ innings. O'Neill also played three games in the outfield and topped the NL with 12 pinch-hit ABs. He was successful in only one of those attempts, but he made it count. On June 3 O'Neill hit the first pinch grand slam in ML history as St. Louis beat the Boston Beaneaters 11–9. Stan Yerkes ranked second on the Cardinals' rookie-laden staff with 12 wins and 272⅔ innings. Freshmen, in fact, accounted for 118 of the Redbirds' wins and losses, going 46–72 and in the process setting a post-1893 rookie record by registering a gargantuan 88 percent of the team's 134 decisions.

The Cards relied so heavily on rookies in 1902 owing to massive raids on their roster over the previous winter by renegade AL teams. Following a first-division finish in 1901, the Redbirds would not finish within ten games of first place again until 1921, but the Chicago Colts, who were first called the Cubs on March 27, 1902, had a much quicker journey to contention. A 68–69 showing in 1902 preceded the team's .594 winning percentage the following year and four NL pennants by 1910. In 1902 Chicago launched the ML careers of two future Hall-of-Fame infielders who later were linked with first baseman Frank Chance in Franklin P. Adams's immortal poem on the trio. Joe Tinker was the team's shortstop, hitting a respectable .263 and leading the NL in shortstop assists. However, he also paced the loop in errors. On September 1 Tinker's keystone partner, Johnny Evers, debuted. Evers batted only .222 in 90 ABs but would be the regular second baseman on five NL champions, including four in the Windy City. In 1914, with the Boston Braves, he won the Chalmers Award as the senior circuit's MVP.

Also aiding in the Cubs' ascension in the standings was Carl Lundgren, whose 1.97 ERA was fourth best in the loop. Lundgren won 41 games for the Cubs from 1906 through 1908. Due to Chicago's abundance of top-notch pitchers in that period, he never appeared in a World Series game, a fate shared by Addie Joss, whose postseason absence sprang from both Cleveland's ill luck in close races and his own personal tragedy.

The Cleveland Blues cut veteran shortstop Frank Scheibeck at the close of the 1901 season when he hit just .213. In his stead they acquired John Gochnauer, a minor leaguer who showed well in a three-game trial with Brooklyn the previous September.

Gochnauer soon made fans in the Forest City yearn for Scheibeck. Not only did he hit a paltry .185 as a rookie in 1902, but he matched that exact same figure the following year after he somehow contrived to convince the Blues to give him another chance. The Blues, meanwhile, were about to become known as the Naps in honor of Gochnauer's keystone partner, Nap Lajoie, who had been presented to Cleveland early in the 1902 season when legal difficulties made it impossible for him to stay with the Philadelphia A's after he had won the initial AL batting crown with them the previous year.

Lajoie repeated as the AL bat titlist in 1902 with a .378 BA even though the crown was mistakenly awarded at the time to Ed Delahanty for a mark that was actually two points lower than Lajoie's. Hard as it may be to believe, the 193-point BA difference between Lajoie and Gochnauer in 1902 is not a record for the largest disparity between two keystone partners. The previous year, for one, Lajoie had outhit A's shortstop Joe Dolan by 210 points. Furthermore, it is not even the largest disparity involving a keystone partnership in which at least one of the members was a rookie. In 1884 second baseman Fred Dunlap of the Union Association St. Louis Maroons topped recruit shortstop Milt Whitehead by 201 points, .412 to .211.

Other Highlights

April 17—Stan Yerkes of the Cardinals is the first NL rookie pitcher in the twentieth century to get the nod on Opening Day when he loses 1–0 to Deacon Phillippe of the Pirates; frosh hurlers will proceed to start the first 12 games of the season for the Redbirds before the club's lone veteran pitcher, Ed Murphy, finally gets the ball in Game 13 at Chicago on May 5.

April 19—Bob Ewing yields ten walks in his ML debut, including an NL record-tying seven in one inning, and the Chicago Cubs best his Cincinnati Reds 9–5.

April 25—Gene Wright permits but two singles for the Cleveland Blues, who destroy the St. Louis Browns 10–0.

May 1—Pat Carney hits his only two homers of the season for the Beaneaters in their 5–0 topping of the Brooklyn Superbas.

1902 ROOKIE LEADERS

Batting	Pitching
G—AL 127, John Gochnauer, CLE	W—AL 17, Addie Joss, CLE
NL 140, Ed Gremminger, BOS	NL 16, Mike O'Neill, STL
AB—AL 459, John Gochnauer, CLE	L—AL 16, George Mullin, DET
NL 543, George Barclay, STL	**NL 21, Stan Yerkes, STL**
H—AL 150, Patsy Dougherty, BOS	PCT—AL .567, Addie Joss, CLE
NL 163, George Barclay, STL	NL .516, Mike O'Neill, STL
2B—AL 16, John Gochnauer, CLE	GP—AL 35, George Mullin, DET
NL 20, Ed Gremminger, BOS	NL 39, Stan Yerkes, STL
3B—AL 8, Danny Murphy, PHI	GS—AL 30, George Mullin, DET
NL 12, Ed Gremminger, BOS	NL 37, Stan Yerkes, STL
HR—AL 2, Harry Arndt, DET/BAL	CG—AL 28, Addie Joss, CLE
Harry Gleason, BOS	NL 29, Mike O'Neill, STL
NL 3, George Barclay, STL	IP—AL 269.1, Addie Joss, CLE
Tim Flood, BRO	NL 288.1, Mike O'Neill, STL
Homer Smoot, STL	H—AL 282, George Mullin, DET
R—AL 77, Patsy Dougherty, BOS	NL 341, Stan Yerkes, STL
NL 79, George Barclay, STL	BB—AL 95, George Mullin, DET
RBI—AL 48, Danny Murphy, PHI	NL 84, Henry Thielman, NY/CIN
NL 65, Pat Carney, BOS	K—AL 106, Addie Joss, CLE
Ed Gremminger, BOS	NL 106, Ham Iburg, PHI
WK—AL 42, Patsy Dougherty, BOS*	ERA—AL 2.77, Addie Joss, CLE
NL 42, Pat Carney, BOS*	NL 1.97, Carl Lundgren, CHI
SO—AL NA	SHO—**AL 5, Addie Joss, CLE**
NL NA	NL 3, Clarence Currie, CIN/STL
SB—AL 20, Patsy Dougherty, BOS	SV—AL 1, Charlie Shields, BAL/STL
NL 30, George Barclay, STL	Gene Wright, CLE
BA—AL .342, Patsy Dougherty, BOS	NL 2, Mike O'Neill, STL
NL .311, Homer Smoot, STL	
SLG—AL .397, Patsy Dougherty, BOS	
NL .380, Homer Smoot, STL	
OBP—AL .411, Patsy Dougherty, BOS	
NL .351, Homer Smoot, STL	

*Though not a league leader, Davy Jones led all ML rookies with 44 bases on balls, splitting his time between the AL St. Louis Browns and the NL Chicago Colts.

June 30—Rookie gardener Jim Jones guns down three runners at home plate for the New York Giants, but the Boston Beaneaters win 8–0.

July 8—Danny Murphy of the Philadelphia Athletics goes 6-for-6 including a three-run home run off Cy Young as Philadelphia beats the Boston Somersets 22–9.

August 4—Clarence Currie yields only two singles in his 1–0 shutout and also scores the game's only run as the Cardinals nip the Beaneaters in a rain-shortened seven-inning contest.

September 4—Alex Hardy of the Cubs limits Brooklyn to two singles and wins 1–0 in his ML debut; Hardy will collect just two more victories in his career.

September 10—Addie Joss blanks Chicago 12–0 on two hits, marking the fourth time in 1902 that Joss pitches a complete-game win in which he permits two or fewer safeties.

1903

In the first World Series game between the American and National leagues, Pittsburgh's Jimmy Sebring almost single-handedly beat the Boston Pilgrims. Sebring, the Pirates right fielder, hit a two-run single in the first inning to give Pittsburgh an early 4–0 lead. Two innings later, he singled again for another RBI, and in the seventh frame Sebring made history by hitting a solo home run, the first round tripper in "modern" World Series play. The Pirates won the game 7–3 but lost the series, despite Sebring batting .367 and leading all hitters with 11 safeties.

Sebring played 19 late-season games for Pittsburgh in 1902, driving in 15 runs and becoming one of only five rookie batters ever to have as many as four doubles and four triples in fewer than 100 ABs. In his official rookie season he hit .277, an undistinguished mark in most years, but by 1903 the Deadball Era had taken such firm hold that just two other freshmen were able to bat as high as .250 (minimum 400 ABs). The top figure in the AL belonged to Charlie Carr of Detroit, who rapped .281 and drove in 79 runs. Patience, though, was not the young first sacker's forte as he drew just ten walks in 135 games to set a negative mark that has since been topped by only two other rookies with as much playing time.

FEWEST WALKS BY ROOKIE WITH 500 ABs

9 BB/523 AB, Buck Weaver, 1912 Chi AL
9 BB/541 AB, Tito Fuentes, 1966 SF NL
10 BB/548 AB, Charlie Carr, 1903 Det AL
10 BB/533 AB, John Leary, 1914 StL AL
12 BB/543 AB, Damaso Garcia, 1980 Tor AL

Second baseman Johnny Evers of the Chicago Cubs hit .293 to pace all rookie batsmen and also slashed 27 doubles, just five behind the NL leaders. Evers was lucky not to have to face his Cubs teammates, especially recruit southpaw Jake Weimer, who limited batters to a league-low .225 average. Weimer, nicknamed "Tornado Jake," was 20–8 for Chicago, which continued its upward climb by winning 14 more games than the year before. His .714 winning percentage was third in the loop as was his 2.30 ERA. Weimer tossed three shutouts, two of them besting Christy Mathewson and the New York Giants.

Two novice Brooklyn hurlers topped Weimer in the whitewashes category. Henry Schmidt had five for the

Superbas and Oscar Jones four. Schmidt began a streak of three consecutive scoreless outings on April 25 versus the Philadelphia Phillies. He won 22 games but had an ERA of 3.83, more than a half run higher than the NL norm.

HIGHEST ERA BY ROOKIE WITH 5 OR MORE SHUTOUTS

3.83 ERA/5 SHO, Henry Schmidt, 1903 Brk NL
3.70 ERA/5 SHO, Dazzy Vance, 1922 Brk NL
3.43 ERA/5 SHO, Paul Dean, 1934 StL NL
3.37 ERA/5 SHO, Matt Kilroy, 1886 Bal AA
3.26 ERA/5 SHO, Larry Jaster, 1966 StL NL

Jones was stingier than his teammate, posting a 2.94 ERA with 19 victories. He also outhit Schmidt, batting a solid .256 and driving in 13 runs, compared with Schmidt's .196 BA and ten RBI.

While the Brooklyn duo debuted in April when the season opened, a pair of Cleveland twirlers did not appear until the campaign was well past the midpoint and

Until recently Brooklyn was credited with having two rookie 20-game winners in 1903, Henry Schmidt and Oscar "Flip Flap" Jones. Jones's win total has been reduced to 19, but he and Schmidt continue to hold the post-1901 record for the most wins by two rookie teammates on a second-division team after bagging 42 victories with the fifth-place Superbas. In addition, Schmidt holds a number of One Year Wonder pitching records. Rather surprisingly, one record that eluded him is the mark for the most wins by a pitcher who served almost entirely as a starter and made fewer than 50 career starts.

Here are the all-time top ten in wins, excluding pitchers who appeared in more than ten games in relief.

Rank	Name	Years	G	GS	Wins
1	Jim Gardner	1895–1902	59	49	25
2	Tom Walker	1902–05	48	44	24
	Harry Salisbury	1879, 1882	48	48	24
	Will Calihan	1890–91	50	47	24
	Bill Wise	1882–86	54	45	24
	Bobby Wallace	1894–1902	57	48	24
7	Walter Thornton	1895–98	56	48	23
	Jocko Flynn	1886–87	32	29	23
	Charlie Case	1901–06	54	46	23
10	Henry Schmidt	1903	40	36	22

yet still found ample time to impress AL batsmen. Ed Killian first took the mound for the Naps on August 25 and a week later blanked the St. Louis Browns. The lefty tossed two more shutouts through September 11. Killian collected just three wins overall in 1903 and remains the only rookie to register more than two victories with each being a shutout. Jesse Stovall, who debuted on August 31, pitched 11 scoreless innings in beating Detroit 1–0 on September 3. When he fired another shutout five days later, it meant that during an 11-day period, from September 1 through 11, the two Cleveland latecomers had notched five whitewashes.

Chief Bender may not have held as many teams scoreless as Killian, but he won considerably more games. The Philadelphia Athletics righty claimed 17 triumphs for the junior circuit's runner-up club, which also enjoyed a dozen yearling wins from Weldon Henley. But their success was not enough for Philadelphia to defend its AL flag against the onrushing Pilgrims, who had only one frosh hurler of consequence, 13-game winner Norwood Gibson, but got 49 combined victories from veteran Bill Dinneen and the redoubtable Cy Young.

Other Highlights

April 19—Mordecai "Three-Finger" Brown throws five innings of one-hit ball for the St. Louis Cardinals in his major league debut, shutting out Chicago 3–0 in a rain-shortened game.

May 4—Henry Schmidt pitches his third consecutive shutout for the Brooklyn Superbas in their 5–0 win versus the Philadelphia Phillies.

1903 ROOKIE LEADERS

Batting	Pitching
G—AL 138, Lee Tannehill, CHI	W—AL 17, Chief Bender, PHI
NL 136, Ed Abbaticchio, BOS	NL 22, Henry Schmidt, BRO
AB—AL 548, Charlie Carr, DET	L—AL 14, Chief Bender, PHI
NL 506, Jimmy Sebring, PIT	NL 19, Chappie McFarland, STL
H—AL 154, Charlie Carr, DET	PCT—AL .548, Chief Bender, PHI
NL 140, Jimmy Sebring, PIT	NL .714, Jake Weimer, CHI
2B—AL 23, Charlie Carr, DET	GP—AL 36, Chief Bender, PHI
NL 27, Johnny Evers, CHI	NL 40, Henry Schmidt, BRO
3B—AL 11, Charlie Carr, DET	GS—AL 33, Chief Bender, PHI
NL 15, Dave Brain, STL	NL 36, Oscar Jones, BRO
HR—AL 2, Charlie Carr, DET	Henry Schmidt, BRO
Danny Hoffman, PHI	CG—AL 29, Chief Bender, PHI
Jake Stahl, BOS	NL 31, Oscar Jones, BRO
Lee Tannehill, CHI	IP—AL 270.0, Chief Bender, PHI
NL 4, Jimmy Sebring, PIT	NL 324.1, Oscar Jones, BRO
R—AL 59, Charlie Carr, DET	H—AL 239, Chief Bender, PHI
NL 71, Jimmy Sebring, PIT	NL 321, Henry Schmidt, BRO
RBI—AL 79, Charlie Carr, DET	BB—AL 67, Weldon Henley, PHI
NL 64, Jimmy Sebring, PIT	NL 120, Henry Schmidt, BRO
WK—AL 33, Charles Moran, WAS	K—AL 127, Chief Bender, PHI
Rabbit Robinson, WAS	NL 128, Jake Weimer, CHI
NL 52, Ed Abbaticchio, BOS	ERA—AL 2.97, Barney Wolfe, NY
SO—AL NA	NL 2.30, Jake Weimer, CHI
NL NA	SHO—AL 3, Ed Killian, CLE
SB—AL 16, Rabbit Robinson, WAS	NL 5, Henry Schmidt, BRO
NL 25, Johnny Evers, CHI	SV—AL 1, Doc Adkins, NY
BA—AL .281, Charlie Carr, DET	Barney Pelty, STL
NL .293, Johnny Evers, CHI	Ed Pinnance, PHI
SLG—AL .374, Charlie Carr, DET	NL 2, Henry Schmidt, BRO
NL .383, Jimmy Sebring, PIT	
OBP—AL .296, Charlie Carr, DET	
NL .337, Charlie Babb, NY	

May 30—Weldon Henley tosses a 10-inning three-hit shutout of the New York Highlanders as the Philadelphia Athletics win the opener of a doubleheader 1–0.

June 2—Chappie McFarland permits only two Philadelphia hits as the Cardinals edge the Phillies 1–0.

June 4—Kaiser Wilhelm keeps Pittsburgh's shutout streak alive with a 5–0 blanking of the Beaneaters; it is the third successive whitewashing by the Pirates, who are on their way to an all-time record 56 consecutive shutout innings that will end on June 9 when Wilhelm holds the Phillies scoreless for the first three innings before proving human in the fourth frame.

June 17—Barney Wolfe fires a one-hitter for the Highlanders and New York nips the Chicago White Stockings 1–0.

June 29—Jake Weimer allows only two hits and no runs for the Cubs, but the game with the Boston Beaneaters ends 0–0 after nine innings because of darkness.

July 11—Oscar Jones of Brooklyn allows only one Chicago Cub to reach second base in his three-hit 2–0 triumph.

August 12—Joe Stanley hits one of two Beaneater grand slams in Boston's 11–10 second-game win against the Colts.

September 14—Red Ames becomes the third hurler in history to toss a no-hitter in his first big league appearance (the previous two were George Nicol and Bumpus Jones) when he leads the Giants to a 5–0 win over the Cardinals in the finale of a twinbill that darkness limits to five frames.

October 2—Bucky Veil pitches seven innings of one-run relief for Pittsburgh, but the Boston Pilgrims win 3–0 to even the 1903 World Series at one game apiece.

 1904

Hooks Wiltse was unbeatable in 1904—for most of the season anyway. Of Wiltse's first 20 appearances for the New York Giants, 12 were starts and he won them all, becoming the only freshman ever to do so.* Finally, in

---

*In 1976 Butch Metzger got off to a 12–0 career start, but all his wins came in relief.

the second game of a September 22 doubleheader, Wiltse proved fallible, losing to the Cincinnati Reds. New York had clinched the NL flag in the opener, so Wiltse never lost when the pennant race was extant. He also dropped his next two starts before rebounding with a three-hit shutout on October 8 to finish the year 13–3.

Getting two of Brooklyn's hits that October day was Harry Lumley, whose power production was most unique. Lumley, the Superbas right fielder, topped the NL with 18 triples and nine home runs to join Harry Stovey as one of only two rookies among the handful of hitters who have led their league in both these categories. All told, Lumley ripped 50 extra base hits, at the time an NL rookie record for the Deadball Era.

MOST EXTRA BASE HITS BY NL ROOKIE, 1901–19

53 (36 2B/15 3B/2 HR), Zack Wheat, 1910 Bro NL
50 (23 2B/18 3B/9 HR), Harry Lumley, 1904 Bro NL
48 (21 2B/25 3B/2 HR), Tom Long, 1915 StL NL
47 (31 2B/13 3B/3HR), Dots Miller, 1909 Pit NL
43 (37 2B/4 3B/2 HR), George Burns, 1913 NY NL

More symbolic of this era than the slugging Lumley was Miller Huggins of Cincinnati. The scrappy second baseman scored 96 runs and had a .377 OBP, both fourth best in the NL. The 88 walks Huggins amassed were second only to leadoff man extraordinaire Roy Thomas and would not be surpassed by another NL freshman until 1943. On October 8 in a Cincinnati win at St. Louis, the fleet Huggins became the first rookie in the twentieth century to leg out three triples in a game.

ROOKIES WITH THREE TRIPLES IN ONE GAME, 1901–2003

Miller Huggins, Cin NL, October 8 (2), 1904
Jack Lewis, Pit FL, May 7, 1914
Jackie Tavener, Det AL, September 12, 1925
Carlos Bernier, Pit NL, May 2, 1953
Al Bumbry, Bal AL, September 22, 1973

Two of Huggins's teammates achieved something no other tandem in Cincinnati history could claim. Tom Walker and Win Kellum both won 15 games, the only Reds rookie pair ever to notch that many victories in the same season. Walker's performance was slightly superior as he lost only eight games while tossing two shutouts and posting a 2.24 ERA. Kellum, who had started the first game in Boston Red Sox history three years earlier, was 15–10 with a slightly less imposing 2.60 ERA.

A pair of St. Louis Browns hurlers did the Reds freshmen duo one better—make that three better. Fred Glade and Barney Pelty, both right-handers, combined to win 33 games, or more than half of the team's total output of 65. On July 15 Glade fanned 15 Washington Senators and walked none in his 7–2 triumph. He tossed six shutouts, including three in September, and went 18–15, the opposite record of Pelty. In 1904 Glade won the most games by a Browns rookie in the team's 52-year tenure in St. Louis, and Pelty is tied for third.

MOST WINS BY ST. LOUIS BROWNS ROOKIE, 1902–53

18, Fred Glade, 1904
16, Bobo Newsom, 1934
15, Barney Pelty, 1904
15, Jack Ogden, 1928
14, Allen Sothoron, 1917

Bad as the 1904 Browns were, they far outshone the Senators, who at 38–113 finished 23½ games out of—seventh place! The team did have a number of rookie high points, however. On July 29 Beany Jacobson pitched a 12-inning shutout of Cleveland, winning 1–0. Jacobson won only five games that year and dropped 23, still the second most by an AL freshman. Meanwhile, shortstop Joe Cassidy legged out 19 triples, earning him a piece of the loop's frosh record standard.

The Senators found Chicago White Sox righty Frank Smith to be particularly bothersome. Of Smith's four whitewashes, three were against the D.C. boys. He won 16 games and worked his way into the league's top five in winning percentage (.640) and OBA (.215).

Smith's 2.09 ERA was well below the league average of 2.60 but still fell far short of Otto Hess's recruit performance for Cleveland. Hess finished third at 1.67 and tossed four blankings. The Cleveland rookie, who made 21 appearances, didn't throw the first of his shutouts until September 17. Oddly, three were abbreviated five-inning games against the Detroit Tigers.

In 1904 the Washington Senators fielded one of the worst teams in history but, judging at least from the rookie leader board, they would seem to have produced the richest yearling crop in the majors that year as no less than three D.C. recruit hitters, including outfielder Frank Huelsman, who actually played with a rookie-record four different teams, appear on the offensive side of the ledger.

The Senators' real gem in 1904 was 21-year-old shortstop Joe Cassidy. After setting an AL record for triples by a rookie, in 1905 Cassidy slipped significantly in most offensive categories but came to the fore on defense, leading all AL performers in fielding runs with 34. Just how good a player Cassidy would have become if his career had been allowed to proceed in normal fashion will forever remain an unanswerable question.

On the eve of what would have been his third season, Cassidy died of typhoid fever at his home in Chester, Pennsylvania.

Other Highlights

April 22—Art Devlin collects four hits, including a grand slam, and scores four runs in the New York Giants' 18–3 pasting of the Philadelphia Phillies.

May 10—Miller Huggins hits a grand slam in a seven-run second inning for Cincinnati as the Reds beat the Brooklyn Superbas 9–7.

May 19—Ed Walsh throws the first shutout of his Hall-of-Fame career for the White Sox, beating Washington 5–0 and permitting just two hits—doubles to fellow freshmen Joe Cassidy and Jake Stahl.

May 21—Outfielder Bill O'Neill commits six errors for the Boston Pilgrims in their 5–3 13-inning loss to the St. Louis Browns.

June 19—Fred Glade of the Browns strikes out ten New York Highlanders and wins 1–0.

June 22—John McPherson earns his only major league victory—a 13-inning shutout for the Phillies; McPherson, who will finish the season 1–12 and his career 1–13, tops Brooklyn 1–0.

September 9—Rookies Red Ames of the Giants and the Phillies' Frank Corridon battle to a scoreless tie in the

1904 ROOKIE LEADERS

Batting	Pitching
G—AL 152, Joe Cassidy, WAS	W—AL 18, Fred Glade, STL
NL 150, Harry Lumley, BRO	NL 15, Win Kellum, CIN
AB—AL 581, Joe Cassidy, WAS	Mike Lynch, PIT
NL 577, Harry Lumley, BRO	Tom Walker, CIN
H—AL 140, Joe Cassidy, WAS	L—AL 23, Beany Jacobson, WAS
NL 161, Harry Lumley, BRO	NL 16, Tom Fisher, BOS
2B—AL 29, Jake Stahl, WAS	PCT—AL .640, Frank Smith, CHI
NL 27, Jim Delahanty, BOS	NL .652, Tom Walker, CIN
3B—**AL 19, Joe Cassidy, WAS**	GP—AL 39, Barney Pelty, STL
NL 18, Harry Lumley, BRO	NL 31, Tom Fisher, BOS
HR—AL 3, Jake Stahl, WAS	Win Kellum, CIN
NL 9, Harry Lumley, BRO	GS—AL 35, Barney Pelty, STL
R—AL 63, Joe Cassidy, WAS	NL 24, Win Kellum, CIN
NL 96, Miller Huggins, CIN	Mike Lynch, PIT
RBI—AL 50, Jake Stahl, WAS	Tom Walker, CIN
NL 78, Harry Lumley, BRO	CG—AL 31, Barney Pelty, STL
WK—AL 31 Frank Huelsman, CHI/DET/STL/WAS	NL 24, Mike Lynch, PIT
NL 88, Miller Huggins, CIN	IP—AL 301.0, Barney Pelty, STL
SO—AL NA	NL 224.2, Win Kellum, CIN
NL NA	H—AL 276, Beany Jacobson, WAS
SB—AL 25, Jake Stahl, WAS	NL 257, Tom Fisher, BOS
NL 36, Danny Shay, STL	BB—AL 77, Barney Pelty, STL
BA—AL .262, Jake Stahl, WAS	NL 91, Mike Lynch, PIT
NL .285, Jim Delahanty, BOS	K—AL 156, Fred Glade, STL
SLG—AL .381, Jake Stahl, WAS	NL 105, Hooks Wiltse, NY
NL .428, Harry Lumley, BRO	ERA—AL 2.09, Frank Smith, CHI
OBP—AL .309, Jake Stahl, WAS	NL 2.24, Tom Walker, CIN
NL .377, Miller Huggins, CIN	SHO—AL 6, Fred Glade, STL
	NL 3, Charlie Case, PIT
	Doc Scanlan, BRO
	SV—AL 1, Walter Clarkson, NY
	Fred Glade, STL
	Ed Walsh, CHI
	NL 3, Red Ames, NY
	Hooks Wiltse, NY

five-inning finale of a doubleheader; Corridon permits only one hit in the darkness-shortened game.

September 25—Fred Glade and the Browns nip the Senators 1–0; it is the third shutout of the month for Glade, giving him a rookie-best six for the year.

October 10—Ambrose Puttman goes the distance for the Highlanders, beating the Pilgrims 1–0 in the ten-inning finale of a doubleheader after Boston had clinched the AL pennant in the opener.

1905

Many players are superstitious about their uniform numbers. But in the Deadball Era when enumerated jerseys were still more than two decades away from becoming part of the game, Ed Reulbach had to have fancied the number 24. Reulbach, who debuted for the Chicago Cubs in mid-May, pitched an 18-inning gem on June 24, beating the St. Louis Cardinals 2–1. Exactly a month later, he tossed a three-shutout at Philadelphia for his fourth of five whitewashes in 1905. On August 24, again in the City of Brotherly Love, Reulbach hooked up in a marathon duel with the Phillies. The Cubs won 2–1 in 20 innings as the two clubs tied the then-existing record for the longest game in ML history. In these three contests, Reulbach allowed but three runs in 47 innings. He led the NL by holding batters to a .201 average and was second only to Christy Mathewson in opponents' OBP and ERA, the latter department with a figure that is second to none among yearling hurlers who carried as heavy a workload.

LOWEST ERA BY ROOKIE (MINIMUM 250 IP)

1.42 ERA/291.2 IP, Ed Reulbach, 1905 Chi NL
1.508 ERA/250.2 IP, Jack Pfiester, 1906 Chi NL
1.509 ERA/334 IP, John Ward, 1878 Pro NL
1.53 ERA/359.2 IP, George McQuillan, 1908 Phi NL
1.64 ERA/301 IP, Ed Summers, 1908 Det AL

Orval Overall matched Reulbach, his future Cubs teammate, with 18 victories for Cincinnati. Overall fanned 173 batters, third most in the loop, and made 42 appearances. On July 17 the Reds rookie ace blanked the Phillies 1–0 in ten innings, the lone hit off him resulting from his failure to cover first base on a grounder to first sacker Shad Barry. Overall, who lost 23 games, was one of three freshmen to endure at least 20 defeats, the largest collection of rookies to do so in any year after 1900. Another future Cub, Harry McIntire, dropped 25 games for Brooklyn while Irv Young performed a unique feat for the Boston Beaneaters. Young won 20 times, but he lost one more, becoming the sole rookie since 1900 to reach 20 in both wins and losses. In topping the senior circuit with 378 innings, the second most for a freshman since 1893 when the current pitching distance was set, Young completed 41 games, seven of them shutouts.

The AL had no such freshman standouts in its pitching ranks. The loop's rookies combined to win a mere 32 games. Bill Hogg set the pace with nine for the New York Highlanders while Jim Buchanan of the St. Louis Browns was the only other junior circuit recruit with more than three victories, copping five.

Although the Browns finished in last place, they showcased an excellent new offensive weapon in George Stone. The rookie left fielder set a new twentieth-century mark for recruits when he delivered 187 hits.

MOST HITS BY ROOKIE, 1900–10

187, George Stone, 1905 StL AL
186, Irv Waldron, 1901 Mil/Was AL
172, Jimmy Barrett, 1900 Cin NL
172, Zack Wheat, 1910 Bro NL
168, Tris Speaker, 1909 Bos AL

Stone's 632 ABs were also the rookie standard until 1928. He led the AL in total bases, was second in homers, and tied for fourth in triples. Stone hit .296, finishing a dozen points behind the loop leader. The next season, he batted .358, taking the title before another 1905 freshman put it on his annual to-do list. Ty Cobb debuted on August 30 for Detroit, going 1-for-3, with his first of over 4,000 safeties being a double off Jack Chesbro. Despite hitting just .240 in 41 games, Cobb would follow Stone's 1906 bat title by grabbing all but one AL hitting crown from 1907 through 1919.

On the surface at least, Ty Cobb would appear to have had a discouraging rookie year, hitting just .240 after a late-season summons to Detroit. Actually, in the entire Deadball Era (1901–19) only one other performer as young as 18 played in as many games as Cobb and outhit him. That was Johnny Lush, whom the Phillies, perhaps wrongly, decided was better suited to pitching after his stellar debut in 1904.

As can be seen from the top-ten Deadball-Era (1901–19) list, in his sophomore year Cobb fashioned far and away the best hitting season by a teenage performer and rated pretty well even as a freshman. The list is limited to teenage seasons of at least 40 games and 100 at bats.

Rank	Name	Age	Year	G	AB	BA
1	Ty Cobb	19	1906	98	358	.316
2	Sherry Magee	19	1904	95	364	.277
3	Johnny Lush	18	1904	106	369	.276
4	Mike Menosky	19	1914	68	140	.264
5	Les Mann	19	1913	120	407	.253
6	Ty Cobb	18	1905	41	150	.240
7	Jack Burnett	17	1907	59	206	.238
8	Harry Heilmann	19	1914	68	182	.225
9	Eddie Ainsmith	19	1911	61	149	.221
10	Charlie Grimm	19	1918	50	141	.220

Even though the NL outhit the AL by 15 points—.256 to .241—the senior loop had no rookie batsmen that approached Stone's magnitude. The best of a relatively inauspicious bunch were Emil Batch, who had 143 hits for Brooklyn; Wildfire Schulte, with eight fewer safeties for the Cubs; Phillies shortstop Mickey Doolan, who legged out 27 doubles and 11 three-baggers; and first sacker Del Howard of Pittsburgh. Howard had the distinction of pacing all NL freshmen in RBI, BA, OBP, and SA.

Other Highlights

May 1—Bill Hogg of the New York Highlanders suffers a tough 4–3 loss to Boston's Cy Young in his first ML start; Hogg will be the lone rookie ERA qualifier in the AL and also both its top recruit winner and loser.

June 10—The 1905 rookie home run king, George Stone, goes yard for the first time in his career against Jack Powell of the New York Highlanders; by the close of the season, the two will be teammates on the St. Louis Browns.

August 3—Charlie Chech of the Cincinnati Reds blanks Brooklyn 5–0.

October 3—When Irv Young of the Boston Beaneaters sustains his 20th loss of the season, 10–2 to Pittsburgh in the first game of a doubleheader, it insures that he will become the only hurler since 1901 both to win and lose 20 games in his rookie season.

October 7—Frank LaPorte hits a grand slam for the New York Highlanders, but the Boston Pilgrims win the first game 7–6 in ten innings.

1905 ROOKIE LEADERS

Batting	Pitching
G—AL 154, George Stone, STL	W—AL 9, Bill Hogg, NY
NL 145, Emil Batch, BRO	NL 20, Irv Young, BOS
AB—AL 632, George Stone, STL	L—AL 13, Bill Hogg, NY
NL 568, Emil Batch, BRO	NL 25, Harry McIntire, BRO
H—AL 187, George Stone, STL	PCT—AL .409, Bill Hogg, NY
NL 143, Emil Batch, BRO	NL .563, Ed Reulbach, CHI
2B—AL 25, George Stone, STL	GP—AL 39, Bill Hogg, NY
NL 27, Mickey Doolan, PHI	NL 43, Irv Young, BOS
3B—AL 13, George Stone, STL	GS—AL 22, Bill Hogg, NY
NL 14, Wildfire Schulte, CHI	**NL 42, Irv Young, BOS**
HR—AL 7, George Stone, STL	CG—AL 12, Jim Buchanan, STL
NL 5, Emil Batch, BRO	**NL 41, Irv Young, BOS**
R—AL 76, George Stone, STL	IP—AL 205.0, Bill Hogg, NY
NL 74, Otis Clymer, PIT	**NL 378.0, Irv Young, BOS**
RBI—AL 52, George Stone, STL	H—AL 178, Bill Hogg, NY
NL 63, Del Howard, PIT	**NL 340, Harry McIntire, BRO**
WK—AL 46, Ike Rockenfield, STL	BB—AL 101, Bill Hogg, NY
NL 32, Wildfire Schulte, CHI	NL 147, Orval Overall, CIN
SO—AL NA	K—AL 125, Bill Hogg, NY
NL NA	NL 173, Orval Overall, CIN
SB—AL 26, George Stone, STL	ERA—AL 3.20, Bill Hogg, NY
NL 23, Otis Clymer, PIT	NL 1.42, Ed Reulbach, CHI
BA—AL .296, George Stone, STL	SH—AL 3, Bill Hogg, NY
NL .292, Del Howard, PIT	NL 7, Irv Young, BOS
SLG—AL .410, George Stone, STL	**SV—AL 2, Jim Buchanan, STL**
NL .370, Del Howard, PIT	NL 1, done by six pitchers
OBP—AL .347, George Stone, STL	
NL .345, Del Howard, PIT	

Chicago benefited from a unique confluence of events in 1906. True, that was the year that Upton Sinclair's *The Jungle* was published, telling the world of the unsavory conditions in the Windy City's meat packing plants. Balancing that blight on the Windy City's reputation, however, was the fact that for the only time in history both of Chicago's baseball teams made it to the World Series.

Spearheading the Cubs' cause was rookie lefthander Jack Pfiester, who authored many memorable games in 1906. On May 30 he pitched all 15 innings and struck out 17 batters, only to lose to the St. Louis Cardinals 4–2. Then Pfiester threw his third of four shutouts on September 25, holding the Brooklyn Superbas to one hit in ten innings and winning 1–0. Nine days later, he chalked up his 20th victory of the season by blanking the Pittsburgh Pirates. That represented the Cubs' 116th win, establishing the mark the 2001 Seattle Mariners matched in ten additional games.

In the World Series, Pfiester ran into the White Sox, dubbed the Hitless Wonders. In Game Three he permitted a three-run triple in the sixth inning and lost 3–0. Pfiester relieved in the fifth contest and permitted four runs while gaining but four outs, again taking the loss. The White Sox took the Series the next day.

Fred Beebe was a teammate of Pfiester's, albeit only for the first half of the season. Beebe was 6–1 for Chicago but posted a 2.70 ERA, well above the miserly 1.76 mark the Cubs would post in 1906. After being traded July 1, the Nebraska-born rookie went a very respectable 9–9 for the seventh-place Cardinals, leading the staff in victories. Beebe in addition topped the NL with 171 strikeouts to become one of only five pitchers to lead his league in that category while dividing the year between two teams.

PITCHERS LEADING LEAGUE IN Ks WHILE PLAYING FOR MORE THAN ONE CLUB

Hugh Daily, 1884 CP/Was UA, 483
Sadie McMahon, 1890 Phi/Bal AA, 291
Fred Beebe, 1906 Chi/StL NL, 171
Claude Passeau, 1939 Phi/Chi NL, 137
Bert Blyleven, 1985 Cle/Min AL, 206

Beebe was not the sole freshman to be a statistical pacesetter in the senior circuit. Jim Nealon, the first baseman for Pittsburgh, tied for the RBI title with 83, and his 82 runs ranked him fourth. Nealon would play only one more season in the majors and then die at age 25 in 1910. His counterpart in Brooklyn was Tim Jordan, the NL's home run leader with a dozen. Jordan, who in 1908 would lead the loop again with the same total, was fourth in RBI in 1906. This meant that rookies represented half of the NL's top four batters in sending runners across home plate.

Beebe's fellow Redbird rookie Pug Bennett played in all but one of the team's 154 contests, making him the lone Cardinal to participate in as many as 100 games. Bennett's patchwork team won just 52 games, but Joe Harris's club was even worse. The Boston Red

By 1906 both major leagues were in the depths of the Deadball Era. The average BA that year was .247 and the average SA was .315, which meant that a rookie who hit .252 and slugged .336 was a valuable commodity, especially if he was a second baseman with decent fielding numbers.

We are talking here about Whitey Alperman, a member for four years of Brooklyn, which was the weakest-hitting team in the majors during that span. In his sophomore year Alperman tied for the NL lead in triples with 16 but declined a bit in most other batting departments. Two years later he played his last innings in the majors despite racking up 12 three baggers, the most ever to that point by an NL or AL player in his final season.

What motivated Brooklyn to cut Alperman after the 1909 campaign? One reason certainly was that he loathed getting a base on balls, and his aversion no doubt contributed heavily to some very low personal run totals. In four seasons and 1,632 at bats, Alperman collected just 30 walks. Among players since 1889 (the year that four balls first constituted a walk) who rapped as many as 35 career triples, he earned the fewest walks and is alone in notching more three-baggers than bases on balls. Note that the even the all-time list of players who collected as many as 35 career triples and registered more three-baggers than bases on balls is very short.

Name	AB	3B	BB
Whitey Alperman	1632	36	30
Sadie Houck	2662	58	48

Sox were 49–105 in 1906, finishing eight games out of seventh place. Saddled with such dismal support, Harris turned in a miserable 2–21 record for a .087 winning percentage that stands as the worst in rookie history according to Major League Baseball, although those who recognize the National Association as a major circuit know otherwise.

LOWEST WINNING PERCENTAGE BY ROOKIE (MINIMUM 20 DECISIONS)

.045, 1W–21L, John Cassidy, 1875 Atl NA
.087, 2W–21L, Joe Harris, 1906 Bos AL
.121, 4W–29L, Tricky Nichols, 1875 NH NA
.133, 4W–26L, Dory Dean, 1876 Cin NL
.136, 3W–19L, Sam Moffett, 1884 Cle NL
.136, 3W–19L, Kirtley Baker, 1890 Pit NL
.136, 3W–19L, Walt Dickson, 1912 Bos NL

Harris had two highlights, however, in his lone full season in the majors. He tossed a four-hit shutout at Cleveland on August 8, winning 1–0. Then on September 1, Harris hooked up in an epic duel with fellow rookie righty Jack Coombs of the Philadelphia Athletics. Both hurlers completed the 24-inning marathon, which took four hours and 47 minutes to play. Harris, who lost 4–1, yielded 16 hits and two walks while fanning 14. Coombs permitted 14 safeties and walked six. He whiffed 18 men, the most until 1998 by a freshman in any single contest, regardless of length.

Two months earlier, on July 5, Coombs had tossed a shutout in his major league debut. Three other frosh pitchers matched Coombs's feat in 1906. Vive Lindaman applied the whitewash for the Boston Beaneaters on April 14, as did Slow Joe Doyle for the New York High-

1906 ROOKIE LEADERS

Batting	Pitching
G—AL 151, Pete O'Brien, STL	W—AL 11, Jimmy Dygert, PHI
NL 154, Jim Nealon, PIT	NL 20, Jack Pfiester, CHI
AB—AL 541, Harry Niles, STL	**L—AL 21, Joe Harris, BOS**
NL 595, Pug Bennett, STL	NL 23, Vive Lindaman, BOS
H—AL 124, Harry Niles, STL	PCT—AL .500, Jack Coombs, PHI
NL 156, Pug Bennett, STL	NL .714, Jack Pfiester, CHI
2B—AL 23, Frank LaPorte, NY	GP—AL 35, Jimmy Dygert, PHI
NL 21, Johnny Bates, BOS	NL 39, Vive Lindaman, BOS
Jim Nealon, PIT	GS—AL 25, Jimmy Dygert, PHI
3B—AL 9, Frank LaPorte, NY	NL 37, Vive Lindaman, BOS
NL 12, Jim Nealon, PIT	CG—AL 20, Joe Harris, BOS
HR—AL 3, Branch Rickey, STL	NL 32, Vive Lindaman, BOS
NL 12, Tim Jordan, BRO	IP—AL 235.1, Charlie Smith, WAS
R—AL 71, Harry Niles, STL	NL 307.1, Vive Lindaman, BOS
NL 82, Jim Nealon, PIT	H—AL 250, Charlie Smith, WAS
RBI—AL 57, Pete O'Brien, STL	NL 303, Vive Lindaman, BOS
NL 83, Jim Nealon, PIT	BB—AL 91, Jimmy Dygert, PHI
WK—AL 50, Harry Schlafly, WAS	NL 100, Fred Beebe, CHI/STL
NL 59, Tim Jordan, BRO	K—AL 106, Jimmy Dygert, PHI
SO—AL NA	**NL 171, Fred Beebe, CHI/STL**
NL NA	ERA—AL 2.50, Jack Coombs, PHI
SB—AL 37, Dave Altizer, WAS	NL 1.51, Jack Pfiester, CHI
NL 20, Pug Bennett, STL	SHO—AL 4, Jimmy Dygert, PHI
Hans Lobert, CIN	NL 4, Jack Pfiester, CHI
BA—AL .308, Claude Rossman, CLE	SV—AL 2, John Eubank, DET
NL .262, Tim Jordan, BRO	Joe Harris, BOS
SLG—AL .368, Frank LaPorte, NY	**NL 7, George Ferguson, NY**
NL .422, Tim Jordan, BRO	
OBP—AL .334, Harry Schlafly, WAS	
NL .350, Tim Jordan, BRO	

landers on August 25. On September 30 Rube Kroh of the Red Sox made it a quartet with a two-hitter against the St. Louis Browns.

Other Highlights

April 12—Johnny Bates homers in his first ML at bat for the Boston Beaneaters, who beat Brooklyn 2–0 on Opening Day.

July 22—Fred Beebe fans 13 Beaneaters and the St. Louis Cardinals win 4–1.

August 30—Slow Joe Doyle of the New York Highlanders fires a two-hit shutout against the Washington Senators as he becomes one of the few pitchers to toss shutouts in their first two big league starts.

August 31—The youngest of the most famous quintet of brothers in baseball lore, Frank Delahanty goes 4-for-5 with a triple and two home runs, driving in seven in the Highlanders 20–5 trouncing of Washington in a game shortened to six innings due to darkness.

September 11—Frank LaPorte hits a grand slam, two triples, and a single for the Highlanders in their 11–3 win against the Boston Red Sox.

September 24—Cards hurler Stoney McGlynn tosses a seven-inning no-hitter against Brooklyn that ends in a 1–1 tie.

October 5—In his only big league start, Henry Mathewson, showing none of his brother Christy's control, permits 14 walks to the Beaneaters while the New York Giants fall 7–1.

1907

Be afraid, be very afraid. Those words from the movie *Alien* could have served as a warning to the Detroit Tigers on August 2, 1907, when Walter Johnson debuted for the Washington Senators. Johnson, with his superhuman fastball, must have seemed from another planet, impressing even the normally disdainful Ty Cobb. Detroit beat the 19-year-old that day, but John-

son would prevail 417 times in his career. He went 5–9 as a rookie for the last-place Senators but had an excellent 1.88 ERA and two shutouts.

Three other pitchers, all from the NL, dazzled fans in 1907 trials that were even briefer than Johnson's. Nick Maddox made six starts for the Pittsburgh Pirates, the first on September 13 when he fanned 11 St. Louis Cardinals in blanking them 4–0. After another win against the Redbirds three days later, Maddox faced the Brooklyn Superbas on September 20. The right-hander held them hitless but permitted an unearned run in the fourth, costing him the shutout. Maddox finished 5–1 with a 0.83 ERA and allowed but 32 hits in 54 innings. Philadelphia Phillie George McQuillan pitched a scoreless inning of relief on May 8 and then didn't work again until September 22. He blanked the Cardinals for nine innings, but the game ended in a scoreless tie. Three days later, McQuillan held the Chicago Cubs to two hits in a six-inning whitewash and permitted the same meager amount of safeties on September 29 in shutting out Cincinnati. McQuillan was now unscathed in his first 25 innings, the longest such skein to begin an ML career. In his next start he surrendered a first-inning run but beat Pittsburgh 4–1. McQuillan yielded only three runs in 41 innings and the following year would win 23 contests for Philadelphia. Fellow Phillie Harry Coveleski set an all-time frosh record of his own when he pitched 20 innings of relief beginning on September 10 and didn't allow a single earned run.

MOST INNINGS BY ROOKIE WITH ERA OF 0.00

20.0, Harry Coveleski, 1907 Phi NL
18.0, Karl Spooner, 1954 Bro NL
17.2, Fernando Valenzuela, 1980 LA NL
16.2, Mike Norris, 1975 Oak AL
16.0, Wayne Twitchell, 1971 Phi NL

Toiling far more than Coveleski were Stoney McGlynn, Glenn Liebhardt, and Nap Rucker. McGlynn led both the Cardinals and the entire senior circuit with 33 complete games and 352⅓ innings. On June 3 he blanked the Reds in the first game of a doubleheader at Cincinnati. McGlynn also started and completed the second contest but fell victim to poor defense and lost 5–1. With 25 losses, he was one of only three freshman hurlers since 1901 to suffer that many defeats. Unlike McGlynn, Liebhardt had the good fortune of being on a contender, fourth-place Cleveland, which landed just eight games back of Detroit. Liebhardt had a 2.05 ERA and contributed 18 victories. His four shutouts included consecutive 5–0 gems on June 6 and 10. Rucker, a southpaw 15-game winner for Brooklyn, twirled his best game as a rookie on June 18, limiting the Cardinals to a pair of singles in his 1–0 triumph.

The Cardinals and Reds had the largest collection of recruit batters to reach 100 safeties. In a year that saw neither league hit .250, 11 freshmen attained this modest hit total, three apiece for the aforementioned clubs. Mike Mitchell batted .292 for Cincinnati and led the way with 163 safeties, a dozen of them triples. St. Louis third baseman Bobby Byrne ended a distant second on the rookie hit list, garnering 20 fewer than Mitchell. Simon Nicholls of the Philadelphia Athletics hit .302, the only time a rookie in the heart of the Deadball Era from 1903 through 1908 topped the .300 plateau with at least 400 at bats. Nicholls, a shortstop, amassed 139 hits, four more than Boston's Denny Sullivan. The Red Sox center fielder knocked 18 doubles but no triples in 551 ABs, the most ever for a rookie without a three-bagger. Sullivan, however, did manage one home run.

MOST ABs BY ROOKIE WITH FEWER THAN TWO COMBINED 3Bs AND HRs

551 AB/0 3B/1 HR, Denny Sullivan, 1907 Bos AL
511 AB/1 3B/0 HR, George Scharein, 1937 Phi NL
510 AB/1 3B/0 HR, Eddie Stanky, 1943 Chi NL
508 AB/1 3B/0 HR, Spook Jacobs, 1954 Phi AL
504 AB/1 3B/0 HR, Steve Mesner, 1943 Cin NL

Other Highlights

June 8—Lew Moren tosses a one-hit shutout for the Philadelphia Phillies, who top the St. Louis Cardinals 3–0.

August 7—Walter Johnson bags the first of his AL-record 417 wins, beating Cleveland 7–2.

In February 1907 the Pirates sold their incumbent right-fielder Bob Ganley to Washington after he could generate only a .295 SA in his rookie season. During Pittsburgh's training camp that spring, Goat Anderson, a 27-year-old rookie who had been purchased from South Bend of the Central League, emerged victorious in the battle for Ganley's old job. Long before the close of the 1907 season, Ganley's .295 SA had begun to look much better to Pirates player-manager Fred Clarke, as Anderson could fashion just 93 total bases in 127 games and a meager .225 SA, the lowest ever by a right fielder with a minimum of 400 at bats.

Clarke could not replace Anderson quickly enough, but he may have made a grave mistake. Along with his negative SA record, in his lone big league season Anderson also established three positive One Year Wonder records: the most steals (27) and the most runs (73) by an NL player, plus the all-time mark for the most bases on balls (80).

In addition, Anderson also set the all-time standard for the highest OPS by any player, rookie or vet, with a sub .250 SA. Note that Anderson's .225 SA is by far the lowest on the list as his OPS is by far the highest.

Rank	Name	Year	AB	SA	OPS
1	Goat Anderson	1907	413	.225	.568
2	Al Bridwell	1907	509	.242	.551
3	Connie Ryan	1943	457	.249	.550
4	Rollie Zeider	1910	498	.243	.548
5	Will Smalley	1890	502	.239	.542
6	Charlie Jamieson	1918	416	.238	.535
7	Sparky Anderson	1959	477	.249	.532
8	Whitey Wietelmann	1943	534	.245	.527
9	Billy Shindle	1891	415	.246	.523
10	Eddie Mayo	1943	471	.244	.523

August 22—Heinie Wagner of the Boston Red Sox hits the only two home runs he collects in his rookie season, but the Detroit Tigers nonetheless prevail behind Bill Donovan 8–7.

August 28—In his first ML start, Tex Neuer of the Highlanders blanks the Red Sox 1–0; in rapid order Neuer will hurl six complete games, including three shutouts, and then disappear mysteriously from the majors.

September 10—Slow Joe Doyle holds Washington to one hit as the visiting New York Highlanders win 1–0.

Batting	Pitching
G—AL 152, Bill Hinchman, CLE	W—AL 18, Glenn Liebhardt, CLE
NL 150, Ed Holly, STL	NL 15, Nap Rucker, BRO
AB—AL 551, Denny Sullivan, BOS	L—AL 14, Glenn Liebhardt, CLE
NL 559, Bobby Byrne, STL	**NL 25, Stoney McGlynn, STL**
H—AL 139, Simon Nicholls, PHI	PCT—AL .563, Glenn Liebhardt, CLE
NL 163, Mike Mitchell, CIN	NL .536, Nap Rucker, BRO
2B—AL 19, Bill Hinchman, CLE	GP—AL 38, Glenn Liebhardt, CLE
NL 18, Ed Holly, STL	NL 45, Stoney McGlynn, STL
3B—AL 9, Joe Birmingham, CLE	GS—AL 34, Glenn Liebhardt, CLE
Bill Hinchman, CLE	**NL 39, Stoney McGlynn, STL**
NL 12, Mike Mitchell, CIN	CG—AL 27, Glenn Liebhardt, CLE
HR—AL 2, Heinie Wagner, BOS	**NL 33, Stoney McGlynn, STL**
NL 7, Red Murray, STL	IP—AL 280.1, Glenn Liebhardt, CLE
R—AL 75, Simon Nicholls, PHI	**NL 352.1, Stoney McGlynn, STL**
NL 73, Goat Anderson, PIT	H—AL 254, Glenn Liebhardt, CLE
RBI—AL 50, Bill Hinchman, CLE	**NL 329, Stoney McGlynn, STL**
NL 54, Larry McLean, CIN	BB—AL 85, Glenn Liebhardt, CLE
WK—AL 47, Bill Hinchman, CLE	**NL 112, Stoney McGlynn, STL**
NL 80, Goat Anderson, PIT	K—AL 110, Glenn Liebhardt, CLE
SO—AL NA	NL 131, Nap Rucker, BRO
NL NA	ERA—AL 2.05, Glenn Liebhardt, CLE
SB—AL 23, Joe Birmingham, CLE	NL 2.06, Nap Rucker, BRO
NL 27, Goat Anderson, PIT	SHO—AL 4, Glenn Liebhardt, CLE
BA—AL .302, Simon Nicholls, PHI	NL 4, Nap Rucker, BRO
NL .292, Mike Mitchell, CIN	SV—AL 3, Bobby Keefe, NY
SLG—AL .337, Simon Nicholls, PHI	Tex Pruiett, BOS
NL .382, Mike Mitchell, CIN	NL 1, done by six pitchers
OBP—AL .338, Simon Nicholls, PHI	
NL .343, Goat Anderson, PIT	

September 20—Nick Maddox hurls the first and only no-hitter prior to 1951 by a member of the Pittsburgh Pirates franchise, edging Brooklyn's Elmer Stricklett 2–1.

September 26—Heinie Berger of the Cleveland Naps blanks the Highlanders 6–0, permitting just one hit.

October 5—Rube Vickers wins both games for the Athletics, pitching 12 innings of relief at Washington in Philadelphia's 15-frame 4–2 win in the opener of a twinbill, and throwing five perfect innings in the darkness-shortened nightcap, which the A's take 4–0.

1908

Ed Summers joined the elite Detroit starting rotation in 1908. Three Tigers pitchers—Bill Donovan, Ed Killian, and George Mullin—had combined to win 70 games for the AL pennant winners in 1907. Summers responded with a magnificent freshman campaign. His 24 victories not only set the twentieth-century record for most wins by a rookie on a first-place team but also made him the only Bengal with at least 20 triumphs.

MOST WINS BY ROOKIE ON PENNANT WINNER, 1901–2003

24, Ed Summers, 1908 Det AL*
21, Johnny Beazley, 1942 StL NL
20, Roy Patterson, 1901 Chi AL
20, Jack Pfiester, 1906 Chi NL
20, King Cole, 1910 Chi NL
20, Hugh Bedient, 1912 Bos AL
20, Buck O'Brien, 1912 Bos AL
20, Cliff Melton, 1937 NY NL
20, Gene Bearden, 1948 Cle AL**

*led his team in victories
**tied for his team lead in wins

Summers, nicknamed Kickapoo Ed, split his first ten decisions but went 19–7 the remainder of the season to finish 24–12. He beat Rube Waddell and the St. Louis Browns on September 16 to earn his 20th victory. Nine days later Summers became the first rookie since Cy Young in 1890 to complete and win both games of a doubleheader. In the opener he beat the Philadelphia Athletics 7–2, permitting only two hits. Summers was even tougher in the nightcap, yielding but one safety and no walks through nine innings. Detroit hadn't scored yet, however, and Summers had to log one more inning before the Tigers got a run for him to win 1–0. On the day Summers, who was 7–0 against Philadelphia in 1908, toiled 19 innings, allowing two runs on eight hits and three walks.

With a 90–63 record, Detroit finished one-half game ahead of Cleveland. Following the custom of the time, the Tigers were not required to make up a postponed game even though a Detroit defeat would have deadlocked the AL pennant race and forced a playoff.

The Tigers again faced the Chicago Cubs in the World Series and did only slightly better than they had against the Bruins in 1907 when Detroit barely averted a sweep by dint of a 3–3 tie in Game One. In 1908 the Cubs lost once in winning their second consecutive Fall Classic. Summers dropped two games, one in relief, although he did well as a starter in Game Four.

Winning only one fewer game than Summers in 1908 was right-hander George McQuillan of the Philadelphia Phillies. McQuillan impressed the team late in 1907, going 4–0 with an 0.66 ERA in 41 innings.

He suffered his first career loss April 14, 1908, in an Opening Day assignment against the New York Giants. On June 9 McQuillan continued his dominance against the St. Louis Cardinals, blanking them 7–0. Dating back to 1907, he had now thrown 28 consecutive scoreless innings versus the Redbirds. St. Louis pushed across a ninth-inning run off the 23-year-old Phillie on July 15, ending their drought after 36 frames but losing nonetheless, 8–1.

On Independence Day McQuillan dueled Hooks Wiltse and the Giants in an epic battle. Through eight innings McQuillan had yet to allow a run, but Wiltse was even better—perfect in fact. Then, with two out in the top of the ninth, Wiltse hit McQuillan with a pitch after a questionable call deprived the Giant of an inning-ending strike three. The controversial hit bats-

George McQuillan, the NL's leading rookie winner in 1908, prefaced his super recruit performance by going 4–0 with three shutouts for the Phils in the final two weeks of the 1907 season. His feat was almost exactly matched the following year by rookie southpaw Harry Coveleski, brother of Hall of Famer Stan, who won four of five starts for the Phils in the final two weeks of the 1908 season and tossed two shutouts. The difference was that Coveleski's work came almost exclusively against the Giants and was an enormous factor in deciding the 1908 NL pennant race.

Between September 28 and October 3, the Giants and Phils met eight times, with New York winning five of the eight contests. All three of the Giants' losses in the eight-game set were to Coveleski and resulted in his being nicknamed "The Giant Killer," as they were the only defeats New York suffered in its final 13 games of the regular-season schedule. Had the Giants managed to beat Coveleski even once, it would have eliminated the need to replay the notorious "Merkle Game" and given them the 1908 NL pennant.

Date	Place	Score	WP	LP
Sept 28	New York	7–6	McGinnity	Corridon
Sept 29	New York	6–2	Mathewson	McQuillan
Sept 29 (2)	New York	0–7	Coveleski	Crandall
Sept 30	New York	2–1	Ames	Moore
October 1	Philadelphia	4–3	Mathewson	Ritchie
October 1 (2)	Philadelphia	2–6	Coveleski	Wiltse
October 2	Philadelphia	7–2	Ames	McQuillan
October 3	Philadelphia	2–3	Coveleski	Mathewson

Batting	Pitching
G—AL 154, Jerry Freeman, WAS	W—AL 24, Ed Summers, DET
NL 144, Chief Wilson, PIT	NL 23, George McQuillan, PHI
AB—AL 560, Harry Lord, BOS	L—**AL 22, Joe Lake, NY**
NL 529, Chief Wilson, PIT	NL 17, George McQuillan, PHI
H—AL 145, Harry Lord, BOS	PCT—AL .667, Ed Summers, DET
NL 127, Joe Delahanty, STL	NL .586, Bob Spade, CIN
2B—AL 18, Eddie Collins, PHI	GP—AL 41, Rube Manning, NY
NL 14, Chappy Charles, STL	NL 48, George McQuillan, PHI
Joe Delahanty, STL	GS—AL 32, Ed Summers, DET
Dode Paskert, CIN	NL 42, George McQuillan, PHI
3B—AL 11, Gavvy Cravath, BOS	CG—AL 23, Ed Summers, DET
NL 11, Joe Delahanty, STL	NL 32, George McQuillan, PHI
HR—AL 2, Harry Lord, BOS	IP—AL 301, Ed Summers, DET
Amby McConnell, BOS	NL 359.2, George McQuillan, PHI
NL 3, Chief Wilson, PIT	H—AL 271, Ed Summers, DET
R—AL 77, Amby McConnell, BOS	NL 263, George McQuillan, PHI
NL 47, Owen Wilson, PIT	BB—AL 86, Rube Manning, NY
RBI—AL 45, Jerry Freeman, WAS	NL 91, George McQuillan, PHI
NL 44, Joe Delahanty, STL	K—AL 118, Joe Lake, NY
WK—AL 40, Gabby Street, WAS	NL 114, George McQuillan, PHI
NL 36, Buck Herzog, NY	ERA—AL 1.64, Ed Summers, DET
SO—AL NA	NL 1.53, George McQuillan, PHI
NL NA	SHO—AL 5, Ed Summers, DET
SB—AL 32, Neal Ball, NY	NL 7, George McQuillan, PHI
NL 25, Dode Paskert, CIN	SV—AL 2, Eddie Cicotte, BOS
BA—AL .279, Amby McConnell, BOS	Ed Foster, CLE
NL .255, Joe Delahanty, STL	NL 2, Billy Campbell, CIN
SLG—AL .335, Amby McConnell, BOS	Bill Malarkey, NY
NL .333, Joe Delahanty, STL	George McQuillan, PHI
OBP—AL .342, Amby McConnell, BOS	
NL .309, Joe Delahanty, STL	

man would prove to be the only flaw in Wiltse's performance as New York won the game in the bottom of the tenth, 1–0. The contest was one of a record-tying five 1–0 defeats McQuillan endured in 1908. On the bright side, two of his seven shutouts were won by that same margin, including a one-hitter facing the Cubs August 16.

Summers posted a 1.64 ERA and McQuillan 1.53, but neither led his league, illustrating the degree to which pitchers ruled the game by 1908. The average hitter in each circuit batted a mere .239. It was in this environment that just four rookie hitters with at least 400 at bats hit .250 or better. Two of them were Boston Red Sox infielders—Amby McConnell and Harry Lord, who hit .279 and .259, respectively. Cardinals leftfielder Joe Delahanty, brother of Hall of Famer Ed, clubbed .255, and Washington Senators first baseman Jerry Freeman batted .252.

While Dode Criss of the Browns saw more limited action than the aforementioned quartet, he hit .341 in 82 at bats, half of which were in the burgeoning pinch-hitting role. Criss had 12 safeties in this capacity, becoming the first player to attain a double-digit season total. Criss, who played first base, the outfield, and also pitched on occasion, would lead the AL in pinch hits and pinch at bats each year from 1908 through 1911.

Other Highlights

August 22—Tom Tuckey works all 15 innings in the Boston Doves' 3–1 victory over the Chicago Cubs; Tuckey is never again the same pitcher and leaves the majors after going 0–9 in 1909.

September 4—Rookie outfielder Warren Gill of Pittsburgh neglects to touch second base as the Pirates' winning run crosses the plate in the bottom of the tenth inning to break a 0–0 deadlock with the Cubs; despite a protest by Cubs second sacker Johnny Evers, Gill is not ruled out by Hank O'Day, the game's lone umpire, but three weeks later, when Evers tries the same tactic in a game against the Giants, O'Day recognizes the validity of Evers's protest, resulting in the famous "Merkle Boner" (see below).

September 4—Frank Arellanes, the first Mexican-American to make the majors, yields a home run and hits a batter but is otherwise perfect for the Boston Red Sox, who beat the Philadelphia Athletics 10–1 in the second game of a doubleheader.

September 15—Pete Wilson makes his ML debut with the New York Highlanders by blanking the Boston Red Sox 1–0.

September 23—Rookie first sacker Fred Merkle of the New York Giants, following usual procedure (see the "Gill Incident" above), doesn't touch second base on an apparent game-winning hit by teammate Al Bridwell; following a protest by Cubs second baseman Johnny Evers that is upheld by plate umpire Hank O'Day, the winning run is nullified, forcing the game to be replayed October 8 after the Giants end the season tied for first with the Cubs.

September 24—Joe Lake allows only one hit for the New York Highlanders in beating the Chicago White Sox 1–0.

Every fan has probably had the pipe dream where it's the seventh game of the World Series and his team calls on him to be its starting pitcher. Babe Adams lived that pipe dream. Adams, the rookie right-hander of the Pittsburgh Pirates, had started and won games one and five against the Detroit Tigers and was summoned forth once again in Game Seven. Adams limited Detroit to six hits and won the deciding contest 8–0. In so doing, he became the first rookie to win three games in one World Series and gave the Pirates their first World Championship.

Adams was no stranger to shutouts, having thrown three in the regular season. On May 4 he limited the Chicago Cubs, who had won the past two World Series, to six hits in 11 innings and won 1–0. That was the longest outing of Adams's 12–3 campaign, in which he fashioned a brilliant 1.11 ERA in 130 innings.

LOWEST ERA BY A ROOKIE (MINIMUM 100 IP)

0.86/105.0 IP, Tim Keefe, 1880 Tro NL	
1.11/130.0 IP, Babe Adams, 1909 Pit NL	
1.21/201.0 IP, Denny Driscoll, 1882 Pit AA	
1.30/104.0 IP, Guy Hecker, 1882 Lou AA	
1.39/213.0 IP, Harry Krause, 1909 Phi AL	
1.42/291.2 IP, Ed Reulbach, 1905 Chi NL	

To complement Adams, freshman second baseman Dots Miller drove in 87 runs for the Pirates, third best in the NL and the second highest total by a senior circuit freshman from 1901 through 1920.

MOST RBI BY NL ROOKIE, 1901–20

91, Kitty Bransfield, 1901 Pit NL	
87, Dots Miller, 1909 Pit NL	
83, Jim Nealon, 1906 Pit NL	
83, Pat Duncan, 1920 Cin NL	
79, Otto Krueger, 1901 StL NL	

Miller led NL second sackers in assists and fielding percentage, and his 222 total bases ranked fifth in the loop. He finished third in doubles and fourth in triples. In the World Series Miller went 7-for-28 with four

RBI, totals very similar to those of Detroit's rookie shortstop Donie Bush, who was 6-for-23 and knocked home three. Teammate Ty Cobb edged Bush for the runs leadership (116 to 114), but only two freshman shortstops have ever scored more often than the young Bengal, who also topped the AL with 88 walks and was third in OBP (.380) and stolen bases (53).

Bush's Tigers won their third straight AL flag, beating out the 95-win Philadelphia Athletics, who were spurred by two rookies, Harry Krause and Frank Baker. Krause, a southpaw, started off 10–0, hurling six shutouts in that span. Included was a masterpiece May 17 at Chicago when Krause yielded but five hits to the White Sox, taking the 12-inning contest 1–0. Krause fired another whitewash in July for a total of seven. He compiled an 18–8 record while his 1.39 ERA not only paced the AL but is fifth best ever among rookies with at least 100 innings (see on p. 89).

Frank Baker, who wouldn't acquire the moniker "Home Run" for another two years, scored the only run in Krause's gem May 17 after having done the same thing for his teammate nine days earlier. On April 24 Baker hit the AL's only grand slam of 1909 as Philadelphia beat the Boston Red Sox 4–1. Then, on May 29, Baker hit the first round tripper in the A's new Shibe Park home in another Krause victory.

Baker spent a lot of time at third base, which was both his defensive position and his destination on a league-leading 19 triples. No AL rookie has ever hit more three-baggers. Baker was third in the AL in RBI and fourth in SA and total bases.

Finishing one rung below Baker in the latter three categories was Red Sox centerfielder Tris Speaker, who led a talented crop of Boston freshmen. Speaker stroked 26 of his eventual ML record 792 career doubles. He hit .309 in 143 games. Joining Speaker in Boston's pasture was Harry Hooper, another future Hall of Famer. Hooper, who would be the everyday right fielder on four Red Sox champions, played most of his games in 1909 in the other outfield corner. Also helping the 1909 club begin its rise toward future dominance was Joe Wood, who went 11–7 with four shutouts.

Like Wood, Washington's Bob Groom would have his best season in 1912. In 1909, however, Groom suffered through 26 losses, the most by a rookie in the

What do Donie Bush and Ted Williams have in common as hitters? Since their career OPS figures differ by a whopping 460-point margin, the answer, seemingly, is not much, apart from the fact that both of them led the AL in walks as rookies. But when it is taken into account that the object in baseball is to score as many runs as possible, the two suddenly take on another very important similarity.

Even though the light-hitting Bush played almost his entire career in the Deadball Era when runs were scarce, he currently is first in runs among all players since 1893 with less than 10,000 career at bats and a sub-.700 OPS. In addition he scored the most runs of any post-nineteenth-century retired player who collected less than 2000 hits.

Much of Bush's offensive value resided in his ability to draw a lot of walks, but there was another equally important factor. He spent all but two of his 16 seasons in Detroit, where he batted ahead of Ty Cobb.

Rank	Name	AB	OPS	Runs
1	Donie Bush	7210	.656	1280
2	Ozzie Smith	9396	.668	1257
3	Bert Campaneris	8684	.655	1181
4	Maury Wills	7588	.662	1067
5	Bobby Wallace	8618	.690	1057
6	Frankie Crosetti	6277	.695	1006
	Roger Peckinpaugh	7233	.672	1006
8	Tony Taylor	7680	.674	1005
9	Dave Concepcion	8723	.682	993
10	Larry Bowa	8418	.621	987

twentieth century. Moreover, Groom tied fellow Senator Jack Townsend's all-time AL loss record set in 1904.

Other Highlights

April 15—Jim Scott of the White Sox shuts out the St. Louis Browns 1–0 in his ML debut.

July 18—After beginning his rookie season with ten straight wins, A's southpaw Harry Krause suffers his first loss, 5–4 to the Browns' Jack Powell in 11 innings.

July 19—Harry Gaspar of the Cincinnati Reds holds the Boston Doves to three hits, beating them 5–0.

1909 ROOKIE LEADERS

Batting	Pitching
G—AL 157, Donie Bush, DET	W—AL 18, Harry Krause, PHI
NL 151, Dots Miller, PIT	NL 19, Harry Gaspar, CIN
AB—AL 544, Tris Speaker, BOS	**L—AL 26, Bob Groom, WAS**
NL 575, Rube Ellis, STL	NL 21, Al Mattern, BOS
H—AL 168, Tris Speaker, BOS	PCT—AL .692, Harry Krause, PHI
NL 159, Dick Hoblitzel, CIN	NL .633, Harry Gaspar, CIN
2B—AL 27, Frank Baker, PHI	GP—AL 44, Bob Groom, WAS
NL 31, Dots Miller, PIT	NL 47, Al Mattern, BOS
3B—AL 19, Frank Baker, PHI	GS—AL 31, Bob Groom, WAS
NL 13, Dots Miller, PIT	NL 32, Al Mattern, BOS
HR—AL 7, Tris Speaker, BOS	CG—AL 21, Jack Warhop, NY
NL 4, Dick Hoblitzel, CIN	NL 24, Al Mattern, BOS
R—AL 114, Donie Bush, DET	IP—AL 260.2, Bob Groom, WAS
NL 76, Rube Ellis, STL	NL 316.1, Al Mattern, BOS
RBI—AL 85, Frank Baker, PHI	H—AL 218, Bob Groom, WAS
NL 87, Dots Miller, PIT	**NL 322, Al Mattern, BOS**
WK—**AL 88, Donie Bush, DET**	BB—**AL 105, Bob Groom, WAS**
NL 66, Steve Evans, STL	**NL 108, Al Mattern, BOS**
SO—AL NA	K—AL 139, Harry Krause, PHI
NL NA	NL 109, Rube Marquard, NY
SB—AL 53, Donie Bush, DET	ERA—**AL 1.39, Harry Krause, PHI**
NL 54, Bob Bescher, CIN	NL 2.01, Harry Gaspar, CIN
BA—AL .309, Tris Speaker, BOS	SHO—AL 7, Harry Krause, PHI
NL .308, Dick Hoblitzel, CIN	NL 4, Harry Gaspar, CIN
SLG—AL .447, Frank Baker, PHI	SV—AL 2, Larry Pape, BOS
NL .418, Dick Hoblitzel, CIN	Jack Warhop, NY
OBP—AL .380, Donie Bush, DET	Ralph Works, DET
NL .364, Dick Hoblitzel, CIN	NL 3, Al Mattern, BOS
	Steve Melter, STL

August 8 –Bill O'Hara steals second, third, and home in the eighth inning, and the New York Giants blank the St. Louis Cardinals 3–0.

August 28—Dolly Gray tosses a one-hitter for Washington but issues an ML single-inning record eight walks, seven consecutively, in the second frame and yields a total of 11 free passes that lead to six runs and result in his Washington Senators losing the opener of a twin-bill, 6–4 to the Chicago White Sox.

September 11—Lew Brockett tosses a one-hitter, and the New York Highlanders beat the Washington Senators 3–0 in the first game of a doubleheader.

September 11—Giants catcher Chief Meyers hits his first ML home run, a second-inning grand slam off Elmer Knetzer of the Dodgers that accounts for all the scoring in the game, as New York beats Brooklyn 4–0 in the initial contest of a double-dip.

September 25—Senators frosh Bob Groom sets a new ML single-season record when he loses his 19th consecutive game, 2–1 to the White Sox, en route to losing an AL record-tying 26 decisions.

5

1910s

1910

Batman and Robin may have formed the most dynamic fictional duo in Gotham City, but a real-life New York Highlanders tandem was no less dazzling in 1910. Combining for 39 wins, Russ Ford and Hippo Vaughn helped the Highlanders reach second in the AL standings after a fifth-place finish the year before.

Following a two-inning relief stint April 15, Ford made his first start six days later and tossed a five-hit shutout while fanning nine Philadelphia Athletics. Two more blankings followed in May as did a like total in June. On July 19, while allowing only one St. Louis Browns hit—on a pop fly misjudged by rookie shortstop Roxey Roach in the ninth—Ford whiffed 11 and won 5–1. In mid-August Ford rattled off three consecutive shutouts, permitting a collective 14 hits and striking out 25. Ford, called by *Sporting Life* "the twirling find of the year," won his last dozen decisions and finished 26–6. His .813 winning percentage ranked second in the AL, and his 209 strikeouts were fourth best.

The Highlanders got eight shutouts from Ford and five more from left-hander Hippo Vaughn, who started

Opening Day for New York. The April 14 contest ended because of darkness after 14 innings in a 4–4 tie. Vaughn went the distance only to earn a no-decision. Nine days later Vaughn registered his first shutout despite the game also resulting in a deadlock, 0–0, called after six innings. Hippo's last four blankings were of the conventional variety—wins—and his 13 victories solidified the Highlanders rotation. Vaughn's 1.83 ERA, coupled with Ford's 1.65, made the duo the only rookie teammates ever to post sub-2.00 ERAs in at least 200 innings apiece.

Vaughn would post only a 14–21 record the next two seasons for New York and Washington before finding stardom with the Chicago Cubs, the team King Cole helped lead to the 1910 NL pennant. Cole fired a six-hit shutout in his debut on October 6, 1909, and joined the fearsome Cubs rotation in 1910, which would be the seventh year in nine seasons that Chicago led the senior circuit in ERA. Cole, who started 7–0, suffered his first defeat on June 15, losing when Brooklyn rookie pitcher Cy Barger hit a game-winning double in the bottom of the 14th. The Superbas won 3–2 as Barger went 4-for-6 with two doubles.

King Cole followed his dazzling rookie showing in 1910 by winning 18 games as a sophomore. He then won only 15 more games in the majors and died before his 30th birthday of testicular cancer. *Transcendental Graphics*

Cleveland's septet also combined for 42 wins, three short of the 45 Highlanders freshman hurlers produced in 1910 to set an AL rookie record to that point that lasted only one season, as the 1911 Cleveland entry established the current mark of 49.

Lest it seem that rookie hurlers had all the fun in 1910, note must be taken of two freshman outfielders on the New York Giants. Fred Snodgrass and Josh Devore both had brief stints with the club the previous two seasons but in 1910 took on full-time responsibilities. Snodgrass played center field and hit .321, fourth in the NL, and his .440 OBP not only was second in the loop but ranks as the sixth highest in rookie history (minimum 100 games). Leftfielder Devore batted .304 and stole 43 bases.

Across the East River, Zack Wheat gave Brooklyn fans a preview of his future diamond brilliance. His 36

On July 31 Cole pitched seven no-hit innings at St. Louis before the second game of a doubleheader was halted so the Cubs could catch a train. This game is not officially considered a no-hitter, however, because it failed to go nine innings. Cole blanked Brooklyn on one hit on August 17, the fourth and final whitewash of his 20–4 campaign. His 1.80 ERA would have earned Cole the NL leadership under current rules because George McQuillan, the recognized leader, fell 1⅔ innings shy of qualifying.

In Game Four of the World Series, Cole prevented a sweep by the Athletics. He got a no-decision, but Chicago rallied for the win. Philadelphia took the Fall Classic the next day.

The Cleveland Naps had seven rookie pitchers throw shutouts—a record for one team in one season. George Kahler tossed two and the following hurlers had one apiece: Fred Blanding, Harry Fanwell, Spec Harkness, Elmer Koestner, Fred Link, and Willie Mitchell.

In 1910 King Cole produced one of the most dazzling rookie pitching performances ever and also one of the wackiest. He set a post-1893 record that will almost certainly never be equaled—for the most walks by a hurler with a sub-2.00 ERA. Additionally, he shattered the all-time mark for the highest winning percentage by a sub-2.00 ERA pitcher who gave up as many as 100 walks.

Rank	Name	Year	BB	ERA	PCT
1	King Cole	1910	130	1.80	.833
2	Mickey Welch	1885	131	1.66	.800
3	Bill James	1914	118	1.90	.788
4	Jack Coombs	1910	115	1.30	.775
5	Cy Young	1892	118	1.93	.750
6	Hal Newhouser	1945	110	1.81	.735
7	Tim Keefe	1885	102	1.58	.711
8	Jeff Tesreau	1912	106	1.96	.708
9	Babe Ruth	1916	118	1.75	.657
10	Billy Rhines	1890	113	1.95	.622

doubles ranked third in the circuit and were the second highest total a freshman had yet stroked. Wheat's 172 safeties tied him for third while he finished fourth in total bases. By playing in each of the Superbas' 156 games, Wheat set an NL rookie record that would be equaled but not surpassed until 1953.

Other Highlights

June 10—Dixie Walker, the father of two future NL batting champs, Dixie and Harry Walker, fires a one-hitter for Washington, beating the Chicago White Sox 1–0.

June 21—Brooklyn outfield rookie Jack Dalton slaps five straight hits off Christy Mathewson in a 12–1 loss to the Giants ace.

September 30—In his lone ML game, Browns third baseman Ray Jansen goes 4-for-5 in a 9–1 loss to Chicago's Fred Olmstead.

October 1—In his first ML appearance, Lefty Russell of the A's blanks the Red Sox 3–0; Russell will never win another game in the majors and finishes 1–5 with a 6.36 ERA.

October 6—Outfielder Bill Collins hits for the cycle and scores four times as the Boston Doves pound the Philadelphia Phillies 20–7.

October 9—Ordered to play deep in a season-closing doubleheader by St. Louis Browns manager Jack O'Connor, rookie third baseman Red Corriden surrenders six bunt singles to Cleveland's Nap Lajoie to help give Lajoie the 1910 AL batting title.

1910 ROOKIE LEADERS

Batting	Pitching
G—AL 151, Duffy Lewis, BOS	W—AL 26, Russ Ford, NY
NL 156, Zack Wheat, BRO	NL 20, King Cole, CHI
AB—AL 541, Duffy Lewis, BOS	L—AL 11, Hippo Vaughn, NY
NL 606, Zack Wheat, BRO	Dixie Walker, WAS
H—AL 153, Duffy Lewis, BOS	NL 15, Cy Barger, BRO
NL 172, Zack Wheat, BRO	PCT—AL .813, Russ Ford, NY
2B—AL 29, Duffy Lewis, BOS	**NL .833, King Cole, CHI**
NL 36, Zack Wheat, BRO	GP—AL 36, Russ Ford, NY
3B—AL 10, Larry Gardner, BOS	NL 35, Cy Barger, BRO
NL 15, Jake Daubert, BRO	GS—AL 33, Russ Ford, NY
Zack Wheat, BRO	NL 30, Cy Barger, BRO
HR—AL 8, Duffy Lewis, BOS	CG—AL 29, Russ Ford, NY
NL 8, Jake Daubert, BRO	NL 25, Cy Barger, BRO
R—AL 68, Bert Daniels, NY	IP—AL 299.2, Russ Ford, NY
NL 92, Josh Devore, NY	NL 271.2, Cy Barger, BRO
RBI—AL 68, Duffy Lewis, BOS	H—AL 194, Russ Ford, NY
NL 55, Doc Miller, CHI/BOS	NL 267, Cy Barger, BRO
Zack Wheat, BRO	BB—AL 70, Russ Ford, NY
WK—AL 62, Rollie Zeider, CHI	NL 130, King Cole, CHI
NL 71, Fred Snodgrass, NY	K—AL 209, Russ Ford, NY
SO—AL NA	NL 151, Louis Drucke, NY
NL 80, Zack Wheat, BRO	ERA—AL 1.65, Russ Ford, NY
SB—AL 49, Rollie Zeider, CHI	NL 1.80, King Cole, CHI
NL 43, Josh Devore, NY	SHO—AL 8, Russ Ford, NY
BA—AL .283, Duffy Lewis, BOS	NL 4, King Cole, CHI
NL .321, Fred Snodgrass, NY	SV—AL 3, Frank Browning, DET
SLG—AL .407, Duffy Lewis, BOS	NL 2, Chick Evans, BOS
NL .432, Fred Snodgrass, NY	Bert Humphries, PHI
OBP—AL .354, Larry Gardner, BOS	Dick Rudolph, NY
NL .440, Fred Snodgrass, NY	

One of the great things about baseball is that talented rookies always seem to appear on the scene, almost like clockwork, to replace fading veteran superstars. On September 7, 1911, Grover "Pete" Alexander of the Philadelphia Phillies tossed a one-hitter, beating the Boston Doves 1–0. His opponent, Cy Young, was winding down a legendary 22-year career that saw him win 511 games. This battle with the venerable and seemingly inexorable Young was the first of four consecutive shutouts for Alexander, who surrendered just 14 hits in the streak. He finished with seven whitewashes, one-fourth of his league-leading 28 wins. Alexander also paced the NL in complete games, innings pitched, and fewest hits per nine innings. Among rookies since 1893, when baseball adopted its current pitching distance, Alexander ranks fifth in strikeouts (227), third in innings (367), and is tied for second in wins.

Alexander would prove to be a worthy successor to the great Young, but a case can be made that he was not the 1911 season's top rookie hurler. Southpaw Vean Gregg won 23 games for the Cleveland Naps, leading the AL with a 1.80 ERA. His .767 winning percentage is third best by a freshman with at least 30 decisions.

HIGHEST ROOKIE WINNING PCT.
(MINIMUM 30 DECISIONS)

.838 (31W/6L), Bill Hoffer, 1895 Bal NL	
.813 (26W/6L), Russ Ford, 1910 NY AL	
.767 (23W/7L), Vean Gregg, 1911 Cle AL	
.754 (43W/14L), Larry Corcoran, 1880 Chi NL	
.742 (23W/8L), Noodles Hahn, 1899 Cin NL	

Gregg, whose season was prematurely shut down after September 4 when his arm went bad, allowed only 6.33 hits per nine innings, more than one hit per game fewer than runner-up Smokey Joe Wood. In third place was another Cleveland rookie, Gene Krapp, whose talent, fortunately, was the antithesis of his surname. Krapp went 13–9 for the Naps, who also got a fine recruit campaign from Ivy Olson. The shortstop scored 89 runs while his 142 hits were fourth highest among rookies—albeit a very distant fourth.

Leading the freshman hit parade was the most spectacular Cleveland yearling of all in 1911, Shoeless Joe

Jackson, who lashed out 233 safeties, including 45 doubles and 19 triples, and scored 126 runs. However, impressive as they were, none of these figures led the AL, as each category was topped by Ty Cobb, who had one of his finest seasons. Jackson also missed out on the batting title despite a rookie-record .408 average. Even if the qualifying total for frosh status is reduced to 75 previous ABs, Jackson still heads the all-time list. His AL-best .468 OBP, combined with a .590 slugging average, produced a 1.058 OPS, the highest in rookie annals.

HIGHEST ROOKIE OPS (MINIMUM 100 GAMES)

1.058 (.468 OBP/.590 SLG), Joe Jackson, 1911 Cle AL	
1.045 (.436 OBP/.609 SLG), Ted Williams, 1939 Bos AL	
1.036 (.415 OBP/.621 SLG), George Watkins, 1930 StL NL	
1.026 (.375 OBP/.651 SLG), Rudy York, 1937 Det AL	
1.017 (.407 OBP/.610 SLG), Albert Pujols, 2001 StL NL	

Jackson, whose 71 extra-base hits would remain the rookie apex until 1929, had many heroic moments along the way. On May 7, for one, with Cleveland and the St. Louis Browns tied at two in the 12th inning, Jackson hit a game-winning grand slam, collecting four of his 83 RBI.

Driving in still more runs was Chicago White Sox centerfielder Ping Bodie, whose solid rookie season was overshadowed by Jackson's. Bodie had 159 hits and knocked home 97 runs, eclipsing the junior circuit's freshman standard of 90, set by Socks Seybold in the league's inaugural season of 1901. Bodie's mark would last until 1924.

Roy Golden also set a record in 1911 but not one that he cared to boast about. Still, Golden, who pitched for the St. Louis Cardinals, could at least brag that he made the rookie leader chart, tying Pete Alexander no less. Both hurlers yielded an NL frosh-high 129 bases on balls, but there the two parted company as Golden did so in 218⅓ fewer innings, producing the worst walk ratio of any rookie in at least 100 innings prior to 1986.

MOST WALKS PER NINE INNINGS BY ROOKIE
(MINIMUM 100 IP)

8.16 (143 BB/157.2 IP), Bobby Witt, 1986 Tex AL	
7.81 (129 BB/148.2 IP), Roy Golden, 1911 StL NL	
7.80 (91 BB/105 IP), Johnny Gray, 1954 Phi AL	
7.63 (102 BB/120.1 IP), Eric Plunk, 1986 Oak AL	
7.42 (89 BB/108 IP), Bill George, 1887 NY NL	

Golden completed only six of his 25 starts, achieving another dubious distinction. By registering 19 "incomplete" games, he set a negative NL rookie record that would be tied twice but not surpassed until 1932 when Van Lingle Mungo raised the bar to 22.

At the opposite end of the continuum, Red Sox newcomer Buck O'Brien completed all five of his starts, beginning with a shutout in his ML debut on September 9. O'Brien, who also made one relief appearance, worked 47⅔ innings, surrendering all of two earned runs. His 0.38 ERA is the lowest ever for a rookie with 30 or more innings of work.

LOWEST ERA BY ROOKIE (MINIMUM 30 IP)

0.38 (47.2 IP), Buck O'Brien, 1911 Bos AL
0.66 (41 IP), George McQuillan, 1907 Phi NL
0.72 (50.1 IP), Rob Murphy, 1986 Cin NL
0.75 (36 IP), Laurie Reis, 1877 Chi NL
0.76 (47.2 IP), Barry Latman, 1958 Chi AL

O'Brien would win 20 games in 1912 but only four more after that, unlike Pete Alexander, who assumed Cy Young's mantle as one of the game's most prolific winners.

The AL record for the most wins by two rookie teammates was set in the loop's very first season when Roscoe Miller and Ed Siever combined to post 41 victories for Detroit, but the junior circuit mark for the most wins received by a team from all its rookie hurlers belongs to the 1911 Cleveland entry. Led by frosh sensation Vean Gregg with 23, the Forest City club saw its recruit hurlers garner 51 of its 80 total wins.

Gregg followed his outstanding recruit performance by registering two more 20-win seasons for Cleveland before falling prey to arm trouble. Though he recovered sufficiently to pitch in the majors as late as 1925 when he was past 40, he never again approached his early promise.

Gene Krapp, Cleveland's second leading rookie winner in 1911 with 13, plummeted even more quickly from prominence than Gregg. Krapp won just two more games for the Forest City club and finished his brief four-season ML sojourn in 1915 with Buffalo of the Federal League.

Other Highlights

April 23—Orlie Weaver blanks the St. Louis Cardinals on two hits as the Chicago Cubs win 7–0; the gem proves to be Weaver's lone ML shutout as he finishes the 1911 season with a 5.30 ERA, the highest of any qualifier in the Deadball Era (1901–19).

July 22—Lefty Marty O'Toole, who had a brief trial in 1908 with Cincinnati, is purchased by Pittsburgh from St. Paul of the American Association for $22,500, a new record amount to be paid for a minor leaguer; O'Toole will go 3–2 for Pittsburgh in 1912 and lead the NL in both shutouts and walks in 1913 before arm trouble forces him back to the minors.

August 2—Charlie Becker tosses a two-hitter in his ML debut for the Washington Senators, who best the Chicago White Sox 3–1.

September 21—Vic Saier of the Cubs, soon to become one of the Deadball Era's premier sluggers, hits his first ML home run, a grand slam in a 9–2 win against the Phillies.

September 24—After a rookie-record 41 straight shutout innings, Phillies phenom Pete Alexander is finally scored on in an 8–2 win over Cincinnati.

October 7—Some ten weeks after appearing at the Giants' hotel in St. Louis on July 28 and begging manager John McGraw for a tryout, Charlie "Victory" Faust pitches in his lone ML game, allowing two hits and a run in a two-inning mop-up role; even though Faust shows little talent, he is retained by McGraw for several years as a good-luck charm.

October 9—First sacker Ben Houser goes 4-for-4 with a grand slam and takes part in a triple play for the Boston Doves, who topple the Phillies 11–5 in the opener of a twinbill.

Batting	Pitching
G—AL 147, Joe Jackson, CLE	W—AL 23, Vean Gregg, CLE
NL 146, Bob Coulson, BRO	**NL 28, Pete Alexander, PHI**
AB—AL 572, Burt Shotton, STL	L—AL 14, Ray Caldwell, NY
NL 521, Bob Coulson, BRO	NL 15, Bill Schardt, BRO
Scotty Ingerton, BOS	PCT—AL .767, Vean Gregg, CLE
H—AL 233, Joe Jackson, CLE	NL .683, Pete Alexander, PHI
NL 133, Jim Doyle, CHI	GP—AL 41, Ray Caldwell, NY
2B—AL 45, Joe Jackson, CLE	NL 48, Pete Alexander, PHI
NL 24, Scotty Ingerton, BOS	GS—AL 27, Ray Caldwell, NY
3B—AL 19, Joe Jackson, CLE	NL 37, Pete Alexander, PHI
NL 12, Jim Doyle, CHI	CG—AL 22, Vean Gregg, CLE
HR—AL 7, Joe Jackson, CLE	**NL 31, Pete Alexander, PHI**
NL 5, Max Carey, PIT	IP—AL 255, Ray Caldwell, NY
Jim Doyle, CHI	**NL 367, Pete Alexander, PHI**
Scotty Ingerton, BOS	H—AL 240, Ray Caldwell, NY
R—AL 126, Joe Jackson, CLE	NL 285, Pete Alexander, PHI
NL 77, Max Carey, PIT	BB—**AL 138, Gene Krapp, CLE**
RBI—AL 97, Ping Bodie, CHI	NL 129, Pete Alexander, PHI
NL 62, Jim Doyle, CHI	Roy Golden, STL
WK—AL 56, Joe Jackson, CLE	K—AL 145, Ray Caldwell, NY
NL 53, Bert Tooley, BRO	NL 227, Pete Alexander, PHI
SO—AL NA	ERA—**AL 1.80, Vean Gregg, CLE**
NL 78, Bob Coulson, BRO	NL 2.57, Pete Alexander, PHI
SB—AL 41, Joe Jackson, CLE	SHO—AL 5, Vean Gregg, CLE
NL 32, Bob Coulson, BRO	**NL 7, Pete Alexander, PHI**
BA—AL .408, Joe Jackson, CLE	SV—AL 2, Fred Blanding, CLE
NL .282, Jim Doyle, CHI	NL 4, George Chalmers, PHI
SLG—AL .590, Joe Jackson, CLE	Bill Schardt, BRO
NL .413, Jim Doyle, CHI	
OBP—**AL .468, Joe Jackson, CLE**	
NL .340, Jim Doyle, CHI	

1912

The fate of the Boston Red Sox fell on the shoulders, or rather on the right arm, of rookie Hugh Bedient. In the 1912 World Series, Boston and the New York Giants had each won three games and tied the second contest in an epic struggle that truly lived up to the name "Fall Classic." Bedient surrendered only one run in his seven innings of work in the eighth and final match before being pinch-hit for by fellow freshman Olaf Henriksen, who promptly doubled in the tying run. Bedient got a no-decision, but Boston won in the tenth inning. He previously had been the victor in Game Five, allowing three hits in his 2–1 win. Bedient was one of three rookie hurlers in the East Coast battle. Buck O'Brien lost games three and six for Boston, despite pitching

well in the former contest. New York's Jeff Tesreau dropped the opener and Game Four, but his gritty complete-game victory in Game Seven kept the Giants alive for one more day.

The trio of freshmen had stellar campaigns preceding the World Series. Bedient and O'Brien each won 20 games for the Red Sox, who copped the AL flag by 14 games. Bedient was fourth in the AL in winning percentage (.690) and opponents' OBP (.288). O'Brien, who started the first game ever at Fenway Park on April 20, 1912, held batters to 7.74 hits per nine innings, fifth fewest in the loop. Tesreau went 17–7 for the Giants and paced the NL with a 1.96 ERA. He was also the stingiest at allowing hits, enemy batters posting a meager .204 BA against the 23-year-old. On September 6 Tesreau pitched a no-hitter at Philadelphia. Phillie centerfielder

Dode Paskert seemingly led off the game with a hit, but the official scorer later reversed his decision after Giants first sacker Fred Merkle said he had touched a popup that he and Art Wilson let drop between them.

Despite the great success of the Red Sox tandem, they were not the winningest rookie duo in 1912. Larry Cheney and Jimmy Lavender combined for 42 triumphs for the Chicago Cubs. Cheney claimed 26 of them, tying for the senior circuit lead, and also completed a league-best 28 games.

MOST WINS BY ROOKIE 1901–2003

28, Pete Alexander, 1911 Phi NL
26, Russ Ford, 1910 NY AL
26, Larry Cheney, 1912 Chi NL
24, Ed Summers, 1908 Det AL
23, (Five tied)

Cheney ranked second in the NL with a .722 winning percentage and trailed Tesreau with a .234 opponents' BA. Lavender won 16 times, four coming in an 11-day stretch starting June 28. That day he blanked the Pittsburgh Pirates 3–0, allowing but one safety while he collected three himself, including a double. Three days later, Lavender whitewashed the Pirates again, winning 1–0 in 12 innings. On July 5 he tossed his third straight shutout, this time picking off the St. Louis Cardinals. Lavender gained national attention on July 8 when he handed Giants lefty Rube Marquard his first defeat of the 1912 season after a record 19–0 start.

Tom Seaton tied Lavender by winning 16 games as a freshman for the Phillies, who also got ten victories from Eppa Rixey. Pittsburgh's recruit lefty, Hank Robinson, took a dozen contests while placing in the league's top five not only in ERA but also in both opponents' batting average and OOBP.

Three AL infielders made sure rookie pitchers would not get all the ink in 1912. Eddie Foster played all 154 Washington games at third base, leading AL third sackers in assists. He topped the circuit with 618 at bats, which would remain the loop's rookie standard for his position until 1957. Foster had 176 hits and scored 98 runs, six fewer than Morrie Rath, the second baseman for the Chicago White Sox. Rath's 95 walks ranked third in the league and were the most by any AL freshman until 1921. Defensively, he led in fielding average and as-

Late in the 1912 season, Rabbit Maranville arrived in Boston and promptly claimed the Braves shortstop slot for the rest of the decade. Maranville hit just .209 that season in 26 games but was still a vast improvement over another rookie shortstop the Braves had employed earlier in the 1912 campaign. For some 59 games in mid-summer the job belonged to 17-year-old Frank O'Rourke, who would survive to play over 1000 games in the majors despite producing just about the most execrable single-season batting stats ever in his frosh season.

Here are both the five worst OPS and BA marks in history among position players with at least 150 at bats.

Rank	Name	Year	AB	BA	OPS
1	Joe Gunson	1884	166	.139	.304
2	Bill Bergen	1909	346	.139	.319
3	Frank O'Rourke	1912	196	.122	.325
4	Bill Bergen	1911	227	.132	.337
5	Bill Killefer	1910	193	.124	.339

Rank	Name	Year	AB	OPS	BA
1	Frank O'Rourke	1912	196	.325	.122
2	Bill Killefer	1910	193	.339	.124
3	Luis Pujols	1978	153	.414	.131
4	Bill Bergen	1911	227	.337	.132
5	Ray Oyler	1968	215	.401	.135
	Doc Lavan	1913	163	.371	.135
	Charlie Bastian	1889	155	.391	.135

sists. Fellow second sacker Del Pratt of the St. Louis Browns hit .302 with 15 triples. On May 5 Pratt tagged his first ML home run, a solo shot at Detroit's new ballpark, then called Navin Field but later renamed Tiger Stadium. It was the first round tripper at the park, which, like Boston's Fenway, opened April 20, less than a week after the sinking of the Titanic.

Other Highlights

April 20—George Baumgardner of the St. Louis Browns fans ten Chicago White Sox in 15 innings, but the game ends in a scoreless tie.

May 18—Protesting the suspension of Ty Cobb for fighting with a New York fan, the Tigers go on strike,

1912 ROOKIE LEADERS

Batting	Pitching
G—AL 157, Morrie Rath, CHI*	W—AL 20, Hugh Bedient, BOS
NL 130, Art Phelan, CIN	Buck O'Brien, BOS
AB—AL 618, Eddie Foster, WAS	**NL 26, Larry Cheney, CHI**
NL 486, Red Smith, BRO	L—AL 17, Mack Allison, STL
H—AL 176, Eddie Foster, WAS	NL 19, Walt Dickson, BOS
NL 139, Red Smith, BRO	PCT—AL .690. Hugh Bedient, BOS
2B—AL 34, Eddie Foster, WAS	NL .722, Larry Cheney, CHI
NL 28, Red Smith, BRO	GP—AL 41, Hugh Bedient, BOS
3B—AL 15, Del Pratt, STL	NL 44, Tom Seaton, PHI
NL 11, Art Phelan, CIN	GS—AL 34, Buck O'Brien, BOS
HR—AL 6, Guy Zinn, NY	NL 37, Larry Cheney, CHI
NL 4, Jay Kirke, BOS	CG—AL 25, Buck O'Brien, BOS
Red Smith, BRO	**NL 28, Larry Cheney, CHI**
R—AL 104, Morrie Rath, CHI	IP—AL 275.2, Buck O'Brien, BOS
NL 75, Red Smith, BRO	NL 303.1, Larry Cheney, CHI
RBI—AL 70, Eddie Foster, WAS	H—AL 237, Buck O'Brien, BOS
NL 62, Jay Kirke, BOS	NL 262, Larry Cheney, CHI
WK—AL 95, Morrie Rath, CHI	BB—AL 90, Buck O'Brien, BOS
NL 54, Red Smith, BRO	NL 111, Larry Cheney, CHI
SO—AL NA	K—AL 122, Hugh Bedient, BOS
NL 51, Red Smith, BRO	NL 140, Larry Cheney, CHI
SB—AL 30, Morrie Rath, CHI	ERA—AL 2.58, Buck O'Brien, BOS
NL 25, Art Phelan, CIN	**NL 1.96, Jeff Tesreau, NY**
BA—AL .302, Del Pratt, STL	SHO—AL 3, Boardwalk Brown, PHI
NL .290, Lee Magee, STL	NL 4, Larry Cheney, CHI
SLG—AL .426, Del Pratt, STL	SV—AL 3, George Mogridge, CHI
NL .393, Red Smith, BRO	NL 3, Jimmy Lavender, CHI
OBP—AL .380, Morrie Rath, CHI	
NL .362, Red Smith, BRO	

*Rookie record for games played prior to the adoption of the 162-game schedule; shared by Donie Bush, Vern Duncan, Al Wickland, and Ray Jablonski.

forcing manager Hughie Jennings to play a lineup against the A's that includes himself, two former catchers whose best days came in the mid-1890s, and six Philadelphia amateurs including divinity student Al Travers, who hurls a complete-game 24–2 loss, and third baseman Ed Irvin, who closes his ML career with a 2.000 SA when he compiles two triples in three at bats.

June 20—In his first ML appearance and the only game he will ever pitch in the NL, Ernie Shore enters the game in the ninth inning for the Giants, who hold a prohibitive 21–2 lead; even though Shore proceeds to give up ten runs in his one inning of work to make the final score 21–12, he is credited in today's record books with a save.

August 15—Yankees rookie Guy Zinn steals home twice in a 5–4 win over Detroit, helping the New Yorkers to notch a record 18 thefts of home in 1912; in addition, Zinn will post an .893 FA in 1912, making him the last outfielder in history to field below .900.

September 6—Jeff Tesreau of the Giants is the first NL rookie in the twentieth century to log a full-game no-hitter when he beats the Phils 3–0.

September 17—Brooklyn centerfielder Casey Stengel makes his ML debut a memorable one when he bags four hits, a walk, two stolen bases, and two RBI in a 7–3 win over Pittsburgh.

September 18—Boardwalk Brown of the Athletics allows only one hit and no walks as he beats the Chicago White Sox 12–0 in the eight-inning nightcap of a doubleheader.

1913

The 16th Amendment to the Constitution, authorizing a federal income tax, was ratified in 1913. That year, AL batters found two rookies pitchers especially taxing. Ewell Albert "Reb" Russell of the Chicago White Sox could do it all—start, relieve, and even hit. Russell, who led the AL with 52 games pitched, hurled a two-hitter April 26 in beating the St. Louis Browns 1–0. On July 14 Russell collected more hits than he allowed, going 2-for-4 with a triple in his one-hit shutout of the Boston Red Sox. Russell applied five more whitewashes for the White Sox, the Cleveland Indians being the only opponents to escape a blanking.

MOST SHUTOUTS BY ROOKIE

9, George Derby, 1881 Det NL
8, Ben Sanders, 1888 Phi NL
8, Russ Ford, 1910 NY AL
8, Reb Russell, 1913 Chi AL
8, Fernando Valenzuela, 1981 LA NL

Russell notched 22 wins while posting a 1.90 ERA in 316.2 innings. All three figures remain the standard for White Sox freshmen. Three of Russell's wins came in relief, and he also saved four games. At the plate Russell batted a respectable .189 with nine extra-base hits, foreshadowing his production when, as a right fielder for the 1922 Pittsburgh Pirates, he hit .368 with 75 RBI in 220 at bats.

The ChiSox left-hander held opposing batters to a .273 OBP, second only to Walter Johnson, who had the finest season in his superlative career. Next to the "Big Train," Joe Boehling had the most wins for the second-place Washington Senators. As Russell did with Chicago, Boehling frequently worked out of the bullpen. Boehling earned two victories in relief before making his first start June 15. The wins continued for the 22-year-old rookie southpaw. With a three-hit shutout of the Red Sox on July 2, Boehling improved to 7–0. His unbeaten streak was stopped at 11–0 by the Browns on July 28. Boehling split his next 12 decisions but still achieved a .708 winning percentage, good for third in the AL.

As impressive as Russell and Boehling were, their seasons did not end as they would have preferred, with a World Series appearance. Instead, that pleasure in 1913 fell to two rookie outfielders on opposing teams. Left-fielder George Burns contributed 40 of the New York Giants' NL-leading 296 stolen bases. Burns's 173 hits placed him third in the loop while his 37 doubles got him a rung higher. But in the Fall Classic, Burns was largely stymied,

Reb Russell and Babe Ruth share the honor of being the two most outstanding southpaw pitchers in the twentieth century who later became formidable run producers. The two main differences between them are that Russell made the transition from pitcher to hitter out of necessity rather than choice after he encountered arm trouble, and secondly, his awesome run production was accomplished over a much shorter period of time.

Some 10 years after Russell tied the post-1893 rookie mark for shutouts in 1913, he became a part-time outfielder with Pittsburgh. In 1922 he had a season like no other hitter in history. Among players with less than 250 at bats but at least 250 plate appearances, Russell ranks first in RBI production and is second only to Mark McGwire in OPS.

Rank	Name	Year	AB	OPS	RBI
1	Reb Russell	1922	220	1.091	75
2	Mark McGwire	2000	236	1.232	73
3	Jack Stivetts	1894	244	.902	64
	Ron Northey	1948	246	.949	64
5	Ty Cobb	1926	233	.918	62
6	Joe Wood	1921	194	1.000	60
7	Gus Mancuso	1930	227	.965	59
8	Jim Leyritz	1994	249	.887	58
	Alex Ochoa	2000	244	.970	58
10	Jocko Milligan	1890	234	.760	57
	Jose Canseco	1989	227	.883	57

hitting .158 in the five-game loss to the Philadelphia Athletics. Eddie Murphy, a right fielder, didn't fare much better for the victors. Murphy went 5-for-22 with two runs. In the regular season, however, he tied for fourth in the AL by scoring 105 runs and had a solid .391 OBP in 137 games.

Playing a larger part than Murphy in Philadelphia's postseason success were rookie battery mates Wally Schang and Joe Bush. Catcher Schang had five hits in the 1913 World Series, including a triple and a homer, while knocking in seven runs. Right-hander Bush, after going 15–6 in the regular season, earned a complete-game victory in the third contest.

The following day, novice righty Al Demaree of the Giants tried to duplicate Bush's 8–2 triumph but instead took the loss and put New York in a three-games-to-one hole from which they would not recover.

While Demaree was adept at preventing hitters from reaching base (his .286 OOBP was fifth in the NL), Pittsburgh's Jimmy Viox excelled at getting aboard. Viox hit .317 and had a .399 OBP, ranking him third and fourth, respectively, in the senior loop. Viox's batting average is the fifth best in history by a freshman second sacker, and only two rookie keystoners have had more success getting on base.

1913 ROOKIE LEADERS

Batting	Pitching
G—AL 141, Ray Chapman, CLE	W—AL 22, Reb Russell, CHI
NL 150, George Burns, NY	NL 14, Chief Johnson, CIN
AB—AL 508, Ray Chapman, CLE	Dick Rudolph, BOS
Eddie Murphy, PHI	L—**AL 20, Carl Weilman, STL**
NL 605, George Burns, NY	NL 16, Chief Johnson, CIN
H—AL 150, Eddie Murphy, PHI	PCT—AL .714, Joe Bush, PHI
NL 173, George Burns, NY	NL .765, Al Demaree, NY
2B—AL 22, Bobby Veach, DET	GP—**AL 52, Reb Russell, CHI**
NL 37, George Burns, NY	NL 44, Chief Johnson, CIN
3B—AL 10, Bobby Veach, DET	GS—AL 36, Reb Russell, CHI
NL 11, Joe Connolly, BOS	NL 31, Chief Johnson, CIN
HR—AL 3, Ray Chapman, CLE	CG—AL 26, Reb Russell, CHI
Hal Janvrin, BOS	NL 17, Dick Rudolph, BOS
Wally Schang, PHI	IP—AL 316.2, Reb Russell, CHI
NL 7, Casey Stengel, BRO	NL 269, Chief Johnson, CIN
R—AL 105, Eddie Murphy, PHI	H—AL 262, Carl Weilman, STL
NL 86, Jimmy Viox, PIT	NL 258, Dick Rudolph, BOS
RBI—AL 64, Bobby Veach, DET	BB—AL 94, Dutch Leonard, BOS
NL 65, Jimmy Viox, PIT	NL 86, Chief Johnson, CIN
WK—AL 70, Eddie Murphy, PHI	K—AL 144, Dutch Leonard, BOS
NL 68, Rabbit Maranville, BOS	NL 109, Dick Rudolph, BOS
SO—AL 51, Ray Chapman, CLE	ERA—AL 1.90, Reb Russell, CHI
Johnny Johnston, STL	NL 2.21, Al Demaree, NY
NL 74, George Burns, NY	SHO—AL 8, Reb Russell, CHI
SB—AL 29, Ray Chapman, CLE	NL 3, Chief Johnson, CIN
NL 57, Hap Myers, BOS	George Pearce, CHI
BA—AL .295, Eddie Murphy, PHI	SV—AL 4, Joe Boehling, WAS
NL .317, Jimmy Viox, PIT	Reb Russell, CHI
SLG—AL .356, Eddie Murphy, PHI	NL 2, Al Demaree, NY
NL .427, Jimmy Viox, PIT	
OBP—AL .391, Eddie Murphy, PHI	
NL .399, Jimmy Viox, PIT	

BEST BA BY ROOKIE SECOND BASEMAN
(MINIMUM 100 GAMES)

.345, Cupid Childs, 1890 Syr AA
.322, Hughie Critz, 1924 Cin NL
.321, Dave Stapleton, 1980 Bos AL
.3174, Duke Kenworthy, 1914 KC FL
.3171, Jimmy Viox, 1913 Pit NL

HIGHEST OBP BY ROOKIE SECOND BASEMAN
(MINIMUM 100 GAMES)

.434, Cupid Childs, 1890 Syr AA
.400, Ken Oberkfell, 1979 StL NL
.399, Jimmy Viox, 1913 Pit NL
.383, Jim Gilliam, 1953 Bro NL
.375, Joe Morgan, 1965 Hou NL

Other Highlights

April 24—Bill James throws a 12-inning shutout and the Boston Braves nip the Brooklyn Dodgers 1–0.

May 1—Dodgers rookie gardener Casey Stengel hits a leadoff home run in the first inning and a two-run shot in the second as Brooklyn beats the Braves 4–2.

August 5—Cy Williams goes 4-for-4 with a grand slam, and southpaw George Pearce goes the distance for the Chicago Cubs, who rip the Dodgers 13–2.

October 3—Dutch Leonard of the Boston Red Sox fires his second two-hit shutout of the season, beating the Washington Senators 2–0 in the opener of a doubleheader.

October 9—A's rookie Joe Bush beats the Giants 8–2 in Game Three of the World Series in front of 36,896 at the Polo Grounds, a new record crowd for a Fall Classic game.

1914

In the year the Great War commenced, baseball experienced its own form of combat—a bitter fight for fans.

The American and National leagues were challenged for turnstile supremacy by the Federal League, which had operated as a minor circuit the previous season. The Feds' leading luminary was Indianapolis outfielder Benny Kauff. The rookie gardener, whose only previous taste of big league action had been five games for the 1912 New York Yankees, topped the FL with a .370 batting average, ripped 211 hits, scored 120 runs, and swiped 75 bases. He also poled 44 doubles for the pennant-winning Hoosiers. On May 19 Kauff had four hits and scored four times in a victory at Brooklyn and later pounded three doubles and two singles on August 9 in an extra-inning win against Baltimore. The Hoosiers rotation featured George Kaiserling, a 31-year-old freshman right-hander who won 17 games, one of them a one-hit shutout at St. Louis. Other notable freshmen for Indianapolis included the .306-hitting rightfielder Al Scheer and eight-game winner Harry Billiard.

In addition to getting a record 53 wins from their rookie pitchers, the Chicago Whales possessed an all-freshman outfield, with Max Flack, Dutch Zwilling, and Al Wickland in left, center, and right, respectively. Wickland led the FL with 81 walks but was overshadowed by Zwilling, who hit .313 with 95 RBI and paced the circuit in homers with 16.

Second baseman Duke Kenworthy of the Kansas City Packers had an excellent all-around campaign, second in the FL only to Kauff's. Kenworthy made the top three in each extra-base-hit category while hitting .317 and leading Fed keystoners in putouts, double plays, and chances per game. His lone negative was a league-high 43 errors. Kenworthy hit two homers in a game three times, including June 13 against the Brooklyn Tip-Tops when he had a grand slam and another circuit blast in a 10–7 Packer win. Joining Kenworthy on the Packers was rightfielder Grover Gilmore, who hit .287 and scored 91 runs. Gilmore's one negative was that he became the first freshman batter to log 100 strikeouts, whiffing 108 times. No rookie until Dick Allen in 1964 would top 100 Ks with a higher batting average.

Other Fed rookies of consequence were Buffalo's Charlie Hanford, who was fifth in total bases, and two Baltimore fly chasers who also made their way onto the leader boards. Vern Duncan of the Terrapins was third in runs with 99, and Benny Meyer had a .395 OBP, good for fourth.

Across the Beltway, a pair of Washington Senators yearling pitchers had noteworthy seasons. "Grunting Jim" Shaw was 15–17 and joined Reb Russell as the only freshmen ever to notch at least four shutouts and four saves. Shaw blanked opponents five times, twice more than Doc Ayers, who had fanned 390 Virginia League batters in 1913 and followed that performance by setting an unpropitious rookie record that lasted until 1944. Ayers started 32 games but completed just eight, giving him 24 "incomplete games," five more than the previous rookie record-holder, Roy Golden, had racked up just three years earlier.

MOST INCOMPLETE GAMES BY ROOKIE PITCHER, 1872–1943

24 (32 GS/8 CG), Doc Ayers, 1914 Was AL
22 (33 GS/11 CG), Van Lingle Mungo, 1932 Bro NL
21 (31 GS/10 CG), Jack Kramer, 1939 StL AL
20 (Four rookies tied)

Kaiserling and Shaw won the most games by a freshman in each of their leagues, but they fell short of the brilliance of Jeff Pfeffer, a right-hander for the Brooklyn Robins. Pfeffer was in peak form September 19 when he blanked Cincinnati, holding the Reds hitless until two were out in the eighth. He settled for a one-hitter in his third whitewashing of a 23-win campaign. Pfeffer was fifth in winning percentage, and only two NL hurlers bettered his 1.97 ERA.

The Federal League's emergence as a rebel major league in 1914 helped to create a host of remarkable rookie achievements. Foremost is Benny Kauff's .370 BA for Indianapolis of the FL, second in history only to Joe Jackson's 1911 mark among freshmen with at least 400 at bats. The most arcane rookie record shattered in 1914 was for the most players older than age 30 making their big league debuts. When twenty-three 30-year-old recruits appeared that season, it broke the old mark of 18 that had been set in 1884 and would stand as the record until 1944.

Perhaps the least-appreciated yearling record that emerged from the FL's initial season was set by the Chicago Whales, the first team to call present-day Wrigley Field home. In 1914 Whales rookie pitchers racked up 53 wins to break the previous ML mark of 51, set first by the 1887 Philadelphia Athletics and later tied by Cleveland in 1911.

Here are the top dozen rookie pitching staffs of all-time in terms of wins.

TEAMS RECEIVING MOST WINS, SEASON, FROM ROOKIES

Rank	Team	Year	Wins	Rookie Pitchers
1	Chi-FL	1914	53	Lange (12), Fiske (12), Johnson (9), Watson (9), McGuire (5), Prendergast (5), Black (1)
2	Phi-AA	1887	52	Weyhing (26), Seward (25), Titcomb (1)
	Cle-AL	1911	51	Gregg (23), Krapp (13), Blanding (7), West (3), James (2), Yingling (1), Paige (1), Baskette (1)
	Bro-NL	1952	51	Black (15), Loes (13), Wade (11), Rutherford (7), Hughes (2), Moore (1), Lehman (1), Landrum (1)
5	Chi-NL	1889	48	Hutchison (16), Gumbert (16), Dwyer (16)
6	Phi-AL	1934	47	Marcum (14), Cascarella (12), Dietrich (11), Benton (7), Caster (3)
	NY-AL	1910	47	Ford (26), Vaughn (13), Fisher (5), Caldwell (1), Frill (2)
8	Chi-NL	1880	46	Corcoran (43), Poorman (2), Guth (1)
	StL-NL	1902	46	O'Neill (16), Yerkes (12), Currie (7), Wicker (5), Dunham (2), Pearson (2), Popp (2)
10	Tex-AL	1986	46	Correa (12), Witt (11), Guzman (9), Williams (8), Mohorcic (2), Loynd (2), Brown (1), Henry (1)
11	Bro-NL	1903	44	Schmidt (22), Jones (19), Thatcher (3)
	Bos-NL	1937	44	Turner (20), Fette (20), Hutchinson (4)

1914 ROOKIE LEADERS

Batting

G—AL 144, John Leary, STL
    Everett Scott, BOS
    FL 157, Vern Duncan, BAL
    Al Wickland, CHI
    NL 147, Butch Schmidt, BOS
AB—AL 539, Everett Scott, BOS
    FL 597, Charlie Hanford, BUF
    NL 537, Butch Schmidt, BOS
H—AL 141, John Leary, STL
    FL 211, Benny Kauff, IND
    NL 153 Butch Schmidt, BOS
2B—AL 28, John Leary, STL
    FL 44, Benny Kauff, IND
    NL 19, Joe Kelly, PIT
3B—AL 7, John Leary, STL
    FL 14, Duke Kenworthy, KC
    NL 11, Zinn Beck, STL
HR—AL 5, George Burns, DET
    FL 16, Dutch Zwilling, CHI
    NL 5, Larry Gilbert, BOS
R—AL 66, Everett Scott, BOS
    FL 120, Benny Kauff, IND
    NL 67, Butch Schmidt, BOS
RBI—AL 57, George Burns, DET
    FL 95, Benny Kauff, IND
    Dutch Zwilling, CHI
    NL 71, Butch Schmidt, BOS
WK—AL 44, Doc Cook, NY
    FL 81, Al Wickland, CHI
    NL 43, Butch Schmidt, BOS
SO—AL 71, John Leary, STL
    FL 108, Grover Gilmore, KC
    NL 77, Bert Niehoff, CIN
SB—AL 26, Doc Cook, NY
    FL 75, Benny Kauff, IND
    NL 21, Joe Kelly, PIT
BA—AL .291, George Burns, DET
    FL .370, Benny Kauff, IND
    NL .285, Butch Schmidt, BOS
SLG—AL .389, George Burns, DET
    FL .534, Benny Kauff, IND
    NL .356, Butch Schmidt, BOS
OBP—AL .356, Doc Cook, NY
    FL .447, Benny Kauff, IND
    NL .350, Butch Schmidt, BOS

Pitching

W—AL 15, Jim Shaw, WAS
    FL 17, George Kaiserling, IND
    NL 23, Jeff Pfeffer, BRO
L—AL 17, Jim Shaw, WAS
    FL 20, Henry Keupper, STL
    NL 18, Phil Douglas, CIN
PCT—AL .469, Jim Shaw, WAS
    FL .630, George Kaiserling, IND
    NL .657, Jeff Pfeffer, BRO
GP—AL 49, Doc Ayers, WAS
    FL 42, Henry Keupper, STL
    NL 45, Phil Douglas, CIN
GS—AL 32, Doc Ayers, WAS
    FL 33, George Kaiserling, IND
    NL 34, Jeff Pfeffer, BRO
CG—AL 15, Jim Shaw, WAS
    FL 20, George Kaiserling, IND
    NL 27, Jeff Pfeffer, BRO
IP—AL 265.1, Doc Ayers, WAS
    FL 275.1, George Kaiserling, IND
    NL 315, Jeff Pfeffer, BRO
H—AL 221, Doc Ayers, WAS
    FL 288, George Kaiserling, IND
    NL 264, Jeff Pfeffer, BRO
BB—**AL 137, Jim Shaw, WAS**
    FL 80, Dave Davenport, STL
    NL 92, Phil Douglas, CIN
K—AL 164, Jim Shaw, WAS
    FL 142, Dave Davenport, STL*
    NL 135, Jeff Pfeffer, BRO
ERA—AL 2.54, Doc Ayers, WAS
    FL 2.01, Doc Watson, CHI/STL
    NL 1.97, Jeff Pfeffer, BRO
SHO—AL 5, Jim Shaw, WAS
    FL 5, Doc Watson, CHI/STL
    NL 3, Raleigh Aitchison, BRO
    Jeff Pfeffer, BRO
    Ben Tincup, PHI
SV—**AL 4, Jack Bentley, WAS**
    Red Faber, CHI
    Jim Shaw, WAS
    FL 4, Dave Davenport, STL**
    NL 4, Jeff Pfeffer, BRO

*Tied for the ML rookie lead with 164 strikeouts, dividing the season between the NL Cincinnati Reds and the FL St. Louis Terriers.
**Led ML rookies with six total saves, dividing the season between the NL Cincinnati Reds and the FL St. Louis Terriers.

Two Chicago White Sox recruit pitchers were among the few bright spots for a club that tied for sixth. Red Faber began his Hall-of-Fame career by winning ten games for the Pale Hose, and Mellie Wolfgang was even better. Wolfgang went 9–5 and sported a 1.89 ERA, well below that of Faber and the rest of the AL. Other significant freshman hurlers were Ernie Shore, who claimed ten triumphs for the Boston Red Sox, and Rube Bressler, who did likewise for the pennant-winning Philadelphia Athletics.

Bressler did not pitch in the Fall Classic against the "Miracle Braves" of Boston, a veteran team that had only one major rookie contributor. First sacker Butch Schmidt topped the Braves club with 153 hits and had 71 RBI. In the World Series he batted .294 with a pair of runs and two RBI in the Beantown entry's sweep of Connie Mack's last pennant-winner until 1929.

Other Highlights

June 17—Red Faber of the White Sox holds the Philadelphia A's to a lone hit, winning 5–0.

July 11—Babe Ruth makes his ML debut at Boston's Fenway Park, beating Cleveland southpaw Willie Mitchell 4–3.

August 29—Al Mamaux of Pittsburgh shuts out the Brooklyn Robins for 13 innings, beating fellow rookie Jeff Pfeffer 1–0.

September 9—Jack Bentley follows up a one-hit shutout of the Athletics two days before with a two-hit blanking of the New York Yankees as Washington again wins 1–0.

September 23—King Lear wins his only game as a rookie and posts his lone career shutout in beating the Braves 3–0 to end Cincinnati's club-record losing streak at 19.

September 27—After beginning his career with a record 13 straight losses, Cleveland's Guy Morton wins his final start of the season, beating New York 5–3 in the first game of a doubleheader.

September 29—Harry Moran whitewashes the Kansas City Packers 4–0, allowing one safety in eight innings as Buffalo wins the darkness-shortened second game of a twinbill.

On May 6, 1915, Babe Ruth lost a 13-inning heartbreaker at New York. Nevertheless the 20-year-old Boston Red Sox freshman went 3-for-5 and smashed his first major league home run off Jack Warhop. Ruth finished the 1915 campaign with a .315 BA and 15 extra base hits in only 92 ABs, a record that stood until 1998.

MOST LONG HITS BY ROOKIE WITH FEWER THAN 100 ABs

16 (6 2B/0 3B/10 HR), Shane Spencer, 1998 NY AL
15 (10 2B/1 3B/4 HR), Babe Ruth, 1915 Bos AL
13 (11 2B/1 3B/1 HR), Cliff Mapes, 1948 NY AL
13 (10 2B/1 3B/2 HR), Mike Kelly, 1994 Atl NL
13 (10 2B/1 3B/2 HR), Rondell White, 1994 Mon NL

In addition, Ruth had an OPS of .952, and incidentally, he also did a pretty fair job as a pitcher, going 18–8. His .692 winning percentage ranked fourth in the AL, behind three of his teammates, as Boston became the first team to win 100 contests without a 20-game winner. Ruth also was second in opponents' BA, limiting hitters to .212—or 103 points less than he himself batted as a pitcher!

Ruth's four round trippers were just three back of the pacesetter, Braggo Roth, who split his season with the Chicago White Sox and Cleveland Indians. Roth was fifth in slugging while his 17 triples tied him for third. Surprisingly, he knocked only ten doubles and thus became one of just three rookies to have as many as seven more triples than two-base hits.

This season's freshman triples king, however, was Tom Long. The St. Louis Cardinals outfielder collected 25 three baggers, eight more than any other NL batsman and three more than any other rookie had achieved since the close of the nineteenth century.

MOST TRIPLES BY ROOKIE

27, Jimmy Williams, 1899 Pit NL
25, Buck Freeman, 1899 Was NL
25, Tom Long, 1915 StL NL
22, Paul Waner, 1926 Pit NL
21, Tom McCreery, 1896 Lou NL

Long batted .294, the same mark achieved by Jim Kelly of the Pittsburgh Rebels in the Federal League. In its second year of competing with the two established major league circuits, the insurgent loop employed only about half as many freshmen as it had in 1914. Besides Kelly, the Rebels received 17 freshman wins and five shutouts from Clint Rogge, including a one-hitter at Newark on June 20, en route to finishing third albeit just a half game out in the closest three-team race in major league history. The Chicago Whales, which fell two games short of completing their schedule in 1915, won the pennant with a .566 percentage, while the St. Louis Terriers, who played a full schedule, were at .565 with Pittsburgh four points in arrears at .562. The Terriers utilized a rookie middle infield consisting of Bobby Vaughn at second and Ernie Johnson at short. The combo swiped 56 bags, and Vaughn hit a neat .280 but nevertheless was squeezed out of the majors the following year when the Federal League collapsed, paring jobs by a third. A much less sympathetic victim of the job squeeze was Baltimore Terrapins rookie outfielder Jack McCandless, a .214 hitter in over 400 ABs. McCandless was joined on the Terrapins late in the 1915 campaign by shortstop Jimmy Smith (.207), a Chicago Whales reject despite having hit two home runs including a grand slam in Chicago's win at Baltimore on June 22. Smith and McCandless became the first two freshmen in ML history with as many as 400 ABs to log as many strikeouts as base hits and remained the only rookies prior to Gair Allie in 1954 to earn that dubious distinction.

In the NL the pennant-winning Phillies boasted future Hall of Famer Dave Bancroft at shortstop. He batted a respectable .254, drawing 77 walks and scoring 85 runs, which placed him second and third in the loop, respectively. Bancroft hit .294 in Philadelphia's five-game loss to the Red Sox in the World Series while Boston's leading rookie batsman, Babe Ruth, went hitless in his only time up. The NL runner-up Boston Braves had midseason call-ups Art Nehf and Jesse Barnes contribute nicely. Nehf, a southpaw, won five games for the Braves, four of them shutouts. On September 4 he faced the minimum 27 batters in blanking Brooklyn, permitting just one hit—a ball lost in the sun by his right fielder. Barnes was 3–0 with a 1.39 ERA in 45⅓ innings. Meanwhile, Sherry Smith won 14

times for third-place Brooklyn, and Wheezer Dell chipped in 11 victories. The rookie duo combined for six shutouts.

In addition to Ruth's multiskilled performance, the Red Sox had a second yearling pitcher, Carl Mays, on board. Mays topped the circuit with seven saves. The Detroit Tigers won 100 games but were the first team in AL history—and just the second overall—to win that many and not take the flag. Novice right-hander Bernie Boland claimed 13 of those victories while

Babe Ruth is of course the most famous graduate of the class of 1915, but its top student that year was arguably a performer who shared Ruth's initials and whose last name differed from the Babe's by only a single letter. On August 15, 1915, Cleveland traded Shoeless Joe Jackson to the White Sox for novice outfielder Braggo Roth, two lesser players, and a reported $31,500. Though the deal is generally regarded as one of the worst ever from a Cleveland perspective, it was actually not nearly as one-sided as it appears. In the 39 games Cleveland had left to play, Roth clouted four home runs to win the AL four-bagger crown with seven as well as posting a .906 OPS. Since he falls narrowly within the restrictions for rookie status, he furthermore became the first freshman to lead the AL in home runs.

For each of the next three seasons before being swapped to the Philadelphia A's, Roth posted OPS totals well above the AL average. He finished in 1921 as a sub outfielder on the first New York Yankees flag winner. His final OPS figure of .783 ranks 11th among the top dozen outfielders who played regularly during the span of his career, 1914–21. All the names ahead of Roth's belong to well-known stars of the period.

Rank	Name	AB	OPS
1	Ty Cobb	3891	.969
2	Tris Speaker	4210	.919
3	Joe Jackson	3195	.895
4	Gavvy Cravath	2657	.858
5	Benny Kauff	3083	.839
6	Bobby Veach	4498	.824
7	Harry Heilmann	3157	.820
8	Edd Roush	3516	.807
9	Zack Wheat	4087	.794
10	Sam Rice	2556	.789
11	Braggo Roth	2831	.783
12	Jack Tobin	3534	.780

1915 ROOKIE LEADERS

Batting	Pitching
G—AL 144, Elmer Smith, CLE	W—AL 18, Babe Ruth, BOS
FL 152, Ernie Johnson, STL	FL 17, Clint Rogge, PIT
NL 153, Dave Bancroft, PHI	NL 14, Sherry Smith, BRO
Fritz Mollwitz, CIN	L—AL 9, Sam Jones, CLE
AB—AL 479, Wally Pipp, NY	Tom Sheehan, PHI
FL 524, Jim Kelly, PIT	Roy Walker, CLE
NL 563, Dave Bancroft, PHI	FL 11, Clint Rogge, PIT
H—AL 118, Wally Pipp, NY	NL 11, Lee Meadows, STL
Elmer Smith, CLE	PCT—AL .692, Babe Ruth, BOS
FL 154, Jim Kelly, PIT	FL .607, Clint Rogge, PIT
NL 149, Tom Long, STL	NL .636, Sherry Smith, BRO
2B—AL 23, Elmer Smith, CLE	GP—AL 48, Sam Jones, CLE
FL 19, Bobby Vaughn, STL	FL 37, Clint Rogge, PIT
NL 26, Doug Baird, PIT	NL 40, Wheezer Dell, BRO
3B—AL 17, Braggo Roth, CHI/CLE	GS—AL 28, Babe Ruth, BOS
FL 17, Jim Kelly, PIT	FL 31, Clint Rogge, PIT
NL 25, Tom Long, STL	NL 26, Lee Meadows, STL
HR—**AL 7, Braggo Roth, CHI/CLE**	CG—AL 16, Babe Ruth, BOS
FL 7, Ernie Johnson, STL	FL 17, Clint Rogge, PIT
NL 7, Dave Bancroft, PHI	NL 14, Lee Meadows, STL
R—AL 67, Braggo Roth, CHI/CLE	IP—AL 217.2, Babe Ruth, BOS
FL 69, Bobby Vaughn, STL	FL 254.1, Clint Rogge, PIT
NL 85, Dave Bancroft, PHI	NL 244.0, Lee Meadows, STL
RBI—AL 67, Elmer Smith, CLE	H—AL 167, Bernie Boland, DET
FL 67, Ernie Johnson, STL	FL 240, Clint Rogge, PIT
NL 61, Tom Long, STL	NL 232, Lee Meadows, STL
WK—AL 66, Wally Pipp, NY	BB—AL 85, Babe Ruth, BOS
FL 58, Bobby Vaughn, STL	FL 93, Clint Rogge, PIT
NL 77, Dave Bancroft, PHI	NL 100, Wheezer Dell, BRO
SO—AL 81, Wally Pipp, NY	K—AL 112, Babe Ruth, BOS
FL 99, Jack McCandless, BAL	FL 93, Clint Rogge, PIT
NL 88, Doug Baird, PIT	NL 104, Lee Meadows, STL
SB—AL 26, Braggo Roth, CHI/CLE	ERA—AL 2.44, Babe Ruth, BOS
FL 38, Jim Kelly, PIT	FL 2.55, Clint Rogge, PIT
NL 29, Doug Baird, PIT	NL 2.34, Wheezer Dell, BRO
BA—AL .268, Braggo Roth, CHI/CLE	SHO—AL 2, George Dumont, WAS
FL .294, Jim Kelly, PIT	FL 5, Clint Rogge, PIT
NL .294, Tom Long, STL	NL 4, Wheezer Dell, BRO
SLG—AL .438, Braggo Roth, CHI/CLE	Art Nehf, BOS
FL .405, Jim Kelly, PIT	SV—**AL 7, Carl Mays, BOS**
NL .446, Tom Long, STL	FL 4, Bill Upham, BRO
OBP—AL .361, Braggo Roth, CHI/CLE	NL 2, Hank Ritter, NY
FL .356, Bobby Vaughn, STL	Sherry Smith, BRO
NL .346, Dave Bancroft, PHI	

dropping only seven to lead the Bengals staff in winning percentage.

On June 28, fresh from the University of Michigan, George Sisler debuted for the St. Louis Browns. He played 81 games, including 15 at what was then considered his primary position, pitcher, where he was 4–4. Sisler would win just one more decision in his career. However, like Ruth, he would soon become one of the most feared hitters in the game, topping .400 twice and retiring with a .340 career average in more than 2000 big league contests.

Other Highlights

April 19—Cardinals right-hander Lee Meadows makes his ML debut and is the first performer to wear corrective lenses regularly on the field since Will White in 1886.

June 23—In his ML debut A's lefty Bruno Haas walks 16 and throws three wild pitches as he goes the route in a 15–7 loss to the Yankees; it will be Haas's lone ML decision, though he plays with distinction in the minors for many years and also stars in the NFL.

June 18—Happy Felsch hits the only AL grand slam in 1915 and doubles up a runner at first after making an impressive running catch in the outfield for the Chicago White Sox, who beat the Philadelphia Athletics 11–4.

July 2—Lee Meadows of the Cardinals one-hits Cincinnati in winning 2–0.

August 16—Bernie Boland holds Cleveland hitless until there are two outs in the ninth and settles for a one-hitter as Detroit knocks off the Indians 3–1.

August 29—Rookie lefty George Sisler of the Browns edges Walter Johnson 2–1; the following year Sisler will begin the conversion to first base, where he will become one of the all-time greats at the position.

October 6—Elmer Myers of the A's sets a new AL record for a pitcher making his ML debut when he fans 12 Senators in winning 4–0.

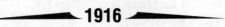
1916

In late May 1916 a 20-year-old St. Louis Cardinals infielder put on a sensational two-day display against the Boston Braves. On May 23 St. Louis won 2–0 after the rookie had singled, stolen second, and scored in the second inning and then accounted for the only other run in the game when he homered three innings later. The next day Boston was leading 4–3 with two outs in the bottom of the ninth before the youngster tripled home the tying run and then scored the winning tally two batters later.

The rookie, Rogers Hornsby, would have many more sparkling diamond moments that year and then continue to shine over the next two decades. On June 28 Hornsby went 5-for-5 with a homer and two triples in the Cardinals' 9–6 win at Cincinnati. Hornsby, who played 83 of his 139 games at third base as a rookie, hit .313 and slugged .444, putting him fourth in the NL in both departments. His 15 triples tied him for second in the loop and vaulted him into the top five all-time among rookies who played primarily the hot corner.

MOST TRIPLES BY ROOKIE THIRD BASEMAN

27, Jimmy Williams, 1899 Pit NL
19, Frank Baker, 1909 Phi AL
18, Bill Joyce, 1890 Bro PL
15, Lefty Marr, 1889 Col AA
15, Rogers Hornsby, 1916 StL NL

Hornsby collected 155 hits, making him one of only three freshmen in 1916 to crack the century mark. In fact, far fewer rookies than usual eclipsed statistical milestones that year, largely because jobs for novices were scarce after the collapse of the Federal League. To illustrate exactly how scarce they were, consider the following table.

THE NUMBER OF ROOKIES REACHING STATISTICAL STANDARDS, 1914–1916

	1914	1915	1916
100 G	34	19	8
400 AB	27	13	4
100 H	28	11	3
10 2B	39	23	7
10 3B	9	8	2
200 IP	9	5	4
10 W	15	6	5
10 L	15	5	9

In 1916, however, several newcomers managed to excel despite the dearth of openings. Two freshman hurlers for the Cleveland Indians, for example, combined for 31 victories. Right-handers Jim Bagby and Stan Coveleski won 16 and 15 games, respectively. It remains the only time that Cleveland has had two freshmen win as many as 15 games apiece. Four years later the same Tribe tandem would combine for 55 wins, leading the Indians to their first World Championship.

The 1916 Philadelphia Athletics were about as far from championship caliber as a team could get. The team won 36 games while losing a whopping 117. Nearly matching the sparse victory total was the sheer number of rookies the Athletics used that year in a vain effort to attain respectability. More than half of the A's wins were earned by freshmen, with Elmer Myers's 14 leading the way. Jing Johnson and Rube Parnham notched two each, and Socks Seibold took another. In 1923 Parnham would win 33 games, 20 consecutively, for Baltimore in the International League, setting loop records for each feat.

Parnham wasn't the only A's yearling whose future far exceeded his present station. Charlie Grimm played the first 12 of his 2,166 big league games. He would hit .290 in 20 seasons and manage three Chicago Cubs teams in the World Series. Val Picinich would play 18 years, catching 935 games. Whitey Witt, the A's shortstop, played 143 games in 1916. He hit a mediocre .245 but in the early 1920s was the regular center fielder on two pennant-winning New York Yankees clubs. Charlie Pick fielded a woeful .899 at the hot corner for the A's, a nadir that would not be reached again until 1978. Pick, however, would hit .389 for the Cubs in the World Series two years later.

Other Highlights

April 17—Rookie right-hander George Cunningham of Detroit is forced at the last minute to make his second ML start when Tigers ace Harry Coveleski balks at pitching against his brother Stan of Cleveland; by mutual agreement, the two Coveleskis will never face one another in the majors, and Cunningham will never

---

A two-hit shutout in his major league debut on October 6, 1915, that was augmented by 12 strikeouts pretty well guaranteed that Elmer Myers would open the following season in the regular rotation for the woeful Philadelphia A's, losers of 109 games. When the 1916 version of the A's was even more hapless, dropping 117 games, Myers, in his role as Connie Mack's newfound ace, set a bundle of negative rookie records. Included was the AL mark for most walks (168). To boot, Myers became both the lone rookie since 1907 to lose as many as 23 games and a member of what will almost certainly be the last pitching staff to number three 20-game losers.

Here is a chronological list of all the teams that shared the 1916 A's ignominious distinction, with rookie contributors in bold.

TEAMS WITH THREE OR MORE 20-GAME LOSERS

Team	Year	Pitchers
NY-AA	1886	Lynch (30), Mays (27), Cushman (21)
Pit-NL	1887	McCormick (23), Morris (22), Galvin (21)
Was-NL	1887	Whitney (21), O'Day (20), **Gilmore** (20)
Ind-NL	1888	Healy (24), Shreve (24), Boyle (22)
StL-NL	1896	Hart (29), Breitenstein (26), **Donahue** (24)
Bro-NL	1898	**Yeager** (22), Kennedy (22), Dunn (21)
StL-NL	1898	Taylor (29), Sudhoff (27), Hughey (24)
Was-AL	1904	Townsend (26), **Jacobson** (23), Patten (23)
StL-AL	1905	Glade (25), Howell (22), Sudhoff (20)
Bos-NL	1905	Willis (29), Wilhelm (23), Fraser (21), **Young** (21)
Bos-NL	1906	Young (25), Dorner (25), **Lindaman** (23), Pfeffer (22)
Phi-AL	1916	Bush (24), **Myers** (23), Nabors (20)

Batting		Pitching	
G—AL 143, Whitey Witt, PHI		W—AL 16, Jim Bagby, CLE	
NL 139, Rogers Hornsby, STL		NL 11, Clarence Mitchell, CIN	
AB—AL 563, Whitey Witt, PHI		L—AL 23, Elmer Myers, PHI	
NL 530, Greasy Neale, CIN		NL 15, Jesse Barnes, BOS	
H—AL 138, Whitey Witt, PHI		Bob Steele, STL	
NL 155, Rogers Hornsby, STL		PCT—AL .536, Stan Coveleski, CLE	
2B—AL 16, Whitey Witt, PHI		NL .524, Clarence Mitchell, CIN	
NL 17, Rogers Hornsby, STL		GP—AL 48, Jim Bagby, CLE	
3B—AL 15, Whitey Witt, PHI		NL 36, Steamboat Williams, STL	
NL 15, Rogers Hornsby, STL		GS—AL 35, Elmer Myers, PHI	
HR—AL 2, Whitey Witt, PHI		NL 24, Clarence Mitchell, CIN	
NL 6, Rogers Hornsby, STL		CG—AL 31, Elmer Myers, PHI	
Jack Smith, STL		NL 17, Clarence Mitchell, CIN	
R—AL 64, Whitey Witt, PHI		IP—AL 315.0, Elmer Myers, PHI	
NL 63, Rogers Hornsby, STL		NL 194.2, Clarence Mitchell, CIN	
RBI—AL 36, Whitey Witt, PHI		H—AL 280, Elmer Myers, PHI	
NL 65, Rogers Hornsby, STL		NL 211, Clarence Mitchell, CIN	
WK—AL 55, Whitey Witt, PHI		BB—**AL 168, Elmer Myers, PHI**	
NL 40, Rogers Hornsby, STL		NL 49, Frank Miller, PIT	
SO—AL 71, Whitey Witt, PHI		K—AL 182, Elmer Myers, PHI	
NL 79, Greasy Neale, CIN		NL 88, Frank Miller, PIT	
SB—AL 25, Charlie Pick, PHI		ERA—AL 2.61, Jim Bagby, CLE	
NL 24, Jack Smith, STL		NL 2.29, Frank Miller, PIT	
BA—AL .245, Whitey Witt, PHI		SHO—AL 3, Jim Bagby, CLE	
NL .313, Rogers Hornsby, STL		NL 3, Jesse Barnes, BOS	
SLG—AL .337, Whitey Witt, PHI		SV—AL 6, Allan Russell, NY	
NL .444, Rogers Hornsby, STL		NL 1, Jesse Barnes, BOS	
OBP—AL .315, Whitey Witt, PHI		Hi Jasper, STL	
NL .369, Rogers Hornsby, STL		Frank Miller, PIT	
		Steamboat Williams, STL	

pitch a better game as he beats Stan Coveleski and Cleveland 3–1 in 12 innings.

April 20—Johnny Beall clubs the first NL home run at the park that is presently called Wrigley Field, but Beall's Cincinnati Reds lose to the Chicago Cubs 7–6 in 11 innings.

May 14—Cards rookie Rogers Hornsby hits his first career home run, an inside-the-parker off Brooklyn's Jeff Pfeffer at St. Louis's Robison Field; Hornsby will become the first infielder (first base excluded) to collect 300 career four-baggers when he retires with 301.

May 31—Frank Gilhooley of the New York Yankees hits the only rookie grand slam in 1916 as the Yankees come back to beat the Philadelphia Athletics 8–7.

September 14—Scott Perry shuts out the Boston Braves as his Cubs win 2–0 in 11 innings.

September 18—In his second ML start, Claude Thomas fires a two-hitter for the Washington Senators to edge the St. Louis Browns 1–0; the gem will prove to be Thomas's lone ML victory.

1917

Remember that scene in *Close Encounters of the Third Kind* where Richard Dreyfuss's character is creating the model of Devils Tower? Dreyfuss rips off the top portion, leaving a much more accurate representation of the landmark. The rookie crop of 1917 is similar to

Dreyfuss's model—the top portion is missing. To be sure, there were some freshmen who produced solid performances, but none reached the summit of the baseball world. In fact, since 1894, only two seasons in which the schedule ran at least 150 games failed to produce a rookie that either won at least 15 games or garnered as many as 150 hits—1917 and 1990.

Leading the 1917 rookie crop with 14 victories was Allen Sothoron of the St. Louis Browns. On April 17, in his first start of the year and second of his career, Sothoron threw a one-hitter, beating the Cleveland Indians 4–0. He tossed two more whitewashes and made 48 appearances, fourth best in the AL.

In 1920 baseball banned the spitball, but Sothoron and 16 other hurlers that regularly employed the pitch were grandfathered and allowed to continue throwing a spitter. Two of the other exempted twirlers were rookies in 1917 along with Sothoron, Marv Goodwin and Burleigh Grimes. Goodwin, despite winning just six games, matched Sothoron with three shutouts for the rival St. Louis Cardinals. He beat the Chicago Cubs and Hippo Vaughn on September 16, allowing only three hits and fanning nine in his 6–0 triumph. Grimes had less success in 1917 than did his spitballing comrades, but it was he who would make the Hall of Fame. Grimes went 3–16 for the Pittsburgh Pirates, but starting in 1918 he won in double figures every year through 1931 en route to amassing 270 career victories.

Grimes's teammate Chuck Ward had the difficult task of replacing a legend. Honus Wagner had been Pittsburgh's regular shortstop since 1903 and a Steel City mainstay since 1900. In 1917 Wagner played his final 74 major league games, mainly at first base. Ward assumed the shortstop duties but found the Flying Dutchman's spikes too tough to fill, batting .236 and fielding at a league-low .912 clip.

Ward, nonetheless, was one of five freshmen to reach 100 hits. The Philadelphia Athletics, who won 19 more games than they had the previous year but still finished eighth, featured two of the quintet. Third baseman Ray Bates had 115 hits and second sacker Roy Grover, 108. The pair of novices batted .237 and .224, respectively, and would not be long for the big time. Bates never again played in the majors while Grover had only 46 more games awaiting him. Joe Harris, however, had a more sanguine fate. Harris batted .304 in 112 Cleveland contests, the first of several years that he topped the .300 plateau. Indeed, Harris posted an excellent .317 career BA in 970 games and played in two World Series.

Appearing in the 1917 Fall Classic was the year's top rookie hitsmith, first baseman Walter Holke of the New York Giants. Holke had 146 safeties for John McGraw's men, who outdistanced the second-place Philadelphia Phillies by ten games. In the third game of the series, Holke doubled in the go-ahead run and scored an insurance tally in the fourth inning as New York won its first contest 2–0. Holke and Rube Benton, who won Game Three, shared some of the responsibility for a fourth-inning fiasco in Game Six. Neither Giant covered home plate on the play in which Chicago's Eddie Collins got caught in a rundown and then outraced Giants third baseman Heinie Zimmeran to the dish and scored the game's first run. Chicago won the game and the series, 4–2.

In 1915 the Portsmouth Cobblers won the pennant in the Class D Ohio State League. The team was managed by first sacker Chet Spencer, a Portsmouth native and a former outfielder with the Boston Braves, and was loaded with young Ohio-bred stars. Foremost among them were two Cleveland-born phenoms, outfielder Ralph Sharman, the Ohio State League bat crown winner that year, and catcher Pickles Dillhoeffer, who led the loop in runs. Also on the club was another Ohio native, outfielder Austin McHenry.

Few Class D teams in that period produced future major leaguers, let alone three. Sharman and Dillhoeffer were both members of the 1917 rookie crop, with the Philadelphia A's and Cubs, respectively, and McHenry broke in a year later with the Cardinals. But if the 1915 Portsmouth Cobblers were an especially blessed team, they were also extraordinarily ill-fated. Some eight months after Sharman appeared in his first ML game, he died in an army boot camp at Camp Sheridan, Alabama. Dillhoefer and McHenry were reunited in 1919 after Dillhoefer was traded to the Cardinals. In 1921 Dillhoefer shared the catching duties with Verne Clemons and McHenry finished third in the NL in batting with a .350 BA. Within a year both were dead at age 27, as Dillhoefer succumbed over the winter to typhoid fever following a routine operation, and McHenry, after being forced to leave the Cardinals in mid-season when his severe headaches were diagnosed as a brain tumor, died on Thanksgiving weekend.

1917 ROOKIE LEADERS

Batting		Pitching	
G—AL 149, Swede Risberg, CHI		W—AL 14, Allen Sothoron, STL	
NL 153, Walter Holke, NY		NL 13, Leon Cadore, BRO	
AB—AL 485, Ray Bates, PHI		**L—AL 19, Allen Sothoron, STL**	
NL 527, Walter Holke, NY		NL 16, Burleigh Grimes, PIT	
H—AL 115, Ray Bates, PHI		PCT—AL .500, Win Noyes, PHI	
NL 146, Walter Holke, NY		NL .500, Leon Cadore, BRO	
2B—AL 22, Joe Harris, CLE		GP—AL 48, Allen Sothoron, STL	
NL 21, Gene Paulette, STL		NL 37, Leon Cadore, BRO	
3B—AL 8, Swede Risberg, CHI		Hod Eller, CIN	
NL 7, Walter Holke, NY		Burleigh Grimes, PIT	
Gene Paulette, STL		GS—AL 32, Allen Sothoron, STL	
HR—AL 2, Ray Bates, PHI		NL 30, Leon Cadore, BRO	
Tod Sloan, STL		CG—AL 17, Allen Sothoron, STL	
NL 6, Jim Hickman, BRO		NL 21, Leon Cadore, BRO	
R—AL 59, Swede Risberg, CHI		IP—AL 276.2, Allen Sothoron, STL	
NL 55, Walter Holke, NY		NL 264.0, Leon Cadore, BRO	
RBI—AL 66, Ray Bates, PHI		H—AL 259, Allen Sothoron, STL	
NL 55, Walter Holke, NY		NL 231, Leon Cadore, BRO	
WK—AL 59, Swede Risberg, CHI		BB—AL 96, Allen Sothoron, STL	
NL 34, Walter Holke, NY		NL 70, Burleigh Grimes, PIT	
SO—AL 65, Swede Risberg, CHI		K—AL 85, Allen Sothoron, STL	
NL 66, Jim Hickman, BRO		NL 115, Leon Cadore, BRO	
SB—AL 16, Swede Risberg, CHI		ERA—AL 2.83, Allen Sothoron, STL	
NL 14, Jim Hickman, BRO		NL 2.45, Leon Cadore, BRO	
BA—AL .304, Joe Harris, CLE		SHO—AL 3, Allen Sothoron, STL	
NL .277, Walter Holke, NY		NL 3, Marv Goodwin, STL	
SLG—AL .385, Joe Harris, CLE		SV—AL 4, Allen Sothoron, STL	
NL .338, Walter Holke, NY		NL 3, Leon Cadore, BRO	
OBP—AL .389, Joe Harris, CLE			
NL .327, Walter Holke, NY			

*Harris had only 435 plate appearances but was within 50 of being a qualifier and still easily led in all three AL major batting departments after 42 hitless at bats were added to his total PAs to reach the requisite 477.

Other Highlights

April 26—Dutch Ruether, primarily a pitcher but pinch-hitting on this occasion, hits a bases-loaded triple, but his Chicago Cubs fall to the Cincinnati Reds 6–4.

June 17—Lee Gooch hits a grand slam for the Philadelphia Athletics, who prevail over the Cleveland Indians 9–5.

August 21—Reds rookie Hod Eller throws 5⅓ innings of scoreless relief and fans the side on nine pitches in the ninth inning to beat the Giants 7–5 and end Slim Sallee's ten-game win streak for the 1917 flag winners.

August 22—Jim Hickman goes 5-for-9 with a double and two runs in the Brooklyn Robins' 6–5 22-inning win against the Pittsburgh Pirates.

September 22—Elmer Ponder of Pittsburgh limits the Giants to two hits and whiffs eight in winning a 1–0 gem that marks his first big league triumph.

1918

From 1911 through 1914, the most valuable player in the American and National leagues was honored with

Charlie Hollocher struggled for several years to recapture his rookie form after debuting with the top BA (.316) of any rookie shortstop in the Deadball Era. In 1922 Hollocher smacked .340, the highest figure to that point in the twentieth century of any shortstop, rookie or otherwise, who was not named Wagner. The following year, seemingly at the height of his career, he quit the game claiming his health was failing. *Transcendental Graphics*

Two years before Hollocher took Chicago by storm, right-hander Scott Perry had served a brief apprenticeship with the Cubs. Perry, who also had stints with the St. Louis Browns in 1915 and the Cincinnati Reds in 1917, finally got an extended opportunity with the Philadelphia Athletics in 1918. On May 4 Perry demonstrated the endurance that would allow him to complete an AL-leading 30 games by pitching an 11-inning shutout against Washington. The Senators got only three hits. A week later against the Chicago White Sox, Perry beat fellow rookie Frank Shellenback, who would win a record 295 games in the Pacific Coast League. Perry permitted all of one hit in winning 1–0.

The Athletics finished last for the fourth consecutive season, going 52–76, meaning Perry's 20 wins represented nearly 40 percent of the club's total. He topped the junior circuit in innings while his 1.98 ERA was fourth in the AL, as was his victory total.

While Perry was near the top in surrendering bases on balls, the best rookie batter in drawing them was Truck Hannah, the catcher for the New York Yankees. Hannah received 51 free passes in 90 games, one of the highest totals for a freshman backstop in so few contests.

MOST WALKS BY ROOKIE CATCHER IN LESS THAN 100 GAMES

58 BB/90 G, Herman Pitz, 1890 Bro/Syr AA
54 BB/96 G, Heinie Peitz, 1893 StL NL
52 BB/83 G, Gus Niarhos, 1948 NY AL
51 BB/90 G, Truck Hannah, 1918 NY AL
51 BB/99 G, Tom Haller, 1962 SF NL

Besides Charlie Hollocher, only two rookies had as many as 100 hits—New York Giant Ross Youngs (143) and Irish Meusel (132) of the Philadelphia Phillies. After Meusel, a left fielder, was traded to the Giants in July 1921, he teamed with rightfielder Youngs on four consecutive NL pennant winners.

Youngs would not survive the decade, however, dying of Bright's disease, a kidney malady, in 1927 at age 30.

the Chalmers Award. Had the prize lasted four more seasons there is a good chance a rookie would have been the NL recipient in 1918. Shortstop Charlie Hollocher led the pennant-winning Chicago Cubs in many categories and topped the senior circuit in at bats, hits, and total bases. He was fourth in batting average and second in OBP.

With the Great War still raging in Europe, it was decided to end the regular season on Labor Day, each team losing approximately 25 games from its schedule. Despite the truncated season, Hollocher banged out 161 hits, the most by a rookie shortstop from 1900 through 1920. Hollocher collected only four more safeties in the World Series against the Boston Red Sox, but in Game Five he starred in the Cubs' 3–0 victory. Hollocher went 3-for-3 with a walk, a stolen base, and two runs as Chicago stayed alive before losing the series the following day.

During the Deadball Era (1901–19), on only 26 occasions did a shortstop in either major league hit .300. The number shrinks to 14 after Honus Wagner's twelve .300 seasons are deducted and to just two when consideration is limited to rookies. In 1907, Simon Nicholls hit .302 for the A's, good enough for fifth place that year in the AL batting race. The following year Nicholls plummeted to .216 and was cut shortly thereafter.

The only other rookie shortstop to crack the .300 barrier in that period was Charlie Hollocher in 1918. His .316 BA ranks fourth among Deadball Era shortstops if Wagner's work is excluded. Tormented by mental problems, Hollocher played just seven years before his personal demons compelled him to quit the game and ultimately drove him to suicide when he was only 44. He took with him a .304 career BA. Among all shortstops with at least 2,500 career at bats prior to World War II, Hollocher's mark stands seventh.

SHORTSTOPS BETWEEN 1871 AND 1941 WITH .300 CAREER BAs

Rank	Name	AB	OPS	BA
1	Honus Wagner	10439	.858	.328
2	Cecil Travis	4191	.817	.327
3	Arky Vaughan	5268	.887	.324
4	Luke Appling	5469	.810	.316
5	Joe Sewell	7132	.804	.312
6	Hughie Jennings	4895	.797	.312
7	Charlie Hollocher	2936	.762	.304
8	Joe Cronin	7224	.859	.303
9	Ed McKean	6890	.781	.302

1918 ROOKIE LEADERS

Batting

G—AL 121, Joe Dugan, PHI
 NL 131, Charlie Hollocher, CHI
AB—AL 411, Joe Dugan, PHI
 NL 509, Charlie Hollocher, CHI
H—AL 85, Merlin Kopp, PHI
 NL 161, Charlie Hollocher, CHI
2B—AL 14, Bob Jones, DET
 George Whiteman, BOS
 NL 25, Irish Meusel, PHI
3B—AL 7, Merlin Kopp, PHI
 NL 8, Ross Youngs, NY
HR—AL 3, Joe Dugan, PHI
 NL 4, Cliff Heathcote, STL
 Irish Meusel, PHI
R—AL 60, Merlin Kopp, PHI
 NL 72, Charlie Hollocher, CHI
RBI—AL 34, Joe Dugan, PHI
 NL 62, Irish Meusel, PHI
WK—AL 51, Truck Hannah, NY
 NL 47, Charlie Hollocher, CHI
SO—AL 55, Joe Dugan, PHI
 Merlin Kopp, PHI
 NL 49, Ross Youngs, NY
SB—AL 22, Merlin Kopp, PHI
 NL 26, Charlie Hollocher, CHI
BA—AL .234, Merlin Kopp, PHI
 NL .316, Charlie Hollocher, CHI
SLG—AL .292, Merlin Kopp, PHI
 NL .397, Charlie Hollocher, CHI
OBP—AL .320, Merlin Kopp, PHI
 NL .379, Charlie Hollocher, CHI

Pitching

W—AL 20, Scott Perry, PHI
 NL 11, Red Causey, NY
L—**AL 19, Scott Perry, PHI**
 NL 12, Bill Sherdel, STL
PCT—AL .513, Scott Perry, PHI
 NL .647, Red Causey, NY
GP—AL 44, Scott Perry, PHI
 NL 35, Bill Sherdel, STL
GS—**AL 36, Scott Perry, PHI**
 NL 18, Red Causey, NY
CG—**AL 30, Scott Perry, PHI**
 NL 10, Red Causey, NY
 Dana Fillingim, BOS
IP—**AL 332.1, Scott Perry, PHI**
 NL 182.1, Bill Sherdel, STL
H—**AL 295, Scott Perry, PHI**
 NL 174, Bill Sherdel, STL
BB—AL 111, Scott Perry, PHI
 NL 69, Jakie May, STL
K—AL 81, Scott Perry, PHI
 NL 61, Jakie May, STL
ERA—AL 1.98, Scott Perry, PHI
 NL 2.60, Roy Sanders, PIT
SHO—AL 3, Scott Perry, PHI
 Mule Watson, PHI
 NL 4, Dana Fillingim, BOS
SV—AL 4, Bob Geary, PHI
 NL 2, Red Causey, NY

May 18—Dana Fillingim tosses his second consecutive shutout for the Boston Braves, besting the St. Louis Cardinals 11–0.

May 22—Hank Thormahlen throws a 14-inning whitewash for the New York Yankees, who edge the Chicago White Sox 1–0.

June 13—Cliff Heathcote hits for the cycle as his Cardinals play a 19-inning 8–8 tie with the Philadelphia Phillies.

July 27—Stationed in Brooklyn, Harry Heitman gets permission to start a game for the Dodgers from his Naval CO and is removed when he gives up four straight hits to the Cardinals after retiring the first batter he faces; Heitman is saddled not only with the loss in his lone ML appearance but also with a 108.00 career ERA.

August 31—Mule Watson of the Philadelphia Athletics pitches two complete games, losing the opener to the Boston Red Sox but holding Boston to one hit in the finale to win 1–0.

September 7—Thirty-five-year-old rookie outfielder George Whiteman scores once and prevents a home run with a terrific catch in left field as the Red Sox beat the Chicago Cubs 2–1 in Game Three of the World Series.

September 11—In his last ML game, George Whiteman emerges as the 1918 World Series hero when his line shot is dropped by rightfielder Max Flack, resulting in the Sox' only two runs in their 2–1 Game Six win to clinch the Series; Whiteman will also lead all Sox hitters in the Series in total bases with a mere seven.

1919

Mention the year 1919 to baseball fans and the disturbing picture of a rigged World Series probably will be envisioned. The year could have conjured thoughts of Babe Ruth breaking the single-season home run record for the first time or the game having its highest attendance figures in years. Instead, what would be called the "Black Sox Scandal" tarnishes the season.

Eight Chicago White Sox players conspired to throw the World Series to the underdog Cincinnati Reds. One of the "clean" Sox was rookie southpaw Dickie Kerr, who went 13–7 for Chicago, which featured largely the same crew that had won the World Series two years earlier. Kerr pitched 39 games, 17 as a starter, and topped the AL with seven wins in relief. He was the only honest starting pitcher for the White Sox in the series. In Game Three, Kerr threw a three-hitter, beating Cincinnati 3–0 and giving Chicago its first victory. It was the first World Series shutout an AL rookie had ever thrown. The Reds won games four and five to take a commanding 4–1 lead in the best-of-nine series. Kerr again did his part in Game Six, winning 5–4 in ten innings for the Sox, who seemed to be playing on the level. Chicago also won Game Seven before Lefty Williams got shelled and lost in the finale. Kerr was 2–0, with 1.42 ERA in 19 innings.

Pitching an effective 7⅓ innings of relief in the series was Kerr's teammate, Roy Wilkinson, who tossed a shutout against the Philadelphia Athletics in his first ML start September 12. The White Sox duo represented two of only five freshmen to whitewash an opponent that season. The quintet had but one apiece, making 1919 the first season lacking a rookie with at least two blankings since 1900, when there was only one major league. Oddly, the first of the five shutouts did not occur until August 25, when George Uhle limited the Athletics to six hits and the Cleveland Indians pounded Philadelphia 12–0. Uhle, who got two hits himself, batted .302 in 43 at bats as a rookie and would compile a .289 lifetime average in 1,360 at bats.

Uhle's future teammate with Detroit in 1929–30, Waite Hoyt of the Boston Red Sox, shut out the New York Yankees September 8, something Kerr also achieved nine days later. On September 18 Harry Courtney became the final member of this exclusive club when his Washington Senators beat the St. Louis Browns 7–0.

None of these hurlers pitched in the NL, which experienced the first of only three years in which no senior circuit rookies would fashion a shutout. (The other seasons were 1961 and 2000.) Freshman hitters in the loop fared little better. Though it was true that the schedule had temporarily been abbreviated to only 140 games in the aftermath of World War I, the offensive figures were nonetheless anemic. Only three NL rookies reached 200 at bats while just two topped 50 safeties.

Over in the AL, the numbers were only slightly more impressive. Two freshmen actually had 95 or more hits.

Ira Flagstead, leading the pack with five home runs, hit .331 in 287 at bats, making him by far the most productive rookie hitter in 1919.

Other Highlights

May 6—George Halas, before embarking on a Hall-of-Fame career in the NFL, makes his ML debut with the New York Yankees, going 1-for-4 in a 3–2 loss to the Philadelphia Athletics.

May 13—Tigers outfielder Ira Flagstead, the top recruit hitter in 1919 and the rookie home run king with five, tags his first career round tripper off Fritz Coumbe of the Indians.

August 7—Sammy Vick hits a grand slam as the Yankees beat the St. Louis Browns 8–2 in the second game of a doubleheader.

September 11—Future Hall of Famer Frankie Frisch hits his first career home run, victimizing Pete Alexander of the Cubs; despite having an abysmal rookie year with the Giants, hitting just .226 in 54 games, Frisch will tie for the NL lead in recruit homers with two and also will lead in RBI with just 24.

September 24—Red Sox frosh Waite Hoyt hurls nine consecutive perfect innings against the Yankees, but alas, they are frames four through 12 in a contest that he loses 2–1 in 13 innings.

Though the 1919 rookie crop was glaringly short on talent, it nonetheless produced its share of oddities. At one extreme was Herman Bronkie, a 34-year-old third baseman with the Browns, and at the other was 17-year-old Phils southpaw Lefty Weinert, who became the first major leaguer born in the twentieth century when he worked four rocky innings in relief on September 24.

Weinert later would develop into a regular starter with the Phils for a couple of years, but most of the others on the list of the first ten twentieth-century born players to make the majors are obscure figures at best. Only Fred Heimach was a significant contributor during the 1920s.

Name	Birth date	Debut date
Lefty Weinert	4/21/02	9/24/19
Emmett McCann	3/4/02	4/19/20
Virgil Cheeves	2/12/01	9/7/20
Fred Heimach	1/27/01	10/1/20
Ted Odenwald	1/4/02	4/13/21
Dutch Henry	5/12/02	9/16/21
Kenny Hogan	10/9/02	10/2/21
Art Merewether	7/7/02	7/10/22
Uel Eubanks	2/14/03	7/20/22
Homer Blankenship	8/4/02	9/6/22

1919 ROOKIE LEADERS

Batting	Pitching
G—AL 106, Sammy Vick, NY	W—AL 13, Dickie Kerr, CHI
NL 88, Verne Clemons, STL	NL 9, Frank Woodward, PHI/STL
AB—AL 407, Sammy Vick, NY	L—AL 18, Rollie Naylor, PHI
NL 239, Verne Clemons, STL	NL 14, Frank Woodward, PHI/STL
H—AL 101, Sammy Vick, NY	PCT—AL .650, Dickie Kerr, CHI
NL 63, Verne Clemons, STL	NL .417, Oscar Tuero, STL
2B—AL 22, Ira Flagstead, DET	GP—AL 43, Walt Kinney, PHI
NL 14, Leo Callahan, PHI	**NL 45, Oscar Tuero, STL**
3B—AL 9, Sammy Vick, NY	GS—AL 23, Rollie Naylor, PHI
NL 4, Leo Callahan, PHI	NL 19, Frank Woodward, PHI/STL
Cliff Lee, PIT	CG—AL 17, Rollie Naylor, PHI
HR—AL 5, Ira Flagstead, DET	NL 8, Frank Woodward, PHI/STL
NL 2, Verne Clemons, STL	IP—AL 212.1, Dickie Kerr, CHI
Pat Duncan, CIN	NL 172.2, Frank Woodward, PHI/STL
Frankie Frisch, NY	H—AL 210, Rollie Naylor, PHI
R—AL 59, Sammy Vick, NY	NL 174, Frank Woodward, PHI/STL
NL 26, Leo Callahan, PHI	BB—AL 91, Walt Kinney, PHI
RBI—AL 41, Ira Flagstead, DET	NL 63, Frank Woodward, PHI/STL
NL 24, Frankie Frisch, NY	K—AL 97, Walt Kinney, PHI
WK—AL 35, Ira Flagstead, DET	NL 45, Oscar Tuero, STL
Sammy Vick, NY	Frank Woodward, PHI/STL
NL 29, Leo Callahan, PHI	ERA—AL 2.88, Dickie Kerr, CHI
SO—AL 55, Sammy Vick, NY	NL 3.20, Oscar Tuero, STL
NL 19, Leo Callahan, PHI	SHO—AL 1, done by five pitchers
SB—AL 9, Sammy Vick, NY	NL No Qualifiers
NL 15, Frankie Frisch, NY	SV—AL 2, Walt Kinney, PHI
BA—AL .248, Sammy Vick, NY	**NL 4, Oscar Tuero, STL**
NL No Qualifiers*	
SLG—AL .344, Sammy Vick, NY	
NL No Qualifiers	
OBA—AL .308, Sammy Vick, NY	
NL No Qualifiers	

*The NL rookie closest to being a qualifier was Verne Clemons of St. Louis, who had 270 plate appearances.

6

1920s

1920

For baseball historians 1920 has become the demarcation point that separates the old-school "inside baseball" exemplified by Ty Cobb and the "modern game" first exemplified by Babe Ruth. Of course, most things are never that simple. While it was certainly true that Ruth nearly doubled his own seasonal home run record in 1920, he was the only batter with more than 19 round trippers. Ruth's rookie teammate, Bob Meusel, smashed 11 home runs—or seven more than the next highest freshman. Meusel split his season between right field and third base, hitting .328 with 40 doubles and setting an all-time rookie record in the process.

FEWEST ABs BY ROOKIE WITH 40 DOUBLES

460 AB/40 2B, Bob Meusel, 1920 NY AL	
505 AB/44 2B, Brad Fullmer, 1998 Mon NL	
528 AB/47 2B, Fred Lynn, 1975 Bos AL	
535 AB/44 2B, Bob Johnson, 1933 Phi AL	
538 AB/40 2B, Chris Sabo, 1988 Cin NL	

On June 4 "the California clouter," as *The Sporting News* called him, had four hits, including a double and homer in New York's 12–5 win over the Philadelphia Athletics. Meusel, with 151 safeties, was one of three rookies to top 150 hits. Edging him for the AL freshman lead was Bucky Harris, the Washington Senators new second baseman. Harris had 152 and trailed only Pat Duncan, the Cincinnati swatter who amassed 170 hits. Duncan played 31 games for the Reds in 1919 before facing the crooked Chicago White Sox in the World Series, where he led Cincinnati hitters with eight RBI. In 1920 Duncan played all 154 games in left field and drove in 83 runs, fourth most in the NL.

Just as Meusel headed the freshman charts in home runs, fellow Yankee Rip Collins did so in victories. Collins went 14–8 for New York, which finished third but only three games back of the flag-winning Indians. On June 26 he tossed a one-hitter in beating the Boston Red Sox 14–0. That same day Jesse Haines of the St. Louis Cardinals pitched his third shutout of the month and fourth of the season. The Cards rookie led the senior circuit in games pitched and was fourth in strikeouts and innings pitched. On October 1 Haines allowed two runs and six hits in the first six innings against the Chicago Cubs at what would later be called Wrigley Field. The game went into extra innings, but Haines would not permit another safety until the 17th, when the Cubs won 3–2. It proved to be the toughest of Haines's 20 defeats in his rookie season.

The Athletics had another dismal year, losing 106 times and finishing 50 games behind Cleveland. They used 24 rookies, including Eddie Rommel and Dave Keefe, who won seven and six games, respectively. Each pitcher had an ERA under 3.00, well below the league's average of 3.79. Keefe and another A's righty, Slim Harriss, each notched two-hit shutouts during the course of the 1920 campaign, but a third A's frosh, Roy Moore, didn't fare quite as well in his introduction to the bigs, going 1–13.

Cleveland's Duster Mails, on the other hand, had a brilliant year, or to be more exact, a brilliant month. Mails, a southpaw, was purchased from Portland on August 21 but didn't make his initial start for Cleve-

land until September. He fired two shutouts down the stretch, the first coming on September 16, when his four-hit blanking of Washington propelled the Indians into first place for good. In the Fall Classic against the Brooklyn Robins, Mails delivered everything his name implied. In Game Three he relieved with one out in the first inning and stranded both inherited runners. Mails pitched another six frames of scoreless ball, but the damage had been done and Brooklyn won 2–1. Four days later Mails limited the Robins to three hits in a starting role, winning Game Six, 1–0. Cleveland won its first World Championship the following day after Mails had demonstrated that even at the dawn of the slugging age, good pitching could still prevail.

Other Highlights

June 2—The 1920 rookie home run king, Bob Meusel, hits his first career four-bagger off Jim Shaw of the Senators; in 1925 Meusel will beat out teammate Babe Ruth for the AL homer crown.

August 26—Bill Hubbell throws a four-hitter for the Philadelphia Phillies, who win at Cincinnati 7–0.

September 1—Pacific Coast League acquisition Duster Mails makes his first start for Cleveland, topping Washington 9–5; in the final month of the season, Mails will go 7–0 in eight starts and play a large hand in the Tribe winning its first pennant.

September 12—Harry Courtney holds the Chicago White Sox to five hits as the Washington Senators win 5–0.

September 26—Buddy Napier of the Cincinnati Reds blanks the Pittsburgh Pirates 8–0.

October 3—On the final day of the regular season, Monty Swartz, a 23-year-old recruit from Farmersville, Ohio, debuts for Cincinnati and tosses a 12-inning complete game, losing 6–3 to the Cardinals; Swartz will never again be seen in the majors.

Who had the best season ever by a rookie first baseman? A convincing argument can be mounted for any one of a dozen candidates. But as to who had the worst season ever by a rookie first baseman there is little disagreement. Ivy Griffin's 1920 campaign with the Philadelphia A's wins every time. The owner of the lowest season OPS of any first baseman since the end of the Deadball Era? Griffin with .555. Who had the fewest RBI of any first baseman with at least 400 at bats? Griffin and Joe Agler (Baltimore FL, 1914) are tied with 20. What performer totaled the fewest runs and RBI combined of any first baseman with at least 400 at bats? Griffin again with just 66.

Griffin was purchased by the A's late in the 1919 season after a decent but in no way spectacular year with Atlanta of the Southern Association in his first taste of pro ball. In 1920 he swiftly demonstrated that he was not ready for quality pitching, but since the A's had paid good money for him, Connie Mack kept him around as a seldom-used sub through the 1921 season before allowing him to return to the minors to acquire some much-needed further seasoning. The shame is that even though Griffin ranked among the better hitters in the high minors for the remainder of the 1920s, memories of his dreadful rookie year prevented him from ever receiving another big league opportunity.

1920 ROOKIE LEADERS

Batting	Pitching
G—AL 136, Bucky Harris, WAS	W—AL 14, Rip Collins, NY
NL 154, Pat Duncan, CIN	NL 13, Jesse Haines, STL
AB—AL 506, Bucky Harris, WAS	L—AL 14, Slim Harriss, PHI
NL 576, Pat Duncan, CIN	NL 20, Jesse Haines, STL
H—AL 152, Bucky Harris, WAS	PCT—AL .636, Rip Collins, NY
NL 170, Pat Duncan, CIN	NL .474, Bill Hubbell, NY/PHI
2B—AL 40, Bob Meusel, NY	GP—AL 37, Harry Courtney, WAS
NL 16, Pat Duncan, CIN	**NL 47, Jesse Haines, STL**
Fred Nicholson, PIT	GS—AL 25, Slim Harriss, PHI
3B—AL 7, Bob Meusel, NY	NL 37, Jesse Haines, STL
Jim O'Neill, WAS	CG—AL 11, Slim Harriss, PHI
NL 11, Pat Duncan, CIN	NL 19, Jesse Haines, STL
HR—AL 11, Bob Meusel, NY	IP—AL 192, Slim Harriss, PHI
NL 4, Fred Nicholson, PIT	NL 301.2, Jesse Haines, STL
R—AL 76, Bucky Harris, WAS	H—AL 226, Slim Harriss, PHI
NL 75, Pat Duncan, CIN	NL 303, Jesse Haines, STL
RBI—AL 83, Bob Meusel, NY	BB—AL 79, Rip Collins, NY
NL 83, Pat Duncan, CIN	NL 80, Jesse Haines, STL
WK—AL 41, Bucky Harris, WAS	K—AL 66, Rip Collins, NY
NL 42, Pat Duncan, CIN	NL 120, Jesse Haines, STL
SO—AL 72, Bob Meusel, NY	ERA—AL 2.85, Eddie Rommel, PHI
NL 42, Pat Duncan, CIN	NL 2.98, Jesse Haines, STL
SB—AL 16, Bucky Harris, WAS	SHO—AL 2, Rip Collins, NY
NL 18, Pat Duncan, CIN	Duster Mails, CLE
BA—AL .328, Bob Meusel, NY	Eddie Rommel, PHI
NL .295, Pat Duncan, CIN	NL 4, Jesse Haines, STL
SLG—AL .517, Bob Meusel, NY	SV—AL 4, Bill Burwell, STL
NL .372, Pat Duncan, CIN	NL 4, Bill Hubbell, NY/PHI
OBA—AL .377, Bucky Harris, WAS	
NL .350, Pat Duncan, CIN	

◄ 1921 ►

Replacing a talented and extremely popular player is a difficult task for any athlete but especially so for a rookie. Joe Sewell faced that challenge in 1921. The previous August 16, Cleveland Indians shortstop Ray Chapman was beaned and subsequently died. Harry Lunte temporarily assumed Chapman's role, but once Sewell debuted September 10, the job was his. Sewell played 22 games in the heat of a three-team pennant race, which Cleveland won. In the World Series Sewell batted only .174 in the seven-game triumph over the Brooklyn Robins.

But 1921 was a new year and Sewell was the Tribe's shortstop from Day One of spring training. He played all 154 games, rapping 182 hits, including 36 doubles and a dozen triples. Sewell, a University of Alabama product, scored 101 runs, knocked in 93, and walked 80 times. He is the sole middle infielder among the 13 freshmen ever to reach 80 in the aforementioned three key offensive categories, and his RBI figure has been surpassed by only two rookie shortstops. On July 21 Sewell had five hits, three of them doubles in Cleveland's 17–8 rout of the New York Yankees, who would beat out the Indians to win their first AL pennant. That performance helped Sewell hit .318.

HIGHEST BA BY ROOKIE SHORTSTOP
(MINIMUM 400 ABs)

.343, Gene DeMontreville, 1896 Was NL
.331, Johnny Pesky, 1942 Bos AL
.329, Bill Keister, 1899 Bal NL
.322, Alvin Dark, 1948 Bos NL
.3182, Joe Sewell, 1921 Cle AL
.3179, Arky Vaughan, 1932 Pit NL

Twelve days before Sewell's hot day against the Yankees, three freshmen helped the Chicago White Sox to edge New York in 16 innings. Leftfielder Bibb Falk went 5-for-6 with a triple and scored in the decisive frame. Falk was driven in by first baseman Earl Sheely, who had tied the score in the ninth. Another rookie, Shovel Hodge, pitched nine innings of relief for the 10–9 win.

Falk and Sheely were the first AL rookie teammates each to have at least 150 hits. Falk, who would coach the University of Texas to College World Series titles in 1949 and 1950, hit the lone grand slam by a freshman in 1921. On May 22 his sixth-inning shot gave the White Sox a 6–2 win versus Washington. Sheely, the only rookie in 1921 with a multi-homer game, hit a pair of two-runners in Chicago's 5–0 victory at Philadelphia on June 10.

Sheely was the White Sox regular first sacker for six seasons, a role that Lu Blue would fill for two years late in his career. As a rookie, however, Blue played for Detroit and exhibited the keen eye that would enable him to exceed 100 walks four times and set a new AL frosh record that would last until Ted Williams's arrival in 1939.

MOST BASES ON BALLS BY ROOKIE HITTER

123, Bill Joyce, 1890 Bro PL
115, Roy Thomas, 1899 Phi NL
107, Ted Williams, 1939 Bos AL
106, Les Fleming, 1942 Cle AL
103, Lu Blue, 1921 Det AL

Only Babe Ruth had more bases on balls in 1921 than Blue, who also scored 103 times. In addition to his walks, Blue collected 180 safeties and was hit by five pitches, giving him a .416 OBP. He was part of a record four rookies in 1921 with a .400-plus OBP (minimum 100 games). Blue's teammate, catcher Johnny Bassler, was at .401 while Sewell registered .412.

The lone senior circuit batsman in the quartet was Ray Grimes of the Chicago Cubs. The first baseman, whose twin brother, Roy, also played briefly in the majors, hit .321 with a .406 OBP, which ranked fourth in the league, as did his 38 doubles. Grimes's 70 walks were only ten back of the leader.

In a down year for freshman hurlers, just five were able to win as many as nine games. For Pittsburgh, Whitey Glazner took 14 contests and fellow righty Johnny Morrison nine. Glazner permitted but 8.23 hits per nine innings, tops in the circuit, and was second in opponents' OBP (.306). Despite ranking third with a 2.77 ERA, he failed to throw a single shutout. Morrison, however, had three whitewashes, including a pair of three-hitters in August.

The Cubs received a combined 20 victories from Virgil Cheeves and Buck Freeman—11 for the former and nine for the latter. The remaining frosh with as many as nine wins was Bill Pertica of the St. Louis Cardinals. In his lone productive season before running into arm trouble, Pertica went 14–10, with two shutouts.

Rookies who collect 100 or more walks are few and far between. In 1921 first sacker Lu Blue of the Tigers became the first twentieth-century yearling to break the century mark in free passes when he earned 103 bases on balls. Blue survived to play 13 seasons in the Lively Ball Era despite tagging just 44 career homers and posting a .401 SA. His longevity can be attributed largely to his skill at drawing walks. Blue's .402 career OBP is fifth among first basemen who played at least ten seasons during the Lively Ball Era, trailing only Hall of Famers Lou Gehrig, Jimmie Foxx, Hank Greenberg, and Johnny Mize.

In addition, he is one of only four men in all of history to play at least 1,000 games at first base and register a career OBP higher than his career SA.

Name	G/1B	AB	SA	OBP
Ferris Fain	1116	3930	.396	.425
Lu Blue	1571	5904	.401	.402
Mike Hargrove	1378	5564	.391	.400
Fred Tenney	1810	7595	.358	.371

Other Highlights

May 26—White Sox first baseman Earl Sheely, the 1921 rookie home run leader with 11, goes deep for the first time in his career, against Red Oldham; in his nine-year

Batting		Pitching	

Batting

G—AL 154, Joe Sewell, CLE
Earl Sheely, CHI
NL 153, Sam Bohne, CIN
AB—AL 585, Lu Blue, DET
Bibb Falk, CHI
NL 613, Sam Bohne, CIN
H—AL 182, Joe Sewell, CLE
NL 175, Sam Bohne, CIN
2B—AL 36, Joe Sewell, CLE
NL 38, Ray Grimes, CHI
3B—AL 12, Joe Sewell, CLE
NL 16, Sam Bohne, CIN
HR—AL 11, Earl Sheely, CHI
NL 6, Ray Grimes, CHI
R—AL 103, Lu Blue, DET
NL 98, Sam Bohne, CIN
RBI—AL 95, Earl Sheely, CHI
NL 79, Ray Grimes, CHI
WK—AL 103, Lu Blue, DET
NL 70, Ray Grimes, CHI
SO—AL 69, Bibb Falk, CHI
NL 81, Frank Parkinson, PHI
SB—AL 13, Lu Blue, DET
NL 26, Sam Bohne, CIN
BA—AL .318, Joe Sewell, CLE
NL .321, Ray Grimes, CHI
SLG—AL .457, Bing Miller, WAS
NL .449, Ray Grimes, CHI
OBP—AL .416, Lu Blue, DET
NL .406, Ray Grimes, CHI

Pitching

W—AL 8, Ray Kolp, STL
NL 14, Whitey Glazner, PIT
Bill Pertica, STL
L—AL 11, Jim Middleton, DET
NL 12, Virgil Cheeves, CHI
PCT—AL .533, Ray Kolp, STL
NL .737, Whitey Glazner, PIT
GP—AL 38, Jim Middleton, DET
NL 40, Lefty York, CHI
GS—AL 18, Ray Kolp, STL
NL 31, Bill Pertica, STL
CG—AL 7, Bert Cole, DET
NL 15, Whitey Glazner, PIT
Bill Pertica, STL
IP—AL 166.2. Ray Kolp, STL
NL 234, Whitey Glazner, PIT
H—AL 208, Ray Kolp, STL
NL 214, Whitey Glazner, PIT
BB—AL 58, Carl Holling, DET
NL 70, Buck Freeman, CHI
Bill Pertica, STL
K—AL 46, Doug McWeeny, CHI
NL 88, Whitey Glazner, PIT
ERA—AL 4.97, Ray Kolp, STL
NL 2.77, Whitey Glazner, PIT
SHO—AL 1, Bert Cole, DET
Fred Heimach, PHI
Ray Kolp, STL
Bill Piercy, NY
NL 3, Johnny Morrison, PIT
SV—**AL 7, Jim Middleton, DET**
NL 3, Buck Freeman, CHI
Rosy Ryan, NY

stint in the majors, Sheely will never again reach double figures in home runs.

June 30—Ray Kolp twirls a four-hitter for the St. Louis Browns as he blanks the Chicago White Sox 1–0 in the second game of a twinbill.

August 8—Luke Stuart of the St. Louis Browns becomes the first player in AL history to homer in his initial big league plate appearance when he hammers a two-run blast off the great Walter Johnson; the four-base blow proves to be Stuart's only big league hit.

August 19—Bert Cole gets two hits and holds the Boston Red Sox to four as the Detroit Tigers win 10–0.

September 15—Appearing in his one and only ML game, Arlas Taylor gives up seven hits and three runs in a two-inning starting assignment for the A's but manages to fan a batter; the hitter Taylor rings up is Joe Sewell, the hardest player in history to strike out.

1922

By the end of the 1922 season, three AL teams were especially tired of seeing Detroit's yearling right-hander, Herman Pillette. The 26-year-old Tiger had beaten Cleveland five times and Philadelphia and Boston four games apiece. Pillette led Detroit with 19 wins, four of them shutouts, including three two-hitters. He tied for fourth in the circuit with a .613 winning percentage and was fifth in Opponents' Batting Average (.258). Pillette's 2.85 ERA was only .04 worse than the loop leader.

Shortstop Topper Rigney played behind Pillette in every inning he pitched; in fact, Rigney participated in all 155 of Detroit's games. The rookie shortstop batted .300 with 161 hits and also drove in 63 runs, scored 68 times, and drew 68 walks. The latter three figures might seem like modest accomplishments, but they made Rigney one of just seven freshmen shortstops ever to amass at least 60 in each category. Also roaming the Tiger infield was third sacker Fred Haney, who hit .352 in 213 ABs. In 42 games a third Tigers frosh batsman, outfielder Bob Fothergill, stroked .322, just three points under the outstanding .325 career average he would attain in 1,106 ML contests.

Rigney was the only AL'er among 1922's top eight rookie hit makers, the two leaders notching 164 apiece for also-ran NL squads. Andy High played 153 games, mostly at third base, for the Brooklyn Robins, who finished sixth. Among his 164 hits, High tagged 27 doubles and ten triples. Hack Miller matched High's hit total in 113 fewer ABs. Miller, the left fielder for the fifth-place Chicago Cubs, batted .352, third highest in the senior circuit, cracking the top ten all-time for rookies with 400 or more ABs. His .511 slugging percentage is the best ever for a Cubs freshman. Miller was one of just two rookies in 1922 to club at least ten home runs, two of them coming on July 14 in an 8–4 win versus the New York Giants. Miller also connected twice on August 25 as the Cubs took a 25–6 fourth-inning lead over the Philadelphia Phillies at Wrigley Field. Despite a ferocious Phillies' comeback, Chicago hung on to win 26–23, with Miller driving in six runs and freshman Marty Krug also getting four hits.

The Cubs weren't as lucky when they faced High's freshman teammate Dazzy Vance, losing five times to the right-hander. The 31-year-old Vance had cups of coffee with Pittsburgh and the New York Yankees in 1915 and again with the latter club three years later. Now with Brooklyn, Vance was in the bigs to stay. He went 18–12 and tied for the loop lead with five shutouts. Vance also copped the strikeout crown for the first of his NL-record seven times. He placed fifth in fewest hits per nine innings with 9.49, a solid figure considering that the league

as a whole batted .293. In consecutive starts in late May, Vance blanked the Cubs and Phillies, the second game taking place at Baker Bowl, a hitter's paradise.

Like Vance, Cincinnati's Johnny Couch was born in March 1891 and had limited major league experience before 1922. Couch relieved three times for the 1917 Detroit Tigers prior to earning a spot in the Reds' rotation. He responded with a 16-win campaign, including two whitewashes. On June 20 Couch was perfect for the first seven innings against the host Boston Braves before settling for a two-hit, no-walk 2–0 triumph.

Charlie Robertson did Couch two innings better, throwing a perfect game for the Chicago White Sox on April 30 at Detroit. Robertson joined Lee Richmond as the only rookies to achieve perfection, but this gem was hardly the only highlight for the 14-game winner. On June 13 Robertson had a no-hitter until the eighth against the Red Sox, who managed to get a pair of singles over the final two frames before losing 5–0. At Cleveland on September 1, Robertson blanked the Indians for five innings and drove in both runs of the rain-shortened contest. The rain erased another two RBI he had in the sixth.

White Sox righty Dixie Leverett in some ways outshone his more famous rookie teammate. Leverett went 13–10 with a fine 3.34 ERA and four shutouts. He also had eight doubles and 12 RBI in 83 ABs. On June 11 Leverett stroked a game-winning double in the 13th inning to beat the Red Sox 7–6. He subsequently blanked the Red Sox 8–0 and went 4-for-4 with two doubles on July 19.

Also adroit at accumulating extra-base hits was Jim Bottomley of the St. Louis Cardinals. Although the first baseman didn't debut until August 18, he racked up eight doubles, five triples, and five home runs in just 151 ABs, offering starving Mound City fans a taste of better times to come.

FEWEST ABs FOR ROOKIES WITH AT LEAST 5 2B, 5 3B, 5 HR

151 AB/8 2B/5 3B/5 HR, Jim Bottomley, 1922 StL NL
156 AB/5 2B/5 3B/5 HR, Adam Piatt, 2000 Oak AL
160 AB/6 2B/6 3B/5 HR, Duke Snider, 1948 Bro NL
192 AB/9 2B/5 3B/13 HR, Willie McCovey, 1959 SF NL
197 AB/5 2B/6 3B/9 HR, Dick Gray, 1958 LA NL

Two significant rookie firsts occurred in 1922. Charlie Robertson's perfect game, the first (and, to date, the only) perfecto by a rookie at the current pitching distance, is well remembered. But few know that Butch Henline of the Phillies in 1922 became the first frosh catcher in history to homer in double figures. Henline's 14 dingers not only set a new rookie mark, it represented a twentieth-century high to that point by a backstopper.

Two years later Henline's twentieth-century record fell when Gabby Hartnett hammered 16 homers for the Cubs, but his rookie mark stood for over 20 years albeit few record books recognized it. Instead most credited Rudy York with the mark for clubbing 35 homers with Detroit in 1937. However, nearly half of York's games in his rookie season were played at third base whereas Henline was a pure catcher. All sources should view him as the record holder for the most home runs by a rookie catcher prior to 1945 when Bill Salkeld went deep 15 times for the Pirates.

Other Highlights

April 30—Charlie Robertson hurls the only perfect game in history by an AL rookie, 2–0 over Detroit, after surviving two long stoppages in play when the Tigers complain to umpires that he is illegally doctoring the ball.

May 7—Pirates rookie gardener Walter Mueller homers off Pete Alexander on the first ML pitch he sees; box scores originally credit the dinger to teammate Ray Rohwer, which anguishes Mueller, who hits only one more career home run.

May 30—Catcher Butch Henline of the Phils, the ML rookie homer king with 14, loses what would have been a 15th four-bagger when he clubs a walk-off three-run homer against the Giants but is credited with only a

1922 ROOKIE LEADERS

Batting	Pitching
G—AL 155, Topper Rigney, DET	W—AL 19, Herman Pillette, DET
NL 153, Andy High, BRO	NL 18, Dazzy Vance, BRO
AB—AL 536, Topper Rigney, DET	L—AL 18, Ray Francis, WAS
NL 579, Andy High, BRO	NL 13, Tony Kaufmann, CHI
H—AL 161, Topper Rigney, DET	PCT—AL .613, Herman Pillette, DET
NL 164, Andy High, BRO	NL .640, Johnny Couch, CIN
Hack Miller, CHI	GP—AL 40, Herman Pillette, DET
2B—AL 21, Joe Hauser, PHI	NL 43, Johnny Couch, CIN
NL 28, Hack Miller, CHI	GS—AL 37, Herman Pillette, DET
3B—AL 7, Goose Goslin, WAS	NL 34, Johnny Couch, CIN
Topper Rigney, DET	CG—AL 21, Charlie Robertson, CHI
NL 12, Pie Traynor, PIT	NL 18, Johnny Couch, CIN
HR—AL 9, Joe Hauser, PHI	IP—AL 274.2, Herman Pillette, DET
NL 14, Butch Henline, PHI	NL 264, Johnny Couch, CIN
R—AL 68, Topper Rigney, DET	H—AL 294, Charlie Robertson, CHI
NL 89, Pie Traynor, PIT	NL 301, Johnny Couch, CIN
RBI—AL 63, Topper Rigney, DET	BB—AL 95, Herman Pillette, DET
NL 81, Pie Traynor, PIT	NL 95, Tiny Osborne, CHI
WK—AL 68, Topper Rigney, DET	K—AL 83, Charlie Robertson, CHI
NL 59, Andy High, BRO	**NL 134, Dazzy Vance, BRO**
SO—AL 46, Beauty McGowan, PHI	ERA—AL 2.85, Herman Pillette, DET
NL 49, Roy Leslie, PHI	NL 3.40, Lefty Weinert, PHI
SB—AL 17, Topper Rigney, DET	SHO—AL 4, Dixie Leverett, CHI
NL 17, Pie Traynor, PIT	Herman Pillette, DET
BA—AL .300, Topper Rigney, DET	**NL 5, Dazzy Vance, BRO**
NL .352, Hack Miller, CHI	SV—AL 7, Hub Pruett, STL
SLG—AL .481, Joe Hauser, PHI	**NL 5, Claude Jonnard, NY**
NL .511, Hack Miller, CHI	
OBP—AL .380, Topper Rigney, DET	
NL .389, Hack Miller, CHI	

double when he mysteriously heads for the Phils' clubhouse after rounding second base.

June 12—Cards infielder Specs Toporcer, the first position player in history to wear glasses on the field, loses his first career home run when he passes teammate Doc Lavan on the bases in a 14–8 win over the Phils.

June 13—John Singleton of the Philadelphia Phillies shuts out the St. Louis Cardinals 14–0 in his first ML start for what will be the only victory in his 1–10 career.

August 20—Dan Boone of the Indians hits a game-winning single as he blanks Washington 2–0 in 12 innings.

September 15—Butch Henline hits three homers, becoming the first rookie to ever do so, including a game-tying shot in the bottom of the ninth for the Phillies, who beat the Cardinals 10–9.

September 17—Browns southpaw Hub Pruett, who will fan Babe Ruth nine of the ten times he faces him in 1922, finally allows Ruth to make contact, which results in a home run and the lone tally in a 5–1 win over the Yankees that puts St. Louis only half a game out of first place; the Browns will finish one game behind the victorious Yankees.

1923

If you like watching talented rookies, Chicago was the place to be in 1923. Both of the Windy City's clubs featured memorable freshmen, the most meteoric being Maurice Archdeacon of the White Sox. Archdeacon debuted on September 17 by getting two hits in each game of a doubleheader at Boston's Fenway Park. Five days later, he went 5-for-5 in the second contest against the Philadelphia Athletics. On October 2 the hits just kept raining off Archdeacon's bat as he got five more, including a triple, all off Detroit veteran Hooks Dauss. Archdeacon scored four times but the Tigers won 6–5. In 22 games he batted .402 and scored 23 runs, becoming the sole freshman since 1900 to own more runs than games played (minimum 20 games). In addition, Archdeacon tallied the most hits ever by a rookie with fewer than 100 at bats.

MOST HITS BY ROOKIE WITH FEWER THAN 100 ABs

35 H/87 AB, Maurice Archdeacon, 1923 Chi AL
34 H/86 AB, Fred Tenney, 1894 Bos NL
34 H/92 AB, Jimmy Barrett, 1899 Cin NL
34 H/93 AB, Olaf Henriksen, 1911 Bos AL
34 H/88 AB, Hector Ortiz, 2000 KC AL

Archdeacon played only 105 more ML games owing largely to a prolonged and debilitating bout with tonsillitis. His teammate, third baseman Willie Kamm, was more fortunate, spending 13 seasons with Chicago and Cleveland and leading the AL in fielding eight times. In 1923 Kamm hit .292 with 39 doubles, the most ever for a rookie third sacker in the junior circuit. He also had 87 RBI, second best on the club, which was still recovering from the Black Sox Scandal. The Pale Hose in addition featured two frosh moundsmen, southpaw Mike Cvengros (12–13) and Sloppy Thurston (7–8); the latter also led the south siders with a 3.05 ERA.

On the north side of town, George Grantham ran right into the hearts of Cubs fans. Grantham tied for second in the loop with 36 doubles. His 43 stolen bases were bettered only by Pittsburgh's Max Carey and are the most by a Cubs rookie since 1900. Grantham was the only freshman from 1915 through 1983 to reach both 35 doubles and 35 stolen bases. He joined Cupid Childs in 1890 as the lone rookie second basemen ever to top 70 in runs, RBI, and walks. Grantham's defense was not quite as sparkling. While he did lead NL keystoners in assists, putouts, and chances per game, his 55 errors nearly doubled the next highest total in the loop. The miscues represent the position's league record since 1900.

MOST ERRORS, NL SECOND BASEMAN (SINCE 1900)

1.	George Grantham, 1923,	55
2.	Johnny Evers, 1904,	54
T3.	Larry Doyle, 1910,	53
T3.	John Farrell, 1903,	53
T3.	John Farrell, 1904,	53
T6.	Jay Partridge, 1927,	52
T6.	Kid Gleason, 1904,	52
8.	Miller Huggins, 1905,	51
9.	Bert Niehoff, 1916,	49
T10.	Don Johnson, 1944,	47
T10.	Billy Gilbert, 1903,	47

Grantham fell short of double figures in triples and home runs, hitting eight of each, but he wasn't alone. Excluding the strike-shortened 1981 campaign, 1922 was the only season subsequent to 1919 that failed to produce any rookies with at least ten triples or round trippers.

Cleveland rightfielder Homer Summa seemed to graduate from hitting school with high honors, or *summa cum laude*. Summa hit .328 with 172 safeties and 92 runs. On August 7 he had four hits including a triple as the Indians demolished Washington 22–2. Rube Lutzke, Cleveland's rookie third baseman, had three hits in the pasting. Southpaw Joe Shaute was not the lucky beneficiary of this offensive explosion, but he did win ten games for the Tribe, who finished a half-game behind second-place Detroit. The Tigers received 11 victories from Ken Holloway, including a four-hit shutout of the Boston Red Sox May 19.

Baseball's top recruit winner was Joe Genewich of the dreadful Boston Braves. Boston was suffering through its second of three consecutive 100-loss seasons and would not see .500 again for nine years. Genewich, nonetheless, was a respectable 13–14 and made 43 appearances, just two off the NL lead. He rated third in fewest walks per nine innings at 1.82. On August 9, seven days after the death of President Warren G. Harding, Genewich edged Cincinnati 1–0, holding the Reds to five hits. Genewich, who batted .247, had a double, but this paled in comparison to his performance later that month. Not only did he limit the St. Louis Cardinals to one run on August 22, but the Braves rookie also had two hits and drove in all three of his team's tallies for a 3–1 victory.

Other Highlights

April 18—Third sacker Willie Kamm, the most expensive minor league purchase ever to that point at $100,000, debuts for the White Sox with a double and two errorless chances afield in a 6–5 loss to Cleveland; Kamm will lead all AL rookies in home runs with six and beginning in 1924 will lead all AL third basemen in FA for six straight years.

April 20—Gabby Hartnett's first career home run, which comes in the ninth inning off reliever Earl

Only two of the top ten second basemen in career OPS who are eligible for the Hall of Fame are not as yet enshrined. One is Joe Gordon, whose case for enshrinement is renowned to most followers of the game. The second man has never had a serious case mounted for his inclusion, and perhaps it's time someone did.

In 1923 George Grantham led all NL rookies in almost every major batting department. It turned out not even to be one of his better years, as his .774 OPS fell a full 80 points below his career mark of .854. The reason Grantham has never gotten anywhere near the recognition his stats would indicate he deserves is twofold. He was apparently not a very good fielder (he owns the post-1901 NL season record for errors by a second baseman) and actually spent about a third of his career at first base. Secondly, Grantham never was a league leader in anything. Yet he had one of the most fantastic seasons in history. In 1929 Grantham played in just 110 games and collected only 349 at bats but nevertheless accumulated 85 runs, 93 walks, and 90 RBI. The first two stats are post-1901 records among players with fewer than 350 at bats, and Grantham's 90 RBI are tied with Roger's Hornsby's 1931 production for the all-time high by a middle infielder with fewer than 400 at bats.

Including only games played at second base, Grantham owns the sixth best career OPS at the position with a figure that is 14 points below his overall career mark.

Rank	Name	AB	OPS
1	Rogers Hornsby	6051	1.080
2	Jackie Robinson	2743	.913
3	Charlie Gehringer	8860	.884
4	Eddie Collins	9904	.855
5	Tony Lazzeri	6133	.848
6	George Grantham	3224	.840
7	Nap Lajoie	8554	.837
8	Bobby Doerr	7093	.823
9	Joe Gordon	5707	.822
10	Joe Morgan	9277	.819

Hamilton, produces a 12–11 Cubs win over Pittsburgh; Hartnett will retire with the career record, since broken, for the most home runs by a catcher.

May 13—Joe Sewell is fanned twice in a game for the first of only two times in his career by Washington rookie Cy Warmoth.

1923 ROOKIE LEADERS

Batting	Pitching
G—AL 149, Willie Kamm, CHI	W—AL 12, Mike Cvengros, CHI
NL 152, George Grantham, CHI	NL 13, Joe Genewich, BOS
AB—AL 544, Willie Kamm, CHI	L—AL 13, Mike Cvengros, CHI
NL 570, George Grantham, CHI	NL 14, Joe Genewich, BOS
H—AL 172, Homer Summa, CLE	PCT—AL .556, Joe Shaute, CLE
NL 160, George Grantham, CHI	NL .481, Joe Genewich, BOS
2B—AL 39, Willie Kamm, CHI	GP—AL 46, Sloppy Thurston, STL/CHI
NL 36, George Grantham, CHI	NL 43, Joe Genewich, BOS
3B—AL 9, Willie Kamm, CHI	GS—AL 26, Mike Cvengros, CHI
NL 8, George Grantham, CHI	NL 24, Joe Genewich, BOS
HR—AL 6, Willie Kamm, CHI	CG—AL 14, Mike Cvengros, CHI
NL 8, George Grantham, CHI	NL 12, Joe Genewich, BOS
Gabby Hartnett, CHI	IP—AL 214.1, Mike Cvengros, CHI
R—AL 92, Homer Summa, CLE	NL 227.1, Joe Genewich, BOS
NL 85, Heinie Sand, PHI	H—AL 232, Ken Holloway, DET
RBI—AL 87, Willie Kamm, CHI	NL 272, Joe Genewich, BOS
NL 70, George Grantham, CHI	BB—AL 107, Mike Cvengros, CHI
WK—AL 62, Willie Kamm, CHI	NL 72, Leo Dickerman, BRO
NL 82, Heinie Sand, PHI	K—AL 86, Mike Cvengros, CHI
SO—AL 82, Willie Kamm, CHI	NL 58, Leo Dickerman, BRO
NL 92, George Grantham, CHI	ERA—AL 3.13, Sloppy Thurston, STL/CHI
SB—AL 17, Willie Kamm, CHI	NL 3.72, Leo Dickerman, BRO*
NL 43, George Grantham, CHI	SHO—AL 1, Claral Gillenwater, CHI
BA—AL .328, Homer Summa, CLE	Ken Holloway, DET
NL .281, George Grantham, CHI	Monroe Mitchell, WAS
SLG—AL .430, Willie Kamm, CHI	Paul Zahniser, WAS
NL .414, George Grantham, CHI	NL 2, Johnny Cooney, BOS
OBP—AL .374, Homer Summa, CLE	Dutch Henry, BRO
NL .360, George Grantham, CHI	SV—AL 4, Sloppy Thurston, STL/CHI
	NL 3, Fred Fussell, CHI
	Johnny Stuart, STL

*Leo Dickerman edged Joe Genewich in ERA, 3.7203 to 3.7214.

June 1—Jimmy O'Connell, soon to become the last player ever banned for taking part in a bribe offer to an opposing player, gets five hits, including three doubles and a homer, driving in four runs in the New York Giants' 22–8 thrashing of the Philadelphia Phillies.

July 7—Lefty O'Doul, later a two-time bat title winner, sets a post-1900 record when he allows 13 runs in the sixth inning for the Boston Red Sox, who are trounced by the Cleveland Indians 27–3 in the first game of a double-dip.

July 10—Cards rookie righty Johnny Stuart hurls two complete-game victories over the Braves, winning 11–1 and 6–3 despite not registering a strikeout in either contest.

August 4—Travis Jackson hits two singles, a double, and a homer, driving in eight runs for the Giants, who win at Cincinnati 14–4.

September 13—The White Sox buy outfielder Maurice Archdeacon for $50,000; in the remaining 23 days of the season, Archdeacon will hit .402 in 22 games.

September 27—Lou Gehrig hits his first career home run off Bill Piercy of the Red Sox; Gehrig will leave the game under tragic circumstances in 1939 with 493 career homers, second at the time only to Babe Ruth.

September 30—Willie Kamm collects nine assists to tie an AL record for third basemen that was set earlier in the season by Bob Jones of the Tigers.

October 6—Ernie Padgett of the Braves is the first rookie and also the first documented NL'er in history to pull an unassisted triple play in a game against the Phils.

1924

"The Four Freshmen" was the name of a popular 1950s vocal group. But the title could also be retroactively applied to the rookie crop of the 1924 Pittsburgh Pirates, who profited richly from perhaps the greatest profusion of outstanding performances ever produced by one team's freshmen. Shortstop Glenn Wright set records with his bat and powerful arm. His 111 RBI tied him for third in the NL and still make him the only rookie shortstop ever to top the century mark. Wright, nicknamed "Buckshot," also had 601 assists, the all-time single-season shortstop record until Ozzie Smith surpassed it 1980.

MOST ASSISTS, SINGLE SEASON, SHORTSTOP

1. Ozzie Smith, 1980, 621
2. Glenn Wright, 1924, 601
3. Dave Bancroft, 1920, 598
4. Tommy Thevenow, 1926, 597
5. Ivan DeJesus, 1977, 595
6. Cal Ripken, 1984, 583
7. Whitey Wietelmann, 1943, 581
8. Dave Bancroft, 1922, 579
9. Rabbit Maranville, 1914, 574
10. Don Kessinger, 1968, 573

In a September 16 doubleheader, Wright had eight consecutive hits in Pittsburgh's split with the Philadelphia Phillies. Last but far from least, the Buccos' new shortstop prize clubbed 18 triples, the most in history by an NL freshman shortstop.

MOST TRIPLES BY A ROOKIE SHORTSTOP

19, Joe Cassidy, 1904 Was AL
18, Jim Canavan, 1891 Cin/Mil AA
18, Glenn Wright, 1924 Pit NL
16, Bill Keister, 1899 Bal NL
15, Frank Fennelly, 1884 Was/Cin AA
15, Dave Brain, 1903 StL NL
15, Whitey Witt, 1916 Phi AL

Hitting only two fewer triples than Wright was Kiki Cuyler, Pittsburgh's recruit left fielder. Cuyler hit .354, cracking the top five in the loop and the top ten all-time for rookies. His daring baserunning netted him 32 of the Pirates' league-leading 181 stolen bases. On August 9 Cuyler hit three doubles, two singles, and a triple as Pittsburgh routed the Phillies 16–4 in the lidlifter of a twinbill. In the nightcap Ray Kremer pitched a five-hit shutout to complete the sweep. Kremer and Emil Yde went a collective 34–13 for the Pirates, with each freshman tossing four shutouts. Yde, in addition, enjoyed the highest winning percentage ever attained by a rookie with at least 15 wins.

BEST WINNING PERCENTAGE BY ROOKIE (MINIMUM 15 WINS)

.842 (16–3), Emil Yde, 1924 Pit NL
.838 (31–6), Bill Hoffer, 1895 Bal NL
.833 (15–3), Henry Boyle, 1884 StL UA
.833 (20–4), King Cole, 1910 Chi NL
.833 (15–3), Hoyt Wilhelm, 1952 NY NL

Among Yde's whitewashings were a two-hitter and a three-hitter, but his season highlight came on June 25 against the Chicago Cubs. Yde hit a ninth-inning double to tie the game at six-all, and in the 14th his two-run triple gave Pittsburgh an 8–7 victory. Yde worked 10⅓ innings of relief for the win, his heroics overshadowing a five-hit performance by Cubs freshman outfielder Denver Grigsby.

Two pitchers who would later be traded for another—Firpo Marberry and Earl Whitehill—had stellar freshman campaigns in 1924. Marberry, a Washington Senators right-hander, led the AL with 50 games and 15 saves. The latter number would remain unmatched by a rookie until 1952 and would not be surpassed for another three years, when Jack Meyer saved 16 games in 1955 for the Phillies. After winning their first AL pennant, the Senators squared off in the World Series against the New York Giants, who had taken their fourth consecutive senior circuit flag. Marberry, who started 14 games in the regular season, got the nod in Game Three. He yielded three runs in three innings, taking the loss as the Giants assumed a 2–1 lead in the series. Marberry, however, was credited with two saves in the Fall Classic, which Washington won in dramatic fashion. In Game Seven, with one out in the bottom of the 12th, rookie centerfielder Earl McNeely hit a bouncer to third base that hopped over fellow rookie Freddie Lindstrom and into left field to give the Senators the title.

Eight years later Marberry would be dealt to the Detroit Tigers for Whitehill, the Bengals' freshman southpaw who went 17–9 in 1924 to pace the contending Tigers in wins and rank third in the loop in winning percentage (.654).

Whitehill's Tigers finished in third place, a level only wished for by the teams of two other rookie standouts. The fifth-place Philadelphia Athletics unveiled out-fielder Al Simmons, who drove in 102 runs. The 1924 campaign was the first of 11 straight 100-RBI seasons for Simmons—the most any batter ever had to start his ML tenure. Simmons, who played in all 152 games, would participate in every Philadelphia A's contest through July 20, 1926. The 394-game skein is the longest streak to begin an AL career—more games, in fact, than Ike Boone played in his entire ML sojourn despite sporting a .321 career BA. Boone, a minor league legend with a .370 career mark, hit .337 as a rookie in 1924 with the lowly Boston Red Sox, who escaped the cellar by a bare half-game. Boone also collected 98 RBI, six of them on May 30 against Washington when his fourth-inning grand slam keyed Boston's 9–4 triumph. After hitting .330 in 1925, Boone played only 88 more big league games, the last with the 1932 Brooklyn Dodgers, whose shortstop ironically was Glenn Wright, then playing in his final season as a regular after sustaining a shoulder injury three years earlier while playing handball that nearly ended his career.

When Ray Kremer arrived at the Pirates' training camp in the spring of 1924, he told manager Bill McKechnie that he was 27 going on 28. Not until years later did it emerge that Kremer actually turned 31 that spring. Though not credited as such at that time, his 1924 season was the best to that point in history by a rookie player past the age of 30.

Despite his belated start, Kremer orchestrated a ten-year career, all spent with Pittsburgh, which resulted in a goodly number of black-ink seasons and several all-time records. Among the marks that Kremer still holds are the most career wins (143) of any pitcher whose major league debut did not occur until he was past 30 and the highest winning percentage (.625 in 1930) by a 20-game winner with an ERA above 5.00.

Kremer also ranks third in career wins among retired pitchers who appeared in less than 2,000 innings.

Rank	Name	Years	IP	W
1	Dizzy Dean	1930–41/47	1967.1	150
2	Dave Foutz	1884–94	1997.1	147
3	Ray Kremer	1924–33	1954.2	143
4	Johnny Allen	1932–44	1950.1	142
5	Ramon Martinez	1988–2001	1895.2	135

Other Highlights

May 1—Earle Combs of the Yankees breaks his leg and will miss most of what otherwise would have been his rookie season; in 35 ABs, Combs posts a 1.004 OPS, the highest mark of his 12-year Hall-of-Fame career.

June 10—Maurice Archdeacon, who had two five-hit games in a brief trial last year, has another for the Chicago White Sox, who beat the Boston Red Sox 3–2 in 13 innings.

July 10—Harvey Hendrick hits a grand slam as the New York Yankees pound the White Sox 18–5 in the second game of a doubleheader.

July 11—Rookie first baseman Hooks Cotter of the Cubs ties an ML record for chances (22) when he collects 21 putouts and one assist in a 9–1 loss to Brooklyn.

July 19—Cards rookie Hi Bell duplicates Johnny Stuart's feat of the previous year when he throws two complete-game twinbill wins against the Braves, 6–1 and 2–1.

Batting	Pitching
G—AL 152, Al Simmons, PHI	W—AL 17, Earl Whitehill, DET
NL 153, Glenn Wright, PIT	NL 18, Ray Kremer, PIT
AB—AL 594, Al Simmons, PHI	L—AL 13, Sarge Connally, CHI
NL 616, Glenn Wright, PIT	NL 12, Wayland Dean, NY
H—AL 183, Al Simmons, PHI	PCT—AL .654, Earl Whitehill, DET
NL 177, Glenn Wright, PIT	**NL .842, Emil Yde, PIT**
2B—AL 31, Ike Boone, BOS	GP—**AL 50, Firpo Marberry, WAS**
Al Simmons, PHI	**NL 41, Ray Kremer, PIT**
NL 28, Glenn Wright, PIT	GS—AL 32, Earl Whitehill, DET
3B—AL 9, Al Simmons, PHI	NL 30, Ray Kremer, PIT
NL 18, Glenn Wright, PIT	CG—AL 16, Earl Whitehill, DET
HR—AL 13, Ike Boone, BOS	NL 17, Ray Kremer, PIT
NL 10, Hack Wilson, NY	IP—AL 233, Earl Whitehill, DET
R—AL 72, Ike Boone, BOS	NL 259.1, Ray Kremer, PIT
NL 94, Kiki Cuyler, PIT	H—AL 279, Ted Lyons, CHI
RBI—AL 102, Al Simmons, PHI	NL 262, Ray Kremer, PIT
NL 111, Glenn Wright, PIT	BB—AL 89, Sam Gray, PHI
WK—AL 54, Max Bishop, PHI	NL 62, Emil Yde, PIT
Ike Boone, BOS	K—AL 68, Firpo Marberry, WAS
NL 44, Hack Wilson, NY	NL 64, Ray Kremer, PIT
SO—AL 60, Al Simmons, PHI	ERA—AL 3.09, Firpo Marberry, WAS
NL 62, Kiki Cuyler, PIT	NL 2.83, Emil Yde, PIT
SB—AL 16, Al Simmons, PHI	SHO—AL 2, Sam Gray, PHI
NL 32, Kiki Cuyler, PIT	Earl Whitehill, DET
BA—AL .337, Ike Boone, BOS	**NL 4, Ray Kremer, PIT**
NL .354, Kiki Cuyler, PIT	**Emil Yde, PIT**
SLG—AL .497, Ike Boone, BOS	SV—**AL 15, Firpo Marberry, WAS**
NL .539, Kiki Cuyler, PIT	NL 1, done by seven pitchers
OBP—AL .404, Ike Boone, BOS	
NL .402, Kiki Cuyler, PIT	

October 4—Just 18 years old, Freddie Lindstrom of the Giants is the youngest man ever to participate in a World Series game when he replaces injured third sacker Heinie Groh in Game One against Washington; in the same game Giants rookie Bill Terry goes 3-for-5 with a home run in New York's 12-inning 4–3 win.

1925

Pee-Wee Wanninger is far from being a household name, yet this obscure rookie had a significant role in bridging the gap between two of baseball's longest endurance streaks. On May 6, 1925, Wanninger played shortstop for the New York Yankees, ending Everett Scott's record skein after 1,307 games. Less than four weeks later, on June 1, Wanninger was pinch-hit for by Lou Gehrig. The following day, Gehrig, replacing the headache-suffering Wally Pipp, went 3-for-4 with a double and would go on to play in every Yankees' contest until 1939 and replace Scott as the new endurance record-holder.

Gehrig hit two home runs and collected seven RBI against the Washington Senators on July 23. Included in the barrage was the first of a record 23 grand slams for the Iron Horse. Gehrig led all rookies in 1925 with 20 round trippers and slugged at a .531 clip, but he was not the only freshman bright spot for the seventh-place Bronx Bombers, who would not finish so low in the standings again until 1966. The previous year, centerfielder Earle Combs had hit .400 in 35 ABs before sustaining a season-ending injury. Now healthy, Combs scored 117 runs in 1925 and had 203 hits. His .342 average is still the best ever for a Yankee rookie.

Also featuring more than one freshman destined for Cooperstown were the Philadelphia Athletics. On April 14, Opening Day, flamethrower Lefty Grove and catcher Mickey Cochrane both debuted against the Boston Red Sox. Grove was removed after 3⅔ innings while Cochrane went 1-for-2. Jim Poole, also receiving his big league baptism in the season opener, homered and scored three times in the Athletics' ten-inning win. Some five weeks later, on May 21, Cochrane became the first AL rookie to hit three home runs in one game. He finished his yearling campaign with a .331 BA, still the all-time standard for a freshman backstop.

HIGHEST BA BY ROOKIE CATCHER
(MINIMUM 400 ABs)

.331, Mickey Cochrane, 1925 Phi AL
.324, Bill Dickey, 1929 NY AL
.318, Mike Piazza, 1993 LA NL
.316, Butch Henline, 1922 Phi NL
.309, Al Lopez, 1930 Bro NL

Grove culminated his freshman year by pacing the AL in strikeouts, the first of seven consecutive seasons he would do so. He also walked a loop-high 131 batters and went 10–12, the only time in his 17-year ML career that he would finish below .500. Grove was one of five rookie southpaws to win at least ten games. The Cleveland Indians joined a select group of just five teams when they had two of the quintet—Garland Buckeye, who won 13 times, and Jake Miller, a victor on three fewer occasions.

TEAMS WITH TWO ROOKIE LEFT-HANDERS
WINNING 10+ GAMES

1901 Phi AL, Eddie Plank (17), Snake Wiltse (13)
1901 Was AL, Case Patten (18), Watty Lee (16)
1925 Cle AL, Garland Buckeye (13), Jake Miller (10)
1979 Chi AL, Ross Baumgarten (13), Steve Trout (11)
1986 Mil AL, Juan Nieves (11), Dan Plesac (10)

On September 10 Buckeye became the first rookie pitcher since John Clarkson in 1884 to hit two homers

in a game as Cleveland beat Detroit 7–2. Relieving for the Tigers that day was Jess Doyle, who soon duplicated Buckeye's feat. Doyle emerged from the bullpen in the sixth inning on September 28 at New York and homered in his only two times up, accounting for three Detroit tallies. In the ninth, however, Doyle was plagued by wildness and the Yankees won 7–6.

Two more southpaws who won in double figures toiled in St. Louis. Joe Giard of the Browns went 10–5 and tossed four shutouts, posting a 5.04 ERA, the highest ever for a rookie with at least four whitewashes. Art Reinhart was 11–5 for the Cardinals, who also had freshman Les Bell at third base. Bell, the only NL rookie to play more than 124 games in 1925, drove in 88 runs and scored 80 times.

Even though Bell hit .285, he failed to reach the ML average of .292. Not surprisingly, given the times, the 1925 season produced a swarm of recruit batters who scaled the .300 plateau, albeit some in modest playing time. Ben Paschal hit .360 with 56 RBI in only 247 ABs while the Athletics' Walter French, who doubled in the off-season as an NFL running back, went 37-for-100.

If Rookie of the Year Awards had been handed out in 1925, Earle Combs undoubtedly would have won the prize in the AL, and the NL winner probably would have been Brooklyn rightfielder Dick Cox. But in the 1920s outfielders who hit under .300 were expendable, especially if they lacked power, and that became Cox's fate after he sagged to .296 in 1926 with a .367 SA.

Two other rookie hitters who made the 1925 leaders chart suffered an even swifter terminus to their big league ambitions. Both played for a Windy City entry. On Memorial Day weekend in 1925, the Cubs sent recent call-up Mandy Brooks to center field for the first time and then left him in the lineup when he proceeded to set a new club rookie home run record. The following spring Brooks lost his job to Hack Wilson, failed to impress as a pinch hitter, and was gone after just 48 at bats.

Even more puzzling was the story on the south side of Chicago where Ike Davis became only the second shortstop in the twentieth century to score 100 or more runs as a rookie. Davis was rewarded by the White Sox with his release. To this day, he remains one of only four shortstops in Pale Hose history to score as many as 100 runs in a season.

Two Red Sox outfielders, Roy Carlyle and Tex Vache, both topped .300, as did future Hall of Famer Chick Hafey for the Cardinals. Dick Cox of Brooklyn and the Braves' Jimmy Welsh each played 122 games and hit .329 and .312, respectively.

Going 6-for-9 (.667) was a 17-year-old catcher who would soon be switched to first base, where he would team with Lefty Grove and Mickey Cochrane on some of the best teams in history. The backstop, Jimmie Foxx of the Athletics, would drive in more than 100 runs 13 consecutive years, tying the record set by another of this year's rookies—Lou Gehrig.

Other Highlights

June 15—In his second and final ML game, rookie righty Tom Glass is ordered by A's manager Connie Mack to mop up when Philadelphia trails Cleveland 15–4 after seven innings, but the A's stagger the Tribe by mounting one of the greatest comebacks in history and rallying for 13 runs in the eighth to give Glass a shocking 17–15 victory.

July 14—Lefty Grove hurls one of the finest games in his career, only to lose 1–0 to the Yankees' Herb Pennock in 15 innings.

1925 ROOKIE LEADERS

Batting	Pitching
G—AL 150, Earle Combs, NY	W—AL 13, Garland Buckeye, CLE
NL 153, Les Bell, STL	NL 12, Kent Greenfield, NY
AB—AL 593, Earle Combs, NY	L—AL 19, Ted Wingfield, BOS
NL 586, Les Bell, STL	NL 13, Flint Rhem, STL
H—AL 203, Earle Combs, NY	PCT—AL .619, Garland Buckeye, CLE
NL 167, Les Bell, STL	NL .600, Kent Greenfield, NY
2B—AL 36, Earle Combs, NY	GP—AL 45, Jess Doyle, DET
NL 29, Les Bell, STL	Lefty Grove, PHI
3B—AL 13, Earle Combs, NY	NL 34, Skinny Graham, BOS
NL 10, Dick Cox, BRO	GS—AL 27, Red Ruffing, BOS
HR—AL 20, Lou Gehrig, NY	NL 23, Skinny Graham, BOS
NL 14, Mandy Brooks, CHI	Flint Rhem, STL
R—AL 117, Earle Combs, NY	CG—AL 18, Ted Wingfield, BOS
NL 80, Les Bell, STL	NL 15, Art Reinhart, STL
RBI—AL 68, Lou Gehrig, NY	IP—AL 254.1, Ted Wingfield, BOS
NL 88, Les Bell, STL	NL 171.2, Kent Greenfield, NY
WK—AL 71, Ike Davis, CHI	H—AL 267, Ted Wingfield, BOS
NL 43, Les Bell, STL	NL 204, Flint Rhem, STL
SO—AL 60, Jackie Tavener, DET	BB—**AL 131, Lefty Grove, PHI**
NL 47, Les Bell, STL	NL 64, Kent Greenfield, NY
SB—AL 19, Ike Davis, CHI	K—**AL 116, Lefty Grove, PHI**
NL 11, Doc Gautreau, BOS	NL 66, Kent Greenfield, NY
Billy Zitzmann, CIN	Flint Rhem, STL
BA—AL .342, Earle Combs, NY	ERA—AL 3.31, Jake Miller, CLE
NL .329, Dick Cox, BRO	NL 3.88, Kent Greenfield, NY
SLG—AL .531, Lou Gehrig, NY	SHO—AL 4, Joe Giard, STL
NL .477, Dick Cox, BRO	NL 1, Freddie Fitzsimmons, NY
OBP—AL .411, Earle Combs, NY	Art Reinhart, STL
NL .382, Dick Cox, BRO	Flint Rhem, STL
	Dutch Ulrich, PHI
	SV—AL 8, Jess Doyle, DET
	NL 3, Jack Knight, PHI

July 21—Roy Carlyle hits for the cycle as the Boston Red Sox win the opener of a twinbill against the Chicago White Sox 6–3.

August 15—Red Ruffing throws his second straight shutout for the Red Sox, who beat the Philadelphia Athletics 5–0 in the nightcap of a doubleheader.

September 12—Shortstop Jackie Tavener of Detroit hits three triples, but Cleveland nonetheless wins the game 4–1 in 13 innings; Tavener will amass 53 triples overall, the most by any player since 1901 with fewer than 2500 career at bats.

1926

Two hitters who rewrote the Pacific Coast League record book the previous year unleashed their bats on major league pitchers in 1926. San Francisco's Paul Waner led the PCL in hitting with a .401 average in 1925 and set the loop standard by ripping 75 doubles. Tony Lazzeri, a member of the heavy-hitting Salt Lake City club, became the first player in organized ball to hit 60 home runs. He set additional PCL records in 1925 by driving in 222 runs and scoring a minor league high 202 times. For good measure, Lazzeri also topped the circuit with 512 total bases.

Waner, Pittsburgh's right fielder in 1926, hit .336, which would have topped the NL had today's criteria for determining the batting title been in effect at the time. He did lead the loop with a .413 OBP and 22 triples. The latter figure ranks fourth in rookie annals. Waner collected one of his three-baggers on August 26 against the New York Giants. He also had two doubles and three singles, giving him a 6-for-6 day. Waner was one of only two performers in the senior circuit to reach 100 runs, plus he finished third in slugging average and fourth in total bases.

Lazzeri played in all 155 of the New York Yankees' games, almost exclusively at second base. He drove in 114 runs, tying him for second in the league as he became the only freshman second baseman ever to reach the century mark in ribbies. In addition, Lazzeri ranked third in the AL with 18 home runs and set a new four-bagger standard for second baseman that has since been surpassed only twice.

MOST HR BY ROOKIE SECOND BASEMAN

25, Joe Gordon, 1938 NY AL
19, Ron Gant, 1988 Atl NL
18, Tony Lazzeri, 1926 NY AL
18, Alfonso Soriano, 2001 NY AL
17, Jim Baxes, 1959 LA NL/Cle AL*

*also played third base

On May 18, with New York down 3–1 in the eighth, Lazzeri hit a grand slam to give the Yankees a win over the Chicago White Sox. However, it is not for Lazzeri's regular-season success but for his postseason failure that his rookie campaign is remembered best. The Yankees faced the St. Louis Cardinals in the World Series and the teams split the first four contests. In Game Five Lazzeri hit a go-ahead sacrifice fly in the top of the tenth and the Bronx Bombers took a 3–2 lead in the series. St. Louis won Game Six and led the finale 3–2 going into the bottom of the seventh inning. New York then loaded the bases with two out, giving Lazzeri another chance to be the hero. Facing reliever Pete Alexander, Lazzeri narrowly missed a grand slam with a foul drive down the leftfield line and then struck out on the next pitch. The Cardinals held on, wrapping up their first championship as an NL club.

The Yankees teamed Lazzeri with another rookie, Mark Koenig, at shortstop, a rare middle-infield combo for a pennant winner. Koenig slashed 167 hits, five more than Lazzeri, making them the only freshman double-play partners each to amass 150 or more safeties.

Another minor league standout of the previous season made good in the bigs in 1926. Tommy Thomas had led the International League with 32 wins and 268 strikeouts for the 1925 Baltimore Orioles, who won their seventh consecutive pennant. Now with the White Sox, Thomas went 15–12 and was third in strikeouts. He held opponents to a .244 average, beating out Lefty Grove for the league low by a slim margin, and tossed two shutouts, one of them a two-hit gem June 13 versus Washington.

Cleveland's Dutch Levsen edged Thomas for the rookie lead in victories. Levsen snared 16, two of them in a doubleheader on August 28 against the Boston Red Sox. Levsen completed both games of the twinbill, winning 6–1 and 5–1. At the time Levsen's effort did not seem anything special, but for more than three quarters of a century now, he has remained the last pitcher to win two route-going efforts in one day, making it likely that his feat is not one that we can expect ever to see again.

Levsen lost his only two relief appearances in 1926, a disappointment that southpaw Joe Pate of the Philadelphia Athletics did not experience all season. Pate, a Texas League graduate, saved six games to lead all freshmen and went a perfect 9–0.

ROOKIES WITH MOST WINS WITHOUT A LOSS

10, Howie Krist, 1941 StL NL
9, Joe Pate, 1926 Phi AL
8, Kirk Rueter, 1993 Mon NL
7, Duster Mails, 1920 Cle AL
7, Mike Wallace, 1974 Phi NL/NY AL
7, Tom Filer, 1985 Tor AL

While Pate's Athletics had to be taken seriously in 1926, the Brooklyn Robins were renowned for inducing laughs. Babe Herman, Brooklyn's first baseman-outfielder, was involved in a notoriously bizarre play on August 15 in the first game of a doubleheader when the Robins had three runners on third base at one time. Despite the baserunning fiasco, Herman's double did drive in the go-ahead run for Brooklyn, which captured this game as well as the nightcap from the Boston Braves. In 1926 Herman batted .319 with 35 doubles, 11 triples, and the same number of home runs. He drove in 81 runs for the worst offensive—but easily the most hilarious—club in the NL.

Other Highlights

May 1—Joe Munson hits two home runs, one a tie-breaking three-run shot, for the Chicago Cubs, who beat the St. Louis Cardinals 11–8.

May 25—Doc Farrell hits a grand slam as his New York Giants top the Brooklyn Robins 5–1 in the first game of a doubleheader.

August 4—Former Stanford star and future pro football Hall of Famer Ernie Nevers pitches his first complete-game win for the Browns, topping the A's 3–1; Nevers

Nowhere on our 1926 leaders chart is the name of the rookie who at the end of the 1926 season was regarded as the frosh leader in both BA and OBP. The explanation is simply that the qualifications for eligibility were much more liberal at that time. In 1926 the Reds platooned rookie Cuckoo Christensen in left field with veteran Rube Bressler. Consequently, Christensen collected only 329 at bats. However, the fact that he appeared in 114 games made his .350 BA eligible for the bat title, which went that year to Reds catcher Bubbles Hargrave, who had just 326 at bats.

Christensen also posted a .426 OBP, 13 points higher than that of the acknowledged leader, Paul Waner. Like so many rookie hitters who appear on the frosh leader charts in the 1920s, Christensen's ML career was abruptly truncated when his BA slipped nearly 100 points to .254 the following year.

will win only five more games in the majors before quitting to concentrate solely on football.

August 7—Johnny Werts drives in the first run of the game for the Boston Braves and shuts out the Pittsburgh Pirates 2–0 in the opener of a twinbill.

August 11—Dodgers rookie Babe Herman flies out to Kiki Cuyler of Pittsburgh to end his consecutive hit streak at nine, one short of the NL record.

August 16—Sam Gibson of the Detroit Tigers pitches three-hit ball for ten innings, but the game ends in a scoreless tie when both Detroit and Cleveland have to catch trains.

August 28—Cleveland uses an identical lineup in both ends of a doubleheader, including pitcher Dutch Levsen, who hurls two complete-game wins over the Red Sox, 6–1 and 5–1, despite not fanning a single batter in either game.

August 31—Rookie second sacker Ray Morehart of the White Sox ties an ML record when he collects nine hits in a doubleheader at Detroit as the Sox and Tigers split a pair.

September 11—Pete Scott's seventh-inning grand slam keys the Cubs' 10–6 comeback victory against the Philadelphia Phillies.

Batting		Pitching	
G—AL 155, Tony Lazzeri, NY		W—AL 16, Dutch Levsen, CLE	
NL 147, Johnny Butler, BRO		NL 11, Johnny Werts, BOS	
AB—AL 617, Mark Koenig, NY		L—AL 15, Hal Wiltse, BOS	
NL 536, Paul Waner, PIT		NL 12, Claude Willoughby, PHI	
H—AL 167, Mark Koenig, NY		PCT—AL .556, Tommy Thomas, CHI	
NL 180, Paul Waner, PIT		NL .550, Johnny Werts, BOS	
2B—AL 28, Tony Lazzeri, NY		GP—AL 47, Joe Pate, PHI	
NL 35, Babe Herman, BRO		NL 47, Claude Willoughby, PHI	
Paul Waner, PIT		GS—AL 32, Tommy Thomas, CHI	
3B—AL 17, Charlie Gehringer, DET		NL 23, Johnny Werts, BOS	
NL 22, Paul Waner, PIT		CG—AL 18, Dutch Levsen, CLE	
HR—AL 18, Tony Lazzeri, NY		NL 7, Johnny Werts, BOS	
NL 11, Babe Herman, BRO		IP—AL 249, Tommy Thomas, CHI	
R—AL 93, Mark Koenig, NY		NL 189.1, Johnny Werts, BOS	
NL 101, Paul Waner, PIT		H—AL 235, Dutch Levsen, CLE	
RBI—AL 114, Tony Lazzeri, NY		NL 218, Claude Willoughby, PHI	
NL 81, Babe Herman, BRO		BB—AL 110, Tommy Thomas, CHI	
WK—AL 54, Tony Lazzeri, NY		NL 71, Claude Willoughby, PHI	
NL 66, Paul Waner, PIT		K—AL 127, Tommy Thomas, CHI	
SO—AL 96, Tony Lazzeri, NY		NL 65, Johnny Werts, BOS	
NL 53, Babe Herman, BRO		ERA—AL 3.41, Dutch Levsen, CLE	
SB—AL 24, Bill Hunnefield, CHI		NL 3.28, Johnny Werts, BOS	
NL 11, Paul Waner, PIT		SHO—AL 2, Sam Gibson, DET	
BA—AL .304, Buddy Myer, WAS		Dutch Levsen, CLE	
NL .336, Paul Waner, PIT		Tommy Thomas, CHI	
SLG—AL .462, Tony Lazzeri, NY		NL 1, Don Songer, PIT	
NL .528, Paul Waner, PIT		Johnny Werts, BOS	
OBP—AL .370, Buddy Myer, WAS		SV—AL 6, Joe Pate, PHI	
NL .413, Paul Waner, PIT		NL 2, Bunny Hearn, BOS	
		Don Songer, PIT	

1927

It was the year most often associated with the Jazz Age. Top stories for 1927 featured Charles Lindbergh, Sacco and Vanzetti and, of course, Babe Ruth and the New York Yankees' Murderers' Row. The Bronx Bombers lost only 44 games all season, but their top two foes were a pair of rookie right-handers. Hod Lisenbee of the Washington Senators beat the Yankees five times, the most by any AL pitcher. Right behind Lisenbee was Willis Hudlin, who gave the Cleveland Indians four victories against New York.

Lisenbee won 18 games and collected a league-leading four shutouts, albeit none against the Yankees.

Lisenbee and his freshman teammate Bump Hadley both ranked in the top four in opponents' batting average. Hadley went 14–6 for third-place Washington, and the two rookies more than made up for the soon-retiring Walter Johnson, who won his fewest games since 1907.

Hudlin, like Lisenbee, led his club with 18 wins. He was the third busiest pitcher in the loop, working 264⅔ innings. Hudlin surrendered only three home runs in 1927, including the 51st of Ruth's record-breaking campaign.

Besides Lisenbee and Hudlin, only one other freshman hurler was able to slay the Yankee beast. On August 4 Detroit's Ownie Carroll beat New York 6–2, one of ten wins for the Tiger righty. Returning the favor for the Yankees was George Pipgras, who notched his tenth win with a three-hit shutout of Detroit September 24. It was the 106th victory for New York, breaking the AL record set by the 1912 Red Sox.

Wilcy Moore, however, was by far the Yankees most valuable hurler, rookie or veteran. The freshman won 19 games and saved 13 others. Moore and Joe Black in 1952 are the only rookies to reach a baker's dozen in each category. Moore's 2.28 ERA was the lowest in the junior circuit, as were the .234 BA and .289 OBP opposing batters mustered against him. In the first game of the World Series against the Pittsburgh Pirates, Moore relieved in the eighth inning. Pittsburgh was down 5–3 but had runners at first and second with only one out. Moore permitted one of the runners to score but retired the Pirates in order in the ninth to preserve the victory and earn the save. Pipgras went the distance in the second contest, winning 6–2. The Yankees also took the third game and Moore started the next day. He permitted just one earned run in his 4–3 win, giving New York a sweep of what some historians believe was the most one-sided World Series in history.

The first batter Moore faced in the finale was Pittsburgh's center fielder, Paul Waner's younger brother Lloyd, who had a run and three hits in a losing effort. In due time the two siblings would become known as "Big Poison" and "Little Poison." In the 1927 Series, "Little Poison" Lloyd went 6-for-15 and scored five times to cap a brilliant freshman season. He collected seven hits in a May 30 doubleheader versus the Chicago Cubs and on July 20 made five successive safeties and scored twice in Pittsburgh's 6–5 win at Philadelphia. The newest Waner tied Rogers Hornsby for the NL lead in runs with 133, the most ever by a rookie since the close of the nineteenth century.

MOST RUNS SCORED BY ROOKIE

144, Billy Hamilton, 1889 KC AA
142, Mike Griffin, 1887 Bal AA
137, Herman Long, 1889 KC AA
137, Roy Thomas, 1899 Phi NL
133, Lloyd Waner, 1927 Pit NL

Waner's 223 hits are the most ever for a senior circuit freshman and the third best among all rookies. As

per his nickname of "Little Poison," only 25 of those hits went for extra bases, giving him a freshman-record 198 singles.

MOST SINGLES BY ROOKIE

198, Lloyd Waner, 1927 Pit NL
192, Ichiro Suzuki, 2001 Sea AL
168, Bill Everitt, 1895 Chi NL
167, Harvey Kuenn, 1953 Det AL
165, Johnny Pesky, 1942 Bos AL

St. Louis Cardinals catcher Johnny Schulte played considerably less than Waner but put up extraordinarily impressive numbers nonetheless. In 64 games Schulte posted a .456 OBP and walked 47 times.

On April 12, 1927, Cubs outfielder Earl Webb became the first rookie to homer twice on Opening Day and only the third player to perform this feat, following Herman Long in 1890 and Sherry Magee in 1914. Webb proved to be the lone frosh to post a double-digit home run figure that year. Interestingly, the frosh leader in total bases, Lloyd Waner with 258, produced fewer extra bases on long hits (35) than Webb did on his home runs alone (42).

Of Waner's NL rookie-record 223 hits, 198 were singles, only eight short of Willie Keeler's all-time one-base-hit mark of 206, set in 1898. Waner also set the post-1901 rookie record for runs (133) as well as the post-1901 mark for the greatest differential between runs and RBI (106). What's more, his 27 RBI in 1927 represent the fewest ever by a player who hit as high as .300 in 600 at bats, let alone .355.

THE 10 LOWEST RBI TOTALS BY .300 HITTERS WITH AT LEAST 400 AT BATS

Rank	Name	Year	AB	BA	RBI
1	Luis Castillo	2000	539	.334	17
2	Ron Hunt	1973	401	.309	18
3	Simon Nicholls	1907	460	.302	23
4	Frankie Baumholtz	1953	520	.306	25
	Ross Youngs	1918	474	.302	25
6	Nemo Leibold	1919	434	.302	26
7	Lloyd Waner	1927	629	.355	27
	Matty Alou	1966	535	.342	27
	Lenny Randle	1977	513	.304	27
	Josh Devore	1910	490	.304	27
	Roy Thomas	1903	477	.327	27

MOST WALKS BY ROOKIE WITH FEWER THAN 200 ABs

47, Johnny Schulte, 1927 StL NL
45, Herman Pitz, 1890 Bro AA
44, Frank Thomas, 1990 Chi AL
41, Babe Borton, 1913 Chi AL/NY AL
41, Sammy Esposito, 1956 Chi AL

While Ruth was the hottest Babe in 1927, Babe Ganzel also attracted a fair amount of attention. Ganzel debuted September 19 for Washington and two days later went 4-for-4 with two doubles and a triple. In 13 games he racked up 21 hits, batting .438. Unlike the Bambino, however, Ganzel's fame was fleeting. In 1928 he got but two hits in 26 ABs helping to make that season his last in the majors.

Other Highlights

April 12—Earl Webb hits two home runs on Opening Day for the Chicago Cubs, who beat the defending world champion St. Louis Cardinals 10–1.

April 29—Jumbo Elliott doubles in the first two runs for Brooklyn and then shuts out the Philadelphia Phillies 7–0 on four hits.

May 1—Senators rookie Hod Lisenbee blanks the Red Sox 6–0 in his first ML start; Lisenbee will go 18–9 with four shutouts as a frosh and then go 19–49 in the remaining seven years of his career and never throw another shutout.

May 31—Jimmie Foxx of the Philadelphia Athletics hits a solo home run, his first in the majors, but the New York Yankees take the nightcap of a twinbill 18–5.

1927 ROOKIE LEADERS

Batting	Pitching
G—AL 134, Alex Metzler, CHI	W—AL 19, Wilcy Moore, NY
NL 153, Fresco Thompson, PHI	NL 7, Watty Clark, BRO
AB—AL 543, Alex Metzler, CHI	L—AL 12, Willis Hudlin, CLE
NL 629, Lloyd Waner, PIT	NL 13, Jumbo Elliott, BRO
H—AL 173, Alex Metzler, CHI	PCT—AL .731, Wilcy Moore, NY
NL 223, Lloyd Waner, PIT	NL .316, Jumbo Elliott, BRO
2B—AL 29, Alex Metzler, CHI	GP—AL 50, Wilcy Moore, NY
NL 32, Fresco Thompson, PHI	NL 30, Jumbo Elliott, BRO
3B—AL 11, Alex Metzler, CHI	GS—AL 34, Hod Lisenbee, WAS
NL 14, Fresco Thompson, PHI	NL 21, Jumbo Elliott, BRO
HR—AL 5, Johnny Hodapp, CLE	CG—AL 18, Willis Hudlin, CLE
NL 14, Earl Webb, CHI	NL 12, Jumbo Elliott, BRO
R—AL 87, Alex Metzler, CHI	IP—AL 264.2, Willis Hudlin, CLE
NL 133, Lloyd Waner, PIT	NL 188.1, Jumbo Elliott, BRO
RBI—AL 61, Alex Metzler, CHI	H—**AL 291, Willis Hudlin, CLE**
NL 70, Fresco Thompson, PHI	NL 188, Jumbo Elliott, BRO
WK—AL 61, Alex Metzler, CHI	BB—AL 86, Bump Hadley, WAS
NL 48, Earl Webb, CHI	NL 60, Jumbo Elliott, BRO
SO—AL 53, Bobby Reeves, WAS	K—AL 105, Hod Lisenbee, WAS
NL 52, Randy Reese, NY	NL 99, Jumbo Elliott, BRO
SB—AL 15, Alex Metzler, CHI	ERA—**AL 2.28, Wilcy Moore, NY**
NL 24, Lance Richbourg, BOS	NL 3.30, Jumbo Elliott, BRO
BA—AL .319, Alex Metzler, CHI	SHO—**AL 4, Hod Lisenbee, WAS**
NL .355, Lloyd Waner, PIT	NL 2, Jumbo Elliott, BRO
SLG—AL .429, Alex Metzler, CHI	SV—**AL 13, Wilcy Moore, NY**
NL .410, Lloyd Waner, PIT	NL 3, Jumbo Elliott, BRO
OBP—AL .396, Alex Metzler, CHI	
NL .396, Lloyd Waner, PIT	

June 21—Shanty Hogan gets four hits, including a homer in the ninth inning to tie the score followed by a go-ahead two-run shot in the tenth as the Boston Braves win 7–5 against the New York Giants.

July 18—Mel Ott of the Giants hits the first of his 511 career homers, an inside-the-park job against Hal Carlson of the Cubs.

September 5—Rookie outfielder Pid Purdy of the Reds taps Pittsburgh's Lee Meadows for his first career home run; some six weeks later, on October 23, Purdy will become the first athlete to homer in the majors and score a touchdown in the NFL in the same calendar year when he crosses the goal line for the Green Bay Packers in a game against New York.

1928

Pat Malone was at his best on June 18 at Boston. The Chicago Cubs freshman right-hander held the Braves to a solitary hit as he cruised to a 12–0 victory in the second game of a doubleheader. The shutout was one of 18 wins for the 25-year-old Malone, who was the lone NL rookie to fan 100 or more batters. His 155 whiffs put him in select company for the era.

MOST STRIKEOUTS BY ROOKIE PITCHER, 1917–52

191, Dizzy Dean, 1932 StL NL
161, Bill Voiselle, 1944 NY NL
155, Pat Malone, 1928 Chi NL
151, Allie Reynolds, 1943 Cle AL
150, Paul Dean, 1934 StL NL

Malone held opponents to a .236 average, third best in the senior circuit, but he was topped by an ex-Cub for the rookie lead in wins. Ed Morris had pitched 12 innings of relief for Chicago in 1922 and didn't resurface in the majors until 1928 with the Boston Red Sox. Morris won 19 and saved 5 games for Boston, which posted only 57 victories. He suffered 15 defeats, giving him 34 decisions, the most by a rookie in the 1920s. Four other BoSox freshmen combined for a 0–14 record, the chief culprit being Merle Settlemire, who dropped all six of his ML decisions, and

the Boston staff as a whole, minus Morris, was an aggregate 38–81.

Settlemire could take solace in that he wasn't the worst winless rookie in 1928. Russ Miller had a historically wretched season for the Philadelphia Phillies, going 0–12 to set a new ML yearling mark for futility that remained the standard until 1982.

WINLESS ROOKIES WITH THE MOST LOSSES

13, Terry Felton, 1982 Min AL
12, Russ Miller, 1928 Phi NL
12, Steve Gerkin, 1945 Phi AL
10, William Stecher, 1890 Phi AA
9, Stump Wiedman, 1880 Buf NL

While Miller and fellow rookie Ray Benge, who was 8–18, had their difficulties, not all the news was bad on the Phillies' freshmen front. Third baseman Pinky Whitney drove in 103 runs and made 176 hits, 35 of them doubles. Denny Sothern, a center fielder, scored 82 times and swiped 17 bases. After debuting in mid-May, first baseman Don Hurst ripped 19 homers and drew 68 walks in only 107 games. Hurst would lead the NL in RBI in 1932, a feat that Chuck Klein had performed the year before and would do again the season after Hurst. Klein joined the Phils at the end of July in 1928 and immediately took a liking to his new home ballpark, Baker Bowl. Klein, a right fielder, hit .386 with nine home runs in 37 home games. No soft touch on the road, he batted .324 with two round trippers during his 27 away bouts. From 1930 through 1933, however, Klein's home average would top his road figure by well over 100 points each season. Klein played 17 years, one more than catcher Spud Davis. After two games with the St. Louis Cardinals in 1928, Davis was dealt to Philadelphia, where he hit .282 in 67 games. He retired with a .308 career average, among the best ever by a backstopper.

The year's top offensive freshman did not represent the City of Brotherly Love even though his name might suggest otherwise. Del Bissonette, whose full first name was Delphia, was the first baseman for the Brooklyn Dodgers. He stroked 30 doubles, 13 triples, and 25 home runs, placing in the loop's top five with the latter two numbers. Bissonette hit .320, ranked fourth with 319 total bases, and had 106 RBI.

107, Gus Suhr, 1930 Pit NL
106, Del Bissonette, 1928 Bro NL
106, Frank McCormick, 1938 Cin NL
101, Babe Young, 1940 NY NL
97, Todd Helton, 1998 Clr NL

Two recruit middle infielders topped the junior circuit's hit list. Cleveland second baseman Carl Lind hit 42 doubles, tying him for the most ever for a freshman second sacker, and just one rookie keystoner in all of history has exceeded Lind's 191 hits. Meanwhile, shortstop Red Kress had 153 hits for the St. Louis Browns, and his 81 RBI led all ML shortstops.

The Browns featured two rookies who combined for 25 wins. Jack Ogden took 15 games for the third-place Brownies while George Blaeholder added ten. However, it was a pitcher who made far fewer appearances that was destined for greatness. Carl Hubbell went 10–6 with a 2.83 ERA in 124 innings for the New York Giants. Hubbell would have five 20-win seasons, cop three ERA titles, and total 253 victories in his Hall-of-Fame career.

Along with dominating the NL rookie hitting leaders chart in 1928, Del Bissonette also tied Buck Freeman's frosh home run record and was the first yearling without any previous ML experience to hammer as many as 20 four baggers. Bissonette never again approached his rookie numbers. His career as a result lasted less than five seasons, but the career of Carl Lind, the AL's top all-around rookie performer in 1928, was even shorter.

Lind began Cleveland's training camp in 1928 as a backup shortstop to Joe Sewell. He appeared certain to be cut by manager Roger Peckinpaugh until second baseman Lew Fonseca was injured in a collision with first sacker Eddie Morgan. Lind moved across the diamond, teamed with Sewell, and led AL second basemen in double plays and chances per game. The following spring Sewell was switched to third base, putting incumbent Johnny Hodapp out of a job. Hodapp battled Lind for the second-base slot and won out when he outhit Lind in 1929 by nearly 100 points. In 1930 Lind tried to return to shortstop but lost out to rookie Jonah Goldman and was released.

Other Highlights

April 20—Rookie leftfielder Paul Easterling of Detroit slugs his third home run in three days; after his hot start, Easterling will go homerless for the rest of the season and hit just one more four-bagger in his brief ML career.

April 26—Ed Brandt tosses a two-hitter for the Boston Braves, who best Brooklyn 4–0.

May 1—Rookie centerfielder Sam Langford of Cleveland ties an ML record when he bags four assists in a game against the Browns; Langford will notch just one more assist in 1928 and then depart from the majors.

June 26—Less than a month after receiving a $6,000 signing bonus, a record at the time, former St. Mary's College football star Larry Bettencourt hits a sixth-inning grand slam, giving the St. Louis Browns a 6–3 win over the Cleveland Indians.

July 20—George Earnshaw of the Philadelphia Athletics fires his second three-hitter of the month, striking out ten Browns in a 4–0 win.

July 26—Detroit rookie Vic Sorrell holds the powerful Yankees to a 1–1 tie through 11 innings, only to collapse in the 12th frame and watch the Bombers pile up 12 hits and 11 runs in the biggest extra-frame explosion prior to 1983.

August 11—The Giants' Carl Hubbell, arguably the greatest NL southpaw of the first half of the twentieth century, makes his first ML victory a 4–0 whitewash of the heavy-hitting Phillies.

August 20—First sacker Art "The Great" Shires smacks four hits, including a triple, in his ML debut for the Chicago White Sox, who win at Boston 6–4.

September 8—Earl Caldwell blanks the Braves 4–0 in his first ML game for the Philadelphia Phillies in the nightcap of a doubleheader.

September 30—Bob Weiland, making his ML debut for the White Sox, whitewashes the Athletics 1–0, beating rookie Carroll Yerkes, who permits but four hits in eight innings.

1928 ROOKIE LEADERS

Batting	Pitching
G—AL 154, Carl Lind, CLE	W—AL 19, Ed Morris, BOS
NL 155, Del Bissonette, BRO	NL 18, Pat Malone, CHI
AB—**AL 650, Carl Lind, CLE**	L—AL 16, Grady Adkins, CHI
NL 587, Del Bissonette, BRO	Jack Ogden, STL
H—AL 191, Carl Lind, CLE	**NL 21, Ed Brandt, BOS**
NL 188, Del Bissonette, BRO	PCT—AL .559, Ed Morris, BOS
2B—AL 42, Carl Lind, CLE	NL .581, Pat Malone, CHI
NL 35, Pinky Whitney, PHI	GP—AL 47, Ed Morris, BOS
3B—AL 15, Red Barnes, WAS	NL 42, Pat Malone, CHI
NL 13, Del Bissonette, BRO	GS—AL 31, Jack Ogden, STL
HR—AL 10, Otis Brannan, STL	NL 31, Ed Brandt, BOS
NL 25, Del Bissonette, BRO	CG—AL 20, Ed Morris, BOS
R—AL 102, Carl Lind, CLE	NL 16, Pat Malone, CHI
NL 90, Del Bissonette, BRO	IP—AL 257.2, Ed Morris, BOS
RBI—AL 81, Red Kress, STL	NL 250.2, Pat Malone, CHI
NL 106, Del Bissonette, BRO	H—AL 257, Jack Ogden, STL
WK—AL 60, Otis Brannan, STL	NL 234, Ed Brandt, BOS
NL 70, Del Bissonette, BRO	BB—AL 100, George Earnshaw, PHI
SO—AL 70, Red Kress, STL	NL 109, Ed Brandt, BOS
NL 75, Del Bissonette, BRO	K—AL 117, George Earnshaw, PHI
SB—AL 18, Bill Cissell, CHI	NL 155, Pat Malone, CHI
NL 17, Denny Sothern, PHI	ERA—AL 3.53, Ed Morris, BOS
BA—AL .305, Red Barnes, WAS	NL 2.84, Pat Malone, CHI
NL .320, Del Bissonette, BRO	SHO—AL 3, George Earnshaw, PHI
SLG—AL .472, Red Barnes, WAS	NL 2, Pat Malone, CHI
NL .543, Del Bissonette, BRO	SV—AL 5, Ed Morris, BOS
OBP—AL .391, Red Barnes, WAS	**NL 5, Hal Haid, STL**
NL .396, Del Bissonette, BRO	

1929

Their names might be unfamiliar to many of today's fans, but the 1929 rookie crop was the first in history to feature three 200-hit men. The lone NLer from this group was Johnny Frederick, the center fielder of the Brooklyn Robins. In the first game of a May 18 twin-bill, Frederick had five hits, including two doubles and a home run, and scored five times as Brooklyn beat the Philadelphia Phillies 20–16 at Baker Bowl. On September 25 he added another five safeties to his collection, this time in a losing cause at Philadelphia. Frederick totaled 206 hits and scored 127 runs. He hit 24 homers and a rookie-record 52 doubles, the most two-baggers in the senior circuit since 1899. Frederick's 82 extra base hits were the loop's freshman standard until 2001.

Detroit's Dale Alexander topped Frederick by one more long hit, amassing 43 doubles, 15 triples, and 25 round trippers. Alexander's 137 RBI are the fourth-most a rookie has attained, six coming on August 7 when the first baseman hit a homer, two doubles, and a single in the Tigers' win at Cleveland. Only Al Simmons prevented Alexander from leading the AL with 363 total bases.

While Brooklyn enjoyed the hitting heroics of only one freshman swatter, the Motor City had twice the fun. Joining Alexander in the Detroit lineup was Roy Johnson, who played mostly in left field but also spent considerable time in the other two pasture positions. The Tigers' tandem are the only rookie teammates to reach the 200-hit milestone, Alexander netting 215 and Johnson 201. Of the two, Johnson possessed less power, but he still tied for the league lead in doubles with 45 and legged out 14 triples. Johnson tallied 128 times, the fifth highest total by a freshman since 1901.

Earl Averill, center fielder for the Cleveland Indians, fell just shy of making the 1929 200-hit triumvirate a quartet. Averill gathered 198 hits, the first of which came in his initial big league at bat. On April 16 he ripped a solo homer off Earl Whitehill in the first inning. Whitehill's future teammate on Washington's last pennant winner in 1933, General Crowder, at that time with the Browns, keenly felt Averill's power, surrendering five of his 18 home runs in 1929. In addition, Averill had 43 doubles, making him one of the record four rookies to reach 40 two-baggers in 1929.

Averill scored 110 runs and drove in 96 for third-place Cleveland, whose pitching staff was headed by Wes Ferrell, a 21-year-old right-hander. On September 29 Ferrell earned his 20th victory with a two-hit shutout against the Browns. He achieved a .677 winning percentage that ranked third in the league and finished second in wins while posting the highest frosh victory total since Jeff Pfeffer in 1914.

MOST WINS BY ROOKIE, 1915–31

21, Wes Ferrell, 1929 Cle AL
20, Scott Perry, 1918 Phi AL
19, Herman Pillette, 1922 Det AL
19, Wilcy Moore, 1927 NY AL
19, Ed Morris, 1928 Bos AL

Ferrell was also a dangerous hitter, batting .237 with nine extra base hits and 12 RBI in 93 ABs. He compiled a .280 career average and hit the first of his record 37 home runs as a pitcher on July 10 off Washington's Bump Hadley.

Ferrell actually outhomered his brother Rick, a catcher with the Browns. The elder Ferrell hit only .229 in 1929 but displayed a good eye, walking 32 times in 64 games. Rick would go on to play 18 seasons and would eventually join another of that season's freshman backstops in Cooperstown. The New York Yankees' Bill Dickey hit .324 in 1929 and pounded ten home runs. His 145 hits are the second highest total ever by an AL rookie receiver.

MOST HITS BY ROOKIE CATCHER

174, Mike Piazza, 1993 LA NL
164, Benito Santiago, 1987 SD NL
155, Johnny Bench, 1968 Cin NL
146, Bob Rodgers, 1962 LA AL
145, Bill Dickey, 1929 NY AL

For the first time since 1925, the Yankees failed to win the AL flag, being supplanted by Connie Mack's Philadelphia Athletics. Bill Shores won 11 games for the Mackmen, joining Wes Ferrell as the only freshmen in either league to win at least ten times. Shores also saved seven contests, third best in the AL, but did not play in the Athletics' five-game victory over the Chicago Cubs in the World Series.

The Cincinnati Reds were ten years removed from their last appearance in the Fall Classic and another ten away from their next one. In 1929 they finished seventh but benefited from Evar Swanson's flying feet. A four-sport star at Lombard College, where he won 16 varsity letters, Swanson stole 33 bases, the most by a rookie from 1924 through 1949. He scored 100 runs, tops on the club, and batted .300 with 172 hits, including 35 doubles and 12 triples.

Only twelve players since 1872 have scored 100 runs in their rookie seasons and never again reached that figure. Off his 1929 season, Dale Alexander would become the third performer in a five-year span to make that select list, joining Ike Davis (1925) and Carl Lind (1928). In addition, Alexander tied the rookie home run record and then, like Del Bissonette, who had tied the mark the previous year, began a slow but steady decline in power and production that brought his ML career to a halt after less than five full seasons.

100 RUNS, ROOKIE YEAR, NEVER AGAIN SCORING 100 RUNS

Name	Team	Year	C/R	R/R
Ted Scheffler	Roc-AA	1890	128	111
Dale Alexander	Det-AL	1929	369	110
Kevin Seitzer	KC-AL	1987	739	105
Ike Davis	Chi-AL	1925	110	105
Morrie Rath	Chi-AL	1912	291	104
Jim Burns	KC-AA	1889	131	103
Irv Waldron	Mil/Was-AL	1901	102	102
Carl Lind	Cle-AL	1928	131	102
Hersh Martin	Phi-NL	1937	331	102
Walt Dropo	Bos-AL	1950	478	101
John Farrell	Was-AL	1901	329	100
Kiddo Davis	Phi-NL	1932	281	100

Considering that 1929 is regarded as one of the most fertile seasons ever for rookies, it is something of a surprise that the frosh leader that year in shutouts was able to notch only two. Even more surprising is that Al Grabowski, the leader, did not make his initial appearance until there were less than four weeks left in the season. Commencing on September 11, Grabowski made six starts in the final 25 days of the campaign. His two shutouts were the only shutouts of his career and came in back-to-back appearances. On September 22 he beat Ray Moss of the Dodgers 4–0, and then, three days later, he blanked Ray Kolp of the Reds 8–0. In 1930 Grabowski remained with the Cardinals all season as a middle reliever and occasional starter. Though reasonably effective, he was dropped prior to the 1931 season.

Other Highlights

April 27—Dodgers relief pitcher Clise Dudley is the first NLer in the twentieth century to homer in his first plate appearance; moreover, Dudley homers off Claude Willoughby of the Phils on the first pitch he sees.

May 27—Rookie pinch-hit specialist Pat Crawford of the Giants makes his first career homer a pinch grand slam in a 15–9 win against Bob Smith of the Braves; in the same game Les Bell of Boston also hits a pinch slam, making the contest the only one in history to feature two pinch four-run dingers.

July 9—"Fidgety" Phil Collins stops Cardinals star Chick Hafey's NL-tying consecutive hit streak at ten in

1929 ROOKIE LEADERS

Batting	Pitching
G—AL 155, Dale Alexander, DET	W—AL 21, Wes Ferrell, CLE
NL 148, Johnny Frederick, BRO	NL 9, Phil Collins, PHI
Evar Swanson, CIN	L—AL 10, Wes Ferrell, CLE
AB—AL 640, Roy Johnson, DET	NL 14, Clise Dudley, BRO
NL 628, Johnny Frederick, BRO	PCT—AL .677, Wes Ferrell, CLE
H—AL 215, Dale Alexander, DET	NL .300, Clise Dudley, BRO
NL 206, Johnny Frederick, BRO	GP—AL 43, Wes Ferrell, CLE
2B—AL 45, Roy Johnson, DET	NL 43, Phil Collins, PHI
NL 52, Johnny Frederick, BRO	GS—AL 25, Wes Ferrell, CLE
3B—AL 17, Russ Scarritt, BOS	NL 21, Clise Dudley, BRO
NL 12, Evar Swanson, CIN	CG—AL 18, Wes Ferrell, CLE
HR—AL 25, Dale Alexander, DET	NL 8, Clise Dudley, BRO
NL 24, Johnny Frederick, BRO	IP—AL 242.2, Wes Ferrell, CLE
R—AL 128, Roy Johnson, DET	NL 156.2, Clise Dudley, BRO
NL 127, Johnny Frederick, BRO	H—AL 256, Wes Ferrell, CLE
RBI—AL 137, Dale Alexander, DET	NL 202, Clise Dudley, BRO
NL 75, Johnny Frederick, BRO	BB—AL 109, Wes Ferrell, CLE
WK—AL 67, Roy Johnson, DET	NL 83, Phil Collins, PHI
NL 51, Charlie Gelbert, STL	K—AL 100, Wes Ferrell, CLE
SO—AL 63, Dale Alexander, DET	NL 61, Phil Collins, PHI
NL 47, Evar Swanson, CIN	ERA—AL 3.60, Wes Ferrell, CLE
SB—AL 20, Roy Johnson, DET	NL 5.69, Clise Dudley, BRO
NL 33, Evar Swanson, CIN	SHO—AL 1, Wes Ferrell, CLE
BA—AL .343, Dale Alexander, DET	Chief Hogsett, DET
NL .328, Johnny Frederick, BRO	Hal McKain, CHI
SLG—AL .580, Dale Alexander, DET	Bill Shores, PHI
NL .545, Johnny Frederick, BRO	NL 2, Al Grabowski, STL
OBP—AL .398, Earl Averill, CLE	SV—AL 7, Bill Shores, PHI
NL .372, Johnny Frederick, BRO	NL 5, Phil Collins, PHI
	Steve Swetonic, PIT

a 7–4 loss to St. Louis; Collins will lead all NL rookies in wins with nine but fall two-thirds of an inning short of qualifying as the senior loop's rookie winning percentage leader.

September 15—In a "Field Day" event, rookie Reds left-fielder Evar Swanson, a former college sprinter, circles the bases in a record 13.3 seconds; two years later Swanson will shave the mark to 13.2.

September 24—Brooklyn's Johnny Frederick strokes his all-time rookie record 52nd double in an 8–6 loss to the Phillies.

1930s

1930

The hitting started Opening Day for the St. Louis Cardinals and didn't stop until October. The 1930 Cards batted .314 and scored 1,004 runs, the most by any NL team since 1897, thanks in no small part to the team's freshman class. Showboat Fisher got four hits in St. Louis's 9–8 Opening Day loss to the Chicago Cubs. The next day he did it again, driving in four runs as St. Louis earned its first victory. Fisher batted .374 and drove in 61 runs in 254 ABs. He outhit fellow Redbirds outfielder George Watkins, but not by much. Watkins smote .373, the highest mark ever by an NL rookie with 300 or more ABs. The same was true of Watkins's .621 slugging average, a result of obtaining 56 extra-base hits in 391 times up. Watkins scored five runs on May 7 and had four-hit games twice in early July and again on September 19, when catcher Gus Mancuso also had a banner day. Mancuso drove in three runs for the Cardinals, who won 7–3 at Philadelphia. The frosh backstopper knocked home 59 runs in only 227 AB.

MOST RBI BY ROOKIE WITH FEWER THAN 250 ABs

59 RBI/227 AB, Gus Mancuso, 1930 StL NL	
56 RBI/247 AB, Ben Paschal, 1925 NY AL	
53 RBI/226 AB, Frank Colman, 1944 Pit NL	
50 RBI/239 AB, Vince Barton, 1931 Chi NL	
47 RBI/245 AB, Ryan Klesko, 1994 Atl NL	

Fisher, Watkins, and Mancuso all hit better than .365, giving the 1930 Cardinals a one-of-a-kind rookie trifecta.

HIGHEST BA BY ROOKIE, 1901–2003 (MINIMUM 150 ABs)

.408/571 AB, Joe Jackson, 1911 Cle AL	
.374/254 AB, Showboat Fisher, 1930 StL NL	
.373/391 AB, George Watkins, 1930 StL NL	
.370/571 AB, Benny Kauff, 1914 Ind FL	
.366/227 AB, Gus Mancuso, 1930 StL NL	

The trio went 5-for-21 in the World Series against the Philadelphia Athletics, who held St. Louis to a .200 average in beating the Cardinals four games to two.

Naturally, in a season known as "The Year of the Hitter," teams other than the Cardinals featured hard-hitting freshmen, too. Boston Braves leftfielder Wally Berger batted .310 and drove in 119 runs, the eighth best in rookie history. Berger smashed 38 home runs to set a new mark for the most ever by a senior circuit freshman, a record tied in 1956 by Frank Robinson. Berger had four multi-homer games, including the first game of a May 17 doubleheader. He hit his sixth and seventh round trippers in the Braves' 4–3 win at New York. In the nightcap Berger homered again as Boston won by the same score. On July 20 he went 4-for-4 with two triples and his 26th home run in a second-game victory versus Cincinnati.

Berger was one of a record four rookies in 1930 to tally at least ten in each extra-base-hit category; the other three were Smead Jolley, Gus Suhr, and Ben Chapman. Jolley, who won six minor league batting titles, hit .313 for the Chicago White Sox. The outfielder set still existing team freshman records with 193 hits and 114 RBI. In late May Jolley homered in three straight games at Cleveland, collecting a total of four safeties in two of them. Suhr, Pittsburgh's first baseman, sent 107 runners home and drew 80 bases on balls, fifth most in the loop. Suhr's walk total was the highest for an NL rookie from 1924 through 1942. He legged out 14 triples, an exceptional number for a first

Granted, 1930 was one of the most sanguine years ever for hitters, especially in the NL, where the average team smoked the ball for a .304 BA. But that still does not diminish George Watkins's extraordinary performance. The Cards sensational rookie outfielder is absent from many of the departments on the 1930 rookie leaders chart in which he actually led according to the eligibility rules in vogue at the time. Today, because he fell short of 400 at bats, his .373 BA, .415 OBP, and .621 SA are not recognized as the top rookie figures in the NL.

In actuality, Watkins had 391 at bats and 424 plate appearances. His 1.037 OPS ranks as one of the top 15 in history among player seasons that fall between the same two parameters: more than 400 plate appearances but less than 400 at bats.

Rank	Name	Year	PA	AB	BA	OPS
1	Frank Thomas	1994	517	399	.353	1.223
2	Ted Williams	1955	417	320	.356	1.204
3	Ted Williams	1954	526	386	.345	1.151
4	Bill Joyce	1894	459	355	.355	1.143
5	Mark McGwire	1995	422	317	.274	1.132
6	Ted Williams	1950	416	334	.317	1.099
7	Mickey Mantle	1962	502	377	.321	1.093
8	Mike Schmidt	1981	434	354	.316	1.083
9	Barry Bonds	1994	474	391	.312	1.076
10	Paul O'Neill	1994	443	368	.359	1.067
11	Kal Daniels	1987	430	368	.334	1.046
12	Hank Aaron	1973	465	392	.301	1.048
13	George Watkins	1930	424	391	.373	1.037
14	Mel Ott	1939	508	396	.308	1.030
	J.D. Drew	2001	443	375	.323	1.030

Following the custom of his time, George Watkins shaved two years off his birth date when he began playing professionally in 1925. As a result, his actual age was pushing 30 in 1930 when the Cardinals recalled him early in the season from their Rochester farm club. Watkins proceeded to post the top BA of any NL rookie in the twentieth century who had at least 400 plate appearances. *Transcendental Graphics*

sacker and the most by any freshman NL gateway guardian since the close of the Deadball Era.

MOST TRIPLES BY ROOKIE FIRST BASEMAN

16, Harry Davis, 1896 NY NL/Pit NL
16, Kitty Bransfield, 1901 Pit NL
15, Jake Daubert, 1910 Bro NL
15, Dale Alexander, 1929 Det AL
14, Gus Suhr, 1930 Pit NL

Chapman played third and second bases for the New York Yankees, batting .316 with ten home runs—or ten more than Tom Oliver hit. Oliver played all 154 Boston Red Sox games in center field, getting 189 hits. But in 646 ABs, he failed to hit a single home run, breaking the former freshman standard of 599 without a long ball set by Jimmy Slagle in 1899.

Though hitters got most of the headlines in 1930, a handful of freshman hurlers grabbed their share of glory, too. Ray Phelps went 14–7 for Brooklyn, which hung in the NL race longer than expected, while Bud Teachout took 11 games for the second-place Chicago Cubs. On August 29 the only two AL rookies who won at least ten games battled each other into extra innings. Pat Caraway of the White Sox and Cleveland's Clint Brown each hurled shutout ball for 12 frames. Brown was the first to crack, surrendering three runs in the top of the 13th, the first of which was doubled in by Caraway himself. The White Sox lefty won, blanking the Indians on three hits.

1930 ROOKIE LEADERS

Batting	Pitching
G—**AL 154, Tom Oliver, BOS**	W—AL 11, Clint Brown, CLE
NL 151, Wally Berger, BOS	NL 14, Ray Phelps, BRO
Gus Suhr, PIT	L—AL 15, Ed Durham, BOS
AB—**AL 646, Tom Oliver, BOS**	**NL 18, Benny Frey, CIN**
NL 578, Footsie Blair, CHI	PCT—AL .458, Clint Brown, CLE
H—AL 193, Smead Jolley, CHI	NL .667, Ray Phelps, BRO
NL 172, Wally Berger, BOS	GP—AL 40, Charlie Sullivan, DET
2B—AL 38, Smead Jolley, CHI	NL 44, Benny Frey, CIN
NL 32, George Watkins, STL	GS—AL 31, Clint Brown, CLE
3B—AL 12, Smead Jolley, CHI	NL 28, Benny Frey, CIN
NL 14, Wally Berger, BOS	CG—AL 16, Clint Brown, CLE
Gus Suhr, PIT	NL 14, Benny Frey, CIN
HR—AL 16, Smead Jolley, CHI	IP—AL 213.2, Clint Brown, CLE
NL 38, Wally Berger, BOS	NL 245, Benny Frey, CIN
R—AL 86, Tom Oliver, BOS	H—AL 271, Clint Brown, CLE
NL 98, Wally Berger, BOS	NL 295, Benny Frey, CIN
RBI—AL 114, Smead Jolley, CHI	BB—AL 63, Chief Hogsett, DET
NL 119, Wally Berger, BOS	NL 63, Glenn Spencer, PIT
WK—AL 43, Ben Chapman, NY	K—AL 83, Pat Caraway, CHI
NL 80, Gus Suhr, PIT	NL 64, Ray Phelps, BRO
SO—AL 61, Dusty Cooke, NY	ERA—AL 3.86, Pat Caraway, CHI
NL 69, Wally Berger, BOS	NL 4.11, Ray Phelps, BRO
SB—AL 14, Ben Chapman, NY	SHO—**AL 3, Clint Brown, CLE**
NL 11, Gus Suhr, PIT	NL 2, Benny Frey, CIN
BA—AL .316, Ben Chapman, NY	Ray Phelps, BRO
NL .312, Tony Cuccinello, CIN	Spades Wood, PIT
SLG—AL .492, Smead Jolley, CHI	SV—AL 5, Charlie Sullivan, DET
NL .614, Wally Berger, BOS	NL 6, Joe Heving, NY
OBP—AL .371, Ben Chapman, NY	
NL .380, Tony Cuccinello, CIN*	

*Cuccinello's OBA was .38008, edging Gus Suhr's .37981.

May 7—Benny Frey of the Cincinnati Reds blanks the Boston Braves on three hits, beating them 1–0.

May 24—Gordon Slade homers in his first major league AB for the Brooklyn Robins, who beat the Braves 5–2 in 11 innings, as Ray Phelps goes the distance for the win.

July 21—Both Hal Lee of Brooklyn and Pooch Puccinelli of the Cardinals make their first ML hits pinch home runs as a record four pinch taters are hit in a twinbill between the Dodgers and St. Louis.

August 25—Former minor league strikeout-king Tommy Bridges of Detroit walks 12 St. Louis Browns but still wins 7–5; wild streaks will plague Bridges throughout his otherwise outstanding ML career.

September 27—In a 7–1 win over Brooklyn, Wally Berger of the Braves clubs his 38th homer to establish a rookie record that will remain the standard until 1987.

1931

Think of the St. Louis Cardinals in the 1930s and the image of a hungry, hustling ballplayer craving the next base springs to mind. Perhaps no one better exemplified this persona than Johnny Leonard Roosevelt "Pepper" Martin. After totaling 45 games in the 1928 and 1930 seasons, Martin became the Cardinals regular center fielder after the June 15, 1931, trade of Taylor Douthit to the Cincinnati Reds. Martin responded with a .300 average, 75 RBI, and 16 stolen bases, the latter figure tying him for third best in the National League.

His regular season accomplishments pale, however, in comparison to his World Series exploits. The Fall Classic was a rematch of the 1930 edition, with the Cardinals hoping to dethrone the Philadelphia Athletics. In the opener Martin went 3-for-4 with an RBI double, but St. Louis lost 6–2. The next day, Pepper scored the first run after doubling and stealing third in the second inning and later singled, stole second, and scored an insurance tally. St. Louis won 2–0 and evened the series at a game apiece. After scoring twice in Game Four and collecting St. Louis's only two safeties, in the following contest Martin went 3-for-4 with four RBI. On the strength of their 5–1 victory, the Cardinals took a 3–2

lead in the series. Despite going hitless in the final two contests, Martin finished with a .500 BA, 12 hits, four doubles, and a homer. He also collected five runs, five RBI, and five stolen bases.

Joining Martin on the victorious Cards was rookie right-hander Paul Derringer, who started two games in the World Series. Derringer was not inserted into the Redbirds' rotation until May 31 but then preceded to go 18–8 (14–8 as a starter). His achievement was accomplished in the first season that the National League did not have a 20-game winner. Derringer led the NL with a .692 winning percentage, tossed four shutouts, and saved two games. On August 23 he whitewashed the Boston Braves 1–0 in 11 innings. A week later, Derringer fanned ten Pittsburgh Pirates, blanking them 5–0 and earning his 15th victory. On September 7 the 24-year-old Derringer made it three shutouts in a row, this time whiffing eight Chicago Cubs and winning 1–0.

The Athletics proved tougher for Derringer in the World Series. He started Game One, the first rookie hurler since Jeff Tesreau in 1912 to be so honored, but was tagged for six runs in seven innings and took the loss. In Game Six Derringer met a similar fate after permitting four unearned runs.

Martin and Derringer were not the only freshman contributors to St. Louis's world championship. Ripper Collins and Allyn Stout also chipped in valuable work. Collins hit .301, drove home 59 runs, and hit 20 doubles and 10 triples in only 89 games. His 279 at bats are the fewest ever for a rookie who had such high totals in those two extra-base-hit categories. Stout fashioned a 6–0 record with an NL rookie-high three saves; in addition, he made three starts, winning twice.

While the American League rookie crop in 1931 had no one nearly as colorful as Martin or as significant to his team's pennant chances as Derringer, it did produce the top "local boy makes good" story of the 1930s in Joe Vosmik. A graduate of Cleveland's East Tech High School, Vosmik was signed by the Indians at the behest of former shortstop Roger Peckinpaugh, himself an East Tech alumnus, after being observed "socking the ball all over the municipal lots" in the Forest City. A two-year minor league apprenticeship, culminating in the 1930 Three I League batting crown, earned Vosmik the Cleveland left-field slot in 1931. At the season's end he stood atop the rookie leader board in every major hitting department save home runs. Nicknamed "The Blond Bohemian," Vosmik remained the Tribe's fair-haired boy for six full seasons in the 1930s before an unpopular trade sent him to the St. Louis Browns.

Other Highlights

April 19—Joe Vosmik hits his first career home run off Earl Whitehill of the Tigers; in 1931 Vosmik will set a new frosh record for the most RBI (117) on fewer than ten home runs as he hits just seven taters.

August 23—Lefty Grove fails in his bid to win a record-breaking 17th consecutive game when rookie outfielder Jimmy Moore, subbing for Al Simmons, misjudges a fly ball that leads to the lone run in the A's 1–0 loss to Dick Coffman of the Browns.

Minor league legend Buzz Arlett received his one and only big league chance in 1931 at age 32. It can hardly be said that the Phils let him go after the season because he flopped. Among men who played only one season in the majors, Arlett set the following records:

BUZZ ARLETT'S RECORDS AMONG PLAYERS WITH ONLY ONE ML SEASON

Highest BA all-time by an NL player: .313
Highest SA all-time: .538
Most home runs all-time: 18
Most RBI since 1901: 72
Most hits all-time by an NL player: 131
Most doubles all-time (tied with two others): 26
Most triples all-time by an NL player: 7
Most total bases all-time: 225

1931 ROOKIE LEADERS

Batting	Pitching
G—AL 149, Joe Vosmik, CLE	W—AL 13, Carl Fischer, WAS
NL 152, Johnny Vergez, NY	Vic Frasier, CHI
AB—AL 591, Joe Vosmik, CLE	NL 18, Paul Derringer, STL
NL 565, Johnny Vergez, NY	L—AL 16, Tommy Bridges, DET
H—AL 189, Joe Vosmik, CLE	NL 12, Stew Bolen, PHI
NL 157, Johnny Vergez, NY	PCT—AL .591, Carl Fischer, WAS
2B—AL 36, Joe Vosmik, CLE	**NL .692, Paul Derringer, STL**
NL 32, Pepper Martin, STL	GP—AL 46, Carl Fischer, WAS
3B—AL 14, Joe Vosmik, CLE	Vic Frasier, CHI
NL 12, Estel Crabtree, CIN	NL 38, Frank Watt, PHI
HR—AL 9, Urbane Pickering, BOS	GS—AL 29, Vic Frasier, CHI
NL 18, Buzz Arlett, PHI	NL 23, Paul Derringer, STL
R—AL 80, Joe Vosmik, CLE	CG—AL 13, Vic Frasier, CHI
NL 70, Estel Crabtree, CIN	NL 15, Paul Derringer, STL
RBI—AL 117, Joe Vosmik, CLE	IP—AL 254, Vic Frasier, CHI
NL 81, Johnny Vergez, NY	NL 211.2, Paul Derringer, STL
WK—AL 47, Joe Kuhel, WAS	H—AL 258, Vic Frasier, CHI
NL 45, Buzz Arlett, PHI	NL 225, Paul Derringer, STL
SO—AL 83, Jim Levey, STL	BB—AL 127, Vic Frasier, CHI
NL 65, Johnny Vergez, NY	NL 65, Paul Derringer, STL
SB—AL 19, Jack Burns, STL	K—AL 105, Tommy Bridges, DET
NL 16, Pepper Martin, STL	NL 134, Paul Derringer, STL
BA—AL .320, Joe Vosmik, CLE	ERA—AL 4.38, Carl Fischer, WAS
NL .313, Buzz Arlett, PHI	NL 3.36, Paul Derringer, STL
SLG—AL .464, Joe Vosmik, CLE	SHO—AL 2, Tommy Bridges, DET
NL .538, Buzz Arlett, PHI	Vic Frasier, CHI
OBP—AL .363, Joe Vosmik, CLE	NL 4, Paul Derringer, STL
NL .387, Buzz Arlett, PHI	SV—AL 4, Vic Frasier, CHI
	NL 3, Allyn Stout, STL

September 7—In his ML debut Van Lingle Mungo of the Dodgers blanks Boston 2–0 while fanning seven and hitting a home run and a single.

September 22—Rookie receiver Hal Finney of the Pirates registers no putouts in teammate Heinie Meine's 13-inning 3–2 win over the Phillies when Meine fails to fan a single batter; Finney will conclude his ML career in 1936 by going 0-for-35 to shatter Ed Whiting's old record of 21 (set in 1886) for the most hitless ABs in a season by a position player.

1932

For the St. Louis Cardinals, 1932 was not a good year. The defending world champions finished tied for sixth place with a .468 winning percentage that would be the club's worst until 1955. But the Redbirds did have one bright spot—22-year-old flamethrower Jay Hanna "Dizzy" Dean. Dean fired a late-season three-hitter in 1930 and was the Texas League's MVP the following season. In 1932 Dean went 18–15 for the Cards and led the National League in innings pitched, shutouts, and strikeouts. His 191 whiffs were the most by a rookie from 1912 through 1954.

On August 14 Dean fanned six straight Chicago Cubs in a 2–1 victory in ten innings. A week later Diz whiffed ten batters in six innings of relief, but the Cards lost to Boston. In late August he started and won three games in five days, and on September 3 Dean blanked the Cubs, ending Chicago's 14-game winning streak.

In addition to his pitching talent, Dean possessed strong baserunning and hitting skills, batting .258 with five doubles, two homers, and 12 RBI for the year. Dean's notable on-field accomplishments, coupled with his boastful nature and penchant for playing pranks, provided a necessary diversion for a nation facing the worst depression in its history.

Another rookie right-hander, as fiery as Dean was flaky, helped the New York Yankees return to the apex of the baseball world. Johnny Allen gave manager Joe McCarthy added flexibility, starting 21 games and relieving in 12 more. Allen threw four shutouts and saved three contests. On May 21 he not only whitewashed the Wash-

ington Senators on five hits but also homered, doubled, and drove in three runs in New York's 8–0 win. Allen, who had a ten-game winning streak snapped in mid-September, posted a 17–4 record, good for an AL-best .810 winning percentage. Only one AL rookie with at least 15 wins ever had a higher success rate—Russ Ford in 1910 (.813).

The Yankees won the junior circuit flag by 13 games and took the first three World Series contests against the Cubs. Allen started for New York in Game Four but was pounded for four runs (three earned) in only two-thirds of an inning. The Bronx Bombers overcame Allen's rough start, however, to win 13–6 and sweep Chicago.

One of the two hitters Allen retired in the Fall Classic was Billy Herman, the Cubs rookie second baseman. Herman played with Chicago the final month of the 1931 campaign, batting .327 in 98 at bats. In 1932 he

Monte Weaver received a master's degree in mathematics and was teaching analytical geometry before the stock market crash in 1929 made him redo his math and decide that he could gain more financial security playing baseball. He began his rookie year in 1932 by losing four of his first five decisions with Washington but then proceeded to go 22–6 the rest of the way. His 22 wins were the most by a rookie hurler since 1914, when Jeff Pfeffer collected 23 victories with Brooklyn. They also represent the most wins since 1913 by a rookie who never again won 20 games in a season.

MOST WINS, 20-GAME WINNER ROOKIE YEAR ONLY

Rank	Name	Team	Year	Wins
1	Jesse Duryea	Cin-AA	1889	32
2	George Derby	Det-NL	1881	29
3	Ed Daily	Phi-NL	1885	26
4	Gus Krock	Chi-NL	1888	25
	Mickey Hughes	Bro-AA	1888	25
6	Ed Summers	Det-AL	1908	24
	Tom Vickery	Phi-NL	1890	24
8	Bill Wise	Was-UA	1884	23
	Jocko Flynn	Chi-NL	1886	23
	Roscoe Miller	Det-AL	1901	23
	George McQuillan	Phi-NL	1908	23
12	Reb Russell	Chi-AL	1913	22
	Henry Schmidt	Bro-NL	1903	22
	Monte Weaver	Was-AL	1932	22

appeared in all 154 games, clubbed 42 doubles, and collected 206 hits. The latter two figures are still team rookie records and remain unsurpassed by any freshman keystoner.

Herman, a superb hit-and-run man, was also a masterful bunter. Despite committing an NL-high 38 errors, Herman flashed his defensive skills by topping his position in assists and total chances per game. Chicago scored 19 runs in losing the World Series, and Herman tallied five of them and drove in another. This season established a pattern for Herman—playing in the Fall Classic every three years. He was a vital cog for the Cubs in 1935 and 1938 and then in 1941 for the Brooklyn Dodgers, where he teamed with an old nemesis, Johnny Allen.

Other Highlights

July 10—A's rookie Lew Krausse is knocked out in the first inning of a game at Cleveland, forcing Eddie Rommel to pitch the remainder of the contest since the A's brought only two pitchers to save on train fare; Rommel labors 17 innings in relief and gives up a record 29 hits before winning 18–17 when the A's score a fluke run in the 18th inning.

August 11—Rookie shortstop Arky Vaughan's tenth-inning error allows the Cubs to top the Pirates 3–2 and take over first place from the Corsairs; the Cubs will proceed to win the NL flag.

August 31—A's rookie Tony Freitas's ten-game winning streak is ended when his mound rival that day,

1932 ROOKIE LEADERS

Batting	Pitching
G—AL 146, Bruce Campbell, CHI/STL	W—AL 22, Monte Weaver, WAS
NL 154, Billy Herman, CHI	NL 18, Dizzy Dean, STL
AB—AL 611, Bruce Campbell, CHI/STL	L—AL 10, Monte Weaver, WAS
NL 656, Billy Herman, CHI	NL 15, Dizzy Dean, STL
H—AL 173, Bruce Campbell, CHI/STL	PCT—**AL .810, Johnny Allen, NY**
NL 206, Billy Herman, CHI	NL .545, Dizzy Dean, STL
2B—AL 36, Bruce Campbell, CHI/STL	GP—AL 43, Monte Weaver, WAS
NL 42, Billy Herman, CHI	NL 46, Dizzy Dean, STL
3B—AL 13, Harry Davis, DET	GS—AL 30, Monte Weaver, WAS
NL 10, Arky Vaughan, PIT	NL 33, Dizzy Dean, STL
	Van Lingle Mungo, BRO
HR—AL 14, Bruce Campbell, CHI/STL	CG—AL 13, Johnny Allen, NY
NL 5, Dave Barbee, PIT	Monte Weaver, WAS
Kiddo Davis, PHI	NL 16, Dizzy Dean, STL
R—AL 92, Harry Davis, DET	Ed Holley, PHI
NL 102, Billy Herman, CHI	
RBI—AL 87, Bruce Campbell, CHI/STL	IP—AL 234, Monte Weaver, WAS
NL 61, Arky Vaughan, PIT	**NL 286, Dizzy Dean, STL**
WK—AL 61, Marv Olson, BOS	H—AL 236, Monte Weaver, WAS
NL 44, Kiddo Davis, PHI	NL 280, Dizzy Dean, STL
SO—**AL 104, Bruce Campbell, CHI/STL**	BB—AL 112, Monte Weaver, WAS
NL 56, Kiddo Davis, PHI	**NL 115, Van Lingle Mungo, BRO**
SB—AL 12, Harry Davis, DET	K—AL 109, Johnny Allen, NY
NL 16, Kiddo Davis, PHI	**NL 191, Dizzy Dean, STL**
BA—AL .283, Bruce Campbell, CHI/STL	ERA—AL 3.52, Ivy Andrews, NY/BOS
NL .318, Arky Vaughan, PIT	NL 3.30, Bob Brown, BOS*
SLG—AL .447, Bruce Campbell, CHI/STL	SH—AL 3, Johnny Allen, NY
NL .424, Kiddo Davis, PHI	**NL 4, Dizzy Dean, STL**
OBP—AL .347, Marv Olson, BOS	SV—AL 4, Johnny Allen, NY
NL .375, Arky Vaughan, PIT	NL 4, Bill Swift, PIT

*Brown's ERA of 3.296 edged Dizzy Dean's 3.304.

Chief Hogsett, hammers two home runs to give Detroit a 5–4 victory.

September 2—In his final big league start, Lew Krausse of the A's blanks the Red Sox 15–0; 29 years later his son, Lew Jr., will debut with a shutout for the A's, by then based in Kansas City.

◄ 1933 ►

Al Simmons was the first to go. The Philadelphia Athletics, holding their second fire sale in the last 20 years, dealt the future Hall of Famer just after the 1932 season ended. Over the next few years, three more eventual Cooperstown honorees—Lefty Grove, Mickey Cochrane, and Jimmie Foxx—would be discarded along with other vital cogs of the Athletics' machine that won three pennants and two World Series from 1929 through 1931.

Helping to fill the resulting vacuum was Bob Johnson, who replaced Simmons as the A's left fielder. While not able to duplicate Bucketfoot Al's staggering statistics, in 1933 Johnson did drive in 93 runs and hit 21 home runs, fourth highest in the AL. Combining a .290 average with 85 walks, he produced a solid .387 OBP. Johnson's 44 two-baggers not only ranked second in the league but also made him one of only three rookies ever to have at least 40 doubles and 80 bases on balls (Ted Williams and Ben Grieve are the other two).

A's teammate Pinky Higgins drove in even more runs than Johnson. Higgins, who inherited the hot corner after Jimmy Dykes was traded to the White Sox with Simmons, had 99 RBI, the most in the majors by a third sacker. On August 6 Higgins hit for the cycle, scored three times, and knocked in five as Philadelphia beat the Washington Senators 12–8. He is one of an exclusive quartet of freshman third basemen to have at least 10 doubles, triples, and home runs.

ROOKIE THIRD BASEMEN WITH TEN DOUBLES, TRIPLES, AND HOME RUNS

Ben Chapman, 1930 NY AL, 31 2B/10 3B/10 HR
Pinky Higgins, 1933 Phi AL, 35 2B/11 3B/13 HR
Harlond Clift, 1934 StL AL, 30 2B/10 3B/14 HR
Dick Allen, 1964 Phi NL, 38 2B/13 3B/29 HR

After 1933 the Athletics would not finish better than .500 again until 1947. The Detroit Tigers, however, were about to give Motor City fans much to celebrate, thanks in large part to four members of their 1933 rookie harvest. First baseman Hank Greenberg hit .301 and drove in 87 runs in only 117 games, foreshadowing the massive productive he would contribute to four Bengal pennant winners in the next 12 years. Outfielder Pete Fox, who teamed with Greenberg on the first three of those championship clubs, had 154 hits, including 13 triples in 1933. Right-handers Schoolboy Rowe and Elden Auker totaled only ten wins as frosh but combined for 76 victories over the next two seasons when Detroit took the AL flag in 1934 and then won its first World Championship in 1935.

As late as the 1930s it was still a common practice for players to shave a few years off their true age when they turned professional. "Indian" Bob Johnson got an especially belated start. The Cherokee outfielder was 22 years old by the time he played his first professional game with Wichita of the Western League in 1929 but claimed he was only 20. Though already past 26 when he joined the A's in 1933, Johnson is rated by some observers to have been the top graduate of that year's class, even better than its two most illustrious members, Hank Greenberg and Joe Medwick. The career hitting profiles for each of the three gives considerable support to that contention. Moreover, although all three were regarded as fairly good fielders, Johnson had a decided edge. Note that Greenberg's career stats are slimmer than Medwick's and Johnson's because he was the only one of the three who lost time to military service during World War II.

Name	G	AB	R	H	2B	3B	HR	HR%	RBI	BB	SO	BA	SA	OBP	OPS
Greenberg	1394	5193	1051	1628	379	71	331	6.37	1276	85 2	844	.313	.605	.412	1.017
Johnson	1863	6920	1239	2051	396	95	288	4.16	1283	1075	851	.296	.506	.393	.899
Medwick	1984	7635	1198	2471	540	113	205	2.69	1383	437	551	.324	.505	.362	.867

Greenberg, Fox, and Rowe first experienced winning together for the 1932 Texas League champion Beaumont Exporters, taking the MVP, batting crown, and ERA title, respectively. Fox hit .357, edging Houston's Joe Medwick, who finished at .354. Medwick was called up by the St. Louis Cardinals for the final month of the 1932 season and responded with a .349 average with 12 doubles in 26 games. In 1933 the Hungarian bammer from Carteret, New Jersey, picked up where he had left off by ranking in the top five in doubles (40), homers (18), RBI (98), runs (92), total bases (296), and slugging percentage (.497). In the succeeding years Medwick got only better, culminating in 1937 when he won the Triple Crown and became the last senior circuit player to do so.

Other Highlights

April 25—Russ Van Atta pitches a five-hit shutout in his ML debut, going 4-for-4 with two runs and an RBI for the New York Yankees, who pummel the Washington Senators 16–0.

May 15—Sugar Cain scores the only Philadelphia Athletics run as he blanks the Cleveland Indians 1–0.

May 16—Cecil Travis gets five singles for Washington in his first big league game as the Senators beat the Indians 11–10 in 12 innings.

September 11—Johnny Marcum, who four days earlier debuted with a shutout, in his second start tosses another whitewash effort for the Athletics and beats the White Sox 8–0.

1933 ROOKIE LEADERS

Batting	Pitching
G—AL 152, Pinky Higgins, PHI	W—AL 13, Sugar Cain, PHI
NL 148, Joe Medwick, STL	NL 8, Hal Smith, PIT
AB—AL 567, Pinky Higgins, PHI	L—AL 12, Sugar Cain, PHI
NL 595, Joe Medwick, STL	NL 7, Hal Smith, PIT
H—AL 178, Pinky Higgins, PHI	PCT—AL .750, Russ Van Atta, NY
NL 182, Joe Medwick, STL	NL No Qualifiers
2B—AL 44, Bob Johnson, PHI	GP—AL 38, Sugar Cain, PHI
NL 40, Joe Medwick, STL	NL 28, Hal Smith, PIT
3B—AL 13, Pete Fox, DET	GS—AL 32, Sugar Cain, PHI
NL 10, Joe Medwick, STL	NL 19, Hal Smith, PIT
HR—AL 21, Bob Johnson, PHI	CG—AL 16, Sugar Cain, PHI
NL 18, Joe Medwick, STL	NL 8, Hal Smith, PIT
R—AL 103, Bob Johnson, PHI	IP—AL 218, Sugar Cain, PHI
NL 92, Joe Medwick, STL	NL 145, Hal Smith, PIT
RBI—AL 99, Pinky Higgins, PHI	H—AL 244, Sugar Cain, PHI
NL 98, Joe Medwick, STL	NL 149, Hal Smith, PIT
WK—AL 85, Bob Johnson, PHI	BB—AL 137, Sugar Cain, PHI
NL 26, Otto Bluege, CIN	NL 35, John Jackson, PHI
Joe Medwick, STL	K—AL 76, Russ Van Atta, NY
SO—AL 78, Hank Greenberg, DET	NL 40, Hal Smith, PIT
NL 62, Blondy Ryan, NY	ERA—AL 4.18, Russ Van Atta, NY
SB—AL 15, Billy Werber, NY/BOS	NL No Qualifiers*
NL 7, Buzz Boyle, BRO	SHO—AL 2, Johnny Marcum, PHI
BA—AL .314, Pinky Higgins, PHI	Russ Van Atta, NY
NL .306, Joe Medwick, STL	NL 2, Hal Smith, PIT
SLG—AL .505, Bob Johnson, PHI	SV—AL 3, Don Brennan, NY
NL .497, Joe Medwick, STL	NL 1, Leroy Herrmann, CHI
OBP—AL .387, Bob Johnson, PHI	Hal Smith, PIT
NL .337, Joe Medwick, STL	

*Hal Smith of Pittsburgh had a stellar 2.86 ERA but worked only 145 innings, nine short of qualifying.

October 4—Alex McColl, at age 39, becomes the oldest rookie besides Satchel Paige ever to appear in a World Series game when he hurls two scoreless innings in relief for Washington in the Senators' 6–1 loss to the Giants in Game Two.

1934

Posting a winning record with the Philadelphia Phillies in the 1930s was never easy. The team wallowed below the .500 mark in all but one season from 1918 though 1948 and failed to have a single 20-game winner in that 31-year span. Rookie right-hander Curt Davis was one of the few Phillies to thrive in this barren climate. In 1934, Davis went 19–17 for Philadelphia while the rest of the Phils hill staff went 37–76 to land the team in seventh place. Only one other Phillies pitcher, rookie or veteran, won as many games during the aforementioned drought.

MOST WINS BY A PHILLIES PITCHER, 1918–48

19, Jumbo Elliott, 1931
19, Curt Davis, 1934
18, Jimmy Ring, 1923
17, Hal Carlson, 1926
17, Dutch Leonard, 1947

Davis's 2.95 ERA, which was bettered by only three pitchers in the NL, assumes added luster when his home park is considered. To say Baker Bowl was hitter friendly is like saying Babe Ruth had a bit of talent. The park, with its short porch in right field, was a major contributor to the Phillies having the worst ERA in the NL for 17 straight seasons from 1918 through 1934.

Like Davis, Paul "Daffy" Dean fell one victory shy of entrance into the charmed 20-win circle as a yearling. However, Dean won several games in the heat of a taut pennant race. On September 13 he pitched a 12-inning shutout against the first-place New York Giants. Three days later, Dizzy Dean's younger brother was slightly more human but still beat the host Giants for the sixth time in 1934. He permitted one run in 11 innings to win 3–1. On the 21st Paul Dean fired a no-hitter at Brooklyn

with only a first-inning walk to rookie Len Koenecke keeping him from perfection.

The Cardinals came back to win the flag and faced the Detroit Tigers in the World Series. Paul Dean won games three and six for the victorious Redbirds, who got their other two wins from his brother Dizzy. The younger Dean allowed only two earned runs in 18 innings.

The Philadelphia Athletics had a trio of right-handers who didn't approach 20 wins but all nonetheless exceeded ten. Johnny Marcum, who topped the staff with 14 victories and also served as a pinch hitter, had tossed shutouts in his first two ML starts the previous September. He fashioned two more whitewashes in 1934, a total matched by Joe Cascarella and doubled by Bill Dietrich. The latter two flingers won 12 and 11 games, respectively, for the 1934 Athletics, one of only four clubs to have three freshmen win at least ten games.

TEAMS WITH THREE ROOKIES WINNING TEN GAMES

1884 StL UA: Henry Boyle (15), Charlie Hodnett (12), Perry Werden (12)
1889 Chi NL: Frank Dwyer (16), Ad Gumbert (16), Bill Hutchison (16)
1934 Phi AL: Johnny Marcum (14), Joe Cascarella (12), Bill Dietrich (11)
1952 Bro NL: Joe Black (15), Billy Loes (13), Ben Wade (11)

On June 14 the trio of Athletics freshman hurlers witnessed the power of a rival rookie, Hal Trosky. The Cleveland first baseman hit two home runs, including a grand slam, and drove in six runs in the Indians' 11–7 win over the A's. Well before then AL hurlers in every city had grown accustomed to Trosky's lethal stroke. On May 30 he homered three times in the finale of a doubleheader with the Chicago White Sox. Trosky wound up with 35 round trippers, part of the rookie-record 89 extra-base hits he amassed. His 374 total bases stood alone as the rookie apex until 1964 when Tony Oliva duplicated the sum. Trosky finished in the top five of numerous offensive categories in 1934, but his 142 RBI and 206 hits gained him admission into a select group of five freshman hitters.

Note that four of the five on this elite list performed their feats between 1929 and 1938, which most authorities consider the most hitter friendly ten-year span in history.

ROOKIES WITH 200+ HITS AND 100+ RBI

Jimmy Williams, 1899 Pit NL: 220 H/116 RBI
Dale Alexander, 1929 Det AL: 215 H/137 RBI
Hal Trosky, 1934 Cle AL: 206 H/142 RBI
Joe DiMaggio, 1936 NY AL: 206 H/125 RBI
Frank McCormick, 1938 Cin NL: 209 H/106 RBI

Lost in the blizzard of Trosky's accomplishments were Zeke Bonura and Ray Pepper. Playing for the last-place White Sox, Bonura drove in 110 runs while Pepper plated 101 for the worst offensive club in the AL. Pepper's St. Louis Browns touched home only 674 times, with rookie third baseman Harlond Clift doing the honors on 104 occasions to lead the club.

Paying the price for the Brownies' woeful offense was Bobo Newsom, whose 4.01 ERA was well under the league average of 4.50. Newsom nevertheless went 16–20 and discovered, as Curt Davis did with the Phillies, that winning for an also-ran can be a very difficult task.

Other Highlights

May 7—Bill Lee of the Cubs shuts out the Phillies in his first ML start, winning 2–0.

June 7—Len Koenecke leads off the game with a home run and Dutch Leonard pitches a seven-hitter for the Brooklyn Dodgers, who beat the Phillies 1–0.

June 14—Johnny Broaca fires a one-hitter and strikes out ten St. Louis Browns for the New York Yankees, who win 7–0.

June 25—Johnny Broaca ties a record by fanning five straight times but pitches the Yankees to an easy 11–2 win over the White Sox.

July 8—Harlin Pool hits a grand slam and drives in five runs for the Cincinnati Reds, who top the St. Louis Cardinals 8–4 in the second half of a doubleheader.

Zeke Bonura's rookie slugging achievements were eclipsed in 1934 by Hal Trosky, but he still established several new highs for White Sox freshmen including home runs (27) and RBI (110). Additionally, Bonura took part in a significant record-setting performance on Opening Day, April 17, when he joined with five other Sox rookies—Frenchy Uhalt, Frenchy Bordagaray, Joe Chamberlain, John Pomorski, and Lee Stine—to establish the post-1901 mark for the most players on one team (six) making their ML debuts in the same game.

A far more significant record was set in 1934 by A's rookie Frankie Hayes when he caught 89 games while still just 19 years old to go to the head of the list for most games caught in a season by a teenage catcher. Note that the first teenage catching regular, Pop Snyder of the 1872 Washington Nationals, is not on the list because his team played only 39 games, of which he worked behind the plate in 28.

Rank	Name	Year	Age	G
1	Frankie Hayes	1934	19	89
2	Ivan Rodriguez	1991	19	88
3	Del Crandall	1949	19	63
4	Lew Brown	1877	19	55
5	Fred Carroll	1884	19	54
6	Eddie Ainsmith	1911	19	47
7	Lew Brown	1876	18	45
	Kid Baldwin	1884	19	45
9	Val Picinich	1916	19	37
10	Doggie Miller	1884	19	36

August 19—Moose Solters hits for the cycle, but his Boston Red Sox fall to Detroit 8–6 in the first game of a twinbill.

September 18—Bobo Newsom of the Browns permits a run but no hits for $9\frac{2}{3}$ innings, only to lose 2–1 to Rube Walberg of the Red Sox, who scratch out a hit and a run for Walberg with two out in the tenth.

September 21—The Dean brothers take turns shutting out the Dodgers in a twinbill when Paul Dean fashions a 3–0 no-hitter after Dizzy wins the opener with a 13–0 three-hitter and reportedly later says, "If'n Paul had told me he was gonna pitch a no-hitter, I'd of throwed one too."

1934 ROOKIE LEADERS

Batting		Pitching	
G—**AL 154, Hal Trosky, CLE**		W—AL 16, Bobo Newsom, STL	
NL 134, Dolph Camilli, CHI/PHI		NL 19, Curt Davis, PHI	
Lou Chiozza, PHI		Paul Dean, STL	
AB—AL 625, Hal Trosky, CLE		L—**AL 20, Bobo Newsom, STL**	
NL 498, Dolph Camilli, CHI/PHI		NL 17, Curt Davis, PHI	
H—AL 206, Hal Trosky, CLE		PCT—AL .444, Bobo Newsom, STL	
NL 147, Lou Chiozza, PHI		NL .633, Paul Dean, STL	
Len Koenecke, BRO		GP—AL 47, Bobo Newsom, STL	
2B—AL 45, Hal Trosky, CLE		**NL 51, Curt Davis, PHI**	
NL 31, Len Koenecke, BRO		GS—AL 32, Bobo Newsom, STL	
3B—AL 10, Harlond Clift, STL		NL 31, Curt Davis, PHI	
NL 7, Len Koenecke, BRO		CG—AL 17, Johnny Marcum, PHI	
HR—AL 35, Hal Trosky, CLE		NL 18, Curt Davis, PHI	
NL 16, Dolph Camilli, CHI/PHI		IP—AL 262.1, Bobo Newsom, STL	
R—AL 117, Hal Trosky, CLE		NL 274.1, Curt Davis, PHI	
NL 79, Len Koenecke, BRO		H—AL 259, Bobo Newsom, STL	
RBI—AL 142, Hal Trosky, CLE		NL 283, Curt Davis, PHI	
NL 87, Dolph Camilli, CHI/PHI		BB—**AL 149, Bobo Newsom, STL**	
WK—AL 84, Harlond Clift, STL		NL 74, Bill Lee, CHI	
NL 70, Len Koenecke, BRO		K—AL 135, Bobo Newsom, STL	
SO—**AL 100, Harlond Clift, STL**		NL 150, Paul Dean, STL	
NL 94, Dolph Camilli, CHI/PHI		ERA—AL 3.12, Johnny Murphy, NY	
SB—AL 9, Moose Solters, BOS		NL 2.95, Curt Davis, PHI	
NL 11, Lonny Frey, BRO		SHO—AL 4, Bill Dietrich, PHI	
BA—AL .330, Hal Trosky, CLE		NL 5, Paul Dean, STL	
NL .320, Len Koenecke, BRO		SV—AL 5, Bobo Newsom, STL	
SLG—AL .598, Hal Trosky, CLE		NL 5, Curt Davis, PHI	
NL .509, Len Koenecke, BRO		Dutch Leonard, BRO	
OBP—AL .388, Hal Trosky, CLE		Al Smith, NY	
NL .411, Len Koenecke, BR			

◄— 1935 —►

If any nickname can lead to high expectations for a pitcher, it is the sobriquet borne by the greatest winner of all time, Denton True "Cy" Young. Darrell Elijah Blanton did not disappoint Pittsburgh fans in 1935. Cy Blanton dropped his major league debut on September 23, 1934, despite permitting only three runs in eight innings. He began 1935 on a better note, however. On April 19 Blanton tossed a one-hit shutout against the defending world champion St. Louis Cardinals, fanning six. He also drove in the game's go-ahead run and won 3–0. Two weeks later, Blanton topped Brooklyn 1–0, allowing but three hits and lowering his ERA to 0.80 in five games.

Blanton's ERA would rise over the summer but not enough to prevent him from leading the National League in that department. His 142 strikeouts remain unsurpassed in Pittsburgh rookie annals since 1887 when the club first joined the National League, while his four shutouts tied for the loop high and also matched the Pirates' rookie record.

Two of Blanton's victories came against the Chicago Cubs, who were greatly aided in their pennant-winning season by Chicago natives Phil Cavarretta and Roy Henshaw. Cavarretta, a graduate of Lane Technical High School just a few miles west of Wrigley Field, succeeded Charlie Grimm as the Cubs' first baseman. He negated some defensive shortcomings (a league-worst 20 miscues) by driving in 82 runs, third most on the

It was said of Cy Blanton that he possessed "a sinkerball that wears no parachute." In 1935 Blanton not only led all rookies in the majors in wins with 18, but he fashioned stats that would one day earn *Total Baseball*'s accolade as the best pitcher in the NL that season. Blanton's 4.6 TPI topped even that of 28-game winner Dizzy Dean (4.2). The premier rating stemmed mostly from the fact that the new Pirates ace paced the NL in OBA and OOBP as well as ERA. *Transcendental Graphics*

team. Four of those RBI came in the second game of an August 21 doubleheader when he went 5-for-6 with a double in the Cubs' 19–5 pounding of the Philadelphia Phillies at Baker Bowl.

Henshaw, a University of Chicago alumnus, narrowly missed baseball immortality June 28 when he fired a one-hitter against the Pirates. Rookie pitcher Mace Brown doubled off the glove of Cubs centerfielder Freddie Lindstrom for the Bucs' only safety. Henshaw's 8–0 win was one of three shutouts in the southpaw's 13–5 season. His last two victories came

during the Cubs' 21-game winning streak in which they wrapped up the NL flag.

The two freshman Bruins fell on harder times in the World Series. Cavarretta went 3-for-24 and Henshaw surrendered three earned runs in fewer than four innings of relief.

Besides Cy Blanton, only two freshman pitchers topped 200 innings pitched, and both played for the AL Chicago White Sox. A pair of right-handers, John Whitehead and Vern Kennedy, threw 222.1 and 211.2 innings, respectively. Whitehead went 13–13 and Kennedy finished 11–11, which made them the two winningest rookies in the junior circuit in 1935.

But rookie hurlers were not the whole story that year. Only one team from 1915 through 1981 featured four recruits with at least 100 hits—the 1935 Cincinnati Reds. Leading the way was rightfielder Ival Goodman with 159. Third baseman Lew Riggs was second with 148 while second sacker Alex Kampouris (123) and shortstop Billy Myers (119) completed the foursome.

Other Highlights

May 30—Vito Tamulis blanks the Washington Senators 4–0; it is the third shutout for the New York Yankees southpaw in the last two weeks.

In addition to Cy Blanton, the Pirates had a second outstanding rookie in keystoner Pep Young. Despite getting into only 128 games in his frosh season and collecting less than 500 at bats, Young drove in 82 runs, the third highest total ever for a National League rookie second baseman and the most since 1909. But Young was the first of what in the next few years would become a long parade of Pittsburgh rookies who would never again match their freshman RBI totals. Apart from 1935, his RBI high was 79 in 1938, which was also his final season as a regular.

MOST RBI BY A NATIONAL LEAGUE ROOKIE SECOND BASEMAN

Name	Team	Year	RBI
Bill Lange	Chicago	1893	88
Dots Miller	Pittsburgh	1909	87
Pep Young	Pittsburgh	1935	82
Heinie Reitz	Baltimore	1893	76
Ace Stewart	Chicago	1895	76

1935 ROOKIE LEADERS

Batting	Pitching
G—AL 151, Mel Almada, BOS	W—AL 13, John Whitehead, CHI
NL 148, Ival Goodman, CIN	NL 18, Cy Blanton, PIT
Alex Kampouris, CIN	L—AL 13, John Whitehead, CHI
AB—AL 623, Rip Radcliff, CHI	NL 15, Orville Jorgens, PHI
NL 592, Ival Goodman, CIN	PCT—AL .667, Vito Tamulis, NY
H—AL 178, Rip Radcliff, CHI	NL .714, Slick Castleman, NY
NL 162, Phil Cavarretta, CHI	GP—AL 55, Jim Walkup, STL
2B—AL 28, Rip Radcliff, CHI	**NL 53, Orville Jorgens, PHI**
NL 34, Terry Moore, STL	GS—AL 27, John Whitehead, CHI
3B—AL 10, Jake Powell, WAS	NL 31, Cy Blanton, PIT
NL 18, Ival Goodman, CIN	CG—AL 18, John Whitehead, CHI
HR—AL 10, Rip Radcliff, CHI	NL 23, Cy Blanton, PIT
NL 12, Ival Goodman, CIN	IP—AL 222.1, John Whitehead, CHI
R—AL 95, Rip Radcliff, CHI	NL 254.1, Cy Blanton, PIT
NL 86, Ival Goodman, CIN	H—AL 226, Jim Walkup, STL
RBI—AL 98, Jake Powell, WAS	NL 220, Jim Bivin, PHI
NL 82, Phil Cavarretta, CHI	Cy Blanton, PIT
Pep Young, PIT	BB—AL 104, Jim Walkup, STL
WK—AL 56, Babe Dahlgren, BOS	NL 96, Orville Jorgens, PHI
NL 43, Lew Riggs, CIN	K—AL 80, Whitey Wilshere, PHI
SO—AL 97, Boze Berger, CLE	NL 142, Cy Blanton, PIT
NL 84, Alex Kampouris, CIN	ERA—AL 3.72, John Whitehead, CHI
SB—AL 20, Mel Almada, BOS	**NL 2.58, Cy Blanton, PIT**
NL 18, Frenchy Bordagaray, BRO	SH—AL 3, Vito Tamulis, NY
BA—AL .312, Jake Powell, WAS	Whitey Wilshere, PHI
NL .302, Jim Bucher, BRO	**NL 4, Cy Blanton, PIT**
SLG—AL .428, Jake Powell, WAS	SV—AL 3, Leon Pettit, WAS
NL .429, Ival Goodman, CIN	NL 2, Clay Bryant, CHI
OBP—AL .360, Jake Powell, WAS	Ed Heusser, STL
NL .334, Lew Riggs, CIN	Orville Jorgens, PHI
	Bobby Reis, BRO

June 5—White Sox recruit John Whitehead, a winner in all of his first eight starts in the majors, suffers his first loss when Jack Knott of the Browns shuts out the Sox 2–0 at Sportsman's Park; Whitehead will not win again until the first game of a July 4 doubleheader at Sportsman's Park when he gets his revenge, beating Knott 11–6.

June 6—Henry Coppola throws a shutout for the Senators in his first ML start, beating the Boston Red Sox 3–0.

July 5—Rookie second sacker Al Cuccinello of the Giants and his brother Tony of the Reds are the first pair of siblings in ML history to homer for opposing teams in the same game.

August 31—Vern Kennedy hurls the first American League no-hitter in four years as the Chicago White Sox top the Cleveland Indians 5–0; Kennedy also hits a three-run triple in his gem.

September 5—Centerfielder Terry Moore goes 6-for-6 with a double, two runs, and two RBI as the Cardinals destroy the Boston Braves 15–3.

September 29—Catcher Aubrey Epps of Pittsburgh goes 3-for-4 with a triple and three RBI in his only major league game, but the Pirates lose nonetheless to the Cincinnati Reds 9–6 in the second game of a doubleheader to ring down the curtain on the 1935 season.

◄ 1936 ►

The first elections for the Baseball Hall of Fame were in 1936, and four of that year's rookies eventually would be immortalized in the shrine. The Cooperstown-bound quartet comprised one outfielder, an infielder, a pitcher, and a future manager.

The fly hawk, Joe DiMaggio, was well known to baseball fans before joining the New York Yankees. DiMaggio had hit in 61 consecutive games in the Pacific Coast League in 1933, and two years later he led that circuit with 154 RBI and was named MVP. In 1936 DiMaggio was out of the Yankee lineup until May 3 because of a bad foot but immediately made up for lost time by going 3-for-6 with a triple and three runs in his debut. In mid-May DiMaggio had back-to-back four-hit games, collecting five doubles. On June 24 the 21-year-old made history. DiMaggio hit a record-tying two home runs in a ten-run Yankees fifth inning, five of the runs scoring on the rookie's blasts. He also ripped two doubles in New York's 18–11 victory against the Chicago White Sox.

On July 7, at Braves Field in Boston, DiMaggio became the first rookie to start in an All-Star Game. (The St. Louis Cardinals' recruit second baseman, Stu Martin, was on the National League squad but did not play.) The Yankee went 0-for-5 with an error in right field. He also misplayed another ball in the NL's 4–3 win, the first senior circuit triumph in a Midsummer Classic. That was one of DiMaggio's few low points in a freshman campaign that saw him produce these staggering statistics:

JOE DIMAGGIO'S ROOKIE STATS

637 at bats (team rookie record)
206 hits (sixth in AL; team rookie record)
44 doubles (seventh in AL; team rookie record)
15 triples (tied for tops in AL; team rookie record)
29 home runs (fourth in AL; team rookie record)
132 runs (sixth in AL; team rookie record)
125 RBI (tied for eighth in AL; team rookie record)
.576 SA (team rookie record)

DiMaggio accomplished all this while playing in only 138 games, and these stats don't even take into account his seemingly effortless defense while patrolling the outfield.

In the Yankees' World Series victory over the crosstown Giants, Joltin' Joe went 9-for-26 with three doubles, three runs, and a trio of RBI.

While DiMaggio would become an icon of his era, another symbol of that time was amazing fans in Cleveland. Bob Feller broke into the bigs with a scoreless inning of relief on July 19 at Washington. The 17-year-old flamethrower remained in the bullpen until August 23. That day, in his first start, Feller blew away 15 St. Louis Browns, beating them 4–1 and earning his first major league win. Three weeks later, he set an AL record by fanning 17 Philadelphia Athletics. Feller allowed only two hits but walked nine, hit another, and made a wild pitch.

Feller finished 5–3 and despite working only 62 innings had 76 strikeouts, third best among rookies in 1936. Not since Toad Ramsey in 1885 had a rookie averaged more than a strikeout per inning (minimum 50 IP).

Before making his major league debut, Feller had pitched an exhibition game against the St. Louis Cardinals, the team of first baseman Johnny Mize. By driving in 93 runs, Mize shattered Chick Stahl's 1897 record for fewest at bats by an NL freshman who topped the 90 RBI plateau. Stahl had 469 ABs, Mize 414. The lefty-batting Mize had a .577 slugging average, third best in the NL, and 57 extra-base hits. Only one senior circuit rookie has ever surpassed 55 long hits in fewer at bats than did Mize—fellow Cardinal George Watkins in 1930.

On September 27, in the final game of the season, Mize made remarks that umpire Ziggy Sears found objectionable. Sears ejected Mize, who was replaced at first base by a rookie that was playing his only major league game. The replacement, who struck out against Lon Warneke in his only at bat, would win seven pennants and four World Series as a major league manager. He thus became the fourth Hall of Famer who debuted in 1936. His name was Walter Alston.

After taking over the White Sox centerfield post midway through the 1936 season, Larry Rosenthal notched 71 runs and 89 hits. Both of these modest rookie figures turned out to be personal highs for him in a seemingly undistinguished eight-year career that was extended only by the manpower shortage in the majors during World War II. But Rosenthal, although never again more than a part-time player after his rookie season, was actually a much more valuable asset than any of his numerous managers in the majors realized. He ranks first in walks and second in runs among all retired players active since 1901 who collected less than 1,500 career at bats. Note that many of the names on these lists are renowned either as terrific role players or for one or two outstanding seasons whereas Rosenthal, to most followers of the game, is a total nonentity. Here are both top-ten lists.

MOST WALKS, POST-1901 RETIRED PLAYERS (LESS THAN 1,500 ABs)

Rank	Name	AB	BB
1	Larry Rosenthal	1483	251
2	Pat Collins	1204	235
3	Phil Weintraub	1382	232
4	Les Fleming	1330	226
5	Jack Hiatt	1142	224
	Ron Hodges	1426	224
7	Dave Nicholson	1419	219
8	Tony Solaita	1316	214
9	Don Lenhardt	1481	214
10	Sandy Amoros	1311	211
	Al Wingo	1326	211

MOST RUNS, POST-1901 RETIRED PLAYERS (LESS THAN 1,500 ABs)

Rank	Name	AB	R
1	Dave Harris	1447	243
2	Larry Rosenthal	1483	240
3	Lefty Davis	1296	232
4	Milt Cuyler	1386	227
5	Al Wingo	1326	224
6	Fred Brickell	1448	221
7	George Myatt	1345	220
8	Denny Sothern	1355	219
9	Phil Weintraub	1382	215
	Sandy Amoros	1311	215

Other Highlights

April 14—Eddie Morgan homers on the first major league pitch he sees, but the Chicago Cubs beat Morgan's St. Louis Cardinals 12–7.

April 28—Leo Norris goes 5-for-5 with a homer, a double, and three RBI as the Philadelphia Phillies top Pittsburgh 9–7.

June 27—Cleveland's Roy Weatherly ties the ML rookie record by clubbing two triples in his debut; Weatherly drives in four, and the Tribe pounds the Boston Red Sox 14–5.

August 25—Gene Moore goes 5-for-7 with three doubles and 5 RBI for the Braves, who maul the Cardinals 20–3 in the first game of a doubleheader.

August 29—Les Scarsella collects five hits, one a home run, plus three runs and three RBI as the Cincinnati Reds beats Brooklyn 12–2.

September 11—Mike Kreevich is 5-for-6, scores four times, and knocks in three with two doubles and a triple as his Chicago White Sox annihilate the Athletics 17–2.

September 23—Cleveland's Bob Feller breaks Rube Waddell's 28-year-old single-game nine-inning AL record when he fans 17 A's.

October 3—Jimmy Ripple homers, accounting for the New York Giants' only run in their 2–1 loss to the New York Yankees in Game Three of the World Series.

1936 ROOKIE LEADERS

Batting	Pitching
G—AL 143, Buddy Lewis, WAS	W—AL 15, Harry Kelley, PHI
NL 156, Buddy Hassett, BRO	NL 11, Harry Gumbert, NY
AB—AL 637, Joe DiMaggio, NY	Claude Passeau, PHI
NL 637, Gene Moore, BOS	Jim Winford, STL
H—AL 206, Joe DiMaggio, NY	L—AL 16, Herman Fink, PHI
NL 197, Buddy Hassett, BRO	NL 15, Claude Passeau, PHI
2B—AL 44, Joe DiMaggio, NY	PCT—AL .556, Harry Kelley, PHI
NL 38, Gene Moore, BOS	NL .524, Jim Winford, STL
3B—AL 15, Joe DiMaggio, NY	GP—AL 36, Denny Galehouse, CLE
NL 12, Gene Moore, BOS	NL 49, Claude Passeau, PHI
HR—AL 29, Joe DiMaggio, NY	GS—AL 27, Harry Kelley, PHI
NL 19, Johnny Mize, STL	Buck Ross, PHI
R—AL 132, Joe DiMaggio, NY	NL 23, Jim Winford, STL
NL 91, Gene Moore, BOS	CG—AL 20, Harry Kelley, PHI
RBI—AL 125, Joe DiMaggio, NY	NL 10, Jim Winford, STL
NL 102. Bill Brubaker, PIT	IP—AL 235.1, Harry Kelley, PHI
WK—AL 61, Mike Kreevich, CHI	NL 217.1, Claude Passeau, PHI
NL 50, Bill Brubaker, PIT	H—AL 253, Buck Ross, PHI
Johnny Mize, STL	NL 247, Claude Passeau, PHI
SO—AL 46, Mike Kreevich, CHI	BB—AL 83, Buck Ross, PHI
Buddy Lewis, WAS	NL 68, Jim Winford, STL
NL 96, Bill Brubaker, PIT	K—AL 82, Harry Kelley, PHI
SB—AL 10, Mike Kreevich, CHI	NL 85, Claude Passeau, PHI
NL 17, Stu Martin, STL	ERA—AL 3.86, Harry Kelley, PHI
BA—AL .323, Joe DiMaggio, NY	NL 3.48, Claude Passeau, PHI
NL .329, Johnny Mize, STL	SHO—AL 1, Harry Kelley, PHI
SLG—AL .576, Joe DiMaggio, NY	Buck Ross, PHI
NL .577, Johnny Mize, STL	Jake Wade, DET
OBP—AL .378, Mike Kreevich, CHI	NL 2, Claude Passeau, PHI
NL .402, Johnny Mize, STL	Roy Weir, BOS
	SV—AL 3, Herman Fink, PHI
	Harry Kelley, PHI
	NL 5, Peaches Davis, CIN

◄— 1937 —►

"Trip aces" sounds like a winning poker hand—but in 1937 it described a trio of rookie pitchers. Two of the freshmen, right-handers Jim Turner and Lou Fette, pitched for the Boston Braves while southpaw Cliff Melton twirled for the pennant-winning New York Giants. The triumvirate all won 20 games and dotted the NL leader boards, each finishing in the top five in wins, winning percentage, and ERA.

Fette and Turner both tossed five shutouts, becoming just the second rookie tandem to reach that total. (The 1910 New York Highlanders received eight blank-

ings from Russ Ford and five from Hippo Vaughn.) On June 29 Fette threw his third whitewash of the month, driving in the winning run in the 12th inning to beat Brooklyn 1–0. Less than two weeks later, he shut out the Philadelphia Phillies 1–0, going the full 13 frames. On October 2 Turner picked up his 20th win, a 7–1 besting of the Phillies. The following day, in Boston's final game of the season, the Phils became Fette's patsies as well when he joined Turner in the charmed circle by blanking them 6–0.

Coincidentally, the Phillies also had suffered the defeat five days earlier on September 29 that gave Melton his 20th triumph. Unlike the Braves duo, Melton did a lot of bullpen work, winning four games and topping the league with seven saves in 19 relief appearances. It was in this role that Melton had his best success in the World Series against the Bronx-based Yankees. In Game Three he pitched two scoreless innings of relief, but the Giants still lost 5–1. Melton was roughed up in his two starts, losing both, and the Yanks took the series in five games.

While the three aces all fashioned ERAs well below the league average of 3.92, Wayne LaMaster of the lowly Phils far exceeded the norm. He won 15 games, albeit with 19 defeats, posting a 5.31 ERA, the worst ever for a freshman who had 15 or more wins.

HIGHEST ERA BY ROOKIE WITH 15 WINS

5.31 ERA/15 W, Wayne LaMaster, 1937 Phi NL
5.10 ERA/15 W, Jeriome Robertson, 2003 Hou NL
5.02 ERA/15 W, Bob Hooper, 1950 Phi AL
4.74 ERA/18 W, Danny Friend, 1896 Chi NL
4.65 ERA/16 W, Bill Carrick, 1899 NY NL
4.57 ERA/17 W, Sid Hudson, 1940 Was AL

The NL produced no less than five freshmen who won in double figures—the aforementioned four and Russ Bauers, a 13-game winner for the Pittsburgh Pirates. The junior circuit featured only two such hurlers, and both toiled for the Detroit Tigers. George Gill and Boots Poffenberger won 11 and ten games, respectively, but it was their powerful teammate who won the yearling accolades in the AL. Rudy York hit 18 home runs— in August alone! That remains the most any AL slugger ever amassed in one month and was the overall standard until Sammy Sosa ripped 20 round trippers in June 1998 for the Chicago Cubs. York's "august" August included three multi-homer games and his second grand slam of the season. On August 31 he drove in seven runs and pounded his 17th and 18th circuit shots of the month, eclipsing the previous ML record of 17, established by Babe Ruth in September 1927.

York hit "only" five homers in the final month of the season, giving him 35 for the year. Of the nine rookies to amass that amount, York's 375 ABs are by far the fewest. Ron Kittle in 1983 is second with 520—or 145 more. York was also the lone freshman in the twentieth century to compile 100 RBI in fewer than 500 ABs. Not bad for a guy who played the majority of his games as a catcher.

Ace Parker and Gene Hasson combined to hit 30

The luckiest rookie in 1937 might have been Rudy York, who snared 103 RBI and 37 home runs on just 115 hits. Then again, it might have been the Boston Bees hill tandem of Jim Turner or Lou Fette, the only two 30-year-old rookies since Henry Schmidt in 1903 to bag 20 wins. Or it might have been Earle Brucker who, at age 36, became the oldest frosh ever to serve as his team's regular catcher when he won the A's backstopping job, but there is no doubt as to that year's unluckiest rookie. It was one of Brucker's frequent battery mates, a 23-year-old southpaw named Eddie Smith. For his work in 1937, *Total Baseball* awards Smith a 1.6 TPI rating despite the fact that he had a .190 winning percentage and led all AL rookies with 17 losses.

Much of TB's high rating is based on Smith's excellent .242 OBA and 3.94 ERA, which was .69 runs below the league average. Smith never did get lucky. He finished with a career TPI rating of 5.2, higher than some pitchers who have received serious Hall of Fame consideration, but just a .392 winning percentage.

fewer homers than did York, but each left his mark in the record books. On April 30 Parker had a two-run pinch-hit homer in his first big league AB. Hasson followed Parker's lead on September 9, ripping a three-runner off Senators rookie Dick Lanahan in his initial ML AB. They were the first of three such teammate duos in history.

TEAMS WITH TWO ROOKIES HOMERING IN THEIR FIRST ABs

1937 Phi AL, Ace Parker (April 30), Gene Hasson (September 9)
1997 Mon NL, Dustin Hermanson (April 16), Brad Fullmer (September 2)
2000 StL NL, Keith McDonald (July 4), Chris Richard (July 17)

Parker would hit only one additional career home run but had greater success on the gridiron, so much in fact that he would be inducted into both the college and pro football halls of fame. This fourth "Ace" helped make the 1937 season one of the best ever for rookies.

Other Highlights

April 25—Rookie southpaw Cliff Melton sets a new NL record for the most Ks in his first ML start with 13—and

1937 ROOKIE LEADERS

Batting		Pitching	
G—AL 123, Buster Mills, BOS		W—AL 11, George Gill, DET	
NL 146, George Scharein, PHI		NL 20, Lou Fette, BOS	
AB—AL 505, Buster Mills, BOS		Cliff Melton, NY	
NL 579, Hersh Martin, PHI		Jim Turner, BOS	
H—AL 149, Buster Mills, BOS		L—AL 17, Eddie Smith, PHI	
NL 164, Hersh Martin, PHI		**NL 19, Wayne LaMaster, PHI**	
2B—AL 25, Buster Mills, BOS		PCT—AL .348, Bud Thomas, PHI	
NL 35, Hersh Martin, PHI		NL .690, Cliff Melton, NY	
3B—AL 8, Buster Mills, BOS		GP—AL 38, Eddie Smith, PHI	
NL 12, Lee Handley, PIT		NL 50, Wayne LaMaster, PHI	
HR—AL 35, Rudy York, DET		GS—AL 26, Bud Thomas, PHI	
NL 13, Vince DiMaggio, BOS		NL 33, Lou Fette, BOS	
R—AL 85, Buster Mills, BOS		CG—AL 14, Eddie Smith, PHI	
NL 102, Hersh Martin, PHI		**NL 24, Jim Turner, BOS**	
RBI—AL 103, Rudy York, DET		IP—AL 196.2, Eddie Smith, PHI	
NL 74, Don Padgett, STL		NL 259, Lou Fette, BOS	
WK—AL 48, Earle Brucker, PHI		H—AL 208, Bud Thomas, PHI	
NL 69, Hersh Martin, PHI		NL 255, Wayne LaMaster, PHI	
SO—AL 66, Chet Laabs, DET		BB—AL 90, Eddie Smith, PHI	
NL 111, Vince DiMaggio, BOS		NL 82, Wayne LaMaster, PHI	
SB—AL 11, Buster Mills, BOS		K—AL 79, Eddie Smith, PHI	
NL 13, George Scharein, PHI		NL 142, Cliff Melton, NY	
BA—AL .295, Buster Mills, BOS		ERA—AL 3.94, Eddie Smith, PHI	
NL .314, Don Padgett, STL		**NL 2.38, Jim Turner, BOS**	
SLG—AL .418, Buster Mills, BOS		SH—AL 2, Spud Chandler, NY	
NL .457, Don Padgett, STL		**NL 5, Lou Fette, BOS**	
OBP—AL .361, Buster Mills, BOS		**Jim Turner, BOS**	
NL .362, Hersh Martin, PHI		SV—AL 5, Eddie Smith, PHI	
		NL 7, Cliff Melton, NY	

also a new NL mark for the most Ks in a losing effort when he's beaten 3–1 by Guy Bush of the Boston Bees.

August 29—Ray Harrell of the St. Louis Cardinals fires a one hitter against the Boston Bees, stinging them 3–0 in the second game of a twinbill.

September 6—Bill Phebus allows only one Boston Red Sox hit and his Washington Senators win 2–0.

September 9—Joe Krakauskas wins his ML debut, pitching seven innings of one-hit scoreless relief for the Senators, who beat the Philadelphia Athletics 13–6 in a twinbill opener that was also highlighted by Gene Hasson's debut feat (see 1937 summary).

September 29—Eddie Smith of the Athletics pitches a seven-inning shutout, yielding but one safety to the New York Yankees, who drop the abbreviated nightcap of a twinbill 3–0.

1938

In the early years of baseball, when the rules were still in flux and almost every pitcher or batter had his own unique style, there was a saying that every game would provide something that had never been seen before on the ballfield. That was certainly true on April 19, 1938, when not one but *two* batters homered in their first ML at bats in the same game—the only such occurrence in baseball history. Brooklyn's Ernie Koy and the Phillies' Heinie Mueller performed the feat in the Dodgers' 12–5 Opening Day win. Mueller finished the season batting a lackluster .250 in 136 games, but Koy teamed with Goody Rosen to give Brooklyn two speedy freshmen. Koy rapped .299, led all rookies with 15 steals, and beat out 13 triples. He also hit 11 home runs. Rosen collected 11 three-baggers and in early May had eight consecutive hits over a three-game span.

But these Flatbush fly chasers weren't even close to being the top rookie tandem in 1938. Cleveland's Jeff Heath and Ken Keltner are the only rookie teammates each to drive in 110 or more runs, with 112 and 113, respectively. Heath also hit an AL-leading 18 triples and banged out 31 two-baggers plus 21 round trippers. He joined Buck Freeman (1899) as the only freshmen to rack up as many as 18 in each extra-base-hit department. It also bears mentioning that Heath boasted a .343 average and scored 104 times. All that—and he played only 126 games!

FEWEST GAMES BY ROOKIE WITH 100 RUNS AND 100 RBI

126 (104 R/112 RBI), Jeff Heath, 1938 Cle AL
128 (130 R/114 RBI), Jimmy Bannon, 1894 Bos NL
135 (107 R/104 RBI), Bug Holliday, 1889 Cin AA
136 (101 R/144 RBI), Walt Dropo, 1950 Bos AL
138 (132 R/125 RBI), Joe DiMaggio, 1936 NY AL

Keltner, meanwhile, powdered 66 extra-base hits, and his RBI total was the most by an AL freshman third baseman until his successor in Cleveland, Al Rosen, surpassed it in 1950. Keltner's best season came in 1948, when the world champion Indians had Joe Gordon at second base. In 1938, however, Gordon was a New York Yankees rookie, and an outstanding one at that. He hit 25 home runs, the most ever for a rookie second sacker, and contributed 97 runs to the high-powered Bronx Bomber offense. Gordon slugged two homers and a triple, driving in six runners in Monte Pearson's no-hitter against Cleveland on August 27. Eight days later, Gordon blasted two more round trippers, along with a pair of doubles in New York's 7–4 besting of Washington. In the World Series he batted a nifty .400 and knocked in six mates during the Yankees' sweep of the Chicago Cubs.

Before joining the Yankees, Gordon had grown accustomed to playing for dominant teams, having been on the 1937 Newark Bears, considered one of the best clubs in minor league history. Also on that Yankees farm team was first baseman George McQuinn, whose way to the parent club was blocked by Lou Gehrig. Consequently, McQuinn was sold to the St. Louis Browns over the winter. In 1938 the Brownies new gateway guardian hit .324, lashing 195 hits, including 42 doubles, second best in the loop. Late in the season McQuinn also batted safely in a rookie-record 34 straight games, capping what many authorities believe to have been the finest year ever by a Browns' yearling.

The 1937 Newark team had won the International League pennant by 25½ games, gone 8–0 in the IL playoffs, and then beaten the American Association's Columbus club in the Junior World Series. Like Newark, Columbus, part of the Cardinals chain, showcased two players who would shine in the big leagues the following year. Johnny Rizzo, sold to Pittsburgh, set a new Pirates' franchise record with his 20th home run, an 11th-inning game-winning shot on September 16, 1938. He finished with 23, hitting a round tripper at every league playing field, including both that were used that season in Philadelphia once the Phils gave up the Baker Bowl and joined the A's in playing at Shibe Park. Rizzo topped the Corsairs, which were in first place as late as September 27, with 111 RBI. Rizzo's former Columbus teammate, fellow outfielder Enos Slaughter, batted .276 with ten triples in 112 Cardinals contests.

In 1938 Rizzo was not the only rookie to place among the NL's top RBI men. Frank McCormick sent home 106 Reds runners while collecting a league-leading 209 hits to launch what would become an NL-record three straight seasons in which he paced the loop in safeties. The first baseman batted .327, third highest in the circuit, and had 40 two-baggers, second most in the league. In the All-Star Game McCormick played the entire contest as the senior circuit's first sacker, getting a single off Lefty Grove and scoring once in the NL's 4–1 victory. On August 22 McCormick got five hits and four runs at St. Louis and later had a 5-for-5 day at Chicago on September 10. McCormick shared a room on the road and an apartment at home in Cincinnati with fellow Reds freshman Harry Craft, who collected 83 RBI and 165 hits in his own right.

Last but far from least among the many exciting new rookie offensive tandems in 1938 were Washington outfielders George Case and Taffy Wright. After tying for the AL rookie lead in steals as a freshman, Case would pace the majors in thefts in each of the next four seasons. Wright celebrated his recruit season by hitting an AL high .350 and also topping the junior circuit with 13 pinch hits. Wright played in 100 games, the unwritten eligibility standard at that time for the batting title, but notched only 263 at bats, forcing an impromptu ruling that named Jimmie Foxx, with a .349 BA, the league's official batting champion.

Although all of the year's top rookies were hitters, there were a healthy number of reasonably successful new pitchers as well, including four who won in double figures. Jim Bagby logged 15 wins for the Red Sox, including a three-hit blanking of the Athletics on August 18. Bob Klinger took twelve for Pittsburgh, Lefty Mills ten for the Browns, and Tot Pressnell shut out the Phillies in his ML debut on April 21 en route to winning 11 times for Brooklyn.

Other Highlights

June 10—Bill Lefebvre homers in his first ML at bat and only plate appearance of the season but gets no decision in a relief role in the Chicago White Sox' 15–2 romp over his Red Sox.

June 22—Hank Steinbacher gets five singles and a double, scoring thrice and driving in two as the White Sox thrash Washington 16–3.

August 5—Still technically a rookie, 44-year-old Fred Johnson, who will win over 250 games in the minors over his long career, earns his first major league win since 1923 when he hurls the Browns to a 9–2 triumph over the Athletics.

August 6—Vance Page finally reaches the majors with the Cubs a month short of his 33rd birthday after toiling in the minors for 13 years; despite his belated entry, Page will pitch four seasons with the Cubs.

The A's had a string of execrable teams in the late 1930s. In consequence, even good rookie pitchers with Connie Mack's club, like Eddie Smith in 1937, tended to fare poorly. Hence it was no surprise when Nels Potter could win just two of 14 decisions in 1938 given his 6.47 ERA with the last-place A's. The shocker was that Mack kept Potter in the rotation after he posted an even more hideous 6.60 ERA in his sophomore season. It was one of the few times in the twilight years of Mack's long managerial career that his patience paid dividends.

Potter completed his ML tenure ten years later in 1949 as the only pitcher in history to post a career ERA below 4.00 after boasting an ERA above 6.50 for his first 300 innings of hill duty. Making his climb to respectability even more remarkable is the fact that his 6.60 ERA in 1939, his first year as a qualifier, is one of the ten worst ERAs since 1901. Note that five new names have joined the list just since 1994.

WORST ERAS BY QUALIFIERS SINCE 1901

Rank	Name	Team	Year	ERA
1	Les Sweetland	Phi-NL	1930	7.71
2	Jim Deshaies	Min-AL	1994	7.39
3	Jack Knott	StL-AL	1936	7.29
4	LaTroy Hawkins	Min-AL	1999	6.66
5	Jose Lima	Hou-NL	2000	6.65
	Greg Harris	Col-NL	1994	6.65
7	Chubby Dean	Phi-AL	1940	6.61
	Darryl Kile	Col-NL	1999	6.61
9	Nels Potter	Phi-AL	1939	6.60
10	Ernie Wingard	StL-AL	1927	6.56

August 25—Browns first sacker George McQuinn's 34-game hitting streak, which remains a rookie record (though since tied by Benito Santiago), is stopped by Athletics hurlers just seven games short of the then-existing AL record of 41 games, held by a former Browns first sacker also named George—Sisler.

September 17—Merv Connors hits three homers and a double and knocks in five runs for the White Sox, who top the Athletics 7–4 in the nightcap of a twinbill.

Batting		Pitching	
G—AL 149, Ken Keltner, CLE		W—AL 15, Jim Bagby, BOS	
NL 151, Harry Craft, CIN		NL 12, Bob Klinger, PIT	
Frank McCormick, CIN		L—AL 12, Lefty Mills, STL	
AB—AL 602, George McQuinn, STL		Nels Potter, PHI	
NL 640, Frank McCormick, CIN		NL 14, Tot Pressnell, BRO	
H—AL 195, George McQuinn, STL		PCT—AL .577, Jim Bagby, BOS	
NL 209, Frank McCormick, CIN		NL .706, Bob Klinger, PIT	
2B—AL 42, George McQuinn, STL		GP—**AL 45, Johnny Humphries, CLE**	
NL 40, Frank McCormick, CIN		NL 47, Bill McGee, STL	
3B—**AL 18, Jeff Heath, CLE**		GS—AL 27, Lefty Mills, STL	
NL 13, Ernie Koy, BRO		NL 25, Bill McGee, STL	
HR—AL 26, Ken Keltner, CLE		CG—AL 15, Lefty Mills, STL	
NL 23, Johnny Rizzo, PIT		NL 10, Bill Klinger, PIT	
R—AL 104, Jeff Heath, CLE		Bill McGee, STL	
NL 97, Johnny Rizzo, PIT		IP—AL 210.1, Lefty Mills, STL	
RBI—AL 113, Ken Keltner, CLE		NL 216.0, Bill McGee, STL	
NL 111, Johnny Rizzo, PIT		H—AL 218, Jim Bagby, BOS	
WK—AL 58, George McQuinn, STL		NL 216, Bill McGee, STL	
NL 65, Goody Rosen, BRO		BB—AL 116, Lefty Mills, STL	
SO—AL 94, Sam Chapman, PHI		NL 78, Bill McGee, STL	
NL 76, Johnny Hudson, BRO		K—AL 134, Lefty Mills, STL	
Ernie Koy, BRO		NL 104, Bill McGee, STL	
SB—AL 11, George Case, WAS		ERA—AL 4.21, Jim Bagby, BOS	
Joe Gordon, NY		NL 2.99, Bob Klinger, PIT	
NL 15, Ernie Koy, BRO		SHO—AL 1, Jim Bagby, BOS	
BA—AL .343, Jeff Heath, CLE		Emerson Dickman, BOS	
NL .327, Frank McCormick, CIN		Joe Krakauskas, WAS	
SLG—AL .602, Jeff Heath, CLE		Lefty Mills, STL	
NL .514, Johnny Rizzo, PIT		NL 1, done by seven pitchers	
OBP—AL .384, George McQuinn, STL		SV—AL 6, Johnny Humphries, CLE	
NL .368, Johnny Rizzo, PIT		NL 6, Dick Errickson, BOS	

1939

Imagine being a rookie third baseman who drives in 95 runs. Now picture that you not only fail to lead your team's rookies in that category but you finish a full 50 RBI behind another freshman. Jim Tabor of the Boston Red Sox lived that scenario. On July 4 Tabor singled, doubled, and homered in the first game of a doubleheader at Philadelphia. In the nightcap he hit three more round trippers, two of them grand slams. Tabor drove in nine runs—for 11 on the day—and scored five times as Boston completed the sweep by a combined score of 35–19.

Tabor had a fine season, batting .289 with 55 extra base hits, but teammate Ted Williams relegated him to the sidelines of history. Williams, one year removed from winning the American Association Triple Crown, put up breathtaking numbers as a 20-year-old Red Sox freshman. He batted .327 with 44 doubles, 11 triples, and 31 home runs. Moreover, Williams walked 107 times and led the AL in both total bases and RBI with 145.

MOST RBI BY ROOKIE

145, Ted Williams, 1939 Bos AL
144, Walt Dropo, 1950 Bos AL
142, Hal Trosky, 1934 Cle AL
137, Dale Alexander, 1929 Det AL
130, Albert Pujols, 2001 StL NL

On April 23 Williams hit his first ML home run, part of a four-hit day. After April Williams never had fewer than 22 RBI in any month, his high being 36 in August. He and Tabor combined for 240 RBI, the most ever for freshman teammates. Williams connected twice and drove in five runs on May 4 at Detroit, one of his shots a tape-measure blast to right-center.

Barney McCosky of the Tigers had three hits in that same game, raising his average to .361. While the recruit center fielder wasn't able to maintain that heady pace, he did hit .311. In addition, McCosky laced 190 safeties, scored 120 runs, and legged out 14 triples, making the loop's top five in each department. His hot start was bolstered by a four-hit showing against the Chicago White Sox on April 20, when he collected two of his 33 doubles.

A solid all-around performer, McCosky also stole 20 bases and drew 70 bases on balls. His .384 OBP would have led the freshman ranks in most seasons, but 1939 was far from a normal season for rookies, particularly in the AL. McCosky could finish no better than a distant third on the freshman OBP list as Williams posted a .436 mark and Yankees yearling Charlie Keller reached a stratospheric .447 in the process of setting an all-time record for the fewest games by a rookie who exceeded 80 runs, RBI, and walks.

FEWEST GAMES BY ROOKIE WITH 80 + RUNS, RBI, AND BB

111 G (87 R/83 RBI/81 BB), Charlie Keller, 1939 NY AL
134 G (84 R/81 RBI/86 BB), Elmer Flick, 1898 Phi NL
136 G (84 R/88 RBI/87 BB), Joe Ferguson, 1973 LA NL
142 G (103 R/93 RBI/85 BB), Bob Johnson, 1933 Phi AL
142 G (93 R/95 RBI/82 BB), Tim Salmon, 1993 Cal AL

In the World Series against Cincinnati, Keller went 7-for-16 with eight runs and six RBI. In the first game

Charlie Keller, shown here scoring, was second only to Joe DiMaggio among Yankees rookies who debuted during the Joe McCarthy era when the club won eight pennants in a 16-year span. At drawing walks, Keller was second to none, however, among Yankees rookies of any era. His .447 OBP in 1939 set a new club frosh record that has never been approached since. *Transcendental Graphics*

Ted Williams had a memorable rookie season in what would be an even more memorable career. One of its most remarkable features was that even though he hit .327 and set the post-1900 rookie record for walks, he failed to lead all AL frosh in OBP. The 1939 pace setter, Charlie Keller, would never again match his rookie BA of .334 but would continue to be one of the most prolific walk collectors in modern history.

At the time of Keller's retirement, in 1952, he was only the fifth performer to play 1,000 games and finish with a .400+ OBP and a sub-.300 BA. Ironically, the fourth player to accomplish this feat also debuted in 1939, albeit to little acclaim. That year, as a combination pinch hitter and sub outfielder with Detroit, Roy Cullenbine hit just .240 in 179 at bats but registered a .362 OBP when he collected nearly as many walks as hits. It was a pattern he would repeat for the remainder of his ten-year career. In 1947 Cullenbine set the all-time record for the most walks by a player in his final season when he snagged 137 free passes as opposed to just 104 hits. That year, he also established a second mark that is unlikely ever to be surpassed: for the highest OPS (.823) by a sub-.230 hitter.

Here, in order of their retirement, are the only batsmen no longer active in 2004 to play 1,000 games and achieve a .400 career OBP despite posting a sub-.300 BA.

Name	Retired	Games	AB	BA	OBP
Roy Thomas	1911	1470	5296	.290	.413
Lu Blue	1933	1615	5904	.287	.402
Max Bishop	1935	1338	4494	.271	.423
Roy Cullenbine	1947	1181	3879	.276	.408
Charlie Keller	1952	1170	3790	.286	.410
Eddie Stanky	1953	1259	4301	.268	.410
Ferris Fain	1955	1151	3930	.290	.425
Joe Cunningham	1966	1141	3362	.291	.406
Mickey Mantle	1968	2401	8102	.298	.423
Mike Hargrove	1985	1666	5564	.290	.400
Rickey Henderson	2003	3081	10961	.279	.401

he tripled and scored the game-winning run in the bottom of the ninth. The next day Keller hit an RBI double and scored in the third inning. He gave the Yanks a quick 2–0 lead in Game Three with a homer to right, scored his second run in the third inning, and followed with another two-run circuit shot in the fifth. In Game Four, the series finale, Keller broke a scoreless tie in the seventh inning with his third homer of the series. The Reds managed to take a 4–2 lead into the ninth, but

Keller singled and scored as New York forced extra frames. In the tenth Keller reached on an error and tallied an insurance run as the Yankees scored three times and went on to sweep the Fall Classic.

Two glittering freshman hurlers chafed at having to sit idle on the bench in the postseason after helping the Yankees get there—Atley Donald and Marius Russo. Donald won his first dozen decisions in 1939 and had two shutouts before tailing off a bit to finish 13–3. Russo likewise dropped just three games while winning eight. In 116 innings the fledgling southpaw sported a dazzling 2.41 ERA, far shy of the AL average of 4.62; Russo also logged the lowest OBA (.210) and the second lowest OOBP (.283) among all big league hurlers in 1939 who worked a minimum of 100 innings.

Unlike Donald and Russo, Junior Thompson did see postseason action for Cincinnati, losing Game Three after a fine 13–5 rookie campaign. Thompson had a 2.54 ERA and, despite making just 11 starts in his 42 appearances, tossed three shutouts. Brooklyn's Hugh Casey topped all rookies in both circuits with 15 wins and ranked fourth in the NL in ERA. Mort Cooper and Bob Bowman each cracked double figures in wins for the Cardinals. Cooper copped 12 victories and Bowman, a combination starter and reliever, bagged 13 along with leading all rookies in saves and finishing second in the NL in ERA and OBA only to Cincinnati's Bucky Walters, the top hurler in the game in 1939.

Other Highlights

May 10—Rip Sewell homers and blanks the New York Giants, his Pittsburgh Pirates winning 5–0.

May 12—Jack Kramer of the St. Louis Browns shuts out Detroit on two hits to win 1–0.

May 28—A's rookie reliever Bob Joyce surrenders the fourth of four consecutive homers by Yankees outfielder George Selkirk in four at bats over a two-day period.

June 10—Frank Croucher hits two home runs, one of them a grand slam, as Detroit pounds Washington 17–5.

July 25—Unbeaten rookie Atley Donald of the Yankees wins his 12th game in a row, topping the Browns 5–1.

1939 ROOKIE LEADERS

Batting	Pitching
G—AL 149, Jim Tabor, BOS	W—AL 13, Atley Donald, NY
Ted Williams, BOS	NL 15, Hugh Casey, BRO
NL 143, Rip Russell, CHI	L—AL 16, Jack Kramer, STL
AB—AL 611, Barney McCosky, DET	NL 15, Kirby Higbe, CHI/PHI
NL 542, Rip Russell, CHI	PCT—AL .813, Atley Donald, NY
H—AL 190, Barney McCosky, DET	NL .600, Hugh Casey, BRO
NL 148, Rip Russell, CHI	GP—AL 40, Alex Carrasquel, WAS
2B—AL 44, Ted Williams, BOS	Jack Kramer, STL
NL 27, Pinky May, PHI	NL 52, Rip Sewell, PIT
3B—AL 14, Barney McCosky, DET	GS—AL 31, Jack Kramer, STL
NL 8, Fern Bell, PIT	NL 28, Kirby Higbe, CHI/PHI
HR—AL 31, Ted Williams, BOS	CG—AL 11, Atley Donald, NY
NL 9, Rip Russell, CHI	NL 15, Hugh Casey, BRO
R—AL 131, Ted Williams, BOS	IP—AL 211.2, Jack Kramer, STL
NL 59, Pete Coscarart, BRO	NL 227.1, Hugh Casey, BRO
RBI—AL 145, Ted Williams, BOS	H—AL 269, Jack Kramer, STL
NL 79, Rip Russell, CHI	NL 228, Hugh Casey, BRO
WK—AL 107, Ted Williams, BOS	BB—AL 127, Jack Kramer, STL
NL 46, Pete Coscarart, BRO	**NL 123, Kirby Higbe, CHI/PHI**
SO—AL 86, Bill Nagel, PHI	K—AL 72, Dizzy Trout, DET
NL 56, Pete Coscarart, BRO	NL 130, Mort Cooper, STL
Rip Russell, CHI	ERA—AL 3.61, Dizzy Trout, DET
SB—AL 20, Barney McCosky, DET	NL 2.60, Bob Bowman, STL
NL 10, Pete Coscarart, BRO	SH—AL 2, Bill Beckmann, PHI
BA—AL .334, Charlie Keller, NY	Atley Donald, NY
NL .287, Pinky May, PHI	Jack Kramer, STL
SLG—AL .609, Ted Williams, BOS	Marius Russo, NY
NL .386, Rip Russell, CHI	NL 3, Junior Thompson, CIN
OBP—AL .447, Charlie Keller, NY	SV—AL 2, Alex Carrasquel, WAS
NL .354, Pete Coscarart, BRO	Marius Russo, NY
	Dizzy Trout, DET
	NL 9, Bob Bowman, STL

July 26—Tom Sunkel fans nine Giants and limits them to two hits in a10–0 win for the St. Louis Cardinals.

September 16—Joe Haynes of the Senators fires a two-hit shutout against the Browns, besting them 4–0.

1940s

1940

Some years are marked by an especially outstanding rookie full-season achievement such as Bill Hoffer's 31 wins in 1895 or Lloyd Waner's 223 hits and 133 runs in 1927. Other years, like 1892, which culminated with Bumpus Jones's no-hitter in his first big league appearance on the final day of the season, are distinguished by a single-game memorable effort. In 1940 there was a generous mix of both significant rookie full-season performances and single-game memorable efforts.

In the American League 19-year-old Bob Kennedy of the White Sox established the all-time season record for the most games by a teenage player when he held down third base in all but one of Chicago's 155 contests. Meanwhile the New York Yankees, aiming for a record fifth straight pennant, finished a disappointing third but fell only two games short of overtaking first-place Detroit at the wire after pitcher Tiny Bonham was recalled from their Kansas City farm club on August 5, just 11 days shy of his 27th birthday. Despite debuting with less than two months left in the season, Bonham won nine of 12 starts and logged ten complete games,

the exact number needed at the time to qualify as an ERA leader. Thus it was that Bonham was able to lay claim to the 1940 AL ERA crown with his 1.90 mark, albeit his title has since been rescinded because he logged only 99.1 innings. Bonham's relatively short stint at the apex of the Yankees rotation, sensational as it was, prevented him from gaining general recognition as the top freshman in the junior loop. The unofficial honor went instead to Browns outfielder Wally Judnich, who a few years earlier had been rated a better prospect than Ted Williams in the opinion of Yankees scout Joe Devine.

While the National League lacked for a rookie whose achievements stood out as prominently as Judnich's or Bonham's, it suffered no shortage of quality freshman performances. Either first sacker Babe Young, who led the Giants in RBI with 101, or outfielder Chet Ross, the Braves leader in almost every major offensive department including home runs and OPS, would have been a worthy choice as the top senior-circuit frosh, but the best overall recruit crop in 1940 clearly belonged to Pittsburgh. Joining lefty Ken Heintzelman, who tied for the NL rookie lead in both strikeouts and saves, were 20-year-old second baseman

Frankie Gustine and two hard-hitting outfielders, Bob Elliott and Maurice Van Robays. The 1940 campaign also featured the debuts of the two shortstops—Pee Wee Reese of the Dodgers and Marty Marion of the Cardinals—who would vie for fielding titles and All-Star game selections in the elder loop for the next decade. In addition to Marion, the Cards introduced several other freshmen destined to become prominent contributors to the four pennants the team would win in the 1940s. Among them were Harry Brecheen, Johnny Hopp, Creepy Crespi, Harry Walker, and Walker Cooper. The last named enjoyed a particularly auspicious entry to the majors. After joining the Cardinals on September 25, Cooper caught the club's last six games of the season. In addition, on the 25th, he became only the 11th receiver in history to catch his brother when he teamed with his elder sibling Mort, pitching in relief in the Cards' 4–3 win over the pennant-bound Reds. Then, in the season finale on September 29 at St. Louis, the Cooper brothers played their first of many full games together when Mort bested Dizzy Dean of the Cubs in a 6–0 shutout.

But as exquisite as Walker Cooper's experience on September 29 might have been, it was no match for the experience another rookie had been given to treasure forever just two days earlier. In 1940 the defining freshman moment—and indeed the defining moment of the entire season—occurred in Cleveland on Friday September 27 when Floyd Giebell, an obscure 30-year-old yearling right-hander with Detroit, paired off against Tribe ace Bob Feller. With three games left to play, Detroit led Cleveland by two games and needed to win just one of its final three contests to wrap up the pennant. The cushion induced Tigers manager Del Baker to concede the opening game to Feller and save his two aces, Bobo Newsom and Schoolboy Rowe, by starting Giebell, whose only previous outing in 1940 had come eight days earlier against the last-place Philadelphia A's. Rather than sustaining the expected shellacking at Feller's expense, in a script that not even a Hollywood writer would have dared to craft, Giebell blanked the Indians 2–0 and clinched the pennant for Detroit. It proved to be not only the most important game of Giebell's career but the only game of any consequence in which he ever appeared. Following his pennant-clinching shutout win, Giebell never figured in another decision in the major leagues.

CHRONOLOGICAL LIST OF BROTHER BATTERIES

Rank	Names	Team	Year
1	Will & Deacon White	Bos-NL	1877
2	Ed & Bill Dugan	Vir-AA	1884
3	Pete & Fred Wood	Buf-NL	1885
4	Dick & Bill Conway	Bal-AA	1886
5	John & Buck Ewing	NY-PL	1890
6	Mike & Jack O'Neill	StL-NL	1902
7	Homer & Tommy Thompson	NY-AL	1912
8	Lefty & Fred Tyler	Bos-NL	1914
9	Milt & Alex Gaston	Bos-AL	1929
10	Wes & Rick Ferrell	Bos-AL	1934
11	Mort & Walker Cooper	StL-NL	1940
12	Elmer & John Riddle	Cin-NL	1941
13	Bobby & Billy Shantz	Phi-AL	1954
14	Jim & Ed Bailey	Cin-NL	1959
15	Larry & Norm Sherry	LA-NL	1960

The Pittsburgh Pirates have long had a penchant for producing rookies who never again came even remotely close to matching their superlative yearling seasons. In 1899 it was third baseman Jimmy Williams, still the owner of the all-time frosh mark for triples. Eight years later it was outfielder Goat Anderson, arguably the most underrated One Year Wonder in history. The 1924 campaign brought Emil Yde, whose glittering 16–3 pitching log enabled him to top the National League in both winning percentage and shutouts.

In 1936 the Pirates embarked on a brief but truly strange skein that saw them produce a freshman hitter in alternate years who would collect 100 RBI only in his initial season. First it was Bill Brubaker, the replacement at third base for longtime fixture Pie Traynor. After netting 102 RBI in 1936, Brubaker never again had more than 48 ribbies in a season. Two years later, in 1938, frosh left-fielder Johnny Rizzo garnered 111 RBI along with setting a new Pittsburgh franchise record for home runs with 23. Rizzo finished his career four years later with just 289 career RBI. The third and final member of the skein was Maurice Van Robays, who generated 116 RBI as Rizzo's replacement in left field in 1940 and then collected just 171 more RBI in his remaining four seasons. The odd string was broken in 1942 when Johnny Barrett, who shared left field that year with Van Robays, led all Pirates rookies in RBI with just 26.

Batting	Pitching

Batting

G—AL 154, Bob Kennedy, CHI
NL 149, Chet Ross, BOS
Babe Young, NY
AB—AL 606, Bob Kennedy, CHI
NL 572, Maurice Van Robays, PIT
H—AL 157, Wally Judnich, STL
NL 161, Bob Elliott, PIT
2B—AL 32, Dom DiMaggio, BOS
NL 34, Bob Elliott, PIT
3B—AL 7, Wally Judnich, STL
NL 14, Chet Ross, BOS
HR—AL 24, Wally Judnich, STL
NL 17, Chet Ross, BOS
Babe Young, NY
R—AL 97, Wally Judnich, STL
NL 88, Bob Elliott, PIT
RBI—AL 89, Wally Judnich, STL
NL 116, Maurice Van Robays, PIT
WK—AL 54, Wally Judnich, STL
NL 69, Babe Young, NY
SO—AL 77, Ray Mack, CLE
NL 127, Chet Ross, BOS
SB—AL 8, Wally Judnich, STL
NL 15, Pee Wee Reese, BRO
BA—AL .303, Wally Judnich, STL
NL .305, Bama Rowell, BOS
SA—AL .520, Wally Judnich, STL
NL .460, Chet Ross, BOS
OBP—AL .368, Wally Judnich, STL
NL .383, Joe Orengo, STL

Pitching

W—AL 17, Sid Hudson, WAS
NL 13, Vern Olsen, CHI
L—AL 16, Sid Hudson, WAS
NL 9, Vern Olsen, CHI
Ken Raffensberger, CHI
PCT—AL .515, Sid Hudson, WAS
NL .591, Vern Olsen, CHI
GP—AL 38, Sid Hudson, WAS
NL 43, Ken Raffensberger, CHI
GS—AL 31, Sid Hudson, WAS
NL 20, Vern Olsen, CHI
CG—AL 19, Sid Hudson, WAS
NL 9, Vern Olsen, CHI
IP—AL 252.0, Sid Hudson, WAS
NL 172.2, Vern Olsen, CHI
H—AL 272, Sid Hudson, WAS
NL 193, Ken Heintzelman, PIT
BB—AL 84, Herb Hash, BOS
NL 65, Ken Heintzelman, PIT
K—AL 96, Sid Hudson, WAS
NL 71, Ken Heintzelman, PIT
Vern Olsen, CHI
ERA—AL 4.33, Johnny Gorsica, DET
NL 2.97, Vern Olsen, CHI
SHO—AL 3, Tiny Bonham, NY
Sid Hudson, WAS
NL 4, Vern Olsen, CHI
SV—AL 3, Herb Hash, BOS
NL 3, Ken Heintzelman, PIT
Ken Raffensberger, CHI

Other Highlights

April 30—Art Mahan debuts at first base for the Phillies joining rookie second baseman Herm Schulte, who debuted two weeks earlier on Opening Day; Mahan and Schulte will become the only pair of One Year Wonder qualifiers in history to play side by side in the same infield for an entire season.

August 6—Sid Hudson, the season's surprise rookie star who leaped all the way to the Washington Senators from the Class D Florida State League, continues his march toward being the top frosh hurler in 1940 with a one-hit win over the A's.

August 10—Recent minor league call-up Tiny Bonham lifts the defending champion Yankees above .500 when he notches his first ML win, beating the A's 13–0; after being at 51–51 on August 9, the Yankees will go 37–15 the rest of the way with Bonham playing a huge role in their resurgence.

September 11—Tiny Bonham puts the rampaging Yankees in first place when he beats Cleveland's Bob Feller 3–1 in the first game of a doubleheader; however, the Yankees will lose the nightcap and never regain the lead.

September 16—Switch-hitter Johnny Lucadello of the Browns is the first rookie ever to homer from both sides of the plate in the same game in a 16–4 win over the Yankees; the two dingers are the only homers Lucadello will hit all season as he appears in just 17 games and retains his rookie status for the following year when he will lead all AL frosh in walks.

September 17—Phils rookie Danny Litwhiler's hitting streak is stopped at 21 games by Whitey Moore of Cincinnati; notwithstanding his long hitting skein, Litwhiler will finish the season with just 142 ABs and, like Lucadello, retain rookie status for the 1941 season when he will top all incoming frosh in several batting departments.

September 29—The game's most heralded rookie in 1940, Giants' outfielder Johnny Rucker, who was featured on the cover of *Life* magazine prior to the season, finally begins to live up to his press clippings when he drives in seven runs in two consecutive innings as New York whips the hapless Braves 14–0 in the season finale; Rucker will finish his frosh campaign with just 23 RBI in 86 games.

1941

The period between 1935 and 1945 was not a fun time to be a baseball fan in Philadelphia. In that 11-year stretch, the two Quaker City entries, the Phillies and the A's, collected a staggering total of 16 last-place finishes between them, and 1941 was no different. Both Philadelphia clubs not only finished in the cellar but were in the midst of a three-year skein in which last place in the majors was the exclusive province of the Quaker City. Yet, in 1941 at least, each team offered its fans a modicum of hope in the form of a munificent supply of exciting new talent. The A's unveiled three performers who would become major contributors to the team's return to respectability later in the decade, third sacker Pete Suder, outfielder Elmer Valo, and pitcher Phil Marchildon. Their Shibe Park co-tenant likewise turned out a trio of promising newcomers in the person of leftfielder Danny Litwhiler, second baseman Danny Murtaugh, and rightfielder Stan Benjamin. Litwhiler paced all rookies in home runs, RBI, and SA as well as in fielding runs with 17.1. The following year

he would shatter Harry Craft's FA record for an outfielder (.997 in 1940) when he became the first gardener in major league history to go through an entire season without making an error. Murtaugh also set a new record as a frosh by leading the NL in stolen bases despite hitting just .219, the lowest BA by a pacesetter in thefts since the current scoring rule for what constitutes a stolen base was introduced in 1898.

LOWEST BA, SEASON, LEAGUE LEADER IN STOLEN BASES

Rank	Name	Team	Year	SB	BA
1	Hugh Nicol	Cin-AA	1887	138	.215
2	Danny Murtaugh	Phi-NL	1941	18	.219
3	George Case	Cle-AL	1946	28	.225
4	Vince Coleman	StL-NL	1986	107	.232
5	Tommy Harper	Sea-AL	1969	73	.235
	Omar Moreno	Pit-NL	1978	71	.235

At the opposite end of the flagpole in the NL, the pennant-winning Brooklyn Dodgers presented no rookies of consequence and only one, Tom Drake, a spot starter and reliever, who appeared in as many as ten games. In sharp contrast the New York Yankees, back in the driver's seat in the AL after a year away, turned out a plenteous crop of newcomers, including half their starting infield. Skipper Joe McCarthy began the campaign by moving incumbent second sacker Joe Gordon to first base to make room at the keystone sack for Jerry Priddy. But McCarthy's plan to pair Priddy with his 1940 minor league teammate at Kansas City, shortstop Phil Rizzuto, was ditched when Priddy failed to hit. By June Gordon had been restored at second base, and the first base slot was handed to another graduate of the 1940 Kansas City club, Johnny Sturm. Although McCarthy's juggling paid a rich dividend as the Yankees romped to an easy pennant, it is difficult, in retrospect, to follow his logic, at least when it came to his choice of Sturm. In 524 at bats Sturm generated only 36 RBI, the fewest ever by a first baseman on a flag winner. Furthermore, he scored just 58 runs, and his .592 OPS is the lowest in history among first basemen on pennant-winning teams who had as many as 500 at

In September 1937 the Cardinals brought up Howie Krist, a 21-year-old right-hander, from their Rochester farm club and watched him win three of four late-season starts. Krist then returned to the minors where he apprenticed for three more years. Winning 22 games for Houston of the Texas League in 1940 finally earned him a permanent spot on the Cardinals varsity in 1941. Krist spent most of his rookie season in the bullpen, where he collected six wins but also made eight starts, winning four of them and not being involved in the decision in the other four. On the year, he was a perfect 10–0, breaking Joe Pate's 15-year-old record for the most wins without a defeat by a rookie hurler.

Krist followed his rookie campaign by going 24–8 in his next two seasons before his career was interrupted by military service. Returning to the Cardinals in 1946, he was not the same pitcher. Before being released he appeared in 15 games and lost his only two decisions. The two losses shaved his career winning percentage from .804 to .771, which is still the highest in history among pitchers involved in at least 25 decisions. In addition, Krist continues to hold the rookie mark for the most wins without a loss.

HIGHEST WINNING PERCENTAGE, ROOKIE, MINIMUM EIGHT WINS

Rank	Name	Year	Team	Record	PCT
1	Howie Krist	1941	StL-NL	10–0	1.000
2	Joe Pate	1926	Phi-AL	9–0	1.000
3	Kirk Rueter	1993	Mon-NL	8–0	1.000
4	Jim Nash	1966	KC-AL	12–1	.923
	Perry Werden	1884	StL-UA	12–1	.923
6	Larry Twitchell	1887	Det-NL	11–1	.917
7	Whitey Ford	1950	NY-AL	9–1	.900
8	Al Orth	1895	Phi-NL	8–1	.889
	Don Bessent	1955	Bro-NL	8–1	.889
	Tim Wakefield	1992	Pit-NL	8–1	.889
	Brad Clontz	1995	Atl-NL	8–1	.889

bats. Sturm's final big league innings came in the 1941 World Series in which he hit .286 and led the Yankees in at bats but failed to score so much as a single run. After the season, like many other rookies from the 1941 class, he was inducted into the military and did not return to the majors when the war concluded.

But if McCarthy was wrong on Sturm, he hit the bull's-eye when he installed Rizzuto at shortstop in 1941 ahead of nine-year veteran Frankie Crosetti. In 1994 Rizzuto became the second member of the 1941 rookie class to be selected for the Hall of Fame, joining Early Wynn.

Other Highlights

April 15—Cubs shortstop Lou Stringer makes a record four errors in his ML debut, but the Bruins survive his bobbles to beat Pittsburgh 7–4.

May 3—Hank Gornicki of the Cardinals one-hits the Phils in his first ML start; rookie Stan Benjamin's single is the lone Philadelphia hit in Gornicki's 6–0 win.

June 28—White Sox rookie Don Kolloway is a one-man gang, stealing second, third, and home in the ninth inning after previously hitting two key home runs in Chicago's 6–4 win over Cleveland.

September 16—Johnny Schmitz is the first documented pitcher to notch a win in his ML debut on just one pitch as the Cubs rally in the bottom of the ninth to beat Brooklyn 5–4 after Schmitz's single relief toss closed the top of the inning.

September 17—Stan Musial makes his ML debut by going 2-for-4 for the Cardinals in a win over the Braves; Musial will hit .426 with the Cards after beginning the season in the Class C Western Association.

September 28—In the season finale A's rookie Fred Caligiuri allows Ted Williams's final two hits in Williams's .406 campaign but nevertheless beats Lefty Grove 7–1 in the game that will spell Grove's ML coda; the victory also proves to be Caligiuri's last in the bigs.

Batting	Pitching
G—AL 139, Pete Suder, PHI	W—AL 19, Dick Newsome, BOS
NL 151, Danny Litwhiler, PHI	NL 19, Elmer Riddle, CIN
AB—AL 531, Pete Suder, PHI	L—AL 15, Phil Marchildon, PHI
NL 590, Danny Litwhiler, PHI	NL 15, Art Johnson, BOS
H—AL 158, Phil Rizzuto, NY	PCT—AL .655, Dick Newsome, BOS
NL 180, Danny Litwhiler, PHI	**NL .826, Elmer Riddle, CIN**
2B—AL 23, George Archie, WAS/STL	GP—AL 36, Tom Ferrick, PHI
NL 31, Lou Stringer, CHI	Bob Muncrief, STL
3B—AL 9, Phil Rizzuto, NY	Dick Newsome, BOS
Pete Suder, PHI	NL 43, Art Johnson, BOS
NL 7, Stan Benjamin, PHI	GS—AL 29, Dick Newsome, BOS
HR—AL 5, Pat Mullin, DET	NL 25, Ernie White, STL
NL 18, Danny Litwhiler, PHI	CG—AL 17, Dick Newsome, BOS
R—AL 65, Phil Rizzuto, NY	NL 15, Elmer Riddle, CIN
NL 85, Creepy Crespi, STL	IP—AL 214.1, Bob Muncrief, STL
RBI—AL 53, George Archie, WAS/STL	NL 216.2, Elmer Riddle, CIN
NL 66, Danny Litwhiler, PHI	H—AL 235, Dick Newsome, BOS
WK—AL 48, Johnny Lucadello, STL	NL 191, Johnny Podgajny, PHI
NL 59, Lou Stringer, CHI	BB—AL 118, Phil Marchildon, PHI
SO—AL 50, Johnny Sturm, NY	NL 82, Tommy Hughes, PHI
NL 86, Lou Stringer, CHI	K—AL 74, Phil Marchildon, PHI
SB—AL 14, Phil Rizzuto, NY	NL 117, Ernie White, STL
NL 18, Danny Murtaugh, PHI	ERA—AL 3.57, Phil Marchildon, PHI
BA—AL .307, Phil Rizzuto, NY	**NL 2.24, Elmer Riddle, CIN**
NL .305, Danny Litwhiler, PHI	SHO—AL 2, Bob Muncrief, STL
SLG—AL .398, Phil Rizzuto, NY	Dick Newsome, BOS
NL .466, Danny Litwhiler, PHI	NL 4, Elmer Riddle, CIN
OBP—AL .343, Phil Rizzuto, NY	SV—AL 7, Tom Ferrick, PHI
NL .355, Creepy Crespi, STL	NL 7, Bill Crouch, PHI/STL

1942

The 1942 season was the first to be affected appreciably by the war effort. By Opening Day several of the game's leading luminaries, including Hank Greenberg and Bob Feller, had been siphoned from their teams, and by the close of the year, many other prominent performers would join them in the various branches of the military service. But despite the pronounced attrition in overall talent, the 1942 rookie class ranks near the top in the decade of the 1940s.

Highlighting the hitting side of the ledger were four budding stars who not only fashioned outstanding frosh seasons but would generate stats throughout the remainder of their careers that would indelibly etch their names in every history of the postwar game. In Boston, Red Sox player-manager Joe Cronin, surrendering to age, turned his shortstop post over to Johnny Pesky and then glowed when Pesky became the first performer in American League history to lead the loop in hits in each of his first three seasons. Braves manager Casey Stengel meanwhile boasted the best new center fielder in the majors in the person of Tommy Holmes, who would set a new post-1900 senior loop hitting-streak record three years later as well as win the home run crown with just nine strikeouts, the fewest of any four-bagger kingpin since the close of the Deadball Era.

Each of the two St. Louis teams likewise introduced a future black-ink batsman. The Browns new shortstop, Vern Stephens, provided a taste of his future prowess when he led all members of the 1942 rookie class in RBI and tied for the frosh lead in homers. Before the decade was out, Stephens would set a new season record for the most home runs by a shortstop that has since been broken and a second mark for the most RBI by a shortstop with 159 that still stands. The Cardinals, seldom outdone by their Sportsman's Park co-tenants during the 34 seasons the two clubs shared the same home ground, were not about to take a back seat in 1942, either. Manager Billy Southworth's new left fielder was none other than Stan Musial. The 1942 rookie leader in SA would really begin to gather momentum the following year when he topped the NL in BA, SA, and OBP.

Supporting Musial's effort to propel the Cardinals to the NL pennant in 1942 was fellow rookie Whitey Kurowski. Like Musial, Kurowski did not fully begin to come into his own until the following season when he seized the mantle as the top third baseman in the senior loop and held it through the 1947 campaign, after which his career was abruptly halted by a crippling shoulder injury. But the real catalyst of the Cardinals' flag run in 1942 was yet a third freshman, Johnny Beazley. Easily the most ephemeral rookie pitching star in history with the possible exception of Jocko Flynn, Beazley spent three undistinguished seasons in the lower echelons of the Cardinals farm system before logging a 16–12 record in 1941 for New Orleans of the Southern Association. Called up to St. Louis after the Southern Association campaign ended, Beazley launched his ML career on September 28, 1941, by beating Chicago 3–1 in the Cards' season finale. The following spring, Beazley made the parent club as a reliever and did not gain a spot in the starting rotation until several weeks into the season. As a result, Beazley made just 23 starts, the second-fewest in history to that point by a 20-game winner. His magnificent 21–6 regular-season mark was followed by two complete-game wins in the 1942 World Series, making him the putative MVP of the first Fall Classic since 1926 that found the Yankees on the losing end.

After the season Beazley enlisted in the Army Air Force and was commissioned a second lieutenant the following spring. He was not released from the service until March 17, 1946. With spring training already half over, Beazley hurried to get into condition, hurt his arm, and saw his career quickly go down the tube after collecting only 31 wins. Among rookie 20-game winners since 1901, only Henry Schmidt, Brooklyn's 1903 One Year Wonder, owns fewer career victories than Beazley.

Although rookies from the two-team cities of Boston and St. Louis claimed most of the yearling honors in 1942, the hidden freshman nugget that year played in Cleveland. Released by Detroit after six lackluster seasons in the Bengals farm system, first sacker Les Fleming suddenly got everyone's attention in 1941 when he hit .414 for Nashville to set the all-time Southern Association BA record. Like fellow SA product Johnny Beazley, Fleming was called up to the majors late in the 1941 season and then won the Cleveland first-base slot the following spring when migraine headaches forced veteran Hal Trosky into temporary retirement.

In the process of leading all freshman hitters in OBP in 1942, Fleming snared 106 walks to set a Cleveland franchise record that lasted until 1980. Again like Beazley, Fleming's career was interrupted after the 1942 season by the war effort. Returning to Cleveland late in the 1945 campaign, Fleming was already 30 years old and on the downhill side of his career. He finished in 1949 with Pittsburgh after never again putting in a full season as a regular following his rookie year and as a result is the only performer in major league history to collect 100 walks in the lone season he played enough to qualify for a batting title.

CHRONOLOGY OF CLEVELAND FRANCHISE SEASON RECORD FOR BASES ON BALLS

Name	Year	BB
Ollie Pickering	1901	58
Billy Lush	1904	72
Josh Clarke	1908	76
Joe Jackson	1913	80
Jack Graney	1916	102
Jack Graney	1919	105
Les Fleming	1942	106
Mike Hargrove	1980	111
Jim Thome	1996	123
Jim Thome	1999	127

Other Highlights

May 31—Reds outfielder Clyde Vollmer is only the fourth documented player to homer on the first pitch he sees in the majors in leading Cincinnati to a 3–0 win over Pittsburgh's Max Butcher; Vollmer will not hit another dinger in the majors until 1947.

August 26—Johnny Beazley tops Brooklyn 2–1 in ten innings for his 16th win of the season, capping the Cardinals sweep of a four-game series with the Dodgers that revives their fading pennant hopes.

Batting	Pitching
G—AL 156, Les Fleming, CLE	W—AL 15, Hank Borowy, NY
NL 154, Bert Haas, CIN	NL 21, Johnny Beazley, STL
AB—AL 620, Johnny Pesky, BOS	L—AL 15, Roger Wolff, PHI
NL 585, Bert Haas, CIN	NL 14, Hi Bithorn, CHI
H—AL 205, Johnny Pesky, BOS	PCT—AL .789, Hank Borowy, NY
NL 155, Tommy Holmes, BOS	NL .778, Johnny Beazley, STL
2B—AL 29, Johnny Pesky, BOS	GP—AL 34, Hal White, DET
NL 32, Stan Musial, STL	NL 43, Johnny Beazley, STL
3B—AL 10, Ned Harris, DET	GS—AL 25, Hal White, DET
Elmer Valo, PHI	Roger Wolff, PHI
NL 10, Stan Musial, STL	NL 23, Johnny Beazley, STL
HR—AL 14, Les Fleming, CLE	CG—AL 15, Roger Wolff, PHI
Vern Stephens, STL	NL 13, Johnny Beazley, STL
NL 12, Ray Lamanno, CIN	IP—AL 216.2, Hal White, DET
R—AL 105, Johnny Pesky, BOS	NL 215.1, Johnny Beazley, STL
NL 87, Stan Musial, STL	H—AL 212, Hal White, DET
RBI—AL 92, Vern Stephens, STL	NL 191, Hi Bithorn, CHI
NL 72, Stan Musial, STL	BB—AL 99, Russ Christopher, PHI
WK—AL 106, Les Fleming, CLE	NL 81, Hi Bithorn, CHI
NL 64, Tommy Holmes, BOS	K—AL 94, Roger Wolff, PHI
SO—AL 57, Les Fleming, CLE	NL 91, Johnny Beazley, STL
NL 61, Nanny Fernandez, BOS	ERA—AL 2.52, Hank Borowy, NY
SB—AL 13, Elmer Valo, PHI	NL 2.13, Johnny Beazley, STL
NL 15, Nanny Fernandez, BOS	SHO—AL 4, Hank Borowy, NY
BA—AL .331, Johnny Pesky, BOS	Hal White, DET
NL .315, Stan Musial, STL	NL 3, Johnny Beazley, STL
SLG—AL .433, Vern Stephens, STL	SV—AL 3, Roger Wolff, PHI
NL .490, Stan Musial, STL	NL 6, Johnny Sain, BOS
OBP—AL .412, Les Fleming, CLE	
NL .397, Stan Musial, STL	

September 11—In his ML debut Eddie Freed of the Phillies hammers a single, two doubles, and a triple in an 8–5 loss to the Reds; Freed will collect just six more hits in the bigs.

September 27—Johnny Beazley closes the regular season for the Cardinals with his 21st win and sixth in September alone as St. Louis tops the Cubs 4–1 to give the Cards 12 wins in their last 13 games of the campaign and a two-game final edge over the Dodgers.

October 5—Johnny Beazley holds the Yankees to just seven hits in his 4–2 Game Five victory to seal the 1942 World Series win for the Cardinals.

◄ 1943 ►

In reclaiming their customary throne as the top team in the game after a year's absence, the 1943 edition of the New York Yankees also matched the achievement of Joe McCarthy's 1941 squad by harvesting the finest rookie yield in the majors. Butch Wensloff led all AL yearlings in wins, Bud Metheny did the same in home runs, and third sacker Billy Johnson topped the entire rookie class in both leagues in RBI. In addition, Johnny Lindell, although technically no longer a rookie after logging 52.2 innings as a pitcher the previous year, was an AL co-leader in triples in his first season after converting from the mound to the outfield.

Because his spectacular rookie season occurred in 1943 and was never equaled during the remainder of his career, some historians view Dick Wakefield as little more than a wartime fluke. Those who played with him, however, regarded him as a major talent that for the most part went unrealized. Wakefield's attitude toward the game was perceived by his managers as being somewhere between casual and indifferent. *Transcendental Graphics*

The most outstanding rookie on a flag winner in 1943 was not a member of the Yankees, however, but the St. Louis Cardinals new second baseman, Lou Klein. After a mediocre year at Columbus in 1942, Klein inherited the Cards' keystone sack when incumbent Creepy Crespi was lost to military service, and he exceeded all expectations by leading NL freshmen in games, at bats, hits, doubles, triples, and SA before being called to duty in the Coast Guard in November 1943 for the duration of World War II. Upon returning to the Cardinals late in the 1945 season, Klein quickly became embroiled in conflict on another front. After a series of disputes with the St. Louis organization regarding his salary and playing time, Klein jumped to the Mexican League shortly after the 1946 season commenced and was subsequently banned from organized baseball until 1949. The lengthy sojourn in Mexico eroded his skills. Following his superb rookie year, Klein played just 151 more games in the majors and hit a miserable .217 in 410 at bats.

Whereas Klein's failure to fulfill his rookie potential can be explained, at least in part, by his ill-advised flirtation with the Mexican League, the failure of the AL's top freshman performer in 1943 to ever again tap into his gargantuan potential remains one of the game's greatest enigmas. In July 1941, while attending the University of Michigan, 20-year-old Dick Wakefield was given a reported $52,000 by Detroit to sign with the Tigers. At that time $52,000 was not only an enormous sum, it was more than the aggregate amount that the entire starting lineup for many major league teams earned in a season. The windfall made Wakefield, in effect, the first Bonus Baby. Following his signing with the Tigers, Wakefield finished out the 1941 season with Winston-Salem of the Piedmont League and then moved up to Beaumont in the Double A Texas League in 1942, where he led the loop in batting and total bases and was named the circuit's MVP. Wakefield more than lived up to the hoopla accompanying his arrival in Detroit the following spring. In 1943 he led all freshmen in at bats, hits, BA, and SA. That October he entered a naval aviation pre-flight program but was discharged on July 7, 1944. After a week of "spring training" in midsummer, Wakefield returned to the Detroit lineup on July 13, 1944, and hammered AL pitchers for 98 hits in the remaining 78 games to finish with a 1.040 OPS, the highest in the majors that season among players with at least 200 at bats.

Wakefield then returned to naval duty in November 1944 and was discharged in January 1946. His eagerly anticipated reemergence as one of the top hitters in the majors never materialized. Instead, Wakefield settled into a disappointing role as a part-time left fielder and pinch hitter for the remainder of his nine-year career. His rookie year and the superlative partial season that followed it glitter so brightly in contrast to the rest of his stats that they seem almost as if they were appended to his career profile by mistake. After leading all AL performers in hits and at bats as a freshman in 1943, Wakefield never again had a season in which he played enough games to qualify for a batting title.

By the spring of 1943, so many players had been lost to the war effort that teams were forced, in desperation, to seek replacements wherever they could find them. One of the results was an enormous age gap in wartime rosters. For example, in 1943, 16-year-old Carl Scheib, not even old enough for military service, competed for a spot on the Philadelphia A's mound staff with 33-year-old career minor leaguer Orie "Old Folks" Arntzen. By the end of the war, Scheib would lose his status as the youngest pitcher to date in the twentieth century to 15-year-old Joe Nuxhall, and numerous rookies, senior even to Arntzen, would find roster spots on teams in both leagues.

A second offshoot of the voracious need for replacements was the emergence of several performers as significant contributors during the 1940s and early 1950s who would otherwise in all probability have been doomed to spend the rest of their baseball lives in the minors. Among the most salient of this group was right-hander Allie Reynolds, the rookie leader in strikeouts at age 28 after never having previously pitched above Class A. Another late bloomer who might have never reached the majors if it were not for the exigencies imposed by the war was Eddie Stanky. In 1943, his rookie year with the Cubs, the 26-year-old Stanky collected just 142 total bases in 142 games and 510 at bats but nevertheless managed to score 92 runs when he also collected 92 walks. Stanky's highly respectable .363 OBP surpassed his anemic SA by 85 points, calling to mind the performance of another 27-year-old rookie in 1907, Goat Anderson. But unlike Anderson, whose limited but nonetheless invaluable talents went unappreciated in his time, Stanky was recognized for his. Nicknamed "The Walking Man," Stanky finished an 11-year career in 1953 third among all players in history with at least 3,000 at bats whose OBPs exceeded their SAs.

TOP 10 WITH OBP HIGHER THAN SA
(MINIMUM 3,000 ABs)

Rank	Name	AB	OBP	SA	Diff
1	Roy Thomas	5296	.413	.333	80
2	Miller Huggins	5558	.382	.314	68
3	Eddie Stanky	4301	.410	.348	62
4	Donie Bush	7210	.356	.300	56
5	Al Bridwell	4169	.347	.295	52
	Mike Tresh	3169	.335	.283	52
7	Yank Robinson	3428	.375	.324	51
8	Paul Radford	4979	.351	.308	43
	Ralph Young	3643	.339	.296	43
	Bill North	3900	.366	.323	43

Other Highlights

April 25—In his first start with the Braves, Nate Andrews tops Van Lingle Mungo of the Giants 8–3; Andrews will proceed to lead all rookies in both wins and losses in 1943.

May 4—Braves outfielder Chuck Workman hits his first career dinger off Bill Lohrman of the Giants; owing to the deader ball that was introduced prior to the season, Workman, with ten round trippers, will be the lone frosh in 1943 to reach double figures in jacks.

July 2—After hitting safely in 26 straight games, White Sox outfielder Guy Curtright has his skein stopped by Milo Candini and Alex Carrasquel of Washington.

September 6—Carl Scheib is the youngest player ever to appear in an AL game at the age of 16 years and 248 days as he hurls two-thirds of an inning in relief for the A's in an 11–4 loss to the Yankees in the second game of a doubleheader.

September 6—Rookie Woody Williams of the Reds ties an NL record when he collects his tenth straight hit before being stopped by fellow frosh Ed Hanyzewski of the Cubs.

September 24—Andy Pafko, one of the most popular players in Cubs' lore, makes his ML debut with Chicago in front of 314 fans, the smallest crowd in Wrigley Field history to that point; Pafko goes 2-for-3 with four RBI in a 7–4 win over the Phils shortened by rain to just five innings.

October 3—Billy Johnson completes his rookie year with the distinction of having played third base for the Yankees in every inning of every one of the team's 155 games.

October 11—Billy Johnson's streak continues in the 1943 World Series as he plays every inning at third base for the Yankees in all five games of the Fall Classic and, moreover, leads all series participants in hits with six.

1943 ROOKIE LEADERS

Batting	Pitching
G—AL 155, Billy Johnson, NY	**W—AL 13, Butch Wensloff, NY**
Dick Wakefield, DET	NL 14, Nate Andrews, BOS
NL 154, Lou Klein, STL	L—AL 16, Don Black, PHI
AB—AL 633, Dick Wakefield, DET	**NL 20, Nate Andrews, BOS**
NL 627, Lou Klein, STL	PCT—AL .688, Mickey Haefner, WAS
H—AL 200, Dick Wakefield, DET	NL .562, Hank Wyse, CHI
NL 180, Lou Klein, STL	GP—AL 37, Gordon Maltzberger, CHI
2B—AL 38, Dick Wakefield, DET	NL 38, Red Barrett, BOS
NL 28, Lou Klein, STL	Al Gerheauser, PHI
3B—AL 8, Ralph Hodgin, CHI	Hank Wyse, CHI
Joe Hoover, DET	GS—AL 27, Jesse Flores, PHI
Dick Wakefield, DET	Butch Wensloff, NY
NL 14, Lou Klein, STL	NL 34, Nate Andrews, BOS
HR—AL 9, Bud Metheny, NY	CG—AL 18, Butch Wensloff, NY
NL 10, Chuck Workman, BOS	NL 23, Nate Andrews, BOS
R—AL 91, Dick Wakefield, DET	IP—AL 231.1, Jesse Flores, PHI
NL 92, Eddie Stanky, CHI	NL 283.2, Nate Andrews, BOS
RBI—AL 94, Billy Johnson, NY	H—AL 208, Jesse Flores, PHI
NL 67, Chuck Workman, BOS	NL 253, Nate Andrews, BOS
WK—AL 79, Thurman Tucker, CHI	BB—AL 110, Don Black, PHI
NL 92, Eddie Stanky, CHI	NL 78, Jack Kraus, PHI
SO—AL 101, Joe Hoover, DET	**K—AL 151, Allie Reynolds, CLE**
NL 72, Chuck Workman, BOS	NL 92, Al Gerheauser, PHI
SB—AL 29, Thurman Tucker, CHI	ERA—AL 2.29, Mickey Haefner, WAS
NL 13, Peanuts Lowrey, CHI	NL 2.57, Nate Andrews, BOS
BA—AL .316, Dick Wakefield, DET	SHO—AL 3, Milo Candini, WAS
NL .292, Peanuts Lowrey, CHI	Stubby Overmire, DET
SLG—AL .434, Dick Wakefield, DET	Allie Reynolds, CLE
NL .410, Lou Klein, STL	NL 3, Nate Andrews, BOS
OBP—AL .382, Guy Curtright, CHI	Red Barrett, BOS
NL .363, Eddie Stanky, CHI	**SV—AL 14, Gordon Maltzberger, CHI**
	NL 5, Hank Wyse, CHI

1944

On the surface 1944 would appear to have been a fallow year for rookies. No recruit hitters were able to bat .280, post a .400 SA, or reach a .325 OBP—modest figures that in an average year would have been achieved by several freshmen. Furthermore, only one newcomer, Pat Seerey of Cleveland, reached double figures in home runs, and the rookie leaders in each league in games played and at bats were both second basemen with the two Chicago entries who were on the wrong side of age 30.

In actuality, however, 1944 was a watershed season. For one, Seerey, the rookie home run king, became only

the ninth player in history and the first recruit since Charlie Duffee in 1889 to slug as many as 15 four-baggers on a sub .250 batting average. Seerey's dubious feat would soon become commonplace. Whereas only eight hitters in the 73 major league seasons prior to 1944 had compiled as many as 15 homers while batting below .250, by 1950 the list had grown to 28. In the following decade the number would swell to 79, as more and more batters began swinging for the fences without concern for their averages or strikeout totals.

A second new phenomenon in major league history emanated from the career performance of the 1944 pu-

By 1944 wartime conditions had such a pervasive influence on the nature of the game on the field that it would consume several pages to document the many oddities that occurred in the rookie class alone. For one, the Tigers' 41-year-old freshman outfielder, Chuck Hostetler, began his pro career before several of his recruit classmates were even born. Among them were 15-year-old Joe Nuxhall and 16-year-old Tommy Brown, who the following year became the youngest performer ever to homer in a major league game. The St. Louis Browns, meanwhile, in the process of winning their only pennant in their 52-year existence, joined the very short list of postseason qualifiers that have entrusted the bulk of their catching load to rookies, as Frank Mancuso and Red Hayworth, both of them brothers of prominent backstoppers in the 1930s, shared the duty for manager Luke Sewell, himself a former catching bulwark.

But no team brought more wacky rookie feats, facts, and firsts to the table than Connie Mack's A's. In addition to Joe Berry, the A's unveiled a second top-notch recruit in third sacker George Kell, who leaped all the way to the majors from Lancaster of the Class B Interstate League after leading the minors in hitting in 1943 with a .396 BA. Accompanying Kell was his Lancaster teammate Lew Flick, a 29-year-old singles hitter, and 26-year-old Ed Busch, another singles hitter who had spent the 1943 season with Elmira of the Eastern League. Flick was soon dropped when he proved unable to hit major league pitching, but Busch held down the A's shortstop post for the remainder of the war years. His career stats reflect that he was a decent hitter by wartime standards with a .262 career BA but had absolutely no power, as he logged just 27 extra-base hits and no home runs in 917 at bats. They also reflect something about Busch that has never before been noted. He was quite simply one of the best contact hitters in history. Since 1912, when batter strike-outs began being faithfully recorded every season in both leagues, only one performer who collected as many as 900 at bats in the majors (roughly the equivalent of Busch's two seasons as a regular) has fanned fewer than 45 times. That man heads the list found below.

FEWEST Ks SINCE 1912, MINIMUM 900 CAREER ABs

Rank	Name	AB	SO
1	Ed Busch	917	28
2	Benny Bengough	1125	45
3	Bill Cunningham	945	48
	Benny Zientara	906	48
5	Charlie Hargreaves	1188	49
6	Cliff Bolton	962	50
	Pinky Pittinger	959	50
8	Bennie Tate	1560	51
9	Woody Williams	1255	52
10	Alan Strange	947	54

tative AL ROY, "Jittery" Joe Berry. Slight of build at just 145 pounds and, in his own words, "the nervous type," Berry lied about his age in order to induce A's manager Connie Mack to purchase him after he went 18–10 for Milwaukee of the American Association in 1943 and completed 18 of his 28 starts. Berry was actually 39 when he joined the A's in the spring of 1944, making him the oldest putative ROY in history. Unconvinced that the wispy-looking Berry had the stamina to be a starter, Mack put him in the bullpen, and the results astounded even the usually unflappable Mack. In 1944 Berry permitted only 8.35 enemy baserunners per nine innings, the best ratio of any hurler in a minimum of 100 innings during the entire decade of the 1940s. What's more, Berry finished his career in 1946 with Cleveland at age 41 as the first hurler in big league history to appear in as many as 100 games without ever making a start. Gordon Maltzberger, the White Sox rookie bullpen whiz in 1943, joined Berry a year later by retiring with 135 career appearances, all in relief. Berry and Maltzberger would remain the only two hurlers who collected 100 career appearances without making a start until 1963 when Frank Funk became just the third of what today is a list that has grown to include a multitude of pitchers with well over 500 appearances, all in relief, led by Kent Tekulve at 1,050.

The unofficial ROY in the National League performed a feat equally as auspicious as Berry's. Whereas the A's novice bullpen ace proved to be the first of a new breed, the Giants new hill stalwart, Bill Voiselle, was the last of a kind. In 1943 Voiselle was just 10–21 with Jersey City of the International League, but Giants player-manager Mel Ott was so enamored of Voiselle's four late-season outings with his club that he named the rookie his Opening Day starter in 1944. After topping Al Javery of the Braves 2–1 in the season lidlifter, Voiselle, who wore number 96 to commemorate the name of his hometown in South Carolina, went on to log 21 wins and become the last rookie to date to log as many as 300 innings pitched.

Other Highlights

April 18—The A's and Senators join in setting an Opening Day record when the combined ages of the two hurlers who gain decisions in the A's 3–2 triumph is 79;

1944 ROOKIE LEADERS

Batting		Pitching	
G—AL 146, Roy Schalk, CHI		W—AL 13, Monk Dubiel, NY	
NL 154, Don Johnson, CHI		Sig Jakucki, STL	
AB—AL 587, Roy Schalk, CHI		NL 21, Bill Voiselle, NY	
NL 608, Don Johnson, CHI		L—AL 14, Rufe Gentry, DET	
H—AL 140, Gil Torres, WAS		NL 16, Hal Gregg, BRO	
NL 169, Don Johnson, CHI		Charley Schanz, PHI	
2B—AL 20, Gil Torres, WAS		Bill Voiselle, NY	
NL 37, Don Johnson, CHI		PCT—AL .591, Sig Jakucki, STL	
3B—AL 9, Hal Epps, STL/PHI		**NL .810, Ted Wilks, STL**	
NL 5, Frank Colman, PIT		GP—AL 53, Joe Berry, PHI	
Nap Reyes, NY		NL 43, Bill Voiselle, NY	
HR—AL 15, Pat Seerey, CLE		GS—AL 30, Rufe Gentry, DET	
NL 9, Buddy Kerr, NY		**NL 41, Bill Voiselle, NY**	
R—AL 63, Ford Garrison, BOS/PHI		CG—AL 19, Monk Dubiel, NY	
NL 70, George Hausmann, NY		NL 25, Bill Voiselle, NY	
RBI—AL 60, Eddie Carnett, CHI		IP—AL 232, Monk Dubiel, NY	
NL 71, Don Johnson, CHI		**NL 312.2, Bill Voiselle, NY**	
WK—AL 45, Roy Schalk, CHI		H—AL 217, Monk Dubiel, NY	
NL 52, Hal Luby, NY		Ed Lopat, CHI	
SO—**AL 99, Pat Seerey, CLE**		NL 276, Bill Voiselle, NY	
NL 50, Buck Etchison, BOS		BB—**AL 108, Rufe Gentry, DET**	
SB—AL 10, Ford Garrison, BOS/PHI		**NL 137, Hal Gregg, BRO**	
Gil Torres, WAS		K—AL 79, Monk Dubiel, NY	
NL 14, Buddy Kerr, NY		**NL 161, Bill Voiselle, NY**	
BA—AL .276, Eddie Carnett, CHI		ERA—AL 3.26, Ed Lopat, CHI	
NL .278, Don Johnson, CHI		NL 2.64, Ted Wilks, STL	
SLG—AL .357, Eddie Carnett, CHI		SHO—AL 4, Sig Jakucki, STL	
NL .387, Buddy Kerr, NY		NL 4, Ted Wilks, STL	
OBP—AL .322, Eddie Carnett, CHI		SV—**AL 12, Joe Berry, PHI**	
NL .324, George Hausmann, NY		NL 5, Freddy Schmidt, STL	

39-year-old rookie Joe Berry, working in relief of starter Lum Harris, bests 40-year-old Johnny Niggeling.

August 3—Tommy Brown epitomizes wartime baseball when he debuts with Brooklyn by playing shortstop in both games of a doubleheader loss to the Cubs at the age of 16 years and eight months; the following year, on August 20, Brown will become the youngest player in ML history to rap a home run when he goes yard against Preacher Roe of the Pirates.

August 29—Ted Wilks of the Cardinals is 14–1 and stands on the threshold of the greatest rookie pitching season in history when he wins his 11th straight game by blanking the Reds 3–0; in the final month of the season, Wilks will go just 3–3 to finish 17–4.

October 1—Rookie right-hander Sig Jakucki brings the St. Louis Browns their one and only pennant when he beats the Yankees 5–2 on the final day of the season in front of 37,815, the Browns' first home sellout crowd in 20 years.

October 9—The Cards win the first World Series to be played entirely west of the Mississippi as rookie Emil Verban drives in all three runs in the Redbirds' 3–1 Game Six win over the Browns that is saved by recruit Ted Wilks's 3⅓ shutout innings in relief of Max Lanier.

1945

Prior to the 1945 World Series, Warren Brown, a Chicago sports editor, was asked whether he fancied the

Among the hitters Don Fisher faced in his shutout classic on September 30, 1945, was that season's rookie leader in both batting and OBP, Braves centerfielder Carden Gillenwater. In addition to being the top recruit hitter in either league, Gillenwater also led all NL outfielders in putouts and assists and tied for second in double plays. Fast, with a good arm and some power, Gillenwater had pushed the Braves centerfield incumbent, Tommy Holmes, into right field in the spring of 1945. The following year, after Billy Southworth took over as Braves manager, Gillenwater fell into disfavor when he got off to a slow start and eventually lost his job to Mike McCormick. The remainder of his career was spent in the minors save for a short ML stint in 1948.

The AL rookie batting leader in 1945 was also a center fielder, George Binks of Washington. After finishing last the previous year, the Senators still had a shot at the 1945 AL pennant going into their final game of the season against the Philadelphia A's. Both the game and Washington's pennant chances hinged on a fly ball hit in Binks's direction by A's rookie Ernie Kish that Binks failed to catch, reputedly because he'd neglected to don sunglasses after the sun broke through while the inning was in progress.

Binks never again approached his rookie form and began his final ML season in 1948, somewhat ironically, in the uniform of the Philadelphia A's. Gillenwater's big league coda also came that same season after he occupied the centerfield spot for a couple of months in Washington.

Here are the hitting profiles for the top two rookie hitters in the final wartime campaign. In an average year they would seem decent but hardly exceptional. However, 1945 was not a typical year. Pitchers so dominated the game that Gillenwater finished 15th among all NL batting title qualifiers while Binks, whose BA was ten points lower, ranked 14th in the AL, where offense in 1945 was so depressed that Snuffy Stirnweiss led all hitters with a .309 figure.

1945 STATS, CARDEN GILLENWATER (BRAVES) & GEORGE BINKS (SENATORS)

YEAR	TEAM	AGE	G	AB	R	H	2B	3B	HR	RBI	BB	SO	SB	CS	AVG	SLG	OBA	OPS
1945	Braves	27	144	517	74	149	20	2	7	72	73	70	13	NA	.288	.375	.379	.755
1945	Senators	28	145	550	62	153	32	6	6	81	34	52	11	7	.278	.391	.324	.715

Tigers or his hometown Cubs. Brown's reply that he didn't think either club had enough talent to win has since become the defining statement on the last wartime season, and the 1945 rookie class definitely indicates that there was a fair amount of truth in it. Neither the Cubs nor the Tigers had so much as a single player on the freshman leader board, and only one rookie member of either team, third baseman Bob Maier of Detroit, appeared in enough games to be a qualifier for either a batting or pitching title. Furthermore, no fewer than 50 members of the 1945 rookie class, including Maier, were age 30 or older by the end of the calendar year. They ranged from Pete Gray, a one-armed outfielder with the St. Louis Browns, to Paul Schreiber, a 42-year-old batting-practice pitcher for the Yankees, whose last ML appearance had come a record 22 years earlier. Significantly, only one of the 50 oldster recruits, catcher Aaron Robinson, stuck around the majors long enough to become part of the player pension plan that was spawned immediately after the war.

Yet not all rookies in 1945 were ancients. The Phillies briefly teamed 18-year-old shortstop Granny Hamner with his brother Garvin, a 21-year-old second baseman, as well as with 18-year-old Don Hasenmayer. Brooklyn's 19-year-old right-hander, Ralph Branca, topped all NL recruit pitchers in strikeouts, and at Comiskey Park another 19-year-old, Cass Michaels, landed the White Sox shortstop job. Michaels, who had debuted two years earlier at age 17 under his real name of Casimir Kwietniewski, would blossom into a first-rate player after the war, as would Branca and Granny Hamner, but the same could not be said of the White Sox' other three infield regulars in 1945. As a rookie, Michaels had the novel experience of anchoring an inner perimeter that, in addition to himself, included a trio of 30-year-olds—third baseman Tony Cuccinello, second baseman Roy Schalk, and first baseman Kerby Farrell—none of whom would ever again play in the majors.

The marginal quality of many roster regulars coupled with the use of a deader ball during the wartime campaigns gave pitchers a decided advantage, and it was never more evident than in 1945. While for the second year in a row no rookie hitters were able to approach the .300 barrier, both rookie ERA leaders, Boo Ferriss of the Red Sox and Ken Burkhart of the Cardinals, allowed fewer than three earned runs per game. Exempted from military service because of a severe asthma condition, Ferriss established a new AL record for the most consecutive shutout innings at the start of an ML career—22.1—and progressed from there to defeat each of the other seven AL teams the first time he faced them. When he added to his 21 rookie wins by posting 25 victories in 1946, he tied Wes Ferrell's junior loop record of logging 46 wins in his first two years in the majors.

Along with leading all rookies in their respective leagues in wins and ERA, Ferriss and Burkhart also paced their fellow recruits in shutouts, but neither of them fashioned a whitewash effort that could match that of Giants rookie Don Fisher. Signed off the Cleveland sandlots in the summer of 1945, Fisher debuted on August 25 with a five-inning relief stint and then sat idle on the Giants bench until September 30, the final day of the season. Given the ball by manager Mel Ott in the opening game of a campaign-ending doubleheader against the Braves, Fisher had to labor for 13 innings before he was finally provided with the run that enabled him to shut out Boston 1–0. It was not only Fisher's first start, it was also his final big league appearance.

Other Highlights

April 17—One-armed outfielder Pete Gray is 1-for-4 for the Browns on Opening Day in his ML debut.

April 29—In his ML debut BoSox right-hander Dave "Boo" Ferriss throws 17 balls in the first inning and loads the bases but survives to blank the A's 2–0 and go 3-for-3; Ferriss will reel off a second consecutive shutout—giving him an AL-record 22⅓ straight scoreless innings at the start of a career—and eight straight victories before

1945 ROOKIE LEADERS

Batting	Pitching
G—AL 145, George Binks, WAS	W—AL 21, Boo Ferriss, BOS
NL 144, Carden Gillenwater, BOS	NL 18, Ken Burkhart, STL
AB—AL 550, George Binks, WAS	L—AL 13, Marino Pieretti, WAS
NL 565, Red Schoendienst, STL	NL 13, Howie Fox, CIN
H—AL 153, George Binks, WAS	PCT—AL .677, Boo Ferriss, BOS
NL 157, Red Schoendienst, STL	NL .692, Ken Burkhart, STL
2B—AL 32, George Binks, WAS	GP—AL 44, Marino Pieretti, WAS
NL 27, John Antonelli, STL/PHI	NL 45, Howie Fox, CIN
3B—AL 9, Hal Peck, PHI	GS—AL 31, Boo Ferriss, BOS
NL 9, Al Gionfriddo, PIT	NL 25, Bob Logan, BOS
HR—AL 13, Russ Derry, NY	CG—AL 26, Boo Ferriss, BOS
NL 18, Danny Gardella, NY	NL 12, Ken Burkhart, STL
R—AL 62, George Binks, WAS	IP—AL 264.2, Boo Ferriss, BOS
NL 89, Red Schoendienst, STL	NL 217.1, Ken Burkhart, STL
RBI—AL 81, George Binks, WAS	H—**AL 263, Boo Ferriss, BOS**
NL 72, Carden Gillenwater, BOS	NL 213, Bob Logan, BOS
WK—AL 44, Felix Mackiewicz, CLE	BB—AL 91, Marino Pieretti, WAS
NL 73, Carden Gillenwater, BOS	NL 86, Vic Lombardi, BRO
SO—AL 52, George Binks, WAS	K—AL 94, Boo Ferriss, BOS
NL 70, Carden Gillenwater, BOS	NL 69, Ralph Branca, BRO
SB—AL 11, George Binks, WAS	ERA—AL 2.96, Boo Ferriss, BOS
NL 26, Red Schoendienst, STL	NL 2.90, Ken Burkhart, STL
BA—AL .278, George Binks, WAS	SHO—AL 5, Boo Ferriss, BOS
NL .288, Carden Gillenwater, BOS	NL 4, Ken Burkhart, STL
SLG—AL .399, Hal Peck, PHI	SV—AL 4, Johnny Johnson, CHI
NL .426, Danny Gardella, NY	NL 5, Cy Buker, BRO
OBP—AL .331, Hal Peck, PHI	Don Hendrickson, BOS
NL .379, Carden Gillenwater, BOS	

sustaining his first defeat, 3–2 on June 10 to Hank Borowy of the Yankees.

June 15—Boo Ferriss makes Washington the seventh and final AL team he beats in his first attempt when he wins a 6–5 squeaker in the first game of a double-header.

July 21—Detroit and the Philadelphia A's stagger to a 1–1 tie in 24 innings as Tigers rookie Les Mueller hurls $19\frac{2}{3}$ innings, the longest mound stint in the past 75 years.

August 4—Wounded war hero Bert Shepard pitches $5\frac{1}{3}$ innings for the Senators with an artificial leg in his ML debut and allows just one run; because the Senators, for the final time in their history, are embroiled in a pennant race, Shepard is never given another opportunity by Washington pilot Ossie Bluege.

August 10—A's rookie Steve Gerkin drops his final career start 14–13 to the St. Louis Browns in the first game of a doubleheader; the loss saddles Gerkin with an 0–12 record, the worst ever by a One Year Wonder.

September 4—Batting practice pitcher Paul Schreiber, who pitched briefly in the majors in the early 1920s, returns after a 22-year hiatus to hurl $3\frac{1}{3}$ hitless relief innings for the Yankees at age 42 in a 10–0 loss to the Tigers.

1946

If the Brooklyn Dodgers had won just one more game during the regular season in 1946, they would be remembered today as one of the most rookie-laden flag winners ever. Instead, the Dodgers finished the season tied with the Cardinals and then lost the first pennant playoff series in history, two games to none. The list of Brooklyn performers who had rookie status in 1946 includes well over a dozen names that are immediately recognizable to 1940s aficionados. Among them are Carl Furillo, Joe Hatten, Rex Barney, Gene Hermanski, Eddie Miksis, Hank Behrman, Harry Taylor, Bob Ramazzotti, Paul Minner, Jack Graham, Stan Rojek, and Dick Whitman. In addition, manager Leo Durocher entrusted the bulk of his catching load to a pair of recruit receivers, Bruce Edwards and Ferrell Anderson. Finally, the Dodgers were saddled in 1946

with Joe Tepsic, the first of what would soon become a horde of Bonus Babies who fizzled rather than sizzled. That year a new rule required any player who received a bonus of $5,000 or more to remain on the roster of his signing team for the entire season. After getting into just 15 games in 1946, mostly as a pinch runner, Tepsic balked when the Dodgers attempted to farm him out prior to the 1947 season and chose to quit the game and pocket his bonus rather than undergo a minor league apprenticeship.

But while the Dodgers fielded the richest rookie crop, several other NL teams were not far behind. Led by third baseman Grady Hatton and second sacker Bobby Adams, Cincinnati in some games displayed an all-rookie infield with the sole exception of veteran first baseman Bert Haas. The world champion Cardinals turned over their first-string catching post to rookie Joe Garagiola and employed two other recruits, Dick Sisler and Erv Dusak, as their main subs. Phils leftfielder Del Ennis shared honors with Cubs first baseman Eddie Waitkus as the first two first recruit hitters since 1943 to top .300. In addition to edging Waitkus out for the yearling BA title, .313 to .304, Ennis also led all freshmen in SA, hits, runs, and total bases. In Pittsburgh Ralph Kiner, slated prior to spring training for further minor league seasoning, instead won the Pirates' left-field slot when he went on a slugging rampage in Grapefruit League action that continued all season as he proceeded to become the first rookie since Braggo Roth in 1915 to win a loop home run crown.

As for the AL, the most illustrious graduate of its sparse 1946 rookie class was Cleveland's Opening Day center fielder who hit all of .180. Nevertheless, he is not only generally regarded as having been the loop's most outstanding freshman in 1946 but in 1976 he made the Hall of Fame, albeit not for his work as an outfielder. His name was Bob Lemon.

Other Highlights

April 18—Pirates rookie Ralph Kiner, the surprise NL home run king, collects his first career jack, victimizing St. Louis's ace lefty, Howie Pollet.

May 6—Rookie shortstop Jeff Cross, kept on the roster all season only because roster sizes have been expanded to 30 to accommodate returning servicemen, is in-

No other season has seen a greater disparity between the rookie crops in two different major leagues than was evidenced in 1946. Whereas the NL had two freshmen who hit .300 and a third freshman who led the loop in homers, Browns first baseman Chuck Stevens was not only the leading AL rookie hitter with a lowly .248 BA, he was the *lone* yearling bat-title qualifier. The pitching side of the ledger was no better, as only Bob Savage (3–15) worked enough innings to be an ERA qualifier.

Why was there such a huge disparity between the two leagues that year? No one has ever offered a plausible explanation. It apparently just happened, and moreover, the 1946 season was a one-time phenomenon. In every other year the rookie crops in the two major leagues have been, if not of equal strength, at least reasonably close to it.

Exactly how enormous the disparity was in 1946 is best illustrated by comparing each league's rookie "All-Star" team.

	NATIONAL LEAGUE					AMERICAN LEAGUE				
Pos	Name	Team	AB	HR	BA	Name	Team	AB	HR	BA
1B	Eddie Waitkus	Chi	441	4	.304	Chuck Stevens	StL	432	3	.248
2B	Buddy Blattner	NY	420	11	.255	Gene Handley	Phi	251	0	.251
SS	Billy Cox	Pit	411	2	.290	Jack Wallaesa	Phi	194	5	.196
3B	Grady Hatton	Cin	436	14	.271	Bob Dillinger	StL	225	0	.280
Inf	Bill Rigney	NY	360	3	.236	Jack Conway	Cle	258	0	.225
Inf	Bobby Adams	Cin	311	4	.244	Steve Souchock	NY	86	2	.302
Inf	Claude Corbitt	Cin	274	1	.248	Jake Jones	Chi	79	3	.266
Inf	Jack Graham	Bro/NY	275	14	.218	Eddie Pellagrini	Bos	71	2	.211
Inf	Benny Zientara	Cin	280	0	.289	Don Richmond	Phi	62	1	.290
OF	Del Ennis	Phi	540	17	.313	Hoot Evers	Det	304	4	.266
OF	Ralph Kiner	Pit	502	23	.247	Whitey Platt	Chi	247	3	.251
OF	Carl Furillo	Bro	335	3	.284	Gene Woodling	Cle	133	0	.188
OF	Marv Rickert	Chi	392	7	.263	Gil Coan	Was	134	3	.209
OF	Eddie Lukon	Cin	312	12	.250	Anse Moore	Det	134	1	.209
OF	Erv Dusak	StL	275	9	.240	Dave Philley	Chi	68	0	.353
C	Bruce Edwards	Bro	292	1	.267	Hank Helf	StL	182	6	.192
C	Joe Garagiola	StL	211	3	.237	Sherm Lollar	Cle	62	1	.242
C	Ferrell Anderson	Bro	199	2	.256	Tom Jordan	Chi/Cle	50	1	.220

	Name	Team	IP	W-L	ERA	Name	Team	IP	W-L	ERA
P	Joe Hatten	Bro	222	14–11	2.84	Bob Savage	Phi	164	3–15	4.06
P	Hank Behrman	Bro	150.2	11–5	2.93	Cliff Fannin	StL	86.2	5–2	3.01
P	Ewell Blackwell	Cin	194.1	9–13	2.45	Bob Lemon	Cle	94	4–5	2.49
P	Ken Trinkle	NY	151	7–14	3.87	Ralph Hamner	Chi	71.1	2–7	4.42
P	Monte Kennedy	NY	186.2	9–10	3.42	Ellis Kinder	StL	86.2	3–3	3.32
P	Warren Spahn	Bos	125.2	8–5	2.94	Cuddles Marshall	NY	81	3–4	5.33
P	Emil Kush	Chi	129.2	9–2	3.05	Bill Wight	NY	40.1	2–2	4.46
P	Ed Bahr	Pit	136.2	8–6	2.63	Bill Kennedy	Was	39	1–2	6.00
P	Johnny Hetki	Cin	126.1	6–6	2.99	Fred Sanford*	StL	22	2–1	2.05

*The AL rookie leader in shutouts despite making only three starts all season.

serted as a pinch runner in the tenth inning and steals home to give the Cardinals a 9–8 win over the Braves; the game is critical as St. Louis ends the regular schedule in a tie with Brooklyn.

June 23—Cubs rookie teammates Eddie Waitkus and Marv Rickert hit back-to-back inside-the-park homers in the fourth inning at the Polo Grounds, but Chicago still loses 15–10 to the Giants.

September 4—Cliff Fannin of the Browns wins his first career start, topping Ed Lopat of the White Sox 5–1; despite not making his ML debut with the

Batting		Pitching	
G—AL 122, Chuck Stevens, STL		W—AL 5, Cliff Fannin, STL	
NL 144, Ralph Kiner, PIT		NL 14, Joe Hatten, BRO	
AB—AL 432, Chuck Stevens, STL		L—AL 15, Bob Savage, PHI	
NL 540, Del Ennis, PHI		NL 14, Ken Trinkle, NY	
H—AL 107, Chuck Stevens, STL		PCT—AL .167, Bob Savage, PHI	
NL 169, Del Ennis, PHI		NL .560, Joe Hatten, BRO	
2B—AL 17, Chuck Stevens, STL		GP—AL 40, Bob Savage, PHI	
NL 30, Del Ennis, PHI		**NL 48, Ken Trinkle, NY**	
3B—AL 5, Gene Handley, PHI		GS—AL 19, Bob Savage, PHI	
Whitey Platt, CHI		NL 30, Joe Hatten, BRO	
NL 8, Eddie Lukon, CIN		CG—AL 7, Bob Savage, PHI	
HR—AL 6, Hank Helf, STL		NL 13, Joe Hatten, BRO	
NL 23, Ralph Kiner, PIT		IP—AL 164.0, Bob Savage, PHI	
R—AL 53, Chuck Stevens, STL		NL 222.0, Joe Hatten, BRO	
NL 70, Del Ennis, PHI		H—AL 164, Bob Savage, PHI	
RBI—AL 33, Hoot Evers, DET		NL 207, Joe Hatten, BRO	
NL 81, Ralph Kiner, PIT		BB—AL 93, Bob Savage, PHI	
WK—AL 47, Chuck Stevens, STL		**NL 116, Monte Kennedy, NY**	
NL 74, Ralph Kiner, PIT		K—AL 78, Bob Savage, PHI	
SO—AL 62, Chuck Stevens, STL		NL 100, Ewell Blackwell, CIN	
NL 109, Ralph Kiner, PIT		ERA—AL 4.06, Bob Savage, PHI	
SB—AL 8, Bob Dillinger, STL		NL 2.45, Ewell Blackwell, CIN	
Gene Handley, PHI		SHO—AL 2, Fred Sanford, STL	
NL 16, Bobby Adams, CIN		**NL 5, Ewell Blackwell, CIN**	
BA—AL .248, Chuck Stevens, STL		SV—AL 3, Bill Kennedy, WAS	
NL .313, Del Ennis, PHI		NL 4, Hank Behrman, BRO	
SLG—AL .326, Chuck Stevens, STL			
NL .485, Del Ennis, PHI			
OBP—AL .324, Chuck Stevens, STL			
NL .369, Grady Hatton, CIN			

Browns until September 2, Fannin will lead all AL rookies in wins with five.

September 22—Browns rookie Fred Sanford joins the short list of hurlers who have hurled shutouts in each of their first two ML starts when he blanks the White Sox 2–0 a week to the day after whitewashing the Yankees 1–0 in his first ML starting assignment.

1947

When Brooklyn rookie Jack Roosevelt Robinson took the field against the Boston Braves on Opening Day in 1947, it was arguably the most electrifying moment in the game's long history. Robinson's ML debut marked the first appearance in 63 years by an African-American on a major league diamond and punctured an ugly cloud that had hung over baseball ever since 1885 when draconian owners celebrated the collapse of the Union Association and a concomitant reduction in ML jobs by establishing an unofficial color barrier. Some three months later, on July 5, 1947, the AL was likewise integrated when Larry Doby of Cleveland stepped to the plate as a pinch hitter against Earl Harrist of the White Sox.

Doby's adjustment to ML pitching was painfully slow—he hit just .156 in 1947—but Robinson was an instant sensation. A middle infielder by trade, in his rookie year Robinson was installed instead at first base where the Dodgers had a gaping hole. Along with leading all NL rookies in batting, he established a new post-

Deadball Era record for senior loop first sackers when he swiped 29 bases. When Robinson's contributions helped bring the Dodgers both the NL pennant and a new league attendance record, he deservedly was voted the first winner of the newly established Baseball Writers Association of America (BBWAA) Rookie of the Year Award or the J. Louis Comiskey Memorial Award, as it was then called. During the 1987 Hall of Fame induction ceremony, Commissioner Peter Ueberroth announced that the award would henceforth be known as the Jackie Robinson Award.

But if the Dodgers had the top individual rookie in 1947, the Giants had by far the most outstanding rookie class. In addition to Larry Jansen (21–5), the NL winning-percentage champ, and slugging third sacker Bobby Thomson, the frosh home run king, skipper Mel Ott also had the services of Lucky Lohrke, one of the few "lucky" members of his Spokane minor league team to escape a catastrophic bus crash the previous year unscathed, and Clint Hartung, a yearling pitcher-outfielder whose prodigious skills were so multifaceted that he seemed a real-life incarnation of Ozark Ike, a comic-strip baseball hero of the 1940s.

Even with all that yearling talent, plus a record-shattering 221 homers, the Giants finished a distant fourth in 1947. The defending AL champion Red Sox did only slightly better, finishing third despite flourishing the junior loop's best rookie hitting tandem in first sacker Jake Jones, the frosh RBI leader, and Sam Mele, the AL's yearling pacesetter in runs and SA. Much of Boston's failure to repeat in 1947 could be traced to the Yankees producing an even stronger recruit assemblage. Two midseason additions, outfielder Allie Clark (.373 in 24 games) and Vic Raschi (7–2 in 14 starts), joined with catcher Yogi Berra, who had 54 RBI in just 293 at bats, and pitcher Spec Shea, to help launch the Bronx Bombers on a 19-game winning skein that tied the AL record set by the 1906 White Sox and rocketed Bucky Harris's men into an insurmountable lead that brought them home 12 games ahead of the Tigers.

Had there been a dual J. Louis Comiskey Award for both leagues in 1947, the vastly underappreciated Shea ought to have been an easy winner in the AL. He topped all junior loop pitchers in OBA, a title that he would bag again the following year, won the All-Star game, and then won two games against the Dodgers in the 1947

On June 14, 1947, the Chicago White Sox and Boston Red Sox swapped first basemen as rookie Jake Jones, a World War II pilot credited with shooting down seven enemy planes, went from cavernous Comiskey Park to friendly Fenway in return for aging Rudy York. It was regarded as a major trade at the time and a potentially bad one for Chicago—York was nearly finished and Jones seemingly had a fine career ahead of him. As it turned out, the deal had little long-range impact on the fortunes of either team and is no longer remembered as a particularly significant transaction. With a slight reordering of events, however, it might now be very memorable, at least in rookie annals. Had Jones been traded a week or two earlier, it seems likely that he would have collected another home run or two given Fenway's short leftfield porch. Even just one more home run would have raised him to 20, an important figure in that the current record for the fewest career homers by a performer who had 20 as a rookie stands at 29. Jones finished his short ML tour of duty midway through the 1948 season with just 23 career dingers.

But if Jones missed out on one dubious record owing to the mistiming of his trade in 1947, he did manage to set another equally dubious mark. His 96 RBI in 1947 were the most in AL history to that point, as well as the most in the twentieth century, by a player with a sub-.250 batting average. Second to Jones after the 1947 season was none other than Rudy York, who collected 91 ribbies with Boston and Chicago combined. Below is the list of the top ten RBI producers on a sub-.250 BA prior to 1953 when Eddie Robinson became the first to reach 100 RBI (102) while hitting less than .250. It suggests that, in effect, the Jones-York trade, rather than being a major one, was almost irrelevant, as the two players involved in the deal almost exactly canceled each other out in 1947.

Rank	Name	Year	BA	RBI
1	Jake Beckley	1892	.236	96
	Jake Jones	1947	.237	96
3	Rudy York	1947	.233	91
4	Babe Dahlgren	1939	.235	89
5	Vince DiMaggio	1943	.248	88
	Bill Nicholson	1945	.243	88
7	Reddy Mack	1889	.241	87
	Jim Canavan	1891	.238	87
9	Charlie Duffee	1889	.244	86
	Ed Delahanty	1891	.243	86

World Series. But for the fact that Shea missed seven weeks in midseason with a pulled neck muscle, he otherwise might also have led the AL in victories. A second neck injury ultimately ruined his career with the Yankees

Batting	Pitching
G—AL 154, Jake Jones, CHI/BOS	W—AL 14, Spec Shea, NY
NL 151, Frankie Baumholtz, CIN	NL 21, Larry Jansen, NY
Jackie Robinson, BRO	L—AL 16, Fred Sanford, STL
AB—AL 575, Jake Jones, CHI/BOS	NL 13, Kent Peterson, CIN
NL 643, Frankie Baumholtz, CIN	PCT—AL .737, Spec Shea, NY
H—AL 156, Dale Mitchell, CLE	**NL .808, Larry Jansen, NY**
NL 182, Frankie Baumholtz, CIN	GP—AL 41, Harry Dorish, BOS
2B—AL 28, Ferris Fain, PHI	NL 42, Larry Jansen, NY
NL 32, Frankie Baumholtz, CIN	GS—AL 23, Fred Sanford, STL
3B—AL 11, Dave Philley, CHI	Spec Shea, NY
NL 9, Frankie Baumholtz, CIN	NL 30, Larry Jansen, NY
HR—AL 19, Jake Jones, CHI/BOS	CG—AL 13, Spec Shea, NY
NL 29, Bobby Thomson, NY	NL 20, Larry Jansen, NY
R—AL 71, Sam Mele, BOS	IP—AL 186.2, Fred Sanford, STL
NL 125, Jackie Robinson, BRO	NL 248.0, Larry Jansen, NY
RBI—AL 96, Jake Jones, CHI/BOS	H—AL 186, Fred Sanford, STL
NL 85, Bobby Thomson, NY	NL 241, Larry Jansen, NY
WK—AL 95, Ferris Fain, PHI	BB—AL 89, Spec Shea, NY
NL 82, Earl Torgeson, BOS	NL 83, Harry Taylor, BRO
SO—AL 85, Jake Jones, CHI/BOS	K—AL 89, Spec Shea, NY
NL 78, Bobby Thomson, NY	NL 104, Larry Jansen, NY
SB—AL 21, Dave Philley, CHI	ERA—AL 3.07, Spec Shea, NY
NL 29, Jackie Robinson, BRO	NL 3.11, Harry Taylor, BRO
BA—AL .316, Dale Mitchell, CLE	SHO—AL 3, Spec Shea, NY
NL .297, Jackie Robinson, BRO	NL 2, Harry Taylor, BRO
SLG—AL .448, Sam Mele, BOS	SV—AL 5, Pete Gebrian, CHI
NL .508, Bobby Thomson, NY	NL 2, Kent Peterson, CIN
OBP—AL .414, Ferris Fain, PHI	
NL .403, Earl Torgeson, BOS	

when it was misdiagnosed as an arm problem. Although Shea's ailment was eventually cured by a chiropractor, by then he had drifted to the Senators where a series of second-division clubs would enable him only partially to retrieve his early success before retiring in 1955.

Other Highlights

April 15—Jackie Robinson, the first black performer to appear in an ML game in 63 years, is 0-for-3 in his debut with Brooklyn as the Dodgers top the Braves 5–3 under interim manager Clyde Sukeforth, the man credited by some with first having scouted Robinson for the Dodgers.

April 17—Jackie Robinson collects his first ML hit off Glenn Elliott in a 12–6 Brooklyn win over the Braves.

May 9—Clint Hartung, the game's most vaunted rookie at the start of the season, makes his first mound appearance with the Giants and hurls six shutout innings; Hartung will hit .309 and go 9–7 in 1947 as a combination pitcher-outfielder.

June 18—Reds rookie Frankie Baumholtz, who doubles as a pro basketball player in the off-season with the Cleveland Rebels, chips in four hits as teammate Ewell Blackwell no-hits the Braves 6–0.

July 17—Hank Thompson is the second black player in AL history when he plays second base for the St. Louis Browns.

July 20—When Thompson is joined on the Browns by veteran Negro League centerfielder Willard Brown, it marks the first time in ML history that two black players have appeared in the same ML game.

August 13—Willard Brown is the first black American to homer in an AL game when he hits a pinch inside-the-park dinger in a 6–5 Browns' win over Tigers ace Hal Newhouser.

August 26—Dan Bankhead of the Dodgers is the first black American to hurl in an ML game; in the process of being rocked for ten hits by Pittsburgh in a 3⅓ inning relief stint, Bankhead also becomes the first black player to homer in his first ML at bat when he goes deep against Fritz Ostermueller.

September 1—Jack "Lucky" Lohrke, so nicknamed because he got off a Spokane team bus in 1946 just minutes before it careened off a mountain road and killed nine club members, hits the Giants' 183rd home run in 1947 to break the former team record of 182 set by the 1936 Yankees; the Giants will finish with 221 homers, 11 by Lohrke.

September 3—Rookie Bill McCahan of the A's, like Baumholtz a pro basketball player in the winter, no-hits the Senators 3–0; McCahan loses his bid for a perfect game in the second inning when fellow rookie Ferris Fain, considered one of the slickest fielding first basemen of his era, feeds him an errant toss as he races from the mound to cover first on a routine grounder.

September 25—Giants rookie ace Larry Jansen wins his 21st game and his tenth in a row, beating the Braves 2–1 in his final start of the season

October 4—Spec Shea wins Game Five of the World Series for the Yankees 2–1 on a four-hitter and aids his own cause with two hits.

━ 1948 ━

The 1948 campaign was the last season in which the BBWAA selected only one Rookie of the Year. Although the runaway winner was a shortstop, Alvin Dark of the Boston Braves, and the runner-up in many minds was either centerfielder Richie Ashburn of the Phils or outfielder-first baseman Billy Goodman of the Red Sox, the 1948 season, insofar as the overall rookie class

is concerned, should be remembered as "The Year of the Southpaw." In the spring attention focused on Billy Pierce, a 21-year-old Detroit native who was expected to combine with Tigers kingpin Hal Newhouser to give the Bengals one of the most formidable southpaw starting duos in AL history. But when Pierce proved unready and was designated instead for bullpen duty, the spotlight fell on rookie portsider Bill Wight, who had almost immediately been installed as the White Sox ace after coming to Chicago from the Yankees over the winter in a trade for veteran southpaw Eddie Lopat.

As April ended and May began, yet to make their presence felt were three other AL rookie southpaws who would each leave a distinctive footprint on the 1948 season. One was Lou Brissie of the A's, a 24-year-old war vet who had required 23 operations after being wounded in Italy. Despite having a steel plate in his head and being forced to wear a steel brace and shin

Bill Wight was regarded as the most promising pitcher in the Yankees' farm system in 1947 after he won 16 games for Kansas City. Part of the steep price the New York club paid the White Sox in February 1948 in exchange for lefty Ed Lopat, Wight was expected to contend for Rookie of the Year honors. Instead he led all hurlers in the majors in walks surrendered, was second in the AL in losses, and posted the third-worst ERA among AL qualifiers. *Transcendental Graphics*

guard on his left leg when he pitched, Brissie won 14 games in 1948. Another southpaw who did not begin to emerge until the season was several weeks old was Cleveland's Gene Bearden, also a wounded war vet, and the third novice lefty lurking in the wings was "Terrible" Tommy Byrne of the Yankees.

Byrne's control problems were so severe that prior to 1948 he had pitched a total of 45.1 innings in the majors over parts of three seasons and given up 49 walks. As a result, Yankees pilot Bucky Harris was loath to use him except in desperation. Injuries to other New York pitchers finally drove Harris to start Byrne for the first time in 1948 on June 27 at Detroit. Byrne blanked the Tigers 7–0 but nonetheless finished with just an 8–5 record as he became the first hurler in history to surrender 100 walks (101) in a season despite working less than 140 innings (133⅔). Byrne's wildness masked a second historic feat that he performed in 1948. He allowed just 5.31 enemy hits per nine innings, at that time a record 3.88 hits below the league average for a pitcher in a minimum of 125 innings. The following year, even though he gave up 179 walks in just 196 innings, Byrne officially led the AL in OBA and allowed 3.28 hits below the league average, a record among ERA qualifiers that stood until 1991.

HITS/NINE IP BELOW LEAGUE AVERAGE, MINIMUM 125 IP

Rank	Name	Year	IP	H/9 IP	LA	Diff
1	Pedro Martinez	2000	217	5.31	9.66	4.35
2	Tommy Byrne	1948	133.2	5.31	9.19	3.88
3	Goose Gossage	1977	133	5.28	8.97	3.69
4	Nolan Ryan	1991	173	5.31	8.92	3.61
5	Jim Hearn	1950	134	5.64	9.06	3.42
6	Tommy Byrne	1949	196	5.74	9.02	3.28
7	Randy Johnson	1997	213	6.21	9.48	3.27
8	Hideo Nomo	1995	191.1	5.83	9.06	3.23
9	Nolan Ryan	1977	299	5.96	9.16	3.20
10	Pedro Martinez	1997	241.1	5.89	8.97	3.08

But if Byrne's remarkable rookie accomplishments were obscured for many years by his legendary wildness, Bearden's frosh achievements have stood out in sharp relief ever since the final curtain was drawn on the 1948 season. On the morning of September 16, Bearden sported a 14–7 record and was vying with Brissie for the lead in rookie wins. In the next 18 days, Bearden put on

The National League had no one like the AL's three B's—Bearden, Byrne, and Brissie—to contribute to "The Year of the Southpaw," but it still had an intriguing assortment of rookie lefties. Foremost among them was Phillies Bonus Baby Curt Simmons, who led all NL frosh in walks and tied for the lead in losses. Brooklyn debuted 32-year-old Willie Ramsdell, the NL frosh saves leader and one of the first portsiders to rely mainly on the knuckleball. The Cubs organization, perhaps remembering their fiasco several years earlier when they failed to care properly for the talented left arm of minor league sensation Boyd Tepler and thereby lost the services of what might have been one of the greatest pitchers in franchise history, opted to keep Dutch McCall on the parent club in 1948 despite his abysmal 5–12 season with Los Angeles of the PCL the previous year. A converted outfielder, McCall was nearly as wild as Tommy Byrne, but like Byrne, he also had great stuff when he was on his game and in 1946 had tied the Southern Association single-game strikeout record when he fanned 17 on April 30.

McCall won his first ML start on April 27, 1948, beating Reds ace Ewell Blackwell, 7–2. He then embarked on a club-record 13-game losing streak that carried him to September 22 with a 1–13 log. That afternoon, in the second game of a doubleheader at New York, McCall broke his horrendous skid by staggering to an 11–7 win. A week later he beat the Reds top lefty, Johnny Vander Meer, and in the Cubs' final game of the season, on October 3 at St. Louis, he edged Murray Dickson, 4–3. Thus, McCall finished his rookie campaign on quite a roll, winning his last three starts after suffering 13 straight losses. He also finished his ML career on quite a roll, for he never threw another pitch in the bigs after his win at St. Louis in the 1948 season finale.

the greatest finishing spurt of any rookie pitcher in history, especially in the heat of a pennant race. He made six starts and won them all, including four in the final nine days of the season. The culmination was his 8–3 triumph at Boston's Fenway Park on October 4 in the first pennant playoff game in AL history.

Bearden's iron-man effort in the closing days of the 1948 season brought him 20 wins as well as the AL ERA crown, but he was still not finished. In Game Three of the World Series, he blanked the Braves 2–0 on five hits. Slated to start Game Seven if it was necessary, Bearden was brought out of the bullpen instead three days later to save a 4–3 Cleveland lead in Game Six, giving him a perfect 0.00 ERA for 10.2 innings of work in the series.

Batting		Pitching	
G—AL 150, Al Kozar, WAS		W—AL 20, Gene Bearden, CLE	
NL 149, Virgil Stallcup, CIN		NL 14, Bob Chesnes, PIT	
AB—AL 577, Al Kozar, WAS		L—AL 20, Bill Wight, CHI	
NL 584, Whitey Lockman, NY		NL 13, Dutch McCall, CHI	
H—AL 144, Al Kozar, WAS		Curt Simmons, PHI	
NL 175, Alvin Dark, BOS		PCT—AL .741, Gene Bearden, CLE	
2B—AL 27, Billy Goodman, BOS		NL .700, Bob Chesnes, PIT	
NL 39, Alvin Dark, BOS		GP—AL 49, Al Widmar, STL	
3B—AL 9, Larry Doby, CLE		NL 54, Jess Dobernic, CHI	
George Vico, DET		GS—AL 32, Bill Wight, CHI	
NL 10, Whitey Lockman, NY		NL 24, Herm Wehmeier, CIN	
HR—AL 14, Larry Doby, CLE		CG—AL 15, Gene Bearden, CLE	
NL 18, Whitey Lockman, NY		NL 15, Bob Chesnes, PIT	
R—AL 83, Larry Doby, CLE		IP—AL 229.2, Gene Bearden, CLE	
NL 117, Whitey Lockman, NY		NL 194.1, Bob Chesnes, PIT	
RBI—AL 66, Larry Doby, CLE		H—AL 238, Bill Wight, CHI	
Billy Goodman, BOS		NL 180, Bob Chesnes, PIT	
NL 81, Nippy Jones, STL		BB—**AL 135, Bill Wight, CHI**	
WK—AL 74, Billy Goodman, BOS		NL 108, Curt Simmons, PHI	
NL 68, Whitey Lockman, NY		K—AL 127, Lou Brissie, PHI	
SO—AL 77, Larry Doby, CLE		NL 89, Dutch McCall, CHI	
NL 77, Johnny Blatnik, PHI		ERA—**AL 2.43, Gene Bearden, CLE**	
SB—AL 9, Larry Doby, CLE		NL 3.57, Bob Chesnes, PIT	
NL 32, Richie Ashburn, PHI		SHO—AL 6, Gene Bearden, CLE	
BA—AL .310, Billy Goodman, BOS		NL 1, Vern Bickford, BOS	
NL .333, Richie Ashburn, PHI		Cliff Chambers, CHI	
SLG—AL .490, Larry Doby, CLE		SV—AL 8, Howie Judson, CHI	
NL .454, Whitey Lockman, NY		NL 4, Willie Ramsdell, BRO	
OBP—AL .414, Billy Goodman, BOS			
NL .410, Richie Ashburn, PHI			

Other Highlights

April 19—In his ML debut World War II vet Lou Brissie, who has a metal plate in one leg, is felled when he is struck on the game leg by a hard line drive off the bat of Ted Williams but recovers to give the A's a 4–2 win over the Red Sox.

April 20—First baseman Sam Vico of the Tigers joins the select group of players who homered on the first pitch they saw in the majors when he goes the distance on Joe Haynes of the White Sox.

June 5—Phils speedster Richie Ashburn hits safely in his 23rd straight game to set a new twentieth-century record for NL rookies; Ashburn's mark will be matched a few weeks later by Braves rookie shortstop Alvin Dark.

June 30—Johnny Antonelli, an 18-year-old southpaw from Rochester, New York, is given a record $75,000 bonus by the Boston Braves; later that summer the Tigers will hand roughly the same staggering amount to teenage catcher Frank House.

July 13—At Sportsman's Park in St. Louis, centerfielder Richie Ashburn of the Phils becomes the first NL rookie to start an All-Star Game and goes 2-for-4.

August 13—The last-place White Sox draw 51,013 to Comiskey Park to watch recently signed Cleveland rookie Satchel Paige hurl the first shutout in ML history by a black pitcher as the Tribe wins 5–0.

After seeing the initial two official Rookie of the Year awards go to senior loop freshmen, the American League was assured of having its first winner in 1949 when the BBWAA instigated the custom of choosing the best yearling in each league. The same three writers in each league city who selected the MVP winners participated in the voting.

At the beginning of the 1949 season, the National League was without a clear favorite for the award, as its two leading freshmen in the eventual balloting, Brooklyn pitcher Don Newcombe and 19-year-old Braves catcher Del Crandall, both began the year in the minors. Virtually every AL writer had the same preseason choice, however: centerfielder Johnny Groth of the Tigers. Touted as a potential combination of Ty Cobb and Harry Heilmann, Groth seemed capable of living up to his advance billing when he slugged two home runs on Opening Day. But soon after that he fell prey to a string of nagging injuries that held him to only 348 at bats. Groth's favorite role then shifted to slugging outfielder Gus Zernial of the White Sox, but Zernial also became an injury victim when he broke his collarbone diving for a fly ball. By September the winner of the first AL ROY Award, if only by default, seemed likely to be A's southpaw Alex Kellner, who was zeroing in on 20 wins. When the final ballots were counted, however, the victor was Browns outfielder Roy Sievers. Prior to the season, Sievers had been a long shot even to make the Browns' roster after spending most of the 1948 campaign in the Class B Three I League. But an unexpected opening occurred when veteran outfielders Paul Lehner, Stan Spence, and Whitey Platt all had poor years, and Sievers made the most of his opportunity as he topped all rookies in BA, SA, OBP, and RBI and also paced the Browns with a .869 OPS.

Third in the AL rookie balloting behind Sievers and Kellner was second baseman Jerry Coleman, the principal graduate of yet another strong rookie class produced by the Yankees. In 1949, their first season with Casey Stengel at the helm, along with Coleman the Bombers brought in Hank Bauer as their new right fielder, installed a third recruit, Charlie Silvera, as the backup catcher to Yogi Berra, and tested no less than four recruit first basemen—Dick Kryhoski, Joe Collins,

The 1949 season was one of a kind, especially in the American League. Led by Tommy Byrne with 179, no less than 19 pitchers surrendered 100 or more walks. All but three of the 19 were AL hurlers, including two rookies, 20-game winner Alex Kellner of the A's and three-game winner Dick Weik of the last-place Senators.

Just one year after Byrne had become the first hurler ever to reach triple figures in walks in less than 140 innings, Weik became the first and only hurler to date to top 100 walks despite pitching less than 100 innings. Rather incredibly, second to Weik on the all-time list for the most walks in a season in less than 100 innings is a teammate of his on the 1949 Senators, Dick Welteroth.

MOST WALKS, SEASON, LESS THAN 100 IP

Rank	Name	Year	IP	BB
1	Dick Weik	1949	95.1	103
2	Dick Welteroth	1949	95.1	89
3	Steve Blass	1973	88.2	84
4	Ken Wright	1973	80.2	82
5	Mitch Williams	1986	98	79

Jack Phillips, and Fenton Mole—with Collins emerging as the eventual winner of the job.

In postseason play Coleman led the Yankees in at bats and was second on the club in hits and RBI. Newcombe, meanwhile, endeavored to become the first rookie in history to win Game One of a World Series via a shutout but received no cooperation from his Brooklyn teammates. After the Dodgers had scraped together just two hits all day off Yankees ace Allie Reynolds, Newcombe entered the bottom of the ninth at Yankee Stadium in a scoreless tie, only to see it rudely shattered by Tommy Henrich's leadoff homer.

Other Highlights

May 6—In his second ML appearance (his first lasted only a third of an inning five days earlier), A's rookie Bobby Shantz relieves starter Carl Scheib in the fourth inning with a runner on third and none out and proceeds to hurl nine hitless innings before surrendering a run in the top of the 13th, but then he gains his first ML win, 5–4 over the Tigers, when Wally Moses slugs a two-run pinch homer in the bottom of the frame.

Batting	Pitching
G—AL 140, Roy Sievers, STL	**W**—AL 20, Alex Kellner, PHI
NL 149, Willie Jones, PHI	NL 17, Don Newcombe, BRO
AB—AL 471, Roy Sievers, STL	**L**—AL 12, Alex Kellner, PHI
NL 532, Willie Jones, PHI	Dick Weik, WAS
H—AL 144, Roy Sievers, STL	NL 13, Bill Werle, PIT
NL 130, Willie Jones, PHI	**PCT**—AL .737, Mike Garcia, CLE
2B—AL 28, Roy Sievers, STL	NL .680, Don Newcombe, BRO
NL 35, Willie Jones, PHI	**GP**—AL 44, Max Surkont, CHI
3B—AL 6, Hank Bauer, NY	NL 48, Jack Banta, BRO
Chuck Kress, CHI	**GS**—AL 27, Alex Kellner, PHI
NL 6, Stan Hollmig, PHI	NL 31, Don Newcombe, BRO
HR—AL 16, Roy Sievers, STL	**CG**—AL 19, Alex Kellner, PHI
NL 19, Willie Jones, PHI	NL 19, Don Newcombe, BRO
R—AL 84, Roy Sievers, STL	**IP**—AL 245.0, Alex Kellner, PHI
NL 71, Willie Jones, PHI	NL 244.1, Don Newcombe, BRO
RBI—AL 91, Roy Sievers, STL	**H**—AL 243, Alex Kellner, PHI
NL 77, Willie Jones, PHI	NL 243, Bill Werle, PIT
WK—AL 70, Roy Sievers, STL	**BB**—AL 129, Alex Kellner, PHI
NL 65, Willie Jones, PHI	NL 73, Don Newcombe, BRO
SO—AL 75, Roy Sievers, STL	**K**—AL 94, Mike Garcia, CLE
NL 66, Willie Jones, PHI	Alex Kellner, PHI
SB—AL 8, Jerry Coleman, NY	NL 149, Don Newcombe, BRO
NL 5, Tom Saffell, PIT	**ERA**—**AL 2.36, Mike Garcia, CLE**
Hank Thompson, NY	NL 3.17, Don Newcombe, BRO
BA—AL .306, Roy Sievers, STL	**SHO**—AL 5, Mike Garcia, CLE
NL .268, Pete Castiglione, PIT	**NL 5, Don Newcombe, BRO**
SLG—AL .471, Roy Sievers, STL	**SV**—AL 4, Max Surkont, CHI
NL .421, Willie Jones, PHI	NL 3, Jack Banta, BRO
OBP—AL .398, Roy Sievers, STL	
NL .328, Willie Jones, PHI	

June 15—Dino Restelli joins the Pirates after being re-called from San Francisco of the PCL; in his first 39 at bats with Pittsburgh, Restelli will pound seven home runs and seem destined for certain ROY honors, but his career instead will come to a quick halt when he collects only six more homers in his next 231 at bats and sags to a .241 BA.

June 16—Nineteen-year-old Del Crandall is recalled by the Braves from their Evansville farm club and becomes the youngest NL player since 1876 to serve as his team's regular catcher.

July 8—Monte Irvin and Hank Thompson make the Giants the fourth team in the majors to feature two black players in the same game; the previous three, in order, were the Browns, the Dodgers, and the Indians.

August 26—Rookie lefty Bob Kuzava of the White Sox ties a then-existing AL record when he fans six Red Sox hitters in a row in the first two innings of the second game of a doubleheader at Comiskey Park.

September 14—Phils outfielder Eddie Sanicki socks a three-run homer off Rip Sewell of the Pirates in his first ML at bat; two weeks later, on September 28 at Shibe Park, Sanicki will collect his third and final hit of the season, and also his third home run, when he goes yard against Sheldon Jones of the Giants; the blow will give

Sanicki a 1.209 OPS for the 1949 season on just a .231 BA (3-for-13).

October 1—Rookie southpaw Alex Kellner bags his 20th win, making him the first A's hurler to win 20 since Lefty Grove in 1933.

October 2—On the closing day of the season, in the second game of a doubleheader that is abbreviated to five innings, Ed Albrecht of the Browns tosses a one-hitter in his ML debut to edge Mickey Haefner of the White Sox 5–3; Albrecht's victory, following his 29 wins that year with Pine Bluff of the Class C Cotton States League, enables him to become the last hurler in history to post a 30-win season in the minors and majors combined and represents his only ML win.

October 19—The A's make what may be their worst deal ever when they give up on rookie second baseman Nellie Fox after he posts just a .296 SA and ship him to the White Sox for backup catcher Joe Tipton.

9

1950s

1950

The first chink in the system of selecting the game's top rookies appeared in 1950. Previously all of the ROY winners had been, if not unanimous, at least free of controversy. In 1950, however, it grew evident that allowing each voter to use his individual judgment to determine the eligibility of candidates for the ROY prizes could create serious problems. The conflict that year erupted around Cleveland's Al Rosen, who not only paced the AL in homers but set what is now regarded as a new AL frosh four-bagger mark with 37, only to be denied the top rookie honor because he had 58 previous ML at bats. Selected instead was Red Sox first baseman Walt Dropo despite having collected 41 ML at bats prior to 1950. Accusations, especially from Cleveland followers, that the voters were employing arbitrary criteria tainted Dropo's prize, perhaps unfairly inasmuch as Dropo was without question a plausible winner. Although Rosen led all rookies in home runs and OBP, Dropo posted the top freshman BA and SA and finished with 144 RBI, just one short of Ted Williams's all-time rookie record.

Second to Dropo in the official AL rookie balloting was Yankees southpaw Whitey Ford on the basis of the dazzling 9–1 record he logged after he was called up from New York's Kansas City affiliate just before the All-Star break. Had Ford played for an NL team in 1950, he might well have won the loop's top frosh prize, as AL clubs, for the first season since the war, owned the bulk of the game's novice talent. The irony is that, notwithstanding the fact that the AL's rookie crop was far superior to the NL's, the 1950 season is best remembered for "The Whiz Kids," the conglomerate of youthful Philadelphia Phillies who, to the surprise of everyone, walked off with the club's first pennant since 1915. In actuality, although the Phillies indeed were young, they were not the youngest team in the majors in 1950—the Browns were. Moreover, skipper Eddie Sawyer had no rookie position players of consequence and only two freshmen in all, pitchers Bob Miller and Bubba Church, who contributed anything significant to the club's pennant effort.

By the closing weeks of the season, both Miller and Church were on the disabled list, although Miller did remain active long enough to lead all NL freshman hurlers in wins. The overall frosh win leader played for the

Phillies' Shibe Park co-tenant, as for the second year in a row Connie Mack's A's produced the game's top yearling mound bulwark. But whereas Alex Kellner had bagged 20 wins in 1949 despite surrendering a rookie-high 129 walks, in 1950 the A's newest rotation member, Bob Hooper, survived a 5.02 ERA and a dismal bases on balls–to–strikeouts ratio of 1.57 (91/58) to register a .600 winning percentage (15–10), the highest by a recruit pitcher with a 5.00+ ERA prior to 2003, when Jeriome Robertson carved out a .625 winning percentage despite a 5.10 ERA. Of even more importance to historians, Hooper's rookie performance made him what is likely to be the last hurler ever to win as many as 15 games with a bases on balls–to–strikeouts ratio worse than 1.50.

MOST WINS WITH BB/K RATIO WORSE THAN 1.5, MINIMUM 90 WALKS, SINCE 1901

Rank	Name	Year	SO	BB	Ratio	Wins
1	Ted Lyons	1926	51	106	2.1	18
	Jimmie DeShong	1936	59	96	1.6	18
3	Jack Coombs	1915	56	91	1.6	15
	Claude Willoughby	1929	50	108	2.2	15
	Dick Fowler	1949	43	115	2.7	15
	Bob Hooper	1950	58	91	1.6	15
7	Bert Husting	1902	48	99	2.1	14
	Tom Zachary	1926	53	97	1.8	14
	Charlie Wagner	1942	52	95	1.8	14
10	Sugar Cain	1933	43	137	3.2	12

When centerfielder Sam Jethroe of the Boston Braves copped the NL ROY Award in 1950 at age 32, he became the oldest BBWAA rookie honoree to date. But Jethroe was by no means the oldest freshman that season. The distinction belonged to Senators pitcher Connie Marrero, who admitted to being 35 in 1950 but later was discovered to have actually been just ten days short of 39 when he made his big league debut.

A stockily built 5′5″ junk baller, the Cuban-born Marrero started his pro career in 1947 with Havana of the Florida International League. After three consecutive 20-win seasons for Havana, Marrero followed in the tradition of many previous Latino hurlers by joining the Senators. He survived a rocky rookie season that brought him only six wins in 19 starts to make the AL All-Star team the following year and lead the Senators in victories. Marrero finished his ML career in 1954 with 39 wins and 735.1 innings. Both figures are highs among pitchers who did not make their ML debuts until they had celebrated their 35th birthdays, let alone were fast approaching their 39th.

Sam Jethroe, probably the only Rookie of the Year honoree who was already past his prime when he won the award. Jethroe celebrated his 32nd birthday some three months before he made his ML debut with the Boston Braves. The long-time Negro leagues star did not accompany the Braves in 1953 when they moved to Milwaukee, returning to the minors instead. Along with advancing age, Jethroe began experiencing vision problems in the early 1950s. When he returned to the majors briefly in 1954 with the Pirates, he was wearing glasses. *Transcendental Graphics*

Other Highlights

January 31—The Pirates make high-school pitcher Paul Pettit the first $100,000 Bonus Baby.

April 18—Sam Jethroe is the first black to play for a Boston ML entry when he goes 2-for-4 and homers in his debut with the Braves; the other Boston team, the Red Sox, will be the last ML team to integrate.

April 18—When Yankees second baseman Billy Martin doubles in the eighth inning against the Red Sox and then singles later in the frame, he becomes the first performer ever to collect two base hits in one inning in his first ML game.

May 1—Walt Dropo is recalled by the Red Sox from their Louisville farm club when regular first baseman

Batting

G—AL 155, Al Rosen, CLE
    NL 141, Sam Jethroe, BOS
AB—AL 559, Walt Dropo, BOS
    NL 582, Sam Jethroe, BOS
H—AL 180, Walt Dropo, BOS
    NL 159, Sam Jethroe, BOS
2B—AL 28, Walt Dropo, BOS
    NL 28, Sam Jethroe, BOS
3B—AL 10, Irv Noren, WAS
    NL 11, Gus Bell, PIT
HR—**AL 37, Al Rosen, CLE**
    NL 18, Sam Jethroe, BOS
R—AL 101, Walt Dropo, BOS
    NL 100, Sam Jethroe, BOS
RBI—**AL 144, Walt Dropo, BOS**
    NL 66, Monte Irvin, NY
WK—AL 100, Al Rosen, CLE
    NL 65, Bill Serena, CHI
SO—AL 95, Luke Easter, CLE
    NL 93, Sam Jethroe, BOS
SB—AL 7, Tom Upton, STL
    NL 35, Sam Jethroe, BOS
BA—AL .322, Walt Dropo, BOS
    NL .273, Sam Jethroe, BOS
SLG—AL .583, Walt Dropo, BOS
    NL .442, Sam Jethroe, BOS
OBP—AL .405, Al Rosen, CLE
    NL .339, Bill Serena, CHI

Pitching

W—AL 15, Bob Hooper, PHI
    NL 11, Bob Miller, PHI
L—AL 12, Bob Cain, CHI
    NL 10, Bill MacDonald, PIT
PCT—AL .600, Bob Hooper, PHI
    NL .647, Bob Miller, PHI
GP—AL 45, Bob Hooper, PHI
    NL 41, Dan Bankhead, BRO
GS—AL 23, Bob Cain, CHI
    NL 22, Bob Miller, PHI
CG—AL 11, Bob Cain, CHI
    NL 8, Bubba Church, PHI
IP—AL 171.2, Bob Cain, CHI
    NL 174.0, Bob Miller, PHI
H—AL 181, Bob Hooper, PHI
    NL 190, Bob Miller, PHI
BB—AL 109, Bob Cain, CHI
    NL 88, Dan Bankhead, BRO
        Bill MacDonald, PIT
K—AL 77, Bob Cain, CHI
    NL 96, Dan Bankhead, BRO
ERA—AL 3.93, Bob Cain, CHI
    NL 3.57, Bob Miller, PHI
SHO—AL 2, Sandy Consuegra, WAS
        Whitey Ford, NY
    NL 2, Bubba Church, PHI
        Bill MacDonald, PIT
        Bob Miller, PHI
SV—AL 5, Bob Hooper, PHI
    NL 3, Dan Bankhead, BRO
        Frank Smith, CIN

Billy Goodman is injured; Dropo will be the first AL player to win a ROY Award after beginning the season in the minors.

May 23—Pirates rookie Bill MacDonald blanks the Phils 6–0 in his first ML start; MacDonald will win eight games in his rookie year but will never win another after his career is interrupted for two years by military service.

July 19—The Yankees purchase their first black players, Elston Howard and pitcher Frank Barnes, from the Negro League Kansas City Monarchs; Howard will be the first black to don Yankees pinstripes but not until five years later, long after most of the other ML teams have integrated.

July 23—The 1951 AL ERA champ, rookie Saul Rogovin, wins his own game when he hits a grand slam off Ed Lopat to help the Tigers top the Yankees 6–5.

September 14—When pinch hitter Ted Tappe, who homered two months earlier for Charleston of the Central League in his first minor league at bat, homers for Cincinnati in his first ML at bat off Erv Palica of the Dodgers, he becomes the first and, to date, only documented player in history to go yard in both his first major and minor league at bats in the same season.

September 24—Brother of future Senators pitching star Camilio Pascual, Carlos "Little Potato" Pascual, who began the year as a 20-year-old third baseman with Big

Springs of the Class D Longhorn League and subsequently became a pitcher-infielder, completes his meteoric rise from Class D to the majors by debuting for Washington with a five-hit 3–1 win over the A's; the elder Pascual will make only one more hill appearance in the majors, a losing one.

October 7—Whitey Ford gives the Yankees a four-game sweep of the World Series when he beats the Phils 5–2 for his first of what will be a record ten wins in the Fall Classic.

1951

If ever there was a season when both major leagues were in near perfect sync with respect to the rookie crop each harvested, it was 1951. The two most renowned graduates of the class of 1951 both were just 19 years old when spring training began, played for teams representing the same city, and went on not only to oppose one another in the World Series that year but to vie with each other for the remainder of their careers for recognition as arguably the greatest center fielder of all-time. But if even casual fans of the game know that 1951 marked the debuts of both Mickey Mantle and Willie Mays, only the most dedicated students know that it also marked the lone season in history that the ERA leader in each league was a rookie.

The NL ERA champ, Braves lefty Chet Nichols Jr., was the son of a former ML pitcher. Soon after the 1951 season ended, he was drafted into the military for two years. Upon returning to the game in 1954, Nichols struggled for the next decade to regain his rookie form without ever again fashioning a season in which he pitched enough to qualify for another ERA crown. Saul Rogovin, the AL ERA leader, began the year with Detroit but was traded on May 16 to the White Sox for Bob Cain, a journeyman left-hander who would gain a measure of immortality three months later when he faced the most famous pinch hitter in ML history, Eddie Gaedel, the 3'7" midget brainchild of Browns owner Bill Veeck. After foundering in Detroit and failing to complete any of his four starts, Rogovin completed 17 of 22 starts with the White Sox and paced the AL not only in ERA but also in adjusted pitching runs. Like Nichols, Rogovin did far

and away his best work in his frosh season. Long before the end of the decade of the 1950s, he was gone from the majors and had launched the career that would carry him through the remainder of his life as a public school teacher in his home city of Brooklyn.

Rogovin was not the only White Sox rookie to top the AL in a major batting or pitching department in 1951. Minnie Minoso, who, like Rogovin, had been acquired by the White Sox in an early-season trade, paced the junior loop in both triples and stolen bases and was also the runner-up for the batting title. In conjunction with fellow rookie speedster Jim Busby, who finished second in steals, Minoso sparked sportswriters to dub the long dormant Comiskey Park residents the "Go-Go White Sox," as the Pale Hose, in their initial season under the direction of ex-Tigers catcher Paul Richards, finished in fourth place, their loftiest perch since the end of the war.

Other Highlights

May 1—Minnie Minoso becomes the first black to play for a Chicago ML entry when he holds down third base for the White Sox against the Yankees; in the same game Yankees rookie Mickey Mantle hits his first career home run off Randy Gumpert.

May 6—Braves rookie George Estock, normally a reliever, picks the wrong day to make his one and only ML start as he hooks up with Pirates lefty Cliff Chambers, who hurls only the second no-hitter in Pittsburgh franchise history in winning 3–0; the loss is not only Estock's lone start but also his lone decision in the majors.

May 25—Rookie centerfielder Willie Mays joins the Giants after hitting a torrid .477 with Minneapolis and goes 0-for-5 in his ML debut against the Phillies; Mays will start out 0-for-12 before homering off Warren Spahn of the Braves for his first ML hit.

May 29—Cleveland signs lefty high-school star Billy Joe Davidson for a reported $150,000, the highest sum ever handed to a Bonus Baby; Davidson will never throw a single pitch in the majors.

June 5—Lefty Paul LaPalme of the Pirates hurls a shutout in his first ML start, whitewashing the Braves 8–0.

Neither Mantle nor Mays had a particularly distinguished rookie season, albeit Mays, in somewhat of a down year in the NL, was selected the senior loop's best novice in 1951. In the AL, however, for the second year in a row, the BBWAA vote for the top rookie was marred by controversy. Whereas in 1950 the lack of firm eligibility rules had been the root of the problem, the charge on this occasion was that 13 of the 24 writers who cast ballots for the AL's rookie prize were either unduly enamored of any player who wore Yankees pinstripes or else were downright blind. In retrospect, the charge is difficult to counter. Yankees third baseman Gil McDougald, the 1951 AL ROY winner with 13 votes, finished among the top ten in the AL in just two batting departments. He was seventh in BA with a .306 figure and tied for seventh in sacrifice hits with 11. In contrast, White Sox third baseman-outfielder Minnie Minoso, the runner-up with 11 votes, in addition to leading all rookies in the game in BA, SA, OBP, stolen bases, RBI, hits, total bases, runs, doubles, and triples topped the AL in three major departments—steals, triples, and hit by pitches—and also finished second in runs and BA, third in OPS, and fifth in SA.

A strong case can certainly be made that Minoso was robbed. At the very least, he is the poster boy for our All-Star team of deserving performers who, for one reason or another, were denied the ultimate rookie prize.

THE "OVERLOOKED" ROOKIE ALL-STAR TEAM SINCE 1948

Pos	Name	Team	Year	Runs	RBI	BA
1B	Todd Helton	Col-NL	1998	78	97	.315
2B	Juan Samuel	Phi-NL	1984	105	69	.272
3B	Kevin Seitzer	KC-AL	1987	105	83	.323
SS	Dick Howser	KC-AL	1961	108	45	.280
LF	Minnie Minoso	Cle/Chi-AL	1951	112	76	.326
CF	Richie Ashburn	Phi-NL	1948	78	40	.333
RF	Jim Rice	Bos-AL	1975	92	102	.309
C	Jason Kendall	Pit-NL	1996	54	42	.300
Sub	Al Rosen	Cle-AL	1950	100	116	.287
Sub	Vada Pinson	Cin-NL	1959	131	84	.316
Sub	Frank Malzone	Bos-AL	1957	82	103	.292
Sub	Tim Raines	Mon-NL	1981	61	37	.304
Sub	Mitchell Page	Oak-AL	1977	85	75	.307
Sub	Pete Ward	Chi-AL	1963	80	84	.295
Sub	Jim Finigan	Phi-AL	1954	57	51	.302
Sub	Willie Horton	Det-AL	1965	69	104	.273

Pos	Name	Team	Year	IP	W	ERA
P	Larry Jansen	NY-NL	1947	248	21	3.16
P	Gene Bearden	Cle-AL	1948	229.2	20	2.43
P	Alex Kellner	Phi-AL	1949	245	20	3.75
P	Harvey Haddix	StL-NL	1953	253	20	3.06
P	Dick Radatz	Bos-AL	1962	124.2	9	2.24
P	Jerry Koosman	NY-NL	1968	263.2	19	2.08
P	Tom Browning	Cin-NL	1985	261.1	20	3.55
P	Mark Eichhorn	Tor-AL	1986	157	14	1.72

August 19—In the first inning of the nightcap of a doubleheader with the Tigers at Sportsman's Park, 3'7" midget Eddie Gaedel, wearing number 1/8, is sent up as a pinch hitter for Frank Saucier; after walking on four pitches, Gaedel strolls to first base and then gives Jim Delsing a pat on the rump when Delsing is sent into the game to run for him; three nights later Gaedel will be arrested in Cincinnati by a policeman who mistakes him for a boy, too young to be abroad so late at night.

August 26—Niles Jordan of the Phils is the second NL rookie in 1951 to hurl a shutout in his first ML start when he blanks the Reds 2–0; on September 21 Jackie

Batting		Pitching	
G—AL 147, Bobby Young, STL		W—AL 12, Saul Rogovin, DET/CHI	
NL 145, Randy Jackson, CHI		NL 11, Chet Nichols, BOS	
AB—AL 611, Bobby Young, STL		L—AL 11, Julio Moreno, WAS	
NL 557, Randy Jackson, CHI		NL 13, Tom Poholsky, STL	
H—AL 173, Minnie Minoso, CLE/CHI		PCT—AL .600, Saul Rogovin, DET/CHI	
NL 153, Randy Jackson, CHI		NL .714, George Spencer, NY	
2B—AL 34, Minnie Minoso, CLE/CHI		GP—AL 35, Morrie Martin, PHI	
NL 24, Randy Jackson, CHI		NL 57, George Spencer, NY	
3B—AL 14, Minnie Minoso, CLE/CHI		GS—AL 26, Saul Rogovin, DET/CHI	
NL 9, Solly Hemus, STL		NL 26, Tom Poholsky, STL	
HR—AL 14, Gil McDougald, NY		CG—AL 17, Saul Rogovin, DET/CHI	
NL 20, Willie Mays, NY		NL 12, Chet Nichols, BOS	
R—AL 112, Minnie Minoso, CLE/CHI		IP—AL 216.2, Saul Rogovin, DET/CHI	
NL 78, Randy Jackson, CHI		NL 195.0, Tom Poholsky, STL	
RBI—AL 76, Minnie Minoso, CLE/CHI		H—AL 189, Saul Rogovin, DET/CHI	
NL 76, Randy Jackson, CHI		NL 204, Tom Poholsky, STL	
WK—AL 72, Minnie Minoso, CLE/CHI		BB—AL 80, Julio Moreno, WAS	
NL 75, Solly Hemus, STL		NL 90, Turk Lown, CHI	
SO—AL 74, Mickey Mantle, NY		K—AL 82, Saul Rogovin, DET/CHI	
NL 83, George Strickland, PIT		NL 71, Chet Nichols, BOS	
SB—AL 31, Minnie Minoso, CLE/CHI		**ERA—AL 2.78, Saul Rogovin, DET/CHI**	
NL 14, Randy Jackson, CHI		**NL 2.88, Chet Nichols, BOS**	
BA—AL .326, Minnie Minoso, CLE/CHI		SHO—AL 3, Saul Rogovin, DET/CHI	
NL .281, Solly Hemus, STL		NL 3, Chet Nichols, BOS	
SLG—AL .500, Minnie Minoso, CLE/CHI		SV—AL 4, Johnny Kucab, PHI	
NL .472, Willie Mays, NY		NL 6, George Spencer, NY	
OBP—AL .422, Minnie Minoso, CLE/CHI			
NL .395, Solly Hemus, STL			

Collum of the Cardinals will be the third NL rookie to debut with a shutout as he two-hits the Cubs 6–0.

September 13—Browns rookie Bob Nieman becomes the first player to homer in both his first and second ML at bats, but his club loses the game anyway 9–6 to Mickey McDermott of the Red Sox.

1952

Judging from the leaders board alone, 1952 would seem to have been an off year for rookies inasmuch as Bob Nieman, the leading frosh hitter, batted just .289, and no recruit hurlers were able to collect more than 15 wins. But actually the 1952 season brimmed with so many groundbreaking, eye-popping, and genuinely

bizarre rookie feats that our capsule report can only begin to do them justice. For one, the voting for the AL ROY was the closest in history—so close that if just one of the writers who voted for A's pitcher Harry Byrd, the winner, had instead tapped Red Sox catcher Sammy White, the third-place finisher, there would have been an unprecedented three-way tie for the prize. Secondly, Joe Black of the Dodgers became the first relief pitcher to nail a ROY Award when he won the NL's top recruit honor. Furthermore, the balloting for the NL ROY for the first time was touched by controversy when Black nabbed 19 of the 24 votes despite the fact that another rookie bullpenner, Hoyt Wilhelm of the Giants, tied Black for the loop frosh lead in wins and, in addition, not only paced the NL in winning percentage but also earned the distinction of being the only relief pitcher in history to bag a loop ERA crown.

But the significance of these vagaries in the voting for the two 1952 ROY winners would emerge only after the fact. What caught the attention of followers of the game at the time were developments on the playing field. In Boston, the Braves commemorated their last year in the Hub before moving to Milwaukee by unveiling third baseman Eddie Mathews, who set a new franchise record for home runs by a left-handed-hitting rookie with 25, while the Red Sox embarked on a radical youth movement that was nearly derailed when 22-year-old shortstop Jimmy Piersall had to be hospitalized after suffering a dramatic nervous breakdown. Meanwhile Pirates GM Branch Rickey made the Red Sox' youth movement seem little more than a token effort by employing at various times in the season a total of 21 performers who had rookie status in 1952. Rickey's Baby Buccos ranged from Dick Groat, a former All-American basketball player at Duke University who received a vote for ROY and would later win a batting title, to a string of promising pitchers barely out of high school like Bill Bell, Ron Necciai, and Jim Waugh, whose raw talents wound up on the scrap heap when they were rushed into ML livery prematurely and either had their arms destroyed or their confidence shattered. Bell and Necciai were especially tragic stories. Before being yanked up to the parent Pirates, the 18-year-old Bell threw three no-hitters in 1952 for Class D Bristol in the Appalachian League, two of them in succession, and Necciai, also with Bristol, on May 23 no-hit Welch and fanned an Organized Baseball single-game record 27 batters. In his 43 innings with Bristol, before moving on to Burlington in the Carolina League, Necciai recorded a phenomenal 109 strikeouts, an average of 2.5 per inning.

Another rookie in 1952 who became an early burnout victim was Eddie Yuhas of the Cardinals. Eclipsed in spring training by fellow rookie hurler Wilmer Mizell, whose hometown of Vinegar Bend, Arkansas, sparked one of the greatest nicknames in baseball lore, Yuhas was relegated to the bullpen where he quietly fashioned a dazzling 12–2 log in 54 appearances. Yuhas was then eclipsed in the ROY balloting by fellow frosh relievers Black and Wilhelm. When he was felled by arm trouble the following spring, his sudden descent from rookie prominence called to mind an-

other recent Cards frosh whiz of Eastern European heritage named Eddie. In 1949, after being chosen as the NL's All-Star Game third baseman and going 2-for-2 in the Midsummer Classic, Eddie Kazak severely injured his ankle sliding and never regained regular duty with the Cardinals, let alone All-Star status.

Even the lavishly promoted Mizell had to take a backseat in the 1952 preseason to a rookie with the Cardinals' stepbrother in St. Louis, the Browns. Customarily ignored in the spring by the media, the Browns put themselves squarely in the eye of the storm when their new manager, the blunt Rogers Hornsby, proclaimed that the

Rivera was not the only "hard case" Rogers Hornsby welcomed to the Browns in 1952. In some ways Rivera was actually rather mild in comparison to Clint Courtney, who came to the Browns over the previous winter from the Yankees in a trade for pitcher Jim McDonald. Courtney was aptly nicknamed "Scrap Iron." He also happened to be a fine catcher whose way was blocked in New York by Yogi Berra. In 1952 Courtney led ML catchers in fielding average (.996) and also paced all receivers who had a minimum of 400 at bats in BA. If he had played for a better team than the Browns or had a slightly more ingratiating personality, he almost undoubtedly would have gotten another vote or two for AL ROY. Even just one more vote would have swung the honor his way.

Yet Courtney was not the only rookie catcher in 1952 who missed out on the full recognition he deserved. Indeed, three of the top four BAs by receivers who appeared in at least 100 games belonged to rookies. Among the trio was Toby Atwell, an obscure name today but all the rage for a brief time in 1952. After vying for the NL batting crown for a while early in the season, Atwell was selected for the All-Star squad, the only catcher ever to be so honored and then subsequently not to receive even so much as a single vote for ROY. To add insult to the snub Atwell suffered, in late September 1952 he became the first rookie receiver in NL history to catch 100 or more games.

THE TOP 5 CATCHER BAs IN 1952 WITH A MINIMUM 350 PAs (ROOKIES IN BOLD)

Rank	Name	AB	OPS	BA
1	Smoky Burgess	371	.809	.296
2	**Toby Atwell**	362	.730	.290
3	**Clint Courtney**	413	.743	.286
4	**Sammy White**	381	.732	.281
5	Yogi Berra	534	.835	.273

only professional ballplayer in the land that he would pay to see play was his recruit center fielder, Jim Rivera. The PCL bat-title winner and MVP in 1951, Rivera had not begun his professional career until he was released from prison at age 26 after serving a five-year sentence stemming from a court-martial conviction for the rape of an Army nurse who happened to be the daughter of an Army officer. As a result of his dubious background, when Rivera finally made the majors at age 30, he faced, according to sportswriter Milton Gross, "the cruelest, most vicious bench jockeying ever spewed at a player." Gross further contended, "Nobody had it tougher cracking the big leagues, not even Jackie Robinson, the first to break through the color barrier." In midseason Hornsby was fired by the Browns, and Rivera, minus his leading advocate, was traded to the White Sox. On the final day

of the 1952 campaign, the police hauled him off from Comiskey Park in response to a Chicago housewife's charge that he had raped her the night before. Rivera admitted having relations with the woman but maintained that it was consensual. After lie-detector tests, a grand jury concluded that the evidence against Rivera was insufficient to justify a criminal indictment.

Other Highlights

March 24—Promising rookie southpaw Bobby Slaybaugh of the Cardinals loses his left eye when he is struck by a line drive while pitching batting practice in spring training; despite the handicap, Slaybaugh mounts a comeback in the minors but is never able to reach the majors.

1952 ROOKIE LEADERS

Batting

G—AL 150, Jim Rivera, STL/CHI
    NL 145, Eddie Mathews, BOS
AB—AL 537, Jim Rivera, STL/CHI
    NL 540, Davey Williams, NY
H—AL 138, Bob Nieman, STL
    NL 137, Davey Williams, NY
2B—AL 24, Clint Courtney, STL
    NL 26, Davey Williams, NY
3B—AL 9, Jim Rivera, STL/CHI
    NL 5, Eddie Mathews, BOS
HR—AL 19, Dick Gernert, BOS
    NL 25, Eddie Mathews, BOS
R—AL 72, Jim Rivera, STL/CHI
    NL 80, Eddie Mathews, BOS
RBI—AL 74, Bob Nieman, STL
    NL 58, Eddie Mathews, BOS
WK—AL 50, Jim Dyck, STL
    Jim Rivera, STL/CHI
    NL 59, Eddie Mathews, BOS
SO—AL 86, Jim Rivera, STL/CHI
    NL 115, Eddie Mathews, BOS
SB—AL 21, Jim Rivera, STL/CHI
    NL 9, Brandy Davis, PIT
BA—AL .289, Bob Nieman, STL
    NL .254, Davey Williams, NY
SLG—AL .456, Bob Nieman, STL
    NL .447, Eddie Mathews, BOS
OBA—AL .352, Bob Nieman, STL
    NL .324, Davey Williams, NY

Pitching

W—AL 15, Harry Byrd, PHI
    NL 15, Joe Black, BRO
    Hoyt Wilhelm, NY
L—AL 15, Harry Byrd, PHI
    NL 11, Lew Burdette, BOS
PCT—AL .500, Harry Byrd, PHI
    NL .833, Hoyt Wilhelm, NY
GP—AL 41, Dave Madison, STL/DET
    NL 71, Hoyt Wilhelm, NY
GS—AL 28, Harry Byrd, PHI
    NL 30, Vinegar Bend Mizell, STL
CG—AL 15, Harry Byrd, PHI
    NL 8, Billy Loes, BRO
IP—AL 228.1, Harry Byrd, PHI
    NL 190.0, Vinegar Bend Mizell, STL
H—AL 244, Harry Byrd, PHI
    NL 171, Vinegar Bend Mizell, STL
BB—AL 98, Harry Byrd, PHI
    NL 103, Vinegar Bend Mizell, STL
K—AL 116, Harry Byrd, PHI
    NL 146, Vinegar Bend Mizell, STL
ERA—AL 3.31, Harry Byrd, PHI
    NL 2.43, Hoyt Wilhelm, NY
SH—AL 3, Harry Byrd, PHI
    NL 4, Billy Loes, BRO
SV—AL 5, Ike Delock, BOS
    NL 15, Joe Black, BRO

April 19—Eddie Mathews, destined to become the first third baseman in ML history to club 500 homers, hits his first career dinger off Ken Heintzelman of the Phils to help his Braves win 4–0.

April 23—Giants reliever Hoyt Wilhelm homers in his first ML at bat and then pitches five innings to gain his first win, 9–5 over the Braves.

April 29—Outfielder Jim Fridley, the sensation of the Cactus League in the spring of 1952, goes 6-for-6 for Cleveland in a 21–9 rout of the A's; Fridley will collect only 44 hits total in his rookie season and post a weak .642 OPS.

August 12—Stu Miller of the Cards nips the Cubs 1–0 in his ML debut; five days later Miller will be on the verge of joining the elite club of hurlers who have debuted with two consecutive shutouts, only to watch Cards shortstop Solly Hemus make an error with two out in the ninth that allows a run in what turns out to be a 2–1 win over the Reds.

September 2—Mike Fornieles tosses a one-hit 5–0 shutout against the A's in his ML debut with Washington; three days later a second Senators rookie, Raul Sanchez, will match Fornieles by whitewashing the Red Sox 2–0 in his first ML start.

September 27—Three home runs by rookie third sacker Eddie Mathews spark fellow rookie Virgil Jester to an 11–3 win over Brooklyn; Jester's victory is not only the third and final win of his career but also the final game won by the Boston Braves before they become the first ML team since 1903 to relocate by moving to Milwaukee.

September 28—When Dodgers rookie reliever Jim Hughes fans Sid Gordon in the 12th inning of a 5–5 tie with the Braves, the Brooklyn pitching staff logs its 773rd K of the season to set a new NL record.

1953

In the spring of 1953, Brooklyn manager Chuck Dressen took a bold gamble when he moved All-Star second baseman Jackie Robinson to the outfield to make room at second base for the Dodgers' top minor league prospect, Jim Gilliam. The move paid a rich dividend as Gilliam became the first NL rookie since 1899 to collect 100 walks and, more importantly, tallied 125 runs, only eight short of Lloyd Waner's post-1901 rookie record. Since Gilliam also led the NL in triples, not surprisingly he copped the NL ROY honor, but it was not without a struggle. In 1953 the NL boasted an especially large crop of talented freshmen as six newcomers, in addition to Gilliam, garnered votes for the loop's top rookie prize. Among the also-rans were 20-game winner Harvey Haddix of the Cardinals and two 100-RBI recruits, Reds outfielder Jim Greengrass and Cards third sacker Ray Jablonski.

Remarkably, the Cards had a third rookie that vied for the prize, centerfielder Rip Repulski, as the 1953 season launched a run of three consecutive years in which the St. Louis NL entry produced an outstanding recruit center fielder. In 1954 the emergence of ROY Award–winner Wally Moon pushed Repulski from center to left field. The following year Bill Virdon succeeded Moon as the NL ROY and bumped Moon into right field, so that by 1955 the Cards outer perimeter consisted of a trio of gardeners who for three years in succession had achieved recognition as outstanding recruit center fielders. Sadly for the Cards, only Virdon of the three would return for an encore performance in center field with the club before being traded to the Pirates early in the 1956 season for long-forgotten journeyman Bobby Del Greco. Indeed, by 1959 all three of the Cards' recruit outfield stars had moved on to other teams as, for that matter, had both Haddix and Jablonski.

Only Detroit's sensational freshman shortstop, Harvey Kuenn, prevented the AL's 1953 rookie crew from being as undistinguished as the class of 1946. Kuenn led AL recruit hitters in 11 major departments and topped the majors in hits with 209. Meanwhile, Don Bollweg, a 32-year-old backup first baseman with the Yankees, paced all junior-loop frosh in homers with just six, and Boston outfielder Tom Umphlett, who garnered the lone ROY vote that did not go to Kuenn, was the RBI leader with a mere 59. The pitching side of the ledger was even more lackluster. Had there been a separate award in 1953 for the

In 1953 the Pirates' ill-conceived youth movement produced the second of what would become a franchise-record four straight cellar finishes, but it did generate one memorable highlight: the first set of twins who performed as a keystone combination in the majors. On April 19 second baseman Johnny O'Brien, a former Seattle University basketball star, made his ML debut; six days later he was joined on the club by his twin brother, Eddie, a shortstop and also a former member of the Seattle hoop squad, and on May 10 the twins played their first game together. Between them, however, the highly ballyhooed O'Briens appeared in just 570 games in the majors.

Another even more publicized Pirates rookie in 1953, pitcher Paul Pettit, hurled just 30.2 innings in the majors. The first of what would soon be a rush of $100,000 Bonus Babies who flopped, Pettit won only one game for the Pirates before receding to the minors where he finished his career as a first baseman.

On September 13, 1953, the Phils gave the ball for the first time to their answer to Pettit, 18-year-old Tom Qualters. Nicknamed "Money Bags," the long-forgotten Quaker City Bonus Baby hit a batter, walked a batter, and gave up four hits including a home run in just a third of an inning, thereupon ending his horrific ML debut with a 162.00 ERA. Qualters eventually trimmed his career ERA to 5.64 but never won a game in the majors.

At the other end of the continuum in 1953 was Bobo Holloman of the Browns. No rookie pitcher ever received less attention than Holloman prior to making his first major league start. Knowing that he was slated to be sent back to the minors when the Browns' roster was reduced to the legal limit of 25 at the May 15 deadline, Holloman begged manager Marty Marion for a start before he was given his walking papers. On May 6, 1953, he got his chance against the Philadelphia A's. Nine innings later Holloman had joined George Nicol, Ted Breitenstein, Bumpus Jones, and Red Ames as the only five hurlers in history to register no-hitters in their first ML starts. Three months later, however, Holloman was back in the minors anyway after never logging another complete game in the majors and finishing with just three wins in ten decisions.

AL's best frosh hurler, the vote would probably have been split about evenly between two non-qualifiers, Cleveland's Dave Hoskins (9–3 in 112.2 innings) and Bob Keegan, the White Sox 32-year-old novice righthander who was 7–5 in 98.2 innings.

Other Highlights

April 14—Rookie centerfielder Bill Bruton hits the first home run in Milwaukee County Stadium to give the transplanted Braves a 3–2 win over the Cardinals in ten innings; it will be the lone dinger that Bruton hits all season in 613 at bats.

May 2—Rookie centerfielder Carlos Bernier collects three triples for the Pirates in their 12–4 win over the Reds; Bernier will hit just .213 in his lone ML season but will lead Pittsburgh in three-baggers with eight.

June 18—Red Sox rookie outfielder Gene Stephens, used almost exclusively in his first few seasons to spell Ted Williams in the late innings, is the first player in ML history to log three hits in an inning as Boston tallies 17 runs in the fourth frame on the way to a 23–3 romp over Detroit; Stephens's record will belong solely to him until 2003 when it is tied by BoSox centerfielder Johnny Damon.

July 11—Al Worthington of the Giants ties an ML record when he posts his second consecutive shutout in his first two big league starts by blanking Brooklyn 6–0; Worthington's whitewash will prove to be the lone time all season that the flag-winning Dodgers are shut out.

August 1—Red Sox rookie Ben Flowers is the first relief pitcher in ML history to appear in eight straight games; four days later, Flowers will blank the Browns 5–0 in his first ML start.

August 30—Jim Pendleton belts three homers in the first game of a doubleheader leading the Braves to a 19–4 drubbing of the Pirates; Pendleton's feat makes him the first African-American to hit a trio of jacks in a senior loop contest.

September 13—A's rookie Bob Trice is the first black performer to play with a Philadelphia ML entry when he loses to the Browns 5–2 in his big league mound debut.

September 20—Three days after making his debut as the Cubs first black player, Ernie Banks hits his first of 512 career home runs in an 11–6 loss to Gerry Staley of the Cards.

September 26—Rookie shortstop Billy Hunter's first career home run, which comes in a 6–3 loss to the White

1953 ROOKIE LEADERS

Batting	Pitching
G—AL 155, Harvey Kuenn, DET	W—AL 9, Marion Fricano, PHI
NL 157, Ray Jablonski, STL	Dave Hoskins, CLE
AB—**AL 679, Harvey Kuenn, DET**	NL 20, Harvey Haddix, STL
NL 613, Bill Bruton, MIL	L—AL 14, Charlie Bishop, PHI
H—**AL 209, Harvey Kuenn, DET**	NL 11, Jackie Collum, STL/CIN
NL 173, Jim Greengrass, CIN	Ruben Gomez, NY
2B—AL 33, Harvey Kuenn, DET	PCT—AL .429, Marion Fricano, PHI
NL 31, Jim Gilliam, BRO	NL .690, Harvey Haddix, STL
3B—AL 7, Harvey Kuenn, DET	GP—AL 43, Sonny Dixon, WAS
NL 17, Jim Gilliam, BRO	Ray Herbert, DET
HR—AL 6, Don Bollweg, NY	NL 48, Jim Hughes, BRO
NL 21, Ray Jablonski, STL	GS—AL 23, Marion Fricano, PHI
R—AL 94, Harvey Kuenn, DET	NL 33, Harvey Haddix, STL
NL 125, Jim Gilliam, BRO	CG—AL 10, Marion Fricano, PHI
RBI—AL 59, Tom Umphlett, BOS	NL 19, Harvey Haddix, STL
NL 112, Ray Jablonski, STL	IP—AL 211, Marion Fricano, PHI
WK—AL 50, Harvey Kuenn, DET	NL 253, Harvey Haddix, STL
NL 100, Jim Gilliam, BRO	H—AL 206, Marion Fricano, PHI
SO—AL 56, Gene Stephens, BOS	NL 220, Harvey Haddix, STL
NL 100, Bill Bruton, MIL	BB—AL 90, Marion Fricano, PHI
SB—AL 6, Harvey Kuenn, DET	NL 101, Ruben Gomez, NY
NL 26, Bill Bruton, MIL	K—AL 96, Don Larsen, STL
BA—AL .308, Harvey Kuenn, DET	NL 163, Harvey Haddix, STL
NL .285, Jim Greengrass, CIN	ERA—AL 3.88, Marion Fricano, PHI
SLG—AL .386, Harvey Kuenn, DET	NL 2.97, Bob Buhl, MIL
NL .444, Jim Greengrass, CIN	SHO—AL 2, Bob Keegan, CHI
OBP—AL .356, Harvey Kuenn, DET	Don Larsen, STL
NL .383, Jim Gilliam, BRO	**NL 6, Harvey Haddix, STL**
	SV—AL 6, Ray Herbert, DET
	NL 9, Jim Hughes, BRO

Sox, is not only his lone four-bagger in 1953 in 567 at bats but the last homer hit by a player wearing a St. Louis Browns uniform, as the Browns move to Baltimore prior to the 1954 season.

1954

Only the presence of the Browns in their last year in St. Louis prevented the Philadelphia A's from sliding into the AL cellar in 1953. The following spring the A's new manager, Eddie Joost, welcomed the deepest rookie crop in the game to training camp in West Palm Beach, Florida. Among Joost's newcomers were a pair of pitchers who would turn out to be the A's top

two winners in 1954 and a trio of novice regulars that would rank first, second, and third on the club in batting.

Probably no other club in the past half century was so dominated by the contributions of its recruits and certainly no other club ever benefited less from such an influx of new talent. In 1954 the A's finished dead last with the worst record in the majors—worse even than that of the perennial doormat Pirates. The problem was that the club's five rookies, with one exception, performed decently but were hardly noteworthy, while its veteran cast, without exception, was an unmitigated disaster. In 1954 the A's two leading winners were Arnie Portocarrero and Bob Trice, with nine and seven victories, respectively, and the club's top three hitters were

The Pirates and the Cubs, two of the NL's most dominant teams in the first decade of the twentieth century, by 1954 had firmly established that they were the senior loop's two worst teams in the first decade of the second half of the twentieth century. While the upper-echelon teams in the NL were introducing newcomers like Hank Aaron and Wally Moon, the Pirates were still stubbornly trying to make a major league catcher out of Vic Janowicz, whose credentials for the job consisted of little more than a Heisman Trophy for being the best college football player in 1950. But the Pirates at least had company when it came to the Janowicz experiment, as the Red Sox in 1954 gave their first base slot to Harry Agganis, a former All-American quarterback at Boston University, and even the NL flag-winning Giants forked over a sizable bonus to yet a third former All-American back, Paul Giel, in the vain hope that he could be honed into a big league pitcher.

Pittsburgh had no company, however, not even the Cubs, when it came to unearthing execrable middle infielders. Following the fiasco with the O'Brien twins in 1953, the Pirates found two more rookies to fill their keystone slots in 1954. The Cubs also came up with two rookie keystoners that same year. There is no comparison between the two teams. Here are the 1954 rookie batting profiles for the recruit keystoners on both clubs.

TEAM	AGE	G	AB	R	H	2B	3B	HR	RBI	BB	SO	SB	CS	AVG	SLG	OBA	OPS
Pirates	22	121	418	38	83	8	6	3	30	56	84	1	1	.199	.268	.296	.564
Pirates	24	134	496	47	115	18	7	1	36	55	49	6	3	.232	.302	.311	.613
Cubs	29	135	541	68	149	32	5	13	61	47	55	4	5	.275	.425	.336	.761
Cubs	23	154	593	70	163	19	7	19	79	40	50	6	10	.275	.427	.328	.755

In order, the profiles belong to shortstop Gair Allie, followed by second sacker Curt Roberts and then Gene Baker, the Cubs rookie second sacker, and finally, of course, the runner-up for the NL ROY Award in 1954, Ernie Banks, who set a new record for the most homers by a recruit shortstop in the course of posting a higher BA than his Pittsburgh shortstop counterpart's SA.

Jim Finigan (.302), Spook Jacobs (.258), and Vic Power (.255). Finigan was voted the runner-up for the AL ROY Award after topping all junior-loop freshmen in batting, SA, and OBP, but only Power of the five members of the A's 1954 youth corps would assemble a ML career of any substance.

At the other end of the AL flagpole in 1954 were the Cleveland Indians and New York Yankees. That year the Yankees had their best season ever under Casey Stengel's tutelage, winning 103 games. But all it earned them was second place and an end to their record string of five straight pennants, as Cleveland stormed to 111 victories and a .721 winning percentage, the highest in junior-loop history. Though the Yankees garnered the ROY Award behind Bob Grim, the only pitcher prior to Pedro Martinez in 2002 to win 20 games despite hurling less

In 1955 Al Kaline, at age 20, became the youngest performer in ML history to win a batting title. To 23 of the 24 BBWAA voters in 1954, Kaline's sudden emergence was completely unexpected. The 24th writer was the lone committee member to select Kaline as the AL ROY ahead of both Bob Grim and Jim Finigan. It would be nice to report that this writer saw something in Kaline that none of his 23 colleagues was able to perceive, but the evidence that there was anything special about Kaline to see in 1954 has yet to emerge. What has come forward is the unalterable fact that on the all-time list of outfielders with 500 or more at bats in a season, Al Kaline ranks stone cold last in the most critical statistic in baseball—the number of runs scored.

Indeed, there was absolutely nothing in Kaline's rookie season that foreshadowed his quantum leap to stardom in 1955. Not only did his runs total jump from 42 to 121, but his

walks increased by 60, his SA went up 199 points, and his OPS increased a record 318 points.

FEWEST RUNS, OUTFIELDER, 500 ABs

Rank	Name	Year	AB	Runs
1	Al Kaline	1954	504	42
2	Harry Rice	1933	510	44
3	Eddie Brown	1928	523	45
	Joe Pepitone	1967	501	45
5	Hal Lee	1936	565	46
	Del Howard	1906	545	46
	Bunk Congalton	1907	518	46
8	Chief Wilson	1908	529	47
	Joe Kelly	1914	508	47
	Morrie Arnovich	1938	502	47

than 200 innings, Cleveland enjoyed the services of Ray Narleski and Don Mossi, the finest righty-lefty rookie relief duo in history. Narleski led the club in saves with 13 and was second in the league in overall relief ranking, but Mossi was even more spectacular as he not only led the AL in relief ranking but topped all pitchers in the majors in fewest BR/9 with 9.29.

Nearly forgotten today, except in Cleveland, is the rookie who was a household name for all too brief a time in the spring of 1954, Rudy "The Red Hot Rapper" Regalado. The scourge of the Cactus League that spring, Regalado put up slugging numbers so electrifying that he forced Tribe manager Al Lopez to move Al Rosen, the 1953 AL MVP, to first base so that room could be made for him at third. But an early-season injury to Regalado put Rosen back on third base and consigned "The Red Hot Rapper" to being no more than a footnote in baseball lore.

Other Highlights

April 13—Curt Roberts, the first black to play for the Pirates, debuts on Opening Day with a first-inning triple against Robin Roberts as the Pirates open the season at home for the first time since 1893 by topping the Phils 4–2.

April 17—Nino Escalera is the first black to play for Cincinnati when he nails a pinch single in the Reds' 5–1 loss to the Braves; minutes later Chuck Harmon, often mistakenly credited for having been the Reds' first black player, also appears as a pinch hitter for Cincinnati.

May 9—Rookie A's catcher Billy Shantz, brother of former AL MVP Bobby Shantz, makes the first homer of his professional career a grand slam and accounts for

1954 ROOKIE LEADERS

Batting	Pitching
G—AL 147, Bill Tuttle, DET	W—AL 20, Bob Grim, NY
NL 154, Ernie Banks, CHI	NL 15, Brooks Lawrence, STL
AB—AL 530, Bill Tuttle, DET	L—AL 18, Arnie Portocarrero, PHI
NL 635, Wally Moon, STL	NL 11, Corky Valentine, CIN
H—AL 147, Jim Finigan, PHI	PCT—AL .769, Bob Grim, NY
NL 193, Wally Moon, STL	NL .714, Brooks Lawrence, STL
2B—AL 25, Jim Finigan, PHI	GP—AL 48, Camilo Pascual, WAS
NL 32, Gene Baker, CHI	NL 47, Dave Jolly, MIL
3B—AL 11, Bill Tuttle, DET	GS—AL 33, Arnie Portocarrero, PHI
NL 9, Wally Moon, STL	NL 29, Art Fowler, CIN
Bob Skinner, PIT	CG—AL 16, Arnie Portocarrero, PHI
HR—AL 17, Bill Wilson, CHI/PHI	NL 12, Gene Conley, MIL
NL 19, Ernie Banks, CHI	IP—AL 248.0, Arnie Portocarrero, PHI
R—AL 64, Bill Tuttle, DET	NL 227.2, Art Fowler, CIN
NL 106, Wally Moon, STL	H—AL 233, Arnie Portocarrero, PHI
RBI—AL 58, Bill Tuttle, DET	NL 256, Art Fowler, CIN
NL 79, Ernie Banks, CHI	BB—AL 114, Arnie Portocarrero, PHI
WK—AL 64, Jim Finigan, PHI	NL 85, Art Fowler, CIN
NL 71, Wally Moon, STL	K—AL 134, Jack Harshman, CHI
SO—AL 69, Billy Consolo, BOS	NL 113, Gene Conley, MIL
NL 84, Gair Allie, PIT	ERA—AL 2.95, Jack Harshman, CHI
SB—AL 17, Spook Jacobs, PHI	NL 2.96, Gene Conley, MIL
NL 18, Wally Moon, STL	SHO—AL 4, Jack Harshman, CHI
BA—AL .302, Jim Finigan, PHI	NL 3, Corky Valentine, CIN
NL .304, Wally Moon, STL	SV—AL 13, Ray Narleski, CLE
SLG—AL .421, Jim Finigan, PHI	NL 10, Dave Jolly, MIL
NL .447, Hank Aaron, MIL	
OBP—AL .383, Jim Finigan, PHI	
NL .375, Wally Moon, STL	

all the Philadelphia A's runs in a 7–4 loss to the Yankees' Harry Byrd.

May 12—Rookie centerfielder Wally Moon of the Cards has his second five-hit game of the young season and scores five runs in a 13–5 blasting of the Pirates.

July 1—Joe Cunningham of the Cardinals homers twice against Milwaukee to make him the last performer to date to collect as many as three home runs in his first two ML games.

September 5—In the second game of a doubleheader with the Cubs, Braves rookie Hank Aaron breaks his ankle and is lost for the rest of the season after going 4-for-4 in the opener.

September 6—Cuban gardener Carlos Paula is the first black performer to play for the Washington franchise, going 2-for-4 against the Philadelphia A's.

September 21—Bob Grim becomes only the second Yankees rookie to win 20 games and the first hurler in ML history to bag 20 victories while working less than 200 innings when he tops Washington 3–1.

September 22—Dodgers lefty Karl Spooner shatters Charlie Geggus's 70-year-old rookie record when he fans 15 Giants, including six in a row, in his first ML mound appearance.

September 26—Karl Spooner follows his 3–0 shutout of the Giants four days earlier by whitewashing Pittsburgh 1–0 and fanning 12 to give him a record total of 27 in his first two ML games.

September 26—After going winless all season, rookie Art Ditmar tops the Yankees 8–6 in the last game the A's franchise will play representing Philadelphia before it moves to Kansas City.

1955

By 1955 the Bonus Baby problem had grown so dire that virtually every team in the majors had at least one player who was occupying a roster spot solely because the bonus rule required that he be kept with his parent club. For every success story like Johnny Antonelli, a 20-game winner in 1954 after years of struggling to justify the $65,000 windfall the Braves had handed him as an 18-year-old in 1948, there were a dozen failures. Several, such as Yankees washout Ed Cereghino and Cleveland's $150,000 bust, Billy Joe Davidson, never played a single inning in the majors. Many others were thrust into big league livery right out of high school and either failed egregiously or else never progressed beyond substitute status. From the 1955 rookie class, most of the Bonus Babies are long forgotten names such as J.W. Porter, Kenny Kuhn, Jim Small, and Tom Carroll. One that is not belongs to Sandy Koufax, a 19-year-old southpaw the Dodgers signed for $25,000 off the University of Cincinnati campus, where he was attending school on a basketball scholarship.

In due time Koufax would break a ton of strikeout records. Ironically, many of the marks he would surpass were owned by a fellow member of the 1955 rookie class, the ill-fated Herb Score. Three years earlier, Score had been signed by the Indians for a $60,000 bonus at a juncture when the bonus rule had temporarily been liberalized to allow him to start his professional career in the minors. Also inked by the Tribe was Score's high-school battery mate in Lake Worth, Florida, catcher Dick Brown. It took Brown until June of 1957 to reach the majors, but Score was more than ready by 1955 following a Triple Crown pitching season at Indianapolis of the American Association. Score's frosh year with Cleveland not only earned him the AL ROY Award but also resulted in both a new freshman strikeout record and a new all-time season record for the most strikeouts per nine innings. The following year Score nearly toppled his own record when he again averaged more than nine strikeouts per nine innings. In 1957, after allowing just 18 hits in his first 36 innings, he seemed destined for his most remarkable year yet, only to have it shattered abruptly when he was struck in the face by a line drive in just his fifth appearance of the season. Forced to change his delivery in order to avert a second such catastrophic injury, Score showed only intermittent flashes of his early brilliance in the remaining five years of his career.

MOST STRIKEOUTS PER 9 INNINGS PITCHED, SEASON, 1871–1956

Rank	Name	Year	IP	Ks	K/9
1	Herb Score	1955	227.1	245	9.70
2	Herb Score	1956	249.1	263	9.49
3	Hugh Daily	1884	500.2	483	8.68
4	Hal Newhouser	1946	292.2	275	8.46
5	Bob Feller	1946	371.1	348	8.43
6	Sam Jones	1956	188.2	176	8.40
7	Rube Waddell	1903	324	302	8.39
8	Rube Waddell	1904	383	349	8.20
9	Johnny Vander Meer	1941	226.1	202	8.03
10	Matt Kilroy	1886	583	513	7.92

Oddly enough, Bill Virdon, the 1955 NL ROY, though he sustained no major injuries, otherwise almost exactly paralleled Score's downward spiral. Like Score, Virdon followed his fine rookie season with an even better sophomore year, hiking his BA 38 points to .319. But the bottom then fell out for Virdon, so that by the end of the decade he ranked last in career OPS among all NL outfielders who collected a minimum of 2,000 plate appearances between 1955 and 1960.

Other Highlights

April 14—Elston Howard, the first black player to wear Yankees pinstripes, singles in his first ML at bat in an 8–4 New York win over the Red Sox.

May 5—In his first ML start, Dodgers rookie Tom Lasorda ties a record by throwing three wild pitches in an inning against the Cardinals.

May 12—Cubs rookie fireballer Sam "Toothpick" Jones tosses the first no-hit game in Wrigley Field since the famous double no-hitter in 1917 as he beats the Pirates 4–0.

June 24—Rookie second baseman Harmon Killebrew of the Senators hits his first career home run in an 18–7 loss to Detroit; Killebrew will become the only member of the 500-homer club to date who began his career as a second baseman.

July 17—Dodgers rookie pitchers Roger Craig and Don Bessent, both just called up from the minors, top the Reds in a doubleheader, Craig winning the opener 6–2

Last in runs created and next to last in OPS among NL outfielders with a minimum of 2,000 plate appearances between 1955 and 1960 was a teammate of Bill Virdon's on the 1960 Pirates. If it seems improbable that Pittsburgh could have won a World Championship in 1960 with the two least-productive outfielders in the league over the course of the previous six seasons, learning the identity of Virdon's fellow gardener will make it seem utterly unbelievable.

Yes, it was Roberto Clemente. In November of 1954, the Pirates drafted Clemente from the Brooklyn organization after the Dodgers brass tried unsuccessfully to hide his talents by letting him play only sparingly with their Montreal farm team. Clemente's rookie season in 1955 was something of a disappointment as he hit .255 and scored just 48 runs. Like Virdon, Clemente improved markedly in his sophomore year but then crashed in 1957, producing just 30 RBI, 42 runs, and a .637 OPS. Two more disappointing seasons followed, in which Clemente continued to score few runs, seldom walk—just 15 times in 1959—and rank near the bottom among all NL regulars in RBI. The 1960 season was a breakthrough of sorts for Clemente as he hit .314 and knocked home 94 runs, but after his first six seasons, he nevertheless remained last in runs created among all NL outfielders who collected a minimum of 2,000 at bats during that same period. In the years since, many pundits have boasted that they knew from the outset that Clemente was a cinch Hall of Famer, but all of them were curiously silent until the mid 1960s.

WORST RC VS. LEAGUE, NL OF, 1955–60

Rank	Name	AB	RC	L/RC	DIFF
1	Roberto Clemente	2989	363	407	−44
2	Bill Virdon	3207	418	438	−20
3	Bobby Thomson	2078	276	295	−19
4	Bill Bruton	2899	387	394	−7
5	Del Ennis	2025	278	282	−4

and Bessent the nightcap 8–5; between them, the pair will go 13–4 in the remaining ten weeks of the season.

August 27—Seldom used Dodgers Bonus Baby Sandy Koufax offers fans a taste of what his future will hold when he beats Cincinnati 7–0 and strikes out 14.

September 14—Cleveland's Herb Score breaks Pete Alexander's post-1901 rookie strikeout record of 227 in a 3–2 loss to Washington; Score will make just one more start in the remaining 11 days of the season and

Batting		Pitching	
G—AL 140, Gus Triandos, BAL		W—AL 16, Herb Score, CLE	
NL 147, Ken Boyer, STL		NL 14, Sam Jones, CHI	
AB—AL 541, Billy Klaus, BOS		L—AL 15, Frank Lary, DET	
NL 534, Bill Virdon, STL		**NL 20, Sam Jones, CHI**	
H—AL 153, Billy Klaus, BOS		PCT—AL .615, Herb Score, CLE	
NL 150, Bill Virdon, STL		NL .412, Sam Jones, CHI	
2B—AL 26, Billy Klaus, BOS		GP—AL 46, Ray Moore, BAL	
NL 27, Ken Boyer, STL		NL 50, Jack Meyer, PHI	
3B—AL 7, Elston Howard, NY		GS—AL 32, Herb Score, CLE	
Carlos Paula, WAS		NL 34, Sam Jones, CHI	
NL 13, Dale Long, PIT		CG—AL 16, Frank Lary, DET	
HR—AL 27, Norm Zauchin, BOS		NL 12, Sam Jones, CHI	
NL 18, Ken Boyer, STL		IP—AL 235, Frank Lary, DET	
R—AL 83, Billy Klaus, BOS		NL 241.2, Sam Jones, CHI	
NL 78, Ken Boyer, STL		H—AL 232, Frank Lary, DET	
RBI—AL 93, Norm Zauchin, BOS		NL 189, Larry Jackson, STL	
NL 79, Dale Long, PIT		BB—AL 154, Herb Score, CLE	
WK—AL 69, Norm Zauchin, BOS		**NL 185, Sam Jones, CHI**	
NL 48, Dale Long, PIT		K—**AL 245, Herb Score, CLE**	
SO—AL 105, Norm Zauchin, BOS		**NL 198, Sam Jones, CHI**	
NL 72, Dale Long, PIT		ERA—AL 2.85, Herb Score, CLE	
SB—AL 6, Billy Klaus, BOS		NL 4.10, Sam Jones, CHI	
NL 22, Ken Boyer, STL		SHO—AL 2, Ted Abernathy, WAS	
BA—AL .290, Hector Lopez, KC		Frank Lary, DET	
NL .291, Dale Long, PIT		Duke Maas, DET	
SLG—AL .430, Norm Zauchin, BOS		Herb Score, CLE	
NL .513, Dale Long, PIT		NL 4, Sam Jones, CHI	
OBP—AL .354, Billy Klaus, BOS		SV—AL 9, Dixie Howell, CHI	
NL .365, Dale Long, PIT		**NL 16, Jack Meyer, PHI**	

will finish with a new mark of 245 Ks that will endure until 1984.

October 3—Dodgers lefty Karl Spooner, after beginning the season as one of the most promising rookie hurlers in history, makes his final big league appearance when he is kayoed by a five-run Yankees' first inning in Game Six of the World Series; chronic arm trouble, stemming from a spring-training injury, will abruptly end Spooner's career.

1956

To his great disappointment, Frank Robinson was relegated to spending his second straight year with Columbia of the Class A Sally League in 1955. His career appeared to lose headway when his BA dropped 73 points below his 1954 figure of .336 and, to boot, he was injured and missed almost half the season. Nevertheless, Robinson was invited to Cincinnati's spring training camp in 1956 and showed enough in Grapefruit League action to beat out several veterans for the Reds' leftfield job. Six months later, when the 1956 season ended, Robinson stood first in the NL in runs and had also tied Wally Berger's frosh record for the most home runs. Unnoticed at the time was the fact that the Reds' rookie sensation had not only topped the NL in most times hit by pitches with 20 but in the process had become the first player in ML history to collect as many as 20 home runs and 20 hit by pitches in the same season. Oddly, just a few weeks after Robinson accomplished this feat, he was joined by White Sox outfielder

Minnie Minoso, who finished the 1956 AL season with 21 homers and 23 hit by pitches.

Robinson's massive rookie achievements helped the Reds to escape the second division for the first time since 1944 and vault all the way to third place, just two games behind the pennant-winning Dodgers. The third-place finisher in the AL for the fourth straight season was Chicago. In 1956 the White Sox actually regressed slightly, finishing with six fewer wins than they had notched the previous year. Despite the decline in overall performance, the Sox were able to boast the first ROY Award winner by either Windy City ML entry when the club's new shortstop, Luis Aparicio, grabbed all but two of the 24 BBWAA votes. Aparicio's main credentials were his fielding prowess and, to a lesser extent, the AL stolen-base crown, which he won by a margin of only one theft, edging out teammate Jim Rivera.

In 1956 Aparicio paced all AL shortstops for the first of many times in total chances and thereupon became the first performer to bag a ROY trophy largely for his defensive work. The importance AL BBWAA voters apparently attached to Aparicio's fielding is best illustrated when his offensive achievements in his rookie season are put into perspective. Below are the offensive profiles for four rookie middle infielders who debuted in a seven-year span (1956–62). Three won ROY honors and one did not. Guess which profile belongs to Aparcio and which one was snubbed by the BBWAA.

The profiles belong, in order, to Ron Hansen (1960), Dick Howser (1961), Aparicio (1956), and Ken Hubbs (1962). Howser's, which is arguably the best, was the only one that failed to impress the BBWAA committee sufficiently. Adding to the perspective on Aparicio's profile, among all AL performers in 1956, he finished tied for 35th in runs created with 59. And of the 64 AL players who participated in at least 100 games that year, he ranked 54th in OPS.

In contrast to Frank Robinson, Rocky Colavito had a strong minor league season in 1955 and reported to Cleveland's Tucson spring training camp in 1956 with the assurance that the Tribe's rightfield post was his to lose. Colavito then proceeded to lose it when he got off to such a miserable start that he was shipped to San Diego of the Pacific Coast League in early June over howls of protest from his huge local fan club, which consisted mainly of teenage girls.

After pounding PCL hurlers for 12 homers and a .368 BA in 35 games, Colavito was recalled to Cleveland. The haunting plea that his vast coterie of supporters had coined early in the season when his confidence was at its nadir—"Don't Knock the Rock"—was swiftly forgotten. By end of September, despite missing nearly a month and a half of the season, Colavito was second on the club in homers, third in RBI, and first in OPS.

His torrid finish earned him all of one vote for the AL ROY Award. Amazingly, of the six best OPS figures produced by recruit hitters in the decade of the 1950s, only two of them, for a variety of reasons, were deemed worthy of a first prize in the rookie sweepstakes.

TOP SIX OPS FIGURES BY ROOKIES, 1951–60 (MINIMUM 100 GAMES)

Name	Team	Year	OPS
Frank Robinson	Cin-NL	1956	.939
Minnie Minoso	Cle/Chi-AL	1951	.922
Jim Gentile	Bal-AL	1960	.907
Rocky Colavito	Cle-AL	1956	.906
Gil McDougald	NY-AL	1951	.884
Vada Pinson	Cin-NL	1959	.880

Other Highlights

April 21—Red Murff, the minor league pitcher of the year in 1955, makes his ML debut with the Braves at age 35 after not starting his pro career until he was 29 years old; in Murff's first pro season, 1950, he was 17–4 with Baton Rouge and hit .331 as a pitcher-outfielder to finish sixth in the Evangeline League in batting.

OFFENSIVE PROFILES FOR FOUR ROOKIE MIDDLE INFIELDERS, 1956–62

G	AB	R	H	2B	3B	HR	RBI	BB	SO	SB	CS	AVG	SLG	OBA	OPS
153	530	72	135	22	5	22	86	69	94	3	3	.255	.440	.343	.782
158	611	108	171	29	6	3	45	92	38	37	9	.280	.362	.379	.740
152	533	69	142	19	6	3	56	34	63	21	4	.266	.341	.312	.653
160	661	90	172	24	9	5	49	35	129	3	7	.260	.346	.300	.647

1956 ROOKIE LEADERS

Batting	Pitching
G—AL 152, Luis Aparicio, CHI	W—AL 9, Dave Sisler, BOS
NL 152, Frank Robinson, CIN	NL 7, Lindy McDaniel, STL
AB—AL 533, Luis Aparicio, CHI	L—AL 13, Troy Herriage, KC
NL 587, Don Blasingame, STL	NL 9, Jim Brosnan, CHI
H—AL 142, Luis Aparicio, CHI	Don Kaiser, CHI
NL 166, Frank Robinson, CIN	PCT—AL No Qualifiers
2B—AL 24, Don Buddin, BOS	NL No Qualifiers
NL 27, Frank Robinson, CIN	GP—AL 54, Jack Crimian, KC
3B—AL 7, Whitey Herzog, WAS	NL 42, Vito Valentinetti, CHI
Herb Plews, WAS	GS—AL 16, Troy Herriage, KC
NL 11, Lee Walls, PIT	NL 22, Don Kaiser, CHI
HR—AL 21, Rocky Colavito, CLE	CG—AL 4, Wally Burnette, KC
NL 38, Frank Robinson, CIN	NL 5, Don Kaiser, CHI
R—AL 69, Luis Aparicio, CHI	IP—AL 142.1, Dave Sisler, BOS
NL 122, Frank Robinson, CIN	NL 150.1, Don Kaiser, CHI
RBI—AL 65, Rocky Colavito, CLE	H—AL 135, Troy Herriage, KC
NL 83, Frank Robinson, CIN	NL 144, Don Kaiser, CHI
WK—AL 65, Don Buddin, BOS	BB—AL 76, Hal Griggs, WAS
NL 72, Don Blasingame, STL	NL 52, Don Kaiser, CHI
SO—AL 74, Whitey Herzog, WAS	K—AL 93, Dave Sisler, BOS
NL 95, Frank Robinson, CIN	NL 74, Don Kaiser, CHI
SB—**AL 21, Luis Aparicio, CHI**	ERA—AL No Qualifiers
NL 15, Bill White, NY	NL No Qualifiers*
BA—AL .266, Luis Aparicio, CHI	SHO—AL 1, Hank Aguirre, CLE
NL .290, Frank Robinson, CIN	Charlie Beamon, BAL
SLG—AL .373, Tito Francona, BAL	Wally Burnette, KC
NL .558, Frank Robinson, CIN	Don Ferrarese, BAL
OBP—AL .334, Tito Francona, BAL	NL 1, Tom Acker, CIN
NL .381, Frank Robinson, CIN	Jim Brosnan, CHI
	Don Kaiser, CHI
	SV—AL 3, Jack Crimian, KC
	Dave Sisler, BOS
	NL 2, Taylor Phillips, MIL

*Don Kaiser of the Cubs just missed qualifying with a 3.59 ERA in 150.1 IP.

April 28—Frank Robinson hits the first of his 586 career home runs; his victim is Cubs lefty Paul Minner.

May 2—Outfielder Lee Walls, the Pirates' early-season rookie sensation, goes 5-for-5 in a 10-inning 10–9 loss to the Cardinals.

July 15—Wally Burnette of Kansas City blanks Washington 8–0 in his first ML start; it will prove to be the only shutout of Burnette's brief three-year career.

September 11—Frank Robinson ties the ML record for homers by a rookie when he goes deep for the 38th time in an 11–5 Cincinnati win over the Giants.

September 26—Charlie Beamon of the Orioles is the first African-American hurler in AL history to throw a shutout in his first ML start when he blanks the Yankees 1–0 and in so doing prevents Whitey Ford from posting his first 20-win season.

September 30—White Sox Bonus Baby Jim Derrington becomes the youngest hurler in AL history to start a game when he loses 7–6 to Kansas City at the age of 16 years and ten months.

In 1957 the Yankees, amid yet another lengthy pennant-winning skein that would reach four the following year, spawned yet another stellar rookie class led by their third ROY winner of the decade, outfielder-infielder Tony Kubek. Meanwhile, the Baltimore Orioles undraped a pair of 18-year-old righthanders, Jerry Walker and Milt Pappas, who would be but the first of a long parade of "Baby Birds" (teenage pitchers) the O's would introduce in the course of the next decade. Joining the two 18-year-olds on the Baltimore club in early July was Frank Zupo, a 17-year-old catcher from San Francisco.

But the major rookie story in 1957 centered on whether or not a certain player should be considered a rookie. The player was Red Sox third baseman Frank Malzone, who has since said, "All year {in 1957} I was regarded as a rookie, but in the last month, the New York press managed to get my classification changed so that Yankee shortstop Tony Kubek would win the Rookie of the Year Award. My name was taken off the ballot and Tony won." Malzone's memory is not completely accurate. Early in the 1957 campaign an informal poll taken among BBWAA writers indicated that the majority felt that Malzone, who had 123 at bats prior to the season, should no longer be considered a rookie. Cited as a precedent was the Al Rosen case in 1950.

Nevertheless, Malzone had a valid point in that the eligibility rules for the ROY Award in each league as late as 1957 were still informal. Consequently, one of the 24 AL BBWAA writers voted for Malzone to demonstrate his protest, thereby denying Kubek what otherwise would have been a unanimous victory. To avert further conflicts involving the voting process, on December 4, 1957, the BBWAA guidelines were formally changed to impose strict limitations as to what constituted rookie status. Eligibility ended for position players after 75 at bats (the limit was boosted to 90 shortly thereafter), for pitchers after 45 innings, and for all performers, regardless of playing time, after 45 days on a ML roster before September 1. Fourteen years later, in 1971, further refinements were made to the eligibility rules, setting the limitations at their current criteria of 130 at bats and 50 innings.

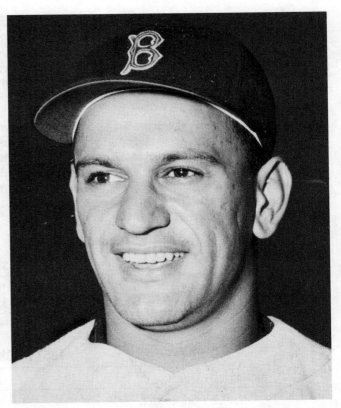

Frank Malzone went public with his beef that he had unfairly been denied the 1957 AL ROY Award. The Malzone incident finally led to badly needed reforms in the way the top rookie honorees in each league were chosen. *Transcendental Graphics*

The controversy still rages today, especially in Boston, as to whether Malzone or Kubek was the true AL ROY of the year in 1957, but Kubek earned an added measure of credibility after the ballots were cast when he had a fine World Series against the Milwaukee Braves while splitting his time between the outfield and third base.

Other Highlights

June 21—Eighteen-year-old Von McDaniel, younger brother of Cards pitcher Lindy McDaniel, blanks Brooklyn 2–0 in his first ML start for the Redbirds; young McDaniel will be a midseason sensation with St. Louis before being shut down by arm trouble after a 7–4 win over Cincinnati on September 7.

July 1—In a 3–2 loss to the Yankees, Bonus Baby catcher Frank "Noodles" Zupo joins with reliever George Zuverink to make the Orioles the first team in history to feature an all "Z" battery.

The NL ROY contest in 1957 was free of controversy as pitcher Jack Sanford was an easy winner over his Phillies teammate, first baseman Ed Bouchee, on the basis of his 19 victories. But in retrospect, a pretty fair argument can be mustered that two other senior loop rookies that year ought to have merited, at the very least, strong consideration for the top prize. One was a third Phillies frosh, reliever Turk Farrell, who not only led all recruit hurlers in saves with ten but also posted a glittering 10–2 record and the second-best ERA in the majors among pitchers in a minimum of 70 innings. For his efforts, Farrell drew a complete blank in the NL ROY balloting.

Milwaukee outfielder Bob Hazle fared a bit better than Farrell, garnering one vote, and at the time not even Hazle could find reason to protest since he collected only 134 at bats. Two years later, however, Hazle must have begun to regret his silence when a frosh hitter with just 58 more at bats than his total in 1957 not only bagged the NL ROY Award but was a unanimous selection.

To add weight to Hazle's case, in 1957 his meteoric batwork after he was recalled in August from Wichita of the American Association helped carry the Braves to their first pennant since moving to Milwaukee. On the other hand, Willie McCovey, for all his heroics in the last two months of 1959 season, could do no better for the San Francisco Giants than third place.

Here are their rookie profiles. The last two figures indicate the league OPS and the difference between Hazle's and McCovey's OPS numbers and the league's.

G	AB	R	H	2B	3B	HR	RBI	BB	SO	SB	CS	AVG	SLG	OBA	OPS	Lg	Diff
41	134	26	54	12	0	7	27	18	15	1	3	.403	.649	.477	1.126	.724	.402
52	192	32	68	9	5	13	38	22	35	2	0	.354	.656	.431	1.087	.727	.350

1957 ROOKIE LEADERS

Batting

G—AL 153, Frank Malzone, BOS
    NL 154, Ed Bouchee, PHI
AB—AL 634, Frank Malzone, BOS
    NL 574, Ed Bouchee, PHI
H—AL 185, Frank Malzone, BOS
    NL 168, Ed Bouchee, PHI
2B—AL 31, Frank Malzone, BOS
    NL 35, Ed Bouchee, PHI
3B—AL 5, Frank Malzone, BOS
    Roger Maris, CLE
    NL 8, Ed Bouchee, PHI
HR—AL 20, Woodie Held, NY/KC
    NL 17, Harry Anderson, PHI
    Ed Bouchee, PHI
R—AL 82, Frank Malzone, BOS
    NL 78, Ed Bouchee, PHI
RBI—AL 103, Frank Malzone, BOS
    NL 76, Ed Bouchee, PHI
WK—AL 60, Roger Maris, CLE
    NL 84, Ed Bouchee, PHI
SO—AL 81, Woodie Held, NY/KC
    NL 91, Ed Bouchee, PHI
SB—AL 14, Jim Landis, CHI
    NL 18, Chico Fernandez, PHI
BA—AL .297, Tony Kubek, NY
    NL .293, Ed Bouchee, PHI
SLG—AL .427, Frank Malzone, BOS
    NL .470, Ed Bouchee, PHI
OBA—AL .338, Tony Kubek, NY
    NL .396, Ed Bouchee, PHI

Pitching

W—AL 7, Bill Fischer, CHI
    Jack Urban, KC
    NL 19, Jack Sanford, PHI
L—AL 12, Ralph Terry, NY/KC
    NL 11, Dick Drott, CHI
PCT—AL No Qualifiers
    NL .704, Jack Sanford, PHI
GP—AL 52, Dick Hyde, WAS
    NL 52, Turk Farrell, PHI
GS—AL 21, Ralph Terry, NY/KC
    NL 33, Jack Sanford, PHI
CG—AL 4, Ralph Terry, NY/KC
    NL 15, Jack Sanford, PHI
IP—AL 151.1, Ralph Terry, NY/KC
    NL 236.2, Jack Sanford, PHI
H—AL 139, Bill Fischer, CHI
    NL 200, Dick Drott, CHI
BB—AL 56, Dick Hyde, WAS
    NL 129, Dick Drott, CHI
K—AL 97, Billy O'Dell, BAL
    NL 188, Jack Sanford, PHI
ERA—AL No Qualifiers
    NL 3.08, Jack Sanford, PHI
SH—AL 2, Ralph Terry, NY/KC
    NL 3, Dick Drott, CHI
    Jack Sanford, PHI
SV—AL 4, Billy O'Dell, BAL
    NL 10, Turk Farrell, PHI

August 27—Hitting a torrid .526 since being recalled from Wichita of the American Association, Bob "Hurricane" Hazle cracks a pair of two-run homers to help Braves ace Warren Spahn beat the Phillies 7–3.

September 24—Rookie lefty Danny McDevitt of the Dodgers blanks the Pirates 2–0 in the last ML game ever played at Brooklyn's Ebbets Field.

October 5—In Game Three of the 1957 World Series, Tony Kubek is only the second rookie in history to clout two home runs in a postseason game as he helps lead the Yankees to a 12–3 win over the Braves.

 **1958**

In 1958 Giants first sacker Orlando Cepeda's domination of the hitting side of the rookie leaders board resulted in his unanimous selection as the NL ROY while Senators outfielder Albie Pearson, who led AL rookie hitters in even more offensive departments than Cepeda—11 to ten—had a tussle for the top honor in the junior circuit before collecting 14 of the 24 ballots to beat out Yankees reliever Ryne Duren (seven) and Cleveland's young right-hander Gary Bell (three). Did Pearson struggle to win the award because the AL had a stronger and deeper rookie crop that year? Far from it. Actually, in 1958, for the first time since 1946, the AL had only one rookie position player who collected as many as 400 at bats, and that, of course, was Pearson. Cepeda, on the other hand, was just one of many NL rookies with 400 at bats.

Most of Cepeda's serious competition for rookie kudos in the NL came from his own teammates, as the Giants celebrated their first year in San Francisco by harvesting the largest and most productive crop of recruit position players in the past half century. In addition to Cepeda, manager Bill Rigney employed three other freshman regulars: catcher Bob Schmidt, third baseman Jim Davenport, and rightfielder Willie Kirkland. What's more, a fifth spot in the lineup, left field, was split among veteran Hank Sauer and two rookies, Leon Wagner and Felipe Alou. In 1958, of the 11 Giants who collected 150 or more at bats, six were freshmen, and only the presence of Willie Mays prevented the six from posting the top figures on the club in every major

By a margin of one-third of an inning, Ryne Duren qualified for rookie status in 1958. In addition to the seven writers who voted him the AL ROY, many observers, including *The Sporting News*, felt he was the junior circuit's leading freshman luminary. He was definitely its most exciting newcomer. Judged incurably wild by both Baltimore and Kansas City in earlier ML trials, Duren came to the Yankees from the A's in a midseason trade in 1957. After being farmed out to Denver, he led the American Association in winning percentage and for the first time in his career seemed finally, at age 28, to master his control problems, walking just 33 batters in 114 innings.

In the spring of 1958, Casey Stengel decided to make Duren the Yankees' new closer, replacing Bob Grim. Even though Duren's wildness instantly reappeared, it was a stroke of genius. Despite surrendering 43 walks in 75.2 innings and also hitting seven batters, Duren paced the AL in saves with 20 and posted a 2.02 ERA. Moreover, he allowed just 4.7 hits per nine innings, the fewest of any hurler in a minimum of 45 innings between 1946, the first postwar season, and 1960, the last year prior to expansion.

Interestingly, two of the other names among the top ten on that same list belong to pitchers who first emerged in 1958. One was White Sox rookie Barry Latman. In addition to giving up just 5.1 hits per nine innings, Latman registered both the lowest BR/9 ratio of any hurler in 45 innings between 1946 and 1960 (8.4) and the lowest ERA (0.76). The second hurler was ex-Braves Bonus Baby Joey Jay. Though no longer considered a rookie because he had languished on the Braves roster off and on for four seasons prior to 1958, Jay nonetheless had appeared in only 47.2 innings before his breakthrough season.

Note that two other list members were rookies featured earlier in this book, Don Mossi of the 1954 Indians and 1948's unrecognized rookie sensation, Tommy Byrne.

FEWEST HITS PER NINE INNINGS, MINIMUM 45 IP (1946–1960)

Rank	Name	Year	IP	ERA	BR/9	H/9
1	Ryne Duren	1958	75.2	2.02	10.66	4.74
2	Ryne Duren	1960	49	4.96	15.24	4.96
3	Barry Latman	1958	47.2	0.76	8.44	5.06
4	Junior Thompson	1946	62.2	1.29	10.86	5.14
5	Tommy Byrne	1948	133.2	3.30	12.69	5.31
6	Don Mossi	1954	93	1.94	9.29	5.42
7	Red Ruffing	1946	61	1.77	8.85	5.46
8	Ray Narleski	1956	59	1.52	8.54	5.49
9	Willie Ramsdell	1952	67	2.42	9.40	5.51
10	Joey Jay	1958	96.2	2.14	9.65	5.57

batting department except walks, where the runner-up to Mays was veteran shortstop Daryl Spencer. Not surprisingly, Rigney's hand of six rookie aces played a vital role in the Giants' vault to third place after a sixth-place finish in their last year in New York.

What distinguished the Giants' 1958 frosh yield even more than its extraordinary immediate impact on the club's fortunes was the longevity of most of its members and their overall influence on the game's history in the second half of the twentieth century. Only Schmidt of the six played less than nine years in the majors and never again had a season as good as his frosh year. Each of the other five played over 1,000 games, ranging from Kirkland's 1,149 to Cepeda's 2,124. Moreover, Cepeda is in the Hall of Fame, Alou was but the first to reach the majors of the most famous trio of brothers with the lone exception of the DiMaggios, and both Davenport and Alou later managed the Giants. Indeed, in 2004 Alou, by then nearing 70, was still going strong and piloting his original team.

Other Highlights

May 18—Former college football star Carroll Hardy pinch hits for Roger Maris and clouts his first career

1958 ROOKIE LEADERS

Batting	Pitching
G—AL 146, Albie Pearson, WAS	W—AL 12, Gary Bell, CLE
NL 148, Orlando Cepeda, SF	NL 13, Ray Semproch, PHI
AB—AL 530, Albie Pearson, WAS	L—AL 11, Mudcat Grant, CLE
NL 603, Orlando Cepeda, SF	NL 11, Ray Semproch, PHI
H—AL 146, Albie Pearson, WAS	PCT—AL .545, Gary Bell, CLE
NL 188, Orlando Cepeda, SF	NL .543, Ray Semproch, PHI
2B—AL 25, Albie Pearson, WAS	GP—AL 52, Murray Wall, BOS
NL 38, Orlando Cepeda, SF	NL 55, Glen Hobbie, CHI
3B—AL 5, Albie Pearson, WAS	GS—AL 28, Mudcat Grant, CLE
NL 9, Johnny Roseboro, LA	NL 30, Ray Semproch, PHI
HR—AL 7, Dick Brown, CLE	CG—AL 11, Mudcat Grant, CLE
Billy Harrell, CLE	NL 12, Ray Semproch, PHI
Marv Throneberry, NY	IP—AL 204, Mudcat Grant, CLE
NL 25, Orlando Cepeda, SF	NL 204.1, Ray Semproch, PHI
R—AL 63, Albie Pearson, WAS	H—AL 173, Mudcat Grant, CLE
NL 88, Orlando Cepeda, SF	NL 211, Ray Semproch, PHI
RBI—AL 33, Albie Pearson, WAS	BB—AL 104, Mudcat Grant, CLE
NL 96, Orlando Cepeda, SF	NL 93, Glen Hobbie, CHI
WK—AL 64, Albie Pearson, WAS	K—AL 111, Mudcat Grant, CLE
NL 43, Willie Kirkland, SF	NL 92, Ray Semproch, PHI
SO—AL 43, Gary Geiger, CLE	ERA—AL 3.31, Gary Bell, CLE
NL 93, Tony Taylor, CHI	NL 3.74, Glen Hobbie, CHI
SB—AL 12, Billy Harrell, CLE	SHO—AL 1, Mudcat Grant, CLE
NL 21, Tony Taylor, CHI	Barry Latman, CHI
BA—AL .275, Albie Pearson, WAS	**NL 4, Carl Willey, MIL**
NL .312, Orlando Cepeda, SF	SV—**AL 20, Ryne Duren, NY**
SLG—AL .358, Albie Pearson, WAS	NL 5, Billy Muffett, STL
NL .512, Orlando Cepeda, SF	
OBP—AL .356, Albie Pearson, WAS	
NL .346, Orlando Cepeda, SF	

home run, a three-run shot, that helps give Cleveland a 7–4 win over Chicago's Billy Pierce; two years later the otherwise obscure Hardy will become doubly renowned when he pinch hits for Ted Williams.

July 6—Giants rookie Jim Davenport drives in the winning run when Cards reliever Larry Jackson hits him with a pitch in the ninth inning with the bases loaded; the previous day, in an almost identical situation, another Giants rookie, Willie Kirkland, had driven home the winning run when Jackson walked him in the bottom of the ninth with the bases jammed.

July 13—Giants rookies Orlando Cepeda and Felipe Alou put San Francisco into first place in the NL when Cepeda hits his third home run in three days, and Alou follows with a run-scoring single in the ninth inning to hang a 6–5 loss on Milwaukee, the former first-place tenant.

August 27—Orlando Cepeda is the third Giants rookie in 1958 to drive in the winning run on a final-inning bases-loaded walk or hit-by-pitch when Braves reliever Bob Trowbridge walks him with the sacks full in the 12th inning to give San Francisco, literally, a walk-off 4–3 win.

September 12—In a doubleheader sweep of the Phillies, rookie third baseman Jim Davenport leads the Giants with seven hits, including an inside-the-park homer, and also tallies seven runs.

September 28—In an 11–4 win over Kansas City, White Sox catcher Chuck Lindstrom, the son of Hall of Famer Freddie Lindstrom, appears in his lone ML game; after walking in his first ML plate appearance, Lindstrom then triples his next time up to finish with perfect 1.000 career BAs and OBPs—and a 3.000 SA!

October 6—Braves rookie right-hander Carl Willey, the NL shutout leader, pitches a perfect eighth inning in relief in Game Five of the World Series; it will be Willey's lone postseason appearance as Milwaukee manager Fred Haney opts to go with veteran hurlers and thereby becomes the first NL pilot to lose a World Series after holding a seemingly prohibitive 3–1 lead.

Only two rookies have ever made a clean sweep of all 14 offensive departments on the frosh leaders board, and both accomplished this unparalled feat astonishingly enough in the same year—1959. Had one of the pair, Vada Pinson, performed his dazzling exploits in recent years rather than in 1959, he would unquestionably have been a unanimous ROY selection. But it was Pinson's ill luck to collect six too many at bats with Cincinnati early in the 1958 season before the Reds farmed him out to Seattle of the Pacific Coast League. Numerologists will not be alone in finding it ironic that Pinson's 96 at bats were not only six more than the allowable limit in 1959 to retain rookie status, but they were also exactly half the number logged in 1959 by Willie McCovey, the man who won a unanimous NL ROY Award in 1959 in Pinson's stead.

Yet it was not that McCovey was undeserving of the prize. Even though he did not join the Giants from their Phoenix farm club until July 30, leaving him time to play in just 52 games, his .354 BA and .656 SA were pivotal factors in San Francisco's surge to what seemed a certain pennant going into the final week of the season. But the Giants then proceeded to lose seven of their final eight games to finish in third place, enabling another senior loop rookie instead of McCovey to become the major story of the Fall Classic. After netting just three saves during the regular season, reliever Larry Sherry made the Los Angeles Dodgers the first team west of the Rockies to win a World Championship when he almost single-handedly stymied the White Sox in the 1959 World Series. In his four appearances Sherry allowed just one earned run in 12.2 innings and became the only man ever to lead all series hurlers in both wins and saves, with two apiece.

Sherry was not Dodgers pilot Walter Alston's only rookie series hero. Frosh outfielder Chuck Essegian set a new postseason record, since tied, with two pinch-hit home runs, and Alston also got valuable work from recruit gardeners Don Demeter and Ron Fairly. White Sox skipper Al Lopez, in contrast, relied almost exclusively on his veterans in the series but received plenty of help from recruits during the regular season. In driving to their first pennant in 40 years, the Pale Hose introduced a welter of newcomers who would be major contributors to the game in the next decade, including Johnny Callison, Ken McBride, John Romano, Gary Peters, J. C. Martin, and Norm Cash. Unhappily for Sox fans, only Peters and Martin did their best work in Chicago as the rest all drifted away in trades before they reached their peak years.

Other Highlights

July 21—Pumpsie Green is the first black to play for the Boston Red Sox when he pinch runs in a game against the White Sox; Green's appearance signifies that the majors are now completely integrated as all 16 teams have now had at least one black player.

July 30—Willie McCovey marks his ML debut with the Giants by going 4-for-4 with two triples in a 7–2 win over the Phillies.

July 31—After becoming the Red Sox first black pitcher three days earlier, Earl Wilson holds Detroit hitless in his first start but leaves the game after just 3⅔ innings when he walks his ninth batter.

September 10—In the second game of a doubleheader against the Cubs, rookie southpaw Jim Bailey starts for the Reds and is caught by his brother Ed; Jim will be charged with a 6–3 loss in his ML debut and then make just two more appearances, both in relief, before disappearing from the scene.

September 28—In the opening game of a best-of-three playoff for the NL pennant, Dodgers rookie reliever Larry Sherry hurls 7⅔ scoreless innings to beat the Braves 3–2; Sherry will rightfully be best remembered for his stellar work in the 1959 postseason but must also be remembered as the last pitcher to date to be caught by his brother in an ML game.

October 8—Dodgers rookie Chuck Essegian establishes a new record when he clouts his second pinch homer in the 1959 World Series; Essegian's distinction will be equaled in 1975 by Bernie Carbo of the Red Sox.

The White Sox had yet another newcomer in 1959, Jim McAnany, who was their lone recruit to appear in more than 60 games. Actually, by the end of season McAnany was serving as Al Lopez's regular right fielder. After seeing spot duty in the 1959 World Series, McAnany never again played a full game in the majors. Even at that, he fared much better than Jim Baxes, the lone rookie regular position player on Cleveland, the White Sox' chief rival in 1959.

A San Francisco native and long time Coast League performer, Baxes was 30 at the beginning of the 1959 season when he finally made the Dodgers roster for the first time. In midseason, after 11 games with the Dodgers, he was sold to Cleveland. Although Baxes's natural position was third base, Tribe manager Joe Gordon installed him at second base to replace Billy Martin, who had suffered a season-ending injury. Playing beside Baxes at shortstop was Woodie Held, a converted center fielder, and at third base for Cleveland in 1959 was George Strickland, whose best position was shortstop although he also had experience at second base. Whatever possessed Gordon, himself a former second baseman, to have Baxes fill in for the injured Martin rather than occupy third base while Strickland moved to second has never been unearthed. In any case, despite having an infield with everyone, including first baseman Vic Power, playing out of his original position, Cleveland, a consistent contender ever since World War II, somehow contrived to make its final serious pennant bid until 1994. At the close of the season, feeling that he had contributed significantly to the team's performance, Baxes, who was making the big league minimum, felt justified in seeking a raise. He was rewarded instead with his release and never again donned a major league uniform.

Was the curse that spelled the Indians' doom for the next 35 years really spurred by the ill-advised Rocky Colavito trade following the 1959 season? Or was it, conceivably, the rude way in which Baxes was treated? In his one and only major league season, Baxes hammered 17 home runs to lead AL second sackers. Even more significantly, Baxes ranks first in home runs among all retired players in ML history with fewer than 300 career at bats.

CAREER HOME RUNS, RETIRED PLAYERS WITH FEWER THAN 300 ABs

Rank	Name	AB	HR
1	Jim Baxes	280	17
2	Ron Jones	239	13
	Jose Oliva	242	13
	Dino Restelli	270	13
5	Paul Ratliff	297	12
6	Adrian Garrett	276	11
7	Luis Medina	150	10
	Randy Johnson	254	10
	Joe Frazier	282	10

1959 ROOKIE LEADERS

Batting	Pitching
G—AL 150, Bob Allison, WAS	W—AL 13, Jerry Casale, BOS
NL 154, Vada Pinson, CIN	NL 12, Jim Owens, PHI
AB—AL 570, Bob Allison, WAS	L—AL 10, Jim Perry, CLE
NL 648, Vada Pinson, CIN	Jerry Walker, BAL
H—AL 149, Bob Allison, WAS	NL 12, Ernie Broglio, STL
NL 205, Vada Pinson, CIN	Jim Owens, PHI
2B—AL 18, Bob Allison, WAS	PCT—AL .619, Jerry Casale, BOS
NL 47, Vada Pinson, CIN	NL .500, Jim Owens, PHI
3B—**AL 9, Bob Allison, WAS**	GP—AL 44, Jim Perry, CLE
NL 9, Vada Pinson, CIN	NL 46, Orlando Pena, CIN
HR—AL 30, Bob Allison, WAS	GS—AL 26, Jerry Casale, BOS
NL 20, Vada Pinson, CIN	NL 30, Jim Owens, PHI
R—AL 83, Bob Allison, WAS	CG—AL 9, Jerry Casale, BOS
NL 131, Vada Pinson, CIN	NL 11, Jim Owens, PHI
RBI—AL 85, Bob Allison, WAS	IP—AL 182.0, Jerry Walker, BAL
NL 84, Vada Pinson, CIN	NL 221.1, Jim Owens, PHI
WK—AL 60, Bob Allison, WAS	H—AL 162, Jerry Casale, BOS
NL 55, Vada Pinson, CIN	NL 203, Jim Owens, PHI
SO—AL 92, Bob Allison, WAS	BB—AL 89, Jerry Casale, BOS
NL 98, Vada Pinson, CIN	NL 89, Ernie Broglio, STL
SB—AL 13, Bob Allison, WAS	K—AL 100, Jerry Walker, BAL
NL 21, Vada Pinson, CIN	NL 135, Jim Owens, PHI
BA—AL .261, Bob Allison, WAS	ERA—AL 2.92, Jerry Walker, BAL
NL .316, Vada Pinson, CIN	NL 3.21, Jim Owens, PHI
SLG—AL .482, Bob Allison, WAS	SHO—AL 3, Jerry Casale, BOS
NL .509, Vada Pinson, CIN	NL 3, Ernie Broglio, STL
OBP—AL .334, Bob Allison, WAS	SV—AL 4, Jim Perry, CLE
NL .371, Vada Pinson, CIN	Jerry Walker, BAL
	NL 5, Orlando Pena, CIN

1960s

━━ 1960 ━━

In 1959 the Washington Senators matched the remarkable feat first performed by the 1954–55 Cardinals when for the second straight year they generated a recruit center fielder who won the loop ROY Award. But unlike Albie Pearson, the 1958 victor, who never again played a full season with the Senators, the team's 1959 winner, Bob Allison, followed the franchise to Minnesota in 1961 and not only spent his entire 13-year ML career with the organization but currently ranks third on the franchise in home runs behind only Harmon Killebrew and Kent Hrbek.

Pearson, meanwhile, was with Baltimore in 1960 when the Orioles perpetrated an equally remarkable rookie exploit. In the final year prior to expansion, the Orioles became the only team to date to have in its stable the win, place, and show horses in a ROY derby, as shortstop Ron Hansen took the blue ribbon by dint of his 22 votes and first baseman Jim Gentile and pitcher Chuck Estrada both shared the red and white ribbons after tying for second in the AL balloting with one vote apiece. The NL ROY winner in 1960 was likewise one of

a kind thus far. Towering 6′7″ Frank Howard became the only former college All-American in another sport to cop his loop's top rookie prize just three years after he left the Ohio State hoop squad for a professional baseball career following his junior season. Moreover, Howard, who had received a reported $108,000 to sign with the Dodgers, was the first six-digit Bonus Baby to claim a ROY honor. His 23 home runs not only led all rookies in 1960 but also topped the Dodgers and ranked second among NL right fielders only to Hank Aaron's 40.

Second and third to Howard in the NL balloting were two members of the Phillies, first baseman Pancho Herrera and pitcher Art Mahaffey. A scattering of votes also went to Cubs third baseman Ron Santo and another Dodgers rookie outfielder, Tommy Davis. But even with two outstanding newcomers in Howard and Davis, Los Angeles was unable to defend its 1959 pennant successfully, let alone its World Championship. Instead, the long moribund Pittsburgh Pirates claimed their first flag in 33 years and culminated their wondrous season by toppling the Yankees in the seventh game of the World Series on Bill Mazeroski's famous walk-off home run. Often neg-

PIRATES ROOKIE PITCHERS, 1960

	W	L	PCT	G	GS	CG	SV	GF	IP	H	R	ER	BB	SO	ERA
Fred Green	8	4	.667	45	0	0	3	18	70	61	26	25	33	49	3.21
Joe Gibbon	4	2	.667	27	9	0	0	6	80.1	87	40	36	31	60	4.03
Jim Umbricht	1	2	.333	17	3	0	1	5	40.2	40	23	23	27	26	5.09
Tom Cheney	2	2	.500	11	8	1	0	0	52	44	25	23	33	35	3.98
Earl Francis	1	0	1.000	7	0	0	0	3	18	14	5	4	4	8	2.00
Diomedes Olivo	0	0	.000	4	0	0	0	2	9.2	8	3	3	5	10	2.79
	16	10	.615	111	20	1	4	34	269.1	254	122	114	133	188	3.81

lected in historical summaries of the 1960 season are the contributions the Pirates received throughout the summer from a wide assortment of rookie hurlers. Six moundsmen with recruit status saw action with the surprise world champions. Though none garnered attention for ROY, they collected an aggregate total of 16 wins, led by lefty Fred Green at 8–4 with a 3.21 ERA in 45 relief appearances. Green, Joe Gibbon, another lefty, and Tom Cheney, renowned for his 21 strikeouts for Washington two years later in a 16-inning game at Baltimore, were all in the Pirates bullpen in the series, along with the team's veteran closer, Roy Face. And all, including Face, were hammered, as the Yankees posted a record .338 team BA but nonetheless lost. Green's treatment was especially brutal; in his four innings of work, he surrendered ten earned runs and never really recovered from

the shelling. Following his stellar recruit season, Green pitched just 35 more innings in the majors without ever again recording either a win or a save. Unhappily for Pittsburgh, for a variety of reasons none of its other talented frosh prospects, with the sole exception of Gibbon, were able to fashion careers of any great substance either.

Other Highlights

April 24—Rookie catcher Jimmie Coker of the Phils hits the fourth grand slam of the day in big league action to tie a one-day ML record; Coker's four-run shot gives the Phils a 9–5 win over the Reds.

May 7—Dodgers rookie Norm Sherry becomes the 15th and last receiver to date to catch his brother in an ML game; moreover, his 11th-inning homer gives brother Larry a 3–2 win over the Phils.

June 17—Cleveland rookie Wynn Hawkins, among the greatest baseball names of all-time, has his handle indelibly engraved in the game's lore when his gopher ball in a 3–1 loss to the Red Sox makes Ted Williams only the fourth player in history to collect 500 career home runs.

July 19—Juan Marichal of the Giants fans 12 and in addition is the first NL pitcher in the twentieth century to debut with a nine-inning one-hitter when only a seventh-inning single by catcher Clay Dalrymple mars his otherwise hitless 2–0 win over the Phils.

September 13—In an 8–6 loss to the Reds at Cincinnati, 18-year-old Danny Murphy is the youngest member of the Cubs to hit a home run; Murphy will hit just two more homers for the Cubs before returning to the

In 1955 Don Bessent of the then Brooklyn Dodgers became the first pitcher to gain recognition in a ROY contest despite being on a big league roster less than half the season when he bagged two votes after going 8–1 as a combination starter-reliever despite not joining Brooklyn until July 17. Five years later Art Mahaffey of the Phillies surpassed Bessent's feat when he acquired three ROY votes for his 7–3 mark in 12 starts after not arriving in Philadelphia until July 30.

Mahaffey's achievement followed immediately on the heels of Willie McCovey's selection as the NL ROY in 1959 after he too did not make his ML debut until July 30. In all the years since, no rookie whose ML entry came after July 4, which is customarily viewed as the midway point in the season, has even come close to bagging the top frosh prize. The latest debut date of any ROY winner subsequent to McCovey belongs to Bob Horner, who made his first appearance with the Atlanta Braves on June 16, 1978.

Batting	Pitching
G—AL 153, Ron Hansen, BAL	**W**—**AL 18, Chuck Estrada, BAL**
NL 145, Pancho Herrera, PHI	NL 9, Ray Sadecki, STL
AB—AL 551, Marv Breeding, BAL	**L**—AL 11, Chuck Estrada, BAL
NL 512, Pancho Herrera, PHI	Dick Stigman, CLE
H—AL 147, Marv Breeding, BAL	NL 13, Dick Ellsworth, CHI
NL 144, Pancho Herrera, PHI	**PCT**—AL .621, Chuck Estrada, BAL
2B—AL 25, Marv Breeding, BAL	NL .500, Ray Sadecki, STL
NL 26, Pancho Herrera, PHI	**GP**—AL 51, Marty Kutyna, KC
3B—AL 5, Lou Clinton, BOS	NL 45, Fred Green, PIT
Ron Hansen, BAL	**GS**—AL 27, Steve Barber, BAL
NL 8, Julian Javier, STL	NL 27, Dick Ellsworth, CHI
HR—AL 22, Ron Hansen, BAL	**CG**—AL 12, Chuck Estrada, BAL
NL 23, Frank Howard, LA	NL 7, Ray Sadecki, STL
R—AL 72, Ron Hansen, BAL	**IP**—AL 208.2, Chuck Estrada, BAL
NL 61, Pancho Herrera, PHI	NL 176.2, Dick Ellsworth, CHI
RBI—AL 98, Jim Gentile, BAL	**H**—AL 162, Chuck Estrada, BAL
NL 77, Frank Howard, LA	NL 170, Dick Ellsworth, CHI
WK—AL 69, Ron Hansen, BAL	**BB**—**AL 113, Steve Barber, BAL**
NL 51, Pancho Herrera, PHI	NL 86, Ray Sadecki, STL
SO—AL 94, Ron Hansen, BAL	**K**—AL 144, Chuck Estrada, BAL
NL 136, Pancho Herrera, PHI	NL 95, Ray Sadecki, STL
SB—AL 10, Marv Breeding, BAL	**ERA**—AL 3.22, Steve Barber, BAL
NL 19, Julian Javier, STL	NL 3.72, Dick Ellsworth, CHI
BA—AL .292, Jim Gentile, BAL	**SH**—AL 2, Jack Kralick, WAS
NL .281, Pancho Herrera, PHI	NL 1, done by six pitchers
SLG—AL .500, Jim Gentile, BAL	**SV**—AL 9, Dick Stigman, CLE
NL .464, Frank Howard, LA	NL 9, Ron Piche, MIL
OBA—AL .407, Jim Gentile, BAL	
NL .352, Pancho Herrera, PHI	

majors in 1969 with the crosstown White Sox—as a pitcher!

September 25—Phils rookie first sacker Pancho Herrera sets a new NL record when he fans for the 135th time in a 5–3 win over the Braves.

1961

Just once in the century-long battle between the American and National leagues have the two circuits scheduled a different number of games. The year was 1961, when the AL expanded to ten teams and played 162 contests while the senior circuit retained the old eight-team configuration and 154-game slate. Perhaps it was the eight additional games, but more likely it was the

slightly watered down competition in the AL that led to almost every top rookie in 1961 coming from a junior loop team.

The chief exception was Billy Williams, the sweet-swinging left fielder of the Chicago Cubs. Williams hit 25 home runs, still the team's freshman standard, and drove in 86 runs while batting .278. He hit two grand slams, both against San Francisco, the first coming on May 2 when he drove in five runs and collected four hits. On August 20 Williams experienced his greatest rookie highlight when he drove in the winning run with two out in the 11th inning for a 1–0 Cubs win.

Jack Curtis, also a Bruin, was the league's top rookie winner, notching ten for a team that won just 64 games. One of his 13 defeats was to Warren Spahn on August 11, when the southpaw earned his 300th victory. Spahn's

Dick Howser lost the AL ROY Award by one vote in 1961. Many observers, including your authors, feel that he should have been a unanimous winner. Howser was a pleasant surprise to the Kansas City organization. If there had been a free-agent draft in 1954 when he graduated from Palm Beach High School in West Palm Beach, Florida, he never would have been selected. In his senior year Howser was moved from shortstop to second base because his coach felt his arm was weak. He began his final high-school season batting leadoff but was dropped to the bottom of the order when he hit under .200.

Howser did not really begin to mature as a player until late in his collegiate career at Florida State. After graduation in 1958, he signed with Kansas City for a modest $21,000 bonus and spent the better part of three seasons in the Class B Three I League before the A's saw fit to move him up in class to their Shreveport farm club. In 1960 Howser led all minor leaguers in runs with 137. His 108 tallies with Kansas City in 1961 was second among AL rookie shortstops only to Donie Bush until 1997 when Nomar Garciaparra set the current mark of 122.

and also leading with a .991 fielding percentage. Schilling committed only eight errors, setting a new AL-record low for second basemen playing 150 or more games. Yet another Boston frosh, catcher Jim Pagliaroni, hit 16 round trippers, one of them a two-run pinch blast on June 17 that gave the Red Sox a 6–5 lead and victory. The next day Pag's grand slam in the bottom of the ninth tied the score at 12, Boston winning the opener of a twinbill moments later. In the second game Pagliaroni connected leading off the bottom of the 13th for another win. Finally, there was Tracy Stallard, who went just 2–7 for the Red Sox but gained immortality by surrendering Roger Maris's record 61st home run of the campaign October 1.

The expansion Los Angeles Angels also got their share of freshman help. Ken Hunt and Lee Thomas hit 25 and 24 home runs, respectively. Hunt, not to be confused with the Reds rookie of the same name who won nine games in 1961, drove in 84 runs. Thomas garnered eight of his 70 RBI in the second game of a September 5

catcher that day was Joe Torre, who hit ten homers, knocked in 42 runs, and finished with a .2783 batting average but lost the senior loop frosh batting crown to Billy Williams (.2779) because he fell short of the requisite number of plate appearances.

In 1961 the NL did not witness a single shutout thrown by a freshman, but the AL, in contrast, had eight rookie hurlers throw whitewashes, five of them tying for the lead with two each. One of the quintet, Don Schwall, started the year in Seattle, going 3–1 for the PCL club before debuting with Boston on May 21. A week later he blanked Baltimore. Schwall pitched three solid innings in the season's second All-Star Game, and on August 3 he improved to 12–2 with a three-hit shutout of the Angels. The rookie right-hander finished 15–7 with a .682 winning percentage that was the highest for a BoSox freshman with at least 20 decisions since Babe Ruth in 1915.

Schwall had plenty of rookie company in the Hub. Carl Yastrzemski performed admirably as Boston's left fielder, inheriting the post from the retired Ted Williams. Yaz had 155 hits, including 31 doubles, and 80 RBI despite having to face constant comparisons to the legendary Teddy Ballgame. Chuck Schilling scored 87 times and drew 78 walks in addition to playing an excellent second base for the BoSox, topping the loop in assists

Dick Howser broke in with the Kansas City A's and 25 years later piloted the KC Royals to their only World Championship to date. Injuries prevented him from reaching his full potential as a player, and a brain tumor brought a tragic early end to what promised to be an outstanding managerial career. *Transcendental Graphics*

twinbill against the Athletics. In the opener he went 5-for-5 with a double before ripping three homers, one a grand slam, and a single in the nightcap. Thomas tied the record that day for most hits in a double-dip, but Kansas City nonetheless swept the Angels. In addition to the important offensive contributions received from Hunt and Thomas, the Halos also showcased a rookie hurler who was second in 1961 only to Don Schwall—Ken McBride won 12 games and struck out 180 batters, fifth most in the circuit.

Two infielders who played for very different clubs tied for the AL frosh lead in hits with 171 apiece. Second sacker Jake Wood, in addition, slapped a league-leading 14 triples for second-place Detroit and unfortunately also led the loop with 141 whiffs, the most by a rookie prior to 1966. Dick Howser, on the 100-loss Kansas City Athletics, was a speedy shortstop who pilfered 37 bases and scored 108 runs. His 92 walks in 1961 are still the most ever for a rookie short-fielder.

A cut below Ken McBride were Kansas City's Norm Bass and Cleveland's Frank Funk, who each finished 11–11, with Funk continuing the numerical theme by saving 11 games. After being called up from Auburn in the NY-Penn League, Rollie Sheldon, the last player to be summoned directly from Class D to the majors, also bagged 11 victories against only five defeats for the flag-winning Yankees; two of Sheldon's wins were consecutive shutouts in early July, enabling him to tie for the 1961 frosh lead in that department.

1961 ROOKIE LEADERS

Batting	Pitching
G—AL 162, Jake Wood, DET	W—AL 15, Don Schwall, BOS
NL 146, Billy Williams, CHI	NL 10, Jack Curtis, CHI
AB—AL 663, Jake Wood, DET	L—AL 18, Joe McClain, WAS
NL 529, Billy Williams, CHI	NL 13, Jack Curtis, CHI
H—AL 171, Dick Howser, KC	PCT—AL .682, Don Schwall, BOS
Jake Wood, DET	NL .435, Jack Curtis, CHI
NL 147, Billy Williams, CHI	GP—AL 58, Bill Kunkel, KC
2B—AL 31, Carl Yastrzemski, BOS	**NL 65, Jack Baldschun, PHI**
NL 21, Joe Torre, MIL	GS—AL 36, Ken McBride, LA
3B—**AL 14, Jake Wood, DET**	NL 27, Jack Curtis, CHI
NL 7, Billy Williams, CHI	CG—AL 11, Ken McBride, LA
HR—AL 25, Ken Hunt, LA	NL 6, Jack Curtis, CHI
NL 25, Billy Williams, CHI	IP—AL 241.2, Ken McBride, LA
R—AL 108, Dick Howser, KC	NL 180.1, Jack Curtis, CHI
NL 75, Billy Williams, CHI	H—AL 229, Ken McBride, LA
RBI—AL 84, Ken Hunt, LA	NL 220, Jack Curtis, CHI
NL 86, Billy Williams, CHI	BB—AL 110, Don Schwall, BOS
WK—AL 92, Dick Howser, KC	NL 66, Ken Hunt, CIN
NL 45, Billy Williams, CHI	K—AL 180, Ken McBride, LA
SO—**AL 141, Jake Wood, DET**	NL 75, Ken Hunt, CIN
NL 82, Charley Smith, LA/PHI	ERA—AL 3.20, Jim Archer, KC
SB—AL 37, Dick Howser, KC	NL 4.89, Jack Curtis, CHI
NL 12, Willie Davis, LA	SHO—AL 2, Jim Archer, KC
BA—AL .310, Floyd Robinson, CHI	Norm Bass, KC
NL .278, Billy Williams, CHI	Joe McClain, WAS
SLG—AL .491, Lee Thomas, NY/LA	Don Schwall, BOS
NL .484, Billy Williams, CHI	Rollie Sheldon, NY
OBP—AL .389, Floyd Robinson, CHI	NL No Qualifiers
NL .340, Billy Williams, CHI	SV—AL 12, Terry Fox, DET
	NL 6, Ron Perranoski, LA

Other Highlights

April 14—In his big league debut Joe McClain earns the expansion Washington Senators' first win when he edges Cleveland 3–2.

April 15—Al Heist of the Chicago Cubs hits a game-ending grand slam, beating the Milwaukee Braves 9–5.

June 16—Kansas City Bonus Baby Lew Krausse Jr., son of a former big league pitcher, debuts with a 4–0 shutout of the expansion Angels just days after he finishes high school.

June 18—Don Leppert homers for Pittsburgh in his first ML at bat as the Pirates top the St. Louis Cardinals 5–3.

July 13—Mack Jones ties a post-1901 NL record when he raps four hits for the Braves in his ML debut, a 6–5 win over St. Louis.

September 1—Cubs catcher Cuno Barragan hits his only ML homer off Dick LeMay in his first ML at bat in a 4–3 loss in 14 innings to the Giants.

October 1—Red Sox rookie Tracy Stallard makes certain his name will always be remembered when he surrenders Roger Maris's record 61st home run in a 1–0 loss to the Yankees.

1962

In the second game of a September 9 twinbill at Yankee Stadium, Dick Radatz pitched nine innings for Boston, allowing just one run and fanning nine. What elevated Radatz's performance from merely outstanding to truly exceptional was that he entered the game in relief in the eighth inning and hurled the final nine innings in the Red Sox' 16-inning win over the Yankees. In 1962 Radatz, although just a rookie, was quite simply the best reliever in the game. He saved a frosh record 24 games, a standard that would endure until 1986. His saves total topped the junior circuit as did his 62 appearances. Furthermore, the 6'6" right-hander struck out 144 hitters and compiled a 2.24 ERA in 124⅔ innings to earn *The Sporting News* AL Fireman of the Year Award.

Radatz garnered just one point in the ROY voting, tying for third behind winner Tom Tresh of the Yankees. With Tony Kubek in the military, Tresh manned shortstop for the Bronx Bombers for the first two-thirds of the season before shifting to left field. A switch-hitter, Tresh showed power from both sides of the plate, hitting 13 home runs off righties and seven versus southpaws. He scored 94 runs, knocked in 93, and batted .286. Eligible for both All-Star games (in the final year of the two-game format), Tresh had an RBI double off Bob Gibson in the second Midsummer Classic as the AL won 9–4.

The Yankees, as was their habit in that era, took the pennant, on this occasion facing the San Francisco Giants in the World Series. Tresh hit .321, and his three-run homer in the bottom of the eighth in Game Five gave the Bronx Bombers a key victory. New York then repeated as world champs two games later.

All of the top five freshmen in hits in 1962 were infielders, with Tresh's 178 earning him the second slot to Rich Rollins. The Minnesota third baseman collected 186 safeties, including 16 circuit shots, and both drove in and scored 96 runs for the second-place Twins. As further evidence that Rollins almost certainly would have been the ROY had the Twins and not the Yankees won the flag, he was selected as the starting third baseman in both All-Star games, going a combined 2-for-5 with one run.

Ken Hubbs of the Chicago Cubs amassed 172 hits to lead NL recruits. Five of them came on April 17 in a 10–6 win against Pittsburgh that featured an inside-the-park home run by Hubbs's swift rookie teammate Lou Brock. On May 20 Hubbs hit safely eight times in a doubleheader at Philadelphia, but it was the second baseman's defense that really turned heads. Hubbs set a record by playing 78 consecutive errorless games, flawlessly handling 418 chances. The senior circuit ROY was awarded the NL Gold Glove but unfortunately would not live to see age 23 as he died in a private plane crash February 13, 1964.

Another keystoner, Bernie Allen, gave Minnesota two hot freshman infielders. Allen batted .269, comfortably ahead of the loop's .255 average, and accumulated 154 hits, matching Ed Charles of the Kansas City Athletics. Charles, a hot-corner guardian, smashed 17 long balls and swiped a rookie-leading 20 bases. He was just the second rookie third sacker since 1916 to pilfer so many bags. Outfielder Manny Jimenez hit .301 in 139 games for KC, which finished one rung above cellar-dwelling

Washington. The Senators won 60 verdicts, 11 belonging to Dave Stenhouse. The righty twirled two shutouts, the second coming in the finale of a July 17 double-dip, when he held the Chicago White Sox to three hits and Washington won 1–0 as Don Lock homered in his debut. Stenhouse was subsequently the AL's starting hurler in the All-Star rematch at Wrigley Field, permitting one tally in his two-inning stint. He won just five more verdicts after 1962, however, earning him a record no pitcher would want to own.

FEWEST CAREER WINS BY ALL-STAR GAME STARTING PITCHER

16, Dave Stenhouse, 1962 Was AL
29, Mark Fidrych, 1976 Det AL
37, Jerry Walker, 1959 Bal AL
40, Ken McBride, 1963 LA AL
40, Jack Armstrong, 1990 Cin NL

Like the Senators, the Los Angeles Angels were in their second season after joining the AL in 1961. But the Angels were remarkably competitive, winning 86 times and finishing just ten games behind New York in third place. Dean Chance attached his name to 14 of those triumphs and Bo Belinsky collected ten. Chance was fourth in the AL with a 2.96 ERA, saved eight games, and had two shutouts. On August 10 he bested Minnesota 1–0, allowing just five safeties in his 11-inning gem. Exactly a month later, Chance fired a one-hitter, again picking on the Twins. Belinsky, a world-class playboy, was under .500 at 10–11, but he too had his moments. Facing Baltimore on May 5, he tossed a 2–0 no-hitter, the first ever sported by a Los Angeles hurler—Angel or Dodger. Bob Rodgers caught Belinsky that day and was behind the plate in 149 other contests, setting the record for most games caught by an AL freshman. Rodgers smacked 34 doubles and had 61 RBI. He was runner-up to Tresh in ROY balloting but finished ahead of Rollins, Chance, and even the reliever who worked overtime in the Bronx, Dick Radatz.

Other Highlights

April 12—Pete Richert of the Dodgers sets a new record in his ML debut when he enters the game in relief in the third inning and fans the first six Cincinnati Reds he faces.

May 6—Jim Bouton spins a whitewash in his first ML start for the New York Yankees, topping Washington 8–0.

May 23—Yankees rookie Joe Pepitone is the sixth player in AL history to hammer two home runs in one inning as New York tramples Kansas City 13–7.

June 17—Rookie outfielder Lou Brock of the Cubs becomes only the second player ever to hit a fair ball into the centerfield bleachers at the Polo Grounds in an 8–7 Chicago win over the expansion Mets.

June 22—Al Jackson, who will throw the only four shutouts the Mets register in 1962, one-hits Houston, winning 2–0.

June 24—Rookie outfielder Jack Reed's only ML home run gives the Yankees a 9–7 win over the Tigers in a 22-inning marathon.

July 13—Cal Koonce of the Cubs holds the Cincinnati Reds to one hit in Chicago's 1–0 triumph.

July 15—Some 11 days after signing for a record $150,000 bonus, Bob Garibaldi debuts with the Giants in relief; Garibaldi will be the last of a long string of $100,000 Bonus Baby hurlers who never win a game in the majors.

Where there had been 16 major league teams for 60 years, on Opening Day in 1962, owing to expansion in both leagues, there were now 20, which made for some 100 new jobs at the major league level. Several of them went to longtime minor leaguers like Pidge Browne and Tom Burgess, who were both well past 30. But Browne and Burgess were youngsters compared to Pirates freshman Diomedes Olivo.

In 1962 Olivo became one of the first natives of the Dominican Republic to reach the majors. More importantly, he fashioned the finest rookie season to date by a 40-year-old. At age 43 Olivo went 5–1 with a 2.77 ERA in addition to collecting seven saves in 62 appearances with the Pirates. His numbers were superior to those of his two chief competitors for 40-year-old rookie honors, Chuck Hostetler, a 40-year-old recruit outfielder with the 1944 Tigers, and Alex McColl, a 40-year-old novice pitcher with Washington in 1934.

Batting	Pitching
G—AL 159, Bernie Allen, MIN	W—AL 14, Dean Chance, LA
Rich Rollins, MIN	NL 12, Ray Washburn, STL
NL 160, Ken Hubbs, CHI	L—AL 14, Dan Pfister, KC
AB—AL 624, Rich Rollins, MIN	NL 20, Al Jackson, NY
NL 661, Ken Hubbs, CHI	PCT—AL .583, Dean Chance, LA
H—AL 186, Rich Rollins, MIN	NL .571, Ray Washburn, STL
NL 172, Ken Hubbs, CHI	**GP—AL 62, Dick Radatz, BOS**
2B—AL 34, Bob Rodgers, LA	NL 62, Diomedes Olivo, PIT
NL 24, Lou Brock, CHI	GS—AL 31, Bo Belinsky, LA
Ken Hubbs, CHI	NL 33, Al Jackson, NY
3B—AL 7, Bernie Allen, MIN	CG—AL 9, Dave Stenhouse, WAS
Ed Charles, KC	NL 12, Al Jackson, NY
NL 9, Ken Hubbs, CHI	IP—AL 206.2, Dean Chance, LA
HR—AL 20, Tom Tresh, NY	NL 231.1, Al Jackson, NY
NL 18, Tom Haller, SF	H—AL 195, Dean Chance, LA
R—AL 96, Rich Rollins, MIN	NL 244, Al Jackson, NY
NL 90, Ken Hubbs, CHI	**BB—AL 122, Bo Belinsky, LA**
RBI—AL 96, Rich Rollins, MIN	**NL 107, Jack Hamilton, PHI**
NL 55, Tom Haller, SF	K—AL 145, Bo Belinsky, LA
WK—AL 75, Rich Rollins, MIN	NL 118, Al Jackson, NY
NL 51, Tom Haller, SF	ERA—AL 2.96, Dean Chance, LA
SO—AL 82, Bernie Allen, MIN	NL 3.97, Cal Koonce, CHI
NL 129, Ken Hubbs, CHI	SHO—AL 3, Bo Belinsky, LA
SB—AL 20, Ed Charles, KC	NL 4, Al Jackson, NY
NL 16, Lou Brock, CHI	**SV—AL 24, Dick Radatz, BOS**
Donn Clendenon, PIT	NL 10, Claude Raymond, MIL
Ted Savage, PHI	
BA—AL .301, Manny Jimenez, KC	
NL .260, Ken Hubbs, CHI	
SLG—AL .454, Ed Charles, KC	
NL .412, Lou Brock, CHI	
OBP—AL .379, Rich Rollins, MIN	
NL .322, Lou Brock, CHI	

August 4—Tommie Aaron of the Milwaukee Braves hits a game-ending grand slam for a 7–3 victory over the Philadelphia Phillies in the finale.

September 5—After going a record 78 consecutive games in which he also handled a record 418 chances without an error, rookie second baseman Ken Hubbs of the Cubs makes an errant throw in a 4–1 loss to Cincinnati.

September 26—Dave McNally tosses a two-hit shutout in his ML debut for Baltimore, beating Kansas City 3–0 in the opener.

1963

"Good things sometimes take time," said Hal Holbrook's character Lou Mannheim in the movie *Wall*

Street, and these words perfectly describe southpaw Gary Peters's sudden emergence in 1963 as the ace of the Chicago White Sox pitching staff. Between minor league stints Peters threw a total of 21 innings in relief for the Sox from 1959 through 1962 but did not make his first ML start until May 6, 1963, some two weeks after his 26th birthday. On that memorable day he both earned his initial big league triumph and hit his first home run. Peters was just 5–4 through the end of June, but beginning on July 11 he went 11–0 in his next 12 starts, including six victories in August, his third straight month with a sub-2.00 ERA. The second win in Peters's streak was a one-hit shutout in which he whiffed 13 Baltimore batters en route to setting a new club frosh season K record. Despite dropping his final two decisions in 1963, Peters finished 19–8 with an AL-best 2.33 ERA. He also tied for fourth with 189 strikeouts and was fifth in both opponents' batting average and OOBP. What's more, Peters, who would frequently be used as a pinch hitter during his 14-year career, batted .259 in his rookie season, 11 points better than the average AL hitter in 1963.

MOST STRIKEOUTS BY WHITE SOX ROOKIE PITCHER

189, Gary Peters, 1963
138, Lefty Williams, 1916
138, Melido Perez, 1988
135, Jim Scott, 1909
134, Jack Harshman, 1954

Peters was AL ROY but faced strong competition from his teammate, third baseman Pete Ward. Like Peters, Ward started slowly, hitting just .229 through May 3. In June, however, Ward exploded with a .364 average, six homers, and 17 RBI. A poor July was followed with averages well over .300 in the final two months. Ward, acquired in a trade with Baltimore, smashed 34 doubles and 22 round trippers while driving in 84 runs.

Third sacker Max Alvis equaled Ward's home run total for Cleveland. On August 19 at Boston, Alvis pounded a pair of circuit shots and knocked in six runs as the Indians beat the Red Sox 8–3. Both Alvis and

Ward exceeded the NL's top rookie sluggers by a margin of ten home runs, but centerfielder Jimmie Hall was by far the year's overall freshman slugging sensation, blasting 33 dingers for the power-laden Minnesota Twins. Hall was particularly lethal in August, with 13 long balls and 27 RBI, more than pulling his weight in the Twins' 225-homer campaign.

While Hall finished third in ROY balloting, New York Yankees left-hander Al Downing was totally ignored by AL voters despite matching Peters with four shutouts and holding hitters to a league-low .184 average. On July 2 Downing limited the White Sox to one hit as he notched the first of his eight double-digit strikeout performances. He tossed two-hit whitewashes in the first

In the spring of 1963, Cleveland sportswriters bragged that the Indians had the finest rookie crop in the majors. Indeed, on Opening Day the Tribe started new faces at three key positions, third base, shortstop, and center field. Third sacker Max Alvis turned out to be the prize newcomer, at least initially, as he led AL frosh in several batting departments, but centerfielder Vic Davalillo would develop into the most significant contributor over the long haul. Unhappily for the Indians, the third newcomer, shortstop Tony Martinez, who began the campaign as the most highly touted of the trio, proved to be among the biggest busts in all of rookie history.

When Martinez could generate just 26 total bases in his first 141 at bats, Cleveland sent him down to the minors. Although he resurfaced several times over the next few years, his hitting never improved. Martinez finished his ML career in 1966 with the eighth lowest OPS since 1901 among positions players with at least 150 career at bats.

LOWEST OPS, POSITION PLAYERS SINCE 1901 (MINIMUM 150 CAREER ABs)

Name	G	AB	OPS
John Black	54	186	.374
Lou Camilli	107	151	.386
Brian Doyle	110	199	.392
Joe Cannon	148	227	.395
Bill Bergen	947	3028	.395
Jul Kustus	53	173	.395
Tony Martinez	73	175	.399
Archie Yelle	87	199	.404
Dick Smith	70	186	.421
Bill McCabe	106	199	.423

game of June 10 and August 25 doubleheaders, the latter featuring 13 strikeouts against the White Sox. In addition to his OBA crown, Downing also topped the junior circuit with 8.76 strikeouts per nine innings. In Game Two of the World Series, he allowed three Los Angeles runs in five frames, suffering the defeat, as the Dodgers finished the day halfway to becoming the first team ever to sweep the Bronx Bombers in postseason play.

Philadelphia's Ray Culp may not have equaled the winning percentages of Peters or Downing—both of which were above .700—but he did top his AL rivals in shutouts. Culp blanked the opposition five times, the most whitewashes by a Phils frosh since Pete Alexander in 1911, and was selected for the All-Star Game at Cleveland, where he tossed a scoreless fifth inning as the senior circuit won the contest 5–3. In the course of leading NL rookies as well as the Phils in wins, Culp

twirled a two-hit shutout and a trio of three-hitters, one on May 26 at Cincinnati when he fanned 12 Reds.

Going hitless that day against Culp was NL ROY Pete Rose, who had previously taken the collar in his first three ML games. Before the year was out, however, Rose would amass the first 170 of his record-setting 4,256 safeties and score 101 runs for Cincinnati along with providing solid work at second base. Ron Hunt of the New York Mets was another rookie second sacker who would one day be a record-breaker, although he took a less conventional route. In 1963 Hunt hit .272 with ten home runs, tops among NL keystone guardians, and collected 13 hit by pitches, second in the NL only to Frank Robinson's 14. Eight years later Hunt, by then with the Montreal Expos, staked his own claim to baseball immortality when he was hit by the staggering total of 50 pitches to set a new post-1901 season record.

1963 ROOKIE LEADERS

Batting		Pitching	
G—AL 158, Max Alvis, CLE		W—AL 19, Gary Peters, CHI	
NL 157, Pete Rose, CIN		NL 14, Ray Culp, PHI	
AB—AL 602, Max Alvis, CLE		L—AL 13, Dave Morehead, BOS	
NL 623, Pete Rose, CIN		NL 11, Ray Culp, PHI	
H—AL 177, Pete Ward, CHI		PCT—AL .704, Gary Peters, CHI	
NL 170, Pete Rose, CIN		NL .560, Ray Culp, PHI	
2B—AL 34, Pete Ward, CHI		GP—AL 57, Julio Navarro, LA	
NL 28, Ron Hunt, NY		NL 58, Larry Bearnarth, NY	
3B—AL 7, Max Alvis, CLE		GS—AL 30, Gary Peters, CHI	
NL 9, Pete Rose, CIN		NL 30, Ray Culp, PHI	
HR—AL 33, Jimmie Hall, MIN		CG—AL 13, Gary Peters, CHI	
NL 12, Bob Bailey, PIT		NL 10, Ray Culp, PHI	
Ellis Burton, CHI		IP—AL 243.0, Gary Peters, CHI	
R—AL 88, Jimmie Hall, MIN		NL 203.1, Ray Culp, PHI	
NL 101, Pete Rose, CIN		H—AL 192, Gary Peters, CHI	
RBI—AL 84, Pete Ward, CHI		NL 148, Ray Culp, PHI	
NL 59, John Bateman, HOU		BB—AL 99, Dave Morehead, BOS	
WK—AL 63, Jimmie Hall, MIN		**NL 102, Ray Culp, PHI**	
NL 59, Rusty Staub, HOU		K—AL 189, Gary Peters, CHI	
SO—AL 109, Max Alvis, CLE		NL 176, Ray Culp, PHI	
NL 103, John Bateman, HOU		ERA—**AL 2.33, Gary Peters, CHI**	
SB—AL 15, Tommy McCraw, CHI		NL 2.97, Ray Culp, PHI	
Al Weis, CHI		SHO—AL 4, Al Downing, NY	
NL 13, Pete Rose, CIN		Gary Peters, CHI	
BA—AL .295, Pete Ward, CHI		NL 5, Ray Culp, PHI	
NL .273, Pete Rose, CIN		SV—AL 12, Julio Navarro, LA	
SLG—AL .521, Jimmie Hall, MIN		NL 11, Ron Taylor, STL	
NL .396, Ron Hunt, NY			
OBP—AL .356, Pete Ward, CHI			
NL .338, Ron Hunt, NY			

Other Highlights

April 13—After going hitless in his first 11 ML at bats, Pete Rose of the Reds notches the first of what will one day be a record 4,256 ML hits, a triple off Pittsburgh's Bob Friend.

April 21—Jim Roland, despite issuing nine walks, blanks the Chicago White Sox, allowing only three hits as Minnesota wins 7–0.

May 3—In his first and only ML at bat in 1963, Orioles pitcher Buster Narum homers off Detroit's Don Mossi; Narum will return to the majors in 1964 and retire with a .059 career BA.

June 16—Nick Willhite tosses a five-hit shutout in his ML debut as the Los Angeles Dodgers top the Chicago Cubs 2–0.

August 1—Ellis Burton homers from both sides of the plate for the Cubs, who win 10–2 at Milwaukee.

August 20—In his first ML start, Grover Powell of the Mets blanks the Phillies 4–0; Powell will never win another game in the majors.

September 16—Bob Veale two-hits the Cubs, fanning nine in Pittsburgh's 1–0 victory.

September 18—Dodgers rookie Dick Nen collects his only hit in 1963, a ninth-inning game-tying homer off Cards reliever Ron Taylor that helps spell an end to St. Louis's pennant hopes when the Dodgers go on to win 6–5 in 13 innings.

September 27—The Houston Colt 45s start an all-rookie lineup and use a total of 16 freshmen in a 10–3 loss to the Mets; the losing pitcher is 17-year-old starter Jay Dahl, who will die in an auto accident two years later without ever appearing in another ML game.

September 29—In his lone ML game, John Paciorek of Houston is 3-for-3 with two walks, three RBI, and four runs scored, making him the greatest ML one-gamer in history.

◄— 1964 —►

The 1960s marked the first expansion in major league baseball since the beginning of the twentieth century, with eight new franchises joining the 16 existing clubs during that decade. Most of these newcomers struggled for years before achieving respectability. In fact, a team made up solely of the rookie class of 1964 would have posed a formidable challenge for any of them. Even a cursory look at the 1964 crop reveals remarkable depth. Take starting pitchers, for example. In 1964 Wally Bunker, just 19, matched his age in victories and spun two one-hitters en route to holding batters to a .269 OBP. Bunker lost only five games, producing an AL-best .792 winning percentage and enrolling him in an exclusive fraternity.

ROOKIES WINNING 19+ GAMES WHILE LOSING FEWER THAN SIX

King Cole, 1910 Chi NL, 20–4
Elmer Riddle, 1941 Cin NL, 19–4
Larry Jansen, 1947 NY NL, 21–5
Wally Bunker, 1964 Bal AL, 19–5

Two other starters who combined nearly to replicate Bunker's win-loss totals didn't arrive until midseason. Luis Tiant pitched a four-hit shutout in his debut with Cleveland on July 19, striking out 11 New York Yankees in the Tribe's 3–0 win in the Bronx. Tiant would go 10–4 in 1964 with three shutouts. Mel Stottlemyre was called up to the majors by the Yankees on August 12 and ten days later shut out Boston to improve to 3–0 on his way to a 9–3 ledger. On September 26 he blanked Washington 7–0 on two hits—three fewer than he had as a batter. Stottlemyre went 5-for-5 that day, including a double and a two-run single. In the World Series he became the last rookie to date to start as many as three games. Stottlemyre won the second game, going the distance. He took a no-decision in Game Five after seven solid innings. In the finale Stottlemyre surrendered three runs in four innings and lost as the St. Louis Cardinals won their first World Series since 1946.

In the fifth World Series contest, Yankees rookie reliever Pete Mikkelsen was tagged for a three-run homer in the tenth and subsequently took the loss. Mikkelsen, however, saved a dozen games in the regular season and was one of three freshman bullpenners to reach double figures. Foremost was Bob Lee of the Los Angeles Angels. Opposing batters hit just .182 off Lee, who had 19 saves and a 1.51 ERA in 137 innings. Two Cincinnati firemen also excelled. Right-hander Sammy Ellis and lefty Billy McCool combined for 21 saves and together struck out 212 batters in 211⅔ innings.

While all these pitchers had seasons many veterans would envy, none of them was the top freshman in his league. That honor in both circuits went to hitters who had historic campaigns. Tony Oliva of the Minnesota Twins and Dick Allen, the third baseman of the Philadelphia Phillies, each had a .557 slugging average that ranked third in his respective league. Oliva, a right fielder, won the AL batting title with a .323 mark and also paced the loop in runs, hits, and doubles. Oliva's 217 safeties are the fifth most ever by a rookie while his 374 total bases not only topped the circuit by 55 but also tied him with Hal Trosky for the highest amount in freshman annals.

Allen got off to a torrid start, especially for a rookie, driving in 13 runs in the Phillies' first 12 games, and unlike the rest of his teammates, most of whom folded badly under the pressure of the September pennant run, he finished well, batting .341 with five homers and 17 RBI from September 1 on to finish with 25 runs and 201 hits. Both figures represent the most since 1899 by a freshman third baseman, as does Allen's total of 162 games at the hot corner in 1964.

Of Allen's 201 knocks, 80 went for extra bases, including 29 homers. Rather amazingly, Allen's dongs were not even the most by a rookie third sacker in 1964. Jim Ray Hart smashed 31 round trippers for the San Francisco Giants, tying for third-best in the NL. Hart also had 81 RBI, seven fewer than yearling leftfielder Rico Carty of the Milwaukee Braves, whose .330 average made him the runner-up in the NL batting race. Carty also ranked fourth in the league in both slugging and OBP. On August 24 he went 5-for-5 with a homer, three doubles, and four runs. Six days later Carty's bat turned savage again in the second game of a doubleheader when he got another five hits, including a double and one home run.

Baltimore's Sam Bowens matched Carty's 22 circuit shots, but Tony Conigliaro of the Boston Red Sox did them both two better. Conigliaro powered 24 pitches into the seats in only 404 ABs, as a broken arm in late July cost him more than a month of playing time and an untold number of round trippers. Cleveland first sacker Bob Chance also made the most of limited action, driving in 75 runs in only 390 ABs.

Tony Conigliaro established a new home run mark for teenagers in 1964 when he went deep 24 times for the Red Sox. The following year, at age 20, Conigliaro became the youngest four-bagger king in history when he topped the AL with 32 jacks. He reached his 100th career home run in 1967 at age 22, only to have his season prematurely ended in July by a near fatal beaning.

Though Conigliaro eventually recovered from his catastrophic injury, he was never the same hitter. Prior to the beginning of the 2003 season, 26 players who were no longer active had achieved as many as 100 home runs before age 25. Conigliaro is the only one of the 26 who never reached 200. Here are the five youngest performers to crack the 100-homer barrier.

YOUNGEST TO REACH 100 HOME RUNS

Name	Age
Mel Ott	22.132
Tony Conigliaro	22.197
Eddie Mathews	22.292
Alex Rodriguez	23.016
Andruw Jones	23.063

Playing all his team's contests was second baseman Bobby Knoop of the Los Angeles Angels, who, like Dick Allen, is one of only seven rookies to play 162 games in a season. Knoop's teammate Willie Smith offered a dash of both Wally Bunker and Tony Oliva, doing double duty as a pitcher and an outfielder. Smith hit 11 homers with 51 RBI and also sported a 2.84 ERA in 15 mound efforts. He became just the third rookie ever to play at least 100 games and pitch in as many as ten, following Yank Robinson in 1884 and Hall of Famer Jesse Burkett six years later in 1890.

Like Smith, the remarkably deep and versatile 1964 freshman class had all the bases covered.

Other Highlights

May 7—Tony Oliva of Minnesota numbers two homers among his four hits, one of them a grand slam, and drives in six of his 94 RBI.

May 17—Ron Herbel of the San Francisco Giants shuts out the New York Mets 1–0 in his first major league start.

1964 ROOKIE LEADERS

Batting	Pitching
G—AL 162, Bobby Knoop, LA NL 162, Dick Allen, PHI	**W**—AL 19, Wally Bunker, BAL NL 10, Sammy Ellis, CIN
AB—AL 672, Tony Oliva, MIN NL 632, Dick Allen, PHI	**L**—AL 15, Buster Narum, WAS NL 9, Dennis Bennett, PHI Ron Herbel, SF
H—**AL 217, Tony Oliva, MIN** NL 201, Dick Allen, PHI	**PCT**—**AL .792, Wally Bunker, BAL** NL .462, Dennis Bennett, PHI
2B—**AL 43, Tony Oliva, MIN** NL 38, Dick Allen, PHI	**GP**—AL 64, Bob Lee, LA NL 62, Bill Wakefield, NY
3B—AL 9, Tony Oliva, MIN **NL 13, Dick Allen, PHI**	**GS**—AL 32, Buster Narum, WAS John O'Donoghue, KC NL 24, Dennis Bennett, PHI
HR—AL 32, Tony Oliva, MIN NL 31, Jim Ray Hart, SF	**CG**—AL 12, Wally Bunker, BAL NL 7, Dennis Bennett, PHI Ron Herbel, SF
R—**AL 109, Tony Oliva, MIN** **NL 125, Dick Allen, PHI**	**IP**—AL 214, Wally Bunker, BAL NL 174.2, Dennis Bennett, PHI
RBI—AL 94, Tony Oliva, MIN NL 91, Dick Allen, PHI	**H**—AL 202, John O'Donoghue, KC NL 162, Ron Herbel, SF
WK—AL 46, Don Buford, CHI Bobby Knoop, LA NL 67, Dick Allen, PHI	**BB**—AL 73, Buster Narum, WAS NL 68, Dennis Bennett, PHI
SO—AL 109, Bobby Knoop, LA **NL 138, Dick Allen, PHI**	**K**—AL 144, Sonny Siebert, CLE NL 149, Dennis Bennett, PHI
SB—AL 12, Don Buford, CHI Tony Oliva, MIN NL 12, Billy Cowan, CHI	**ERA**—AL 2.69, Wally Bunker, BAL NL 3.81, Dennis Bennett, PHI
BA—**AL .323, Tony Oliva, MIN** NL .330, Rico Carty, MIL	**SHO**—AL 3, Luis Tiant, CLE NL 2, Dennis Bennett, PHI Ron Herbel, SF
SLG—AL .557, Tony Oliva, MIN NL .557, Dick Allen, PHI	**SV**—AL 19, Bob Lee, LA NL 14, Sammy Ellis, CIN
OBP—AL .361, Tony Oliva, MIN NL .391, Rico Carty, MIL	

June 24—University of Wisconsin star outfielder Rick Reichardt signs the largest pre-free-agent-draft bonus contract in ML history, as the Angels fork over an estimated $200,000.

June 26—Gerry Arrigo, in the first game of a doubleheader against the Chicago White Sox, pitches a one-hitter in the Twins' 2–0 victory.

July 2—Willie Smith hits a tie-breaking grand slam in the ninth to give the Angels a 10–6 win in Baltimore; on that day, Smith had four hits and drove in six runs.

July 3—Wally Bunker throws his second one-hitter of the season in blanking the Kansas City Athletics as host Baltimore wins 4–0.

July 5—Former Ohio State quarterback Joe Sparma hits a two-run triple in the fifth inning and later scores as he shuts out the Senators 3–0 for Detroit, whiffing ten.

July 10—Jesus Alou of the Giants goes 6-for-6 with a homer in a 10–3 win against the Chicago Cubs at Wrigley Field.

July 23—A's shortstop Bert Campaneris is only the third player in ML history to club two home runs in his initial ML game, the first coming on the first pitch served him by Jim Kaat of the Twins.

September 1—Southpaw reliever Masanori Murakami of the Giants is the first ML player from Japan as he debuts in a 4–1 loss to the Mets; Murakami will begin his career by hurling 11 consecutive scoreless innings.

September 11—The Athletics' Blue Moon Odom fires a two-hitter at Baltimore, becoming the only rookie to register a shutout in a season while having an ERA worse than 10.00.

September 12—Frank Bertaina of Baltimore and Kansas City's Bob Meyer each allow only one hit in the Orioles 1–0 besting of the Athletics; the dueling freshmen combine for 11 walks and 11 strikeouts.

September 15—Boston's Ed Connolly fans 12 Athletics and permits only two hits in an 8–0 win.

September 21—Reds rookie Chico Ruiz steals home to beat the Phillies 1–0 in a game that ultimately signals doom for Philadelphia's once-bright pennant hopes.

September 23—Don Loun of Washington blanks visiting Boston in his major league debut, allowing five hits and no walks and winning 1–0.

September 26—Angels reliever Bill Kelso tosses a four-hit shutout in his first big league start, beating the Twins 2–0.

September 30—Tigers first baseman Bill Roman homers as a pinch hitter in his first ML at bat in a 7–6 loss to the Yankees; Roman will never hit another homer in the bigs and will collect only five hits total.

1965

Always on the lookout for mystery and controversy, Oliver Stone might well decide to focus on the strange NL ROY voting in 1965 if he should ever make a movie about baseball. That year, Houston's Joe Morgan lost out to Jim Lefebvre of Los Angeles despite possessing far superior numbers. The two second basemen each played 157 games but had little else in common as Morgan accumulated 27 additional hits and drew 26 more walks to lead the senior loop with 97.

MOST WALKS BY ROOKIE SECOND BASEMAN

100, Jim Gilliam, 1953 Bro NL
97, Joe Morgan, 1965 Hou NL
96, Jack Crooks, 1890 Col AA
95, Morrie Rath, 1912 Chi AL
92, Eddie Stanky, 1943 Chi NL

Joe Morgan was one of a rare breed, a hitter who exhibited excellent control of the strike zone from the first day of his major league career. Like Bill Joyce, another batsman who paced his loop in walks as a rookie, Morgan also soon learned to hit with exceptional power, especially for a middle infielder. *Transcendental Graphics*

Morgan also had better totals in every extra-base hit category. Although he trailed Lefebvre in RBI, 69 to 40, he tallied 100 runs and stole 20 bases compared to the three thefts and 57 runs registered by his rookie rival. Both played in pitcher's parks—the Astrodome and Dodger Stadium—but Morgan produced an OPS of .793, more than 100 points above the league average, while Lefebvre's OPS was .708. Defensively, Morgan committed three additional errors but topped his Dodgers counterpart in assists and chances per game. Lefebvre no doubt was given extra credit for playing on a championship team, but the better stats were clearly Morgan's—and the sharply diverse career paths that both men followed after their rookie campaigns only heighten the sense that Morgan was the vastly superior player in 1965.

A lefty batter, "Little Joe" did anything but fold when encountering a southpaw on the mound, even if that southpaw happened to be the best in the game at the time. On July 3 Morgan banged three hits, one a home run, off Sandy Koufax. Five days later Morgan tied the rookie single-game record when he had six hits, including two homers and a double, as his Astros lost at Milwaukee 9–8 in 12 innings.

Houston, in its fourth season, finished ninth even with Morgan, but L.A. won the pennant and faced Minnesota in the World Series. Lefebvre went 4-for-10 and scored twice before injuring his heel in Game Three, which the Dodgers won en route to their second World Championship in three seasons. Morgan and Lefebvre ranked two and three in at bats among rookies in 1965. The leader was yet a third NL second baseman, Glenn Beckert of the Chicago Cubs. Beckert hit only three home runs all year but two came on July 1 against the Dodgers as he drove in four in Chicago's 6–3 win.

The AL ROY decision was more clear-cut if only because the rules for determining rookie eligibility differed from today's guidelines. Willie Horton had 123 previous ABs, pushing him over what was then the cutoff of 90 and making Baltimore's Curt Blefary an easy selection. But Horton's season, had it come a few years later, would have made him an almost certain ROY winner. He pounded 29 home runs for Detroit and drove in 104 runs. The Bengals newest slugger also had four multi-homer games, including two consecutive road contests in May. On the 13th at Washington and the next day in Boston, he went a combined 7-for-9 with seven runs and ten RBI.

Blefary was only slightly less adept at going yard, propelling 22 balls over the fence and driving home 70 runs. He also drew an Orioles' freshman-record 88 walks. Blefary, an ex-Yankees' farmhand, did especially well against the Bronx Bombers, hitting .375 with five homers and 11 RBI in his first 13 games versus New York. Other clubs felt his power as well. Blefary connected twice on April 17 at Boston and hit a seventh-inning grand slam on September 5, breaking a 5–5 tie for a 9–5 win over Cleveland.

The senior circuit's top two recruit home run threats were both New York Mets outfielders. Ron Swoboda hit 19 jacks and Johnny Lewis 15 for the still con-siderably less-than-amazing Mets, losers in 1965 of 112 games. In the opener of a July 5 doubleheader, Swoboda knocked a three-run blast in New York's 3–2 win against the Cubs. He had a two-run shot in the nightcap, giving Tom Parsons all the runs he needed to win 3–0. Parsons tossed a six-hitter that day for his only victory in a 1–10 rookie campaign.

Just one freshman cracked double digits in victo-

By 1965 it was painfully clear that something had gone terribly awry in the balance between hitters and pitchers. Whereas the average hitter just three years earlier in 1962, the first year that both leagues expanded to 20 teams, batted .258, in 1965 the ML batting average was down to .246 and was destined to plummet even more dramatically in the years ahead.

The impact on rookie hitters was especially harsh. In 1965 Yankees freshman outfielder Roger Repoz hit just .220 and posted a lowly .300 OBP. Numbers like that would ordinarily have earned a sure ticket back to the minors, but in the mid-1960s they bordered on respectability. In fact, Repoz was able to mount a successful nine-year career as a major league outfielder even though he never broke .250. It is easy to see why when the following list is examined. Here are the top ten OPS figures among outfielders with at least 2,000 at bats and sub-.250 BAs during the period between 1961, the first expansion season, and 1976, the last season there were less than 25 ML teams. All of the names on the list, with the sole exception of Repoz's, are immediately recognizable to students of the period, and two of its members, Tresh and Blefary, were ROY Award winners.

TOP TEN OPS, OUTFIELDERS, MINIMUM 2,000 ABs AND SUB-.250 BA, 1961–1976

Name	AB	BA	OPS
Don Lock	2695	.238	.751
Tom Tresh	4251	.245	.748
Curt Blefary	2947	.237	.745
Jim King	2209	.235	.735
Bill Robinson	2430	.249	.707
Roger Repoz	2145	.224	.706
Ron Swoboda	2581	.242	.704
Jim Landis	2482	.239	.703
Willie Kirkland	2098	.225	.685
Mickey Stanley	4649	.248	.675

ries—Marcelino Lopez of the California Angels. Lopez went 14–13, his lone shutout coming in the second game of a July 9 doubleheader against Cleveland. The Cuban-born southpaw permitted only two hits and no walks in blanking the Indians 2–0.

Three rookies were nine-game winners, Jim Lonborg of Boston (who was also the rookie loss leader with 17), Bruce Howard of the Chicago White Sox, and Frank Linzy of the Giants. In addition to his nine wins, Linzy saved a rookie-high 21 games and fashioned a dazzling 1.43 ERA in his 57 hill appearances, enabling San Francisco to finish second in the NL, just two games back of L.A.

Other Highlights

April 17—In his first full ML game, Curt Blefary hits two homers, but his Orioles nonetheless lose 12–9 to the Red Sox.

April 18—In his ML debut Angels lefty Rudy May carries a no-hitter into the eighth inning before Tigers second baseman Jake Wood doubles; May is lifted after hurling nine innings of one-hit ball, and Detroit eventually wins the game in 13 frames.

June 8—The Kansas City A's make Arizona State University sophomore Rick Monday the first player chosen in the first free-agent amateur draft in ML history.

1965 ROOKIE LEADERS

Batting	Pitching
G—AL 157, Ken Berry, CHI	W—AL 14, Marcelino Lopez, CAL
NL 157, Jim Lefebvre, LA	NL 9, Frank Linzy, SF
Joe Morgan, HOU	L—AL 17, Jim Lonborg, BOS
AB—AL 512, Jose Cardenal, CAL	NL 10, Tom Parsons, NY
Willie Horton, DET	PCT—AL .519, Marcelino Lopez, CAL
NL 614, Glenn Beckert, CHI	NL No Qualifiers
H—AL 140, Willie Horton, DET	GP—AL 68, Jim Dickson, KC
NL 163, Joe Morgan, HOU	NL 59, Gary Wagner, PHI
2B—AL 23, Curt Blefary, BAL	GS—AL 32, Marcelino Lopez, CAL
Jose Cardenal, CAL	NL 19, Larry Dierker, HOU
NL 22, Joe Morgan, HOU	CG—AL 8, Marcelino Lopez, CAL
3B—AL 4, Ken Berry, CHI	NL 3, Larry Jaster, STL
Curt Blefary, BAL	IP—AL 215.1, Marcelino Lopez, CAL
Jim Gosger, BOS	NL 146.2, Larry Dierker, HOU
Roger Repoz, NY	H—AL 193, Jim Lonborg, BOS
NL 12, Joe Morgan, HOU	NL 135, Larry Dierker, HOU
HR—AL 29, Willie Horton, DET	BB—AL 82, Marcelino Lopez, CAL
NL 19, Ron Swoboda, NY	NL 49, Gary Wagner, PHI
R—AL 72, Curt Blefary, BAL	K—AL 122, Marcelino Lopez, CAL
NL 100, Joe Morgan, HOU	NL 109, Larry Dierker, HOU
RBI—AL 104, Willie Horton, DET	ERA—AL 2.93, Marcelino Lopez, CAL
NL 69, Jim Lefebvre, LA	NL No Qualifiers
WK—AL 88, Curt Blefary, BAL	SHO—AL 2, Catfish Hunter, KC
NL 97, Joe Morgan, HOU	NL 1, Tom Parsons, NY
SO—AL 101, Willie Horton, DET	Dick Selma, NY
NL 117, Johnny Lewis, NY	SV—AL 3, Jack Aker, KC
SB—AL 37, Jose Cardenal, CAL	Ed Sukla, CAL
NL 20, Joe Morgan, HOU	NL 21, Frank Linzy, SF
BA—AL .273, Willie Horton, DET	
NL .271, Joe Morgan, HOU	
SLG—AL .490, Willie Horton, DET	
NL .418, Joe Morgan, HOU	
OBP—AL .382, Curt Blefary, BAL	
NL .375, Joe Morgan, HOU	

June 22—Yankees rookie Ray Barker ties an ML record when he hits his second consecutive pinch homer in a 6–2 loss to the A's in the first game of a doubleheader.

July 8—Joe Morgan is the first player in the history of the Houston franchise to collect six hits in a game, but his Astros still lose to the Braves 9–8 in 12 innings.

August 20—Jack Cullen of the New York Yankees fires a three-hitter at Baltimore, winning 1–0.

September 6—Adolfo Phillips hits three doubles and a homer and scores four runs for the Philadelphia Phillies, who beat St. Louis 10–5.

September 12—Dick Selma pitches a ten-inning shutout and fans 13 Braves as the New York Mets win 1–0.

September 12—Washington pinch hitter Brant Alyea homers off Rudy May of the Angels on the first ML pitch he sees.

September 24—Catfish Hunter tosses a two-hit shutout for the Kansas City Athletics, beating Boston 8–0.

September 29—Seldom-used rookie catcher Pat Corrales of the Phils ties an ML single-game record when he reaches base twice against the Cubs on catcher's interference; in the process Corrales, despite collecting just 174 at bats in 1965, shatters the all-time season record for most times reaching base on catcher's interference, with six.

◄ 1966 ►

The Los Angeles Dodgers may have been the property of Walter O'Malley, but in 1966 Larry Jaster *owned* them. The St. Louis Cardinals rookie left-hander tossed a complete-game shutout in each of the five contests he faced L.A., surrendering just 24 hits—all singles—and ten walks in 45 innings, while fanning 35. The most recent of five hurlers to blank one opponent as many as five times in one season, Jaster is also the lone pitcher to do so in five consecutive starts versus that team. Overall, Jaster went 11–5 with a 3.26 ERA, and his five whitewashes against L.A. enabled him to tie for the NL lead in that department. As a further illustration of how severely Jaster's mastery of the Dodgers skewed his season stats, against the other eight NL teams the St. Louis southpaw logged a very mediocre 4.64 ERA in 106⅔ innings.

Four rookies exceeded Jaster's win total, each by one victory. Of the quartet of 12-game winners, Jim Nash of the Kansas City Athletics lost by far the fewest games. Nash started off the season 7–0 for the eighth-place A's before dropping the first game of an August 19 twinbill. He then won his last five decisions to tie the all-time record for the most wins by a recruit with only a single loss.

MOST WINS BY ROOKIE WITH ONLY ONE LOSS

12, Perry Werden, 1884 StL UA
12, Jim Nash, 1966 KC AL
11, Larry Twitchell, 1887 Det NL
9, Whitey Ford, 1950 NY AL
8, (Four tied)

Woodie Fryman, Fritz Peterson, and Don Sutton also garnered a dozen wins, losing nine, eleven, and twelve games, respectively. Pittsburgh's Fryman racked up three consecutive road shutouts starting in late June. He tossed three-hitters at Philadelphia and Chicago and a one-hit gem at Shea Stadium, allowing no walks and fanning eight Mets. Peterson tied for the most wins on the Yankees staff as the Bronx Bombers endured their first last-place finish since 1912. Sutton's winning percentage was just .500, but he fashioned a 2.99 ERA and fanned 209 batters for the pennant-winning Dodgers. He was on Los Angeles's World Series roster but saw no action as Baltimore swept to notch its first World Championship.

Two senior circuit rookie relievers saved 13 games, and one AL freshman nailed ten saves. NL co-leader Joe Hoerner worked 76 innings out of the St. Louis pen, posting a 1.54 ERA. Darold Knowles, another southpaw, made 69 appearances for the Phillies, the third-most games in the loop, and California's Minnie Rojas had a 2.88 ERA with a 7–4 record to go with his ten saves.

Tommie Agee "saved" his share of games for the Chicago White Sox but achieved them all with his bat and glove. From late August to mid-September, Agee was responsible for bringing home the winning tally an inordinate number of times, capping an amazingly balanced rookie season. He scored 98 runs and drove in 86. Agee hit 22 home runs while stealing 44 bases, becoming the first freshman ever to have a 20/40 season. (Mitchell Page, in 1977, is the only other rookie to match Agee's feat.) In center field Agee earned a Gold Glove, leading all AL fly chasers in putouts and double plays. He was the sole White Sox player to make the All-Star team, albeit he did not see action in the Midsummer Classic until the ninth inning when he was used as a defensive replacement.

In contrast, Boston's George Scott started at first base for the AL in the All-Star contest, going 0-for-2 in the National League's stirring 2–1 10-inning victory. Scott hammered 27 round trippers and had 90 RBI while playing in all of the Red Sox' 162 games. His lone negative in an otherwise exceptional rookie dossier was that he fanned 152 times to shatter the previous yearling record. Scott's mark, which seemed astronomical at the time, would last just two years. Another Boston rookie infielder, Joe Foy, achieved a much better walk/strikeout ratio. The BoSox third baseman had 91 bases on balls while going down on strikes on 80 occasions. Foy scored 97 runs and clubbed eight triples and 15 home runs, in all a fine season that nevertheless failed to earn him a single vote for the AL ROY.

Apart from Foy, Cincinnati's Tommy Helms was the only freshman third sacker in either league to get more than 73 at bats. In his lone year at the hot corner before moving to second base after Pete Rose was switched to the outfield, Helms copped the NL's top frosh prize on the strength of his .284 BA and 154 hits, third-most among rookies behind Agee and the yearling leader, shortstop Sonny Jackson of Houston. The lefty-swinging Jackson had five of his 174 hits on September 16 when Houston beat Philadelphia 6–4, thanks in large part to rookie Chuck Harrison's fourth-inning grand slam. Jackson also stole 49 bases, the most by a freshman since 1914. But power wasn't the slightly built Jackson's forte. He garnered just 14 extra-base hits in 596 at bats and his six doubles tied Bill Collins's 1910 output for the fewest ever by a rookie who came to bat 500 or more times. Randy Hundley was Jackson's opposite. The Cubs backstop was far from speedy, swiping just one base in four attempts, but hit 19 home runs, the most by an NL frosh receiver prior to 1971. Hundley's apex in his rookie season came in the opener of a twin-bill on August 11 when he hit for the cycle and scored the game-winning tally in the 11th inning.

When the Yankees finished in the second division for the first time in 40 years in 1965, it sent shock waves throughout the entire organization. But wiser heads in the Bombers' front office understood that 1965 was not simply an aberration and that the team was destined for hard times. Thus it was that when the Yankees broke training camp in the spring of 1966, manager Ralph Houk, figuring he had little to lose, kept a 27-year-old rookie right-hander with mediocre minor league credentials on the final roster largely because many of the team's beat writers had fallen in love with his charismatic name.

The pitcher was Dooley Womack. Given little chance of making the fabled Yankees when he journeyed to their St. Petersburg camp in February, he was the team's most celebrated rookie come October. Womack initially was used in mop-up roles, but by midseason he had graduated to Houk's first choice out of the bullpen in middle relief. He finished the year as the AL rookie leader in OBA and ranked fourth in the entire league among pitchers in at least 50 innings only to Sam McDowell and the game's two premier relievers in 1966, Hoyt Wilhelm and Moe Drabowsky.

The kind of rookie that the Yankees never would have given a second look in their glory years, Womack remained an effective bullpen operative for the rest of the decade.

Other Highlights

April 19—Angels rookie Rick Reichardt hits the first home run in Anaheim Stadium to account for the lone California run in a 3–1 loss to the White Sox.

April 30—Rick Reichardt ties a rookie mark when he hits two home runs in the eighth inning for the Angels, who top the Boston Red Sox 16–9.

August 7—Atlanta rookie Lee Bales ties the NL record, first set by evangelist Billy Sunday in 1883, when he fans four times in his first ML game as the Braves beat the Phillies 3–0; Bales will post an .093 career BA in 43 at bats.

September 11—In a 4–2 victory over the Red Sox, John Miller is the first member of the New York Yankees to homer in his first ML at bat; Miller's only other ML homer will come three years later with the Los Angeles Dodgers in his final career at bat.

September 20—Tom Phoebus of the Orioles is the last hurler to date to toss a complete-game shutout in his

1966 ROOKIE LEADERS

Batting	Pitching
G—AL 162, George Scott, BOS	**W**—AL 12, Jim Nash, KC
NL 150, Sonny Jackson, HOU	Fritz Peterson, NY
AB—AL 629, Tommie Agee, CHI	NL 12, Woodie Fryman, PIT
NL 596, Sonny Jackson, HOU	Don Sutton, LA
H—AL 172, Tommie Agee, CHI	**L**—AL 11, Fritz Peterson, NY
NL 174, Sonny Jackson, HOU	NL 16, Ken Holtzman, CHI
2B—AL 27, Tommie Agee, CHI	**PCT**—AL .522, Fritz Peterson, NY
NL 23, Chuck Harrison, HOU	NL .688, Larry Jaster, STL
Tommy Helms, CIN	**GP**—AL 66, Casey Cox, WAS
3B—AL 8, Tommie Agee, CHI	NL 69, Darold Knowles, PHI
Joe Foy, BOS	**GS**—AL 32, Fritz Peterson, NY
NL 7, Byron Browne, CHI	NL 35, Don Sutton, LA
HR—AL 27, George Scott, BOS	**CG**—AL 11, Fritz Peterson, NY
NL 19, Randy Hundley, CHI	NL 9, Woodie Fryman, PIT
R—AL 98, Tommie Agee, CHI	Ken Holtzman, CHI
NL 80, Sonny Jackson, HOU	**IP**—AL 215, Fritz Peterson, NY
RBI—AL 90, George Scott, BOS	NL 225.2, Don Sutton, LA
NL 63, Randy Hundley, CHI	**H**—AL 196, Fritz Peterson, NY
WK—AL 91, Joe Foy, BOS	NL 194, Ken Holtzman, CHI
NL 42, Sonny Jackson, HOU	**BB**—AL 76, Ken Sanders, BOS/KC
SO—**AL 152, George Scott, BOS**	NL 68, Ken Holtzman, CHI
NL 143, Byron Browne, CHI	**K**—AL 102, Eddie Watt, BAL
SB—AL 44, Tommie Agee, CHI	NL 209, Don Sutton, LA
NL 49, Sonny Jackson, HOU	**ERA**—AL 3.31, Fritz Peterson, NY
BA—AL .273, Tommie Agee, CHI	NL 2.99, Don Sutton, LA
NL .292, Sonny Jackson, HOU	**SHO**—AL 2, Darrell Brandon, BOS
SLG—AL .447, Tommie Agee, CHI	Blue Moon Odom, KC
NL .397, Randy Hundley, CHI	Fritz Peterson, NY
OBP—AL .368, Joe Foy, BOS	Tom Phoebus, BAL
NL .342, Sonny Jackson, HOU	**NL 5, Larry Jaster, STL**
	SV—AL 10, Minnie Rojas, CAL
	NL 13, Joe Hoerner, STL
	Darold Knowles, PHI

first two ML appearances when he blanks Kansas City 4–0.

September 28—Larry Jaster of the Cards ties an ML record when he blanks the pennant-winning Dodgers for the fifth time in 1966.

October 2—Jorge Rubio of California blanks Cleveland 2–0, striking out 15; the glittering shutout win is Rubio's second and last in the majors.

October 2—Jim Cosman tosses a two-hitter versus the Chicago Cubs in his ML debut as his St. Louis Cardinals win 2–0; the whitewash will prove to be Cosman's next-to-last ML win and only complete game.

1967

The New York Mets had experienced so few good times in their first five years of existence that in 1966 their modest win total of 66 had set a team high. However, a pitcher nicknamed "The Franchise" appeared on the scene in the Mets' sixth season and would soon lead the club to baseball's promised land. Tom Seaver debuted April 13, 1967, getting a no-decision despite fanning eight Pittsburgh hitters. A week later, Seaver picked up his first ML win, beating the Chicago Cubs at Shea Stadium. Another 310 wins would follow before Seaver's career was completed.

Seaver was the Mets' sole representative at the 1967 All-Star Game in Anaheim. He pitched a scoreless 15th inning to earn the save for the NL, which won 2–1. Seaver won 16 games, more than one-fourth of his team's total, and completed 18 contests, tied for second in the league. He struck out 170 batters, had a 2.76 ERA, and was named ROY.

While Seaver toiled for a tenth-place club in 1967, Dick Hughes helped bring the St. Louis Cardinals a World Championship. Hughes earned a staff-high 16 victories, dropped only six, and topped the loop with a .727 winning percentage. He held opposing batsmen to a .203 average and a .252 OBP, leading in both departments. Hughes is the only NL freshman subsequent to 1908 to log more innings than walks and hits combined (minimum 150 IP). In the World Series he started two games against the miraculous Boston Red Sox. Hughes took the loss in Game Two despite pitching well and got a no-decision in the sixth contest, which Boston also won before it dropped the finale the next day to Bob Gibson. Another rookie right-hander, reliever Ron Willis, aided the Redbirds' cause nearly as much as Hughes by appearing in 65 games and saving ten.

It had taken Hughes until his late 20s to make the majors. On a much faster track was Gary Nolan of the Cincinnati Reds. Nolan, just 19 and with all of 12 minor league games in his portfolio, fired five shutouts in 1967, including a ten-inning effort on July 14 against the Mets. His 8.18 strikeouts per nine innings paced the senior loop. Of Nolan's 206 whiffs, 15 came on June 7 against the San Francisco Giants. He walked none in 7⅔ innings but surrendered three runs and wasn't involved in the decision.

Including Nolan, six rookie hurlers in 1967 bagged 150 or more strikeouts, the most in any season since 1884 when there were three major leagues and pitchers were first allowed to throw overhand. Less than two weeks after Nolan's dominating performance, Houston righty Don Wilson was even more formidable, no-hitting Atlanta 2–0 and blowing away 15 Braves. Two other members of the 150-strikeout sextet were Los Angeles's Bill Singer and Tom Phoebus of the Baltimore Orioles. Singer notched a dozen Ks on August 21 in holding Atlanta scoreless. Phoebus had thrown shutouts in his first two starts the previous September and tossed four more in 1967. Three of them were in succession, including a two-hitter on May 22, when he fanned 11 New York Yankees. Phoebus won a team-best 14 games for the defending world champs.

Baltimore fell to sixth place, but Rod Carew and the Minnesota Twins narrowly missed taking the AL flag, finishing just one game off the pace. Carew, the AL ROY, batted .292, outhitting the league by 56 points. On May 8 he had five hits, but the Twins nonetheless lost to Washington. First-place Boston featured two rookies in its regular lineup—centerfielder Reggie Smith and second baseman Mike Andrews. Smith smashed 15 home runs, including two in the opener of an August 20 doubleheader against the California Angels. That day he be-

The 1961–76 era was strewn with the dead arms of young pitchers who experienced sensational rookie seasons and then enjoyed little, if any, more success in the majors. Bookending the period were two AL ROYs, the 1961 winner, Red Sox righty Don Schwall, and the 1976 victor, Tigers phenom Mark Fidrych. After leading all frosh hurlers in wins as yearlings, neither lasted long enough to achieve even as many as 50 career victories.

Perhaps the most short-lived rookie mound star of all from the period debuted almost squarely in the middle of the era. In 1967 Dick Hughes of the Cardinals not only was the rookie co-leader in wins with 16, but he topped all NL hurlers in both OBA and OOBP as well as in winning percentage. Hughes contracted arm trouble early in the 1968 campaign, tried to work out of it in spot relief roles, and won just two more games after his superb inaugural season.

STARTING PITCHERS, FEWER THAN 50 CAREER WINS, WHO WON IN DOUBLE FIGURES AS ROOKIES (1961–1976)

Name	Team	Year	R/W	C/W
Don Schwall	Bos-AL	1961	15	49
Ken McBride	LA-AL	1961	12	40
Rollie Sheldon	NY-AL	1961	11	38
Wayne Simpson	Cin-NL	1970	14	36
Ernie McAnally	Mon-NL	1971	11	30
Mark Fidrych	Det-AL	1976	19	29
Bill Parsons	Mil-AL	1971	13	29
Les Cain	Det-AL	1970	12	23
Mike Nagy	Bos-AL	1969	12	20
Dick Hughes	StL-NL	1967	16	20
Dennis Blair	Mon-NL	1974	11	19
Pat Darcy	Cin-NL	1975	11	14
Santo Alcala	Cin-NL	1976	11	14
Norm Bass	KC-AL	1961	11	13
Jerry Janeski	Chi-AL	1970	10	11

came the first Red Sox hitter to homer from both sides of the plate in the same game, driving in five in Boston's 12–2 victory. In the Fall Classic against St. Louis, Smith connected twice more. Andrews, who paced all rookies with 79 runs, batted .263 in Boston's first campaign in 21 years to culminate with a postseason berth and then stroked .308 in the World Series.

Also having a resurgent year were the Cubs, who for the first time since 1912 had two rookies win in double figures. Rich Nye, the only freshman southpaw in 1967 to win more than four times, took a baker's dozen and Joe Niekro garnered ten triumphs. In addition, Chuck Hartenstein gave the Cubs nine relief victories and ten saves.

While the NL offered a swarm of freshman hurlers at whom to marvel, Lee May of Cincinnati was the lone senior loop yearling to put up even modest offensive numbers. The Reds new first sacker was the only NL recruit to surpass any of the following paltry totals:

At bats—231
Hits—57
Doubles—12
Home runs—4
Runs—24
RBI—26
Strikeouts—44
Stolen bases—3

The low productivity in 1967 of NL rookies in particular and the rest of the league's hitters in general was a harbinger of what little offense the 1968 season would bring, but it also can be partly blamed on the likes of

1967 ROOKIE LEADERS

Batting	Pitching
G—AL 158, Reggie Smith, BOS	W—AL 14, Tom Phoebus, BAL
NL 127, Lee May, CIN	NL 16, Dick Hughes, STL
	Tom Seaver, NY
AB—AL 565, Reggie Smith, BOS	L—AL 11, Rickey Clark, CAL
NL 438, Lee May, CIN	NL 13, Tom Seaver, NY
H—AL 150, Rod Carew, MIN	PCT—AL .609, Tom Phoebus, BAL
NL 116, Lee May, CIN	NL .727, Dick Hughes, STL
2B—AL 24, Reggie Smith, BOS	GP—AL 69, Bill Kelso, CAL
NL 29, Lee May, CIN	NL 65, Ron Willis, STL
3B—AL 7, Rod Carew, MIN	GS—AL 33, Tom Phoebus, BAL
NL 4, Doug Rader, HOU	NL 34, Tom Seaver, NY
HR—AL 15, Reggie Smith, BOS	CG—AL 7, Tom Phoebus, BAL
NL 12, Lee May, CIN	NL 18, Tom Seaver, NY
R—AL 79, Mike Andrews, BOS	IP—AL 208, Tom Phoebus, BAL
NL 54, Lee May, CIN	NL 251, Tom Seaver, NY
RBI—AL 61, Reggie Smith, BOS	H—AL 177, Tom Phoebus, BAL
NL 57, Lee May, CIN	NL 224, Tom Seaver, NY
WK—AL 62, Mike Andrews, BOS	BB—AL 114, Tom Phoebus, BAL
NL 25, Dick Dietz, SF	NL 78, Tom Seaver, NY
SO—AL 107, Rick Monday, KC	K—AL 179, Tom Phoebus, BAL
NL 80, Lee May, CIN	NL 206, Gary Nolan, CIN
SB—AL 16, Reggie Smith, BOS	ERA—AL 2.59, Rickey Clark, CAL
NL 4, Lee May, CIN	NL 2.58, Gary Nolan, CIN
BA—AL .292, Rod Carew, MIN	SHO—AL 4, Tom Phoebus, BAL
NL .265, Lee May, CIN*	NL 5, Gary Nolan, CIN
SLG—AL .409, Rod Carew, MIN	SV—AL 12, Dave Baldwin, WAS
NL .422, Lee May, CIN	NL 10, Chuck Hartenstein, CHI
OBP—AL .348, Mike Andrews, BOS	Ron Willis, STL
NL .310, Lee May, CIN	

*Technically there were no rookie qualifiers in the NL in 1967 in any of the three major hitting departments. May, with 468 PAs, came the closest to qualifying, close enough that for our purposes in this book we deem him the leader.

Seaver, Hughes, Nolan, and their many hard-throwing freshman counterparts.

Other Highlights

April 14—Red Sox rookie Billy Rohr is on the verge of hurling a no-hitter in his first ML start—against the Yankees at Yankee Stadium, no less—when New York catcher Elston Howard lines a 3–2 pitch to center field for a single with two out in the bottom of the ninth; Rohr gets the next out to win his debut start 3–0 but will collect only two more victories in his brief ML career.

July 4—Cubs rookie Joe Niekro loses 8–3 to brother Phil of the Braves in the first of numerous career matchups between the two sibling starters.

July 13—Mike Epstein hits two homers and a triple and drives in four Washington runs as the Senators best Detroit 8–3 in the opener of a twinbill.

September 14—Cisco Carlos of the Chicago White Sox blanks Cleveland for ten innings, winning 4–0.

September 16—Rick Joseph blasts a pinch-hit grand slam in the bottom of the 11th as the Philadelphia Phillies beat the Los Angeles Dodgers 8–4.

◄ 1968 ►

It may not have been reminiscent of the late 1940s to late 1950s when New York City was the undisputed capital of the baseball world, but considering the rank showing of the two New York teams in the previous two seasons, 1968 represented a breath of fresh air for Big Apple baseball kranks. The Mets and Yankees combined for 156 wins, the most by the pair since the Mets joined the NL in 1962. Thirty-six of those victories came from two rookies who more than held their own in what many historians have dubbed "The Year of the Pitcher." Yankees right-hander Stan Bahnsen won 17 games, with 13 of those coming against Boston, California, and Washington. It was the most wins by a Yankees freshman since 1954 when Bob Grim won 20, and only Russ Ford in 1910 has ever garnered more recruit "Ws" for the Yankees as a starter. On August 1 Bahnsen began a five-win month by tossing his only shutout, a three-

hitter with a season-high 12 strikeouts against the Red Sox. Only one club—Baltimore—pinned an ERA higher than 2.45 on him, the Orioles more than doubling that figure. Bahnsen fanned 162 hitters and posted a 2.05 ERA, the sixth lowest in the AL in 1968 and the best by any rookie hurler in as many as 200 innings since the close of the Deadball Era.

LOWEST ERA BY ROOKIE WITH 200+ IP (1920–2003)

2.05 ERA/267.1 IP, Stan Bahnsen, 1968 NY AL
2.08 ERA/263.2 IP, Jerry Koosman, 1968 NY NL
2.13 ERA/215.1 IP, Johnny Beazley, 1942 StL NL
2.24 ERA/216.2 IP, Elmer Riddle, 1941 Cin NL
2.28 ERA/213.0 IP, Wilcy Moore, 1927 NY AL

Koosman, second only to Bahnsen on the above list, was fourth in the NL ERA race, albeit far behind leader Bob Gibson with his legendary 1.12 mark. The Mets southpaw set a new team record by winning 19 games, a figure that is still the club's rookie standard. Koosman tossed shutouts in his first two starts in 1968 and had seven overall, the most by a rookie hurler since 1913. On July 21 he blanked the pennant-bound St. Louis Cardinals 1–0, whiffing 12 while permitting just four hits. Twelve days earlier Koosman had earned a save in the All-Star Game, finishing the NL's 1–0 win by striking out Carl Yastrzemski, who was en route to leading the AL with a record-low .301 batting average.

Behind the plate for the senior circuit in the ninth inning of the Midsummer Classic was Johnny Bench, Cincinnati's strong-armed receiver. Bench, who beat out Koosman for the loop's ROY prize, had an excellent freshman campaign, serving ample notice of his future as the game's dominant backstop by hitting 15 home runs with 82 RBI and setting a new standard for rookie catchers by rapping 40 doubles, 25 more than the total produced by the recruit two-bagger runner-up in 1968.

MOST DOUBLES BY ROOKIE CATCHER

40, Johnny Bench, 1968 Cin NL
34, Bob Rodgers, 1962 LA AL
33, Benito Santiago, 1987 SD NL
33, A.J. Pierzynski, 2001 Min AL
30, Bill Dickey, 1929 NY AL

Bench also excelled defensively, topping NL catchers in putouts and assists while working 154 games behind the plate, the most ever for a freshman, and winning his first Gold Glove. Nine more would follow.

Koosman was not the only senior loop rookie caught by Bench in the All-Star contest. Atlanta righty Ron Reed recorded the first two outs in the ninth inning en route to an 11-win season. Reed worked the third most innings among freshmen in 1968, but the number-three man in strikeouts was a pitcher who would not take a backseat to anyone in that category for very long. Nolan Ryan blew away 133 batters in 134 innings, compiling a 6–9 record for the Mets. Opposing hitters batted just .200 off the flame-throwing Texan.

In 1983 Ryan would become baseball's career pitching strikeout king. Ironically, the record-holder for batters, Reggie Jackson, also celebrated his rookie season in 1968 and led the AL with 171 whiffs in the process of setting a new recruit record for batter Ks. The Oakland right fielder scored 82 runs and blasted 29 homers, a total exceeded by only three other AL sluggers. At the other end of the power spectrum was rookie centerfielder Del Unser, who hit just one round tripper in 635 ABs for Washington. Unser's solitary circuit shot was launched on August 20 when he went 5-for-5 and scored three runs as the Senators beat Jackson's Oakland A's 7–5.

Although Unser hit a meager .230, his BA was only a point below the AL norm of .231, illustrating the extent to which pitchers dominated the 1968 campaign. Vicente Romo, for example, sported a 1.60 ERA overall in 84⅓ innings after coming to Cleveland from the Los Angeles Dodgers early in the season. In addition, the long-forgotten Romo saved 12 games for the Indians to lead all recruits while Jack Billingham notched eight saves for Los Angeles to pace senior loop yearlings. Only a notch behind these two frosh bullpenners was another recruit hurler whose name has long since lapsed into obscurity, Daryl Patterson. In 1968 Patterson collected seven saves for Detroit with a 2.12 ERA and then contributed three scoreless innings in the Tigers' comeback from a 3–1 deficit in games to beat St. Louis in the 1968 World Series.

Other Highlights

May 6—Dave Leonhard of Baltimore holds Detroit to one hit as he blanks the Tigers 4–0.

A rookie hurler who allows only six runs in his first four starts generally begins his career 4–0, but Jim McAndrew of the Mets had the opposite experience in 1968. In his debut on July 21 at St. Louis in the first game of a doubleheader, he dropped a tight 2–0 decision to the 1968 Pitcher of the Year, Bob Gibson. McAndrew then waited nearly two weeks before making his second career start on August 4 at Los Angeles. Once again he lost 2–0, this time to journeyman lefty Mike Kekich. Six days later McAndrew dropped his third career start 1–0 to Bobby Bolin of San Francisco. When he again was blanked 1–0 the following week by Don Wilson of the Astros, he established a new record for the most consecutive shutout losses.

McAndrew held sole possession of the mark until 1999 when Arizona's Randy Johnson also suffered four straight whitewash defeats.

June 14—Pittsburgh's Bob Moose limits Houston to two hits in his 3–0 win.

June 25—Bobby Bonds is only the second player in ML history to blast a grand slam in his first ML game when he goes yard with the sacks jammed against John Purdin of the Dodgers in his third at bat of the contest.

July 12—Rookie reliever Tom Dukes of the Astros ties a post-1893 ML record when he pitches in his ninth straight game as Houston loses 8–1 to St. Louis.

August 4—Mike Kekich fires a one-hitter for Los Angeles, beating the New York Mets 2–0.

August 26—Luckless Mets rookie Jim McAndrew turns the tables after suffering a record four straight shutout losses to begin his career when he nips Steve Carlton of the Cardinals 1–0.

September 6—Andy Messersmith of the Angels blanks the Boston Red Sox 4–0 as he surrenders just two safeties.

September 11—Mets rookie Jim McAndrew follows his gem against Steve Carlton two weeks earlier by edging another future Hall of Famer, Fergie Jenkins of the Cubs, 1–0 to saddle Jenkins with his ML record-tying fifth 1–0 loss in 1968.

Batting		Pitching	
G—AL 156, Del Unser, WAS		**W**—AL 17, Stan Bahnsen, NY	
NL 154, Johnny Bench, CIN		NL 19, Jerry Koosman, NY	
AB—AL 635, Del Unser, WAS		**L**—AL 14, Cisco Carlos, CHI	
NL 564, Johnny Bench, CIN		NL 12, Jerry Koosman, NY	
H—AL 146, Del Unser, WAS		Bob Moose, PIT	
NL 155, Johnny Bench, CIN		**PCT**—AL .586, Stan Bahnsen, NY	
2B—AL 15, Bobby Cox, NY		NL .613, Jerry Koosman, NY	
NL 40, Johnny Bench, CIN		**GP**—AL 56, Tom Burgmeier, CAL	
3B—AL 7, Del Unser, WAS		NL 50, Jack Billingham, LA	
NL 5, Bobby Bonds, SF		**GS**—AL 34, Stan Bahnsen, NY	
HR—AL 29, Reggie Jackson, OAK		NL 34, Jerry Koosman, NY	
NL 15, Johnny Bench, CIN		**CG**—AL 10, Stan Bahnsen, NY	
R—AL 82, Reggie Jackson, OAK		NL 17, Jerry Koosman, NY	
NL 67, Johnny Bench, CIN		**IP**—AL 267.1, Stan Bahnsen, NY	
RBI—AL 74, Reggie Jackson, OAK		NL 263.2, Jerry Koosman, NY	
NL 82, Johnny Bench, CIN		**H**—AL 216, Stan Bahnsen, NY	
WK—AL 50, Reggie Jackson, OAK		NL 221, Jerry Koosman, NY	
NL 38, Bobby Bonds, SF		**BB**—AL 68, Stan Bahnsen, NY	
SO—**AL 171, Reggie Jackson, OAK**		NL 75, Nolan Ryan, NY	
NL 96, Johnny Bench, CIN		**K**—AL 162, Stan Bahnsen, NY	
SB—AL 23, Dave Nelson, CLE		NL 178, Jerry Koosman, NY	
NL 18, Freddie Patek, PIT		**ERA**—AL 2.05, Stan Bahnsen, NY	
BA—AL .250, Reggie Jackson, OAK		NL 2.08, Jerry Koosman, NY	
NL .275, Johnny Bench, CIN		**SHO**—AL 2, Dave Leonhard, BAL	
SLG—AL .452, Reggie Jackson, OAK		NL 7, Jerry Koosman, NY	
NL .433, Johnny Bench, CIN		**SV**—AL 12, Vicente Romo, CLE	
OBP—AL .317, Reggie Jackson, OAK		NL 8, Jack Billingham, LA	
NL .315, Johnny Bench, CIN			

1969

What will posterity decide was the most remarkable event of 1969—man landing on the moon or the New York Mets winning the World Series? Certainly many Gothamites who suffered through the first seven seasons of Mets baseball would opt for the latter. Rookie right-hander Gary Gentry played a large hand in the Amazins' march to their first postseason berth, winning 13 games, three of them shutouts. In Gentry's two-hitter on June 17 at Philadelphia, he struck out nine, winning the first game of a twinbill 1–0. In September he went 4–0 with a 2.19 ERA and added his final two whitewashes as the Mets overtook the Chicago Cubs in the NL East race. Gentry started against the Atlanta Braves in Game Three of the first NLCS but yielded a pair of runs in two-plus innings. However, New York rallied for a 7–4 victory to advance to the World Series where Gentry held the Baltimore Orioles, winners of 109 games in the regular season, to just three hits in 6⅔ scoreless innings in Game Three, earning the win in the Mets' 5–0 triumph. New York won the next two contests, completing an improbable season with the World Championship.

The Mets had compiled a 24–6 record against the two NL expansion teams—the Montreal Expos and San Diego Padres—both of which chose to build with youth, thereupon giving rookies ample playing time. One of them, Coco Laboy, homered in his ML debut, which was also the first game in Expos history, in an 11–10 win against the Mets at Shea Stadium. Laboy, a third baseman, had 83 RBI and 18 round trippers for Montreal. Reliever Dan McGinn also connected for the Expos in that game, hitting the first circuit shot in team

In 1969 Gary Gentry earned a slot in the Mets starting rotation in spring training and held his place all season. Gentry's 35 starts tied Tom Seaver for the team lead and, in addition, tied Clay Kirby of the Padres for the rookie lead. The apex of Gentry's season, and probably his career as well, came on September 24, 1969, when he blanked St. Louis 6–0 to clinch the NL East crown for the Mets. *Transcendental Graphics*

Oliver enjoyed a six-hit game that featured a double and a circuit blast on May 4, as Kansas City thumped California 15–1. Piniella, Oliver, and Kelly are recognizable names to fans of that era in every city, but not even the most rabid K.C. rooter is likely to recall the rookie who led the 1969 Royals in OPS with an .842 mark: record-setting first sacker Mike Fiore, who walked 84 times in just 107 games to post a splendid .421 OBP to go with a .428 SA that was second on the team only to veteran Ed Kirkpatrick.

MOST BASES ON BALLS BY ROOKIE WITH FEWER THAN 350 ABs

84 BB/339 AB, Mike Fiore, 1969 KC AL
65 BB/348 AB, Johnny Groth, 1949 Det AL
61 BB/347 AB, Gerald Perry, 1984 Atl NL
60 BB/295 AB, Fred McGriff, 1987 Tor AL
59 BB/317 AB, Larry Rosenthal, 1936 Chi AL

history. McGinn then proceeded to win seven games and save six more in 74 appearances. First baseman Nate Colbert was San Diego's main power source, blasting 24 home runs for the Padres who, like Montreal, lost 110 games. Colbert saved his best day for the season finale when he tripled and homered, driving in five runs in a 9–4 Padres' win at San Francisco on October 1.

Baltimore also feasted on the two new clubs in their league, the Orioles going 20–4 versus the Seattle Pilots and Kansas City Royals, both of which were placed in the AL West. Seattle went the opposite course of most expansion teams, using freshmen very sparingly, with only two playing more than 23 games. Outfielder Steve Hovley hit .277 in 91 contests while John Gelnar was 3–10. Kansas City, in contrast, had four rookies who played at least 100 games and three freshman pitchers who made 20 or more starts. Lou Piniella started his ROY campaign with four hits on Opening Day for K.C. against the ultimate division winner, Minnesota, as the Royals won in 12 innings. The left fielder batted .282 with 68 RBI. Fellow outfielders Bob Oliver and Pat Kelly joined Piniella in the Royals' attack, the former ripping 13 home runs and the latter swiping 40 bags.

On the pitching side of the ledger, Dick Drago was a respectable 11–13 for the Royals, who led the four expansion teams with 69 wins. Southpaw Bill Butler copped nine victories, four of them shutouts, including a one-hit whitewash at Cleveland August 9. Another Royals lefty, Jim Rooker, went just 4–16 but had a fine 3.75 ERA. Rooker also led all rookie pitchers with four home runs, two coming on July 7 in a 6–5 defeat at Minnesota.

Second baseman Ted Sizemore joined Piniella as a ROY, taking the NL award for the Los Angeles Dodgers. Sizemore played all but three of L.A.'s games and accumulated 160 hits, four on June 28, when he tallied three times at San Diego. Pittsburgh's Al Oliver tied Laboy as runner-up to Sizemore. Oliver, Richie Hebner, and Manny Sanguillen all played 129 games for Pittsburgh in 1969 and would each play a major role on what would become the strongest team in the NL East during the decade to come. Oliver, a future bat titlist, led the trio with 17 round trippers but was the only one of the three to hit less than .300 (.285), as Hebner swatted .301 and Sanguillen .303, the highest mark by a yearling backstop since 1930 (minimum 400 ABs).

On the other side of Pennsylvania, the Philadelphia Phillies got 18 stolen bases and 20 home runs from centerfielder Larry Hisle. Don Money, one of the Phils' most highly touted rookies in the past half century, did not fare nearly as well. A shortstop before shifting permanently to the hot corner the following year, Money hit two homers on Opening Day in the Phils' loss to the Cubs at Wrigley Field but then hit only four more jacks the rest of the year and batted just .229.

In the nightcap of a June 24 twinbill, White Sox third baseman Bill Melton rapped three solo shots among his four safeties at Seattle. Melton would connect 23 times in 1969 while another Sox rookie, outfielder Carlos May, went deep on 18 occasions and batted .281. Either May and Melton would probably have been as reasonable a choice for AL ROY as Piniella, but the top junior loop recruit of all, in the estimation of many observers, was Bobby Murcer of the New York Yankees. Like Mickey Mantle, Murcer began as a shortstop and was turned into an outfielder his rookie season. Murcer resembled a young Mantle at the plate also, scoring 82 runs, driving in a like amount, and hitting 26 circuit blasts in 152 games.

Houston hurler Tom Griffin topped all rookies with 200 strikeouts and tossed three five-hit shutouts. Griffin made seven starts in which he whiffed at least ten hitters, including all three of his whitewashes. Further marking one of the most fertile years for rookies since the close of World War II, Boston's Mike Nagy went 12–2, ending up second only to Gentry in wins. But arguably the best rookie pitcher of all in 1969 was reliever Ken Tatum. After debuting for California in late May, Tatum yielded just one run in his first 27⅔ innings. He not only saved 22 games and finished with an amazing 1.36 ERA but also easily led all hurlers in 1969 with at least 70 innings pitched in fewest hits per nine innings.

H/9 IP, 1969 (MINIMUM 70 IP)

	Name	H/9 IP	IP
1	Ken Tatum	5.53	86.1
2	Hoyt Wilhelm	5.77	78
3	Nolan Ryan	6.03	89.1
4	Andy Messersmith	6.08	250
5	Jim Roland	6.16	86.1
6	Eddie Watt	6.21	71
7	Moe Drabowsky	6.24	98
8	Pete Mikkelsen	6.32	81.1
9	Ron Perranoski	6.39	119.2
10	Jim Palmer	6.51	181

It was never the intention of the expansion Montreal Expos to open their inaugural season in 1969 with 29-year-old career minor leaguer Coco Laboy as their third baseman. However, when manager Gene Mauch was unable to unearth anyone better in spring training, he opted to go with the elderly rookie as a stopgap. The decision proved a sound one as Laboy led the club in RBI with 83, but when Mauch attempted to extend his good fortune the following year, the roof caved in on the Expos. In 1970, Laboy slipped to .199 and became the last NL third sacker to date to post a sub-.200 BA in at least 400 at bats. Ironically, that same year, Jerry Kenney of the Yankees became the last third sacker to perform the identical negative feat in the AL.

Other Highlights

April 14—Expos rookie reliever Dan McGinn wins the first ML game ever played in Canada as Montreal nips the Cardinals 8–7.

April 22—Rollie Fingers twirls a shutout in his first ML start for Oakland, beating Minnesota 7–0.

May 17—Jerry Nyman fires a one-hitter in the Chicago White Sox' 6–0 victory over the Washington Senators.

May 24—In a 7–5 San Diego win over the Cubs, Padres second baseman John Sipin is only the fourth player in history to hammer two triples in his first ML game; Sipin will play 67 more games in the majors without ever hitting another triple.

June 11—Joe Lahoud hits three home runs for Boston, knocking in four runs, as the Red Sox top Minnesota 13–5.

July 9—Cubs rookie outfielder Jim Qualls shatters Mets ace Tom Seaver's hopes when he hits a bloop single with one out in the ninth to mar what would otherwise have been a perfect-game 4–0 win by Seaver.

September 10—Mike Wegener fans 15 New York Mets in 11 innings and allows no earned runs but takes a no-decision as the Montreal Expos lose 3–2 in 12 frames.

1969 ROOKIE LEADERS

Batting	Pitching
G—AL 157, Bill Melton, CHI	W—AL 12, Mike Nagy, BOS
NL 159, Ted Sizemore, LA	NL 13, Gary Gentry, NY
AB—AL 564, Bobby Murcer, NY	L—AL 16, Jim Rooker, KC
NL 590, Ted Sizemore, LA	**NL 20, Clay Kirby, SD**
H—AL 146, Bobby Murcer, NY	PCT—AL .857, Mike Nagy, BOS
NL 160, Ted Sizemore, LA	NL .714, Mike Torrez, STL
2B—AL 26, Bill Melton, CHI	GP—AL 60, Rollie Fingers, OAK
NL 29, Coco Laboy, MON	NL 74, Dan McGinn, MON
3B—AL 6, Lou Piniella, KC	GS—AL 29, Bill Butler, KC
NL 9, Nate Colbert, SD	NL 35, Gary Gentry, NY
HR—AL 26, Bobby Murcer, NY	Clay Kirby, SD
NL 24, Nate Colbert, SD	CG—AL 10, Dick Drago, KC
R—AL 82, Bobby Murcer, NY	NL 6, Gary Gentry, NY
NL 75, Larry Hisle, PHI	Tom Griffin, HOU
RBI—AL 87, Bill Melton, CHI	IP—AL 200.2, Dick Drago, KC
NL 83, Coco Laboy, MON	NL 233.2, Gary Gentry, NY
WK—AL 84, Mike Fiore, KC	H—AL 190, Dick Drago, KC
NL 53, Richie Hebner, PIT	NL 204, Clay Kirby, SD
SO—AL 106, Bill Melton, CHI	BB—AL 106, Mike Nagy, BOS
NL 152, Larry Hisle, PHI	NL 100, Clay Kirby, SD
SB—AL 40, Pat Kelly, KC	K—AL 156, Bill Butler, KC
NL 18, Larry Hisle, PHI	NL 200, Tom Griffin, HOU
BA—AL .282, Lou Piniella, KC	ERA—AL 3.11, Mike Nagy, BOS
NL .301, Richie Hebner, PIT	NL 3.43, Gary Gentry, NY
SLG—AL .454, Bobby Murcer, NY	SHO—AL 4, Bill Butler, KC
NL .482, Nate Colbert, SD	Mike Kilkenny, DET
OBP—AL .356, Wayne Comer, SEA	NL 3, Gary Gentry, NY
NL .383, Richie Hebner, PIT	Tom Griffin, HOU
	SV—AL 22, Ken Tatum, CAL
	NL 6, Dan McGinn, MON
	Frank Reberger, SD
	Bill Wilson, PHI

September 21—Mike Kilkenny of Detroit throws the fourth shutout in his last seven starts, besting Boston 9–0.

September 24—Rookie Gary Gentry clinches the NL East title for the "Amazing" Mets when he blanks the Cardinals 6–0 on just four hits.

1970s

1970

The 1970s were very good to the Cincinnati Reds and the Pittsburgh Pirates. Each team won six division titles and two World Series during that decade. Both clubs launched their lengthy span of success by introducing players in 1970 who would be instrumental to their postseason ambitions. That season, pitchers Wayne Simpson, Don Gullett, and Milt Wilcox combined for a 22–6 record for Cincinnati. Simpson started 13–1, including a two-hitter in his debut on April 9 and a one-hitter ten days later. He made the All-Star team but did not see action in the game and then tore his rotator cuff in late July, limiting him to two starts the rest of the way. Nonetheless, Simpson led the NL with a .198 OBA. Gullett, a 19-year-old southpaw, won five games, logged a rookie-high six saves, and fanned 76 hitters in just 77⅔ innings. He then allowed just one earned run in 10⅓ postseason frames with two saves, both in the NLCS. Wilcox, a September call-up from Indianapolis, where he had led the American Association in shutouts, went 3–1 down the stretch and won Game Three of the NLCS, when the Reds completed a sweep of Pittsburgh.

The Reds also featured two impressive freshman position players in 1970. Dave Concepcion, who would play more than 2,000 games at shortstop for Cincinnati, batted .260 in 101 games, and Bernie Carbo, who platooned in left field with fellow rookie Hal McRae, stroked 21 home runs in 125 games while hitting .310 and drawing 94 walks to give him the highest freshman OBP since 1911.

HIGHEST OBP BY ROOKIE (MINIMUM 100 GAMES)

.468, Joe Jackson, 1911 Cle AL
.457, Roy Thomas, 1899 Phi NL
.456, Bernie Carbo, 1970 Cin NL
.4470, Benny Kauff, 1914 Ind FL
.4468, Charlie Keller, 1939 NY AL

Pittsburgh, the Reds' opposition in four league championship series in the 1970s, followed its rich rookie crop of the previous year that featured Al Oliver, Richie Hebner, and Manny Sanguillen by unveiling slugging first baseman Bob Robertson, who blasted 27 homers and drove in 82 runs in just 117 games. On August 1 Robertson went 5-for-6 with four runs and three

RBI in the Pirates' 20–10 rout at Atlanta. Joining Robertson in the 1970 Pirates' freshman class was Dave Cash, .314 in 64 games, who was being groomed to take over at second base the following season from Pittsburgh legend Bill Mazeroski.

Los Angeles's Billy Grabarkewitz, like Carbo, was exceptionally deft at getting on base, sporting a .403 OBP. Grabarkewitz's rookie campaign unfortunately was the lone season in his seven-year career that he was fully healthy. In the 156 games he played, he walked 95 times, making 1970 the only season in NL history to feature two freshmen who each collected over 90 bases on balls.* The versatile Grabarkewitz, who played third, short, and second, hit .289 with 84 RBI and 45 extra-base hits. He went 1-for-3 in the Midsummer Classic, where Cleveland's recruit catcher, Ray Fosse, experienced the full gamut of baseball's highs and lows. Fosse singled and scored in the sixth inning and hit a sacrifice fly in the seventh. In the 12th frame, however, he was flattened in a violent collision at home plate as Pete Rose scored the winning run for the NL. Though Fosse sustained a career-threatening injury in the crash, he nonetheless batted .307 and had a 23-game hitting streak in which he hit .376. He also connected for 18 round trippers and won the Gold Glove for the Indians, who had a second noteworthy freshman in left field, Roy Foster. Foster led AL rookies with 23 home runs and 26 doubles, one more two-bagger than Thurman Munson hit.

Munson, the hardscrabble backstop for the New York Yankees, was named AL ROY despite going hitless in his first 24 ABs of the season. The Kent State product finished at .302 and would quickly emerge as the Yankees on-field leader until dying at age 32 in 1979 when his private plane crashed.

Carl Morton, the ROY in the senior circuit, also died much too young, a heart attack claiming his life in 1983 when he was only 39. As a rookie in 1970, Morton won

---

* The only other two seasons that produced two rookies who each collected as many as 90 bases on balls were 1890, when Bill Joyce of Brooklyn in the PL posted a rookie-record 123 walks and Jack Crooks of Columbus in the AA had 96 walks, and 1950, when Al Rosen of Cleveland had 100 free passes and Don Lenhardt of the St. Louis Browns had exactly 90.

When Cesar Cedeno made his ML debut with Houston on June 20, 1970, he was just four months past his 19th birthday. Cedeno held the Astros' centerfield post for the rest of the season and looked like a near certain future Hall of Famer. Although he never quite fulfilled his early promise, his .310 BA is still the highest in history by a teenage rookie who had a minimum of 200 at bats. Moreover, his BA ranks third only to Mel Ott (1928) and Ty Cobb (1906) among all teenage hitters.

THE TOP TEN TEENAGE BATSMEN

Name	Year	AB	OPS	BA
Mel Ott	1928	435	.921	.322
Ty Cobb	1906	358	.749	.316
Cesar Cedeno	1970	355	.792	.310
Edgar Renteria	1996	431	.760	.309
Buddy Lewis	1936	601	.746	.291
Tony Conigliaro	1964	404	.883	.290
Scott Stratton	1889	229	.747	.288
Chubby Dean	1936	342	.711	.287
Freddie Lindstrom	1925	356	.761	.287
John Ward	1879	364	.648	.286

18 games, nearly one-fourth of Montreal's total. He tossed four shutouts, two in September. On the 11th of that month, Morton held Philadelphia to two hits in a 1–0 win. Sixteen days later, Morton outdueled St. Louis rookie Harry Parker, who threw nine scoreless innings of his own, as the Expos won 1–0 in 11 frames.

Bob Johnson could relate to the challenges Morton faced toiling for a second-year expansion team. Johnson made two scoreless relief appearances for the world champion Mets in 1969 before being dealt to the Kansas City Royals prior to the 1970 season. Even though he blew away 206 batters and had a fine 3.07 ERA, his record with the 65–97 Royals was only 8–13, giving him a frosh distinction that he would rather have avoided.

FEWEST WINS BY ROOKIE WITH 200+ KS

8 W/206 K, Bob Johnson, 1970 KC AL
10 W/225 K, Tom Hughes, 1901 Chi NL
11 W/200 K, Tom Griffin, 1969 Hou NL
12 W/209 K, Don Sutton, 1966 LA NL
13 W/236 K, Hideo Nomo, 1995 LA NL
13 W/233 K, Kerry Wood, 1998 Chi NL

1970 ROOKIE LEADERS

Batting		Pitching	
G—AL 139, Roy Foster, CLE		W—AL 12, Les Cain, DET	
NL 156, Billy Grabarkewitz, LA		NL 18, Carl Morton, MON	
AB—AL 477, Roy Foster, CLE		L—AL 17, Jerry Janeski, CHI	
NL 581, Dave Campbell, SD		NL 14, Dave Roberts, SD	
H—AL 138, Ray Fosse, CLE		PCT—AL .632, Les Cain, DET	
NL 153, Billy Grabarkewitz, LA		NL .621, Carl Morton, MON	
2B—AL 26, Roy Foster, CLE		GP—AL 48, Fred Scherman, DET	
NL 28, Dave Campbell, SD		NL 44, Don Gullett, CIN	
3B—AL 4, Elliott Maddox, DET		GS—AL 35, Jerry Janeski, CHI	
Thurman Munson, NY		NL 37, Carl Morton, MON	
NL 8, Billy Grabarkewitz, LA		CG—AL 10, Bob Johnson, KC	
HR—AL 23, Roy Foster, CLE		NL 10, Carl Morton, MON	
NL 27, Bob Robertson, PIT		Wayne Simpson, CIN	
R—AL 66, Roy Foster, CLE		IP—AL 214, Bob Johnson, KC	
NL 92, Billy Grabarkewitz, LA		NL 284.2, Carl Morton, MON	
RBI—AL 66, Danny Walton, MIL		H—AL 247, Jerry Janeski, CHI	
NL 84, Billy Grabarkewitz, LA		NL 281, Carl Morton, MON	
WK—AL 57, Thurman Munson, NY		BB—AL 98, Les Cain, DET	
NL 95, Billy Grabarkewitz, LA		**NL 125, Carl Morton, MON**	
SO—AL 126, Danny Walton, MIL		K—AL 206, Bob Johnson, KC	
NL 149, Billy Grabarkewitz, LA		NL 154, Carl Morton, MON	
SB—AL 5, Thurman Munson, NY		ERA—AL 3.07, Bob Johnson, KC	
NL 24, Larry Bowa, PHI		NL 3.02, Wayne Simpson, CIN	
BA—AL .307, Ray Fosse, CLE		SHO—AL 2, Vida Blue, OAK	
NL .289, Billy Grabarkewitz, LA		NL 4, Carl Morton, MON	
SLG—AL .468, Roy Foster, CLE		SV—AL 4, Jerry Crider, CHI	
NL .551, Bernie Carbo, CIN		Bob Johnson, KC	
OBP—AL .389, Thurman Munson, NY		Dave LaRoche, CAL	
NL .456, Bernie Carbo, CIN		NL 6, Don Gullett, CIN	

In addition to Johnson and Morton, two other freshmen topped 150 punch-outs. Les Cain fanned 156 while going 12–7 for Detroit, and Ken Brett had 155 for Boston to go with his eight wins.

Other Highlights

June 28—Jack Heidemann gets five hits and scores twice in Cleveland's 8–2 win at Detroit.

July 19—Jim Hutto hits a ninth-inning pinch-hit grand slam to break a 4–4 tie at Los Angeles as the Phillies win 9–4.

September 2—Future big league manager Gene Lamont homers in his first ML at bat to account for the Tigers' lone run in their 10–1 loss to the Red Sox.

September 2—Catcher Hal King hits his second grand slam of the season and the Atlanta Braves hang on to beat Los Angeles 4–3.

September 11—Eight days after being recalled from the minors by the Oakland A's, lefty Vida Blue hurls a one-hit 8–0 shutout against the Royals.

September 21—Ten days after his one-hitter against Kansas City, Vida Blue no-hits the Minnesota Twins, fanning nine and winning 6–0.

1971

There is little question that a league has produced a weak rookie crop when a batter with only 82 hits and lackluster power numbers finishes third in ROY voting.

That was case for the AL in 1971 when Angel Mangual batted .286 with four home runs in 94 games. The Oakland A's outfielder trailed only Cleveland first baseman Chris Chambliss and Milwaukee right-hander Bill Parsons in his loop's freshman-of-the-year balloting. Chambliss paced junior circuit recruits with nine home runs and hit .275. Parsons won 13 games and threw 244⅔ innings to set a Brewers' frosh record, but also lost 17 times, setting a second club rookie standard. In addition, Parsons tossed four shutouts to join with Jim Slaton, another Suds City rookie righty in 1971, to establish yet a third Brewers' freshman mark.

MOST SHUTOUTS BY MILWAUKEE BREWERS ROOKIE (1970–2003)

4, Bill Parsons, 1971
4, Jim Slaton, 1971
3, Jerry Augustine, 1976
3, Juan Nieves, 1986
2, Kevin Kobel, 1974
2, Andy Replogle, 1978
2, Ted Higuera, 1985

Slaton won ten times, giving the rookie duo one-third of the last-place club's 69 wins. Steve Arlin of San Diego matched the Brewsome twosome in shutouts but won just five additional games the rest of the season. He did, however, pace rookies with 156 strikeouts. The freshman victory leaders in the NL were Reggie Cleveland, Ernie McAnally, and Ross Grimsley, who won 12, 11, and ten, respectively. Cleveland was a .500 pitcher for St. Louis despite his 4.01 ERA, which was more than a half run higher than the loop norm. Montreal's McAnally was only a tad better at 3.90 but duplicated Cleveland's two shutouts. Grimsley went 10–7 with three whitewashes for Cincinnati, as the Reds suffered their only sub-.500 campaign from 1967 through 1981.

But future help for the Reds arrived with the May 29 acquisition of George Foster from San Francisco. The outfielder hit ten home runs in 104 games after the trade, giving him 13 for the season. His booming bat would play a key part in the success of the Big Red Machine beginning the following year. In 1971 Foster was third among rookies in circuit shots—a distant third, to be sure, as Earl Williams and Willie Montanez became the

In 1971 the Braves rotated Earl Williams at three different positions—third base, catcher, and first base—before finally deciding catching was what he did best. That decision might have been a mistake. Williams's defensive skills as a catcher were inadequate, causing the position to distract him from his hitting. After clouting 83 dongs in his first three seasons, including a personal high of 33 as a rookie, Williams finished his career four years later with just 138. *Transcendental Graphics*

only pair of NL freshmen each to reach the seats at least 30 times in the same season. Williams had five multi-homer games for Atlanta, one coming on April 17 in a Braves' win at Philadelphia. Primarily a catcher in 1971, Williams also saw plenty of action at the hot corner and first base. He totaled 33 round trippers and amassed 87 RBI as the first Brave ROY since Sam Jethroe in 1950 when the franchise was still based in Boston.

Montanez, an outfielder, had been reluctantly turned over to Philadelphia the previous year by the St. Louis Cardinals as a replacement for Curt Flood after Flood set into motion the chain of events that would result in free agency when he refused to report to the Phillies following a trade between the two teams. The 23-year-old Montanez hit just .255 but powered 30 long balls and drove in 99 runs, fifth most in the league. On September

13 at St. Louis, Montanez tied the game 5–5 with a two-run circuit clout in the seventh and then hit a solo shot in the tenth, capping a five-hit day and providing the Phillies a 6–5 lead and win. Montanez led all rookies with 153 safeties and 67 bases on balls and was runner-up in the NL ROY derby.

Six recruit shortstops played at least 100 games in 1971, five of them members of NL West clubs. Future managers Toby Harrah and Bobby Valentine played for Washington and Los Angeles, respectively, with the former being the sole AL freshman among the sextet. Ironically all of the six hit below .250 with Valentine leading the way at .249. Harrah clocked in at .230 while Marty Perez batted just .227 for Atlanta and Houston's Roger Metzger stroked .235, although Metzger did tie his double-play partner, veteran Joe Morgan, for the NL lead in triples with 11. Chris Speier of division-winning San Francisco matched Metzger's average, but his slick defensive play considerably aided the Giants' cause during the regular season. Then in the postseason Speier batted .357 and scored four times in a four-game NLCS loss to the Pittsburgh Pirates. Enzo Hernandez's .222 BA brought up the rear among the sextet, but the San Diego Padres new shortfielder's main claim to fame was the fact that he somehow contrived to drive in a record-low 12 runs in 549 at bats.

FEWEST RBI BY ROOKIE WITH 500+ ABs

12 RBI/549 AB, Enzo Hernandez, 1971 SD NL
19 RBI/591 AB, Morrie Rath, 1912 Chi AL
20 RBI/530 AB, Greasy Neale, 1916 Cin NL
25 RBI/596 AB, Sonny Jackson, 1966 Hou NL
26 RBI (Four tied)*

---

*One of the four tied at 26 was Metzger, who had 562 ABs in 1971

Pirates recruit Bruce Kison faced Speier's Giants in the postseason, winning the decisive fourth game with 4⅔ innings of scoreless relief. Kison entered Game Four of the World Series with two outs in the first inning and yielded just one Baltimore hit in 6⅓ frames, allowing no runs and earning the victory as the Pirates knotted the series at two games apiece. Pittsburgh won the Fall Classic in seven games, proving that it was the senior circuit's year for producing both the most quality newcomers and the best overall team.

Nearly a third of Steve Arlin's 34 career wins were shutouts. Every one of Arlin's 11 whitewash efforts came in the uniform of a last-place team as his career with San Diego almost exactly spanned the Padres' record six straight last-place finishes in the NL West from 1969 through 1974. In 1971, Arlin's official rookie season, he lost 19 games. When he dropped 21 decisions the following year, he became the last pitcher to date to collect 40 losses over a two-year period. Only four other hurlers have suffered Arlin's fate since 1933–34 when both Si Johnson and Paul Derringer tasted defeat some 40 times.

PITCHERS WITH 40 OR MORE LOSSES IN TWO-YEAR PERIOD, POST-1934

Pitcher	Years	Losses
Steve Arlin	1971–72	40
Jack Fisher	1964–65	41
Roger Craig	1962–63	46
Robin Roberts	1956–57	40
Murray Dickson	1952–53	40

Other Highlights

June 20—Steve Stone fans 11 Padres, allowing San Diego just three hits, as he and the San Francisco Giants win the second game 2–0.

July 9—In his first ML game, Braves shortstop Leo Foster boots his first chance in the field, then hits into a double play in the fifth inning and follows by hitting into a triple play in the seventh inning.

July 23—Bruce Kison fires a two-hitter at San Diego for Pittsburgh, striking out nine and winning 4–0.

August 1—In his second ML game with the Giants, Dave Kingman slugs a grand slam against the Pirates; the following day Kingman will hit two more dongs in a 5–4 loss to the Dodgers.

August 24—In his first ML start, Padres righty Ed Acosta blanks the Phillies 2–0; it will be the only shutout of Acosta's brief three-year career.

September 5—Astros fireballer J. R. Richard ties the record for the most Ks by a pitcher in his ML debut when he blows away 15 Giants in winning 5–3.

Batting	Pitching
G—AL 128, Steve Braun, MIN	W—AL 13, Bill Parsons, MIL
NL 158, Willie Montanez, PHI	NL 12, Reggie Cleveland, STL
AB—AL 483, Doug Griffin, BOS	L—AL 17, Bill Parsons, MIL
NL 601, Chris Speier, SF	**NL 19, Steve Arlin, SD**
H—AL 118, Doug Griffin, BOS	PCT—AL .433, Bill Parsons, MIL
NL 153, Willie Montanez, PHI	NL .588, Ross Grimsley, CIN
2B—AL 23, Doug Griffin, BOS	GP—AL 57, Denny Riddleberger, WAS
NL 27, Willie Montanez, PHI	NL 59, Al Severinsen, SD
3B—AL 4, Chris Chambliss, CLE	GS—AL 35, Bill Parsons, MIL
NL 11, Roger Metzger, HOU	NL 34, Steve Arlin, SD
HR—AL 9, Chris Chambliss, CLE	Reggie Cleveland, STL
NL 33, Earl Williams, ATL	CG—AL 12, Bill Parsons, MIL
R—AL 51, Steve Braun, MIN	NL 10, Steve Arlin, SD
Doug Griffin, BOS	Reggie Cleveland, STL
NL 78, Willie Montanez, PHI	IP—AL 244.2, Bill Parsons, MIL
RBI—AL 48, Chris Chambliss, CLE	NL 227.2, Steve Arlin, SD
NL 99, Willie Montanez, PHI	H—AL 219, Bill Parsons, MIL
WK—AL 48, Steve Braun, MIN	NL 238, Reggie Cleveland, STL
NL 67, Willie Montanez, PHI	BB—AL 93, Bill Parsons, MIL
SO—AL 83, Chris Chambliss, CLE	NL 103, Steve Arlin, SD
NL 120, George Foster, SF/CIN	K—AL 139, Bill Parsons, MIL
SB—AL 13, Mickey Rivers, CAL	NL 156, Steve Arlin, SD
NL 21, Enzo Hernandez, SD	ERA—AL 3.20, Bill Parsons, MIL
BA—AL .275, Chris Chambliss, CLE	NL 2.53, Ken Forsch, HOU
NL .260, Earl Williams, ATL	SHO—AL 4, Bill Parsons, MIL
SLG—AL .407, Chris Chambliss, CLE	Jim Slaton, MIL
NL .491, Earl Williams, ATL	NL 4, Steve Arlin, SD
OBP—AL .341, Chris Chambliss, CLE	SV—AL 15, Lloyd Allen, CAL
NL .333, Willie Montanez, PHI	NL 8, Al Severinsen, SD

September 15—Larry Yount, brother of Brewers shortstop Robin, is announced as the Astros new relief pitcher against Atlanta but then injures his arm while completing his warm-up tosses and must be removed before he can throw a single pitch in what will be his lone ML appearance.

September 15—Burt Hooton of the Cubs strikes out 15 New York Mets in the second game of a twinbill to pick up his first ML win by a narrow 3–2 margin.

1972

Although the 1972 season will always be remembered as the first to have games lopped off the schedule because of a players' strike, it also produced a host of memorable freshman feats, not the least of which was a rookie leading his league in triples. A rare feat in itself, what made it truly unique was that the leader was a catcher. Boston receiver Carlton Fisk tied for the AL lead with nine three-baggers, becoming the first—and to date only—rookie backstop to pace a major loop in this department.

MOST TRIPLES BY ROOKIE CATCHER, SINCE 1920

9, Johnny Roseboro, 1958 LA NL
9, Carlton Fisk, 1972 Bos AL
8, Bubbles Hargrave, 1921 Cin NL
8, Merritt Ranew, 1962 Hou NL
7, Tim McCarver, 1963 StL NL

Fisk, who had 15 home runs at the All-Star break, singled and scored in the eighth inning of the July 25

Midsummer Classic, but the NL won 4–3 in ten innings. The BoSox backstop ended with 22 circuit shots and 28 doubles, giving him 59 extra-base hits, the second most ever for a rookie receiver. He hit .293 and slugged .538, second best in the junior circuit, and also provided a brand of leadership not commonly offered by a rookie. Everyone's choice for ROY, Fisk added another accolade when he finished fourth in MVP balloting.

Two other rookies, pitchers Lynn McGlothen and John Curtis, also helped to keep Boston in the AL East race. McGlothen went 8–7 while the southpaw Curtis was 11–8 with three shutouts, as the Red Sox finished a mere half game behind Detroit in the strike-shortened season.

Another recruit left-hander, Jon Matlack, sparked the New York Mets in the early going. Matlack was 6–0 through June 1 as the Queens nine raced to a 30–11 start. Neither the pitcher nor his club could maintain that sizzling pace; the Mets ultimately finished third while Matlack went just 9–10 the rest of the way, although he did toss three of his four shutouts after July 11. The 22-year-old southpaw was fourth in the NL with a 2.32 ERA and became the second Mets hurler to be named NL ROY.

The Chicago Cubs finished a rung higher on the NL East ladder after slipping two rookies into the starting rotation. Knuckle-curveballer Burt Hooton, who had dazzled in a brief trial the previous year, got the 1972 campaign off to a sensational start by no-hitting the Philadelphia Phillies on a dreary mid-April day at Wrigley Field. He walked seven but completed the 4–0 whitewash by fanning Greg Luzinski, the Phillies rookie who would slug 18 home runs in 1972. Hooton won another ten games, including two additional shutouts. On September 16 Hooton's bat complemented his arm when he slugged a third-inning grand slam off Tom Seaver, beating the Mets 18–5. The second new member of the Cubs rotation, Rick Reuschel, chipped in ten wins, four of them shutouts, and posted a 2.93 ERA.

Two other newcomers who would be Reuschel's teammates on the Cubs by the late 1970s—Dick Tidrow and Dave Kingman—both had solid novice campaigns. Tidrow won 14 games and posted a 2.77 ERA for Cleveland. In five starts from July 15 through August 4, he went 4–0 with three shutouts, surrendering just three earned runs in 41⅓ innings. Kingman,

who played third, first, and the outfield for San Francisco, survived a .225 BA to remain in the regular lineup by blasting 29 home runs and collecting 83 RBI. On April 16 he hit for the cycle and knocked in six runs in a 10–6 win at Houston. The giant Giant even stole 16 bases, three more than Garry Maddox, the team's fleet center fielder who beat out 26 doubles and hit 12 round trippers. Owning their strongest rookie crop since 1958, the Giants also introduced Dave Rader, who caught 127 games and finished second to Matlack for ROY honors, and two novice hurlers of considerable merit. One, righty Jim Barr, tossed a two-hit shutout on August 23, retiring the last 21 Pittsburgh hitters. Six days later, when Barr was perfect for 6⅔ innings at St.

In 1972 Carlton Fisk was the first AL ROY to be a unanimous selection. Fisk's award was richly deserved as he set a new SA record for rookie catchers that still stands as the AL mark. Subsequent to 1972, OPS, a new stat combining SA and OBP, was invented, and it was retrospectively discovered that Fisk had set a second, equally important mark for yearling catchers. Mike Piazza topped both of Fisk's record-setting figures in 1993, but the BoSox receiver's .909 OPS still remains the AL standard.

Although Fisk unquestionably had the best all-around season of any rookie catcher in the 1961–76 era, he had plenty of competition. In ML history there have been a total of ten rookie catchers who produced an .800 OPS with at least 400 at bats. Significantly, even though the 1960s and early 1970s were one of the most pitcher-dominant periods ever, five of the ten highest OPS figures produced by rookie catchers occurred in that short span. In addition, Joe Torre (1961) and Johnny Bench (1968) also generated OPS figures that rank among the top 15.

ROOKIE CATCHERS WITH .800 OPS (MINIMUM 400 ABs)

Rank	Name	Team	Year	BA	SA	OPS
1	Mike Piazza	LA-NL	1993	.318	.561	.935
2	Carlton Fisk	Bos-AL	1972	.293	.538	.909
3	Matt Nokes	Det-AL	1987	.289	.536	.882
4	Butch Henline	Phi-NL	1922	.316	.479	.859
5	Joe Ferguson	LA-NL	1973	.263	.470	.846
6	Mickey Cochrane	Phi-AL	1925	.331	.448	.845
7	Bill Dickey	NY-AL	1929	.324	.485	.832
8	Ray Fosse	Cle-AL	1970	.307	.469	.832
9	Earl Williams	Atl-NL	1971	.260	.491	.817
10	Thurman Munson	NY-AL	1970	.302	.415	.804

Batting		Pitching	
G—	AL 145, Bobby Darwin, MIN	W—	AL 14, Dick Tidrow, CLE
	NL 150, Greg Luzinski, PHI		NL 15, Jon Matlack, NY
AB—	AL 527, Jack Brohamer, CLE	L—	AL 15, Dick Tidrow, CLE
	NL 563, Greg Luzinski, PHI		NL 16, Bill Greif, SD
H—	AL 137, Bobby Darwin, MIN	PCT—	AL .483, Dick Tidrow, CLE
	NL 158, Greg Luzinski, PHI		NL .600, Jon Matlack, NY
2B—	AL 28, Carlton Fisk, BOS	GP—	AL 61, Chuck Seelbach, DET
	NL 33, Greg Luzinski, PHI		NL 49, Wayne Twitchell, PHI
3B—	**AL 9, Carlton Fisk, BOS**	GS—	AL 34, Dick Tidrow, CLE
	NL 7, Garry Maddox, SF		NL 32, Jon Matlack, NY
HR—	AL 22, Bobby Darwin, MIN	CG—	AL 10, Dick Tidrow, CLE
	Carlton Fisk, BOS		NL 9, Burt Hooton, CHI
	NL 29, Dave Kingman, SF	IP—	AL 237.1, Dick Tidrow, CLE
R—	AL 74, Carlton Fisk, BOS		NL 244.0, Jon Matlack, NY
	NL 66, Greg Luzinski, PHI	H—	AL 200, Dick Tidrow, CLE
RBI—	AL 80, Bobby Darwin, MIN		NL 215, Jon Matlack, NY
	NL 83, Dave Kingman, SF	BB—	AL 73, Don Stanhouse, TEX
WK—	AL 53, Bobby Grich, BAL		NL 81, Burt Hooton, CHI
	NL 56, Tom Hutton, PHI	K—	AL 123, Dick Tidrow, CLE
SO—	**AL 145, Bobby Darwin, MIN**		NL 169, Jon Matlack, NY
	NL 140, Dave Kingman, SF	ERA—	AL 2.77, Dick Tidrow, CLE
SB—	AL 24, Don Baylor, BAL		NL 2.32, Jon Matlack, NY
	NL 16, Dave Kingman, SF	SHO—	AL 3, John Curtis, BOS
BA—	AL .293, Carlton Fisk, BOS		Dick Tidrow, CLE
	NL .281, Greg Luzinski, PHI		NL 4, Jon Matlack, NY
SLG—	AL .538, Carlton Fisk, BOS		Rick Reuschel, CHI
	NL .462, Dave Kingman, SF	SV—	AL 14, Chuck Seelbach, DET
OBP—	AL .370, Carlton Fisk, BOS		NL 4, Randy Moffitt, SF
	NL .334, Greg Luzinski, PHI		Mac Scarce, PHI

Louis, he set a new ML record by retiring 41 batters in a row, with Kingman's three-run double in the ninth giving him a 3–0 win. Barr may have been the club's "Jim-dandy" but another recruit Jim, Willoughby, wasn't far behind, going 6–4 with a 2.36 ERA in 11 starts.

Upon joining the Phils in 1975, Garry Maddox became a perennial Gold Glove recipient, as would fellow 1972 freshmen Buddy Bell and Bobby Grich. Bell, after debuting with the Indians in 1972 as an outfielder, matured into the AL's premier third baseman in the early 1980s while Baltimore's Grich would take home four second-base fielding awards beginning the following season. On April 22 Bell drove in five runs against Grich's Orioles and later had two consecutive four-hit games in mid-August. Grich, who played shortstop for most of his rookie campaign, compiled a fine .777 OPS

to lead all shortfielders in both leagues in 1972, but his Orioles nonetheless sat out the postseason after three straight World Series appearances.

Other Highlights

April 19—Pitcher-turned-outfielder Bobby Darwin homers and drives in five Minnesota runs as the Twins win at California 12–3.

May 24—Angels pitcher Don Rose homers in his first ML at bat and then proceeds to nip the A's 6–5 for what will be both his only homer and his only win in the bigs.

July 20—Bill Slayback of Detroit pitches his third consecutive complete game, fanning 13 in beating Texas 5–1.

August 23—Montreal's Balor Moore strikes out 13 in a four-hit shutout, beating Cincinnati 11–0.

September 2—Dave Downs of Philadelphia fires a shutout in his ML debut for the Phillies, who win the nightcap of a twinbill at Atlanta 3–0.

September 8—John Milner gets five hits, including a double and homer, for the New York Mets in an 8–2 win over St. Louis.

September 16—Balor Moore has his scoreless string of innings ended at 25 when Phils frosh Mike Schmidt hits a three-run shot in the seventh inning to stick Moore with a 3–1 loss; the homer is Schmidt's first of what will eventually be 548.

September 19—Jorge Orta homers with one out in the top of the 15th inning, giving the Chicago White Sox an 8–7 victory at Oakland.

October 3—Orioles rookie Roric Harrison goes deep against Cleveland in the second game of a double-header; with the coming of the DH rule in 1973, Harrison's blow will be the last four-bagger by an AL pitcher until interleague play begins in 1997.

1973

From 1960 through 1984 the Baltimore Orioles were the winningest team in baseball, with their remarkably fertile farm system and their manager, Earl Weaver, perhaps their two biggest assets. The 1973 season saw the Birds win the AL East, thanks in large part to a pair of speedy rookie outfielders who each hit well over .300. Going into June, Baltimore's offense was slumping and the team was below .500, but freshmen Al Bumbry and Rich Coggins were about to see their averages skyrocket as they each became part of a Weaver platoon. The duo was especially hot starting in mid-August when the Orioles launched a 14-game winning streak. Bumbry, who had a five-hit game at Milwaukee June 25, hit three triples on September 22 as Baltimore clinched the division title, also at the Brewers' County Stadium. In the ALCS, Bumbry was hitless in seven at bats, but Coggins went 4-for-9 as the Orioles lost to the Oakland Athletics 3–2 in the best-of-five series.

Bumbry and Coggins each played 110 games, the former batting .337 and tying for the loop lead with 11 triples while Coggins stroked .319 with nine three-baggers, which ranked fourth in the AL. The pair combined to steal 40 bases as Baltimore led the circuit in that department for the first time in ten years. The Orioles fly chasers were two of six freshmen with 300 or more at bats to top .300 in 1973. Pittsburgh's Richie Zisk hit .324 in 103 games and on September 10 had five hits, including a triple, and scored three times as Pittsburgh beat the Chicago Cubs. More difficult than facing big league pitching may have been Zisk's shift from left field to right in early July. The previous New Year's Eve, Pirates' legend Roberto Clemente had perished in a plane crash, leaving a hole in both the team's heart and its lineup. Zisk inherited the position after catcher Manny Sanguillen had been tried there without success in the first part of the season.

Johnny Grubb batted .311 (including .583 as a pinch hitter) for San Diego and Dan Driessen .301 for NL West leader Cincinnati, but Gary Matthews, with an even .300 BA, was the season's rookie hit king. The San Francisco left fielder, who accumulated 162 hits, had an .812 OPS, second only to Bobby Bonds among Giants qualifiers, en route to being Bumbry's counterpart as a ROY winner. Matthews hit 22 doubles, ten triples, and 12 home runs, making him the sole freshman from 1966 through 1983 to reach double figures in each extra-base hit department.

But Matthews was not the only frosh to prosper for the 88-win Giants. Elias Sosa went 10–4 with 18 saves in 71 appearances, all but one out of the bullpen. Sosa was one of four rookies to earn at least ten wins. Doc Medich was 14–9 for the New York Yankees and tied Steve Rogers for the freshman lead in shutouts with three. After beginning the season in the minors and not being called up to the parent Montreal Expos until after the All-Star break, Rogers threw whitewashes in his second and third starts, including a one-hitter on July 26 at Philadelphia. He finished with a magnificent 1.54 ERA in 134 innings, joining Bob Lee in 1964 as the only rookies since 1914 with an ERA less than 1.60 (minimum 100 IP).

Steve Busby won 16 times for Kansas City, striking out 174 batters. He spun a no-hitter at Detroit on April 27, beating the Tigers 3–0 despite allowing six walks. Providing strong relief help for the contending Royals were Doug Bird with 20 saves and Gene Garber with 11. Jim Bibby, who started the season in the NL with St. Louis, joined Busby in the no-hitter club on July 30, when he blew away 13 Oakland batters in his 6–0 win for Texas. Bibby's gem came a month and a day after he had held the Royals to one safety. In addition to seven ten-plus strikeout games, including an August 30 loss when he fanned 15 in 10⅔ innings, Bibby topped the AL in OBA, holding enemy hitters to just a .192 average.

Bob Reynolds, who sported a 1.95 ERA and nine saves for the Orioles, joined Bumbry and Coggins to give Baltimore a triumvirate of productive freshmen, an asset the Los Angeles Dodgers also possessed. Joe Ferguson not only led NL catchers with a .996 fielding percentage but also walked 87 times, the most ever by a rookie back-stop. On September 22 he had four hits, including two of his 25 round trippers, and scored four runs. For the season Ferguson had 88 RBI, eight more than frosh third baseman Ron Cey, who collected ten ribbies in a three-game span in mid-May. The third member of the Dodgers' outstanding rookie trio, second sacker Davey Lopes, swiped 36 bags and scored 77 runs.

Less publicized than the recruit threesomes the contending Orioles and Dodgers displayed, but only slightly less productive, was the triad of hitters new to the Milwaukee Brewers' batting order—catcher Darrell Porter, second baseman Pedro Garcia, and outfielder Bob Coluccio. Porter collected 57 walks, Garcia tied for the AL lead with 32 doubles, and Coluccio ranked fifth with eight triples as all three joined Bumbry and Coggins on the junior circuit leader board.

Other Highlights

June 7—Dave Winfield, a multi-sports star at the University of Minnesota is the first-round pick of the San Diego Padres in the June free-agent draft; Winfield's selection insures that he will become the first college athlete to be taken in the NFL and NBA drafts as well as baseball's amateur draft.

June 27—Twenty-two days after being the first pick in the June free-agent draft, 18-year-old David Clyde, out of Houston's Westchester High School, makes his ML debut with Texas before 35,698, the Rangers' largest crowd of the year, and earns a 4–3 win over the Twins.

June 27—Mike Schmidt hits two home runs and drives in five, giving him 18 RBI in his last dozen games, as the Philadelphia Phillies top the New York Mets 7–1.

July 1—Dick Ruthven pitches a two-hit shutout for Philadelphia, beating St. Louis and Bob Gibson 1–0.

September 9—Charlie Spikes homers twice and knocks in all four Cleveland runs, but the Indians drop the nightcap of a twinbill to Baltimore 13–4.

September 20—Late-season Pirates call-up Dave Augustine hits what appears to be a game-winning homer against the Mets in the 13th inning, but the blast is ruled to have bounced off the top of the wall, and Augustine is credited with only a double; the Mets will proceed to win the game and the NL pennant, and Augustine will never again get an extra-base hit in the majors, let alone a home run.

The 1973 hitting profiles shown below belong to two members of that year's recruit class. One performed for an AL team and the other for an NL team. Neither player received so much as a single vote for his loop's ROY award—and rightfully so—but one of the pair now has a plaque in Cooperstown and the other hit 69 percent of his career home runs in his first two seasons. Could you have predicted that the two would follow such wildly diverse career paths based on their rookie hitting profiles?

Age	G	AB	R	H	2B	3B	HR	RBI	BB	SO	SB	CS	BA	SA	OBP	OPS
22	140	506	68	120	12	3	23	73	45	103	5	3	.237	.407	.306	.715
23	132	367	43	72	11	0	18	52	62	136	8	2	.196	.373	.326	.700

The top profile belongs to Charlie Spikes, owner of the fewest career home runs (65) of any player who compiled at least 20 home runs in each of his first two seasons. Our congratulations if you recognized the bottom profile as belonging to Mike Schmidt, owner of the lowest rookie BA of any future Hall of Famer.

1973 ROOKIE LEADERS

Batting

G—AL 160, Pedro Garcia, MIL
  NL 152, Ron Cey, LA
AB—AL 580, Pedro Garcia, MIL
  NL 540, Gary Matthews, SF
H—AL 142, Pedro Garcia, MIL
  NL 162, Gary Matthews, SF
2B—**AL 32, Pedro Garcia, MIL**
  NL 26, Joe Ferguson, LA
3B—**AL 11, Al Bumbry, BAL**
  NL 10, Gary Matthews, SF
HR—AL 23, Charlie Spikes, CLE
  NL 25, Joe Ferguson, LA
R—AL 73, Al Bumbry, BAL
  NL 84, Joe Ferguson, LA
RBI—AL 73, Charlie Spikes, CLE
  NL 88, Joe Ferguson, LA
WK—AL 57, Darrell Porter, MIL
  NL 87, Joe Ferguson, LA
SO—AL 119, Pedro Garcia, MIL
  NL 136, Mike Schmidt, PHI
SB—AL 23, Al Bumbry, BAL
  NL 36, Davey Lopes, LA
BA—AL .245, Pedro Garcia, MIL
  NL .300, Gary Matthews, SF
SLG—AL .411, Bob Coluccio, MIL
  NL .470, Joe Ferguson, LA
OBP—AL .311, Bob Coluccio, MIL
  NL .376, Joe Ferguson, LA

Pitching

W—AL 16, Steve Busby, KC
  NL 10, Steve Rogers, MON
    Elias Sosa, SF
L—AL 15, Steve Busby, KC
  NL 9, Dick Ruthven, PHI
    Rich Troedson, SD
PCT—AL .516, Steve Busby, KC
  NL No Qualifiers
GP—AL 54, Doug Bird, KC
  NL 71, Elias Sosa, SF
GS—AL 37, Steve Busby, KC
  NL 23, Dick Ruthven, PHI
CG—AL 11, Jim Bibby, TEX
    Doc Medich, NY
  NL 7, Steve Rogers, MON
IP—AL 238.1, Steve Busby, KC
  NL 152.1, Rich Troedson, SD
H—AL 246, Steve Busby, KC
  NL 167, Rich Troedson, SD
BB—AL 106, Jim Bibby, TEX*
  NL 75, Dick Ruthven, PHI
K—AL 174, Steve Busby, KC
  NL 98, Dick Ruthven, PHI
ERA—AL 2.95, Doc Medich, NY
  NL 4.25, Rich Troedson, SD**
SHO—AL 3, Doc Medich, NY
  NL 3, Steve Rogers, MON
SV—AL 20, Doug Bird, KC
  NL 18, Elias Sosa, SF

*Bibby also yielded 17 bases on balls for St. Louis in the National League for a total of 123.
**Troedson worked 152.1 innings, within ten of being a qualifier; Steve Rogers with 134 IP had a glossy 1.54 ERA.

September 26—Don Hood permits just two Detroit safeties as Baltimore wins 4–0.

September 30—September call-up Frank Tanana, who will win 14 games for California in 1974, holds the Minnesota Twins to two hits, fanning nine in his 3–0 victory.

1974

A gross can mean 144, but Greg Gross had far more hits than that as a rookie. In fact, the 185 safeties the Houston Astros outfielder collected led all freshmen in the 1970s—the only decade since 1900–1909 not to witness a rookie topping 200 hits.

MOST HITS BY ROOKIE (1970–1979)

185, Greg Gross, 1974 Hou NL
179, Alfredo Griffin, 1979 Tor AL
175, Fred Lynn, 1975 Bos AL
175, Warren Cromartie, 1977 Mon NL
174, Jim Rice, 1975 Bos AL

Gross, whose hit total actually paced freshmen from 1965 through 1983, collected ten of those knocks over his first three games in 1974 and then kept right on going. He hit .373 in April, reached .380 May 11, and was still above the .350 mark as late as June 23. On August 5 Gross went 5-for-5 in a win at San Francisco before "settling" for a .314 average, third best in the NL.

Greg Gross, the unlikely runner-up for the NL ROY in 1974. That season Gross went homerless in 589 at bats, collected just 36 RBI and was caught stealing 20 times in 32 attempts. Balancing his many negative numbers at least partially, however, were 76 walks and 185 hits. In a 17-year career Gross never again reached such heights in either of those two departments. He also finished with the fewest career homers—just seven—of any outfielder since the close of the Deadball Era with at least 3,500 at bats. *Transcendental Graphics*

Winning his loop's ROY was not among Gross's accomplishments, however, as he lost out to Bake McBride, the swift center fielder of the St. Louis Cardinals. McBride, who stole 30 bases, hit .309 and was just a hit shy from making the above list. In a four-game stretch in mid-September, he had a trio of four-hit games, including September 11, when St. Louis won 4–3, outlasting the New York Mets in 25 innings. But McBride's best game was probably the May 18 contest against the Chicago Cubs. He had two singles, a double, and a home run, scoring three runs and knocking in two as the Cardinals rolled 11–2 at Busch Memorial Stadium.

An ankle injury that forced Bill Madlock onto the disabled list prevented the Cubs third baseman from participating in McBride's highlight-reel day. However, Madlock played enough to qualify for the batting title and finished fifth in the race, only one point behind Gross. The next two seasons Madlock topped the senior circuit and would win four batting crowns in all.

In 1973, before being dealt to the Cubs, Madlock had batted .351 in 21 games for the Texas Rangers, the club with which Mike Hargrove took AL freshman honors in 1974. Hargrove's .323 average and .400 OBP would have ranked second and fourth, respectively, in the junior circuit had he compiled the necessary 25 more plate appearances to be a qualifier. In 131 games the first baseman had 66 RBI but just four home runs in a season that suffered from a dearth of slugging rookies. Just four freshmen hit as many as ten round trippers and, surprisingly, three of them were catchers, with Montreal receiver Barry Foote setting the pace with 11. Cubs first sacker Andre Thornton hit ten while

Here are the hitting profiles of the top three vote getters in the race for the 1974 NL ROY Award. Which of the three would have been your choice? And could you have predicted which of the three would be the only one who would ever be a loop leader in a major offensive department?

Age	G	AB	R	H	2B	3B	HR	RBI	BB	SO	SB	CS	BA	SA	OBP	OPS
25	150	559	81	173	19	5	6	56	43	57	30	11	.309	.394	.372	.766
21	156	589	78	185	21	8	0	36	76	39	12	20	.314	.377	.393	.770
23	128	453	65	142	21	5	9	54	42	39	11	7	.313	.442	.378	.820

In order of their finish in the 1974 vote, the three profiles belong to Bake McBride, Greg Gross, and Bill Madlock. Only Madlock ever garnered black ink, winning four batting titles.

catcher Brian Downing of the crosstown White Sox matched him. Houston backstop Cliff Johnson also pounded ten jacks, but his teammate Greg Gross hit none in 589 at bats, the fourth highest total ever for a rookie who failed to go the distance at least once.

Foote had the pleasure of catching a pair of right-handed rookies who turned in fine seasons. Dennis Blair went 11–7 with a 3.27 ERA and, in the second game of a June 28 twinbill, tossed a two-hitter, beating the Cubs 15–0. Working entirely in relief, Dale Murray saved ten games, won 15, and registered a microscopic 1.03 ERA, the fourth lowest mark ever by a freshman with at least 50 innings.

Another bullpenner, Larry Hardy, broke the then-existing rookie record by pitching in 76 contests and was one of three San Diego Padres freshmen to win

nine games. Starters Dan Spillner and Dave Freisleben joined Hardy in this three-man fraternity. On June 19—nine days before Blair dominated the Cubs—Spillner blanked the Bruins on just one hit, edging Chicago 1–0 at Wrigley Field.

Like Freisleben, who gave up 112 walks, San Francisco's John D'Acquisto was overly generous at issuing free passes. The Giants yearling walked 124 batters but fanned 167 while winning 12 games for the fifth-place team. California flamethrower Frank Tanana showed sharper control, walking 77, less than half his 180 strike-outs. Tanana started 4–13 for the lowly Angels, who finished 16 games behind the next worst team in the AL West, but then won ten games after July 15, ending up 14–19. His 268⅔ innings rank third all-time among AL freshman southpaws.

1974 ROOKIE LEADERS

Batting		Pitching	
G—	AL 154, Bucky Dent, CHI	W—	AL 14, Frank Tanana, CAL
	NL 156, Greg Gross, HOU		NL 12, John D'Acquisto, SF
AB—	AL 496, Bucky Dent, CHI	L—	AL 19, Frank Tanana, CAL
	NL 589, Greg Gross, HOU		NL 14, John D'Acquisto, SF
H—	AL 136, Bucky Dent, CHI		Dave Freisleben, SD
	NL 185, Greg Gross, HOU	PCT—	AL .424, Frank Tanana, CAL
2B—	AL 22, Rick Burleson, BOS		NL .462, John D'Acquisto, SF
	NL 23, Barry Foote, MON	GP—	AL 55, Tom Buskey, NY/CLE
3B—	AL 6, Mike Hargrove, TEX		NL 76, Larry Hardy, SD
	NL 8, Greg Gross, HOU	GS—	AL 35, Frank Tanana, CAL
HR—	AL 10, Brian Downing, CHI		NL 36, John D'Acquisto, SF
	NL 11, Barry Foote, MON	CG—	AL 12, Frank Tanana, CAL
R—	AL 57, Mike Hargrove, TEX		NL 6, Dave Freisleben, SD
	NL 81, Bake McBride, STL	IP—	AL 268.2, Frank Tanana, CAL
RBI—	AL 66, Mike Hargrove, TEX		NL 215.0, John D'Acquisto, SF
	NL 60, Barry Foote, MON	H—	AL 262, Frank Tanana, CAL
WK—	AL 62, Jim Sundberg, TEX		NL 194, Dave Freisleben, SD
	NL 76, Greg Gross, HOU	BB—	AL 80, Vic Albury, MIN
SO—	AL 72, Brian Downing, CHI		NL 124, John D'Acquisto, SF
	NL 74, Barry Foote, MON	K—	AL 180, Frank Tanana, CAL
SB—	AL 29, Herb Washington, OAK		NL 167, John D'Acquisto, SF
	NL 30, Bake McBride, STL	ERA—	AL 3.12, Frank Tanana, CAL
BA—	AL .323, Mike Hargrove, TEX		NL 3.66, Dave Freisleben, SD
	NL .314, Greg Gross, HOU	SHO—	AL 4, Frank Tanana, CAL
SLG—	AL .424, Mike Hargrove, TEX		NL 2, Bob Forsch, STL
	NL .442, Bill Madlock, CHI		Dave Freisleben, SD
OBP—	AL .400, Mike Hargrove, TEX		Dan Spillner, SD
	NL .393, Greg Gross, HOU	SV—	AL 18, Tom Buskey, NY/CLE
			NL 10, Dale Murray, MON
			Oscar Zamora, CHI

MOST IP BY AL ROOKIE LEFT-HANDER

316.2, Reb Russell, 1913 Chi AL
288.2, Ed Siever, 1901 Det AL
268.2, Frank Tanana, 1974 Cal AL
262.0, Watty Lee, 1901 Was AL
260.2, Eddie Plank, 1901 Phi AL

Other Highlights

August 9—George Brett hits three doubles and a single and scores twice for the Kansas City Royals, who beat Milwaukee 13–3.

August 27—Benny Ayala of the New York Mets homers in his first ML at bat in a 4–2 win against the Houston Astros.

September 1—Reggie Sanders, in his initial time up in the bigs, goes deep against Catfish Hunter, who will win the 1974 AL Cy Young Award, but Sanders's Detroit Tigers lose to Oakland 5–3.

September 3—In his ML debut Giants hurler John Montefusco homers in his first at bat and then pitches nine innings in relief to earn a 9–5 win over the Dodgers.

1975

Red Sox fans have witnessed many excellent rookies perform for their Hub City entry. But in 1975 the Fenway faithful were doubly blessed. Centerfielder Fred Lynn and leftfielder/designated hitter Jim Rice formed perhaps the most lethal rookie duo in baseball history. When spring training began, either Juan Beniquez or Rick Miller was expected to play center for Boston, but on Opening Day it was Lynn in the middle of the BoSox pasture. Batting second, Lynn went 0-for-4 against Milwaukee in Hank Aaron's first American League game. He then hit leadoff before settling into the fourth hole. On April 16 Lynn went 3-for-4 with his first two home runs of the season. Not to be outdone, Rice hit his first pair of round trippers two days later against Baltimore.

While producing similar results, the tandem came from very different backgrounds. Rice, Boston's first-round pick out of high school in the 1971 draft, was *The Sporting News* Minor League Player of the Year in 1974. He became the first hitter to win the International League Triple Crown in 15 years when he hit .337 with 25 homers and 93 RBI for Pawtucket. The New York Yankees picked Lynn in the third round in 1970, but he opted to play for Rod Dedeaux at the University of Southern California. Dedeaux hammered home the game's fundamentals, which was evident by Lynn's play early in 1975. Besides his offensive output, Lynn played superb defense. He always hit the cutoff man and also impressed by backing up pickoff throws to second base. Boston suffered a rash of injuries early on, including Carlton Fisk's broken hand, so Lynn's fast start was extremely important. In the first dozen games, Lynn hit .429 with 13 RBI.

Two games best illustrated Lynn's all-around brilliance. On June 18 he destroyed the Detroit Tigers when he hit three homers, a triple, and an infield single, good for a rookie record 16 total bases and ten RBI. The latter figure equaled Norm Zauchin's 1955 single-game freshman mark. Then Lynn used his legs and glove on July 27 to help the Red Sox hold on to beat the Yankees when he made a terrific long running catch of Graig Nettles's potential triple in the ninth inning.

Rice, who had a mediocre spring training, made the Opening Day roster but was the DH the first few months. When Cecil Cooper forced himself into the everyday lineup, Rice shifted to left field. While Rice may not have been in Lynn's class, he provided solid defense and worked hard on improving his game. On July 23 Rice twice robbed Minnesota's Glenn Borgmann with leaping catches in preserving Boston's 4–2 win. On the season Rice didn't commit a single error. Late in the campaign he was receiving serious MVP consideration when his year ended abruptly. On September 21 a Vern Ruhle pitch struck Rice, breaking the fourth metacarpal of the slugger's left hand.

Rice's absence did not adversely affect Boston in the ALCS partly because Lynn hit .364 in Boston's three-game sweep of the Oakland A's. In the World Series against the Cincinnati Reds, however, Rice's bat could have made the difference for the Red Sox as three Cincinnati wins were by one run. Lynn did his part, going 7-for-25 with a homer, a double, and 5 RBI, but

ROOKIE TEAMMATES WITH 100 OR MORE RBI

1938 Cleveland Indians
Ken Keltner (113) Jeff Heath (112)
1950 Cleveland Indians
Al Rosen (116) Luke Easter (107)
1975 Boston Red Sox
Fred Lynn (105) Jim Rice (102)

The Pittsburgh Pirates had their backs against the wall in October 1975. They trailed two games to none in the best-of-five NLCS versus the Cincinnati Reds. The Pirates turned to 21-year-old southpaw John Candelaria to prolong their season. Candelaria began the year at Charleston in the International League, posting a 7–1 record and 1.78 ERA. He lost his big league debut on June 8 to the San Francisco Giants but garnered his first win 12 days later against the Mets. Many of the Brooklyn-born hurler's relatives witnessed the victory at Shea Stadium. In the next three weeks, Candelaria won three more games, including a four-hit shutout of the San Diego Padres. On September 16 he threw seven scoreless innings in a 22–0 pasting of the Cubs at Wrigley Field. Candelaria scored a run and drove in two others in the most lopsided blanking in the twentieth century.

Game Three of the NLCS, however, was a much tighter contest. Through seven innings Candelaria yielded only one hit—a solo home run by Reds shortstop Dave Concepcion in the second. Pittsburgh scored twice in the sixth and needed only six more outs when Candelaria took the mound in the eighth. A two-out walk to Merv Rettenmund preceded Pete Rose's go-ahead two-run homer. A double by Joe Morgan chased the young lefty, who got a no-decision. Cincinnati won in ten innings and met the Boston Red Sox in the World Series. Candelaria fanned 14 batters, still one of the highest postseason totals by a freshman.

MOST STRIKEOUTS BY ROOKIE IN POSTSEASON GAME

15 Livan Hernandez (Fla NL) 10/12/1997 NLCS
14 John Candelaria (Pit NL) 10/7/1975 NLCS
14 Mike Boddicker (Bal AL) 10/6/1983 ALCS
11 Don Newcombe (Bro NL) 10/5/1949 WS
10 Dave Righetti (NY AL) 10/8/1981 ALDS
10 Tim Belcher (LA NL) 10/5/1988 NL

the Reds prevailed in one of the most dramatic Fall Classics ever.

Despite having the season end on a downer, Rice and Lynn had much to show for their play. Lynn became the first rookie to win an MVP Award and also copped a Gold Glove, joining Tommie Agee of the 1966 Chicago White Sox as the only freshman fly chasers so honored (Ichiro Suzuki later joined this elite club in 2001). Rice finished third in MVP balloting, and the tandem became just the third rookie teammates with at least 100 RBI.

One brash right-handed rookie established himself as a legitimate staff ace in 1975. John Montefusco played the final month of the 1974 season with the San Francisco Giants, just long enough to let Bay Area fans know he was as talented as he was confident. The rookie right-hander quickly established himself as the Giants staff ace in 1975 when he blanked Atlanta in his first start and followed by tossing three more whitewashes to lead all freshmen. On May 27 Montefusco battled fellow recruit Tom Underwood in Philadelphia. The Giants scored the game's only run in the top of the tenth and won when Montefusco continued his shutout mastery in the frame's bottom half. In late August, opposing the Montreal Expos, Montefusco fanned 14 hitters, giving him one of a senior circuit's seven best double-digit strikeout performances in 1975. On the year he whiffed 215 batters—the eighth highest freshman total since 1893, when the current pitching distance was established. Montefusco finished fourth in the NL Cy Young race, and his 15 wins topped the San Francisco staff. He was only the sixth Giants rookie to lead the club in victories.

200 OR MORE STRIKEOUTS BY ROOKIE SINCE 1893

276 Dwight Gooden 1984 NY NL
245 Herb Score 1955 Cle AL
236 Hideo Nomo 1995 LA NL
233 Kerry Wood 1998 Chi NL
227 Pete Alexander 1911 Phi NL
225 Tom Hughes 1901 Chi NL
221 Christy Mathewson 1901 NY NL
215 John Montefusco 1975 SF NL
209 Russ Ford 1910 NY AL
209 Don Sutton 1966 LA NL
206 Bob Johnson 1970 KC AL
206 Gary Nolan 1967 Cin NL
204 Mark Langston 1984 Sea AL
200 Tom Griffin 1969 Hou NL

In the 1961–76 era the Cincinnati Reds were the only team that generated as many as three rookie starters who won in double figures as freshmen and then flamed out before they were able to achieve 50 career victories. The Reds had equally poor luck with their bullpenners. In 1975 Reds rookie right-hander Rawly Eastwick tied Al Hrabosky for the NL lead in saves with 22. The following year Eastwick was the solo NL save leader with 26 and in the process became the first closer since Gordon Maltzberger in 1944 to top his loop in saves in each of his first two seasons.

Eastwick compiled just 18 more saves in the remaining five years of his career, but his lefty rookie counterpart with the 1975 Reds, Will McEnaney, had an even shorter stay in the limelight. After tying for fourth in the NL with 15 saves as a frosh, McEnaney slipped to just seven saves in 1976 and departed three years later with a mere 29 career saves.

Other Highlights

April 10—In his ML debut Oakland's Mike Norris blanks the White Sox 9–0.

May 25—Cleveland's Dennis Eckersley tosses a three-hit 6–0 shutout against Oakland in his first ML start.

July 30—Astros reliever Jose Sosa homers in his first ML at bat as Houston tops San Diego 8–4; Sosa will collect just one win in his ML career and only two more hits, neither of them home runs.

August 21—Rookie Cubs reliever Paul Reuschel comes to the aid of his brother Rick and puts the finishing touches on a 7–0 win over the Dodgers, marking the first time in ML history that two brothers have combined to hurl a shutout.

1975 ROOKIE LEADERS

Batting	Pitching
G—**AL 160, Phil Garner, OAK**	W—AL 16, Jim Hughes, MIN
NL 154, Manny Trillo, CHI	NL 15, John Montefusco, SF
AB—AL 569, Jerry Remy, CAL	L—AL 14, Jim Hughes, MIN
NL 545, Manny Trillo, CHI	NL 15, Joe McIntosh, SD
H—AL 175, Fred Lynn, BOS	PCT—AL .682, Dennis Leonard, KC
NL 146, Larry Parrish, MON	NL .625, John Montefusco, SF
2B—**AL 47, Fred Lynn, BOS**	GP—AL 56, Jim Umbarger, TEX
NL 32, Larry Parrish, MON	NL 70, Will McEnaney, CIN
3B—AL 7, Fred Lynn, BOS	GS—AL 34, Jim Hughes, MIN
NL 6, Pete Mackanin, MON	NL 35, Tom Underwood, PHI
HR—AL 22, Jim Rice, BOS	CG—AL 12, Jim Hughes, MIN
NL 17, Gary Carter, MON	NL 10, John Montefusco, SF
R—**AL 103, Fred Lynn, BOS**	IP—AL 249.2, Jim Hughes, MIN
NL 59, Pete Mackanin, MON	NL 243.2, John Montefusco, SF
RBI—AL 105, Fred Lynn, BOS	H—AL 241, Jim Hughes, MIN
NL 70, Manny Trillo, CHI	NL 221, Tom Underwood, PHI
WK—AL 62, Fred Lynn, BOS	BB—AL 127, Jim Hughes, MIN
NL 72, Gary Carter, MON	NL 111, Pete Falcone, SF
SO—AL 122, Jim Rice, BOS	K—AL 152, Dennis Eckersley, CLE
NL 99, Pete Mackanin, MON	NL 215, John Montefusco, SF
SB—AL 34, Jerry Remy, CAL	ERA—AL 2.60, Dennis Eckersley, CLE
NL 12, Rob Andrews, HOU	NL 2.88, John Montefusco, SF
BA—AL .331, Fred Lynn, BOS	SHO—AL 3, Vern Ruhle, DET
NL .274, Larry Parrish, MON	NL 4, John Montefusco, SF
SLG—**AL .566, Fred Lynn, BOS**	SV—AL 8, Tippy Martinez, NY
NL .416, Gary Carter, MON	Dyar Miller, BAL
OBA—AL .405, Fred Lynn, BOS	**NL 22, Rawly Eastwick, CIN**
NL .363, Gary Carter, MON	

September 15—Late-season outfield call-up Mike Vail hits safely in his 23rd consecutive game to tie the then-existing Mets club record as New York tops Montreal 3–1.

1976

It was hardly the kind of beginning that a pitcher with Cy Young Award aspirations would desire. Already more than a month into the season, Mark Fidrych had made only two brief relief appearances, facing a total of six batters. But on May 15, 1976, everything changed as Fidrych, nicknamed "The Bird," got his first ML start. The right-hander tossed a two-hitter to beat Cleveland 2–1. Fidrych lost his next assignment but then won the following eight starts. He took a 9–2 record and 1.78 ERA into the All-Star break and was the AL's starting pitcher in the Midsummer Classic. Fidrych surrendered two runs in two innings and took the loss in the 7–1 NL victory. Three days later, showing no ill effects, he pitched an 11-inning shutout against Oakland. Fidrych finished 19–9 with four shutouts. While his ERA eventually "ballooned" all the way up to 2.34, he still paced the junior circuit. He also led with 24 complete games, four of them requiring him to labor at least 11 innings, an especially high workload for a rookie since the close of the Deadball Era.

MOST COMPLETE GAMES BY ROOKIE (1920–2003)

26, Boo Ferriss, 1945 Bos AL
25, Bill Voiselle, 1944 NY NL
24, Jim Turner, 1937 Bos NL
24, Mark Fidrych, 1976 Det AL
23, Cy Blanton, 1935 Pit NL
23, Lou Fette, 1937 Bos NL
23, Nate Andrews, 1943 Bos NL

The 21-year-old drew fans all across the country not just because of the excellent numbers he posted but also owing to his joyfully nutty behavior, which included standing on the mound prior to each pitch and verbally instructing the ball what to do once it left his hand. The Bird flew away with the AL ROY Award but was runner-up to Baltimore's Jim Palmer in the Cy Young race as the time Fidrych idled in the bullpen in all likelihood cost him another trophy.

The ROY race in the senior circuit was more contentious, if not nearly as entertaining. Cincinnati righty Pat Zachry went 14–7 for the world champion Reds and ranked fifth in the loop with a 2.74 ERA. Zachry worked the first five innings in Game Two of the NLCS versus Philadelphia, yielding two runs. Despite leaving the contest trailing, Zachry got the win after Cincinnati scored four times in the top of the sixth. After the Big Red Machine swept the Phillies in three, they got a new set of brooms out for the New York Yankees in the Fall Classic. In the third game Zachry held the Bronx Bombers to a pair of runs in 6⅔ innings, winning by the same 6–2 margin by which he bested the Phillies. Two days later, Cincinnati repeated as World Series victors and completed a 7–0 postseason run.

Although Santo Alcala wasn't needed by the Reds in fall action, he posted an excellent 11–4 mark during the regular season. Alcala's inauspicious 4.70 ERA removed him from the NL ROY picture, but another pitcher with an 11–4 record contributed to a new chapter in rookie history when he and Zachry wound up in the first dead heat ever in a battle for freshman laurels. Butch Metzger was 1–0 with San Francisco in 1974 and the same in a brief trial with San Diego in 1975. Still a

Rookies who make their marks with their gloves generally draw little attention in ROY balloting, and Chet Lemon was no exception. In 1976 the White Sox' new center fielder finished among the top ten AL outfielders in every major fielding department but came up empty in the annual vote for the AL's best freshman owing largely to his anemic .246 BA.

The following year Lemon hiked his average to .273 and produced perhaps the finest defensive season ever by an AL outfielder. In 1977 the Pale Hose gardener established the junior loop record for putouts with 512 and earned a range factor of 3.52, second at that time only to an earlier-day White Sox center fielder, Thurman Tucker, who clocked a 3.55 figure in 1944.

After his first two seasons, Lemon seemed destined to rank among the top outfield gloves in history. He suffered a severe groin injury, however, in 1978, and though he eventually matured into one of the better-hitting gardeners of his time, he never again approached his spectacular 1977 defensive stats.

member of the Padres, the reliever began the 1976 season 10–0, setting the fireman record for most consecutive wins from the start of a career. Metzger finally lost on August 28 to Montreal. The busiest member of the Padre pen, he made 77 appearances and saved 16 games for the fifth-place club.

While young, Fidrych was not the most junior All-Star in 1976. Minnesota catcher Butch Wynegar, just 20 years old, walked as a pinch hitter his lone time up, an apt result considering that he drew 79 bases on balls in 1976, the most ever by a freshman receiver in the AL. In a sparse season for neophytes looking to make a living with their bats rather than their pitching arms, Wynegar also topped all rookies with 139 hits, ten of them home runs.

Detroit's Jason Thompson, lost in the hoopla surrounding his teammate Fidrych, smashed a rookie-high 17 round trippers in 123 games, albeit on just a .218 batting average. On June 16 the first baseman hit two solo shots in support of his avian fellow Bengal helping him to notch his fifth win. The other main freshman power source was generated in St. Louis, where Hector Cruz led the Cardinals in home runs with 13 but, much like Thompson, was otherwise a disappointment at the plate, hitting just .228 in what would prove to be his only season with enough plate appearances to be a qualifier.

Cruz's career was already on the wane two years later when he briefly roamed the outfield for the Chicago Cubs in Wrigley Field, where he witnessed firsthand the devastating out-pitch employed by Bruce

1976 ROOKIE LEADERS

Batting	Pitching
G—AL 153, Bob Randall, MIN	W—AL 19, Mark Fidrych, DET
NL 151, Hector Cruz, STL	NL 14, Pat Zachry, CIN
AB—AL 534, Butch Wynegar, MIN	L—AL 12, Jerry Augustine, MIL
NL 533, Jerry Royster, ATL	NL 12, Frank LaCorte, ATL
H—AL 139, Butch Wynegar, MIN	PCT—AL .679, Mark Fidrych, DET
NL 132, Jerry Royster, ATL	NL .667, Pat Zachry, CIN
2B—AL 21, Butch Wynegar, MIN	GP—AL 39, Jerry Augustine, MIL
NL 17, Hector Cruz, STL	NL 77, Butch Metzger, SD
3B—AL 10, Tom Poquette, KC	GS—AL 29, Mark Fidrych, DET
NL 5, Jerry Mumphrey, STL	NL 28, Pat Zachry, CIN
Jerry Turner, SD	CG—**AL 24, Mark Fidrych, DET**
Joe Wallis, CHI	NL 9, Joaquin Andujar, HOU
HR—AL 17, Jason Thompson, DET	IP—AL 250.1, Mark Fidrych, DET
NL 13, Hector Cruz, STL	NL 204.0, Pat Zachry, CIN
R—AL 59, Willie Randolph, NY	H—AL 217, Mark Fidrych, DET
NL 65, Jerry Royster, ATL	NL 170, Pat Zachry, CIN
RBI—AL 69, Butch Wynegar, MIN	BB—AL 63, Pete Redfern, MIN
NL 71, Hector Cruz, STL	NL 83, Pat Zachry, CIN
WK—AL 79, Butch Wynegar, MIN	K—AL 97, Mark Fidrych, DET
NL 52, Jerry Royster, ATL	NL 143, Pat Zachry, CIN
SO—AL 72, Jason Thompson, DET	ERA—**AL 2.34, Mark Fidrych, DET**
NL 119, Hector Cruz, STL	NL 2.74, Pat Zachry, CIN
SB—AL 37, Willie Randolph, NY	SHO—AL 4, Mark Fidrych, DET
NL 24, Jerry Royster, ATL	NL 4, Joaquin Andujar, HOU
BA—AL .267, Bob Randall, MIN	SV—AL 4, John Verhoeven, CAL
NL .248, Jerry Royster, ATL	NL 16, Butch Metzger, SD
SLG—AL .363, Butch Wynegar, MIN	
NL .338, Hector Cruz, STL	
OBP—AL .358, Butch Wynegar, MIN	
NL .316, Jerry Royster, ATL	

Sutter, who earned the first ten saves of his brilliant career in 1976. From the very outset of his extraordinary, if all too brief, ML sojourn, Sutter's split-fingered fastball, which had the effect of a pitch rolling off a table at break-neck speed, was his chief weapon in an arsenal that would make him one of the game's premier relievers for the next decade.

Other Highlights

June 6—Joaquin Andujar twirls a two-hitter against the Chicago Cubs in the first game of a twinbill, Houston winning 2–0.

June 15—Tom Poquette scores five runs, tying the Kansas City record, and hits two singles, two doubles, and a homer as the Royals win 21–7 at Detroit.

July 3—Mark Fidrych blanks the Orioles 4–0 for his eighth consecutive win.

August 2—Rick Sawyer of the San Diego Padres fires a shutout in his first ML start at Atlanta, taking the nightcap of a doubleheader 7–0.

August 8—In beating the Astros 4–3, Padres rookie Butch Metzger bags his 12th straight win to start his career, all coming in relief.

1977

Expansion seasons are conducive to offense and 1977 was no exception. The Seattle Mariners and Toronto Blue Jays joined the American League and each featured one of the ten rookies to hit at least ten home runs. (For comparison, just three freshmen cracked double digits in 1976.) Ruppert Jones smashed 24 long balls and provided excellent defense as Seattle's center fielder. He went 0-for-1 as a pinch hitter as the club's first representative in the All-Star Game. Toronto first baseman Doug Ault hit 11 home runs, including a pair on April 7 as the Blue Jays won the first game in team history. In that 9–5 victory against the Chicago White Sox, Jays outfielder Al Woods homered in his first ML at bat when he went deep as a pinch hitter.

Eddie Murray matched Jones as the busiest rookie in 1977, each playing 160 games. Murray, Baltimore's switch-hitting designated hitter, blasted 27 home runs and had 88 RBI. He amassed 173 hits and set a Baltimore frosh record with 611 at bats. On August 3 Murray, the AL ROY, connected from each side of the plate at Oakland—the first of his record-setting 11 such displays.

Oakland also had its fair share of power threats. Left-fielder Mitchell Page had 57 extra-base hits, 21 clearing the fence. On April 13 he homered twice and doubled, driving in six as Oakland beat California 9–3. In addition to bringing new power to the A's lineup, Page also stole 42 bases, including the first 26 consecutively, and was thrown out just five times. Page was fifth in the league with a .407 OBP, thanks to a .307 batting average and 78 walks. He was the first AL freshman since 1962—and just the second subsequent to 1950—to total as many as 75 runs, RBI, and bases on balls. Joining Page on the rebuilding A's were third baseman Wayne Gross, who hit 22 jacks, and future AL home run champ Tony Armas with 13.

Slugging newcomers, though more plentiful in the expansion AL, were also prominent in the senior circuit. Andre Dawson of Montreal took awhile to get his bat untracked but ended up as the NL ROY. Through May 13, the strong-armed center fielder was batting a paltry .225 and would not hit his first home run until five days later. What Dawson really needed, it appeared, was to face his future team, the Chicago Cubs. On June 29 Dawson went 4-for-4 in an Expos' win against the Bruins. Then, in the first game of an Independence Day twinbill, he knocked in five runs in a 19–3 rout at Wrigley Field. The next day Dawson experienced his first multi-homer contest, homering twice with four RBI as Montreal again beat the Cubs. Dawson ended up with 19 circuit shots, 21 steals, and a .282 average that was matched by his rookie teammate, Warren Cromartie. The fleet Montreal left fielder sliced 41 doubles, tying him for third in the league, and collected 175 safeties. Two other noteworthy NL recruits were Jack Clark of San Francisco, who had 13 home runs and 12 stolen bases, and Steve Henderson, who led the New York Mets in RBI with 66 and tied for the club lead in homers with 12.

The Detroit Tigers were the lone club in 1977 to introduce both a meritorious new slugger and a novice hurling ace. Steve Kemp drove in 88 runs and hit 18 round trippers while Dave Rozema paced the Bengals staff with 15 wins. The righty's .682 winning percentage ranked fourth in the loop, right behind fellow rookie Ron Guidry's .696 for the New York Yankees. Guidry tied for the team lead with 16 wins, five of them shutouts, including a two-hitter on August 28 when he fanned eight Texas Rangers. After winning a complete game against the Kansas City Royals in the second ALCS contest, Guidry failed to survive the third inning of Game Five, but New York won nevertheless and advanced to the World Series. With the Yankees already leading Los Angeles two games to one, Guidry beat the Dodgers in Game Four, permitting only four hits in his 4–2 complete game. Three days later the Bronx Bombers were world champions for the first time in 15 years.

Following the 16–7 Guidry and 15–7 Rozema was Dennis Martinez, who was 14–7 for Baltimore. Eight of Martinez's triumphs came in relief, and he also saved four games for the Orioles, who tied Boston for second in the AL East, 2½ games back.

But for every winner there has to be a loser, and the 1977 season was the lone campaign in the past half-century that saw three rookies lose as many as 18 games.

SEASONS WITH THE MOST ROOKIES LOSING 18+ GAMES (1901–2003)

1905	4
1906	3
1909	3
1943	3
1977	3

Rick Langford dropped 19 decisions for Oakland and San Diego's Bob Shirley was on the wrong end 18 times, although he also won a dozen games to lead the Padres in victories. The third beleaguered newcomer was Jerry Garvin, who claimed 18 of Toronto's 107 losses and, in addition, set a still-existing all-time rookie record when he surrendered 33 home runs.

Bob Bailor made the Blue Jays' season a little more palatable, batting a nifty .310 with 154 hits. The San Diego Padres, despite enduring 93 losses of their own, had the first NL rookie tandem with 150 or more hits since 1953. Bill Almon accumulated 160 and Gene Richards 152. In the nightcap of a July 26 doubleheader against Montreal, Richards had six hits, tying the one-

All eyes in the spring of 1977 were focused on the Giants' spring training camp, where unheralded Randy Elliott, who had sat out the previous eighteen months with a string of shoulder and rib injuries, was ripping Cactus League hurlers to the tune of .547 (29-for-53 with an incredible 18 extra base hits) and begging comparison to such earlier-day Arizona spring phenoms as Jim Fridley and Rudy Regalado. So gaudy were Elliott's preseason numbers that the non-roster rookie beat out veterans Gary Thomasson and Darrell Evans for the Giants leftfield post that had been left vacant when Gary Matthews was traded to Atlanta over the winter.

In Elliott's first plate appearance of the regular season, though, he was hit on his weak shoulder by a pitch from the Dodgers' Doug Rau. Then, in his very next at bat, he felt the shoulder pop loose on a swing. When Elliott was still flirting with the .200 mark in May, the Giants' leftfield job went to Thomasson, and Elliott was relegated to pinch-hitting duty, where he was reasonably effective (11-for-31) as opposed to his .213 BA when serving as a regular outfielder. Following the 1977 season, the Giants released Elliott, and he stayed away from the game for the next two years. Then on the eve of spring training in 1980, Elliott decided to spend the night in his van outside of Scottsdale Stadium, the Oakland A's training site at the time, bent on convincing the club's new manager Billy Martin to give him one last shot.

Despite impressing Martin in Cactus League action, Elliott began the 1980 season in the minors when Martin could not convince A's owner Charlie Finley to keep Elliott on the roster. In mid-May, just as he was about to quit the game permanently, Elliott got a call from A's coach Clete Boyer, telling him to join the A's in Kansas City that night. But Elliott's shoulder problem flared up again, holding him to just a .128 BA in 14 games as a DH. Near the end of June, he was let go by the A's. The first-round pick of the Padres in their first-ever amateur draft in 1969, the once-promising Elliott finished his career 11 years later with a lackluster a .215 BA in just 114 games, but with the coming of each spring, his name will forever conjure up a mix of sweet and bitter memories, at least in San Francisco.

game rookie record, but the Padres still lost to the Expos in 15 innings.

Other Highlights

April 7—Al Woods's pinch homer for Toronto in a 9–5 win over the White Sox makes him the first member of a first-year expansion team to go yard on Opening Day in his first ML at bat.

1977 ROOKIE LEADERS

Batting	Pitching
G—AL 160, Ruppert Jones, SEA	W—AL 16, Ron Guidry, NY
Eddie Murray, BAL	NL 12, Bob Shirley, SD
NL 159, Lee Mazzilli, NY	L—**AL 19, Rick Langford, OAK**
AB—AL 611, Eddie Murray, BAL	NL 18, Bob Shirley, SD
NL 620, Warren Cromartie, MON	PCT—AL .696, Ron Guidry, NY
H—AL 173, Eddie Murray, BAL	NL .625, Randy Lerch, PHI
NL 175, Warren Cromartie, MON	GP—AL 68, Bob McClure, MIL
2B—AL 29, Steve Kemp, DET	NL 67, Willie Hernandez, CHI
Eddie Murray, BAL	GS—AL 37, Paul Thormodsgard, MIN
NL 41, Warren Cromartie, MON	NL 35, Bob Shirley, SD
3B—AL 8, Ruppert Jones, SEA	CG—AL 16, Dave Rozema, DET
Mitchell Page, OAK	NL 6, Bob Knepper, SF
NL 11, Bill Almon, SD	IP—AL 244.2, Jerry Garvin, TOR
Gene Richards, SD	NL 214.2, Mark Lemongello, HOU
HR—AL 27, Eddie Murray, BAL	H—AL 247, Jerry Garvin, TOR
NL 19, Andre Dawson, MON	NL 237, Mark Lemongello, HOU
R—AL 87, Bump Wills, TEX	BB—AL 85, Jerry Garvin, TOR
NL 79, Gene Richards, SD	NL 100, Bob Shirley, SD
RBI—AL 88, Steve Kemp, DET	K—AL 176, Ron Guidry, NY
Eddie Murray, BAL	NL 146, Bob Shirley, SD
NL 65, Andre Dawson, MON	ERA—AL 2.82, Ron Guidry, NY
Steve Henderson, NY	NL 3.36, Bob Knepper, SF
WK—AL 86, Wayne Gross, OAK	SHO—AL 5, Ron Guidry, NY
NL 72, Lee Mazzilli, NY	NL 2, Bob Knepper, SF
SO—AL 120, Ruppert Jones, SEA	Paul Moskau, CIN
NL 114, Bill Almon, SD	Bob Owchinko, SD
SB—AL 42, Mitchell Page, OAK	SV—AL 16, Enrique Romo, SEA
NL 56, Gene Richards, SD	NL 13, Dave Campbell, ATL
BA—AL .310, Bob Bailor, TOR	
NL .290, Gene Richards, SD	
SLG—AL .521, Mitchell Page, OAK	
NL .474, Andre Dawson, MON	
OBP—AL .407, Mitchell Page, OAK	
NL .365, Gene Richards, SD	

May 27—Barry Bonnell goes 5-for-5, but Atlanta loses at San Francisco 4–3 in ten innings.

July 1—Joe Zdeb hits two singles, two doubles, and a homer while driving in four runs for the Kansas City Royals, who win 12–2 at Cleveland.

September 5—Bob Owchinko tosses a two-hitter for San Diego, beating Los Angeles 1–0.

September 18—Ted Cox of the Red Sox goes 4-for-4 in his first ML game, a 10–4 win over Baltimore; when Cox gets hits in his first two at bats the following day

against the Yankees, he sets a new ML mark for the most consecutive hits (six) at the start of a career.

1978

Although it took six years to come to fruition, the 1978 Detroit Tigers' rookie crop rewarded the franchise generously. Freshmen Lou Whitaker, Alan Trammell, and Lance Parrish formed the core, and Jack Morris was the ace of the world champion Tigers of 1984. In 1978 second sacker Whitaker hit .285 with seven triples and was named AL ROY. Whitaker had debuted September 9, 1977, the same day that shortstop Trammell also broke in. Subsequently the two would be forever linked as the most prolific pair of keystone teammates in history. Trammell, like his double-play partner, appeared in 139 games in 1978 and batted .268 as Detroit could finish no better than fifth in the tough AL East despite winning 86 times. On July 7 Trammell had five hits and drove in two runs at Texas as the Tigers won 12–7. Parrish, in just 288 at bats, hit 14 home runs, one a grand slam on August 21, when he knocked in six in a Detroit win at Minnesota. In his rookie season Morris was used mainly as a reliever and was just 3–5, offering little hint that he would lead the majors in wins in the 1980s.

While Detroit's "Big Four" would have a fairly lengthy wait before getting their first taste of the postseason, the ambitions of Los Angeles hurler Bob Welch were fulfilled far more quickly. Welch, an Eastern Michigan University product taken in the first round of the 1977 draft, went 5–1 for Albuquerque before debuting for the Dodgers on June 20. He then went 7–4 with three shutouts and a 2.02 ERA. Welch's ERA rose, but only marginally, in the NLCS against Philadelphia. The rookie righty relieved in Game One and earned the victory by limiting the Phillies to one run over the last 4⅓ innings. L.A. dispatched Philadelphia three games to one and faced the New York Yankees in a rematch on the previous year's World Series. The Dodgers won the opener and took a 4–3 lead into the top of the ninth in Game Two. The Yankees, however, had two men on with just one out when Welch was called upon to save the day. After he retired Thurman Munson, Welch had a tense confrontation with Reggie Jackson, striking out the slugger and preserving the victory. Welch, however, lost Game Four as Jackson got his revenge with a key tenth-inning single.

The Yankees, who won the last four games to take the Fall Classic, had beaten Kansas City to get there. The Royals, lacking a reliable fourth starter at the beginning of the 1978 season, received an unexpected bequest from rookie Rich Gale. In crafting a 14–8 campaign in his 30 starts, the righty tossed three shutouts, including a one-hitter on June 13, and allowed just two safeties in his 3–1 win versus Boston on May 15.

Kansas City may have experienced a Gale, but Atlanta got a whirlwind June from Bob Horner. Horner,

The Sporting News college player of the year, was taken first overall out of Arizona State by the Braves on June 6. Ten days later he homered in his first major league game. On August 25 Horner belted two long balls and batted in five runs, but the Braves still lost to St. Louis. In his 89 games Atlanta's prize draftee ripped 23 home runs with 63 RBI, good enough to earn the NL ROY. Rookie first baseman Dale Murphy also pounded 23 round trippers for the Braves, and the Georgia club produced yet a third novice find in 1978 after calling up southpaw Larry McWilliams from their Richmond farm club in mid-July. In his first two starts, both against the New York Mets, McWilliams permitted no runs over 13 innings. He won his initial seven decisions, the third of which came on August 1, when he held Pete Rose hitless in two at bats as the Cincinnati hitter went 0-for-4 to snap his 44-game hitting streak. McWilliams wound up 9–3.

Two hurlers joined Gale atop the frosh leader board with 14 wins: Roger Erickson of Minnesota and Pittsburgh's Don Robinson, the overall rookie winning-percentage leader thanks to his 14–6 effort. Next in line were Steve Comer and John Henry Johnson.

Coming off two straight last-place finishes in the NL West, the Braves had such low expectations in 1978 that they began the campaign with journeyman second sacker Rod Gilbreath at third base. Gilbreath fared so poorly, however, that Atlanta showed no hesitation in throwing its first-round pick in the June free-agent draft, 1978 college player of the year Bob Horner, into the breach even before the ink dried on his signature approving a contract that included a $175,000 signing bonus. The season was already two months old when the Arizona State third sacker debuted on June 16, limiting him to just 89 games. Nevertheless, Horner led all freshmen in home runs and finished second in the NL only to Willie Stargell in HR percent (7.12 to 7.18) among players with at least 350 plate appearances.

Horner's 23 dingers are the most in history among rookies who participated in fewer than 100 games. Second to him with 21 is Kevin Maas (1990) and third with 19 is Adam Dunn (2001). More importantly, Horner's slugging performance prevented the early-season front-runner for the NL ROY Award, shortstop Ozzie Smith of San Diego, from becoming the first freshman in senior loop history to win the top rookie prize primarily on the basis of his glove work.

Texas's Comer went 11–5 with a 2.30 ERA. He tossed a pair of shutouts as did Johnson, an 11-game winner for Oakland.

Though all of these pitchers had fine seasons, none was able to match the wild performance swings that Silvio Martinez produced. After making ten relief appearances in 1977 for the Chicago White Sox, the right-hander was dealt to St. Louis. Converted to a starter, Martinez pitched a no-hitter in the minors on May 26 and four days later fashioned a one-hitter in his first ML start, an 8–2 win versus the Mets. On July 8 he overcame seven walks to fire another one-hitter, this time a shutout against Pittsburgh. Although Martinez later twirled a pair of two-hitters, one being a whitewash, he finished just 9–8 with an uninspiring 3.65 ERA and managed to complete just one other start apart from his four low-hit jewels.

Even more jewels were witnessed by spectators in San Diego, where Ozzie Smith, the Padres new shortstop, was reaching, almost on a daily basis, new heights in infield defensive play. Smith also stole 40 bases and topped rookies with 152 hits, a total that would remain his personal high until his tenth season in the majors.

Other Highlights

June 9—Dennis Lamp tosses a one-hitter for the Chicago Cubs, beating San Diego 5–0.

June 13—Jim Wright limits California to two hits as Boston wins 5–0.

1978 ROOKIE LEADERS

Batting	Pitching
G—AL 152, Dave Revering, OAK	W—AL 14, Roger Erickson, MIN
NL 159, Ozzie Smith, SD	Rich Gale, KC
AB—AL 521, Paul Molitor, MIL	NL 14, Don Robinson, PIT
Dave Revering, OAK	L—AL 15, Matt Keough, OAK
NL 590, Ozzie Smith, SD	NL 15, Dennis Lamp, CHI
H—AL 142, Paul Molitor, MIL	PCT—AL .636, Rich Gale, KC
NL 152, Ozzie Smith, SD	NL .700, Don Robinson, PIT
2B—AL 26, Paul Molitor, MIL	GP—AL 52, Shane Rawley, SEA
NL 17, Bob Horner, ATL	NL 56, Mark Lee, SD
Ozzie Smith, SD	GS—AL 37, Roger Erickson, MIN
3B—AL 7, Lou Whitaker, DET	NL 36, Dennis Lamp, CHI
NL 6, Ozzie Smith, SD	CG—AL 14, Roger Erickson, MIN
HR—AL 16, Dave Revering, OAK	NL 9, Don Robinson, PIT
NL 23, Bob Horner, ATL	IP—AL 265.2, Roger Erickson, MIN
Dale Murphy, ATL	NL 228.1, Don Robinson, PIT
R—AL 73, Paul Molitor, MIL	H—AL 268, Roger Erickson, MIN
NL 69, Ozzie Smith, SD	NL 221, Dennis Lamp, CHI
RBI—AL 58, Lou Whitaker, DET	BB—AL 100, Rich Gale, KC
NL 79, Dale Murphy, ATL	NL 71, Silvio Martinez, STL
WK—AL 61, Lou Whitaker, DET	K—AL 121, Roger Erickson, MIN
NL 47, Ozzie Smith, SD	NL 135, Don Robinson, PIT
SO—AL 84, Clint Hurdle, KC	ERA—AL 3.09, Rich Gale, KC
NL 145, Dale Murphy, ATL	NL 3.30, Dennis Lamp, CHI
SB—AL 46, Willie Wilson, KC	SHO—AL 3, Rich Gale, KC
NL 40, Ozzie Smith, SD	Jim Wright, BOS
BA—AL .294, Carney Lansford, CAL	NL 3, Dennis Lamp, CHI
NL .258, Ozzie Smith, SD	Bob Welch, LA
SLG—AL .415, Dave Revering, OAK	SV—AL 9, Victor Cruz, TOR
NL .394, Dale Murphy, ATL	NL 4, Ed Whitson, PIT
OBP—AL .366, Lou Whitaker, DET	
NL .312, Ozzie Smith, SD	

June 21—Angels second baseman Dave Machemer homers against the Twins in his first ML bat; Machemer will never hit another tater in his brief two-year career.

August 19—Gary Serum two-hits Toronto as Minnesota bests the Blue Jays 5–0.

September 1—En route to a 9–3 win over the White Sox in his ML debut, Orioles right-hander Sammy Stewart sets a new record for a pitcher in his first ML game when he fans seven consecutive batters.

September 4—In his first ML at bat, Dorian Boyland of the Pirates is charged with a strikeout while sitting on the bench when he is replaced by a pinch hitter with a 1–2 count after the Mets change pitchers and the pinch hitter, Rennie Stennett, promptly takes a called third strike.

September 24—Scott Sanderson wins his fourth game of the month for Montreal, a three-hit shutout of Pittsburgh, as he fans nine and wins 4–0.

1979

The Los Angeles Dodgers and New York Yankees had met in the previous two World Series, with the Bronx Bombers taking each in six games. A third straight such matchup seemed a strong possibility in 1979, but neither team even made the postseason. Their absences can hardly be blamed, however, on freshman right-handers Rick Sutcliffe and Ron Davis. Sutcliffe won a team-high 17 games for Los Angeles, who finished third in the NL West. It was the most victories by a Dodgers rookie since Don Newcombe also won 17 in 1949, when the team called Brooklyn home. To find a Dodger frosh with more triumphs, one would need to go all the way back to Dazzy Vance in 1922. Sutcliffe's .630 winning percentage was fourth highest in the league, and his top single-game effort came on September 14 against Cincinnati, the club that eventually dethroned L.A. as division champs, when he turned back the powerful Reds on a three-hit shutout.

Davis saved nine games for the fourth-place Yankees, who suffered a devastating loss with the August 2 death of All-Star catcher Thurman Munson. Davis had

a 2.85 ERA pitching entirely in relief and went 14–2 to set a new rookie standard for the fewest losses with that many wins.

MOST WINS BY ROOKIE WITH TWO OR FEWER LOSSES

14, Ron Davis, 1979 NY AL
12, Perry Werden, 1884 StL UA
12, Charlie Hodnett, 1884 StL UA
12, Eddie Yuhas, 1952 StL NL
12, Jim Nash, 1966 KC AL
12, Mike Nagy, 1969 Bos AL

Davis failed to make the All-Star team, but another AL freshman fireman, California's Mark Clear, pitched two innings in the 1979 Midsummer Classic, giving up one run in the NL's 7–6 come-from-behind victory. Clear was AL Pitcher of the Month in June and overall won 11 games and saved 14 others, lending a hand in more than a quarter of the Angels' 88 wins en route to the AL West title. California faced the Baltimore Orioles in the ALCS but lost in four games. In the second contest Clear relieved in the second inning but only added to the Angels' miseries, giving up three runs in 5⅔ frames as the Orioles won 9–8.

Despite the sterling relief work that Davis and Clear provided their clubs, neither was the AL ROY. That honor was shared by two infielders—Toronto shortstop Alfredo Griffin and John Castino, third baseman for the Minnesota Twins. Griffin, who had played 31 games for Cleveland over the previous three seasons, posted 179 hits, 60 more than any other rookie in 1979. He legged out ten triples, stole 21 bases, and hit .287. Griffin finished strongly, going 41-for-118 (.347) as the AL Player of the Month for September. How Castino made history as one half of the only recruit pair in AL annals to tie for ROY honors is something of a mystery. While the frosh third sacker hit .285, he had just 393 at bats and produced 67 fewer safeties than Griffin. Castino did however top junior circuit third sackers in double plays.

If Major League Baseball had dispensed with the roster-time criterion for determining rookie status prior to the 1979 season, Willie Aikens probably would have taken the AL ROY. Aikens had played 42 games but totaled just 91 at bats for the Angels two years earlier before belting 21 home runs for California in 1979. He had 81 RBI, nine over a two-game span in mid-June. In the nightcap of a June 13 twinbill, Aikens hit a grand slam at Toronto. The next day he repeated the feat, becoming the first AL player in 17 years to hit jackpot wallops in consecutive contests.

Aside from Sutcliffe, it was a rather lean rookie crop in the NL. Steve Nicosia, a backstop for the world champion Pittsburgh Pirates, led NL freshmen in round trippers with the awe-inspiring sum of . . . well, four, and Jeffrey Leonard of Houston had 119 hits, most among NL frosh. After Sutcliffe's 17 triumphs, the next highest total came from John Fulgham and David Palmer, who won ten apiece for St. Louis and Montreal, respectively.

The Chicago White Sox offered just the fourth left-handed rookie tandem—and the first since 1925—each to win at least ten games. Ross Baumgarten copped 13 decisions for the ChiSox and Steve Trout garnered 11. The duo combined for five whitewashes, one a two-hitter by Baumgarten, and Trout saved four games.

Other Highlights

May 31—When Pat Underwood of the Tigers edges his brother Tom of the Blue Jays 1–0, he becomes the only pitcher to date to start against his brother in his ML debut.

June 24—A's outfielder Rickey Henderson marks his ML debut against Texas by going 2-for-4 and stealing the first of what will be a record number of bases before he retires.

July 7—Scot Thompson hikes his average to .347 with a 5-for-5 game against Houston, the Chicago Cubs winning the opener 6–0; Thompson, who will have two four-hit games later this month, will see his average climb as high as .356 before finishing at .289.

August 17—St. Louis's John Fulgham twirls a two-hit shutout against San Francisco.

August 27—Phil Huffman tosses a one-hit shutout for Toronto, beating the Oakland A's 7–0.

In August 1978 the Toronto Blue Jays acquired Phil Huffman, a 20-year-old hurler, from the Oakland A's organization along with Willie Horton in a trade for Rico Carty. Even though Huffman had just 234 innings of minor league experience and sported a career ERA close to 5.00 when he reported to the Jays training camp in the spring of 1979, manager Roy Hartsfield opted to keep him with the parent club and installed him in the regular rotation.

The result was an unmitigated disaster. In 1979 Huffman not only topped all AL rookies in losses with 18, but he also set a junior loop record for the most losses by a freshman pitcher who never figured in another ML decision. Returned to the minors for much needed further seasoning after his horrendous ML introduction, Huffman reappeared with the Orioles in 1985 just long enough to hurl 4.2 innings and post a 15.43 ERA. His 18 career losses tie him for fourth among pitchers who hurled less than 200 innings.

MOST LOSSES, 200 OR FEWER INNINGS

Rank	Name	IP	L
1	Craig Anderson	192	23
2	Archie Stimmel	192.1	19
	Frank Bates	190.2	19
4	Johnny Gray	169	18
	Phil Huffman	177.2	18
	Art Hagan	178	18

September 17—Rickey Henderson hits his initial ML home run and the first of what will become a record 81 leading off a game, but Oakland loses 6–3 to Texas.

September 18—Rookie pitcher Bob Kammeyer of the Yankees reportedly is given $100 by manager Billy Martin after he hits ex-Yankee Cliff Johnson in a game against Cleveland; Johnson had been traded to the Indians earlier in the season after a clubhouse brawl with closer Goose Gossage.

November 26—When John Castino of the Twins and Blue Jays shortstop Alfredo Griffin tie for the AL ROY Award with seven votes apiece, it precipitates a change in the voting system that will prevent future deadlocks.

1979 ROOKIE LEADERS

Batting	Pitching
G—AL 153, Alfredo Griffin, TOR	W—AL 14, Ron Davis, NY
NL 135, Ken Oberkfell, STL	NL 17, Rick Sutcliffe, LA
AB—AL 624, Alfredo Griffin, TOR	L—**AL 18, Phil Huffman, TOR**
NL 411, Jeffrey Leonard, HOU	NL 10, Neil Allen, NY
H—AL 179, Alfredo Griffin, TOR	Rick Matula, ATL
NL 119, Jeffrey Leonard, HOU	Rick Sutcliffe, LA
2B—AL 22, Alfredo Griffin, TOR	PCT—AL .619, Ross Baumgarten, CHI
NL 19, Ken Oberkfell, STL	NL .630, Rick Sutcliffe, LA
3B—AL 10, Alfredo Griffin, TOR	GP—AL 52, Mark Clear, CAL
NL 5, Jeffrey Leonard, HOU	NL 50, Neil Allen, NY
Ken Oberkfell, STL	GS—AL 31, Phil Huffman, TOR
Scot Thompson, CHI	NL 30, Rick Sutcliffe, LA
HR—AL 21, Willie Aikens, CAL	CG—AL 8, Steve McCatty, OAK
NL 4, Steve Nicosia, PIT	NL 10, John Fulgham, STL
R—AL 81, Alfredo Griffin, TOR	IP—AL 190.2, Ross Baumgarten, CHI
NL 53, Ken Oberkfell, STL	NL 242.0, Rick Sutcliffe, LA
RBI—AL 81, Willie Aikens, CAL	H—AL 220, Phil Huffman, TOR
NL 47, Jeffrey Leonard, HOU	NL 217, Rick Sutcliffe, LA
WK—AL 61, Willie Aikens, CAL	BB—AL 83, Ross Baumgarten, CHI
NL 57, Ken Oberkfell, STL	NL 97, Rick Sutcliffe, LA
SO—AL 79, Willie Aikens, CAL	K—AL 98, Mark Clear, CAL
NL 68, Jeffrey Leonard, HOU	NL 117, Rick Sutcliffe, LA
SB—AL 33, Rickey Henderson, OAK	ERA—AL 3.54, Ross Baumgarten, CHI
NL 23, Jeffrey Leonard, HOU	NL 3.46, Rick Sutcliffe, LA
BA—AL .287, Alfredo Griffin, TOR	SHO—AL 3, Ross Baumgarten, CHI
NL .290, Jeffrey Leonard, HOU	NL 2, John Fulgham, STL
SLG—AL .364, Alfredo Griffin, TOR	Randy Niemann, HOU
NL .462, Jeffrey Leonard, HOU	Rick Williams, HOU
OBP—AL .335, Alfredo Griffin, TOR	SV—AL 14, Mark Clear, CAL
NL .364, Jeffrey Leonard, HOU	NL 8, Neil Allen, NY

1980s

1980

Being named ROY can often signal that a very successful career has begun. Eddie Murray in 2003, for instance, was the 12th ROY honoree later to be enshrined in the Baseball Hall of Fame. But for the 1980 season's chosen two, the future was filled with disappointment and scandal. The AL winner, Cleveland's Joe Charboneau, split his time between left field and designated hitter, smashing 23 home runs and driving in 87 for the Indians, who, despite finishing sixth, lost just two more games than they won. On July 23 at Seattle, Charboneau hit two round trippers, one of them an 11th-inning grand slam, and had six RBI in a 12–6 Cleveland victory. He batted .289 for the campaign, but the 25-year-old was not destined for a long big league career, hitting only .211 in 70 more games.

Los Angeles closer Steve Howe played 11 more seasons after his selection as NL ROY in 1980, but his career was marred by numerous suspensions for cocaine use. A first-round pick out of the University of Michigan in 1979, Howe pitched 13 minor league games before debuting with Los Angeles in the second contest of

1980. He saved 17 games, breaking Joe Black's team rookie record of 15. Howe's 2.66 ERA was nearly a full run better than the NL average. The southpaw would do even more superlative work in each of the next three seasons but would then miss all of 1984 as punishment for his drug use and never really recapture his early form that had once made him appear to be a potential Hall-of-Fame candidate.

In 1980 Howe was just one of an impressive class of rookie relievers. Doug Corbett saved 23 games for Minnesota, posting a 1.98 ERA in 73 games, and in the process set a new AL record for frosh bullpenners that would be broken by Mark Eichhorn later in the decade.

MOST IP OF PURE RELIEF BY ROOKIE

159.1, Hoyt Wilhelm, 1952 NY NL
157.0, Mark Eichhorn, 1986 Tor AL
136.1, Doug Corbett, 1980 Min AL
124.2, Dick Radatz, 1962 Bos AL
123.1, Butch Metzger, 1976 SD NL

Jeff Reardon of the New York Mets blew away 101 batters in 61 games, saving six. San Francisco lefty Al

Holland sported a dazzling 1.75 ERA with seven saves for the Giants. Current all-time saves leader Lee Smith pitched his first 18 games for the Chicago Cubs while another rookie Smith, Dave of the Astros, had a 1.93 ERA in more than 100 innings out of the bullpen.

The latter Smith won Game Three of the NLCS, an 11-inning epic against Philadelphia. The visiting Phillies, however, grabbed the next two battles and advanced to the World Series for the first time since 1950. Philadelphia, in the thick of a tense pennant race with Montreal in the NL East, called up Marty Bystrom in September. After a one-inning relief stint, Bystrom made his first

As a Cleveland rookie in 1980, "Super" Joe Charboneau was likened to Rocky Colavito. By the close of the following season, he had revived memories of Dick Wakefield. But Wakefield at least played long enough to collect a pension despite his lackadaisical approach to the game, whereas Charboneau lasted less than three seasons. *Transcendental Graphics*

No ROY Award winner ever fell from prominence more precipitously than Super Joe Charboneau. Along with copping the AL's top yearling accolade, the flaky outfielder led Cleveland in home runs, RBI, slugging, and OPS. Injuries and a lackadaisical training regimen held Charboneau to just 194 more at bats in the majors. As a result, he finished with the fewest career home runs of any player in history who clubbed 20 or more four-baggers as a freshman and is one of only five such performers who finished with less than 50 dingers.

Oddly, one of the other four list members was an Indians rookie who preceded Charboneau by exactly ten years, and a second member performed the feat in 1982, just two years after Charboneau did it.

20 HOMERS AS A ROOKIE, LESS THAN 50 CAREER HOMERS

Rank	Name	Team	Year	R/HR	C/HR
1	Joe Charboneau	Cle-AL	1980	23	29
2	Ken Hunt	LA-AL	1961	25	33
3	Dave Hostetler	Tex-AL	1982	22	37
4	Roy Foster	Cle-AL	1970	23	45
	Sam Bowens	Bal-AL	1964	22	45

start on September 10 and blanked the Mets on five hits. He made four more starts, won them all to finish with a perfect 5–0 log, and was named NL Pitcher of the Month. Bystrom got a no-decision in the deciding game of the NLCS versus Houston and met a similar fate in Game Five against Kansas City in the Fall Classic. However, another Phils rookie hurler had better luck in postseason action. With both Bystrom and staff ace Steve Carlton insufficiently rested, 11-game winner Bob Walk started and won the opener of the World Series, which Philadelphia took in six games. Unfortunately, Bystrom's fabulous September was not a forerunner of a brilliant career as he won just 29 games in the majors, whereas Walk, whose lone postseason appearance in 1980 was almost perforce, went on to pitch in the majors for 14 seasons.

The Phillies had won the 1980 NL East by one game over the Expos, who received an exceptional contribution from Bill Gullickson. The yearling right-hander went 10–5 with two shutouts, but the game for which he is best known wasn't a whitewash. On September 10 Gullickson beat the Chicago Cubs 4–2, striking out 18 to tie the then-existing rookie record for whiffs in one game.

The Chicago White Sox showcased some fancy neophyte pitching of their own. The team possessed the top three freshman winners in the AL, with Britt Burns leading the parade with 15. The southpaw, just 21, worked 238 innings with a 2.84 ERA that ranked third in the loop. Trailing Burns were teammates Richard Dotson, who was victorious 12 times, and LaMarr Hoyt with nine wins, including a two-hitter at Toronto on September 5 in which he blanked the Blue Jays 3–0.

Going hitless against Hoyt that day was Damaso Garcia, who paced rookies with 151 safeties. Fellow second baseman Dave Stapleton of the Red Sox was just seven behind Garcia despite playing in only 106 games. Stapleton had a 19-game hitting streak in August and a five-hit game against Cleveland on September 16. He hit .321 but with too few plate appearances to qualify as the AL rookie leader. Nor was Stapleton even the leader among rookies who played at least 100 games, as Philadelphia's Lonnie Smith appeared in exactly that number and batted .339 with 69 runs for the champion Phils. Like Stapleton, Smith sprinkled a five-hit performance among his highlights, Smith's coming on July 14 against the defending champion Pittsburgh Pirates.

1980 ROOKIE LEADERS

Batting

G—AL 141, Harold Baines, CHI
    NL 128, Rudy Law, LA
AB—AL 543, Damaso Garcia, TOR
    NL 388, Rudy Law, LA
H—AL 151, Damaso Garcia, TOR
    NL 101, Rudy Law, LA
        Lonnie Smith, PHI
2B—AL 33, Dave Stapleton, BOS
    NL 16, Ron Oester, CIN
3B—AL 7, Damaso Garcia, TOR
        Rick Peters, DET
    NL 7, Luis Salazar, SD
HR—AL 23, Joe Charboneau, CLE
    NL 8, Leon Durham, STL
R—AL 79, Rick Peters, DET
    NL 69, Lonnie Smith, PHI
RBI—AL 87, Joe Charboneau, CLE
    NL 42, Leon Durham, STL
WK—AL 54, Rick Peters, DET
    NL 28, Terry Kennedy, STL
SO—AL 92, Rick Sofield, MIN
    NL 55, Leon Durham, STL
SB—AL 27, Bobby Brown, NY
    NL 40, Rudy Law, LA
BA—AL .289, Joe Charboneau, CLE
    NL .339, Lonnie Smith, PHI
SLG—AL .488, Joe Charboneau, CLE
    NL .443, Lonnie Smith, PHI
OBP—AL .371, Rick Peters, DET
    NL .399, Lonnie Smith, PHI

Pitching

W—AL 15, Britt Burns, CHI
    NL 11, Bob Walk, PHI
L—AL 13, Britt Burns, CHI
    NL 9, Steve Howe, LA
        Charlie Liebrandt, CIN
PCT—AL .536, Britt Burns, CHI
    NL .555, Mark Bomback, NY
GP—AL 73, Doug Corbett, MIN
    NL 61, Jeff Reardon, NY
GS—AL 32, Britt Burns, CHI
        Richard Dotson, CHI
    NL 27, Charlie Liebrandt, CIN
        Bob Walk, PHI
CG—AL 11, Britt Burns, CHI
    NL 5, Bill Gullickson, MON
        Charlie Liebrandt, CIN
IP—AL 238.0, Britt Burns, CHI
    NL 173.2, Charlie Liebrandt, CIN
H—AL 213, Britt Burns, CHI
    NL 200, Charlie Liebrandt, CIN
BB—AL 87, Richard Dotson, CHI
    NL 71, Bob Walk, PHI
K—AL 133, Britt Burns, CHI
    NL 120, Bill Gullickson, MON
ERA—AL 2.84, Britt Burns, CHI
    NL 4.09, Mark Bomback, NY
SHO—AL 1, Britt Burns, CHI
        LaMarr Hoyt, CHI
        Alfredo Martinez, CAL
        Paul Mirabella, TOR
    NL 2, Bill Gullickson, MON
        Charlie Liebrandt, CIN
SV—AL 23, Doug Corbett, MIN
    NL 17, Steve Howe, LA

Other Highlights

March 8—Prior to a spring-training game, Cleveland prospect Joe Charboneau is stabbed by a crazed fan; fortunately, the fan's weapon is a ballpoint pen and leaves a wound that sidelines the rookie who will become the 1980 AL ROY for only four days.

April 13—In his first ML start, Cincinnati's Charlie Liebrandt blanks the Braves 5–0.

April 30—Mark Bomback fires a two-hitter for the New York Mets, who beat Philadelphia 2–0.

August 23—A month after driving in 13 runs over a three-game stretch, Baltimore catcher Dan Graham knocks in all four Orioles' runs, homering twice as Baltimore wins at Oakland 4–2.

September 18—Gary Ward of Minnesota hits for the cycle, but the Twins lose 9–8 at Milwaukee.

October 3—San Francisco second sacker Guy Sularz catches a line drive by veteran Dave Cash, starting an all-rookie triple play that goes from Sularz to shortstop Joe Pettini and then to first baseman Rich Murray, but the Giants are nonetheless defeated by the San Diego Padres.

1981

Precious few players—and especially rookies—have captivated the nation to such a degree that a new word was coined on their behalf, but Fernando Valenzuela was among the precious few. The Los Angeles Dodgers southpaw had pitched ten games in relief in 1980, permitting no earned runs in 17⅔ innings, before starting the 1981 opener as a last-minute injury replacement for scheduled starter Jerry Reuss. Valenzuela blanked Houston on five hits and was just getting warmed up. He also completed his next game, allowing one run, and then rattled off three more shutouts. Valenzuela won his first eight starts, five of them whitewashes, permitting all of four runs and giving birth to the term "Fernandomania." He could also hit, as evidenced by his five multi-hit games during the season.

The screwballer started the 1981 All-Star Game, which was delayed due to the 50-day players' strike that

cut the heart out of the season schedule. Valenzuela pitched a scoreless inning in the NL's 5–4 victory. He ended the season 13–7 and led the senior circuit with 180 strikeouts, 11 complete games, and eight shutouts. Valenzuela tossed a league-best 192⅓ innings before going 1–0 with a 1.06 ERA in two games against Houston in the postseason series that determined the NL West champion. This extra round was necessitated by the split-season format baseball adopted after the strike. Valenzuela split two decisions as Los Angeles beat the Montreal Expos in the NLCS. In the third game of the World Series versus the archrival New York Yankees, he earned Los Angeles's first win with a 5–4 route-going stint. The Dodgers took the next three contests to capture their first title since 1965, capping a season that saw Valenzuela win ROY and become the first freshman to cop the Cy Young Award.

In an all-rookie confrontation, Yankees left-hander Dave Righetti had faced Valenzuela in Game Three of the 1981 World Series. Righetti yielded three runs in two-plus innings, taking a no-decision, but it was one of his few poor outings. In the first round of the postseason, he beat the Milwaukee Brewers twice (once as a starter), striking out 13 over nine innings. In the ALCS Righetti tossed six scoreless frames in Game Three as the Yanks knocked the Oakland A's out of the postseason picture. In the regular season Righetti went 8–4 with a 2.05 ERA that would have led the AL had he worked just two more innings.

Righetti was named ROY, the first Yankee so honored since catcher Thurman Munson in 1970. A rookie who would have given Munson, or any of the game's other outstanding receivers of that or any other era, fits played left field for Montreal in 1981. Tim Raines stole 71 bases (topping the loop by 32 thefts) in just 88 games and was caught only 11 times.

MOST STOLEN BASES BY ROOKIE IN FEWER THAN 100 GAMES (SINCE 1898)

71 SB/88 G, Tim Raines, 1981 Mon NL
41 SB/95 G, Bert Daniels, 1910 NY AL
40 SB/63 G, Alex Cole, 1990 Cle AL
36 SB/99 G, Danny Shay, 1904 StL NL
33 SB/89 G, Rickey Henderson, 1979 Oak AL
33 SB/72 G, Alan Wiggins, 1982 SD NL

Raines, who pinch-ran in the All-Star Game, scored 61 runs and had a fine .394 OBP, ranking fifth in the senior circuit. He was third among rookies in hits while two New York Mets finished in the top four. Third baseman Hubie Brooks had 110 safeties in the abbreviated campaign while speedy centerfielder Mookie Wilson collected 89 and swiped 24 bags. San Diego Padres second baseman Juan Bonilla rounded out the top four by amassing 107.

Dave Henderson paced all freshmen in home runs with the enormous sum of six, doing so for Seattle in just 126 at bats. Even considering the shortened schedule, that total was anemic for the times. Also, fewer mound opportunities certainly didn't prevent Valenzuela from grabbing headlines, and Bruce Berenyi was not far behind him. The Cincinnati righty went 9–6, including a pair of two-hit shutouts and a one-hitter on

Two of the most colorful names in baseball's long history debuted with AL teams almost exactly ten years apart and graced the scene for only one season. On April 6, 1971, Gomer Hodge collected the first of what would be a loop-leading 68 pinch-hit at bats for Cleveland. Even though Hodge also topped the AL in pinch hits with 16, the Tribe cut him after the season, leaving him with the all-time record for the most pinch bingles by a One Year Wonder.

Some ten years later, on April 9, 1981, Shooty Babitt made his first of 54 appearances with the Oakland A's. Babitt's lone ML campaign was abbreviated by the long midseason strike and came to an abrupt end on the closing day of the regular campaign. Even though the popular 22-year-old Oakland native saw more duty at second base in 1981 than any other team member, in both the division series battle with Kansas City and the subsequent LCS loss to the Yankees, A's manager Billy Martin used veteran backup infielder Dave McKay at the keystone sack in every game.

1981 ROOKIE LEADERS

Batting

G—AL 85, Gary Ward, MIN
    NL 99, Juan Bonilla, SD
AB—AL 295, Gary Ward, MIN
    NL 369, Juan Bonilla, SD
H—AL 78, Gary Ward, MIN
    NL 110, Hubie Brooks, NY
2B—AL 15, Rich Gedman, BOS
    NL 21, Hubie Brooks, NY
3B—AL 6, Gary Ward, MIN
    NL 8, Mookie Wilson, NY
HR—AL 6, Dave Henderson, SEA
    NL 5, Rufino Linares, ATL
        Tim Raines, MON
R—AL 42, Gary Ward, MIN
    NL 61, Tim Raines, MON
RBI—AL 32, Dave Engle, MIN
    NL 38, Hubie Brooks, NY
WK—AL 28, Gary Ward, MIN
    NL 45, Tim Raines, MON
SO—AL 48, Gary Ward, MIN
    NL 65, Hubie Brooks, NY
SB—AL 8, Von Hayes, CLE
    NL 71, Tim Raines, MON
BA—AL .264, Gary Ward, MIN*
    NL .307, Hubie Brooks, NY
SLG—AL .359, Gary Ward, MIN
    NL .438, Tim Raines, MON
OBP—AL .328, Gary Ward, MIN
    NL .394, Tim Raines, MON

Pitching

W—AL 8, Dave Righetti, NY
        Mike Witt, CAL
    NL 13, Fernando Valenzuela, LA
L—AL 9, Mike Witt, CAL
    NL 8, Tim Lollar, SD
PCT—AL .471, Mike Witt, CAL
    NL .650, Fernando Valenzuela, LA
GP—AL 41, Larry Andersen, SEA
        Kevin Hickey, CHI
    NL 45, Fred Breining, SF
GS—AL 21, Mike Witt, CAL
    NL 25, Fernando Valenzuela, LA
CG—AL 7, Mike Witt, CAL
    NL 11, Fernando Valenzuela, LA
IP—AL 129.0, Mike Witt, CAL
    NL 192.1, Fernando Valenzuela, LA
H—AL 123, Mike Witt, CAL
    NL 140, Fernando Valenzuela, LA
BB—AL 55, Bryan Clark, SEA
    NL 77, Bruce Berenyi, CIN
K—AL 89, Dave Righetti, NY
    NL 180, Fernando Valenzuela, LA
ERA—AL 3.28, Mike Witt, CAL
    NL 2.48, Fernando Valenzuela, LA
SHO—AL 1, John Butcher, TEX
        Brad Havens, MIN
        Mike Witt, CAL
    NL 8, Fernando Valenzuela, LA
SV—AL 5, Larry Andersen, SEA
    NL 7, Rod Scurry, PIT

*Ward had 323 plate appearances but was only 18 short of being a qualifier in the strike-shortened 1981 season; no other AL rookies had as many.

June 7, when he struck out ten Expos, beating Montreal 2–0. Berenyi led all major league pitchers with three low-hit games, something even the inspiration for Fernandomania could not accomplish.

Other Highlights

May 18—After winning his first eight starts in the majors, Fernando Valenzuela suffers his first loss, 4–0 to the Phillies, causing his ERA to balloon to 0.90.

August 24—In his first ML game, first sacker Kent Hrbek homers in the 12th inning to give the Twins a 3–2 win at Yankee Stadium.

August 28—Catcher Tim Laudner is the second Twins player in four days to homer in his first game when he goes deep in a 6–0 win over the Tigers.

September 12—BoSox rookie Bob Ojeda no-hits the Yankees for eight innings at Yankee Stadium before surrendering back-to-back hits to open the ninth and being replaced by reliever Mark Clear, who preserves his 2–1 win.

September 17—Fernando Valenzuela sets a new post-1900 NL rookie record when he notches his eighth shutout, 2–0 over the Braves.

September 21—Rookie Bryn Smith of the Expos enters the game in relief in the top of the 17th inning, retires one batter, and then picks up his first ML win, 1–0, when Montreal scores in the bottom of the inning.

September 21—Chris Welsh fires his second shutout of the year for San Diego, three-hitting Cincinnati 6–0.

September 28—Mike Witt blanks the Chicago White Sox on six hits as the California Angels win 6–0.

1982

Though no one knew it at the time, May 30, 1982, was the beginning of an era. Cal Ripken played third base for the Baltimore Orioles that day and would not miss another game for more than 16 years. During his record-breaking streak of 2,632 consecutive games played, there were four presidential elections, the Berlin Wall crumbled, and Halley's Comet appeared—just once, of course. Ripken

homered on Opening Day in 1982 but then went into a deep slump, the nadir of which would see his average tumble to .117 on May 1. Better days were ahead, however, and on August 22 he went 5-for-5 with a home run in Baltimore's win at Texas. In midseason Ripken was shifted to shortstop, a position he made his own in the succeeding seasons. For the 1982 season, he batted .264 with 28 home runs and 93 RBI as the Orioles finished one game back in the AL East.

Ripken was named ROY in the junior circuit as was Steve Sax in the NL. Sax, who sprinted to first base after drawing a walk a la Pete Rose, was the fourth consecutive Los Angeles Dodger to be named his league's top freshman. The second baseman stole 49 bases and collected 180 hits for the Dodgers, who, like Ripken's Orioles, wound up a solitary game out of first place. Sax singled in his only at bat in the All-Star Game, as the NL won for the 11th straight time, 4–1.

Pittsburgh's Johnny Ray, another second sacker, matched Sax hit for hit, actually garnering two additional safeties. Ray played all 162 Pirate contests and hit 30 doubles while driving in 63 runs.

Like Ripken, Ryne Sandberg started at the hot corner before moving to another spot in the infield. Sandberg became the Chicago Cubs second baseman in early September and treated fans to superb defense for the next decade. Also similar to Ripken, he started slowly, getting one hit in his first 32 times up before rebounding strongly. Sandberg scored 103 runs, the highest rookie total in 1982 and the most by a Cubs freshman since 1895. He hit 33 doubles and stole 32 bases, becoming just the second rookie after 1929 to exceed 30 in each category.

Wade Boggs was another rookie unsettled in his defensive role, almost evenly dividing his season between first and third bases in 1982 before the latter became his diurnal destination in 1983. All Boggs did in his rookie year was hit .349 in 104 games, one of the highest freshman averages since the hitter-happy season of 1930.

BEST BA BY ROOKIE IN 300+ ABs (1931–2003)

.351/342 AB, Dan Gladden, 1984 SF NL
.350/692 AB, Ichiro Suzuki, 2001 Sea AL
.349/338 AB, Wade Boggs, 1982 Bos AL
.343/502 AB, Jeff Heath, 1938 Cle AL
.340/309 AB, Hal Morris, 1990 Cin NL

Again we look at the hitting profiles of two members of a rookie class. Here we have a 1982 pair who were the same age and for most of their careers played the same position in the same league (albeit one of them did not become a full-timer at that position until his sophomore year). Between them, the two would compile over 4,000 career hits and nearly 800 stolen bases, but only one member of the duo would ever be a league leader in a major offensive department.

Could you have predicted from their rookie stats which of the two it would be and what three departments he would lead at one time or another in his career?

Age	G	AB	R	H	2B	3B	HR	RBI	BB	SO	SB	CS	BA	SA	OBP	OPS
22	150	638	88	180	23	7	4	47	49	53	49	19	.282	.359	.335	.694
22	156	635	103	172	33	5	7	54	36	90	32	12	.271	.372	.314	.686

No, neither of the pair ever led in stolen bases, doubles, or strikeouts. The first hitting profile belongs to 1982 NL ROY Steve Sax, who never was a pacesetter in anything. Ryne Sandberg, the owner of the second profile, finished sixth to Sax in the 1982 NL ROY balloting but subsequently led the NL in runs, triples, and also once in home runs.

Boggs would capture five batting crowns, but the freshman hitting leader among qualifiers in 1982 was Kent Hrbek, the Minnesota Twins first baseman. Hrbek batted .301 and swatted 23 round trippers. He knocked in 92 runs and scored 82 times. Two other Twins rookies topped 20 taters. Third baseman Gary Gaetti hit 25, including a pair on Opening Day, and outfielder Tom Brunansky smashed 20.

Another fly chaser, Willie McGee, saved his best performance for the postseason. The St. Louis Cardinal did hit .296 with eight triples, however, prior to facing Atlanta in the NLCS. In St. Louis's three-game sweep, McGee hit a homer, two triples, and a single while scoring four runs and driving in five. McGee went wild in Game Three of the World Series against Milwaukee. He hit two home runs, knocking in four, and made two excellent leaping catches in the outfield, the latter preventing a Gorman Thomas home run.

Chili Davis was one of a trio of San Francisco freshmen to help the Giants' cause. The switch-hitting center fielder had 167 hits, 52 for extra bases, including 19 home runs. Davis also stole 24 bases and scored 86 runs. Bill Laskey and southpaw Atlee Hammaker topped all rookies in wins in 1982 with 13 and 12, respectively, completing 11 games between them as the Giants ended up third but only two games behind Atlanta.

Across the bay, Oakland's Dave Beard won ten games and saved 11 more. Jerry Ujdur also took ten for Detroit, a figure matched by San Diego's Eric Show. The latter was one of four Padres rookies to sport an ERA less than 3.00 while working either 100 innings or 50 games. Luis DeLeon saved 15 contests and had a 2.03 ERA. Dave Dravecky and Floyd Chiffer also impressed, combining to go 9–6 with a half dozen saves.

But the most impressive new Padre of all was a 22-year-old outfielder who joined the club in July, hit .289 in 54 games, and would do much, much better in the future. The ball hawk would take eight NL batting titles and help lead San Diego to two World Series. Like Ripken in Baltimore, Tony Gwynn ushered in a new era in Southern California.

Other Highlights

May 31—Von Hayes drives in five runs in Cleveland's 9–4 win against Minnesota.

June 7—Gene Nelson fires a two-hitter for Seattle at Texas, winning 6–0.

July 31—Jim Gott of the Toronto Blue Jays tosses a ten-inning shutout, fanning eight Detroit Tigers in his 1–0 win.

September 17—Emulating his Seattle teammate's June performance, Bob Stoddard blanks Texas on two hits as the Mariners beat the Rangers 6–0.

October 1—Terry Leach permits just one Philadelphia hit in ten innings as he and the New York Mets win 1–0.

1982 ROOKIE LEADERS

Batting	Pitching
G—AL 160, Cal Ripken, BAL	W—AL 10, Dave Beard, OAK
NL 162, Johnny Ray, PIT	Jerry Ujdur, DET
AB—AL 598, Cal Ripken, BAL	NL 13, Bill Laskey, SF
NL 647, Johnny Ray, PIT	L—AL 14, Mike Moore, SEA
H—AL 160, Kent Hrbek, MIN	NL 12, Bill Laskey, SF
NL 182, Johnny Ray, PIT	PCT—AL .500, Jerry Ujdur, DET
2B—AL 32, Cal Ripken, BAL	NL .600, Atlee Hammaker, SF
NL 33, Ryne Sandberg, CHI	GP—**AL 78, Ed Vande Berg, SEA**
3B—AL 6, Bobby Mitchell, MIN	NL 64, Steve Bedrosian, ATL
Ron Washington, MIN	GS—AL 27, Mike Moore, SEA
NL 8, Willie McGee, STL	NL 31, Bill Laskey, SF
HR—AL 28, Cal Ripken, BAL	CG—AL 7, Jerry Ujdur, DET
NL 19, Chili Davis, SF	NL 7, Bill Laskey, SF
R—AL 90, Cal Ripken, BAL	IP—AL 178.0, Jerry Ujdur, DET
NL 103, Ryne Sandberg, CHI	NL 189.1, Bill Laskey, SF
RBI—AL 93, Cal Ripken, BAL	H—AL 159, Mike Moore, SEA
NL 76, Chili Davis, SF	NL 189, Atlee Hammaker, SF
WK—AL 71, Tim Brunansky, MIN	BB—AL 79, Mike Moore, SEA
NL 49, Steve Sax, LA	NL 90, Charlie Puleo, NY
SO—AL 113, Dave Hostetler, TEX	K—AL 92, Terry Felton, MIN
NL 115, Chili Davis, SF	NL 123, Steve Bedrosian, ATL
SB—AL 32, Von Hayes, CLE	ERA—AL 3.69, Jerry Ujdur, DET
NL 49, Steve Sax, LA	NL 3.14, Bill Laskey, SF
BA—AL .301, Kent Hrbek, MIN	SHO—AL 1, done by six pitchers
NL .282, Steve Sax, LA	NL 2, Eric Show, SD
SLG—AL .485, Kent Hrbek, MIN	SV—AL 21, Salome Barojas, CHI
NL .410, Chili Davis, SF	NL 15, Luis DeLeon, SD
OBP—AL .378, Tom Brunansky, MIN	
NL .335, Steve Sax, LA	

◄ 1983 ►

In September 1983 Ron Kittle figuratively raised the roof twice at cavernous old Comiskey Park when he thrilled the home crowd by hitting two balls onto it. The Chicago White Sox left fielder produced his blasts on September 6 and 19, the latter home run giving him 33 for the season. Kittle would hit two more, extending his team's rookie record.

MOST HOME RUNS BY A WHITE SOX ROOKIE

35, Ron Kittle, 1983
27, Zeke Bonura, 1934
23, Bill Melton, 1969
22, Pete Ward, 1963
22, Tommie Agee, 1966

Earlier in the season, in the All-Star Game at Comiskey, Kittle had an infield single and scored in the seventh inning as the AL rolled to a 13–3 victory. On the year he drove in 100 runs for the AL West champion White Sox, who dominated the division by 20 games. Kittle went 2-for-7 in the ALCS against Baltimore before getting hit by a Mike Flanagan pitch in Game Three that brought a sudden end to his storybook season.

Kittle's abrupt departure allowed another freshman to make the ALCS his personal showcase. After Chicago had won the opener, Mike Boddicker started Game Two for the Orioles and gave a masterful performance, limiting the White Sox to five hits and fanning 14 in his 4–0 win to even the series. After garnering MVP honors in the ALCS, Boddicker continued to shine in the World Series, permitting just three Philadelphia safeties and one unearned run in the second game as Baltimore evened the match at one-all with a 4–1 win. In both postseason series Boddicker followed a Baltimore loss with a victory that helped spur the Orioles to sweep the remaining games. Boddicker had seen limited action in each of the previous three seasons before getting his first real opportunity in 1983. He responded with a 16–8 record and tossed a league-leading five shutouts—a total unmatched by any rookie since. In addition, his 2.77 ERA was second lowest in the AL, and opposing batsmen hit a loop-low .216 off his righty slants. Even more significantly, Boddicker's base-runners-per-nine-innings ratio of 9.70 was second among all rookie hurlers in the 1980s only to Fernando Valenzuela's 9.45 in the strike-shortened 1981 season.

Boddicker finished fifth in winning percentage, as did Atlanta's Craig McMurtry in the NL. McMurtry went 15–9 and had the most wins by a Braves freshman since 1937 when the franchise played in Boston. He threw three shutouts, including a pair of three-hitters, but the Braves were unable to defend their 1982 NL West crown.

While both Boddicker and McMurtry toiled for contending teams that bolstered their won-lost totals, Ken Schrom got little aid from his Minnesota Twins teammates, who produced just 70 wins. Nevertheless, Schrom went 15–8, giving him a .652 winning percentage, seventh-best in the AL, as the rest of the Twins staff went 55–84 (.396).

Darryl Strawberry's New York Mets could not even claim 70 victories, going 68–94, but the rookie right fielder and former first pick in the 1980 free-agent draft helped revitalize a team that would dramatically improve the following year. If Schrom's sterling season for a weak team was vastly underappreciated, Strawberry's efforts were not, as his 26 home runs and 19 stolen bases gained him ROY plaudits. The left-handed slugger, whose swing reminded Ted Williams of his own, registered his top rookie highlight in the first game of a June 28 doubleheader at St. Louis. Strawberry hit two round trippers, driving in five runs in New York's 10–1 romp. Freshman relievers Doug Sisk and Carlos Diaz also worked to give the last-place Mets reason to hope for a brighter 1984. Sisk saved 11 games and had a 2.24

ERA in more than 100 innings while Diaz posted a 2.05 ERA in 54 games.

Mel Hall of the Chicago Cubs enjoyed a frosh season that was nearly the equal of Strawberry's, especially in August, when he was the NL Player of the Month. Of his 17 home runs, nine came in August, including five over the last three games. Hall batted .333 for the month with 17 RBI, nearly one-third of the 56 he accumulated in 1983. Four other freshmen cracked double digits in home runs. First sacker Greg Brock pounded 20 for Los Angeles but went 0-for-9 in the NLCS versus Philadelphia. Cincinnati featured Gary Redus and Nick Esasky, who poled 17 and 12, respectively, and the Reds

A fine .322 season in 1981 with Tucson of the PCL earned outfielder Tim Tolman eight at bats with Houston in September in which he garnered one hit for a .125 BA. The following year, after another excellent season with Tucson, Tolman spent some time with the Astros again and hit .192 in 26 at bats. In 1983 Tolman remained with Houston most of the season and celebrated his rookie year by hitting just .196 in 43 games.

Four years later Tolman finished his ML career with Detroit by hitting .083 in 12 games. It was his seventh straight sub-.200 season and established a new record for the longest ML career by a position player who never hit above the Mendoza line. The record for most years without a season above .200 had previously been six and belonged to Larry Murray, an AL outfielder with the Yankees and A's from 1974 through 1979.

Tolman and Murray are both also prominent on the list of the ten worst career BAs since 1900 among outfielders with a minimum of 200 plate appearances.

TEN WORST CAREER BAs, OUTFIELDERS, POST-1900 (MINIMUM 200 PAs)

Rank	Name	PA	BA
1	Bill McCabe	219	.161
2	Don Bosch	346	.164
3	Tim Tolman	228	.168
4	Joe Cannon	232	.176
5	Larry Murray	471	.177
6	Jay Hankins	224	.184
7	Earl Naylor	318	.186
8	Jack Daniels	256	.187
9	Joe Durham	228	.188
	John Kelly	217	.188

also got nine more from catcher Dann Bilardello. Finally, Kittle's teammate, White Sox first baseman Greg Walker, hit an even ten dongs.

In the 1990s Houston was renowned for its lineup of "Killer Bs," but the 1983 Astros' rookie crop featured the "Killer Ds." Bill Doran hit .271 with 86 walks in 154 games and led NL second basemen in putouts. The Astros also possessed just the fourth rookie tandem in history to save at least ten games each, Frank DiPino notching 20 and Bill Dawley 14. Dawley, who got off to a particularly hot start as a freshman bullpenner, was selected to the NL All-Star squad and pitched 1⅓ scoreless innings in the midsummer contest. The three

Ds were supplemented by yearling lefty Mike Madden, who went 9–5 with a 3.14 ERA as a combination starter-reliever.

Along with the lowly Mets, Astros, and Twins, the AL East basement-dwelling Indians generated one of the year's most outstanding rookies in shortstop Julio Franco, the runner-up for the AL ROY prize. Franco, who was still cranking out hits in 2004, amassed 153 of them in his frosh season as he batted .273 and led the Tribe in both stolen bases with 32 and RBI with 80. Five of his ribbies came on his biggest day of the season, June 18, when he also rapped two doubles and a single to lead Cleveland to a 12–8 win over Detroit.

1983 ROOKIE LEADERS

Batting	Pitching
G—AL 154, Pete O'Brien, TEX	W—AL 16, Mike Boddicker, BAL
NL 154, Bill Doran, HOU	NL 15, Craig McMurtry, ATL
AB—AL 560, Julio Franco, CLE	L—AL 15, Matt Young, SEA
NL 535, Bill Doran, HOU	NL 9, Andy McGaffigan, SF
H—AL 153, Julio Franco, CLE	Craig McMurtry, ATL
NL 145, Bill Doran, HOU	PCT—AL .667, Mike Boddicker, BAL
2B—AL 24, Julio Franco, CLE	NL .625, Craig McMurtry, ATL
Pete O'Brien, TEX	GP—AL 61, Rick Lysander, MIN
NL 23, Mel Hall, CHI	NL 73, Bill Scherrer, CIN
3B—AL 8, Julio Franco, CLE	GS—AL 33, Mike Smithson, TEX
NL 9, Gary Redus, CIN	NL 35, Craig McMurtry, ATL
HR—AL 35, Ron Kittle, CHI	CG—AL 10, Mike Boddicker, BAL
NL 26, Darryl Strawberry, NY	Mike Smithson, TEX
R—AL 75, Ron Kittle, CHI	NL 6, Craig McMurtry, ATL
NL 90, Gary Redus, CIN	IP—AL 223.1, Mike Smithson, TEX
RBI—AL 100, Ron Kittle, CHI	NL 224.2, Craig McMurtry, ATL
NL 74, Darryl Strawberry, NY	H—AL 233, Mike Smithson, TEX
WK—AL 58, Pete O'Brien, TEX	NL 204, Craig McMurtry, ATL
NL 86, Bill Doran, HOU	BB—AL 98, Tim Conroy, OAK
SO—**AL 150, Ron Kittle, CHI**	NL 88, Craig McMurtry, ATL
NL 128, Darryl Strawberry, NY	K—AL 135, Mike Smithson, TEX
SB—AL 32, Julio Franco, CLE	NL 118, Jose DeLeon, PIT
NL 39, Gary Redus, CIN	ERA—AL 2.77, Mike Boddicker, BAL
BA—AL .273, Julio Franco, CLE	NL 3.08, Craig McMurtry, ATL
NL .271, Bill Doran, HOU	SHO—**AL 5, Mike Boddicker, BAL**
SLG—AL .504, Ron Kittle, CHI	NL 3, Craig McMurtry, ATL
NL .512, Darryl Strawberry, NY	Lee Tunnell, PIT
OBP—AL .316, Ron Kittle, CHI	SV—AL 8, Tom Tellmann, MIL
NL .372, Bill Doran, HOU	NL 20, Frank DiPino, HOU

Other Highlights

August 6—Walt Terrell hits two home runs off Fergie Jenkins and drives in four while allowing just one run in 7⅓ innings as the New York Mets beat the Chicago Cubs 4–1.

August 20—Jose DeLeon two-hits Cincinnati, striking out 13, as he and the Pittsburgh Pirates prevail 4–0.

August 22—Carmelo Martinez homers for the Cubs in his initial big league at bat as Chicago bests Cincinnati 2–0.

September 13—Mike Fitzgerald of the Mets hits a home run in his first ML at bat in a 5–1 victory at Philadelphia.

September 16—Tim Teufel hits two homers, a triple, and two singles, scoring five times for the Minnesota Twins, who top the Toronto Blue Jays 11–4.

September 29—Mike Warren of the Oakland A's no-hits the Chicago White Sox, winning 3–0.

◄ 1984 ►

In 1984 Robert Redford starred in *The Natural,* playing a pitcher-turned-outfielder who finally cracks the big leagues at age 34 with the fictional New York Knights. That year Dwight Gooden debuted with the New York Mets and this real-life natural was only 19. Gooden, nicknamed "Doctor K," had a blazing fastball and knee-buckling curve to which he added control and poise uncommon in a pitcher so young. He dominated NL batters, striking out both a loop-best and rookie-record 276 batters. Moreover, his 11.39 whiffs per nine innings set a since-broken ML record. Gooden was NL Pitcher of the Month in September, posting a 4–1 record, which included a one-hit shutout and two other games in which he fanned 16 batters. On the year he held opponents to a .202 BA and a .270 OOBP, both league bests. A 17–9 record and 2.60 ERA earned the right-handed Gooden the runner-up spot for the Cy Young Award.

Not surprisingly, Gooden was NL ROY, but he was far from the only freshman hurler to excel in the year of George Orwell's "Big Brother." Ron Darling, also of the Mets, and Orel Hershiser of the Los Angeles Dodgers preceded Gooden as Pitcher of the Month honorees. In June, Darling was 5–0, while the following month all Hershiser did was throw four shutouts, three of them two-hitters. Hershiser ended the season with opposing hitters registering a .279 OOBP, second best in the league only to Gooden. In August Red Sox fireballer Roger Clemens took his turn winning laurels, going undefeated while picking up four wins as the junior circuit's Pitcher of the Month. On August 21 Clemens whiffed 15 Kansas City Royals while not allowing a walk as his Boston Red Sox won 11–1. An arm injury would end Clemens's season ten days later, but he would win a few hundred more games before all was said and done.

Matching Gooden's 17 wins was Seattle's Mark Langston, who set a new Mariners' victory record in the process. Langston topped the AL with 204 strikeouts but also issued a loop-worst 118 free passes. But while bases on balls were Langston's nemesis, they were welcomed by fellow Mariner Alvin Davis. The first baseman drew 97 of them, tied for eighth best in rookie history. In addition, Davis knocked in 116 runs, the most by a freshman since 1950, and set a new club record. Combining these feats put Davis in tall company and brought him the AL's top rookie honor by a comfortable margin over teammate Langston and Kirby Puckett of the Twins.

ROOKIES WITH 100 RBI AND 90+ WALKS

Ted Williams, 1939 Bos AL, 145 RBI/107 BB
Al Rosen, 1950 Cle AL, 116 RBI/100 BB
Alvin Davis, 1984 Sea AL, 116 RBI/97 BB

Second baseman Juan Samuel also put up historic numbers. The Philadelphia Phillie became just the fifth rookie to compile at least 15 of each variety of extra-base hit.

ROOKIES HITTING 15 DOUBLES, TRIPLES, AND HOME RUNS

Buck Freeman, 1899 Was NL, 19 2B/25 3B/25 HR
Dale Alexander, 1929 Det AL, 43 2B/15 3B/25 HR
Joe DiMaggio, 1936 NY AL, 44 2B/15 3B/29 HR
Jeff Heath, 1938 Cle AL, 31 2B/18 3B/21 HR
Juan Samuel, 1984 Phi NL, 36 2B/19 3B/15 HR

Samuel's 19 triples were the most by a rookie since 1926 and are the high-water mark for freshman second basemen. He also established a pair of NL rookie records with his 72 stolen bases and 168 strikeouts. In 1985 Vince Coleman ran by the thefts figure, but the whiff mark still stands. In addition, Samuel's 701 at bats are the most ever by a freshman and also the highest any NL batter has accumulated.

Another Phillie also had impressive statistics, though for a much briefer period. With a .362 average in 185 ABs, Jeff Stone was the first rookie since 1930 to top .360 (minimum 150 ABs). In addition, Stone swiped 27 bases in just 51 games. Giants outfielder Dan Gladden also brought back memories of 1930. When he hit .351 in 342 ABs, Gladden became the first freshman since that season to top the .350 plateau (minimum 200 ABs).

Other Highlights

April 19—Bret Saberhagen of the Kansas City Royals earns his first ML win, beating the previously unbeaten Detroit Tigers 5–2; Detroit had been 9–0.

May 8—Kirby Puckett gets four hits in his ML debut as his Minnesota Twins beat the California Angels 5–0.

June 29—Ricky Horton tosses a two-hitter for the St. Louis Cardinals, who best the San Diego Padres 5–0.

June 29—Andre David of the Twins homers in his first ML at bat, and Minnesota tops the Tigers 5–3 in the opener of a doubleheader.

July 10—In the All-Star Game Dwight Gooden of the Mets pitches two scoreless innings and fans the side in the fifth frame as the youngest player ever in the Midsummer Classic.

August 24—Frank Williams pitches only a combined 1⅔ innings but earns a victory for the San Francisco Giants in each game of a doubleheader against the New York Mets.

September 12—Dwight Gooden Ks 16 Pirates in a 2–0 win to break Herb Score's old ML rookie strikeout mark of 245.

In 1984 no fewer than five pitchers garnered votes for the AL ROY Award, but none went to the loop's only rookie hurler to set a new positive club record that year. That spring, after Dan Spillner was traded and Neal Heaton was converted to a starter, Cleveland manager Pat Corrales found himself without a closer. It was familiar territory for a Tribe skipper. In 1983 alone, nine ML pitchers produced 22 or more saves. The Cleveland franchise record meanwhile stood at just 21 as late as the spring of 1984, and Spillner had led the club the previous year with a mere eight saves.

Corrales, almost by default, chose as his stopper 29-year-old Ernie Camacho, a career minor leaguer who had flunked two earlier tests with Oakland and Pittsburgh and, furthermore, had been ineffective in a brief trial with the Tribe the previous fall. Camacho proceeded to capture 23 saves for Corrales and set a new club record that stood until 1988. After being injured almost the entire season in 1985, Camacho rebounded the following year to regain the Indians' closer role and notch 20 saves, but his arm was never again completely sound.

REVERSE CHRONOLOGY OF SAVE RECORD FOR CLEVELAND FRANCHISE

Name	Year	Saves
Jose Mesa	1995	46
Doug Jones	1990	43
Doug Jones	1988	37
Ernie Camacho	1984	23
Dan Spillner	1982	21
Dave LaRoche	1976	21
Ray Narleski	1955	19
Russ Christopher	1948	17
Ed Klieman	1947	17
Joe Heving	1944	10
Joe Heving	1943	9
Willis Hudlin	1928	7
Jim Bagby Sr.	1917	7
Jim Bagby Sr.	1916	5
Sad Sam Jones	1915	4
Vean Gregg	1913	3
Otto Hess	1906	3
Bill Hoffer	1901	3

September 26—Juan Samuel of the Phillies breaks Tim Raines's rookie record for thefts when he swipes his 72nd base in a 7–1 loss to the Mets.

1984 ROOKIE LEADERS

Batting	Pitching
G—AL 157, Tim Teufel, MIN	W—AL 17, Mark Langston, SEA
NL 160, Juan Samuel, PHI	NL 17, Dwight Gooden, NY
AB—AL 568, Tim Teufel, MIN	L—AL 16, Jaime Cocanower, MIL
NL 701, Juan Samuel, PHI	NL 15, Jeff Robinson, SF
H—AL 165, Kirby Puckett, MIN	PCT—AL .630, Mark Langston, SEA
NL 191, Juan Samuel, PHI	NL .654, Dwight Gooden, NY
2B—AL 34, Alvin Davis, SEA	GP—AL 69, Ernie Camacho, CLE
NL 36, Juan Samuel, PHI	NL 61, Frank Williams, SF
3B—AL 6, Gary Pettis, CAL	GS—AL 33, Mark Langston, SEA
NL 19, Juan Samuel, PHI	Ron Romanick, CAL
HR—AL 27, Alvin Davis, SEA	NL 33, Ron Darling, NY
NL 20, Kevin McReynolds, SD	Jeff Robinson, SF
R—AL 80, Alvin Davis, SEA	CG—AL 8, Ron Romanick, CAL
NL 105, Juan Samuel, PHI	NL 8, Orel Hershiser, LA
RBI—AL 116, Alvin Davis, SEA	IP—AL 229.2, Ron Romanick, CAL
NL 75, Kevin McReynolds, SD	NL 218.0, Dwight Gooden, NY
WK—AL 97, Alvin Davis, SEA	H—AL 240, Ron Romanick, CAL
NL 68, Carmelo Martinez, SD	NL 195, Jeff Robinson, SF
SO—AL 115, Gary Pettis, CAL	BB—**AL 118, Mark Langston, SEA**
NL 168, Juan Samuel, PHI	NL 104, Ron Darling, NY
SB—AL 48, Gary Pettis, CAL	K—**AL 204, Mark Langston, SEA**
NL 72, Juan Samuel, PHI	**NL 276, Dwight Gooden, NY**
BA—AL .303, Marty Barrett, BOS	ERA—AL 3.40, Mark Langston, SEA
NL .278, Kevin McReynolds, SD	NL 2.60, Dwight Gooden, NY
SLG—AL .497, Alvin Davis, SEA	SHO—AL 2, Mark Gubicza, KC
NL .465, Kevin McReynolds, SD	Mark Langston, SEA
OBP—AL .395, Alvin Davis, SEA	Ron Romanick, CAL
NL .346, Carmelo Martinez, SD	**NL 4, Orel Hershiser, LA**
	SV—AL 23, Ernie Camacho, CLE
	NL 6, Ken Howell, LA

◄ 1985 ►

In 1985 Tom Browning and Ted Higuera accomplished something that had not been seen by major league audiences since Silent Cal resided in the White House. Both southpaws won at least 15 games—the first time since 1924 each league had offered a rookie left-hander who won as often. Browning actually won 20 decisions for Cincinnati, the most by a freshman since Bob Grim took 20 for the 1954 New York Yankees. The Reds hurler tied the "modern" NL record for victories by a freshman southpaw.

MOST WINS BY NL ROOKIE LEFT-HANDER (SINCE 1901)

20, Jake Weimer, 1903 Chi NL
20, Irv Young, 1905 Bos NL
20, Jack Pfiester, 1906 Chi NL
20, Cliff Melton, 1937 NY NL
20, Harvey Haddix, 1953 StL NL
20, Tom Browning, 1985 Cin NL

Browning tossed four shutouts and worked 261⅓ innings, the most by a rookie since 1978. A defeat on August 9 dropped his record to 9–9 with less than eight weeks left in the season, but four days later he launched an 11-game winning streak. On September 28 Browning notched his 20th triumph, beating Houston 5–2.

Higuera went 15–8 for Milwaukee, setting the Brewers' freshman win record. His .652 winning percentage also is tops among Brewers rookies and ranked fourth among all AL hurlers in 1985. Higuera also held hitters to a .235 average, the fifth lowest in the loop.

As fine as their seasons were, neither Browning nor Higuera was named ROY. In the NL Vince Coleman's blazing speed allowed him to run away with freshman laurels. The St. Louis left fielder, the chief thief on a Cardinals team that swiped 314 bags, stole a rookie-record 110 bases all by himself, 40 more than the runner-up in the senior circuit. Coleman's legs also enabled him to score 107 runs and speed to ten triples.

The Cardinals won the NL East by three games and met the Los Angeles Dodgers in the NLCS. Coleman got four hits and scored twice in the first three contests, but during his stretching exercises prior to Game Four, his left leg was badly injured when the automated tarp in Busch Stadium rolled over it, trapping him for about half a minute and ending his season. St. Louis nevertheless beat the Dodgers before losing the World Series to the Kansas City Royals.

Ozzie Guillen of the Chicago White Sox overcame hitting .208 in both May and June to earn honors as the AL's top freshman. Guillen batted .342 in July and .333 the next month to finish at .273. He walked just 12 times in 150 games, the fewest ever by a rookie in that many appearances, but his defense made the difference. Guillen led junior circuit shortstops with a .980 fielding percentage and committed only 12 errors.

Including Guillen, no less than eight rookie shortstops played at least 70 games in 1985, but the real strength of that season's rookie crop was its relief pitchers. Montreal's Tim Burke set a new NL frosh record with 78 appearances, saving eight games. Burke went 9–4, as did Don Carman for Philadelphia. Carman, a southpaw, relieved 71 times and had a 2.08 ERA with seven saves. A sigh of relief could be heard in the Big Apple as Roger McDowell saved 17 games for the Mets, and Brian Fisher earned 14 for the Yankees, each right-hander pacing his loop's freshmen in saves. Middle reliever Steve Ontiveros excelled for Oakland, fashioning a 1.93 ERA in 74⅔ innings, and California's Stew Cliburn

went 9–3 with six saves and a 2.09 ERA in just a shade less than 100 innings.

Yet not every yearling reliever in 1985 has fond memories. Rich Thompson of Cleveland and Curt Wardle, who began with Minnesota before being dealt to the Indians, each suffered through seasons with ERAs worse than 6.00 to join an extremely small list that had only one member prior to 1985.

6.00+ ERA BY ROOKIE WITH 50+ GAMES PITCHED

6.52 ERA/63 GP, Doug Creek, 1996 SF NL
6.30 ERA/57 GP, Rich Thompson, 1985 Cle AL
6.25 ERA/55 GP, Jim Walkup, 1935 StL AL
6.18 ERA/50 GP, Curt Wardle, 1985 Min AL/Cle AL

In addition to Browning and Higuera, rookie starters who performed well included 12-game winner Kirk McCaskill of the Angels and three others who all won ten games. That trio included Montreal's Joe Hesketh, Tim Birtsas of Oakland, and Rick Aguilera on the Mets. Meanwhile, Tom Filer went 7–0 for Toronto in nine late-season starts as the Blue Jays made the postseason for the first time.

Other newcomers of note were Chris Brown, who led NL third basemen in fielding average with a .971 mark while smashing 16 home runs and driving in 61 for San Francisco. On September 6 Brown bagged a homer, two doubles, and a single with six RBI as the Giants beat the Expos. First baseman Glenn Davis pounded 20 round trippers for Houston in just 350 ABs while Baltimore DH Larry Sheets knocked 17 dongs in 22 fewer ABs.

Other Highlights

July 23—Oddibe McDowell goes 5-for-5 and becomes the first member of the Texas Rangers to hit for the cycle in an 8–4 win over Cleveland.

August 1—Vince Coleman of the Cardinals breaks the previous rookie stolen-base record of 72 when he swipes two bases in the first inning of St. Louis's 9–8 loss to the Cubs to run his total to 74.

August 29—Angels rookie Kirk McCaskill takes part in setting a new all-time AL record when he hits Yankees

These pitching profiles belong to two rookies who served for the most part as middle relievers in their yearling seasons.

The 1999 profile, which belongs to Jeff Zimmerman, attracted considerable attention and spurred Zimmerman to a third-place finish in the AL ROY balloting. The 1985 profile not only received zero votes for ROY, but it went almost entirely unnoticed at the time and still has never received its due recognition as one of the finest seasons ever by a rookie working in a relief role. It belongs to Steve Ontiveros.

Year	Team	Age	W	L	Pct	G	GS	CG	SV	IP	H	R	ER	HR	BB	SO	H/9	BR/9
1985	A's	24	1	3	.250	39	0	0	8	74.2	45	17	16	4	19	36	5.42	7.96
1999	Rangers	26	9	72	.750	65	0	0	3	87.2	50	24	23	9	23	67	5.13	7.70

Following his monumental recruit effort, Ontiveros labored in obscurity for nearly a decade before emerging from his seemingly perpetual battle with arm trouble to lead the AL in ERA and OOBP in the strike-shortened 1994 season. A year later, after Ontiveros spent most of the campaign in the A's starting rotation, his arm betrayed him once more, albeit he mounted a brief comeback with the Red Sox in 2000.

1985 ROOKIE LEADERS

Batting

G—AL 150, Ozzie Guillen, CHI
   NL 151, Vince Coleman, STL
AB—AL 491, Ozzie Guillen, CHI
   NL 636, Vince Coleman, STL
H—AL 134, Ozzie Guillen, CHI
   NL 170, Vince Coleman, STL
2B—AL 21, Ozzie Guillen, CHI
   NL 24, Mariano Duncan, LA
3B—AL 9, Ozzie Guillen, CHI
   NL 10, Vince Coleman, STL
HR—AL 18, Oddibe McDowell, TEX
   NL 20, Glenn Davis, HOU
R—AL 71, Ozzie Guillen, CHI
   NL 107, Vince Coleman, STL
RBI—AL 50, Larry Sheets, BAL
   NL 64, Glenn Davis, HOU
WK—AL 36, Oddibe McDowell, TEX
      Ernie Riles, MIL
   NL 50, Vince Coleman, STL
SO—AL 85, Oddibe McDowell, TEX
   NL 115, Vince Coleman, STL
SB—AL 25, Oddibe McDowell, TEX
   NL 110, Vince Coleman, STL
BA—AL .286, Ernie Riles, MIL
   NL .267, Vince Coleman, STL
SLG—AL .431, Oddibe McDowell, TEX
   NL .442, Chris Brown, SF
OBP—AL .342, Ernie Riles, MIL
   NL .345, Chris Brown, SF

Pitching

W—AL 15, Ted Higuera, MIL
   NL 20, Tom Browning, CIN
L—AL 12, Kirk McCaskill, CAL
   NL 10, Zane Smith, ATL
PCT—AL .652, Ted Higuera, MIL
   NL .690, Tom Browning, CIN
GP—AL 57, Rich Thompson, CLE
   NL 78, Tim Burke, MON
GS—AL 30, Ted Higuera, MIL
   NL 38, Tom Browning, CIN
CG—AL 7, Ted Higuera, MIL
   NL 6, Tom Browning, CIN
IP—AL 212.1, Ted Higuera, MIL
   NL 261.1, Tom Browning, CIN
H—AL 189, Kirk McCaskill, CAL
   NL 242, Tom Browning, CIN
BB—AL 91, Tim Birtsas, OAK
   NL 80, Zane Smith, ATL
K—AL 127, Ted Higuera, MIL
   NL 155, Tom Browning, CIN
ERA—AL 3.67, Ken Dixon, BAL
   NL 3.55, Tom Browning, CIN
SHO—AL 2, Ted Higuera, MIL
   NL 4, Tom Browning, CIN
SV—AL 14, Brian Fisher, NY
   NL 17, Roger McDowell, NY

DH Don Baylor with a pitch, giving Baylor 190 HBPs to break Minnie Minoso's former mark of 189.

September 16—Switch-hitter Nelson Simmons homers from both sides of the plate and drives in four, but the Detroit Tigers lose to Baltimore 14–7.

September 25—Boston outfielder Mike Greenwell hits his first ML home run in the top of the 13th inning to lift the Red Sox to a 4–2 win at Toronto.

October 4—Roger Mason tosses a four-hit shutout and strikes out ten Atlanta Braves as the San Francisco Giants win 1–0 on Chris Brown's RBI pinch double in the bottom of the ninth.

1986

Texas Rangers manager Bobby Valentine had to be pulling his hair out in 1986. Chief among most skippers' pet peeves are pitchers who issue a lot of walks and hitters who strike out frequently. Unhappily, the 1986 Rangers featured a host of rookies who committed both of these baseball sins. In 157⅔ innings Bobby Witt walked 143 men, the fourth most in AL rookie history. By comparison, Ed Correa had pinpoint control, yielding "only" 126 bases on balls in more than 200 innings. Not since 1896 had a team endured two freshman pitchers who both topped the 120 mark in free passes. In the bullpen Mitch "Wild Thing" Williams fit right in, issuing 79 freebies in only 98 frames. Despite the infinitely better control of two other frosh, starter Jose Guzman and reliever Dale Mohorcic, Ranger rookies walked an alarming 464 batters in just 775⅔ innings.

Meanwhile, Pete Incaviglia, the free-swinging right fielder for Texas, fanned a rookie record 185 times. However, Incaviglia also hit 30 home runs and was part of a powerful group of freshmen in the class of 1986. Jose Canseco whiffed only ten times fewer than Incaviglia but smashed 33 homers and drove in 117 runs for the Oakland A's. Showing his athletic versatility, he also stole 15 bases.

ROOKIES WITH 30+ HR AND 10+ SB

Bob Allison, 1959 Was AL, 30 HR/13 SB
Tony Oliva, 1964 Min AL, 32 HR/12 SB
Jose Canseco, 1986 Oak AL, 33 HR/15 SB
Nomar Garciaparra, 1997 AL, 30 HR/22 SB

While Canseco would not experience postseason play until 1988, Wally Joyner had to wait only until October of 1986 to do so. Joyner replaced Rod Carew as the first baseman for the California Angels and responded with 100 RBI. In April Joyner hit six homers, tripling the departed Hall of Famer's 1985 production. The following month was even better, with Joyner connecting ten times. By midseason he had 19 taters and was the first rookie elected by the fans to start an All-Star Game. Joyner continued to drive in runs after the break, but his power numbers plummeted. He hit only three homers after June, but then, in the first three games of the ALCS against the Boston Red Sox, Joyner went 5-for-11 with three extra-base hits before a bacterial infection suddenly ended his season and helped cost the Angels their first World Series appearance as well.

Joyner, who had good bat control, became the first rookie since Joe DiMaggio in 1936 to hit at least 20 home runs and strike out in fewer than ten percent of his ABs. Danny Tartabull of the Seattle Mariners, like most freshmen in 1986, could scarcely imagine such discipline. Tartabull, who mainly played right field but also was at second base for 31 games, fanned 157 times but sent 96 runs across the plate.

Overshadowed by the freshman fence busters were three relievers who could each present a convincing argument that he had the best rookie season by a fireman to that point in time. One of the trio, Todd Worrell, had been 3–0 with five saves after a late-season call-up by the St. Louis Cardinals in 1985. Worrell also did well in the 1985 postseason and then took the NL by storm in 1986 with a 2.08 ERA and a league-leading 36 saves that are still the loop record for a freshman. Worrell's best stretch came in July when he was NL Pitcher of the Month, posting a 1.17 ERA and saving eight games.

The second of the trio, Rob Murphy, saved only one game for Cincinnati but was devastating as a middle reliever. Murphy gave up all of four runs in 50⅓ innings, giving him an 0.72 ERA, the best ever for a rookie with at least 50 innings of work.

LOWEST ERA BY ROOKIE (MINIMUM 50 IP)

0.72 ERA/50.1 IP, Rob Murphy, 1986 Cin NL
0.83 ERA/54 IP, Nick Maddox, 1907 Pit NL
0.86 ERA/105 IP, Tim Keefe, 1880 Tro NL
1.03 ERA/69.2 IP, Dale Murray, 1974 Mon NL
1.04 ERA/77.2 IP, Bob Veale, 1963 Pit NL

Worrell and Murphy had top-notch campaigns, to be sure, but Toronto's Mark Eichhorn was absolutely overwhelming. Eichhorn won 14 games and saved ten, pitching 157 innings, the second most ever for a rookie working exclusively in relief. He was only the second freshman hurler since 1910 to notch more innings than hits and walks combined (150). Also since 1910, Eichhorn's 1.72 ERA was the lowest by any rookie who worked as many as 150 innings. A power pitcher, Eichhorn blew away 166 batters and held right-handed hitters to a woeful .135 average.

ROOKIES WITH MORE Ks THAN HITS AND WALKS ALLOWED COMBINED (MINIMUM 150 IP)

Dwight Gooden, 1984 NY NL, 276 K/234 H+W
Mark Eichhorn, 1986 Tor AL, 166 K/150 H+W
Hideo Nomo, 1995 LA NL, 236 K/202 H+W
Kerry Wood, 1998 Chi NL, 233 K/202 H+W

If Eichhorn had toiled just five more innings, he would have been eligible for the ERA crown. Roger Clemens's 2.48 ERA led the AL, but as long as Eichhorn yielded fewer than 14 earned runs in those five extra frames, he would have taken the title. In strikeouts per nine innings, Eichhorn made an even stronger case. If five more innings without even one strikeout are charged to his record, his ratio comes to 9.22 whiffs per nine, edging Mark Langston's official league-leading figure of 9.21.

Despite finishing a disappointing third in ROY voting and a distant sixth in the Cy Young Award race, Eichhorn can rest assured that he had one of the best seasons ever by a reliever—rookie or otherwise.

After Vince Coleman set a new post-1901 rookie mark for stolen bases in 1985, John Cangelosi followed by swiping 50 sacks for the White Sox in 1986 to establish a new AL record. Cangelosi's baserunning mark has since been eclipsed by Kenny Lofton, who pilfered 66 bags with Cleveland in 1992, just six years later, but the diminutive Pale Hose center fielder perpetrated another rookie first in 1986 that appears certain not to be matched again for a much longer while. Batting leadoff for the Sox, Cangelosi picked up 71 walks but just 131 total bases, making him the only rookie outfield qualifier to post a sub-.300 SA and a .350+ OBP. What's more, Cangelosi and Bill North are the lone outfielders to perform this unlikely feat since the end of the Deadball Era.

OUTFIELDERS WITH SUB-.300 SA AND .350+ OBP

Name	Year	PA	SA	OBP
Paul Radford	1893	577	.293	.378
Bill North	1980	500	.292	.374
Bill North	1978	442	.270	.367
Cliff Carroll	1893	531	.276	.360
Ed Hahn	1907	698	.294	.359
Jimmy Slagle	1907	575	.294	.359
John Cangelosi	1986	525	.299	.351
Charlie Hemphill	1910	419	.288	.350
Nemo Leibold	1917	509	.292	.350

Note that the only other rookies, regardless of position, to match Cangelosi's feat are Frank Scheibeck in 1890 (.350 OBP and .295 SA), Jack Crooks in 1890 (.357 OBP and .254 SA), Baldy Louden in 1912 (.352 OBP and .298 SA), and Eddie Stanky in 1943 (.363 OBP and .278 SA).

Other Highlights

April 8—Will Clark homers off Nolan Ryan in his first ML at bat as the San Francisco Giants top the Houston Astros 8–3.

June 4—Barry Bonds gets four hits, including his first ML home run, with Craig McMurtry his victim, and Bonds's Pittsburgh Pirates win 12–3 at Atlanta.

September 21—Jimmy Jones pitches a one-hit shutout in his ML debut for the San Diego Padres, who beat Houston 5–0.

September 23—Jim Deshaies of the Astros beats the Los Angeles Dodgers 4–0, holding them to two hits

1986 ROOKIE LEADERS

Batting		Pitching	
G—AL 157, Jose Canseco, OAK		W—AL 14, Mark Eichhorn, TOR	
NL 149, Robby Thompson, SF		NL 12, Jim Deshaies, HOU	
AB—AL 600, Jose Canseco, OAK		L—AL 15, Jose Guzman, TEX	
NL 549, Robby Thompson, SF		NL 10, Lance McCullers, SD	
H—AL 172, Wally Joyner, CAL		Todd Worrell, STL	
NL 149, Robby Thompson, SF		PCT—AL .700, Mark Eichhorn, TOR	
2B—AL 29, Jose Canseco, OAK		NL No Qualifiers	
NL 27, Will Clark, SF		**GP—AL 80, Mitch Williams, TEX**	
Robby Thompson, SF		NL 74, Todd Worrell, STL	
3B—AL 10, Ruben Sierra, TEX		GS—AL 33, Juan Nieves, MIL	
NL 4, Kal Daniels, CIN		NL 26, Jim Deshaies, HOU	
HR—AL 33, Jose Canseco, OAK		CG—AL 4, Ed Correa, TEX	
NL 16, Barry Bonds, PIT		Juan Nieves, MIL	
R—AL 85, Jose Canseco, OAK		NL 6, Bruce Ruffin, PHI	
NL 73, Robby Thompson, SF		IP—AL 202.1, Ed Correa, TEX	
RBI—AL 117, Jose Canseco, OAK		NL 146.1, Bruce Ruffin, PHI	
NL 48, Barry Bonds, PIT		H—AL 224, Juan Nieves, MIL	
WK—AL 71, John Cangelosi, CHI		NL 139, Greg Mathews, STL	
NL 65, Barry Bonds, PIT		**BB—AL 143, Bobby Witt, TEX**	
SO—AL 185, Pete Incaviglia, TEX		NL 59, Jim Deshaies, HOU	
NL 112, Robby Thompson, SF		K—AL 189, Ed Correa, TEX	
SB—AL 50, John Cangelosi, CHI		NL 128, Jim Deshaies, HOU	
NL 36, Barry Bonds, PIT		ERA—AL 4.23, Ed Correa, TEX	
BA—AL .290, Wally Joyner, CAL		NL No Qualifiers	
NL .271, Robby Thompson, SF		SHO—AL 3, Juan Nieves, MIL	
SLG—AL .489, Danny Tartabull, SEA		NL 1, Jim Deshaies, HOU	
NL .444, Will Clark, SF		Jimmy Jones, SD	
OBP—AL .354, Wally Joyner, CAL		Jamie Moyer, CHI	
NL .329, Robby Thompson, SF		Bob Sebra, MON	
		SV—AL 14, Dan Plesac, MIL	
		NL 36, Todd Worrell, STL	

and setting a twentieth-century record by fanning the first eight batters he faces.

September 29—For the first time in history, rookie brothers oppose each other as starting pitchers, with Greg Maddux of the Chicago Cubs besting Mike Maddux and the Philadelphia Phillies 8–3.

September 29—Jay Bell, recently acquired by Cleveland in a trade for Bert Blyleven, homers off Blyleven in his first ML at bat and thereupon saddles Blyleven with his record 47th dinger surrendered in 1986; Blyleven's Twins nevertheless win the game 6–5.

◄─────── 1987 ─►

For investors, 1987 is remembered for the October stock market crash. For baseball fans, that year stirs memories of the crashing bats of several rookie hitters. Chief among the sluggers was Mark McGwire, the 23-year-old first baseman of the Oakland Athletics. McGwire, who hit three home runs in 18 games in 1986, homered four times in April 1987 but was just getting warmed up. In May McGwire powered 15 baseballs over the fences and had three of the seven multi-homer games he would produce that year.

Going into the June 27 game at Cleveland, the red-headed slugger had just three round trippers that month—a far cry from his previous production. But McGwire's ever-increasing fan club need not have been concerned because that day he ripped three home runs and scored five times. The following day McGwire added two more dongs and scored four runs, giving him a modern record-tying nine tallies over two games.

McGwire had 33 homers at the All-Star break, threatening Roger Maris's round tripper standard of 61. On August 14 Big Mac hit number 39, breaking the freshman record held by Wally Berger of the 1930 Boston Braves and Frank Robinson of the 1956 Cincinnati Reds. While McGwire would have to wait 11 years before overtaking Maris, he finished with 49 home runs and a .618 slugging average, both tops in the AL. The latter figure is the highest ever for a rookie with at least 400 at bats, and McGwire's 118 RBI were the most by a rookie in 37 years and also one more than Jose Canseco's A's freshman record, set just the year before. For his prodigious power display, McGwire earned a sixth-place finish in MVP balloting and was a unanimous selection for AL ROY.

Finishing a distant second for junior circuit rookie laurels was third baseman Kevin Seitzer of the Kansas City Royals. Seitzer inherited the hot corner from George Brett, who had moved to first base, and immediately proved to be a worthy successor, hitting .382 with five triples and 12 RBI in April. Like McGwire, Seitzer earned a berth on the All-Star team in July, a month that saw him bat .346. The Royals new third sacker ended the season tied for the AL lead with 207 hits and batted .323.

Matching Seitzer's rookie-high 33 doubles was Benito Santiago, the rifle-armed catcher of the San Diego Padres. Santiago, a free-swinger from Puerto Rico, walked only 16 times but hit .300 and late in August launched an amazing hitting streak. It began on August 25 with a three-run homer against the Montreal Expos in a 5–1 Padres win. Nearly a month later, Santiago was still at it, hitting in his 26th straight game September 24 to break Tony Gwynn's club record. The streak grew to 34 games before being snapped on October 3 and still represents the longest skein ever by a Padre, a catcher,

Kevin Seitzer rode the wind stirred up by the offensive explosion in 1987 to set personal season highs in just about every major offensive department. But unlike so many hitters who peak in their rookie years, Seitzer remained a potent force throughout his 12-year career. In 1996 he topped his frosh output in two major departments when he hit .326 and racked up a .420 OBP. *Transcendental Graphics*

and a rookie. (Browns freshman George McQuinn also had a 34-gamer in 1938.)

Rookie catcher Matt Nokes of the Detroit Tigers also provided an impressive offensive display, albeit for that one year only. Never again in an 11-year career would Nokes approach his yearling form as he hit 32 home runs, the fourth-highest total ever for a freshman backstop, batted .289, and posted a .536 SA, second among rookies only to McGwire. In addition, Nokes's 87 RBI ranked third among rookies in 1987, following only McGwire and outfielder Mike Greenwell of Boston. The Red Sox benefited from 89 RBI and a .328 batting average from Greenwell, who teamed with Ellis Burks and Sam Horn to form a potent freshman triad. Burks became just the fifth rookie with at least 20 homers and stolen bases, with 20 and 27, respectively.

Benito Santiago properly won the NL ROY award in 1987 on the basis of his rookie-record 34-game hitting streak and fine overall stats that included 18 home runs and a .793 OPS. But that same season a rookie catcher in the AL hammered 16 home runs and posted a .815 OPS and yet failed to receive a single first-place vote for the junior loop ROY prize.

Much of the reason that A's backstopper Terry Steinbach was ignored by balloters rested in the fact that Mark McGwire, the game's top rookie in 1987, was his teammate, but it was Steinbach's fate to remain below the radar for his entire career. Few fans today are even aware that he is a co-holder of the AL season record for home runs by a catcher, largely because in 1996, the year he clubbed 35 homers for the A's, Todd Hundley set the since-broken all-time ML backstoppers mark with 41.

Moreover, Burks's steals were the most by a BoSox rookie since 1909 when Tris Speaker had 35. Horn's stay in Boston was briefer, not beginning until July 25. In 158 at bats, however, Horn ripped 14 home runs and knocked in 34 runs. Sub gardener, Todd Benzinger, with 43 RBI in just 223 ABs, also contributed significantly to the awesome totals posted by the Hub's rookie outfielders.

Other Highlights

June 10—Ellis Burks of the Red Sox hammers two homers, one a grand slam, and drives in seven runs in a 15–4 Boston victory over Baltimore.

July 11—When Billy Ripken joins his brother Cal in the Orioles' starting lineup in a 2–1 loss to the Twins, their

1987 ROOKIE LEADERS

Batting

G—AL 161, Kevin Seitzer, KC
    NL 146, Benito Santiago, SD
AB—AL 641, Kevin Seitzer, KC
    NL 546, Benito Santiago, SD
H—**AL 207, Kevin Seitzer, KC**
    NL 164, Benito Santiago, SD
2B—AL 33, Kevin Seitzer, KC
    NL 33, Benito Santiago, SD
3B—AL 10, Luis Polonia, OAK
    NL 7, Stan Jefferson, SD
HR—**AL 49, Mark McGwire, OAK**
    NL 18, Benito Santiago, SD
R—AL 105, Kevin Seitzer, KC
    NL 64, Benito Santiago, SD
RBI—AL 118, Mark McGwire, OAK
    NL 79, Benito Santiago, SD
WK—AL 80, Kevin Seitzer, KC
    NL 39, Stan Jefferson, SD
SO—AL 158, Bo Jackson, KC
    NL 112, Benito Santiago, SD
SB—AL 29, Luis Polonia, OAK
    NL 34, Stan Jefferson, SD
BA—AL .323, Kevin Seitzer, KC
    NL .300, Benito Santiago, SD
SLG—**AL .618, Mark McGwire, OAK**
    NL .467, Benito Santiago, SD
OBP—AL .400, Kevin Seitzer, KC
    NL .326, Benito Santiago, SD

Pitching

W—AL 12, Jeff Musselman, TOR
    NL 13, Mike Dunne, PIT
L—AL 13, Eric Bell, BAL
    NL 14, Greg Maddux, CHI
PCT—AL .500, Willie Fraser, CAL
    NL .684, Mike Dunne, PIT
GP—AL 68, Jeff Musselman, TOR
    NL 63, John Smiley, PIT
GS—AL 29, Eric Bell, BAL
    NL 27, Greg Maddux, CHI
CG—AL 5, Willie Fraser, CAL
           Bill Long, CHI
    NL 5, Mike Dunne, PIT
IP—AL 176.2, Willie Fraser, CAL
    NL 170.1, Joe Magrane, STL
H—AL 187, Chris Bosio, MIL
    NL 181, Greg Maddux, CHI
BB—AL 78, Eric Bell, BAL
    NL 74, Greg Maddux, CHI
K—AL 150, Chris Bosio, MIL
    NL 101, Greg Maddux, CHI
           Joe Magrane, STL
ERA—AL 3.92, Willie Fraser, CAL
    NL 3.03, Mike Dunne, PIT
SHO—AL 2, Bill Long, CHI
    NL 2, Joe Magrane, STL
SV—AL 17, DeWayne Buice, CAL
    NL 6, Randy Myers, NY
           Jeff Parrett, MON

father, Cal Ripken Sr., becomes the first to manage two sons in a major league game.

July 14—Junior loop rookie stars Mark McGwire, Kevin Seitzer, and Matt Nokes go a collective 0-for-9 in the AL's 2–0 13-inning loss in the All-Star Game.

August 2—In the Royals 13–5 blasting of the Red Sox, KC rookie Kevin Seitzer goes 6-for-6 with two homers and seven RBI to tie the AL record for hits in a nine-inning game.

September 14—Mickey Brantley gets five hits, including three home runs, and drives in seven, but the Seattle Mariners lose to Cleveland 11–8.

October 20—Les Straker of the Minnesota Twins pitches six scoreless innings in Game Three of the World Series, but the St. Louis Cardinals win 3–1.

1988

Chris Sabo was not your prototypical third baseman. Rather than being bulky or slow, the new Cincinnati third sacker was unusually fleet afoot—so fleet, in fact, that he stole 46 bases, the most by a rookie third baseman since the current stolen-base rules went into effect in 1898.

MOST SB BY ROOKIE THIRD BASEMAN, 1898–2003

46, Chris Sabo, 1988 Cin NL
33, Art Devlin, 1904 NY NL
32, Ryne Sandberg, 1982 Chi NL
30, Jimmy Austin, 1909 NY AL
29, Doug Baird, 1915 Pit NL

Sabo also possessed quick reflexes, leading the NL in fielding percentage and tying for the top in double plays. He began his ROY season modestly enough with a .263 average in April. Sabo then improved to .287 in May before really beginning to find his stroke the following month when he batted .373, going 41-for-110 with 14 doubles. In the All-Star Game at his home park, Cincinnati's Riverfront Stadium, Sabo pinch-ran and stole second, but the AL won 2–1. Subsequent to the Midsummer Classic, Sabo fell into a mild slump, and then in September an injury limited his playing time. Nevertheless, he totaled 40 doubles, making him the

first rookie since 1914—and only the third overall—to reach both 40 steals and 40 doubles.

Just five freshmen had more than 113 hits in 1988, all of them in the NL. Jose Lind collected 160 for Pittsburgh, and another second baseman, at least for the moment, Atlanta's Ron Gant, had 146, 55 of which took him beyond first base. Gant smashed 19 home runs, the second highest total by a rookie whose main position was the keystone sack. He also scored 85 runs and swiped 19 bases. Roberto Alomar and Mark Grace were next in line, amassing 145 and 144 hits, respectively. Alomar exhibited his awe-inspiring range as San Diego's second baseman and batted .266, outhitting the loop by 17 points. Cubs first baseman Grace was sixth in batting with a .296 average and drew a rookie-best 60 walks. Defensively, he committed a league-high 17 errors but also made many dazzling plays that foreshadowed his Gold Glove brilliance.

Walt Weiss, en route to becoming the third consecutive Oakland player to be AL ROY, hit just .250 with 113 safeties, but both marks were good enough to lead all AL yearlings. At shortstop Weiss solidified the Athletics' defense and helped Oakland make its first World Series appearance since 1974. In the ALCS he was 5-for-15 with two doubles against the Boston Red Sox. In Game Two Weiss singled in the go-ahead run in the ninth inning as the Athletics won 4–3. After sweeping Boston four straight, Oakland faced the underdog Los Angeles Dodgers in the Fall Classic. The Dodgers stymied the Athletics' potent offense, and especially the so-called "Bash Brothers," Jose Canseco and Mark McGwire, surrendering just 11 runs in their five-game triumph. Weiss scored one of those tallies but had only one hit in 16 at bats as Oakland hit a paltry .177.

Bryan Harvey finished second to Weiss in ROY voting. The California Angels reliever saved a rookie-high 17 games and had a 2.13 ERA in 76 innings before needing a September elbow operation.

Oddly, the NL's freshman saves leader with a mere four was Tim Belcher, who relieved just nine times for Los Angeles. Belcher made 27 starts, completing four of them, and went 12–6, compiling a 2.91 ERA. Starting September 16, he completed three straight starts but went just 1–2 despite yielding only three runs (two earned) in 25 innings. In the NLCS Belcher won games two and five versus the New York Mets. He started the opener of the World Series, but the Athletics tapped him for four runs in two innings and he wound up with a no-decision for the evening. However, Belcher won Game Four, and the Dodgers wrapped up the series the next night.

Don August paced all rookies with 13 wins for the Milwaukee Brewers, and Melido Perez was victorious a dozen times for the Chicago White Sox. Perez ended his season strongly when he fired a two-hitter at Kansas City on October 1, striking out ten Royals and winning 3–0.

Perez's teammate, centerfielder Dave Gallagher, was one of only two freshmen with more than 250 ABs to top the .300 mark. Gallagher batted .303 in 101 games. The unofficial rookie hitting leader, however, was Philadelphia first baseman Ricky Jordan with a .308 BA in 69 games. Although Jordan didn't join the Phils until after the All-Star break, he fashioned an 18-game hitting streak and clubbed 11 home runs, in-

cluding one in his first ML at bat on July 17 against Houston.

Other Highlights

May 31—Jeff Pico of the Chicago Cubs hurls a four-hit shutout in his ML debut, beating Cincinnati 4–0.

August 26—Five days after blanking the Cubs 1–0, Pete Smith of Atlanta whitewashes Chicago again, this time scattering just five hits and winning 4–0.

September 18—Bob Milacki surrenders just one hit in eight innings in his ML debut as Baltimore wins 2–0 at Detroit, beginning a three-game stretch in which Milacki yields only nine hits in 25 innings and posts an 0.72 ERA.

September 25—Dennis Cook tosses a two-hitter as the San Francisco Giants beat Los Angeles's rookie ace Tim Belcher 2–0.

Time once again to examine a pair of hitting profiles from the same rookie class. Here we have two AL outfielders who were both highly touted in the spring of 1988. One had led the International League in home runs in 1987 while playing for the Yankees' top farm team in Columbus, and the other was expected to be the Red Sox center fielder for the next decade.

Age	G	AB	R	H	2B	3B	HR	RBI	BB	SO	SB	CS	BA	SA	OBP	OPS
24	94	325	31	69	13	4	1	21	23	75	10	6	.212	.286	.273	.559
23	85	261	36	56	13	1	13	38	28	93	1	1	.215	.421	.305	.727

After scanning these wretched profiles, will it surprise you to learn that the Yankees farmhand hit only three career homers for the Bombers or that the Red Sox jettisoned their highly ballyhooed center fielder before the 1988 season was finished? Almost certainly not, but it may come as something of a shock to learn that both of these outfielders were still active with other AL teams in the twenty-first century. Even more astonishing, imagine the future kudos a GM could have garnered for himself if he had acquired both men in 1988 on the hunch that one would achieve the third highest career OPS in history among players with a sub-.260 BA and the other would become the first leadoff hitter in history to smack 50 home runs in a season.

The top rookie hitting profile belongs to Brady Anderson, and Jay Buhner owns the other.

HIGHEST CAREER OPS, BA BELOW .260 (4,000 ABS)

Rank	Name	AB	BA	OPS
1	Harmon Killebrew	8147	.256	.887
2	Darryl Strawberry	5418	.259	.865
3	Jay Buhner	5013	.254	.855
4	Bob Allison	5032	.255	.831
5	Cecil Fielder	5157	.255	.829

1988 ROOKIE LEADERS

Batting	Pitching
G—AL 147, Walt Weiss, OAK	W—AL 13, Don August, MIL
NL 154, Jose Lind, PIT	NL 12, Tim Belcher, LA
AB—AL 452, Walt Weiss, OAK	L—AL 15, Jose Bautista, BAL
NL 611, Jose Lind, PIT	NL 15, Pete Smith, ATL
H—AL 113, Walt Weiss, OAK	PCT—AL .650, Don August, MIL
NL 160, Jose Lind, PIT	NL .667, Tim Belcher, LA
2B—AL 23, Jody Reed, BOS	GP—AL 64, Duane Ward, TOR
NL 40, Chris Sabo, CIN	NL 60, Jose Alvarez, ATL
3B—AL 6, Cecil Espy, TEX	GS—AL 32, Melido Perez, CHI
NL 8, Ron Gant, ATL	NL 32, Pete Smith, ATL
HR—AL 13, Jay Buhner, NY/SEA	CG—AL 6, Don August, MIL
NL 19, Ron Gant, ATL	NL 5, Pete Smith, ATL
R—AL 60, Jody Reed, BOS	IP—AL 197.0, Melido Perez, CHI
NL 85, Ron Gant, ATL	NL 195.1, Pete Smith, ATL
RBI—AL 45, Joey Meyer, MIL	H—AL 186, Melido Perez, CHI
NL 60, Ron Gant, ATL	NL 183, Pete Smith, ATL
WK—AL 45, Jody Reed, BOS	BB—AL 72, Melido Perez, CHI
NL 60, Mark Grace, CHI	NL 88, Pete Smith, ATL
SO—AL 93, Jay Buhner, NY/SEA	K—AL 138, Melido Perez, CHI
NL 118, Ron Gant, ATL	NL 152, Tim Belcher, LA
SB—AL 33, Cecil Espy, TEX	ERA—AL 3.79, Melido Perez, CHI
NL 46, Chris Sabo, CIN	NL 2.91, Tim Belcher, LA
BA—AL .250, Walt Weiss, OAK	SHO—AL 1, done by six pitchers
NL .296, Mark Grace, CHI	NL 3, Pete Smith, ATL
SLG—AL .321, Walt Weiss, OAK	SV—AL 17, Bryan Harvey, CAL
NL .439, Ron Gant, ATL	NL 4, Tim Belcher, LA
OBP—AL .317, Walt Weiss, OAK	
NL .374, Mark Grace, CHI	

1989

Dwight Smith did not even start the game that Chicago Cubs fans best remember him for. The Houston Astros led the August 29, 1989, contest 9–0 going into the bottom of the sixth inning, when the Cubs scored twice. Smith entered the game the next inning, and Chicago produced three more runs, partly due to Smith's RBI single. In the eighth Smith's sacrifice fly knotted the game at 9–9, and two innings later he singled in the winning run as the Cubs completed an improbable comeback.

Scoring the winning tally in that game was Jerome Walton, Smith's fellow rookie outfielder. Walton, unlike Smith, was on the Cubs' Opening Day roster and hit in his first seven games. This was just a prelude to a streak Walton would begin July 21. The skein grew to 30 games, the longest for a Cub in the twentieth century. The Cubs went 20–10 in that stretch, surging into first place.

Had a torn hamstring in May not cost him a month of playing time, Walton would have added to his rookie-leading 139 hits. As it was, he batted .293, topped by Smith's .324. Only two Cubs rookies have hit higher than Smith in at least as many at bats—and none since Hack Miller in 1922.

The Cubs became just the sixth team to own the top two slots in a league's ROY voting. The Baltimore Orioles almost saw a pair of their freshmen duplicate Walton and Smith's feat. Gregg Olson, who featured an almost unhittable curveball, was Baltimore's closer, saving 27 games for the revitalized Orioles, which had begun the prior season by dropping their initial 21 contests. Improving by 32½ games in 1989, the Birds finished only two games back in the AL East. Olson, a.k.a. "The Otter," had a 1.69 ERA in 64 games and was named ROY in the junior circuit. Finishing fourth in the balloting was Orioles third baseman Craig Worthington, who drove in 70 runs. Bob Milacki, surprisingly, received nary a vote. Milacki went 14–12 and spun a pair of three-hit shutouts. His 243 innings ranked fifth in the loop and were the most by an AL rookie since 1978. No freshman in either league has equaled Milacki's workload since.

Chris Hoiles, Randy Milligan, and Ben McDonald were also in Baltimore's 1989 rookie stable along with a trio still in the majors in the twenty-first century. Steve Finley would win Gold Gloves patrolling the outfield while Pete Harnisch and, especially, Curt Schilling would prosper on the mound. Unfortunately for the Orioles, most of this success took place after the trio was dealt to Houston in January 1991 when Baltimore felt a pressing, albeit misguided, need to acquire fading first baseman Glenn Davis.

While that transaction might seem like a horror story to Baltimore fans, a pitcher who was later featured in a Stephen King novel terrorized AL batters. In 1988 Tom Gordon went 16–5 at three minor league stops in the Kansas City system, posting a 1.55 ERA, which included a 0.38 showing in 47⅓ innings at AA Memphis. In 1989 Gordon was a valuable swingman for the Royals, starting 16 games and relieving in 33 others. He was 17–9 and finished second to Nolan Ryan in both strikeout ratio and opponents batting average.

A pitcher who would tie Ryan's record for most 300-strikeout seasons was part of an awesome collection of talent surfacing in Seattle. Randy Johnson went 7–9 and whiffed 104 batters, a fraction of his future totals. Edgar Martinez hit only .240 but would win two batting titles in the 1990s as the game's premier designated hitter. Every bit as much as Martinez excelled in the batter's box, Omar Vizquel shined in the field, winning the AL Gold Glove at shortstop for nine straight years from 1993 through 2001. Combining the strengths of Martinez and Vizquel was Ken Griffey Jr. In 1990 the 20-year-old gardener not only became the first performer in big league history to play in a game with his father but, more importantly, first demonstrated the skills that would make him one of the game's superstars for more than a decade.

California Angels pitcher Jim Abbott was not as phys-

When Jerome Walton bagged the 1989 NL ROY Award and Dwight Smith was the runner-up, it made the Chicago Cubs the first NL team with the top two rookies in its loop to qualify for a postseason berth. A loss to San Francisco in the NLCS prevented the Bruins from joining the 1975 Red Sox, which still remains the only club to earn a World Series trip while showcasing its loop's top two rookies.

TEAMS WITH TOP TWO ROY FINISHERS

Team	Year	1	2
Phi-NL	1957	Jack Sanford	Ed Bouchee
Bal-AL	1960	Ron Hansen	Chuck Estrada/ Jim Gentile*
Chi-AL	1963	Gary Peters	Pete Ward
Bos-AL	1975	Fred Lynn	Jim Rice
Sea-AL	1984	Alvin Davis	Mark Langston
Chi-NL	1989	Jerome Walton	Dwight Smith

* The 1960 Orioles swept all 24 votes for AL ROY, as Hansen received 22 and Estrada and Gentile both got one each.

ically blessed as Griffey, or the majority of other people for that matter. Abbott was born without a right hand but despite that handicap fashioned a brilliant collegiate career at the University of Michigan that made him the first baseball player to win the Sullivan Award as the country's best amateur athlete. In the majors in 1989, Abbott won a dozen games, including two shutouts. Abbott, like Dwight Smith and the Cubs on August 29, overcame a rough beginning to reach a superlative end.

Other Highlights

April 18—Tommy Gregg collects three singles and two doubles for the Atlanta Braves, who edge the Houston Astros 5–4 in 11 innings.

May 3—Kevin Brown fires a two-hitter, the Texas Rangers topping the New York Yankees 4–1.

May 16—Randy Kramer allows only one hit as the Pittsburgh Pirates beat the Cincinnati Reds 5–0.

August 23—Lenny Harris of the Dodgers goes 5-for-9 in Los Angeles's 22-inning 1–0 win at Montreal.

September 15—Erik Hanson yields but two hits for Seattle in his 3–1 win over the Yankees.

1989 ROOKIE LEADERS

Batting	Pitching
G—AL 145, Craig Worthington, BAL	W—AL 17, Tom Gordon, KC
NL 141, Gregg Jefferies, NY	NL 8, Greg Harris, SD
AB—AL 497, Craig Worthington, BAL	Derek Lilliquist, ATL
NL 508, Gregg Jefferies, NY	L—AL 12, Jim Abbott, CAL
H—AL 123, Craig Worthington, BAL	Bob Milacki, BAL
NL 139, Jerome Walton, CHI	**NL 15, Ken Hill, STL**
2B—AL 23, Ken Griffey Jr., SEA	PCT—AL .654, Tom Gordon, KC
Randy Milligan, BAL	NL .444, Derek Lilliquist, ATL
Craig Worthington, BAL	GP—AL 73, Kenny Rogers, TEX
NL 28, Gregg Jefferies, NY	NL 59, Jeff Brantley, SF
3B—AL 8, Junior Felix, TOR	**GS—AL 36, Bob Milacki, BAL**
NL 6, Dwight Smith, CHI	NL 33, Ken Hill, STL
HR—AL 16, Ken Griffey Jr., SEA	CG—AL 7, Kevin Brown, TEX
NL 12, Gregg Jefferies, NY	NL 2, Marty Clary, ATL
R—AL 62, Junior Felix, TOR	Dennis Cook, SF/PHI
NL 72, Gregg Jefferies, NY	Ken Hill, STL
RBI—AL 70, Craig Worthington, BAL	Ramon Martinez, LA
NL 56, Gregg Jefferies, NY	IP—AL 243.0, Bob Milacki, BAL
WK—AL 74, Randy Milligan, BAL	NL 196.2, Ken Hill, STL
NL 39, Gregg Jefferies, NY	H—AL 233, Bob Milacki, BAL
SO—AL 114, Craig Worthington, BAL	NL 202, Derek Lilliquist, ATL
NL 100, Rolando Roomes, CIN	BB—AL 88, Bob Milacki, BAL
SB—AL 22, Mike Devereaux, BAL	**NL 99, Ken Hill, STL**
NL 24, Jerome Walton, CHI	K—AL 153, Tom Gordon, KC
BA—AL .264, Ken Griffey Jr., SEA	NL 112, Ken Hill, STL
NL .293, Jerome Walton, CHI	ERA—AL 3.35, Kevin Brown, TEX
SLG—AL .420, Ken Griffey Jr., SEA	NL 3.80, Ken Hill, STL
NL .392, Gregg Jefferies, NY	SHO—AL 2, Jim Abbott, CAL
OBP—AL .331, Ken Griffey Jr., SEA	Bob Milacki, BAL
NL .339, Jerome Walton, CHI	NL 2, Ramon Martinez, LA
	SV—AL 27, Gregg Olson, BAL
	NL 7, Mike Stanton, ATL

1990s

---- **1990** ----

Heading into the 1990s, the Atlanta Braves and Cleveland Indians were the laughingstocks of baseball. The Braves had finished last in the NL West three of the previous four seasons, losing 203 games over the past two years. Cleveland had not breathed first-division air since division play began and had lost more than 100 games in two of the previous five seasons. While neither team would be a factor in the 1990 pennant races, both clubs possessed a rookie who provided hope for the future.

A fractured left cheekbone kept David Justice out of Atlanta's lineup until mid-May, but he hit .352 the remainder of that month. He batted in the low .200s in June and July, but after Dale Murphy was traded to the Philadelphia Phillies, Justice shifted from first base to right field. The move agreed with him. The sweet-swinging Justice was NL Player of the Month in August, topping the loop with 11 home runs and 29 RBI. In an August 7 doubleheader, he went 5-for-9 with three home runs and five RBI. The next day, Justice belted two more round trippers in a 7–1 win against the San Diego

Padres. In September he batted .344 and ripped nine additional taters, giving him 23 after the All-Star break.

Justice took NL ROY honors but could not match the feat of his freshman teammate, catcher Greg Olson, who played in the All-Star Game. Olson went 0-for-1 as a pinch hitter in the NL's 2–0 loss at Wrigley Field. Also participating in that game was another rookie backstopper—Sandy Alomar of the Cleveland Indians. Alomar had his second five-RBI game on May 3, drawing the attention that would result in his being voted the AL's starting receiver in the Midsummer Classic. He did not disappoint, going 2-for-3 and scoring the go-ahead run. Alomar could do more than hit, however, and earned the Gold Glove for his excellent defense behind the plate. He was the unanimous choice for ROY in the junior circuit.

While the Indians would have to wait until 1994 to surpass the .500 mark, the Chicago White Sox flew by that figure in 1990, winning 94 games—25 more than in 1989. Part of the resurgence can be attributed to the August arrival of Frank Thomas. The first baseman became only the fifth rookie with an OBP better than .450 (minimum 50 games). Thomas was on base 109 times in 60

Kevin Maas is remembered today for reaching both ten and 20 career home runs in the fewest at bats of any performer in ML history, but another graduate of the 1990 AL rookie class set an equally interesting, albeit much less publicized, all-time record. On July 11 San Diego and Cleveland swapped minor league players, with the Indians getting centerfielder Alex Cole in return for catcher Tom Lampkin. In the full course of time, Lampkin proved to be the more valuable of the two, but Cole had by far the strongest immediate impact on his team's fortunes.

Although Cole did not join the Tribe until July 27, in the remaining 63 games he compiled 40 stolen bases, the most ever by a player not in the majors prior to the All-Star break. What's more, Cole not only led Cleveland in steals, but he also paced the team in BA and OBP over the second half of the season. Much like Maas, Cole never again approached his rookie form.

games, hitting .330. Between AA Birmingham and the majors, Thomas drew 156 bases on balls in 169 games.

ROOKIES WITH .450 + OBP (MINIMUM 50 GAMES)

.468 OBP/147 G, Joe Jackson, 1911 Cle AL
.460 OBP/60 G, Frank Thomas, 1990 Chi AL
.457 OBP/150 G, Roy Thomas, 1899 Phi NL
.456 OBP/64 G, Johnny Schulte, 1927 StL NL
.456 OBP/125 G, Bernie Carbo, 1970 Cin NL

Had Thomas been called up earlier, he almost certainly would have challenged Alomar for freshman laurels. As it was, finishing second to Alomar was Kevin Maas, the slugging first baseman of the New York Yankees. Maas was a Yankee Doodle Dandy on July 4, hitting his first major league home run. Ten

1990 ROOKIE LEADERS

Batting	Pitching
G—AL 150, Robin Ventura, CHI	W—AL 12, Kevin Appier, KC
NL 144, Todd Zeile, STL	Kevin Tapani, MIN
AB—AL 512, Carlos Quintana, BOS	NL 14, John Burkett, SF
NL 499, Delino DeShields, MON	L—AL 9, Dana Kiecker, BOS
H—AL 147, Carlos Quintana, BOS	NL 11, Steve Avery, ATL
NL 144, Delino DeShields, MON	PCT—AL .600, Kevin Appier, KC
2B—AL 28, Carlos Quintana, BOS	Kevin Tapani, MIN
NL 28, Delino DeShields, MON	NL .667, John Burkett, SF
3B—AL 4, Alex Cole, CLE	GP—AL 62, Scott Radinsky, CHI
NL 6, Delino DeShields, MON	NL 67, Scott Ruskin, PIT/MON
HR—AL 21, Kevin Maas, NY	GS—AL 28, Kevin Tapani, MIN
NL 28, David Justice, ATL	NL 32, John Burkett, SF
R—AL 60, Sandy Alomar, CLE	CG—AL 3, Kevin Appier, KC
NL 76, David Justice, ATL	Alex Fernandez, CHI
RBI—AL 67, Carlos Quintana, BOS	Ben McDonald, BAL
NL 78, David Justice, ATL	NL 3, Pat Combs, PHI
WK—AL 57, John Olerud, TOR	Jose DeJesus, PHI
NL 67, Todd Zeile, STL	Mark Gardner, MON
SO—AL 91, Greg Vaughn, MIL	IP—AL 185.2, Kevin Appier, KC
NL 112, Larry Walker, MON	NL 204.0, John Burkett, SF
SB—AL 40, Alex Cole, CLE	H—AL 179, Kevin Appier, KC
NL 42, Delino DeShields, MON	NL 201, John Burkett, SF
BA—AL .287, Carlos Quintana, BOS	BB—AL 54, Kevin Appier, KC
NL .289, Delino DeShields, MON	Dana Kiecker, BOS
SLG—AL .383, Carlos Quintana, BOS	NL 86, Pat Combs, PHI
NL .535, David Justice, ATL	K—AL 127, Kevin Appier, KC
OBP—AL .355, Carlos Quintana, BOS	NL 135, Mark Gardner, MON
NL .376, Delino DeShields, MON	ERA—AL 2.76, Kevin Appier, KC
	NL 3.26, Mike Harkey, CHI
	SHO—AL 3, Kevin Appier, KC
	NL 3, Mark Gardner, MON
	SV—AL 9, Jeff Gray, BOS
	NL 9, Steve Frey, MON

days later he smashed a pair of circuit clouts and knocked in five runs, but the Yankees lost 8–7 to the White Sox in ten innings. Maas ended July with eight homers, and on August 2 he entered the record books. Two more long balls gave him ten in his first 78 ML at bats, breaking the mark of George Scott, who reached double figures in one more at bat for the 1966 Boston Red Sox.

Other Highlights

July 10—At Chicago's Wrigley Field, in the 61st All-Star Game, Sandy Alomar, of the Cleveland Indians becomes the first rookie catcher to start a Midsummer Classic for either league.

July 12—Mark Gardner throws his second consecutive four-hit shutout for the Montreal Expos, this time striking out ten Atlanta Braves while walking none and winning 3–0.

July 20—Kevin Appier, who tossed a one-hitter earlier in the month, permits only four base runners and fans ten Boston Red Sox in the Kansas City Royals' 5–0 win.

July 21—Baltimore's Ben McDonald marks his first ML start by blanking the Chicago White Sox 2–0.

August 1—Alex Cole steals five bases in the Cleveland Indians' 4–1 win over the Royals.

August 7—Jose DeJesus of the Philadelphia Phillies tosses a two-hitter, whitewashing the New York Mets 9–0.

August 18—Mark Lemke gets five hits, including a double, and Atlanta pounds the Chicago Cubs 17–6.

September 20—Chris Nabholz fires a one-hit shutout as the Montreal Expos beat the Mets 2–0 in the second game of a doubleheader.

1991

A sacrifice bunt may not be the most exciting play in baseball, and some question whether it's even strategically sound. For the Minnesota Twins, however, the successful sacrifice bunt laid down by rookie Chuck

Knoblauch in the bottom of the tenth inning in Game Seven of the 1991 World Series was a memorable moment. Three batters later, the Twins were world champions after having beaten the Atlanta Braves 1–0 in a thrilling Fall Classic that was decided by Gene Larkin's extra-innings pinch single. Knoblauch had collected eight hits and four walks in the series after hitting .350 with five runs in Minnesota's five-game victory over the Toronto Blue Jays in the ALCS. The rookie second sacker, a nephew of former Texas League batting champ Eddie Knoblauch, batted .281, swiped 25 bases in the regular season, and had 159 hits.

Knoblauch was ROY, beating out one of his postseason opponents, Toronto pitcher Juan Guzman. Guzman started off his frosh campaign 0–2 but then won ten in a row to finish 10–3 with a 2.99 ERA. In Game Two of the league championship series, he went 5⅔ innings, yielding just two runs as Toronto enjoyed its only win versus Minnesota. Guzman's 3.18 ERA in the ALCS was duplicated by his rookie teammate, reliever Mike Timlin, who surrendered the decisive run in the tenth inning of Game Three, taking the loss. Timlin made 60 relief appearances and three starts for Toronto, winning 11 games and saving three.

Knoblauch's hometown of Houston witnessed several fine rookie seasons; the best was produced by Astros first baseman Jeff Bagwell, an ex-Boston farmhand. Bagwell hit .294 and drew 75 bases on balls for a .391 OBP that ranked fifth in the NL. He smashed 15 home runs and accumulated 82 RBI en route to ROY honors in the senior circuit. In addition to Bagwell, Luis Gonzalez hit 13 round trippers for Houston, two of them on May 1, when he drove in four runs in a Houston loss, while lefty Al Osuna saved 12 games in 71 relief appearances and Darryl Kile went 7–11 with a 3.69 ERA for the last-place Astros.

Rivaling Bagwell's 1991 performance was that of another Lone Star standout, Texas's Juan Gonzalez. The Rangers' outfielder had used up his "official" rookie status the previous year, a fact bemoaned by *Baseball America* in its March 10, 1991, issue. In his first full season, Gonzalez ripped 27 home runs and had 102 RBI while hitting 34 doubles. Had he not accumulated 20 too many at bats in 1990, Gonzalez would have given Knoblauch a strong challenge for the AL ROY prize.

Two NL East players closely trailed Bagwell for freshman honors in the senior circuit. In third place was Ray Lankford of the St. Louis Cardinals, who led the loop with 15 triples and pilfered 44 bases. On September 15 Lankford hit for the cycle and scored four times in a 7–2 win against the New York Mets. ROY runner-up Orlando Merced hit .275 for Pittsburgh and scored 83 runs in only 120 games. In the NLCS the first baseman went 2-for-9 with a home run as the Pirates lost to Atlanta in seven games. Braves first sacker Brian Hunter, who occupied fourth place in the NL rookie balloting, hit .333 in the NLCS with four RBI, including three in Game Seven, when he hit a two-run homer and a run-scoring double in Atlanta's 4–0 victory. In the Fall Classic Hunter had only four hits but drove in three runs in the Braves' seven-game defeat. He hit 12 home runs in the regular season and knocked in 50 despite not debuting until the campaign was nearly two months old.

Doug Henry also excelled in limited action. After joining the Brewers on July 15, the reliever saved 15 games and sported a nearly invisible ERA of 1.00 in 32 appearances and 36 innings. So stingy was Henry in his frosh endeavor that he allowed the fewest enemy hits per nine innings of any hurler who worked a minimum of 30 innings since the beginning of division play in 1969.

FEWEST HITS PER NINE INNINGS, MINIMUM 30 IP (SINCE 1969)

Rank	Name	YEAR	H/9 IP	G	IP
1	Doug Henry	1991	4.00	32	36
2	Jeff Nelson	2001	4.13	69	65.1
3	Billy Wagner	1999	4.22	66	74.2
4	Goose Gossage	1981	4.24	32	46.2
5	Troy Percival	1995	4.50	62	74

Seattle's Rich DeLucia topped all rookies in 1991 with 12 wins despite a 5.09 ERA. As would be St. Louis's Donovan Osborne in 1992, Omar Olivares of the Cardinals was the lone NL frosh to win at least ten games, going 11–7 for the Redbirds. Charles Nagy was the busiest rookie twirler, throwing 211⅓ innings for Cleveland in winning ten times and topping the entire freshman class with six complete games.

In preparation for the June 1990 free-agent draft, the Oakland A's stockpiled four regular and supplemental first-round picks. They used one on Todd Van Poppel, the projected top pick in the entire draft whom the Atlanta Braves, owners of the pick, ignored in the fear that he would not sign with them. A second pick was spent on Kirk Dressendorfer, a three-time All-American hurler from the University of Texas. The consensus was that the A's June 1990 draft haul would soon be regarded as one for the ages.

Both Van Poppel and Dressendorfer were projected to become part of the A's rotation in 1991. But Van Poppel experienced control problems in the spring and spent most of the season in Double A with the A's Huntsville farm club. Dressendorfer remained with the A's for seven starts and split six decisions, but an ear infection and control problems of his own caused the A's to ship him out to Triple A for further seasoning.

Following the 1991 campaign, the two vaunted rookies won only 18 more games in an Oakland uniform, all of them by Van Poppel. Although it took nearly a decade, Van Poppel eventually developed into a capable middle reliever, but Dressendorfer never again threw a single pitch in the majors after 1991.

But in early August Baltimore unveiled the pitcher who would have the most enduring impact of all the 1991 mound yearlings. In the final eight weeks of the season, Mike Mussina crafted an excellent 2.87 ERA and won the first four of what eventually grew to over 200 career victories.

Other Highlights

June 15—Mike Remlinger fires a three-hit shutout in his ML debut for the San Francisco Giants, who beat Pittsburgh 4–0.

August 2—Bret Barberie of Montreal homers from each side of the plate, but his Expos lose to Philadelphia 6–5 in 11 innings.

August 11—In his first game with the Chicago White Sox—and just his second overall—Wilson Alvarez no-hits the Baltimore Orioles 7–0 while fanning seven.

September 10—Pete Schourek of the New York Mets tosses a one-hitter against Montreal, winning 9–0.

Batting		Pitching
Batting		**Pitching**

Batting	Pitching
G—AL 154, Milt Cuyler, DET	W—AL 12, Rich DeLucia, SEA
NL 156, Jeff Bagwell, HOU	NL 11, Omar Olivares, STL
AB—AL 565, Chuck Knoblauch, MIN	L—AL 15, Charles Nagy, CLE
NL 566, Ray Lankford, STL	NL 11, Darryl Kile, HOU
H—AL 159, Chuck Knoblauch, MIN	PCT—AL .480, Rich DeLucia, SEA
NL 163, Jeff Bagwell, HOU	NL .611, Omar Olivares, STL
2B—AL 34, Juan Gonzalez, TEX	GP—AL 63, Mike Timlin, TOR
NL 28, Luis Gonzalez, HOU	NL 71, Al Osuna, HOU
3B—AL 7, Milt Cuyler, DET	GS—AL 33, Charles Nagy, CLE
Mark Whiten, TOR/CLE	NL 27, Brian Barnes, MON
NL 15, Ray Lankford, STL	CG—AL 6, Charles Nagy, CLE
HR—AL 27, Juan Gonzalez, TEX	NL 4, Frank Castillo, CHI
NL 15, Jeff Bagwell, HOU	IP—AL 211.1, Charles Nagy, CLE
R—AL 78, Juan Gonzalez, TEX	NL 167.1, Omar Olivares, STL
Chuck Knoblauch, MIN	H—AL 228, Charles Nagy, CLE
NL 83, Ray Lankford, STL	NL 148, Omar Olivares, STL
Orlando Merced, PIT	BB—AL 78, Rich DeLucia, SEA
RBI—AL 102, Juan Gonzalez, TEX	NL 84, Brian Barnes, MON
NL 82, Jeff Bagwell, HOU	Darryl Kile, HOU
WK—AL 59, Chuck Knoblauch, MIN	K—AL 123, Juan Guzman, TOR
NL 75, Jeff Bagwell, HOU	NL 117, Brian Barnes, MON
SO—AL 118, Juan Gonzalez, TEX	ERA—AL 4.13, Charles Nagy, CLE
NL 116, Jeff Bagwell, HOU	NL 3.71, Omar Olivares, STL
SB—AL 41, Milt Cuyler, DET	SHO—AL 1, Wilson Alvarez, CHI
NL 44, Ray Lankford, STL	Charles Nagy, CLE
BA—AL .281, Chuck Knoblauch, MIN	NL 1, Mike Remlinger, SF
NL .294, Jeff Bagwell, HOU	Pete Schourek, NY
SLG—AL .479, Juan Gonzalez, TEX	SV—AL 15, Doug Henry, MIL
NL .437, Jeff Bagwell, HOU	NL 12, Al Osuna, HOU
OBP—AL .354, Chuck Knoblauch, MIN	
NL .391, Jeff Bagwell, HOU	

1992

A rookie who aspires to lead his league in a major hitting or pitching department usually faces a monumental challenge. In one department—stolen bases—freshmen seem to have a slightly easier time, probably because of their young legs. In 1992 Kenny Lofton of the Cleveland Indians led the AL in steals with 66 to set a new loop rookie standard. He became the third freshman thefts pacesetter since 1981 and broke Cleveland's overall season mark. Lofton, a member of the University of Arizona's Final Four basketball team in 1988, played 20 games with the Houston Astros in 1991. A December 1991 trade for backup catcher Eddie Taubensee brought Lofton to Cleveland, where he was installed as the team's center fielder when the Indians started to resurrect their long-dormant franchise.

In 1992 Lofton scored 96 runs and slashed 164 hits, including eight triples. His .727 OPS ranked only 46th in the AL, but it topped by 25 points the figure of Milwaukee shortstop Pat Listach, who, much to the surprise of many observers, beat out Lofton for ROY. Listach's positive features were that he hit .290, scored 93 times, and also stole 54 bases, the third highest total in history by an AL frosh and an even dozen behind Lofton's record mark in 1992.

66, Kenny Lofton, 1992 Cle AL
56, Ichiro Suzuki, 2001 Sea AL
54, Pat Listach, 1992 Mil AL
53, Donie Bush, 1909 Det AL
50, John Cangelosi, 1986 Chi AL

10 GS/4 SHO, Art Nehf, 1915 Bos NL
11 GS/4 SHO, Pedro Astacio, 1992 LA NL
13 GS/4 SHO, Dana Fillingim, 1918 Bos NL
15 GS/4 SHO, Mike Kilkenny, 1969 Det AL
16 GS/4 SHO, Otto Hess, 1904 Cle AL

But Listach had an equally prominent downside his frosh season in that he hit just one home run but struck out 124 times, just one K short of Gary Pettis's 1985 record for the most whiffs by a player with less than two home runs. Eric Karros, in contrast, displayed a much more typical rookie profile when he connected for a rookie-high 20 round trippers while fanning 103 times. Moreover, the Los Angeles first baseman drove in 88 runs, slugged 30 doubles, and paced the 1992 freshman class in both SA and total bases. In the NL ROY race, Karros easily outdistanced runner-up Moises Alou of Montreal, who tied for the NL frosh stolen-base lead and also finished second among all 1992 recruits in RBI with just 56 in what, with the exception of Lofton and Karros, was generally a down year for yearling hitters.

On August 25 Lofton prevented Seattle southpaw Dave Fleming from achieving baseball immortality. The outfielder collected the only two hits that day off Fleming, who earned the 15th of his 17 wins in 1992. After dropping his debut start on April 9, Fleming would not lose again for more than two months, winning nine straight decisions in the process. A finesse pitcher, Fleming never fanned more than six in any game, but he walked just 60 hitters in 228.1 innings, the heaviest workload by any rookie since 1989 when Bob Milacki logged 243 frames.

Fleming and the Dodgers' Pedro Astacio both tossed four shutouts, tying Orel Hershiser (1984) and Tom Browning (1985) for the most by a freshman hurler since Mike Boddicker threw five blanks in 1983. In the nightcap of a July 3 twinbill, Astacio limited the Philadelphia Phillies to three hits and struck out ten in his inaugural ML game. After one more start Astacio was sent back to the minors and then returned for good in mid-August. From that point on, the Dodgers rookie made nine more starts, giving him 11 in all, and fired two six-hit shutouts and another three-hit whitewash to put him in very select company.

Astacio, who had a 1.98 ERA in 82 innings, was not the only late-season mound call-up to thrive. Converted infielder Tim Wakefield debuted on July 31 and

Despite not joining the Montreal Expos until July 18, Steve Rogers completed his rookie year in 1973 with ten wins to set a new season record for the most victories by a starting hurler with a sub-2.00 ERA in less than 140 innings. The ill-fated J.R. Richard tied Rogers's mark in 1980 before he suffered a career-ending stroke, but it remained the all-time record standard until 1992 for a partial season hurler with a sub-2.00 ERA. That season, in just 14 starts and 100.1 innings, Brewers frosh Cal Eldred bagged 11 wins on a 1.79 ERA.

Though Eldred lost out on top rookie honors in the AL to teammate Pat Listach and Cleveland's Kenny Lofton, his mark for the most wins by a starter with a sub-2.00 ERA in less than 140 innings remains unchallenged. Furthermore, his 11 victories are just one short of the all-time mark for the most wins by a starter in less than 120 innings, regardless of ERA, which was set by Catfish Hunter in 1978.

MOST WINS, STARTER, LESS THAN 140 IP, ERA BELOW 2.00

Rank	Name	Year	GS	IP	ERA	Wins
1	Cal Eldred	1992	14	100.1	1.79	11
2	J. R. Richard	1980	17	113.2	1.90	10
	Steve Rogers	1973	17	134	1.54	10
4	Tiny Bonham	1940	12	99.1	1.90	9
	George Witt	1958	15	106	1.61	9
	Rube Kroh	1909	13	120.1	1.65	9
7	Stump Wiedman	1881	13	115	1.80	8
	Howie Pollet	1943	14	118	1.75	8
	Chief Bender	1908	17	138.2	1.75	8

Note that a number of pitchers—including Babe Adams in 1909, Sherry Smith in 1920, and Red Munger in 1944—won 11 or more games with sub-2.00 ERAs in less than 140 innings, but in each case several of their wins came in relief.

proceeded to go 8–1 down the stretch as the Pittsburgh Pirates won their third straight NL East title. The knuckleballer fashioned a 2.15 ERA, yielding more than four runs just once in 13 starts. In Game Three of the NLCS, Wakefield held Atlanta to five hits, beating the Braves 3–2 as Pittsburgh won for the first time in the best-of-seven series. With the Pirates facing elimination in Game Six, Wakefield tossed another complete game. Pittsburgh won 13–4 behind the late-season phenom but lost a heartbreaker the next night as Atlanta advanced to the World Series.

In addition to Astacio and Wakefield, after being called up from the minors in July, Cal Eldred won ten consecutive *starts* (not just decisions) for the Milwaukee Brewers beginning on August 8. In September El-dred was the AL Pitcher of the Month, going 6–0 and yielding six earned runs in 46 innings for a 1.17 ERA en route to posting 11 wins overall in just 14 starts.

Other Highlights

April 8—In his ML debut Brian Jordan drives in four runs for the St. Louis Cardinals, who beat the New York Mets 15–7.

June 8—Cubs pitcher Jim Bullinger smacks a homer on the first pitch he ever sees in the majors in the first game of a twinbill.

July 21—Hipolito Pichardo one-hits the Boston Red Sox as the Kansas City Royals win 8–0.

1992 ROOKIE LEADERS

Batting	Pitching
G—AL 157, Gary DiSarcina, CAL	W—AL 17, Dave Fleming, SEA
NL 149, Eric Karros, LA	NL 11, Donovan Osborne, STL
AB—AL 579, Pat Listach, MIL	L—AL 11, Julio Valera, CAL
NL 545, Eric Karros, LA	NL 14, Kyle Abbott, PHI
H—AL 168, Pat Listach, MIL	Anthony Young, NY
NL 140, Eric Karros, LA	PCT—AL .630, Dave Fleming, SEA
2B—AL 22, Andy Stankiewicz, NY	NL .550, Donovan Osborne, STL
NL 30, Eric Karros, LA	GP—AL 66, Jeff Nelson, SEA
3B—AL 8, Kenny Lofton, CLE	NL 55, Denny Neagle, PIT
NL 6, Ruben Amaro, PHI	GS—AL 33, Dave Fleming, SEA
Reggie Sanders, CIN	NL 29, Donovan Osborne, STL
HR—AL 10, Chad Curtis, CAL	CG—AL 7, Dave Fleming, SEA
NL 20, Eric Karros, LA	NL 4, Pedro Astacio, LA
R—AL 96, Kenny Lofton, CLE	Ben Rivera, ATL/PHI
NL 63, Eric Karros, LA	Tim Wakefield, PIT
RBI—AL 47, Pat Listach, MIL	IP—AL 228.1, Dave Fleming, SEA
NL 88, Eric Karros, LA	NL 179.0, Donovan Osborne, STL
WK—AL 68, Kenny Lofton, CLE	H—AL 225, Dave Fleming, SEA
NL 48, Reggie Sanders, CIN	NL 193, Donovan Osborne, STL
SO—AL 124, Pat Listach, MIL	BB—AL 64, Julio Valera, CAL
NL 103, Eric Karros, LA	NL 58, Cliff Brantley, PHI
SB—**AL 66, Kenny Lofton, CLE**	K—AL 113, Julio Valera, CAL
NL 16, Moises Alou, MON	NL 104, Donovan Osborne, STL
Reggie Sanders, CIN	ERA—AL 3.39, Dave Fleming, SEA
BA—AL .290, Pat Listach, MIL	NL 3.77, Donovan Osborne, STL
NL .257, Eric Karros, LA	SHO—AL 4, Dave Fleming, SEA
SLG—AL .372, Chad Curtis, CAL	NL 4, Pedro Astacio, LA
NL .426, Eric Karros, LA	SV—AL 12, Roberto Hernandez, CHI
OBP—AL .362, Kenny Lofton, CLE	NL 15, Anthony Young, NY
NL .307, Eric Karros, LA	

July 25—Tim Fortugno of the California Angels fans 12 Tigers and permits just three hits in whitewashing Detroit 9–0.

August 30—Boston third baseman Scott Cooper hits three doubles and two singles at California, helping the Red Sox to win 4–2 in ten innings.

September 19—Rod Brewer goes 5-for-5 with four runs in St. Louis's 16–4 win over the Chicago Cubs.

1993

The booming bats of two freshman sluggers shook Southern California in 1993 with the intensity of an earthquake. Mike Piazza of the Los Angeles Dodgers and Tim Salmon of the neighboring California Angels each exceeded 30 home runs while also maintaining a healthy OBP en route to being unanimously named his league's respective ROY.

Piazza had the finest offensive season ever for a rookie catcher. Although Rudy York put up similar numbers in 1937, the Detroit freshman played just 54 games back of the plate while Piazza manned baseball's most strenuous position in 146 contests. Piazza batted .318, pounded 35 round trippers, and drove in 112 runs, the fourth most in the NL and the highest total ever for a rookie receiver. His .561 slugging percentage was fourth in the loop while his .935 OPS ranked third. On June 15 Piazza had two homers and two singles and five RBI as the Dodgers won 12–4 at Colorado. A month later he caught two innings in the All-Star Game, but in his only plate appearance, he struck out with two down in the ninth, ending the NL's 9–3 defeat in Baltimore.

Salmon ripped 35 doubles and 31 homers to become the fourth of six rookies ever to reach 30 in each category. Of the sextet, he had by far the fewest at bats, resulting from breaking a finger on September 15. Salmon was hitting .396 that month and had connected for a grand slam in his last at bat before getting hurt. He demonstrated a powerful arm in right field and a veteran's patience at the plate, drawing 82 walks and registering a .387 OBP. In addition, before his season was prematurely ended Salmon collected 95 RBI, 24 in July alone.

Both Salmon and Piazza had freshman teammates who likewise had frequent flashes of brilliance. California's J.T. Snow was hot in April, batting .343 with six homers and 17 RBI. His average plummeted in May, but he finished the season nicely, hitting .297 in the final month. Meanwhile, a slender Dodgers righty, Pedro Martinez, foreshadowed his future Cy Young Award heroics, going 10–5 with a 2.61 ERA. In 107 innings Martinez fanned 119 and yielded just 76 hits, giving him a 6.36 H/9 IP average, second in the NL only to the leader, Sid Fernandez, among hurlers with a minimum of 100 innings.

As with most first-year expansion teams, the Florida Marlins and the Colorado Rockies both were heavily laden with previously untested rookies. A trio of Florida freshmen all logged at least 550 at bats, Jeff Conine heading the pack with 595 while playing all 162 games. The left fielder hit .292 and tied Piazza for the rookie lead with 174 safeties. First baseman Orestes Destrade smashed 20 four-baggers and knocked in 87 runs. Chuck Carr, the Marlins center fielder, topped the circuit with 58 stolen bases. Middle relievers Richie Lewis and Matt Turner also had fine seasons for the Marlins protecting leads so that veteran closer Bryan Harvey was able to notch 45 saves and make mincemeat of the old mark for the most saves with a first-year expansion team.

Yearling right-hander Armando Reynoso was the ace of the expansion Rockies staff, winning a dozen games. His 4.00 ERA not only was less than the league average, but the fact that his home park was hitter-friendly Mile High Stadium caused his accomplishments to take on added luster. Complementing Reynoso were Steve Reed, who won nine games and saved three more out of the Colorado bullpen, and speedy second baseman Eric Young with 42 stolen bases and eight triples.

Though Pittsburgh was not an expansion team, there were times in 1993 when it resembled one, as rookies replaced the many stars who were allowed to leave the Steel City when the Pirates opted to cut their payroll and enter a rebuilding mode. Two new starters, left-hander Steve Cooke and righty Paul Wagner, were .500 pitchers, the former winning ten games, the latter eight. Like the Marlins, the Pirates also had three rookie position players, Carlos Garcia, Al Martin, and Kevin Young, who all played more than 140 games with Martin hitting 18 long balls and Garcia 12.

Jason Bere was more fortunate, playing for the AL West champion Chicago White Sox. On September 8 Bere pitched eight scoreless innings of two-hit ball and struck out 13 Red Sox, beating Boston 8–1. He went 12–5 in the regular season before taking a no-decision after just 2⅓ innings of work in Game Four of the ALCS. The White Sox overcame Bere's ineffective work to rally and win the game, but the Toronto Blue Jays took the series.

Bere's counterpart among rookie pitchers who were significant factors for senior loop postseason qualifiers was Greg McMichael, who saved 19 games for NL West champion Atlanta and had a 2.06 ERA in 74 appearances. In the NLCS, however, McMichael lost the opener to the Phillies and posted an uninspiring 6.75 ERA in four appearances.

Montreal finished only three games out of first in the NL East in large part because of southpaw Kirk Rueter, who was 8–0 after a midseason call-up. Rueter went 9–2 in the minors before debuting on July 7 when he surrendered two hits in 8⅓ innings to top San Francisco 3–0. Two other freshmen—Joe Pate in 1926 and Howie Krist in 1941—won more games without a loss than did Rueter, Pate taking nine and Krist ten. But all of Pate's victories came in relief and Krist bagged only four wins as a starter, enabling Rueter to set a new mark for most wins without a defeat by a rookie who served exclusively in a starting role.

Other Highlights

April 11—Mike Lansing hits four singles and a home run for the Montreal Expos, who pound the hosting Colorado Rockies 19–9.

May 17—Rich Amaral goes 5-for-5 with a double in a 16–9 Seattle win over the Texas Rangers.

Kevin Stocker celebrated his rookie season by playing in a World Series and setting a new post-1900 OPS mark (.828) for NL freshman shortstops with at least 250 at bats. Never again would Stocker play in a postseason game, and by the time he finished his ML career in 2000, his OPS was down to .683. *Transcendental Graphics*

In the June 1991 free-agent draft, the Phillies chose shortstop Kevin Stocker in the second round. The book on Stocker was that he was a decent fielder with good speed whose chances to reach the majors rested on whether he could develop his switch-hitting skills to get on base enough. On July 7, 1993, midway through his third year of pro ball, Stocker was plucked from Triple A after the Phillies had exhausted all their other shortstop options. Displaying little awe of big league pitching, he hit .324 in 70 games, including .395 against left-handers, and established a new twentieth-century record for the highest BA by a switch-hitting shortstop with at least 250 plate appearances.

Even though Stocker helped catapult the Phils to an unanticipated pennant in 1993, manager Jim Fregosi, himself a former shortstop, remained skeptical. At the time Stocker was recalled from Scranton/Wilkes-Barre, he was hitting just .233 and his defense was spotty. Fregosi's skepticism proved to be justified. Stocker never again hit .300 in an eight-year career and finished in 2000 with fielding stats that were dead average. Nonetheless, he currently holds the fifth spot for the all-time highest season BA by a switch-hitting shortstop with at least 250 PAs.

Rank	Name	Year	PA	BA
1	George Davis	1897	571	.353
2	Bob Ferguson	1878	269	.351
3	George Davis	1899	463	.337
4	Omar Vizquel	1999	664	.333
5	Kevin Stocker	1993	302	.324

Batting		Pitching	
G—AL 153, John Jaha, MIL		W—AL 12, Jason Bere, CHI	
NL 162, Jeff Conine, FLA		NL 12, Armando Reynoso, CLR	
AB—AL 535, Brent Gates, OAK		L—AL 8, Eddie Guardado, MIN	
NL 595, Jeff Conine, FLA		NL 15, Tim Pugh, CIN	
H—AL 155, Brent Gates, OAK		PCT—AL No Qualifiers	
NL 174, Jeff Conine, FLA		NL .522, Armando Reynoso, CLR	
Mike Piazza, LA		GP—AL 60, Matt Whiteside, TEX	
2B—AL 35, Tim Salmon, CAL		NL 74, Greg McMichael, ATL	
NL 32, Wil Cordero, MON		GS—AL 24, Jason Bere, CHI	
3B—AL 10, David Hulse, TEX		NL 32, Steve Cooke, PIT	
NL 8, Al Martin, PIT		CG—AL 2, Angel Miranda, MIL	
Eric Young, CLR		Rafael Novoa, MIL	
HR—AL 31, Tim Salmon, CAL		NL 4, Armando Reynoso, CLR	
NL 35, Mike Piazza, LA		IP—AL 142.2, Jason Bere, CHI	
R—AL 93, Tim Salmon, CAL		NL 210.2, Steve Cooke, PIT	
NL 85, Al Martin, PIT		H—AL 131, Mike Trombley, MIN	
RBI—AL 95, Tim Salmon, CAL		NL 207, Steve Cooke, PIT	
NL 112, Mike Piazza, LA		BB—AL 81, Jason Bere, CHI	
WK—AL 82, Tim Salmon, CAL		NL 71, Kent Bottenfield, MON/CLR	
NL 63, Eric Young, CLR		K—AL 129, Jason Bere, CHI	
SO—AL 135, Tim Salmon, CAL		NL 132, Steve Cooke, PIT	
NL 135, Jeff Conine, FLA		ERA—AL No Qualifiers	
SB—AL 29, David Hulse, TEX		NL 3.78, Rene Arocha, STL	
NL 58, Chuck Carr, FLA		SHO—AL 1, Jeff Mutis, CLE	
BA—AL .290, Brent Gates, OAK		NL 1, Steve Cooke, PIT	
NL .318, Mike Piazza, LA		Tim Pugh, CIN	
SLG—AL .536, Tim Salmon, CAL		Paul Wagner, PIT	
NL .561, Mike Piazza, LA		SV—AL 11, Jerry DiPoto, CLE	
OBP—AL .387, Tim Salmon, CAL		NL 19, Greg McMichael, ATL	
NL .374, Mike Piazza, LA			

June 8—Rene Arocha of the Cardinals gains his fifth straight win without a defeat when he tops the Giants 4–3 at San Francisco's Candlestick Park; Arocha will finish the season as the top rookie ERA qualifier in both leagues but, following his 5–0 start, will go just 13–17 for the remainder of his career.

July 9—After getting four hits the previous day, including two home runs and seven RBI, Troy Neel belts two more round trippers as the Oakland Athletics beat Boston 4–2.

July 17—Cleveland's Jeff Mutis nets the lone shutout in 1993 by an AL rookie when he blanks California 3–0;

the gem will turn out to be Mutis's only complete game in the majors as well as his next-to-last win.

September 29—Tim Pugh fires a one-hitter for the Cincinnati Reds, blanking San Diego 8–0.

1994

The 1994 season was progressing nicely. Tight divisional races and impressive showings by both pitchers and hitters—especially San Francisco's Matt Williams, who had a reasonable shot at breaking Roger Maris's home run record—thrilled fans from coast to coast.

Then, on August 12, it all ended when the players went on strike. Despite the truncated season, several rookies compiled impressive numbers.

Dodgers rightfielder Raul Mondesi hit .306 with 133 hits in only 112 games. He had 27 doubles, and his eight triples tied him for third in the NL. Mondesi also pounded 16 home runs, one on April 17 when he also collected a triple and two singles while scoring four runs and driving home three as the Dodgers pulverized Pittsburgh 19–2. Defensively, the rifle-armed Mondesi topped the loop with 16 outfield assists.

Though he had far fewer at bats than Mondesi, Kansas City designated hitter Bob Hamelin ripped just one fewer extra-base hit—50 in 312 times up—and set a record in so doing.

FEWEST ABs BY ROOKIE WITH 50 + LONG HITS

312 AB/50 EXB (25 2B/1 3B/24 HR),
Bob Hamelin, 1994 KC AL
353 AB/50 EXB (28 2B/1 3B/21 HR),
Lance Berkman, 2000 Hou NL
375 AB/56 EXB (18 2B/3 3B/35 HR),
Rudy York, 1937 Det AL
379 AB/50 EXB (31 2B/4 3B/15 HR),
Shawn Green, 1995 Tor AL
381 AB/57 EXB (33 2B/3 3B/21 HR),
Brian Daubach, 1999 Bos AL

Hamelin was fifth in the AL with a .992 OPS and drove in 65 Royals teammates. He knocked in five of those 65 on April 16 and then had four RBI on July 25, when his game-winning three-run homer in the bottom of the 12th erased a 4–3 Chicago White Sox lead.

Other productive freshman hitters included Montreal's Cliff Floyd, who batted .291, and Rusty Greer, who hit .314 with ten homers, including one in his ML debut with Texas on May 16. Manny Ramirez, part of Cleveland's offensive juggernaut, had 60 RBI and 17 round trippers for the revitalized Indians, who stood just one game behind the White Sox in the AL Central when the season came to a depressing halt. Meanwhile, Atlanta's Ryan Klesko scaled 17 pitches over outfield walls in only 245 ABs. On April 15 Klesko went 3-for-3 with three walks and four runs as the Braves thumped the Chicago Cubs 19–5 at Wrigley Field.

The Cubs' Steve Trachsel was one of three rookie hurlers to tie for top frosh honors with a mere nine victories. He was also the freshman leader in innings pitched and had a 3.21 ERA. Joey Hamilton was 9–6 for San Diego. On June 25 he blanked Cincinnati 6–0, holding the Reds to six hits. Seattle bullpenner Bill Risley also went 9–6, surrendering fewer hits and walks combined than innings pitched.

A cut behind this trio was Shane Reynolds, who ranked fifth in the senior circuit with a 3.05 ERA and picked up eight wins for the Astros in the process.

In 1993, for Triple A Omaha, Bob Hamelin hit just .259 but compiled 29 homers and a loop-best 82 walks. Hampered by chronic back problems throughout his pro career, he was viewed as a potential role player and pinch hitter at most when he reported to the Kansas City Royals' spring training site in 1994. But when he began by hitting .361 with six homers and 21 RBI in April, he won the regular DH slot.

Fifty of Hamelin's 88 hits in his rookie season went for extra bases. In addition, even though he had only 312 at bats, he collected 56 walks. Because the season was curtailed by a lengthy strike, Hamelin qualified as a league leader despite his relatively low at-bat total and finished fifth in the AL in OPS. Flare-ups of his back trouble prevented him from ever again approaching the early form that resulted in what was arguably one of the best rookie seasons in history. Hamelin's frosh OPS figure of .992 is tied for fourth on the all-time list of rookie qualifiers.

HIGHEST OPS ALL-TIME, ROOKIE QUALIFIERS

Rank	Name	Year	OPS
1	Joe Jackson	1911	1.058
2	Ted Williams	1939	1.045
3	Albert Pujols	2001	1.013
4	Mark McGwire	1987	.992
	Bob Hamelin	1994	.992
6	Wally Berger	1930	.990
7	Hal Trosky	1934	.987
8	Jeff Heath	1938	.985
9	Benny Kauff	1914	.981
10	Dale Alexander	1929	.977

Note that George Watkins (1.037 in 1930) and Rudy York (1.026 in 1937) both fell short of the number of PAs needed to be qualifiers.

Batting	Pitching

Batting

G—AL 101, Bob Hamelin, KC
    NL 112, Raul Mondesi, LA
AB—AL 338, Matt Walbeck, MIN
    NL 434, Raul Mondesi, LA
H—AL 88, Bob Hamelin, KC
    NL 133, Raul Mondesi, LA
2B—AL 25, Bob Hamelin, KC
    NL 27, Raul Mondesi, LA
3B—AL 3, Domingo Cedeno, TOR
    NL 8, Raul Mondesi, LA
HR—AL 24, Bob Hamelin, KC
    NL 17, Ryan Klesko, ATL
R—AL 64, Bob Hamelin, KC
    NL 63, Raul Mondesi, LA
RBI—AL 65, Bob Hamelin, KC
    NL 56, Raul Mondesi, LA
WK—AL 56, Bob Hamelin, KC
    NL 27, James Mouton, HOU
SO—AL 75, Jose Valentin, MIL
    NL 98, Kurt Abbott, FLA
SB—AL 13, Lee Tinsley, BOS
    NL 24, James Mouton, HOU
BA—AL .314, Rusty Greer, TEX
    NL .306, Raul Mondesi, LA
SLG—AL .599, Bob Hamelin, KC
    NL .516, Raul Mondesi, LA
OBP—AL .393, Bob Hamelin, KC
    NL .335, Cliff Floyd, MON

Pitching

W—AL 9, Bill Risley, SEA
    NL 9, Joey Hamilton, SD
        Steve Trachsel, CHI
L—AL 7, Hector Fajardo, TEX
        Carlos Pulido, MIN
    NL 8, Salomon Torres, SF
PCT—AL No Qualifiers
    NL .615, Shane Reynolds, HOU
GP—AL 43, Darren Oliver, TEX
    NL 51, Johnny Ruffin, CIN
GS—AL 18, Brian Anderson, CAL
    NL 22, Steve Trachsel, CHI
CG—AL 1, done by five pitchers
    NL 1, done by six pitchers
IP—AL 101.2, Brian Anderson, CAL
    NL 146.0, Steve Trachsel, CHI
H—AL 120, Brian Anderson, CAL
    NL 133, Steve Trachsel, CHI
BB—AL 45, Roger Salkeld, SEA
    NL 54, Steve Trachsel, CHI
K—AL 61, Bill Risley, SEA
    NL 110, Shane Reynolds, HOU
ERA—AL No Qualifiers
    NL 3.05, Shane Reynolds, HOU
SHO—AL 1, Rick Helling, TEX
        Albie Lopez, CLE
    NL 1, Joey Hamilton, SD
        Jason Jacome, NY
        Shane Reynolds, HOU
SV—AL 17, Darren Hall, TOR
    NL 16, John Hudek, HOU

Reynolds also authored perhaps the finest pitching performance by a freshman in the strike-abbreviated season when he fanned 11 Pirates in his four-hit 11–0 triumph on July 23.

In addition to Risley, three other recruit relievers posted noteworthy numbers in 1994. Darren Hall saved 17 games for Toronto while Houston's John Hudek notched 16 saves and made the All-Star team. Hudek appeared in six games with Houston's Triple A farm club in Tucson before joining the parent Astros. He then permitted just one run in his first 19 big league outings and was selected for the Midsummer Classic, where he came back to earth for a moment, yielding a pair of runs in the NL's 8–7 win. For their work, Hudek was voted the runner-up for the NL ROY and Hall finished fourth in the AL balloting. A scattering of senior loop votes also went to Hector Carrasco, who fashioned a 2.24 ERA and saved six games in 45 relief stints for Cincinnati.

Other Highlights

July 5—Backup catcher Chris Turner, a .242 hitter on the season with just 36 safeties, goes 5-for-5 with a pair of doubles as California wins 10–3 at Boston.

July 12—John Hudek of Houston is the first hurler in history to pitch in an All-Star Game before notching his first ML win when he toils part of the sixth inning in the NL's 8–7 triumph at Pittsburgh's Three Rivers Stadium.

July 25—Rico Brogna hits three singles and two doubles for the New York Mets, who beat St. Louis 7–1.

August 4—Albie Lopez holds the Tigers to five hits and fans 11 as Cleveland blanks Detroit 5–0.

August 7—Carlos Rodriguez of the Boston Red Sox gets five hits, including three doubles, in a 4–1 win against Cleveland.

1995

They could have been called the Twister and the Blister. Los Angeles's rookie right-handers Hideo Nomo and Ismael Valdes each won 13 games for the division-winning Dodgers, topping the 1995 class of freshman hurlers. Nomo, who employed a twisting corkscrew-like delivery, debuted on May 2, a week after the season opened belatedly when the players' strike that had shut down the 1994 campaign in mid-August was still not resolved by the time the teams were due to report to spring training in 1995. In his first six starts, Nomo suffered one defeat and had five no-decisions. In June, however, Nomo not only broke through into the win column but was also selected the NL Pitcher of the Month on the basis of his 6–0 performance with an 0.89 ERA in 50⅓ innings. In addition to fanning 60 while permitting just 25 hits, the Dodgers' Japanese import tossed shutouts in his last two June starts, including a two-hitter against San Francisco when he struck out 13.

Nomo started the All-Star Game, taking a no-decision after holding the AL scoreless for two innings in the senior circuit's 3–2 win, as many people in his native country stopped work—it was 9 a.m. in Japan at game time—to watch him on TV. He finished at 13–6 with a 2.54 ERA, second only to Greg Maddux. Nomo whiffed 236 batters and logged a stunning .182 OBA and an only slightly less imposing .271 OBP, ranking first and second, respectively, in the NL. He had 11 double-digit strikeout performances, his high coming June 14 at Pittsburgh when he rang up 16 hitters.

Valdes, who suffer periodically from painful blisters on his pitching hand, won his first five June starts before losing on the 28th. Of the Dodgers' 18 wins that month, he and Nomo claimed 11. On September 17 Valdes fired a two-hit shutout at St. Louis, fanning nine

Cardinals in his 8–0 win. He threw seven innings in Game Two of the NLDS and permitted just two unearned runs to Cincinnati. Valdes left with the game tied, but the Reds won 5–4. Nomo lost the next game, and Los Angeles was thereupon swept by the Reds and eliminated from only the second postseason tourney in ML history to feature eight teams and three separate rounds of play.*

Chipper Jones and the Atlanta Braves fared considerably better in fall action. They first knocked off the Colorado Rockies as Jones went 7-for-18 with four extra-base hits. In the NLCS the 23-year-old recruit third baseman did even better, hitting .438 against Cincinnati pitching and scoring three runs while driving in a like amount. Facing Cleveland in the World Series, Jones pounded three doubles, helping the Braves to win their first World Championship since moving to Georgia in 1966. During the regular season Jones drove in 86 runs and smashed 23 home runs, three of them ninth-inning game-winning shots. He also showed remarkable patience for a rookie, drawing 73 walks.

Jones trailed just one other freshman in the round tripper department—Minnesota's Marty Cordova, who smashed eight of his 24 home runs in May. Cordova connected in five straight games beginning May 16. His prodigious power output helped earn him AL player of the week honors, as did his 13 RBI. Cordova finished with 84 RBI and 27 doubles and also ranked second on the Twins in steals with 20.

Even with all that, Cordova narrowly beat out Garret Anderson for AL ROY honors. Anderson crafted a rookie-high .321 BA for the California Angels, with 16 circuit blasts and 69 ribbies, but fell a few plate appearances short of qualifying for the official frosh lead. He was especially hot in July, amassing 43 hits in 105 ABs for a .410 average and eight doubles, seven homers, and 31 RBI. Anderson's slugging average was .686 for the month and .505 overall. Two other AL freshman fly chasers each amassed 31 doubles despite the shortened schedule albeit both, like Anderson, were short the requisite number of plate appearances to qualify for major hitting honors. Shawn Green parlayed his 31

---

*Because the lengthy 1981 strike threw the regular-season schedule into a complete shambles, for that one year only prior to 1995 postseason play included eight teams and three rounds of play.

two-baggers for Toronto into a .509 SA but collected only 379 ABs, and Boston's Troy O'Leary batted .308 in 399 ABs to rank as the unofficial hitting leader on the AL East champs.

Rookie relievers Dave Stevens and Troy Percival had very different seasons in 1995. Stevens saved ten games for Minnesota, but his ERA was 5.07, breaking the 1955 record of Ed Roebuck for the highest ever by a freshman with as many as ten saves. Percival, in sharp contrast, had a 1.95 ERA and whiffed 94 batters in just 74 innings. Even more amazing was Percival's .147 OBA, as he surrendered just 37 hits—or exactly half a hit per inning. But perhaps the most amazing thing of all was that Percival, awesome as his numbers were (see below), finished only fourth in the AL ROY chase.

MOST IP BY ROOKIE WITH 2+ IP PER HIT ALLOWED (MINIMUM 25 IP)

74.0 IP/37 H, Troy Percival, 1995 Cal AL
36.0 IP/16 H, Doug Henry, 1991 Mil AL
27.0 IP/13 H, Frank Biscan, 1942 StL AL
26.1 IP/13 H, Mike Fornieles, 1952 Was AL
25.1 IP/12 H, George Spencer, 1950 NY NL

Third place went to Andy Pettitte, who won 12 games for the New York Yankees, aiding them to make their first postseason appearance since 1981. Despite a 5.32 ERA, Minnesota's Brad Radke managed to bag only one less win than Pettitte, highlighted by a three-hit shutout on August 29 against Texas. Montreal's Carlos Perez and reliever Julian Tavarez of Cleveland also won in double figures, each collecting ten positive verdicts. Perez and Philadelphia's rookie starter, Tyler Green, combined to throw $1\frac{1}{3}$ scoreless innings in the All-Star Game. Though still in the minors when the Midsummer Classic was played, Jason Isringhausen nonetheless found enough time to go 9–2 for the New York Mets after debuting on July 17. Although no pitcher won 20 games in the majors in 1995, Isringhausen bagged 11 victories in the minors as against only two losses prior to his call-up for a sparkling 20–4 composite record. Isringhausen's late-season surge earned him a tie for fourth in the NL ROY balloting, trailing Nomo, Chipper Jones, and Florida's Quilvio Veras. There is perhaps no better illustration of the depth of the 1995 NL rookie crop, as well as the way in

After drafting Jon Nunnally from the Cleveland organization in the fall of 1994 under Rule 5, the Royals were forced either to keep him for the entire 1995 season or offer him back to the Indians. Few Rule 5 draft choices pan out, and no one expected Nunnally to be one of the rare exceptions since in his first three pro seasons he had yet to advance above Class A. But Nunnally won a longer look when he became the first Royals player to homer in his initial major league at bat.

At the close of the 1995 campaign, Nunnally ranked second on the Royals in both home runs and walks and fourth in RBI even though he compiled only 303 at bats. What's more, among his six stolen bases were four thefts of home, the most since Rod Carew's seven in 1969. Finally, despite carrying a lowly .244 BA, he stood fourth in OPS among all rookie hitters.

In the years to follow, Nunnally continued to display excellent power numbers. His partial season stats with Cincinnati in 1997 after coming to the Reds in a trade were among the best in the 1990s. But a penchant for strikeouts and an erratic arm hindered him from ever winning a regular slot.

OPS LEADERS AMONG ROOKIES WHO RECEIVED VOTES FOR 1995 ROY HONORS

Name	BA	OPS
Garret Anderson	.321	.861
Marty Cordova	.277	.842
Shawn Green	.288	.838
Jon Nunnally	.244	.829
Chipper Jones	.265	.805

which the game had changed by the mid-1990s, than Veras. Though the Florida second sacker led the NL with 56 stolen bases and also compiled a rookie-high 80 walks and .384 OBP, the shift in emphasis in recent years from speed to power reduced him in the eyes of most voters to little more than an afterthought and put him some 90 votes behind Chipper Jones and 104 short of Nomo in the final balloting.

Other Highlights

May 10—Kevin Jarvis of Cincinnati holds the Florida Marlins to two hits, winning 3–0.

May 26—Michael Mimbs fires a two-hitter for the Philadelphia Phillies, who top the San Diego Padres 2–0.

1995 ROOKIE LEADERS

Batting	Pitching
G—AL 137, Marty Cordova, MIN	**W**—AL 12, Andy Pettitte, NY
NL 140, Chipper Jones, ATL	NL 13, Hideo Nomo, LA
AB—AL 512, Marty Cordova, MIN	Ismael Valdes, LA
NL 524, Chipper Jones, ATL	**L**—AL 14, Brad Radke, MIN
H—AL 142, Marty Cordova, MIN	NL 11, Ismael Valdes, LA
NL 139, Chipper Jones, ATL	**PCT**—AL .571, Andy Pettitte, NY
2B—AL 31, Shawn Green, TOR	NL .684, Hideo Nomo, LA
Troy O'Leary, BOS	**GP**—AL 62, Troy Percival, CAL
NL 22, Chipper Jones, ATL	NL 63, Jason Christiansen, PIT
3B—AL 6, Ray Durham, CHI	**GS**—AL 28, Brad Radke, MIN
Jon Nunnally, KC	**NL 31, Esteban Loaiza, PIT**
Troy O'Leary, BOS	**CG**—AL 3, Andy Pettitte, NY
NL 7, Scott Bullett, CHI	Steve Sparks, MIL
Quilvio Veras, FLA	NL 6, Ismael Valdes, LA
HR—AL 24, Marty Cordova, MIN	**IP**—AL 202.0, Steve Sparks, MIL
NL 23, Chipper Jones, ATL	NL 197.2, Ismael Valdes, LA
R—AL 81, Marty Cordova, MIN	**H**—AL 210, Steve Sparks, MIL
NL 87, Chipper Jones, ATL	NL 205, Esteban Loaiza, PIT
RBI—AL 84, Marty Cordova, MIN	**BB**—AL 86, Steve Sparks, MIL
NL 86, Chipper Jones, ATL	NL 78, Hideo Nomo, LA
WK—AL 62, Bobby Higginson, DET	**K**—AL 114, Andy Pettitte, NY
NL 80, Quilvio Veras, FLA	**NL 236, Hideo Nomo, LA**
SO—AL 147, Benji Gil, TEX	**ERA**—AL 4.17, Andy Pettitte, NY
NL 99, Chipper Jones, ATL	NL 2.54, Hideo Nomo, LA
SB—AL 22, Curtis Goodwin, BAL	**SHO**—AL 1, Doug Johns, OAK
NL 56, Quilvio Veras, FLA	Brad Radke, MIN
BA—AL .277, Marty Cordova, MIN	**NL 3, Hideo Nomo, LA**
NL .265, Chipper Jones, ATL	**SV**—AL 10, Dave Stevens, MIN
SLG—AL .486, Marty Cordova, MIN	NL 6, Toby Borland, PHI
NL .450, Chipper Jones, ATL	
OBP—AL .355, Marty Cordova, MIN	
NL .386, Quilvio Veras, FLA	

July 11—Hideo Nomo of the Dodgers is the first Japanese national to appear in an All-Star Game and also the first rookie since Fernando Valenzuela in 1981 to receive his league's starting assignment.

September 18—Doug Johns blanks California on two hits as Oakland prevails 4–0.

1996

The 22-year-old-shortstop's team trailed in the opening game of the second postseason round 4–3 with one away in the bottom of the eighth. The rookie then hit a drive to right field that was a few inches short of the wall but was interfered with by a fan. Nonetheless, the freshman, Derek Jeter of the New York Yankees, was credited with a home run, sparking the Bronx Bombers to a highly controversial win in 11 innings. There was no controversy surrounding Jeter's overall postseason performance, however. He had gone 7-for-17 in New York's four-game victory over the Texas Rangers in the ALDS. Then, against Baltimore, he scored five runs and got ten hits in the ALCS. In the World Series Jeter hit .250 off Atlanta Braves hurlers but drew four walks and touched home five more times as the Yankees ended an 18-year drought since their last world title.

Far and away the top freshman in 1996, Jeter was the sole rookie with more than 139 hits, collecting 183 safeties. He scored 104 runs, drove in 78—the most by a frosh shortstop since 1983—and hit .314. Jeter's lone blemish was that he had 102 strikeouts to become just the fourth rookie to top .300 and fan at least 100 times.

ROOKIES WITH .300 BAs AND 100 + STRIKEOUTS

Dick Allen, 1964 Phi NL, .318/138 K
Jim Rice, 1975 Bos AL, .309/122 K
Benito Santiago, 1987 SD NL, .300/112 K
Derek Jeter, 1996 NY AL, .314/102 K

Jeter was the first Yankee chosen as AL ROY since 1981, whereas Los Angeles's Todd Hollandsworth was the record-setting fifth consecutive Dodger to take the top NL frosh honor. Hollandsworth, operating in left field, hit .291 and stole 21 bases while hitting a dozen home runs and 26 doubles. On July 1 he produced five of his 139 hits, a triple and a homer among them, in a 10–2 win at San Diego.

Shortstops Edgar Renteria and Rey Ordonez followed Hollandsworth on the freshman hit list. Renteria garnered 133 bingles for Florida while hitting .309 in 106 games. Ordonez, a New York Met, got 129 safeties. He thrilled fans with his acrobatic defense, compensating for his limited power and patience at the plate. Jason Kendall batted .300 as Pittsburgh's backstop. Moreover, Kendall made the All-Star squad and caught the ninth inning of the NL's 6–0 victory. Considering the difficulty of the position Kendall played and his fine offensive stats, many observers, particularly in Pittsburgh, felt that he would have been a stronger ROY choice than Hollandsworth and deserving of becoming the first Pirate to receive that accolade since the inception of the award in 1947.

Detroit's switch-hitting first baseman Tony Clark had just 94 hits but made them count, as 41 went for extra bases, including 27 home runs, to give him a .503 SA on just a .250 BA. In September Clark had two multi-homer games, but not surprisingly, the 109-loss Tigers dropped both contests. Clark had played a few games with Detroit in 1995, as had Rudy Pemberton with Boston. In 1996 Pemberton returned for another late-season trial with the BoSox and went 21-for-41, hitting .512 with eight doubles, 11 runs, and 10 RBI. Pemberton's overall offensive performance, which featured a

Derek Jeter, the 1996 AL ROY, became only the sixth shortstop in AL history to tally 100 runs in his frosh season. He also topped all rookies with 183 hits. Upon leading the AL with 219 hits in 1999, Jeter had garnered 795 safeties in his first four full seasons to break Johnny Pesky's former all-time mark for the most in that span by an infielder.

MOST HITS, FIRST FOUR FULL SEASONS
(INCLUDING ROOKIE SEASONS)

Name	Years	RH	TH
Paul Waner	1926–29	180	840
Joe Jackson	1911–14	233	809
Derek Jeter	1996–99	183	795
Stan Musial	1942–44/1946	147	792
Joe DiMaggio	1936–39	206	791
Nomar Garciaparra	1997–2000	209	791
Earl Averill	1929–32	198	786
Johnny Pesky	1942/1946–48	205	779
Lloyd Waner	1927–30	223	772
Tony Oliva	1964–67	217	754

1.336 OPS, is the best ever by a rookie with fewer than 50 ABs.

Cardinals right-hander Alan Benes notched 13 wins to pace the 1996 rookie crop. However, his 4.90 ERA was the highest by a freshman with at least that many victories since Bob Hooper in 1950. Baltimore's Rocky Coppinger offered similar numbers, going 10–6 with a 5.18 ERA. Only two other rookies cracked double figures in wins. James Baldwin took 11 games for the Chicago White Sox and Ugueth Urbina one fewer for Montreal.

Nearly half of Urbina's appearances came as a reliever, a role that several key newcomers performed in 1996. Mike Myers set a rookie record that would last just two years when he made 83 hill appearances for Detroit. Terry Adams worked 101 innings of pure relief for the Chicago Cubs, an exceptionally high total for a modern-day bullpenner, let alone a rookie. Francisco Cordova of the Pirates bagged 12 saves to lead all freshmen while Billy Wagner, Houston's flame-throwing southpaw, notched nine. In addition, Wagner posted a 2.44 ERA and struck out 67 helpless batters in just 51⅔ innings.

Batting	Pitching
G—AL 157, Derek Jeter, NY	**W**—AL 11, James Baldwin, CHI
NL 152, F.P. Santangelo, MON	NL 13, Alan Benes, STL
AB—AL 582, Derek Jeter, NY	**L**—AL 11, Don Wengert, OAK
NL 502, Rey Ordonez, NY	NL 13, Osvaldo Fernandez, SF
H—AL 183, Derek Jeter, NY	**PCT**—AL .647, James Baldwin, CHI
NL 139, Todd Hollandsworth, LA	NL .565, Alan Benes, STL
2B—AL 25, Derek Jeter, NY	**GP**—**AL 83, Mike Myers, DET**
NL 26, Todd Hollandsworth, LA	NL 69, Terry Adams, CHI
3B—AL 6, Derek Jeter, NY	**GS**—AL 28, James Baldwin, CHI
NL 7, Ricky Otero, PHI	Bob Wolcott, SEA
HR—AL 27, Tony Clark, DET	NL 32, Alan Benes, STL
NL 15, Butch Huskey, NY	**CG**—AL 2, Jose Rosado, KC
R—AL 104, Derek Jeter, NY	Dennis Springer, CAL
NL 89, Marvin Benard, SF	NL 3, Alan Benes, STL
RBI—AL 78, Derek Jeter, NY	**IP**—AL 169.0, James Baldwin, CHI
NL 60, Butch Huskey, NY	NL 191.0, Alan Benes, STL
WK—AL 52, Ernie Young, OAK	**H**—AL 200, Don Wengert, OAK
NL 59, Marvin Benard, SF	NL 193, Osvaldo Fernandez, SF
SO—AL 127, Tony Clark, DET	**BB**—AL 68, Greg Keagle, DET
NL 93, Todd Hollandsworth, LA	NL 87, Alan Benes, STL
SB—AL 20, Kimera Bartee, DET	**K**—AL 127, James Baldwin, CHI
NL 25, Marvin Benard, SF	NL 131, Alan Benes, STL
BA—AL .314, Derek Jeter, NY	**ERA**—AL 4.42, James Baldwin, CHI
NL .291, Todd Hollandsworth, LA	NL 4.61, Osvaldo Fernandez, SF
SLG—AL .430, Derek Jeter, NY	**SHO**—AL 1, Willie Adams, OAK
NL .437, Todd Hollandsworth, LA	Jose Rosado, KC
OBP—AL .376, Derek Jeter, NY	Dennis Springer, CAL
NL .349, Todd Hollandsworth, LA	Don Wengert, OAK
	NL 1, Alan Benes, STL
	Mike Grace, PHI
	Donne Wall, HOU
	SV—AL 6, Mike Myers, DET
	NL 12, Francisco Cordova, PIT

Other Highlights

May 10—Ernie Young blasts three round trippers and hits a single, driving in six as Oakland pounds Minnesota 15–5.

May 17—Jermaine Dye hits a home run in his first ML at bat for the Atlanta Braves, who top the Cincinnati Reds 8–2.

June 22—Four days after hitting two homers in the nightcap of a doubleheader versus Los Angeles, Brant Brown gets five hits, including a home run, at San Diego, the Chicago Cubs winning 9–6 in 16 innings.

July 3—Alex Ochoa of the New York Mets hits for the cycle, including two doubles, and drives in three in a 10–6 win at Philadelphia.

July 30—Jose Rosado holds Boston to three hits for the Kansas City Royals, who win 7–0.

October 20—Andruw Jones homers in his first two World Series ABs, spurring the Braves to a 12–1 win over the New York Yankees in Game One.

1997

Batting average—.306; runs—122; extra-base hits—85; Nomar Garciaparra's rookie season—priceless. The aforementioned numbers helped Garciaparra to enjoy the best season in history by a freshman shortstop. As the leadoff hitter for the Boston Red Sox, he drove in a rookie record 98 runs in that role and also topped the AL in ABs with 684, hits with 209, and triples with 11.

While other rookie shortstops have produced equally high totals in these categories, it is the power Garciaparra wielded that set him apart from others at his position. His 44 doubles are the most ever for a freshman middle infielder as are his 30 home runs. In addition, Garciaparra eclipsed Ted Williams's total-bases record for a Boston rookie by piling up 365, the fourth most in freshman annals. Those 365 TBs translated into a .534 slugging average, which blew away Cal Ripken's frosh shortstop record set in 1982.

HIGHEST SA BY ROOKIE SHORTSTOP (MINIMUM 400 AB)

.534, Nomar Garciaparra, 1997 Bos AL
.475, Cal Ripken, 1982 Bal AL
.452, Gene DeMontreville, 1896 Was NL
.449, Bill Keister, 1899 Bal NL
.444, Joe Sewell, 1921 Cle AL

Last but not least, from late July to late August, Garciaparra hit in 30 consecutive games, one of the longest streaks in rookie history and tied for second best all-time in the hitter-rich Red Sox annals.

Garciaparra was unanimously selected as ROY, a feat that only a broken bone allowed Scott Rolen to accomplish in the NL. On September 7, 1996, Steve Trachsel of the Chicago Cubs hit Rolen with a pitch, fracturing the third baseman's right ulna. Had Rolen either been retired or gotten a hit in that plate appearance it would have been his 131st AB, making him ineligible for future consideration as a rookie. In 1997 a healthy Rolen played 156 games, scoring 93 runs, one more than he drove in. Showing admirable patience for a 22-year-old hitter, he walked 76 times, becoming the just sixth freshman third baseman to top 75 free passes and 150 safeties.

ROOKIE THIRD BASEMEN WITH 150 + HITS AND 75 + WALKS

Lefty Marr, 1889 Col AA, 167 H/87 BB
Al Rosen, 1950 Cle AL, 159 H/100 BB
Rich Rollins, 1962 Min AL, 186 H/75 BB
Billy Grabarkewitz, 1970 LA NL, 153 H/95 BB
Kevin Seitzer, 1987 KC AL, 207 H/80 BB
Scott Rolen, 1997 Phi NL, 159 H/76 BB

Rolen smashed 59 extra-base hits, 21 of them homers, and like Garciaparra, was his league's unanimous choice for ROY.

Two pitchers tied for second place behind Rolen. One was right-hander Livan Hernandez of the Marlins. Hernandez, a Cuban defector, won his first nine decisions for Florida, who, as the NL's wild-card team, made the postseason for the first time in their five-year existence. Hernandez pitched four effective innings of relief in the NLDS. After Florida swept San Francisco, the Atlanta Braves were up next. In Game Three of the NLCS, Hernandez entered the contest in the sixth and picked up the win. With Alex Fernandez injured, Hernandez started Game Five and was nothing short of incredible. Aided by a strike zone only slightly smaller than Montana, he struck out 15 batters and permitted just three hits in Florida's 2–1 victory. Hernandez was named the NLCS MVP. In the Fall Classic, despite running up a 5.27 ERA, Hernandez beat Cleveland veteran Orel Hershiser twice and again was chosen MVP.

Two other rookies squared off in Game Four of the World Series. Indians righty Jaret Wright pitched six solid innings for the win while southpaw Tony Saunders of the Marlins suffered the defeat. Wright started Game Seven, a daunting task for any pitcher, let alone a rookie. However, the Cleveland yearling allowed just a run in 6⅓ innings in a no-decision. In the bottom of the ninth, Florida rookie second baseman Craig Counsell tied the game at 2-all with a sacrifice fly. Two innings later Counsell scored the winning run and the Marlins were the champions of the world.

The hurler who tied Hernandez for rookie honors was Matt Morris of the St. Louis Cardinals. Morris topped all freshmen in innings and ERA and was second only to Anaheim's Jason Dickson in wins. Like Morris in June, Dickson went 4–1 in April, part of a first half that earned the Angels right-hander a berth on the AL All-Star team. Dickson did not get to play in the contest and then sagged somewhat in the second half, finishing 13–9 after dropping his last four decisions.

While Dickson was tearing up the junior circuit, Jose Cruz Jr. was still in AAA ball. Despite not debuting for the Seattle Mariners until May 31, Cruz quickly

Since his superlative 9–3 debut in 1997, Livan Hernandez has been a less than .500 pitcher. After the 2003 campaign, his career mark stood at 84–79. His counterpart in the 1997 World Series, Cleveland's Jaret Wright, likewise has been a less than .500 pitcher. But while Hernandez has remained a steady contributor, until recently Wright's career was in jeopardy, owing largely to poor mechanics. *Transcendental Graphics*

If closer Jose Mesa had been able to hold Cleveland's precarious 2–1 lead in the ninth inning of the final game in the 1997 World Series, Jaret Wright would have become the first rookie starter since Babe Adams in 1909 to bag a decisive Game Seven World Series victory. As it was, the honor fell instead to John Lackey of the Angels in 2002. Earlier in the series Wright had won Game Four to tie him with Adams for the most postseason wins by a rookie starter with three. Previously Wright had beaten the Yankees twice in the opening round Division Series.

But Wright's rookie heroics, unprecedented as they were prior to 1997, were matched by Florida rookie Livan Hernandez. After going 9–3 in 17 starts during the regular season, Hernandez was thrust into a lead role on the Marlins' postseason staff when Florida ace Alex Fernandez tore his rotator cuff in Game Two of the NLCS. Hernandez responded by winning Game Three in relief and then setting the Braves down 2–1 on just three hits in Game Five. He followed by winning Game One of the World Series. When he bagged a second series win in Game Five and his fourth overall in the 1997 postseason, he eclipsed the all-time mark for the most postseason wins by a rookie, which had been tied by Wright just one night earlier.

Despite the bombardment of Cruz missiles, Jose could finish only a distant second to Garciaparra as the AL's top rookie.

Other Highlights

April 26—Brian Moehler tosses one of the five shutouts rookies will register in 1997, yielding only two hits as his Detroit Tigers best Anaheim 2–0.

April 28—Bobby Abreu hits his first two ML home runs, but his heroics aren't enough to prevent Houston from falling to the Colorado Rockies 7–6 in ten innings.

July 28—Steve Woodard of the Milwaukee Brewers ties an AL record by striking out 12 in his ML debut and he allows only one hit in eight innings, edging the Toronto Blue Jays and Roger Clemens 1–0.

August 31—Andruw Jones of Atlanta hits a grand slam and drives in five runs while the Braves knock off the Boston Red Sox 7–3.

made up for lost time, hitting six home runs in June and also July. He was traded to Toronto at the end of the latter month and then really got hot. In August Cruz ripped nine homers and ended with 26 overall. He is the only rookie to hit more than ten round trippers for each of two teams. Cruz leads all multi-team freshmen in circuit shots.

MOST HRS BY ROOKIE PLAYING FOR MORE THAN ONE TEAM

26, Jose Cruz Jr., 1997 Sea AL (12), Tor AL (14)
24, Lee Thomas, 1961 NY AL (0), LA AL (24)
20, Woodie Held, 1957 NY AL (0), KC AL (20)
19, Jake Jones, 1947 Chi AL (3), Bos AL (16)
19, Carlos Pena, 2002 Oak AL (7), Det AL (12)

Batting	Pitching
G—AL 153, Nomar Garciaparra, BOS	W—AL 13, Jason Dickson, ANA
NL 156, Scott Rolen, PHI	NL 12, Matt Morris, STL
AB—AL 684, Nomar Garciaparra, BOS	L—AL 12, Brian Moehler, DET
NL 641, Tony Womack, PIT	NL 12, Chris Holt, HOU
H—AL 209, Nomar Garciaparra, BOS	PCT—AL .591, Jason Dickson, ANA
NL 178, Tony Womack, PIT	NL .571, Matt Morris, STL
2B—AL 44, Nomar Garciaparra, BOS	GP—AL 71, Aaron Small, OAK
NL 35, Scott Rolen, PHI	NL 72, Rich Loiselle, PIT
3B—AL 11, Nomar Garciaparra, BOS	GS—AL 32, Jason Dickson, ANA
NL 10, Neifi Perez, CLR	NL 33, Matt Morris, STL
HR—AL 30, Nomar Garciaparra, BOS	CG—AL 2, Jason Dickson, ANA
NL 21, Scott Rolen, PHI	Brian Moehler, DET
R—AL 122, Nomar Garciaparra, BOS	NL 3, Matt Morris, STL
NL 93, Scott Rolen, PHI	IP—AL 203.2, Jason Dickson, ANA
RBI—AL 98, Nomar Garciaparra, BOS	NL 217.0, Matt Morris, STL
NL 92, Scott Rolen, PHI	H—AL 236, Jason Dickson, ANA
WK—AL 55, Mike Cameron, CHI	NL 211, Chris Holt, HOU
NL 76, Scott Rolen, PHI	BB—AL 61, Brian Moehler, DET
SO—AL 117, Jose Cruz Jr., SEA/TOR	NL 69, Jeremi Gonzalez, CHI
NL 138, Scott Rolen, PHI	Matt Morris, STL
SB—AL 23, Mike Cameron, CHI	K—AL 116, Glendon Rusch, KC
NL 60, Tony Womack, PIT	NL 149, Matt Morris, STL
BA—AL .306, Nomar Garciaparra, BOS	ERA—AL 4.29, Jason Dickson, ANA
NL .300, Doug Glanville, CHI	NL 3.19, Matt Morris, STL
SLG—AL .534, Nomar Garciaparra, BOS	SHO—AL 1, Chris Carpenter, TOR
NL .469, Scott Rolen, PHI	Jason Dickson, ANA
OBP—AL .345, Nomar Garciaparra, BOS	Brian Moehler, DET
NL .382, Scott Rolen, PHI	NL 1, Jeremi Gonzalez, CHI
	John Thomson, CLR
	SV—AL 14, Kelvim Escobar, TOR
	NL 29, Rich Loiselle, PIT

September 4—Bobby Estalella hits three home runs for the Philadelphia Phillies, who beat the Montreal Expos 6–4.

September 28—Neifi Perez gets five hits, one a double and three RBI, as the Colorado Rockies down the Los Angeles Dodgers 13–9.

1998

On May 6, 1998, Kerry Wood was almost perfect. To a devastating arsenal of blazing fastballs and sharp breaking "slurves," Wood, the rookie right-hander of the Chicago Cubs, added pinpoint control. In only his fifth major league game, the 20-year-old Texan had Houston Astros hitters flailing at pitch after pitch. Wood struck out the side in the first, a feat he matched three times that afternoon. On the day Wood whiffed 20 batters, didn't permit a walk, and surrendered only two base runners. Ricky Gutierrez collected a cheap infield single in the third while Craig Biggio was hit by a pitch in the sixth. Wood exceeded numerous team and rookie strikeout benchmarks, among them the NL single-game record (19) and the rookie standard of 18. The latter was accomplished by Jack Coombs in a 24-inning game in 1906 and matched by Bill Gullickson in nine frames in 1980.

For an encore, on May 11, Wood blew away 13 Arizona Diamondbacks, giving him 33 over consecutive games. Only Dupee Shaw of the 1884 Boston Union Association club whiffed more in back-to-back contests, and that feat occurred in a quasi-major league as well as nine years before the current pitching distance was established. On August 26 Wood added 16 more notches on his strikeout belt against the Cincinnati Reds. A torn elbow ligament forced him to sit out September, but Wood nonetheless held hitters to an NL low .196 average. In addition, he set an ML record by averaging 12.58 strikeouts per nine innings (233K/166.2 IP). The figure has since been surpassed, but it still tops the rookie charts.

MOST Ks PER NINE INNINGS BY ROOKIE (MINIMUM 150 IP)

12.58, Kerry Wood, 1998 Chi NL
11.39, Dwight Gooden, 1984 NY NL
11.10, Hideo Nomo, 1995 LA NL
9.98, Rick Ankiel, 2000 StL NL
9.93, Bobby Witt, 1986 Tex AL

Wood, whose 13 wins were the most by a Cubs freshman since 1967, took NL ROY honors. His AL counterpart was Ben Grieve, the Oakland Athletics right fielder. In his first full ML season, Grieve hit .288 with 41 doubles and 18 round trippers. Perhaps more impressive than his 89 RBI were 85 walks, a solid total for a rookie. On April 29 Grieve had three singles and two doubles and scored four times in Oakland's 11–4 win at Cleveland. In July he walked as a pinch hitter in the AL's 13–8 victory in the All-Star Game.

The Midsummer Classic took place in Colorado, where Todd Helton played for the Rockies. Helton replaced Andres Galarraga as the Rockies first sacker and picked up the slack both offensively and with the glove. Hitting at a .359 clip after the All-Star break increased Helton's average to .315, the sixth best BA ever posted by an NL rookie first baseman.

HIGHEST BA BY NL ROOKIE FIRST BASEMAN (MINIMUM 400 AB)

.329, Johnny Mize, 1936 StL NL
.327, Frank McCormick, 1938 Cin NL
.321, Ray Grimes, 1921 Chi NL
.320, Del Bissonette, 1928 Bro NL
.319, Babe Herman, 1926 Bro NL
.315, Todd Helton, 1998 Clr NL

Helton drove in 97 runs and had a .530 slugging percentage. Although he had a markedly higher batting average at Coors Field than on the road (.354 to .273), Helton's homer totals were more balanced (13 at home, 12 away). Defensively, Helton showed the prowess that would net him the NL Gold Glove Award in 2001 and 2002.

While Helton's first All-Star berth would have to wait a couple years, Tampa Bay's Rolando Arrojo required no such patience. Arrojo earned the first win in Devil Rays' history and went 10–5 in the first half. He became the first Tampa player to make an All-Star team, pitching a scoreless sixth inning for the victorious junior circuit. A 4–7 record in the second half signaled the troubles Arrojo would have in succeeding seasons. Nevertheless, his 14 wins are still Tampa Bay's season record.

Another right-handed Cuban defector played for one of the most dominant teams ever. Orlando Hernandez debuted in early June and made 21 starts, completing three including one shutout. He went 12–4, producing a winning percentage even higher than that of the Bronx Bombers (.750 to .704). Hernandez worked seven-plus scoreless innings in Game Four of

Shortstops who hit .300 as rookies are a rare commodity. So small is their club that most of its members since the inception of the ROY Award in 1947 have been runaway winners of the top frosh honor. Witness Alvin Dark (1948), Harvey Kuenn (1953), and in more recent years, Derek Jeter (1996) and Nomar Garciaparra (1997). Yet there was once a shortstop who hit .300 (.306 actually) and stole 22 bases and not only failed to win his loop's ROY prize—he failed even to get a single first-place vote!

In case you missed it, it happened to Mike Caruso of the White Sox. In 1998 Caruso became the third AL rookie shortstop in three years to stroke .300, following on the heels of Jeter and Garciaparra. But Caruso also topped the junior loop in shortstop boots with 35. A bigger strike against him was a glaring lack of patience at the plate. Once pitchers realized that Caruso would swing at almost anything, his BA toppled to .250 in his sophomore year, and he posted the poorest OPS (.578) of any AL qualifier. The sharp drop-off in hitting, coupled with continued porous glove work, caused the White Sox to cut him after the 1999 season and vindicated all the voters who had snubbed him for rookie honors the previous year.

Batting

G—AL 155, Ben Grieve, OAK
   NL 154, Mark Kotsay, FLA
AB—AL 583, Ben Grieve, OAK
   NL 578, Mark Kotsay, FLA
H—AL 168, Ben Grieve, OAK
   NL 167, Todd Helton, CLR
2B—AL 41, Ben Grieve, OAK
   NL 44, Brad Fullmer, MON
3B—AL 9, Randy Winn, TB
   NL 12, David Dellucci, ARZ
HR—AL 18, Ben Grieve, OAK
   NL 25, Todd Helton, CLR
R—AL 94, Ben Grieve, OAK
   NL 78, Todd Helton, CLR
RBI—AL 89, Ben Grieve, OAK
   NL 97, Todd Helton, CLR
WK—AL 85, Ben Grieve, OAK
   NL 67, Travis Lee, ARZ
SO—AL 123, Ben Grieve, OAK
   NL 123, Travis Lee, ARZ
SB—AL 26, Randy Winn, TB
   NL 16, Terry Jones, MON
BA—AL .306, Mike Caruso, CHI
   NL .315, Todd Helton, CLR
SLG—AL .458, Ben Grieve, OAK
   NL .530, Todd Helton, CLR
OBP—AL .387, Ben Grieve, OAK
   NL .384, Todd Helton, CLR

Pitching

W—AL 14, Rolando Arrojo, TB
   NL 13, Kerry Wood, CHI
L—AL 14, Eric Milton, MIN
   NL 15, Javier Vazquez, MON
PCT—AL .538, Rolando Arrojo, TB
   NL .684, Kerry Wood, CHI
GP—**AL 88, Sean Runyan, DET**
   NL 75, Kerry Ligtenberg, ATL
GS—AL 32, Rolando Arrojo, TB
   Eric Milton, MIN
   NL 32, Javier Vazquez, MON
CG—AL 3, Orlando Hernandez, NY
   NL 1, done by nine pitchers
IP—AL 202.0, Rolando Arrojo, TB
   NL 174.1, Brian Meadows, FLA
H—AL 195, Rolando Arrojo, TB
   Eric Milton, MIN
   NL 222, Brian Meadows, FLA
BB—AL 71, Blake Stein, OAK
   NL 91, Jesus Sanchez, FLA
K—AL 152, Rolando Arrojo, TB
   NL 233, Kerry Wood, CHI
ERA—AL 3.56, Rolando Arrojo, TB
   NL 3.40, Kerry Wood, CHI
SHO—AL 2, Rolando Arrojo, TB
   NL 1, Mark Brownson, CLR
   Kerry Wood, CHI
SV—AL 9, Bob Howry, CHI
   NL 30, Kerry Ligtenberg, ATL

the ALCS. He and the Yankees beat the Cleveland Indians 4–0. In the second game of the World Series against San Diego, Hernandez again pitched seven frames but this time actually allowed one run. He won 9–3.

Joining Hernandez on the Yankees was an outfielder who amassed only 67 at bats in 27 games yet contributed in historic proportions. Shane Spencer hit a rookie-record three grand slams in a ten-day period in late September. In addition, Spencer had two multi-homer games in his brief tenure, the first on August 7, when he also collected two doubles and a single in the nightcap of a doubleheader. In all, Spencer hit ten home runs and six doubles, producing a hefty .910 slugging percentage, the highest ever for a rookie with at least 50 AB.

HIGHEST SA BY ROOKIE (MINIMUM 50 AB)

.910/67 AB, Shane Spencer, 1998 NY AL
.733/60 AB, Mark Quinn, 1999 KC AL
.710/62 AB, Merv Connors, 1938 Chi AL
.679/53 AB, Dave Valle, 1986 Sea AL
.678/59 AB, Jose Oliva, 1994 Atl NL

Other Highlights

May 31—Roger Cedeno of the Los Angeles Dodgers hits five singles in a 10–3 win over the New York Mets.

June 22—Mark Kotsay goes 5-for-6 with a double in the Florida Marlins' 3–2 win at Tampa Bay.

July 21—Mark Brownson pitches a four-hit shutout in his major league debut for the Colorado Rockies, beating the Houston Astros 5–0.

September 14—Juan Encarnacion strokes five hits including a triple and a homer, scores five runs, and drives in four, but the Detroit Tigers lose to the Chicago White Sox 17–16 in 12 innings.

September 26—Brian Simmons homers from each side of the plate—the only two round trippers he will hit in 1998—and the White Sox pound the Kansas City Royals 13–5.

September 27—In his second big league start, Roy Halladay of Toronto leads Detroit 2–0 and is just one out away from a no-no when Tigers pinch hitter Bobby Higginson smacks Halladay's first pitch for a solo home run to make the final score 2–1.

► 1999 ◄

In 1999 Jeff Zimmerman went on a roll that every relief pitcher in the game's long history would have envied. From late May to early August, the Texas Rangers bullpen rookie pitched 30 consecutive scoreless innings. Before the skein ended, Zimmerman had lowered his ERA to 0.75, even more microscopic than the 0.86 he brought to the All-Star Game in Boston, where he pitched a scoreless seventh inning in the AL's 4–1 win. Zimmerman started off 9–0, tying Joe Pate's 1926 junior circuit record for consecutive wins by a rookie reliever. On August 6 Zimmerman tasted defeat for the first time and subsequently finished 9–3 with a 2.36 ERA and three saves. In the ALDS he pitched just once, a scoreless frame in the third game as the New York Yankees completed a sweep of the Rangers.

While impressive, Zimmerman was far from the lone freshman fireman to excel in 1999. Cincinnati's Scott Williamson joined the Rangers righty as an All-Star selectee but was not used by NL skipper Bruce Bochy. Williamson may well have welcomed the rest as he was en route to a 62-appearance season that saw him average more than a strikeout per inning. He went 12–7 with 19 saves and a 2.41 ERA in 93⅓ innings. In May Williamson saved five games and did not allow a single

run, part of a scoreless stretch that eventually reached 23⅔ frames. Two other rookies also starred in relief roles in 1999. Billy Koch took over as Toronto's hard-throwing closer and chalked up 31 saves, the third-most ever by a rookie, and Scott Sauerbeck relieved 65 times and posted a 2.00 ERA for Pittsburgh.

Kris Benson joined Sauerbeck on the Pirates' staff and chipped in 11 wins. Benson, who was on the 1996 U.S. Olympic team and was taken first overall in that year's amateur draft, fanned 139 batters, nearly eclipsing Cy Blanton's post-1900 club record.

MOST STRIKEOUTS BY ROOKIE FOR ANY PITTSBURGH FRANCHISE

189, Fleury Sullivan, 1884 Pit AA
142, Cy Blanton, 1935 Pit NL
139, Kris Benson, 1999 Pit NL
135, Don Robinson, 1978 Pit NL
132, Steve Cooke, 1993 Pit NL

Seattle had two freshmen equal or better Benson's victory total. Freddy Garcia won 17 times and southpaw John Halama 11. Garcia lost just eight games and ranked third in the AL with a .680 winning percentage. He had 170 strikeouts, a dozen of them on August 24, when he blanked Detroit on six hits. Halama spun his own six-hitter on July 4 at Texas, winning 6–0.

Oakland's Tim Hudson matched Benson and Halama with 11 wins while losing only twice. Hudson went a combined 7–0 for Oakland's AA and AAA clubs before debuting on June 8 at San Diego. He fanned 11 Padres in five innings, yielding three runs and receiving a no-decision. Hudson and Garcia were just the second and third AL freshmen subsequent to 1979 to register as many as nine more wins than losses.

Despite these strong pitching performances, it was Kansas City centerfielder Carlos Beltran who was the AL ROY. Beltran, just the second rookie since 1950 to notch both 100 runs and RBI, had 112 runs and 108 ribbies. He collected 194 hits, 56 of the extra-base variety, and also swiped 27 bases. Beltran's 663 ABs in 1999 tied him with Jake Wood for the sixth-highest total in freshmen annals.

Beltran enjoyed five games in which he obtained four hits but never reached five safeties as a rookie, a feat that Chris Singleton of the Chicago White Sox managed to perform twice in his yearling season. Singleton, also a center fielder, hit for the cycle and had a single to spare in a July 6 loss to the Royals. Thirteen days later, he went 5-for-6 again and homered at Milwaukee, the ChiSox taking the interleague game 10–8. Singleton, who batted .373 in June, hit .336 in July before ending at .300 overall with 17 homers and 20 steals. His leftfielder teammate, Carlos Lee, also gave Pale Hose fans considerable hope for the future. Lee homered in his initial time up in the big leagues, connecting on May 7 off Oakland's Tom Candiotti, and then proceeded to drive in 84 runs in only 127 games.

Among the other frosh batsmen who excelled were Florida's Preston Wilson, who smashed 26 home runs and had 71 RBI. Though he struck out 156 times, Wilson hit .280, the highest mark ever by a rookie with 150 or more whiffs. The Marlins also received an unexpected windfall when Alex Gonzalez had eight triples and 14 round trippers, excellent figures for a freshman shortstop. Gonzalez, who went 0-for-1 in the All-Star Game, led NL yearlings with 155 hits. Second to Gonzalez among senior circuit newcomers was Warren Morris of Pittsburgh. Morris first achieved national recognition when his home run won the College World Series for Louisiana State in 1996. Upon reaching the bigs with the Pirates in 1999, he hit 15 circuit blasts and posted 73 RBI, the most by a rookie second baseman since Joe Gordon's 97 in 1938.

Morris was anchored at second for every inning of the 144 games he played, but St. Louis's Joe McEwing roamed the entire ballfield, serving wherever needed. McEwing played the outfield and all four infield positions while hitting .275. On June 8 he began a hitting streak that grew to 25 games, the longest ever by a Cardinal freshman and the best by any Redbird since 1971.

Other Highlights

June 9—Guillermo Mota, a reliever for Montreal, homers in his first ML at bat, and the Expos massacre Boston 13–1.

June 25—Jose Jimenez no-hits the Arizona Diamondbacks, fanning eight as the St. Louis Cardinals beat Randy Johnson 1–0.

Owing to competition from the Players League, a number of ML teams in 1890 were compelled to employ pitchers who were woefully lacking in talent. One such was William Stecher of the American Association Philadelphia Athletics. Stecher not only lost all ten of his starts, but he logged a 10.32 ERA, a figure that stood for over a century as the all-time worst by a hurler making ten or more starts.

In 1999 Stecher's record withstood a severe challenge from Micah Bowie, a rookie left-hander who began the season in Atlanta and then went to the Cubs after being hammered in three relief appearances with the Braves. Chicago pilot Jim Riggleman decided that the solution to Bowie's problem was to make him a starter. In 11 starts with the Cubs, Bowie gave up 73 hits in just 47 innings but somehow contrived to notch two wins in his eight decisions. Not surprisingly, he was not invited back to Wrigley in 2000 for an encore. Remarkably, however, Bowie resurfaced in 2002 in Oakland. Used exclusively in middle relief by A's skipper Art Howe, he won his only two decisions and sported a glittering 1.50 ERA in 13 appearances.

Here are the 10 worst season ERAs among pitchers in at least ten starts. Note that Stecher's record fell just a year after Bowie's challenge and that eight of the ten seasons have occurred since 1994.

TEN WORST SEASON ERAS (MINIMUM 10 STARTS)

Rank	Name	Year	GS	ERA
1	Roy Halladay	2000	13	10.64
2	William Stecher	1890	10	10.32
3	Micah Bowie	1999	11	10.24
4	Aaron Myette	2002	12	10.06
5	Steve Blass	1973	18	9.85
6	Sean Bergman	2000	14	9.66
7	Andy Larkin	1998	14	9.64
8	Todd Van Poppel	1996	15	9.06
9	Bryan Rekar	1996	11	8.95
10	Mark Clark	1999	15	8.60

July 3—Marlon Anderson scores four runs and totals five hits, including a double and a home run as his Philadelphia Phillies maul the Chicago Cubs 21–8.

August 14—Brian Daubach gets four singles and a home run while driving in six Boston runs in the Red Sox' 13–2 pasting of Seattle.

August 29—Kyle Farnsworth two-hits Los Angeles for the Chicago Cubs, who beat the Dodgers 6–0.

1999 ROOKIE LEADERS

Batting	Pitching
G—AL 156, Carlos Beltran, KC	W—AL 17, Freddy Garcia, SEA
NL 152, Joe McEwing, STL	NL 12, Scott Williamson, CIN
AB—AL 663, Carlos Beltran, KC	L—AL 12, Jeff Weaver, DET
NL 560, Alex Gonzalez, FLA	NL 14, Kris Benson, PIT
H—AL 194, Carlos Beltran, KC	Jose Jimenez, STL
NL 155, Alex Gonzalez, FLA	PCT—AL .680, Freddy Garcia, SEA
2B—AL 33, Brian Daubach, BOS	NL .440, Kris Benson, PIT
NL 32, Michael Barrett, MON	GP—AL 65, Mike Venafro, TEX
3B—AL 9, Carlos Febles, KC	Jeff Zimmerman, TEX
NL 8, Alex Gonzalez, FLA	NL 72, Braden Looper, FLA
HR—AL 22, Carlos Beltran, KC	GS—AL 33, Freddy Garcia, SEA
NL 26, Preston Wilson, FLA	NL 31, Kris Benson, PIT
R—AL 112, Carlos Beltran, KC	Matt Clement, SD
NL 81, Alex Gonzalez, FLA	CG—AL 2, Freddy Garcia, SEA
RBI—AL 108, Carlos Beltran, KC	Joe Mays, MIN
NL 73, Warren Morris, PIT	NL 2, Kris Benson, PIT
WK—AL 53, Trot Nixon, BOS	Jose Jimenez, STL
NL 64, Ron Belliard, MIL	IP—AL 201.1, Freddy Garcia, SEA
SO—AL 123, Carlos Beltran, KC	NL 196.2, Kris Benson, PIT
NL 156, Preston Wilson, FLA	H—AL 205, Freddy Garcia, SEA
SB—AL 27, Carlos Beltran, KC	NL 190, Matt Clement, SD
NL 34, Damian Jackson, SD	BB—AL 90, Freddy Garcia, SEA
BA—AL .300, Chris Singleton, CHI	NL 86, Matt Clement, SD
NL .295, Ron Belliard, MIL	K—AL 170, Freddy Garcia, SEA
SLG—AL .490, Chris Singleton, CHI	NL 139, Kris Benson, PIT
NL .502, Preston Wilson, FLA	ERA—AL 4.07, Freddy Garcia, SEA
OBP—AL .342, Carlos Beltran, KC	NL 4.07, Kris Benson, PIT
NL .382, Ron Belliard, MIL	SHO—AL 1, Freddy Garcia, SEA
	John Halama, SEA
	Roy Halladay, TOR
	Joe Mays, MIN
	NL 2, Jose Jimenez, STL
	SV—AL 31, Billy Koch, TOR
	NL 19, Scott Williamson, CIN

October 2—Bruce Chen permits just one hit in his scoreless six-inning stint for Atlanta but gets a no-decision against the Florida Marlins, who prevail 1–0 in ten innings.

14

2000s

◄ 2000 ►

It strikes as a lightning bolt out of a cloudless sky. One day, a pitcher has good control and the next, oftentimes inexplicably, he can't find home plate without a Global Positioning System. Steve Blass is the classic example. Recently, Rick Ankiel suffered the same fate. The 2000 season had gone very well for the St. Louis Cardinals yearling southpaw as he won 11 games with a 3.50 ERA, and his 194 strikeouts shattered Dizzy Dean's 1932 team rookie record. Ankiel, who turned 21 in July, could even hit, batting .250 with two home runs. The Cardinals won the NL Central, and Ankiel started Game One of the NLDS against the Atlanta Braves. He lasted only 2⅔ innings after yielding four earned runs. Worse, Ankiel walked six and threw five wild pitches. St. Louis nonetheless managed to win the game and sweep Atlanta before facing the New York Mets in the NLCS. Ankiel gave up one hit, made two wild pitches and walked three Mets while gaining but two outs in his second-game NLCS start. A relief stint in Game Five was not much better, and Ankiel has yet to recapture the ability to throw strikes consistently.

Facing Ankiel in the division series was Rafael Furcal, the Braves' new shortstop. Furcal swiped 40 bases and walked 73 times. He scored 87 runs in 131 games, becoming just the fourth rookie since 1901 to tally as often in fewer than 460 ABs. Furcal, whose defensive game included a rifle arm, was ROY in the NL, beating out Ankiel.

Vying for freshman honors in the junior circuit were two players from AL West rivals. The Seattle Mariners employed Kazuhiro Sasaki as their closer. Sasaki had played the previous ten years with Yokohama in the Japanese Central League, where he had two seasons with an ERA below 1.00. Now in the States, Sasaki saved a rookie record 37 games, blowing only three of 40 opportunities.

MOST SAVES BY A ROOKIE

37, Kazuhiro Sasaki, 2000 Sea AL
36, Todd Worrell, 1986 StL NL
31, Billy Koch, 1999 Tor AL
30, Kerry Ligtenberg, 1998 Atl NL
29, Rich Loiselle, 1997 Pit NL

Seattle won the AL wild card after finishing half a game behind the Oakland Athletics, and Sasaki saved three games in the postseason, not allowing a run in four appearances. Finishing behind Sasaki in the ROY race was Oakland's Terrence Long, who had been acquired from the New York Mets in July 1999. Long, born Leap Day in 1976, topped rookies with 168 hits, 56 of them for extra bases. In 138 games he drove home 80 runs and scored 104 others, an excellent total for a rookie in less than 140 games.

MOST RUNS BY ROOKIE IN LESS THAN 140 GAMES, 1901–2003

132 R/138 G, Joe DiMaggio, 1936 NY AL
105 R/137 G, Eddie Murphy, 1913 Phi AL
105 R/138 G, Bobby Thomson, 1947 NY NL
104 R/126 G, Jeff Heath, 1938 Cle AL
104 R/138 G, Terrence Long, 2000 Oak AL

Oakland, in addition, brought up a pair of left-handers who would give the team a devastating trio of young starters in the early part of the twenty-first century. Mark Mulder went 9–10 in 2000 but had a 5.44 ERA. However, like Tim Hudson, the previous year's A's rookie sensation, Mulder became a 20-game winner in his soph season in the bigs. Barry Zito began 2000 with Sacramento in the PCL, going 8–5 before debuting with the Athletics on July 22. Zito won seven games for Oakland and had a 2.72 ERA. On September 10 he threw one of the four rookie shutouts of 2000 when he blanked Tampa Bay on five hits.

Giving up quite a few more runs than Zito was Kansas City's Chad Durbin, who had a horrendous 8.21 ERA in 72⅓ innings.

HIGHEST ERA BY ROOKIE, MINIMUM 70 IP

9.64 ERA/74.2 IP, Andy Larkin, 1998 Fla NL
8.32 ERA/114.2 IP, Dewey McDougal, 1895 StL NL
8.29 ERA/89 IP, Jimmy Haynes, 1996 Bal AL
8.21 ERA/72.1, Chad Durbin, 2000 KC AL
8.17 ERA/98 IP, Harry Colliflower, 1899 Cle NL

Durbin's teammate, Hector Ortiz, offered partial consolation to K.C. followers, however, when he went 34-for-88 in a late-season trial. Ortiz's .386 average was the highest by a rookie with at least 75 ABs since

On August 7, 2000, the Rockies made minor league call-up Juan Pierre their new center fielder for the balance of the season. When Pierre hit safely in each of his first 16 games, he established what is currently regarded as the record for the longest hitting streak at the start of an ML career.

Pierre's hitting skein drew a good deal of attention, but another rookie feat that he accomplished went unnoticed. By dint of his .675 OPS in 2000, Pierre tied Simon Nicholls's record for the lowest yearling OPS in history accompanied by a .300 batting average in at least 200 at bats. If sacrifice flies are included in Pierre's plate appearances, as per the custom of many modern statisticians, his OPS is shaved two points to .673, which would make him the sole holder of this negative rookie record.

At the close of the 2003 season, Pierre's fourth in the majors, it began to appear that he might one day challenge another negative mark, as he had the sixth lowest OPS all-time among performers with a .300 career BA in at least 1,000 at bats.

ALL-TIME LOWEST OPS, MINIMUM .300 CAREER BA AND 1,000 ABs

Rank	Name	AB	BA	OPS
1	Patsy Donovan	7505	.301	.702
2	Gene DeMontreville	3615	.303	.712
3	Jay Kirke	1148	.301	.713
4	Stuffy McInnis	7822	.307	.723
5	Matty Alou	5789	.307	.727
6	Juan Pierre	2077	.307	.730
7	Ted Easterly	2020	.300	.732
8	Emmet Heidrick	3047	.300	.732
9	Jack Lelivelt	1154	.301	.735
10	Eddie Brown	2902	.303	.735

Bob Hazle hit .403 in 1957. While Mark Quinn could not hope to match Ortiz's short-term production over a full season, he afforded further consolation for the Durbin disappointment when he hit .294 as the Royals' new left fielder, with 33 doubles, 20 homers, and 78 RBI.

Other Highlights

April 18—Adam Kennedy has a grand slam and a bases-loaded triple and knocks in eight runs as the Anaheim Angels beat the Toronto Blue Jays 16–10.

2000 ROOKIE LEADERS

Batting	Pitching
G—AL 156, Adam Kennedy, ANA	W—AL 12, Mark Redman, MIN
NL 149, Jay Payton, NY	NL 11, Rick Ankiel, STL
AB—AL 598, Adam Kennedy, ANA	Matt Herges, LA
NL 518, Peter Bergeron, MON	L—AL 10, Mark Mulder, OAK
H—AL 168, Terrence Long, OAK	Dan Reichert, KC
NL 142, Jay Payton, NY	NL 11, Jimmy Anderson, PIT
2B—AL 34, Terrence Long, OAK	PCT—AL .571, Mark Redman, MIN
NL 28, Lance Berkman, HOU	NL .611, Rick Ankiel, STL
3B—AL 11, Adam Kennedy, ANA	GP—**AL 83, Kelly Wunsch, CHI**
NL 7, Peter Bergeron, MON	NL 70, Kevin Walker, SD
HR—AL 20, Mark Quinn, KC	GS—AL 27, Mark Mulder, OAK
NL 21, Lance Berkman, HOU	NL 30, Rick Ankiel, STL
R—AL 104, Terrence Long, OAK	CG—AL 2, Ramon Ortiz, ANA
NL 87, Rafael Furcal, ATL	NL 2, Wade Miller, HOU
RBI—AL 80, Terrence Long, OAK	IP—AL 154.0, Mark Mulder, OAK
NL 79, Pat Burrell, PHI	NL 175.0, Rick Ankiel, STL
WK—AL 46, Steve Cox, TB	H—AL 191, Mark Mulder, OAK
NL 73, Rafael Furcal, ATL	NL 169, Jimmy Anderson, PIT
SO—AL 91, Mark Quinn, KC	BB—AL 91, Dan Reichert, KC
NL 139, Pat Burrell, PHI	NL 90, Rick Ankiel, STL
SB—AL 22, Adam Kennedy, ANA	K—AL 117, Mark Redman, MIN
NL 40, Rafael Furcal, ATL	NL 194, Rick Ankiel, STL
BA—AL .294, Mark Quinn, KC	ERA—AL 4.70, Dan Reichert, KC
NL .295, Rafael Furcal, ATL	NL 3.50, Rick Ankiel, STL
SLG—AL .488, Mark Quinn, KC	SHO—AL 1, Brian Cooper, ANA
NL .561, Lance Berkman, HOU	Travis Harper, TB
OBP—AL .344, Mark Quinn, KC	Dan Reichert, KC
NL .395, Rafael Furcal, ATL	Barry Zito, OAK
	NL No Qualifiers
	SV—AL 37, Kazuhiro Sasaki, SEA
	NL 9, Scott Strickland, MON

May 7—Mitch Meluskey gets five hits, including a double, and two RBI for the Houston Astros, who win at Los Angeles 14–8.

June 26—Alex Cabrera homers in his first ML at bat in the Arizona Diamondbacks' 6–1 win against the Astros.

June 30—Brian Cooper fires a three-hit shutout for Anaheim, beating Oakland 7–0.

July 6—Cards catcher Keith McDonald becomes only the second player in history to homer in his first two ML plate appearances when he goes deep against Osvaldo Fernandez of the Reds after hitting a pinch homer against Cincinnati's Andy Larkin in his first plate appearance two days earlier.

September 3—Chris Richard hits a double, a triple, and two home runs, driving in six for the Baltimore Orioles, who fall to the Cleveland Indians 12–11 in 13 innings.

September 4—Juan Pierre goes 5-for-5 for Colorado, who beat the Chicago Cubs 6–2.

September 24—Travis Harper of the Tampa Bay Devil Rays allows only two hits and blanks Toronto 6–0.

2001

Ichiro Suzuki's accomplishments in Japan had become legend. A .350 career hitter, Ichiro had won the last seven Japanese Pacific League batting titles. But in April

2001 Ichiro's immense talent was put to a much sterner test—playing in the major leagues as the Seattle Mariners regular right fielder.

On April 6 Ichiro had his first of six four-hit games in 2001, going 4-for-6 with a two-run homer in the top of the tenth in Arlington, Texas. The long ball, however, wasn't Ichiro's normal modus operandi. Typically he utilized his terrific speed and slashing left-handed stroke to beat out infield hits or stretch singles into doubles. Defensively, he displayed an amazingly accurate arm, which opposing base runners quickly became loath to test.

Ichiro hit .336 in April and .370 in May, proving his Japanese statistics were for real. He was voted to start in the All-Star Game and responded with a single off Randy Johnson before the fans in Seattle's Safeco Field. After a subpar July, Ichiro hit .429 with 51 hits in August. His rookie record 242 hits produced an AL-best .350 batting average, while his 692 at bats broke the junior circuit's freshman standard. Ichiro became only the second rookie in history named MVP, and he also won a Gold Glove for his shining defense.

Other rookies having exceptional seasons in 2001 were Albert Pujols, Alfonso Soriano, and Jimmy Rollins. The 21-year-old Pujols made the St. Louis Cardinals out of spring training and played primarily right field. Soon, however, the versatile Pujols began filling in elsewhere for wounded Redbirds, causing him to end up making at least 30 starts at four positions—left field, right field, and both first and third bases. As if that sort of flexibility were not valuable enough, Pujols's lethal bat established him as a serious MVP candidate. To cement his claim on the National League ROY Award, Pujols hit .329 with 47 doubles, 37 homers, and an NL freshman record 130 RBI. His 360 total bases and 88 extra-base hits also set league rookie marks and helped him cop the Silver Slugger Award for senior circuit third basemen.

The following Cardinals' rookie records were left shattered in Pujols's wake: games, hits, doubles, homers, runs, RBI, batting and slugging average, and on-base percentage. Among the legendary performers eclipsed were Stan Musial, Johnny Mize, and Joe Medwick. Pujols joined Ted Williams as the only freshmen to have a slugging average better than .600 and an on-base percentage above .400 (minimum 400 at bats).

Meanwhile Alfonso Soriano, the second baseman for the three-time defending world champion New York Yankees, demonstrated uncommon power and speed. He was just the fifth freshman to hit at least 15 home runs and steal more than 40 bases.

ROOKIES WITH 15+ HR AND 40+ SB

Bug Holliday, 1889 Cin AA 19 HR, 46 SB
Tommie Agee, 1966 Chi AL 22 HR, 44 SB
Mitchell Page, 1977 Oak AL 21 HR, 42 SB
Juan Samuel, 1984 Phi NL 15 HR, 72 SB
Alfonso Soriano, 2001 NY AL 18 HR, 43 SB

Soriano broke Bert Daniels's 1910 club record for steals by a rookie, and his 156 games at second base broke the team's freshman mark. On the downside, Soriano's 125 strikeouts are also tops among Bronx Bomber rooks.

Jimmy Rollins manned the other side of the keystone sack for the Philadelphia Phillies. Rollins joined Jim Canavan (1891) and Nomar Garciaparra (1997) as the only rookie shortstops to reach double figures in each extra-base hit category. Rollins's 656 at bats not only led the National League but also set a senior circuit record for rookie shortstops. Not since Gene DeMontreville in 1896 had an NL freshman shortstop collected more than Rollins's 180 hits. The young Phillie became only the second rookie to lead his league in both triples and stolen bases.

Unlike Ichiro, Pujols, Soriano, and Rollins, who were full-season rookies, Adam Dunn did not debut for the Cincinnati Reds until July 20, but he quickly made his powerful presence felt. Dunn smashed 11 home runs in August—the highest monthly total ever by an NL rookie. He ended the season with 19 homers, 43 RBI, and 54 runs in only 66 games.

Team USA produced more than an Olympic gold medal in 2000. It also gave baseball two of the best rookie pitchers in 2001—Roy Oswalt and Ben Sheets. The Houston Astros brought up the right-handed Oswalt in early May, putting him in the bullpen. After eight relief appearances, Oswalt made his first start on June 2, beating the Los Angeles Dodgers 2–1. Oswalt went 4–0 in June, and the Astros began their ascent in the National League Central standings. Oswalt featured a mid-90s fastball and a sharp curveball. He combined these pitches with impeccable control to reach a level of dominance not exhibited by a rookie since Chester A. Arthur resided in the White House. To find another freshman hurler who has posted a strikeout-to-walk ratio of six-to-one in a minimum 100 innings, as did Oswalt with 144 whiffs and only 24 bases on balls, one must reach all the way back to 1884. Oswalt sported a 1.99 ERA and another 4–0 mark in August, but the following month the first of what would become a chronic series of groin injuries sidelined the young ace. Still, Oswalt had little to bemoan. He went 14–3, breaking Houston's rookie victory record, and finished second in voting for NL Rookie of the Year.

Also having a fine freshman campaign was Ben Sheets of the Milwaukee Brewers. Sheets, who pitched a three-hit shutout against Cuba to earn Team USA the gold medal, started 2001 slowly. He dropped his first two decisions before earning his first win on April 28 versus the Montreal Expos. By May 13 three more triumphs were under his belt. Sheets sported a 10–4 record by the end of June and made the National League All-Star team. But rotator cuff problems cost him six weeks in the season's second half and forced him to settle for a final mark of 11–10.

Despite their success, neither Oswalt nor Sheets led major league rookies in wins in 2001. That distinction fell to C.C. Sabathia, the physically imposing southpaw of the Cleveland Indians. The 260-pound 6'7″ Sabathia won 17 games—the most by a Tribe rookie since Gene Bearden's 20 in 1948—and his 171 strikeouts in 2001 are topped in Indians' rookie annals only by Herb Score's

245 in 1955. Also, Sabathia's 33 starts are only one short of the record by a Tribe freshman.

Other Highlights

April 17—Gene Stechschulte of the St. Louis Cardinals hits a two-run pinch homer against Arizona in his first major league plate appearance; it was the first pitch Stechschulte, a pitcher, saw in the majors.

June 8—Josh Towers tosses a six-hitter as the Baltimore Orioles blank the visiting Montreal Expos 5–0; the shutout is the first by an Orioles rookie since Arthur Rhodes had one in 1992.

July 10—Four rookies play in the All-Star Game in Seattle—Ichiro Suzuki of the Seattle Mariners, Albert Pujols of the Cardinals, the Phillies' Jimmy Rollins, and Milwaukee's Ben Sheets—as the AL wins 4–1.

August 4—Wes Helms collects seven RBI for visiting Atlanta in Milwaukee; Helms hits a bases-loaded triple and a pair of two-run homers in a 14–2 Braves win.

August 12—Second baseman Junior Spivey has his second five-hit game of the year and scores three times for Arizona as the Diamondbacks beat host Atlanta 9–1.

August 17—Jose Ortiz of Colorado hits home runs off three different Florida pitchers as the hosting Rockies beat the Marlins 12–5.

August 23—Jason Jennings of Colorado throws a five-hit shutout in his major league debut, beating the Mets 10–0; Jennings also went 3-for-5 with two RBI and a ninth-inning home run to make him the only pitcher since 1900 to have both a shutout and a home run in his big league baptism.

August 23—Albert Pujols hits his 30th home run of the season, becoming the 22nd rookie to reach that milestone, but the St. Louis Cardinals fall 12–2 to the Reds.

September 3—Bud Smith no-hits the San Diego Padres, striking out seven as the visiting Cardinals win 4–0; Smith is the first freshman southpaw to throw a no-hitter in the NL since 1880 when Lee Richmond tossed a perfect game for Worcester.

In leading the AL in most times hit by a pitch, Angels shortstop David Eckstein also set a new junior loop rookie HBP record in 2001 with 21. Eckstein fell just one HBP short of the post-1901 frosh mark, which is held by Brooklyn shortstop Charlie Babb, who was nailed 22 times in 1903. The all-time rookie mark is owned by Pete Gilbert. Playing third base for Baltimore in 1891, the American Association's last year as a major league, Gilbert took his base on HBP calls 28 times, this despite hitting just .230 and collecting only 37 walks.

But neither Babb nor Gilbert was ever a loop leader again in HBP. Eckstein, in contrast, became the first man in history to top his loop in HBP in each of his first two seasons when he was hit an AL-high 27 times in 2002.

Batting		Pitching	
G—	AL 158, Alfonso Soriano, NY	W—	AL 17, C.C. Sabathia, CLE
	NL 161, Albert Pujols, STL		NL 14, Roy Oswalt, HOU
AB—	**AL 692, Ichiro Suzuki, SEA**	L—	AL 10, Willis Roberts, BAL
	NL 656, Jimmy Rollins, PHI		Josh Towers, BAL
H—	**AL 242, Ichiro Suzuki, SEA**		NL 15, Chris Reitsma, CIN
	NL 194, Albert Pujols, STL	PCT—	AL .773, C.C. Sabathia, CLE
2B—	AL 34, Alfonso Soriano, NY		NL .318, Chris Reitsma, CIN
	Ichiro Suzuki, SEA	GP—	AL 60, Bob File, TOR
	NL 47, Albert Pujols, STL		NL 67, Gene Stechschulte, STL
3B—	AL 8, Ichiro Suzuki, SEA	GS—	AL 33, C.C. Sabathia, CLE
	NL 12, Jimmy Rollins, PHI		NL 29, Chris Reitsma, CIN
HR—	AL 18, Alfonso Soriano, NY	CG—	AL 1, Chris George, KC
	NL 37, Albert Pujols, STL		Willis Roberts, BAL
R—	AL 127, Ichiro Suzuki, SEA		Josh Towers, BAL
	NL 112, Albert Pujols, STL		NL 3, Roy Oswalt, HOU
RBI—	AL 73, Alfonso Soriano, NY	IP—	AL 180.1, C.C. Sabathia, CLE
	NL 130, Albert Pujols, STL		NL 182.0, Chris Reitsma, CIN
WK—	AL 43, David Eckstein, ANA	H—	AL 165, Josh Towers, BAL
	NL 69, Albert Pujols, STL		NL 209, Chris Reitsma, CIN
SO—	AL 125, Alfonso Soriano, NY	BB—	AL 95, C.C. Sabathia, CLE
	NL 108, Jimmy Rollins, PHI		NL 87, Shawn Chacon, CLR
SB—	**AL 56, Ichiro Suzuki, SEA**	K—	AL 171, C.C. Sabathia, CLE
	NL 46, Jimmy Rollins, PHI		NL 144, Roy Oswalt, HOU
BA—	**AL .350, Ichiro Suzuki, SEA**	ERA—	AL 4.39, C.C. Sabathia, CLE
	NL .329, Albert Pujols, STL		NL 5.29, Chris Reitsma, CIN
SLG—	AL .457, Ichiro Suzuki, SEA	SHO—	AL 1, Josh Towers, BAL
	NL .610, Albert Pujols, STL		NL 1, Jason Jennings, CLR
OBP—	AL .385, Ichiro Suzuki, SEA		Roy Oswalt, HOU
	NL .407, Albert Pujols, STL		Ben Sheets, MIL
			Bud Smith, STL
		SV—	AL 6, Willis Roberts, BAL
			NL 9, Bret Prinz, ARZ

September 4—Roy Oswalt wins his 13th game, breaking Houston's rookie win record, in the Astros' 7–1 victory in Cincinnati.

2002

Canada may experience frigid weather even in the summer, but in the summer of 2002 that country's baseball fans took comfort in the sizzling bats of rookies from both of its teams. Eric Hinske, the third baseman of the Toronto Blue Jays, wasted no time kicking off his ROY campaign. On Opening Day he scored twice and knocked in three runs in his ML debut as the Blue Jays beat Boston 12–11. Hinske connected for his first home run on April 20, a go-ahead shot in the top of the tenth against the New York Yankees. It was Hinske's sole round tripper of the month, but he would smash seven dongs in May and six more in June, including a game-ender on June 29. In all, Hinske hit 24 circuit clouts, setting a new Toronto rookie record, as did his 38 doubles. He also drove in 84 runs and drew 77 walks. Fellow Jays rookie Josh Phelps joined Hinske in the offensive barrage, collecting 58 RBI in just 74 games. In August Phelps, a designated hitter, led all AL hitters with 30 ribbies.

Over in Quebec Brad Wilkerson led NL freshmen in

every main offensive category except steals while he powered 20 home runs, the most ever by a Montreal rookie. Wilkerson, like Hinske, showed excellent patience at the plate, walking 81 times, although he struck out on 161 occasions. The outfielder also set team freshman standards with both of those totals as well as with his 92 runs.

Another recruit fly chaser, Austin Kearns of Cincinnati, had just three fewer RBI than Wilkerson's 59 despite playing only 107 games. Kearns ripped 13 home runs and batted .315 after his mid-April debut. He would have had a strong chance for ROY honors had his season not been ended by injury in late August. Instead, Kearns finished third, behind runner-up Wilkerson and winner Jason Jennings of the Colorado Rockies. "Winner" was the operative word for Jennings, as he was a victor 16 times for the Denver nine, the most ever by a Rockies' freshman and only one short of the overall team mark. The right-hander was 4–0 in May, but his best month was August, when he went 5–1. Jennings finished with an ERA of 4.52 that is more impressive than it might seem considering his home park was Coors Field. In addition, he led all hurlers with a .306 BA and 11 RBI, making him an all-around threat. Note too that in 2002 Colorado for the first time had a pair of double-digit winning freshmen as Dennis Stark was 11–4.

MOST WINS BY COLORADO ROOKIE

16, Jason Jennings, 2002
12, Armando Reynoso, 1993
11, Dennis Stark, 2002
9, Steve Reed, 1993
7, Roger Bailey, 1995
7, John Thomson, 1997
7, Bobby Jones, 1998

Including the Rockies pair, 11 rookies won at least ten decisions, the most since 1986, and one would need to go back some 60 years to 1944 to find a season with more double-digit winning freshmen. Closely trailing Jennings was AL leader Rodrigo Lopez, a 15-game winner for Baltimore. Lopez, who started six games for San Diego in 2000, was 6–0 in July but lost out to Pedro Martinez for Pitcher of the Month laurels. Los Angeles Dodgers southpaw Kazuhisa Ishii took five games in April, and his June 8 win at Balti-

more made him 10–1. Ishii, like Kearns, had his season end prematurely. On September 8, after garnering 14 wins, the Dodger took a line drive off his head, causing a small cranial fracture. Ryan Jensen won a baker's dozen for San Francisco while Josh Fogg won 12 for Pittsburgh and Damian Moss the same number for Atlanta. On May 3 at St. Louis, Moss tossed seven hitless innings in a seven-walk no-decision. Three months and a day later, he yielded just one safety in eight frames but again failed to notch a victory against the Cardinals.

John Lackey fell a win shy of ten, but Anaheim fans forgave him when he became the first rookie in 93 years to start and win Game Seven of a World Series as the Angels completed their first championship season. Reliever Brendan Donnelly posted a 2.17 ERA in just short of 50 frames and then surrendered only one hit and no runs in 7⅔ innings against San Francisco in the Fall Classic. Scot Shields logged similar regular-season numbers to Donnelly's but got roughed up in his lone postseason outing. The jewel of the Angels' postseason pen, however, was Francisco Rodriguez. Despite having just five ML appearances under his belt prior to the commencement of fall play in 2002, Rodriguez domi-

With the AL Central title clinched, Twins manager Ron Gardenhire had the luxury of previewing some of the organization's minor league prospects in the closing weeks of the 2002 season. Thus it was that on September 19 at Detroit, Mike Ryan found his name on an ML lineup card for the first time. The 25-year-old left fielder swiftly set an all-time rookie record when he collected two hits in the first inning and tabulated two RBI and two runs. Minnesota led 9–0 after two innings when the game was abruptly stopped by rain. Since the contest had not gone the necessary five innings, all statistics were erased, including Ryan's sensational record-setting debut. As a result, he refused to keep the game ball he had been given after his first hit and, to add insult, was made to wear a dress by Twins veterans as part of a rookie hazing ritual when the team traveled to Chicago that night.

The following evening, at Comiskey Park, Ryan made what would become his official ML debut in a 10–2 loss to the White Sox. In the space of 24 hours, he descended from the pinnacle of ecstasy to abject embarrassment as he went 0-for-4. Ryan finished the 2002 season with just one hit in 11 at bats.

It finally happened in 2002. Some 113 years after Amos Rusie of the 1889 Indianapolis Hoosiers became the first rookie to win in double figures despite posting an ERA over 5.00, Ryan Drese of the Indians broke the 6.00 ERA barrier when he won his final start of the season to give him ten frosh victories to go with a horrendous 6.55 ERA. Drese's undesired record, 122 years in the setting, lasted all of one year (see list below).

As the list below also indicates, rookies who won in double figures with 5.00+ ERAs were relatively scarce until recent years. Indeed, pitchers who won in double figures with such high ERA numbers were relatively scarce, period. In the 123 years between 1871 and 1993, a total of 161 hurlers collected ten or more wins in a season with a 5.00+ ERA. Between 1994 and 2003, a space of just ten seasons, there were 96. The brutal truth is that of the 257 pitchers in all of history who managed to win ten games in a season despite being saddled with 5.00+ ERAs, 37 percent of them did it in the past ten years alone. What's more, prior to 1994 only ten pitchers ever were able to win in double figures with a 6.00+ ERA. In 2002 Drese became the 11th hurler to do so since 1994, and the list is now at 12.

Here is a chronology of rookies who won in double figures with 5.00+ ERAs. Note that the size of the list has nearly doubled since 1991.

ROOKIES WHO WON IN DOUBLE FIGURES, MINIMUM 5.00 ERA

Name	Year	Wins	ERA
Amos Rusie	1889	12	5.32
Joe Giard	1925	10	5.04
Wayne LaMaster	1937	15	5.31
Lefty Mills	1938	10	5.31
Herm Wehmeier	1948	11	5.86
Bob Hooper	1950	15	5.02
Art Ditmar	1955	12	5.03
Randy Lerch	1977	10	5.07
Bobby Witt	1986	11	5.48
Eric Bell	1987	10	5.45
Chris Bosio	1987	11	5.24
Rich DeLucia	1991	12	5.09
Tim Pugh	1993	10	5.26
Brad Radke	1995	11	5.32
Rocky Coppinger	1996	10	5.18
Brian Meadows	1998	11	5.21
Ryan Drese	2002	10	6.55
Colby Lewis	2003	10	7.30
Jeriome Robinson	2003	15	5.10

nated the Yankees, Minnesota Twins, and Giants, going a combined 5–1 while striking out 28 and allowing just four earned runs in 18⅔ innings. Among Rodriguez, Lackey, and Donnelly, rookies accounted for a record eight of Anaheim's 11 postseason victories.

Other Highlights

April 2—Carlos Pena leads off the bottom of the ninth with a game-winning home run in the Oakland Athletics 3–2 victory against Texas.

June 10—Marcus Thames homers off Randy Johnson on the first ML pitch he faces, helping the New York Yankees best the Arizona Diamondbacks 7–5.

July 25—Kirk Saarloos tosses a six-hitter for Houston in his 8–0 blanking of Pittsburgh.

August 4—Mark Prior fans 13 Colorado Rockies in his complete-game 4–1 win for the Chicago Cubs.

August 27—Joe Crede hits a two-run homer in the bottom of the ninth and follows with the first game-ending grand slam since 1986 in the tenth as he collects seven RBI for the Chicago White Sox, who beat the Toronto Blue Jays 8–4 in ten innings.

September 3—Andy Van Hekken of Detroit twirls a shutout in his ML debut, topping Cleveland 4–0.

September 15—Miguel Olivo hits a home run in his first ML at bat, but the White Sox lose the six-inning contest against the Yankees 8–4.

Batting		Pitching	
G—AL 151, Eric Hinske, TOR		W—AL 15, Rodrigo Lopez, BAL	
NL 153, Brad Wilkerson, MON		NL 16, Jason Jennings, CLR	
AB—AL 566, Eric Hinske, TOR		L—AL 10, Mike Maroth, DET	
NL 507, Brad Wilkerson, MON		NL 12, Josh Fogg, PIT	
H—AL 158, Eric Hinske, TOR		PCT—AL .625, Rodrigo Lopez, BAL	
NL 135, Brad Wilkerson, MON		NL .667, Jason Jennings, CLR	
2B—AL 38, Eric Hinske, TOR		GP—AL 67, Jorge Julio, BAL	
NL 27, Brad Wilkerson, MON		NL 78, Ricky Stone, HOU	
3B—AL 6, Carl Crawford, TB		GS—AL 28, Rodrigo Lopez, BAL	
NL 8, Brad Wilkerson, MON		NL 33, Josh Fogg, PIT	
HR—AL 24, Eric Hinske, TOR		CG—AL 1, five tied	
NL 20, Brad Wilkerson, MON		NL 1, five tied	
R—AL 99, Eric Hinske, TOR		IP—AL 196.2, Rodrigo Lopez, BAL	
NL 92, Brad Wilkerson, MON		NL 194.1, Josh Fogg, PIT	
RBI—AL 84, Eric Hinske, TOR		H—AL 176, Ryan Drese, CLE	
NL 59, Brad Wilkerson, MON		NL 201, Jason Jennings, CLR	
WK—AL 77, Eric Hinske, TOR		BB—AL 66, Justin Miller, TOR	
NL 81, Brad Wilkerson, MON		**NL 106, Kazuhisa Ishii, LA**	
SO—AL 139, Jared Sandberg, TB		K—AL 136, Rodrigo Lopez, BAL	
NL 161, Brad Wilkerson, MON		NL 147, Mark Prior, CHI	
SB—AL 13, Eric Hinske, TOR		ERA—AL 3.57, Rodrigo Lopez, BAL	
George Lombard, DET		NL 3.42, Damian Moss, ATL	
NL 37, Alex Sanchez, MIL		SHO—AL 1, Andy Van Hekken, DET	
BA—AL .279, Eric Hinske, TOR		NL 1, Kirk Saarloos, HOU	
NL .266, Brad Wilkerson, MON		SV—AL 25, Jorge Julio, BAL	
SLG—AL .481, Eric Hinske, TOR		NL 4, T.J. Tucker, MON	
NL .469, Brad Wilkerson, MON			
OBP—AL .367, Eric Hinske, TOR			
NL .373, Brad Wilkerson, MON			

◄— 2003 —►

All ballplayers, especially rookies, yearn to make an instant impact when they join a new team. In 2003 Hideki Matsui and Miguel Cabrera, two freshmen whose paths would converge in October, succeeded in immediately capturing the attention of the home folks in New York and Miami, respectively. Japanese-league graduate Matsui, yet another high-priced Yankees' import, hit a grand slam in the Bronx Bombers' home-opener victory on April 8. He again connected for a bases-filled round tripper on June 28, just one of many highlights in a season replete with shining moments.

While Matsui, who blasted 50 home runs for the Yomiuri Giants in 2002, failed to hit with the same authority against AL hurlers, he still ripped 16 circuit shots along with 42 doubles and 106 RBI. Matsui also demonstrated that his reputation in the Far East for durability was well deserved. After playing in 1,250 consecutive games for Yomiuri, he set a rookie record by appearing in all 163 Yankees' contests in 2003.

The Yankees advanced to the World Series for the 39th time in their 101-year history and, for the second consecutive occasion, found a recently added expansion team barring their path to yet another World Championship, in this instance the Florida Marlins. Though Matsui continued to contribute, finishing the postseason with two home runs and 11 RBI in 17 games, the Marlins unexpectedly earned their second world title in seven years when Florida's Cabrera fared even better in the heightened competition, driving in a dozen runs and connecting for four taters, one of them a three-run shot off Roger Clemens in Game Four of the Fall Classic. But by October dramatic moments were no longer anything new to the 20-year-old Cabrera. In his ML debut on June 20, he hit a game-ending home run in the 11th inning to give the Marlins a 3–1 victory. Only two other players since 1900 had ended their inaugural games in such a spectacular fashion, and of the three only Cabrera found himself batting cleanup for his team in a World Series after hitting seventh in the order for most of the regular season.

The versatile Cabrera, who played third base and left field in the regular season before adding right field to his repertoire in October, was not the only freshman vital to Florida's winning the NL wild-card spot. Through May 20, Dontrelle Willis stood 1–1 and owned an egregious 7.07 ERA in his first three ML starts. Willis, a high-kicking southpaw acquired from the Chicago Cubs in a March 2002 trade, then took off on a remarkable roll. From May 25 through July 13, he went 7–0, including a 5–0 ledger in June. The 21-year-old tossed successive shutouts, one of them a one-hitter against the New York Mets on June 16. Even though Willis slumped in August, he rebounded in September to finish at 14–6 and capture NL ROY laurels.

Willis's natural ebullience and a flamboyant pitching delivery that reminded observers of Vida Blue's style kept him in the forefront of voters' minds when choosing the top NL freshman, but Arizona's Brandon Webb actually outpitched the Marlin. Although Willis possessed the superior won-loss record, 14–6 to Webb's 10–9, the latter tossed 20 more innings and logged a 2.84 ERA, fourth-best in the senior circuit. In addition, Webb held opposing hitters to a .212 average—third lowest in the loop—and just a .605 OPS, 94 points lower than the figure NL hitters achieved against Willis. During the heart of the 2003 season, when the Diamondbacks' twin aces, Randy Johnson and Curt Schilling, were both disabled, Webb's solid work kept his team alive in the NL West race pending their return.

Nonetheless, finishing second to Willis in the NL ROY race was not Webb but Milwaukee centerfielder Scott Podsednik, who provided the Brewers with excellent defense and a fearsome baserunning threat. Podsednik joined Ichiro Suzuki as the only two rookies since Benny Kauff in 1914 to reach 100 runs, 40 stolen bases, and a .300 batting average when he notched figures of 100, 43, and .314, respectively.

Besides the runner-up Matsui, four other recruits garnered points in the AL ROY contest, with Kansas City's Angel Berroa copping the prize. The speedy shortstop hit .287 and tallied 92 times. Of his 163 hits, 52 went for extra bases. On September 16 Berroa went 5-for-5 with a triple and three runs in a 12–8 win at Cleveland. Late in the season, Kansas City's manager Tony Pena called Berroa the team's MVP as the Royals won 83 games, their highest victory total in a decade.

Rocco Baldelli, Jody Gerut, and Mark Teixeira also had memorable campaigns. Baldelli, Tampa Bay's center fielder, had eight multi-hit games by Tax Day, hitting .368 in April and capping the month with a five-RBI showing on April 30. After batting .314 in May, Baldelli tailed off but still finished with 184 safeties and 78 RBI. Gerut, part of a rookie-laden Cleveland roster that logged more freshman at bats and innings pitched combined than any other team in modern history, stroked 57 extra-base hits in just 127 games while slugging .494. The lefty-hitting fly chaser belted two homers and collected five RBI on August 28. Teixeira drove in 84 Texas runs and pounded 29 doubles and 26 home runs. The switch-hitting first baseman even legged out five triples.

Teixeira's teammate, right-hander Colby Lewis, was not nearly as successful. Although Lewis managed to win ten games, his 7.30 ERA presently stands as the worst ever by a freshman cracking double figures in victories. Ironically, Lewis surpassed the record set just one year earlier by Ryan Drese, a fellow Ranger in 2003 after a preseason trade brought him to Texas from Cleveland.

HIGHEST ERA BY ROOKIE WITH 10 + WINS

7.30 ERA/10 W, Colby Lewis, 2003 Tex AL
6.55 ERA/10 W, Ryan Drese, 2002 Cle AL
5.86 ERA/11 W, Herm Wehmeier, 1948 Cin NL
5.48 ERA/11 W, Bobby Witt, 1986 Tex AL
5.45 ERA/10 W, Eric Bell, 1987 Bal AL

In a similar sweet-and-sour vein, Houston's Jeriome Robertson won 15 times, breaking Roy Oswalt's team rookie record, despite a 5.10 ERA, the second highest in history by a rookie with 15 or more wins. Several freshman firemen sported numbers far superior to the two

Everyone expected Hideki Matsui to win the 2003 AL ROY Award and was shocked and outraged when the honor instead went to Kansas City shortstop Angel Berroa. Everyone who lived in New York and rooted for the Yankees, that is. Elsewhere in the country many fans not only felt that Berroa was the more deserving candidate but applauded when two members of the voting committee publicly acknowledged that they did not believe that a longtime veteran of the Japanese major leagues should be considered a rookie and admitted having omitted Matsui altogether from their ballots, thereupon allowing Berroa to claim the AL rookie prize by one of the narrowest margins in the award's history.

The pair of renegade committee members was only echoing the sentiments of Hal Bodley, who wrote the following on September 19, 2003, in *USA Today*:

"When is the Baseball Writers Association of America going to figure out a way to make veteran Japanese players who come to the major leagues ineligible for the Rookie of the Year Award? Former winners were Hideo Nomo, Ichiro Suzuki and Kaz Sasaki. Now the New York Yankees' Hideki Matsui, who's 29 and played 10 years in Japan, is a leading candidate for the American League honor. Is this right?"

Proponents of Matsui's candidacy argued that it is right because each MLB player should have one season in which he is eligible for the Rookie of the Year Award. Furthermore, they pointed to Jackie Robinson and Sam Jethroe, who won ROY honors at Matsui's age or even older after performing for years in the Negro leagues. Their arguments are countered by the fact that many players are first called up to the majors at midseason and, consequently, have little or no realistic chance to compete for a ROY Award. In addition, Robinson, Jethroe, and the other Negro leaguers who won rookie honors, unlike the Japanese leaguers, all apprenticed in the minor leagues before making their ML debuts.

The dispute, in any case, is critical. As baseball becomes increasingly international, more and more Japanese, Taiwanese, Korean, Australian, and European players will leave their native leagues and try to make their way in MLB. Regardless of their age and amount of previous experience in their native leagues, should they or should they not be deemed rookies if they succeed in their quest?

Perhaps the debate, fundamentally, boils down to one single question that MLB, sooner rather than later, must answer: Are the Japanese leagues major or minor? If they are judged to be major leagues, then players like Matsui should be ineligible for ML ROY Awards. If the decision is to fly in the face of international harmony and consider all foreign leagues, regardless of their quality of play, to be minor leagues, then all future graduates of the Japanese leagues should be eligible to win the award.

---

aforementioned starters. Rafael Soriano of the Seattle Mariners held enemy hitters to a lowly .162 average while showing a 1.53 ERA in 53 innings. Arizona's Killer V's—right-handers Oscar Villarreal and Jose Valverde—glistened with equal brilliance. The former made 86 appearances, the most ever by an NL yearling, while Valverde limited batters to a microscopic .137 average and .489 OPS.

Other Highlights

April 24—Chase Utley, in just his second big league game—and his first start—hits a grand slam for the victorious Philadelphia Phillies, who rout Colorado 9–1.

May 1—Zach Day blanks Milwaukee 5–0, holding the Brewers to three hits for Montreal.

June 15—Reed Johnson of Toronto becomes the first rookie ever to lead off the game for his team with a home run and then hit a game-ending homer when his walk-off blast in the bottom of the tenth powers the Blue Jays to a 5–4 win against the Chicago Cubs.

June 29—Robby Hammock hits a two-run homer in the top of the tenth for Arizona, who beats Detroit 5–3 for its 11th consecutive victory.

July 8—Billy Traber permits but one New York Yankee hit and walks none in his 4–0 masterpiece for Cleveland.

August 14—Travis Hafner hits for the cycle in Cleveland's 8–3 win versus Minnesota.

August 28—Jose Reyes of the Mets homers from each side of the plate in a 3–1 win over Atlanta.

September 3—Doug Waechter fires a two-hit shutout for Tampa Bay in his first ML start, beating Seattle 2–0.

September 19—Jason Bay hits two round trippers—including a grand slam—while amassing eight RBI for the Pittsburgh Pirates, who nevertheless drop the first game of a twinbill to the Chicago Cubs 10–9.

2003 ROOKIE LEADERS

Batting	Pitching
G—AL 163, Hideki Matsui, NY	W—AL 10, Colby Lewis, TEX
NL 156, Ty Wigginton, NY	NL 15, Jeriome Robertson, HOU
AB—AL 637, Rocco Baldelli, TB	L—AL 19, Jeremy Bonderman, DET
NL 573, Ty Wigginton, NY	NL 12, Jae Seo, NY
H—AL 184, Rocco Baldelli, TB	PCT—AL .421, Jason Davis, CLE
NL 175, Scott Podsednik, MIL	NL .625, Jeriome Robertson, HOU
2B—AL 42, Hideki Matsui, NY	GP—AL 72, Aquilino Lopez, TOR
NL 36, Ty Wigginton, NY	NL 86, Oscar Villarreal, ARZ
3B—AL 8, Rocco Baldelli, TB	GS—AL 30, Mark Hendrickson, TOR
NL 8, Scott Podsednik, MIL	NL 31, Jeriome Robertson, HOU
HR—AL 26, Mark Teixeira, TEX	Jae Seo, NY
NL 14, Keith Ginter, MIL	CG—AL 1, seven tied
R—AL 92, Angel Berroa, KC	NL 2, Jerome Williams, SF
NL 100, Scott Podsednik, MIL	Dontrelle Willis, FLA
RBI—AL 106, Hideki Matsui, NY	IP—AL 165.1, Jason Davis, CLE
NL 71, Ty Wigginton, NY	NL 188.1, Jae Seo, NY
WK—AL 63, Hideki Matsui, NY	H—AL 207, Mark Hendrickson, TOR
NL 56, Scott Podsednik, MIL	NL 193, Jae Seo, NY
SO—AL 128, Rocco Baldelli, TB	BB—AL 70, Colby Lewis, CLE
NL 124, Ty Wigginton, NY	NL 72, Horacio Ramirez, ATL
SB—AL 27, Rocco Baldelli, TB	K—AL 108, Jeremy Bonderman, DET
NL 43, Scott Podsednik, MIL	NL 172, Brandon Webb, ARZ
BA—AL .289, Rocco Baldelli, TB	ERA—AL 4.68, Jason Davis, CLE
NL .314, Scott Podsednik, MIL	NL 2.84, Brandon Webb, ARZ
SLG—AL .494, Jody Gerut, CLE	SHO—AL 1, R.A. Dickey, TEX
NL .443, Scott Podsednik, MIL	Mark Hendrickson, TOR
OBP—AL .356, Hideki Matsui, NY	Billy Traber, CLE
NL .380, Scott Podsednik, MIL	Doug Waechter, TB
	NL 2, Dontrelle Willis, FLA
	SV—AL 27, Mike MacDougal, KC
	NL 10, Jose Valverde, ARZ

Team Leaders

ANAHEIM ANGELS, AL 1961–2003*

Batting

G—162, Bobby Knoop, 1964
AB—598, Adam Kennedy, 2000
H—172, Wally Joyner, 1986
2B—35, Tim Salmon, 1993
3B—11, Adam Kennedy, 2000
HR—31, Tim Salmon, 1993
R—93, Tim Salmon, 1993
RBI—100, Wally Joyner, 1986
WK—82, Tim Salmon, 1993
SO—135, Tim Salmon, 1993
SB—48, Gary Pettis, 1984
BA—.290, Wally Joyner, 1986
SLG—.536, Tim Salmon, 1993
OBP—.387, Tim Salmon, 1993
SHO—4, Frank Tanana, 1974
SV—22, Ken Tatum, 1969

Pitching

W—14, Dean Chance, 1962
    Marcelino Lopez, 1965
    Frank Tanana, 1974
L—19, Frank Tanana, 1974
PCT—.591, Jason Dickson, 1997
GP—69, Bill Kelso, 1967
GS—36, Ken McBride, 1961
CG—12, Frank Tanana, 1974
IP—268.2, Frank Tanana, 1974
H—262, Frank Tanana, 1974
BB—122, Bo Belinsky, 1962
K—180, Ken McBride, 1961
    Frank Tanana, 1974
ERA—2.59, Rickey Clark, 1967

*Team was called the Los Angeles Angels 1961–64 and California Angels 1965–96.

ALL STARS

Pos	Name	Year	Hits	Runs	HR	RBI	BA	OPS
1B	Wally Joyner	1986	172	82	22	100	.290	.811
2B	Jerry Remy	1975	147	82	1	46	.258	.624
SS	David Eckstein	2001	166	82	4	41	.285	.713
3B	Carney Lansford	1978	133	63	8	52	.294	.750
OF	Tim Salmon	1993	146	93	31	95	.283	.923
OF	Ken Hunt	1961	122	70	25	84	.255	.813
OF	Rick Reichardt	1966	92	48	14	44	.288	.847
C	Bob Rodgers	1962	146	65	6	61	.258	.685

Pit		Year	W	L	Sv	IP	Ks	ERA
	Ken McBride	1961	12	15	1	241.2	180	3.65
	Bob Lee	1964	6	5	19	137.0	111	1.51
	Marcelino Lopez	1965	14	13	1	215.1	122	2.93
	Ken Tatum	1969	7	2	22	86.1	65	1.36

ARIZONA DIAMONDBACKS, NL 1998–2003

Batting

G—146, Travis Lee, 1998
AB—562, Travis Lee, 1998
H—151, Travis Lee, 1998
2B—26, Alex Cintron, 2003
3B—12, David Dellucci, 1998
HR—22, Travis Lee, 1998
R—71, Travis Lee, 1998
RBI—72, Travis Lee, 1998
WK—67, Travis Lee, 1998
SO—123, Travis Lee, 1998
SB—8, Travis Lee, 1998
BA—.317, Alex Cintron, 2003
SLG—.489, Alex Cintron, 2003
OBP—.361, Alex Cintron, 2003

Pitching

W—10, Oscar Villarreal, 2003
     Brandon Webb, 2003
L—9, Brandon Webb, 2003
PCT—.526, Brandon Webb, 2003
GP—86, Oscar Villarreal, 2003
GS—28, Brandon Webb, 2003
CG—1, Brandon Webb, 2003
IP—180.2, Brandon Webb, 2003
H—140, Brandon Webb, 2003
BB—68, Brandon Webb, 2003
K—172, Brandon Webb, 2003
ERA—2.84, Brandon Webb, 2003
SHO—1, Brandon Webb, 2003
SV—10, Jose Valverde, 2003

ALL STARS

Pos	Name	Year	Hits	Runs	HR	RBI	BA	OPS
1B	Travis Lee	1998	151	71	22	72	.269	.775
2B	Matt Kata	2003	74	42	7	29	.257	.738
SS	Alex Cintron	2003	142	70	13	51	.317	.850
3B	Danny Klassen	2000	18	13	2	8	.237	.673
OF	David Dellucci	1998	108	43	5	51	.260	.718
OF	Karim Garcia	1998	74	39	9	43	.222	.643
OF	Jason Conti	2000	21	11	1	15	.231	.667
C	Robby Hammock	2003	55	30	8	28	.282	.823

Pit			W	L	Sv	IP	Ks	ERA
	Brandon Webb	2003	10	9	0	180.2	172	2.84
	Oscar Villarreal	2003	10	7	0	98.0	80	2.57
	Jose Valverde	2003	2	1	10	50.1	71	2.15

ATLANTA BRAVES, NA 1872–1875, NL 1876–2003**

Batting	Pitching
Batting	**Pitching**

Batting

G—153, Chuck Workman, 1943
    Andruw Jones, 1997
AB—637, Gene Moore, 1936
H—185, Gene Moore, 1936
2B—39, Alvin Dark, 1948
3B—14, Wally Berger, 1930
    Chet Ross, 1940
    Bill Bruton, 1953
HR—38, Wally Berger, 1930
R—130, Jimmy Bannon, 1894
    100, Sam Jethroe, 1950*
RBI—119, Wally Berger, 1930
WK—82, Earl Torgeson, 1947
SO—145, Dale Murphy, 1978
SB—57, Hap Myers, 1913
BA—.354, Chick Stahl, 1897
    .330, Rico Carty, 1964*
SLG—.614, Wally Berger, 1930
OBP—.414, Jimmy Bannon, 1894
    .403, Earl Torgeson, 1947*

Pitching

W—31, Jim Whitney, 1881
    20, Irv Young, 1905*
    Lou Fette, 1937*
    Jim Turner, 1937*
L—33, Jim Whitney, 1881
    23, Vive Lindaman, 1906*
PCT—.667, Lou Fette, 1937
GP—75, Kerry Ligtenberg, 1998
GS—63, Jim Whitney, 1881
    42, Irv Young, 1905*
CG—57, Jim Whitney, 1881
    41, Irv Young, 1905*
IP—552.1, Jim Whitney, 1881
    378.0, Irv Young, 1905*
H—548, Jim Whitney, 1881
    337, Irv Young, 1905*
BB—148, Vic Willis, 1898
    109, Lefty Tyler, 1911*
    Ed Brandt, 1928*
K—239, Bill Stemmeyer, 1886
    156, Irv Young, 1905*
ERA—2.07, Bill Sowders, 1888
    2.37, Jesse Barnes, 1916*
SHO—7, Kid Nichols, 1890
    Irv Young, 1905
SV—30, Kerry Ligtenberg, 1998

*Record since 1901.
**Team was based in Boston through 1952 and in Milwaukee 1953–65.

ALL STARS

Pos	Name	Year	Hits	Runs	HR	RBI	BA	OPS
1B	David Justice	1990	124	76	28	78	.282	.909
2B	Ron Gant	1988	146	85	19	60	.259	.757
SS	Alvin Dark	1948	175	85	4	48	.322	.786
3B	Bob Horner	1978	86	50	23	63	.266	.860
OF	Wally Berger	1930	172	98	38	119	.310	.990
OF	Chick Stahl	1897	166	112	4	97	.354	.905
OF	Joe Connolly	1913	120	79	5	57	.281	.788
C	Earl Williams	1971	129	64	33	87	.260	.817

Pit			W	L	Sv	IP	Ks	ERA
	Kid Nichols	1890	27	19	0	424.0	222	2.23
	Vic Willis	1898	25	13	0	311.0	160	2.84
	Jim Turner	1937	20	11	1	256.2	69	2.38
	Lou Fette	1937	20	10	0	259.0	70	2.88
	Kerry Ligtenberg	1998	3	2	30	73.0	79	2.71

BALTIMORE ORIOLES, AL 1901–2003*

Batting	Pitching
G—160, Eddie Murray, 1977	W—19, Wally Bunker, 1964
Cal Ripken, 1982	L—20, Bill Reidy, 1901
AB—632, George Stone, 1905	Carl Weilman, 1913
H—195, George McQuinn, 1938	Bobo Newsom, 1934
2B—42, George McQuinn, 1938	PCT—.792, Wally Bunker, 1964
3B—15, Del Pratt, 1912	GP—67, Jorge Julio, 2002
HR—28, Cal Ripken, 1982	GS—36, Bob Milacki, 1989
R—104, Harlond Clift, 1934	CG—31, Barney Pelty, 1904
RBI—101, Ray Pepper, 1934	IP—301.1, Bill Reidy, 1901
WK—90, Don Lenhardt, 1950	H—364, Bill Reidy, 1901
SO—114, Craig Worthington, 1989	BB—149, Bobo Newsom, 1934
SB—30, Harry Niles, 1906	K—179, Tom Phoebus, 1967
BA—.324, George McQuinn, 1938	ERA—2.27, Fred Glade, 1904
SLG—.520, Wally Judnich, 1940	SHO—6, Fred Glade, 1904
OBP—.398, Roy Sievers, 1949	SV—27, Gregg Olson, 1989

*Team was the Milwaukee Brewers in 1901 and the St. Louis Browns 1902–53.

ALL STARS

Pos	Name	Year	Hits	Runs	HR	RBI	BA	OPS
1B	Eddie Murray	1977	173	81	27	88	.283	.806
2B	Del Pratt	1912	172	76	5	69	.302	.774
SS	Ron Hansen	1960	135	72	22	86	.255	.782
3B	Cal Ripken	1982	158	90	28	93	.264	.795
OF	George Stone	1905	187	76	7	52	.296	.756
OF	Wally Judnich	1940	157	97	24	89	.303	.888
OF	Roy Sievers	1949	144	84	16	91	.306	.869
C	John Orsino	1963	103	53	19	56	.272	.827

Pit			W	L	Sv	IP	Ks	ERA
	Fred Glade	1904	18	15	6	289	156	2.27
	Chuck Estrada	1960	18	11	2	208.2	144	3.58
	Wally Bunker	1964	19	5	0	214.0	96	2.69
	Mike Boddicker	1983	16	8	0	179.0	120	2.77
	Gregg Olson	1989	5	2	27	85.0	90	1.69

BOSTON RED SOX, AL 1901–2003

Batting

G—162, George Scott, 1966
AB—684, Nomar Garciaparra, 1997
H—209, Nomar Garciaparra, 1997
2B—47, Fred Lynn, 1975
3B—17, Russ Scarritt, 1929
HR—34, Walt Dropo, 1950
R—131, Ted Williams, 1939
RBI—145, Ted Williams, 1939
WK—107, Ted Williams, 1939
SO—152, George Scott, 1966
SB—35, Tris Speaker, 1909
BA—.337, Ike Boone, 1924
SLG—.609, Ted Williams, 1939
OBP—.436, Ted Williams, 1939

Pitching

W—21, Boo Ferriss, 1945
L—21, Joe Harris, 1906
PCT—.692, Babe Ruth, 1915
GP—62, Dick Radatz, 1962
GS—34, Buck O'Brien, 1912
CG—26, George Winter, 1901
     Boo Ferriss, 1945
IP—275.2, Buck O'Brien, 1912
H—267, Ted Wingfield, 1925
BB—110, Don Schwall, 1961
K—155, Ken Brett, 1970
ERA—2.18, Joe Wood, 1909
SHO—5, Boo Ferriss, 1945
SV—24, Dick Radatz, 1962

ALL STARS

Pos	Name	Year	Hits	Runs	HR	RBI	BA	OPS
1B	Walt Dropo	1950	180	101	34	144	.322	.961
2B	Chuck Schilling	1961	167	87	5	62	.259	.667
SS	Nomar Garciaparra	1997	209	122	30	98	.306	.878
3B	Frank Malzone	1957	185	82	15	103	.292	.753
OF	Ted Williams	1939	185	131	31	145	.327	1.045
OF	Fred Lynn	1975	175	103	21	105	.331	.971
OF	Jim Rice	1975	174	92	22	102	.309	.845
C	Carlton Fisk	1972	134	74	22	61	.293	.909

Pit			W	L	Sv	IP	Ks	ERA
	Buck O'Brien	1912	20	13	0	275.2	115	2.58
	Hugh Bedient	1912	20	9	2	231.0	122	2.92
	Ed Morris	1928	19	15	0	257.2	104	3.53
	Boo Ferriss	1945	21	10	2	264.2	94	2.96
	Dick Radatz	1962	9	6	24	124.2	144	2.24

CHICAGO CUBS, NA 1874–1875, NL 1876–2003

Batting

G—160, Ken Hubbs, 1962
AB—661, Ken Hubbs, 1962
H—206, Billy Herman, 1932
2B—42, Billy Herman, 1932
3B—16, Marty Sullivan, 1887
    14, Wildfire Schulte, 1905*
HR—25, Billy Williams, 1961
R—129, Bill Everitt, 1895
    103, Ryne Sandberg, 1982*
RBI—95, Charlie Irwin, 1894
    86, Billy Williams, 1961*
WK—92, Eddie Stanky, 1943
SO—143, Byron Browne, 1966
SB—47, Bill Lange, 1893
    Bill Everitt, 1895
    43, George Grantham, 1923*
BA—.358, Bill Everitt, 1895
    .352, Hack Miller, 1922*
SLG—.511, Hack Miller, 1922
OBP—.406, Ray Grimes, 1921

Pitching

W—43, Larry Corcoran, 1880
    26, Larry Cheney, 1912*
L—23, Tom Hughes, 1901
PCT—.833, King Cole, 1910
GP—69, Terry Adams, 1996
GS—60, Larry Corcoran, 1880
    37, Larry Cheney, 1912*
CG—57, Larry Corcoran, 1880
    32, Tom Hughes, 1901*
IP—536.1, Larry Corcoran, 1880
    308.1, Tom Hughes, 1901*
H—404, Larry Corcoran, 1880
    309, Tom Hughes, 1901*
BB—185, Sam Jones, 1955
K—268, Larry Corcoran, 1880
    233, Kerry Wood, 1998*
ERA—1.42, Ed Reulbach, 1905
SHO—5, Ed Reulbach, 1905
SV—10, Chuck Hartenstein, 1967
    Oscar Zamora, 1974
    Bruce Sutter, 1976

*Record since 1901.

ALL STARS

Pos	Name	Year	Hits	Runs	HR	RBI	BA	OPS
1B	Ray Grimes	1921	170	91	6	79	.321	.855
2B	Billy Herman	1932	206	102	1	51	.314	.762
SS	Charlie Hollocher	1918	161	72	2	38	.316	.775
3B	Bill Everitt	1895	197	129	3	88	.358	.839
OF	Billy Williams	1961	147	75	25	86	.278	.824
OF	Hack Miller	1922	164	61	12	78	.352	.899
OF	Earl Webb	1927	100	58	14	52	.301	.897
C	Randy Hundley	1966	124	50	19	63	.236	.685

Pit		Year	W	L	Sv	IP	Ks	ERA
	Larry Corcoran	1880	43	14	2	536.1	268	1.95
	Jake Weimer	1903	20	8	0	282.0	128	2.30
	Jack Pfiester	1906	20	8	0	250.2	153	1.51
	King Cole	1910	20	4	1	293.2	114	1.80
	Larry Cheney	1912	26	10	0	303.1	140	2.85

CHICAGO WHITE SOX, AL 1901–2003

Batting

G—160, Tommie Agee, 1966
AB—629, Tommie Agee, 1966
H—193, Smead Jolley, 1930
2B—39, Willie Kamm, 1923
3B—14, Minnie Minoso, 1951
HR—35, Ron Kittle, 1983
R—109, Minnie Minoso, 1951
RBI—114, Smead Jolley, 1930
WK—95, Morrie Rath, 1912
SO—150, Ron Kittle, 1983
SB—50, John Cangelosi, 1986
BA—.324, Minnie Minoso, 1951
SLG—.545, Zeke Bonura, 1934
OBP—.419, Minnie Minoso, 1951

Pitching

W—22, Reb Russell, 1913
L—20, Bill Wight, 1948
PCT—.704, Gary Peters, 1963
GP—83, Kelly Wunsch, 2000
GS—36, Reb Russell, 1913
CG—30, Roy Patterson, 1901
IP—316.2, Reb Russell, 1913
H—345, Roy Patterson, 1901
BB—135, Bill Wight, 1948
K—189, Gary Peters, 1963
ERA—1.90, Reb Russell, 1913
SHO—8, Reb Russell, 1913
SV—21, Salome Barojas, 1982

ALL STARS

Pos	Name	Year	Hits	Runs	HR	RBI	BA	OPS
1B	Zeke Bonura	1934	154	86	27	110	.302	.925
2B	Morrie Rath	1912	161	104	1	19	.272	.681
SS	Luis Aparicio	1956	142	69	3	56	.266	.653
3B	Pete Ward	1963	177	80	22	84	.295	.838
OF	Minnie Minoso	1951	167	109	10	74	.324	.917
OF	Tommie Agee	1966	172	98	22	86	.273	.775
OF	Smead Jolley	1930	193	76	16	114	.313	.838
C	Ray Schalk	1913	98	38	1	38	.244	.611

Pit			W	L	Sv	IP	Ks	ERA
	Roy Patterson	1901	20	16	0	312.1	127	3.37
	Frank Smith	1904	16	9	4	202.1	107	2.09
	Reb Russell	1913	22	16	4	316.2	122	1.90
	Gary Peters	1963	19	8	1	243	189	2.33
	Britt Burns	1980	15	13	1	238.0	133	2.84

CINCINNATI REDS, AA 1882–1889, NL 1890–2003

Batting	Pitching
G—157, Pete Rose, 1963	W—32, Jesse Duryea, 1889
AB—648, Vada Pinson, 1959	20, Tom Browning, 1985*
H—209, Frank McCormick, 1938	L—23, Orval Overall, 1905
2B—47, Vada Pinson, 1959	PCT—.826, Elmer Riddle, 1941
3B—18, Ival Goodman, 1935	GP—73, Bill Scherrer, 1983
HR—38, Frank Robinson, 1956	GS—48, Jesse Duryea, 1889
R—131, Vada Pinson, 1959	39, Orval Overall, 1905*
RBI—106, Frank McCormick, 1938	CG—45, Billy Rhines, 1890
WK—94, Bernie Carbo, 1970	32, Orval Overall, 1905*
SO—111, Gary Redus, 1983	IP—401.1, Billy Rhines, 1890
SB—54, Bob Bescher, 1909	318.0, Orval Overall, 1905*
BA—.327, Frank McCormick, 1938	H—372, Jesse Duryea, 1889
SLG—.558, Frank Robinson, 1956	301, Johnny Couch, 1922*
OBP—.456, Bernie Carbo, 1970**	BB—147, Orval Overall, 1905
	K—206, Gary Nolan, 1967
	ERA—1.95, Billy Rhines, 1890
	2.01, Harry Gaspar, 1909*
	SHO—6, Billy Rhines, 1890
	5, Ewell Blackwell, 1946*
	Gary Nolan, 1967*
	SV—22, Rawly Eastwick, 1975

* Record since 1901.

** Even though Carbo fell short of the requisite number of plate appearances to qualify as an official league leader in 1970, his OBP of .420 after he is charged with the needed plate appearances still ranks as the club's rookie high.

ALL STARS

Pos	Name	Year	Hits	Runs	HR	RBI	BA	OPS
1B	Dick Hoblitzel	1909	159	59	4	67	.308	.782
2B	Pete Rose	1963	170	101	6	41	.273	.708
SS	Ollie Beard	1889	159	96	1	77	.285	.692
3B	Chris Sabo	1988	146	74	11	44	.271	.730
OF	Bug Holliday	1889	181	107	19	104	.321	.869
OF	Vada Pinson	1959	205	131	20	84	.316	.880
OF	Frank Robinson	1956	166	122	38	83	.290	.939
C	Johnny Bench	1968	155	67	15	82	.275	.748

Pit			W	L	Sv	IP	Ks	ERA
	Jesse Duryea	1889	32	19	1	401.0	183	2.56
	Billy Rhines	1890	28	17	0	401.1	182	1.95
	Noodles Hahn	1899	23	8	0	309	141	2.68
	Harry Gaspar	1909	19	11	2	260	65	2.01
	Elmer Riddle	1941	19	4	1	216.2	80	2.24
	Tom Browning	1985	20	9	0	261.1	155	3.55
	Scott Williamson	1999	12	7	19	93.1	107	2.41

CLEVELAND INDIANS, AL 1901–2003

Batting

G—158, Max Alvis, 1963
AB—650, Carl Lind, 1928
H—233, Joe Jackson, 1911
2B—45, Joe Jackson, 1911
     Hal Trosky, 1934
3B—19, Joe Jackson, 1911
HR—37, Al Rosen, 1950
R—126, Joe Jackson, 1911
RBI—142, Hal Trosky, 1934
WK—106, Les Fleming, 1942
SO—123, Cory Snyder, 1986
SB—66, Kenny Lofton, 1992
BA—.408, Joe Jackson, 1911
SLG—.602, Jeff Heath, 1938
OBP—.468, Joe Jackson, 1911

Pitching

W—23, Vean Gregg, 1911
L—16, Jim Bagby, 1916
PCT—.773, C.C. Sabathia, 2001
GP—69, Ernie Camacho, 1984
GS—34, Glenn Liebhardt, 1907
     Dick Tidrow, 1972
CG—28, Earl Moore, 1901
     Addie Joss, 1902
IP—280.1, Glenn Liebhardt, 1907
H—291, Willis Hudlin, 1927
BB—154, Herb Score, 1955
K—245, Herb Score, 1955
ERA—1.67, Otto Hess, 1904
SHO—6, Gene Bearden, 1948
SV—23, Ernie Camacho, 1984

ALL STARS

Pos	Name	Year	Hits	Runs	HR	RBI	BA	OPS
1B	Hal Trosky	1934	206	117	35	142	.330	.987
2B	Ray Mack	1940	150	60	12	69	.283	.755
SS	Joe Sewell	1921	182	101	4	93	.318	.856
3B	Al Rosen	1950	159	100	37	116	.287	.948
OF	Joe Jackson	1911	233	126	7	83	.408	1.058
OF	Earl Averill	1929	198	110	18	96	.332	.936
OF	Jeff Heath	1938	172	104	21	112	.343	.985
C	Ray Fosse	1970	138	62	18	61	.307	.832

Pit			W	L	Sv	IP	Ks	ERA
	Vean Gregg	1911	23	7	0	244.2	125	1.80
	Wes Ferrell	1929	21	10	5	242.2	100	3.60
	Gene Bearden	1948	20	7	1	229.2	80	2.43
	Mike Garcia	1949	14	5	2	175.2	94	2.36
	Herb Score	1955	16	10	0	227.1	245	2.85

COLORADO ROCKIES, NL 1993–2003

Batting

G—152, Todd Helton, 1998
AB—530, Todd Helton, 1998
H—167, Todd Helton, 1998
2B—37, Todd Helton, 1998
3B—11, Juan Uribe, 2001
HR—25, Todd Helton, 1998
R—82, Eric Young, 1993
RBI—97, Todd Helton, 1998
WK—63, Eric Young, 1993
SO—70, Jason Bates, 1995
SB—42, Eric Young, 1993
BA—.315, Todd Helton, 1998
SLG—.530, Todd Helton, 1998
OBP—.380, Todd Helton, 1998

Pitching

W—16, Jason Jennings, 2002
L—11, Armando Reynoso, 1993
PCT—.667, Jason Jennings, 2002
GP—75, Javier Lopez, 2003
GS—32, Jason Jennings, 2002
CG—4, Armando Reynoso, 1993
IP—189.0, Armando Reynoso, 1993
H—206, Armando Reynoso, 1993
BB—87, Shawn Chacon, 2001
K—134, Shawn Chacon, 2001
ERA—4.00, Armando Reynoso, 1993
SHO—1, John Thomson, 1997
    Mark Brownson, 1998
    Jason Jennings, 2001
SV—3, Steve Reed, 1993

ALL STARS

Pos	Name	Year	Hits	Runs	HR	RBI	BA	OPS
1B	Todd Helton	1998	167	78	25	97	.315	.914
2B	Eric Young	1993	132	82	3	42	.269	.710
SS	Juan Uribe	2001	82	32	8	53	.300	.849
3B	Pedro Castellano	1993	13	12	3	7	.183	.604
OF	Quinton McCracken	1996	82	50	3	40	.290	.774
OF	Juan Pierre	2000	62	26	0	20	.310	.675
OF	Todd Helton	1997	26	13	5	11	.280	.821
C	Ben Petrick	2000	47	32	3	20	.322	.876

Pit		Year	W	L	Sv	IP	Ks	ERA
	Armando Reynoso	1993	12	11	0	189	117	4.00
	Jason Jennings	2002	16	8	0	185.1	127	4.52
	Dennis Stark	2002	11	4	0	128.1	117	4.00

DETROIT TIGERS, AL 1901–2003

Batting

G—162, Jake Wood, 1961
AB—679, Harvey Kuenn, 1953
H—215, Dale Alexander, 1929
2B—45, Roy Johnson, 1929
3B—17, Charlie Gehringer, 1926
HR—35, Rudy York, 1937
R—128, Roy Johnson, 1929
RBI—137, Dale Alexander, 1929
WK—103, Lu Blue, 1921
SO—141, Jake Wood, 1961
SB—53, Donie Bush, 1909
BA—.343, Dale Alexander, 1929
SLG—.580, Dale Alexander, 1929
OBP—.416, Lu Blue, 1921

Pitching

W—24, Ed Summers, 1908
L—19, Jeremy Bonderman, 2003
PCT—.682, Dave Rozema, 1977
GP—88, Sean Runyan, 1998
GS—37, Herman Pillette, 1922
CG—35, Roscoe Miller, 1901
IP—332.0, Roscoe Miller, 1901
H—339, Roscoe Miller, 1901
BB—108, Tommy Bridges, 1931
    Rufe Gentry, 1944
K—156, Les Cain, 1970
ERA—1.64, Ed Summers, 1908
SHO—5, Ed Summers, 1908
SV—14, Chuck Seelbach, 1972

ALL STARS

Pos	Name	Year	Hits	Runs	HR	RBI	BA	OPS
1B	Dale Alexander	1929	215	110	25	137	.343	.977
2B	Lou Whitaker	1978	138	71	3	58	.285	.724
SS	Donie Bush	1909	145	114	0	33	.273	.694
3B	Steve Boros	1961	107	51	5	62	.270	.751
OF	Barney McCosky	1939	190	120	4	58	.311	.814
OF	Roy Johnson	1929	201	128	10	69	.314	.854
OF	Willie Horton	1965	140	69	29	104	.273	.833
C	Rudy York	1937	115	72	35	103	.307	1.026

Pit			W	L	Sv	IP	Ks	ERA
	Roscoe Miller	1901	23	13	3	332.0	79	2.95
	Ed Siever	1901	18	14	2	288.2	85	3.24
	Ed Summers	1908	24	12	1	301.0	103	1.64
	Herm Pillette	1922	19	12	1	274.2	71	2.85
	Mark Fidrych	1976	19	9	0	250.1	97	2.34

FLORIDA MARLINS, NL 1993–2003

Batting

G—162, Jeff Conine, 1993
AB—595, Jeff Conine, 1993
H—174, Jeff Conine, 1993
2B—29, Derrek Lee, 1998
3B—8, Alex Gonzalez, 1999
HR—26, Preston Wilson, 1999
R—86, Quilvio Veras, 1995
RBI—87, Orestes Destrade, 1993
WK—80, Quilvio Veras, 1995
SO—156, Preston Wilson, 1999
SB—58, Chuck Carr, 1993
BA—.292, Jeff Conine, 1993
SLG—.502, Preston Wilson, 1999
OBP—.386, Quilvio Veras, 1995

Pitching

W—14, Dontrelle Willis, 2003
L—13, Brian Meadows, 1998
PCT—.700, Dontrelle Willis, 2003
GP—72, Braden Looper, 1999
GS—31, Brian Meadows, 1998
CG—2, Dontrelle Willis, 2003
IP—174.1, Brian Meadows, 1998
H—222, Brian Meadows, 1998
BB—91, Jesus Sanchez, 1998
K—142, Dontrelle Willis, 2003
ERA—3.30, Dontrelle Willis, 2003
SHO—2, Dontrelle Willis, 2003
SV—8, Antonio Alfonseca, 1998

ALL STARS

Pos	Name	Year	Hits	Runs	HR	RBI	BA	OPS
1B	Orestes Destrade	1993	145	61	20	87	.255	.733
2B	Quilvio Veras	1995	115	86	5	32	.261	.758
SS	Edgar Renteria	1996	133	68	5	31	.309	.760
3B	Mike Lowell	1999	78	32	12	47	.253	.740
OF	Jeff Conine	1993	174	75	12	79	.292	.758
OF	Preston Wilson	1999	135	67	26	71	.280	.856
OF	Mark Kotsay	1998	161	72	11	68	.279	.723
C	Charles Johnson	1995	79	40	11	39	.251	.763

Pit			W	L	Sv	IP	Ks	ERA
	Livan Hernandez	1997	9	3	0	96.1	72	3.18
	Brian Meadows	1998	11	13	1	174.1	88	5.21
	Dontrelle Willis	2003	14	6	0	160.2	142	3.30

HOUSTON ASTROS, NL 1962–2003

Batting

G—157, Joe Morgan, 1965
AB—601, Joe Morgan, 1965
H—185, Greg Gross, 1974
2B—28, Luis Gonzalez, 1991
    Lance Berkman, 2000
3B—12, Joe Morgan, 1965
HR—21, Lance Berkman, 2000
R—100, Joe Morgan, 1965
RBI—82, Jeff Bagwell, 1991
WK—97, Joe Morgan, 1965
SO—116, Jeff Bagwell, 1991
SB—49, Sonny Jackson, 1966
BA—.314, Greg Gross, 1974
SLG—.437, Jeff Bagwell, 1991
OBP—.393, Greg Gross, 1974

Pitching

W—15, Jeriome Robertson, 2003
L—14, Mark Lemongello, 1977
PCT—.625, Jeriome Robertson, 2003
GP—78, Ricky Stone, 2002
    Brad Lidge, 2003
GS—32, Chris Holt, 1997
CG—9, Joaquin Andujar, 1976
IP—214.2, Mark Lemongello, 1977
H—237, Mark Lemongello, 1977
BB—93, Tom Griffin, 1969
K—200, Tom Griffin, 1969
ERA—2.53, Ken Forsch, 1971
SHO—4, Joaquin Andujar, 1976
SV—20, Frank DiPino, 1983

ALL STARS

Pos	Name	Year	Hits	Runs	HR	RBI	BA	OPS
1B	Jeff Bagwell	1991	163	79	15	82	.294	.828
2B	Joe Morgan	1965	163	100	14	40	.271	.793
SS	Sonny Jackson	1966	174	80	3	25	.292	.676
3B	Chris Truby	2000	67	28	11	59	.260	.777
OF	Cesar Cedeno	1970	110	46	7	42	.310	.792
OF	Greg Gross	1974	185	78	0	36	.314	.770
OF	Luis Gonzalez	1991	120	51	13	69	.254	.756
C	Mitch Meluskey	2000	101	47	14	69	.300	.891

Pit			W	L	Sv	IP	Ks	ERA
	Tom Griffin	1969	11	10	0	188.1	200	3.54
	Ken Forsch	1971	8	8	0	188.1	131	2.53
	Charlie Kerfeld	1986	11	2	7	93.2	77	2.59
	Roy Oswalt	2001	14	3	0	141.2	144	2.73

KANSAS CITY ROYALS, AL 1969–2003

Batting	Pitching
G—161, Kevin Seitzer, 1987	W—17, Tom Gordon, 1989
AB—663, Carlos Beltran, 1999	L—16, Jim Rooker, 1969
H—207, Kevin Seitzer, 1987	PCT—.682, Dennis Leonard, 1975
2B—33, Kevin Seitzer, 1987	GP—68, Mike MacDougal, 2003
Mark Quinn, 2000	GS—37, Steve Busby, 1973
3B—10, Tom Poquette, 1976	CG—10, Dick Drago, 1969
HR—24, Bob Hamelin, 1994	Bob Johnson, 1970
R—112, Carlos Beltran, 1999	IP—238.1, Steve Busby, 1973
RBI—108, Carlos Beltran, 1999	H—246, Steve Busby, 1973
WK—84, Mike Fiore, 1969	BB—105, Steve Busby, 1973
SO—158, Bo Jackson, 1987	K—206, Bob Johnson, 1970
SB—46, Willie Wilson, 1978	ERA—2.76, Kevin Appier, 1990
BA—.323, Kevin Seitzer, 1987	SHO—4, Bill Butler, 1969
SLG—.488, Mark Quinn, 2000	SV—27, Mike MacDougal, 2003
OBP—.400, Kevin Seitzer, 1987	

ALL STARS

Pos	Name	Year	Hits	Runs	HR	RBI	BA	OPS
1B	Mike Fiore	1969	93	53	12	35	.274	.849
2B	Carlos Febles	1999	116	71	10	53	.256	.749
SS	Angel Berroa	2003	163	92	17	73	.287	.793
3B	Kevin Seitzer	1987	207	105	15	83	.323	.869
OF	Carlos Beltran	1999	194	112	22	108	.293	.796
OF	Lou Piniella	1969	139	43	11	68	.282	.747
OF	Pat Kelly	1969	110	61	8	32	.264	.737
C	Don Slaught	1983	86	21	0	28	.312	.726

Pit			W	L	Sv	IP	Ks	ERA
	Bob Johnson	1970	8	13	4	214.0	206	3.07
	Dennis Leonard	1975	15	7	0	212.1	146	3.77
	Kevin Appier	1990	12	8	0	185.2	127	2.76
	Jose Rosado	1996	8	6	0	106.2	64	3.21

LOS ANGELES DODGERS, AA 1884–1889, NL 1890–2003**

Batting

G—159, Ted Sizemore, 1969
AB—638, Steve Sax, 1982
H—206, Johnny Frederick, 1929
2B—52, Johnny Frederick, 1929
3B—18, Harry Lumley, 1904
HR—35, Mike Piazza, 1993
R—127, Johnny Frederick, 1929
RBI—112, Mike Piazza, 1993
WK—100, Jim Gilliam, 1953
SO—149, Billy Grabarkewitz, 1970
SB—49, Steve Sax, 1982
BA—.354, Fielder Jones, 1896
    .328, Johnny Frederick, 1929*
SLG—.561, Mike Piazza, 1993
OBP—.411, Len Koenecke, 1934

Pitching

W—25, Mickey Hughes, 1888
    23, Jeff Pfeffer, 1914*
L—35, Adonis Terry, 1884
    25, Harry McIntire, 1905*
PCT—.789, Joe Black, 1952
GP—65, Pedro Martinez, 1993
GS—55, Adonis Terry, 1884
    36, Oscar Jones, 1903*
    Henry Schmidt, 1903*
CG—54, Adonis Terry, 1884
    31, Oscar Jones, 1903*
IP—476.0, Adonis Terry, 1884
    324.1, Oscar Jones, 1903*
H—486, Adonis Terry, 1884
    340, Harry McIntire, 1905*
BB—137, Hal Gregg, 1944
K—236, Hideo Nomo, 1995
ERA—1.97, Jeff Pfeffer, 1914
SHO—8, Fernando Valenzuela, 1981
SV—17, Steve Howe, 1980

*Record since 1901.
**Team was based in Brooklyn through 1957.

ALL STARS

Pos	Name	Year	Hits	Runs	HR	RBI	BA	OPS
1B	Del Bissonette	1928	188	90	25	106	.320	.940
2B	Jim Gilliam	1953	168	125	6	63	.278	.798
SS	Lonny Frey	1934	139	77	8	57	.284	.760
3B	Billy Grabarkewitz	1970	153	92	17	84	.289	.857
OF	Johnny Frederick	1929	206	127	24	75	.328	.917
OF	Harry Lumley	1904	161	79	9	78	.279	.759
OF	Fielder Jones	1896	140	82	3	46	.354	.870
C	Mike Piazza	1993	174	81	35	112	.318	.935

Pit		Year	W	L	Sv	IP	Ks	ERA
	Mickey Hughes	1888	25	13	0	363.0	159	2.13
	Jeff Pfeffer	1914	23	12	4	315.0	159	1.97
	Joe Black	1952	15	4	15	142.1	85	2.15
	Rick Sutcliffe	1979	17	10	0	242.0	117	3.46
	Fernando Valenzuela	1981	13	7	0	192.1	180	2.48

MILWAUKEE BREWERS, AL 1969–1997, NL 1998–2003*

Batting	Pitching
G—160, Pedro Garcia, 1973	W—15, Ted Higuera, 1985
AB—580, Pedro Garcia, 1973	L—17, Bill Parsons, 1971
H—175, Scott Podsednik, 2003	PCT—.652, Ted Higuera, 1985
2B—32, Pedro Garcia, 1973	GP—68, Bob McClure, 1977
3B—8, Bob Coluccio, 1973	GS—35, Bill Parsons, 1971
Scott Podsednik, 2003	CG—12, Bill Parsons, 1971
HR—19, John Jaha, 1993	IP—244.2, Bill Parsons, 1971
R—100, Scott Podsednik, 2003	H—224, Juan Nieves, 1986
RBI—70, John Jaha, 1993	BB—93, Bill Parsons, 1971
WK—64, Ron Belliard, 1999	K—150, Chris Bosio, 1987
SO—126, Danny Walton, 1970	ERA—3.20, Bill Parsons, 1971
SB—54, Pat Listach, 1992	SHO—4, Bill Parsons, 1971
BA—.314, Scott Podsednik, 2003	Jim Slaton, 1971
SLG— .443, Scott Podsednik, 2003	SV—15, Doug Henry, 1991
OBP—.382, Ron Belliard, 1999	

*Team was the Seattle Pilots in 1969.

ALL STARS

Pos	Name	Year	Hits	Runs	HR	RBI	BA	OPS
1B	John Jaha	1993	136	78	19	70	.264	.755
2B	Pedro Garcia	1973	142	67	15	54	.245	.694
SS	Pat Listach	1992	168	93	1	47	.290	.702
3B	Jeff Cirillo	1995	91	57	9	39	.277	.817
OF	Scott Podsednik	2003	175	100	9	58	.314	.823
OF	Wayne Comer	1969	118	88	15	54	.245	.737
OF	Danny Walton	1970	102	32	17	66	.257	.791
C	Darrell Porter	1973	89	50	16	67	.254	.822

Pit			W	L	Sv	IP	Ks	ERA
	Bill Parsons	1971	13	17	0	244.2	139	3.20
	Ted Higuera	1985	15	8	0	212.1	127	3.90
	Dan Plesac	1986	10	7	14	91	75	2.97
	Cal Eldred	1992	11	2	0	100.1	62	1.79

MINNESOTA TWINS, AL 1901–2003*

Batting

G—161, Tony Oliva, 1964
AB—672, Tony Oliva, 1964
H—217, Tony Oliva, 1964
2B—43, Tony Oliva, 1964
3B—19, Joe Cassidy, 1904
HR—33, Jimmie Hall, 1963
R—109, Tony Oliva, 1964
RBI—98, Jake Powell, 1935
    Irv Noren, 1950
WK—79, Butch Wynegar, 1976
SO—145, Bobby Darwin, 1972
SB—37, Dave Altizer, 1906
BA—.323, Tony Oliva, 1964
SLG—.557, Tony Oliva, 1964
OBP—.379, Rich Rollins, 1962

Pitching

W—22, Monte Weaver, 1932
L—26, Bob Groom, 1909
PCT—.708, Joe Boehling, 1913
GP—73, Doug Corbett, 1980
GS—37, Paul Thormodsgard, 1977
    Roger Erickson, 1978
CG—26, Case Patten, 1901
IP—265.2, Roger Erickson, 1978
H—328, Watty Lee, 1901
BB—137, Jim Shaw, 1914
K—164, Jim Shaw, 1914
ERA—1.70, Bill Burns, 1908
SHO—5, Jim Shaw, 1914
SV—23, Doug Corbett, 1980

*Team was the Washington Senators 1901–60.

ALL STARS

Pos	Name	Year	Hits	Runs	HR	RBI	BA	OPS
1B	Kent Hrbek	1982	160	82	23	92	.301	.850
2B	Tim Teufel	1984	149	76	14	61	.262	.751
SS	Joe Cassidy	1904	140	63	1	33	.241	.597
3B	Rich Rollins	1962	186	96	16	96	.298	.807
OF	Tony Oliva	1964	217	109	32	94	.323	.918
OF	Jimmie Hall	1963	129	88	33	80	.260	.864
OF	Bob Allison	1959	149	83	30	85	.261	.816
C	Butch Wynegar	1976	139	58	10	69	.260	.721

Pit			W	L	Sv	IP	Ks	ERA
	Case Patten	1901	18	10	4	254.1	109	3.93
	Joe Boehling	1913	17	7	4	235.1	110	2.14
	Hod Lisenbee	1927	18	9	0	242.0	105	3.57
	Monte Weaver	1932	22	10	2	234.0	83	4.08
	Doug Corbett	1980	8	6	23	136.1	89	1.98

MONTREAL EXPOS, NL 1969–2003

Batting

G—157, Coco Laboy, 1969
AB—620, Warren Cromartie, 1977
H—175, Warren Cromartie, 1977
2B—44, Brad Fullmer, 1998
3B—9, Andre Dawson, 1977
HR—20, Brad Wilkerson, 2002
R—92, Brad Wilkerson, 2002
RBI—83, Coco Laboy, 1969
WK—81, Brad Wilkerson, 2002
SO—161, Brad Wilkerson, 2002
SB—71, Tim Raines, 1981
BA—.289, Delino DeShields, 1990
SLG—.474, Andre Dawson, 1977
OBP—.376, Delino DeShields, 1990

Pitching

W—18, Carl Morton, 1970
L—16, Jerry Robertson, 1969
PCT—.621, Carl Morton, 1970
GP—78, Tim Burke, 1985
GS—37, Carl Morton, 1970
CG—10, Carl Morton, 1970
IP—284.2, Carl Morton, 1970
H—281, Carl Morton, 1970
BB—125, Carl Morton, 1970
K—161, Balor Moore, 1972
ERA—2.49, Joe Hesketh, 1985
SHO—4, Carl Morton, 1970
SV—10, Dale Murray, 1974

ALL STARS

Pos	Name	Year	Hits	Runs	HR	RBI	BA	OPS
1B	Brad Fullmer	1998	138	58	13	73	.273	.773
2B	Delino DeShields	1990	144	69	4	45	.289	.769
SS	Wil Cordero	1993	118	56	10	58	.248	.696
3B	Coco Laboy	1969	145	53	18	83	.258	.721
OF	Tim Raines	1981	95	61	5	37	.304	.832
OF	Andre Dawson	1977	148	64	19	65	.282	.802
OF	Gary Carter	1975	136	58	17	68	.270	.778
C	Barry Foote	1974	110	44	11	60	.262	.737
Pit			**W**	**L**	**Sv**	**IP**	**Ks**	**ERA**
	Carl Morton	1970	18	11	0	284.2	154	3.60
	Steve Rogers	1973	10	5	0	134.0	64	1.54
	Bill Gullickson	1980	10	5	0	141.0	120	3.00
	Tim Burke	1985	9	4	8	120.1	87	2.39

NEW YORK METS, NL 1962–2003

Batting

G—159, Lee Mazzilli, 1977
AB—573, Ty Wiggington, 2003
H—146, Ty Wiggington, 2003
2B—36, Ty Wiggington, 2003
3B—8, Mookie Wilson, 1981
HR—26, Darryl Strawberry, 1983
R—74, Cleon Jones, 1966
RBI—74, Darryl Strawberry, 1983
WK—72, Lee Mazzilli, 1977
SO—128, Darryl Strawberry, 1983
SB—24, Mookie Wilson, 1981
BA—.291, Jay Payton, 2000
SLG—.512, Darryl Strawberry, 1983
OBP—.342, Lee Mazzilli, 1977

Pitching

W—19, Jerry Koosman, 1968
L—20, Al Jackson, 1962
PCT—.654, Dwight Gooden, 1984
GP—67, Doug Sisk, 1983
GS—35, Gary Gentry, 1969
CG—18, Tom Seaver, 1967
IP—263.2, Jerry Koosman, 1968
H—244, Al Jackson, 1962
BB—104, Ron Darling, 1984
K—276, Dwight Gooden, 1984
ERA—2.08, Jerry Koosman, 1968
SHO—7, Jerry Koosman, 1968
SV—17, Roger McDowell, 1985

ALL STARS

Pos	Name	Year	Hits	Runs	HR	RBI	BA	OPS
1B	Jason Phillips	2003	120	45	11	58	.298	.816
2B	Ron Hunt	1963	145	64	10	42	.272	.734
SS	Rey Ordonez	1996	129	51	1	30	.257	.592
3B	Ty Wigginton	2003	146	73	11	71	.255	.714
OF	Steve Henderson	1977	104	67	12	65	.297	.856
OF	Darryl Strawberry	1983	108	63	26	74	.257	.849
OF	Jay Payton	2000	142	63	17	62	.291	.783
C	Mike Fitzgerald	1984	87	20	2	33	.242	.596

Pit			W	L	Sv	IP	Ks	ERA
	Tom Seaver	1967	16	13	2	251.0	170	2.76
	Jerry Koosman	1968	19	12	0	263.2	178	2.08
	Jon Matlack	1972	15	10	0	244.0	169	2.32
	Dwight Gooden	1984	17	9	0	218.0	276	2.60

NEW YORK YANKEES, AL 1901–2003*

Batting

G—163, Hideki Matsui, 2003
AB—637, Joe DiMaggio, 1936
H—206, Joe DiMaggio, 1936
2B—44, Joe DiMaggio, 1936
3B—15, Joe DiMaggio, 1936
HR—29, Joe DiMaggio, 1936
R—132, Joe DiMaggio, 1936
RBI—125, Joe DiMaggio, 1936
WK—81, Charlie Keller, 1939
SO—125, Alfonso Soriano, 2001
SB—43, Alfonso Soriano, 2001
BA—.342, Earle Combs, 1925
SLG—.576, Joe DiMaggio, 1936
OBP—.447, Charlie Keller, 1939

Pitching

W—26, Russ Ford, 1910
L—22, Joe Lake, 1908
PCT—.813, Russ Ford, 1910
GP—55, Brian Fisher, 1985
GS—34, Stan Bahnsen, 1968
CG—29, Russ Ford, 1910
IP—299.2, Russ Ford, 1910
H—252, Joe Lake, 1908
BB—102, Bill Burbach, 1969
K—209, Russ Ford, 1910
ERA—1.65, Russ Ford, 1910
SHO—8, Russ Ford, 1910
SV—20, Ryne Duren, 1958

*Team was the Baltimore Orioles 1901–02.

ALL STARS

Pos	Name	Year	Hits	Runs	HR	RBI	BA	OPS
1B	Lou Gehrig	1925	129	73	20	68	.295	.896
2B	Tony Lazzeri	1926	162	79	18	114	.275	.800
SS	Tom Tresh	1962	178	94	20	93	.286	.803
3B	Billy Johnson	1943	166	70	5	94	.280	.710
OF	Joe DiMaggio	1936	206	132	29	125	.323	.928
OF	Charlie Keller	1939	133	87	11	83	.334	.947
OF	Earle Combs	1925	203	117	3	61	.342	.873
C	Thurman Munson	1970	137	59	6	53	.302	.804

Pit			W	L	Sv	IP	Ks	ERA
	Russ Ford	1910	26	6	1	299.2	209	1.65
	Wilcy Moore	1927	19	7	13	213.0	75	3.28
	Bob Grim	1954	20	6	1	199.0	108	3.26
	Al Downing	1963	13	5	0	175.2	171	2.56
	Stan Bahnsen	1968	17	12	0	267.1	162	2.05

OAKLAND ATHLETICS, AL 1901–2003*

Batting

G—160, Phil Garner, 1975
AB—611, Dick Howser, 1961
H—183, Al Simmons, 1924
2B—44, Bob Johnson, 1933
3B—19, Frank Baker, 1909
HR—49, Mark McGwire, 1987
R—108, Dick Howser, 1961
RBI—118, Mark McGwire, 1987
WK—95, Ferris Fain, 1947
SO—175, Jose Canseco, 1986
SB—42, Mitchell Page, 1977
BA—.334, Socks Seybold, 1901
SLG—.618, Mark McGwire, 1987
OBP—.414, Ferris Fain, 1947

Pitching

W—20, Scott Perry, 1918
          Alex Kellner, 1949
L—23, Elmer Myers, 1916
PCT—.714, Joe Bush, 1913
GP—71, Aaron Small, 1997
GS—36, Scott Perry, 1918
CG—31, Elmer Myers, 1916
IP—332.1, Scott Perry, 1918
H—295, Scott Perry, 1918
BB—168, Elmer Myers, 1916
K—182, Elmer Myers, 1916
ERA—1.39, Harry Krause, 1909
SHO—7, Harry Krause, 1909
SV—12, Joe Berry, 1944
          Rollie Fingers, 1969

*Team was based in Philadelphia 1901–54 and Kansas City 1955–67.

ALL STARS

Pos	Name	Year	Hits	Runs	HR	RBI	BA	OPS
1B	Mark McGwire	1987	161	97	49	118	.289	.992
2B	Brent Gates	1993	155	64	7	69	.290	.752
SS	Dick Howser	1961	171	108	3	45	.280	.740
3B	Frank Baker	1909	165	73	4	85	.305	.790
OF	Mitchell Page	1977	154	85	21	75	.307	.928
OF	Bob Johnson	1933	155	103	21	93	.290	.892
OF	Socks Seybold	1901	150	74	8	90	.334	.901
C	Mickey Cochrane	1925	139	69	6	55	.331	.845

Pit			W	L	Sv	IP	Ks	ERA
	Eddie Plank	1901	17	13	0	260.2	90	3.31
	Harry Krause	1909	18	8	0	213.0	139	1.39
	Scott Perry	1918	20	19	2	332.1	81	1.98
	Joe Berry	1944	10	8	12	111.1	44	1.94
	Alex Kellner	1949	20	12	1	245.0	94	3.75

PHILADELPHIA PHILLIES, NL 1883–2003

Batting

G—162, Dick Allen, 1964
AB—701, Juan Samuel, 1984
H—201, Dick Allen, 1964
2B—39, Kiddo Davis, 1932
3B—19, Juan Samuel, 1984
HR—30, Willie Montanez, 1971
R—137, Roy Thomas, 1899
    125, Dick Allen, 1964*
RBI—103, Pinky Whitney, 1928
WK—115, Roy Thomas, 1899
    84, Ed Bouchee, 1957*
SO—168, Juan Samuel, 1984
SB—72, Juan Samuel, 1984
BA—.333, Richie Ashburn, 1948
SLG—.557, Dick Allen, 1964
OBP—.457, Roy Thomas, 1899
    .410, Richie Ashburn, 1948*

Pitching

W—28, Pete Alexander, 1911
L—48, John Coleman, 1883
    19, Wayne LaMaster, 1937*
    Al Gerheauser, 1943*
PCT—.704, Jack Sanford, 1957
GP—71, Don Carman, 1985
GS—61, John Coleman, 1883
    42, George McQuillan, 1908*
CG—59, John Coleman, 1883
    32, George McQuillan, 1908*
IP—538.1, John Coleman, 1883
    367.0, Pete Alexander, 1911*
H—772, John Coleman, 1883
    286, Ham Iburg, 1902*
BB—184, Tom Vickery, 1890
    129, Pete Alexander, 1911*
K—227, Pete Alexander, 1911
ERA—1.53, George McQuillan, 1908
SHO—8, Ben Sanders, 1888
    7, George McQuillan, 1908*
    Pete Alexander, 1911*
SV—16, Jack Meyer, 1955

*Record since 1901.

ALL STARS

Pos	Name	Year	Hits	Runs	HR	RBI	BA	OPS
1B	Kitty Bransfield	1901	167	92	0	91	.298	.733
2B	Juan Samuel	1984	191	105	15	69	.272	.749
SS	Bob Allen	1890	103	69	2	57	.226	.676
3B	Dick Allen	1964	201	125	29	91	.318	.940
OF	Roy Thomas	1899	178	137	0	47	.325	.819
OF	Del Ennis	1946	169	70	17	73	.313	.849
OF	Richie Ashburn	1948	154	78	2	40	.333	.810
C	Butch Henline	1922	136	57	14	64	.316	.859

Pit		Year	W	L	Sv	IP	Ks	ERA
	Wiley Piatt	1898	24	14	0	306.0	121	3.18
	George McQuillan	1908	23	17	2	359.2	114	1.53
	Pete Alexander	1911	28	13	3	367.0	227	2.57
	Curt Davis	1934	19	17	5	274.1	99	2.95
	Jack Sanford	1957	19	8	3	236.2	188	3.08

PITTSBURGH PIRATES, AA 1882–1886, NL 1887–2003

Batting	Pitching

Batting

G—162, Johnny Ray, 1982
AB—647, Johnny Ray, 1982
H—223, Lloyd Waner, 1927
2B—35, Paul Waner, 1926
3B—27, Jimmy Williams, 1899
    22, Paul Waner, 1926*
HR—27, Bob Robertson, 1970
R—133, Lloyd Waner, 1927
RBI—116, Jimmy Williams, 1899
    Maurice Van Robays, 1940
WK—80, Goat Anderson, 1907
    Gus Suhr, 1930
SO—122, Al Martin, 1993
SB—60, Tony Womack, 1997
BA—.355, Lloyd Waner, 1927
SLG—.539, Kiki Cuyler, 1924
OBP—.416, Jimmy Williams, 1899
    .413, Paul Waner, 1926*

Pitching

W—21, Sam Leever, 1899
    18, Ray Kremer, 1924*
    Cy Blanton, 1935*
L—35, Fleury Sullivan, 1884
    16, Burleigh Grimes, 1917*
PCT—.842, Emil Yde, 1924
GP—72, Rich Loiselle, 1997
GS—51, Fleury Sullivan, 1884
    33, Josh Fogg, 2002*
CG—51, Fleury Sullivan, 1884
    24, Mike Lynch, 1904*
IP—441.0, Fleury Sullivan, 1884
    259.1, Ray Kremer, 1924*
H—496, Fleury Sullivan, 1884
    262, Ray Kremer, 1924*
BB—122, Sam Leever, 1899
    91, Mike Lynch, 1904*
K—189, Fleury Sullivan, 1884
    142, Cy Blanton, 1935*
ERA—1.21, Denny Driscoll, 1882
    2.26, Hank Robinson, 1912*
SHO—4, Sam Leever, 1899
    Ray Kremer, 1924
    Emil Yde, 1924
    Cy Blanton, 1935
SV—29, Rich Loiselle, 1997

*Record since 1901.

ALL STARS

Pos	Name	Year	Hits	Runs	HR	RBI	BA	OPS
1B	Bob Robertson	1970	112	69	27	82	.287	.937
2B	Dots Miller	1909	156	71	3	87	.279	.725
SS	Glenn Wright	1924	177	80	7	111	.287	.744
3B	Jimmy Williams	1899	220	126	9	116	.354	.946
OF	Paul Waner	1926	180	101	8	79	.336	.941
OF	Ed Swartwood	1882	107	86	4	—	.329	.859
OF	Lloyd Waner	1927	223	133	2	27	.355	.806
C	Jason Kendall	1996	124	54	3	42	.300	.776

Pit		Year	W	L	Sv	IP	Ks	ERA
	Sam Leever	1899	21	23	3	379.0	121	3.18
	Hank Robinson	1912	12	7	2	175.0	79	2.26
	Ray Kremer	1924	18	10	1	259.1	64	3.19
	Cy Blanton	1935	18	13	1	254.1	142	2.58
	Mike Dunne	1987	13	6	0	163.1	72	3.03

SAN DIEGO PADRES, NL 1969–2003

Batting

G—159, Ozzie Smith, 1978
AB—613, Bill Almon, 1977
H—164, Benito Santiago, 1987
2B—33, Benito Santiago, 1987
3B—11, Bill Almon, 1977
    Gene Richards, 1977
HR—24, Nate Colbert, 1969
R—84, Roberto Alomar, 1988
RBI—79, Benito Santiago, 1987
WK—68, Carmelo Martinez, 1984
SO—123, Nate Colbert, 1969
SB—56, Gene Richards, 1977
BA—.300, Benito Santiago, 1987
SLG—.482, Nate Colbert, 1969
OBP—.365, Gene Richards, 1977

Pitching

W—12, Bob Shirley, 1977
L—20, Clay Kirby, 1969
PCT—.733, Butch Metzger, 1976
GP—77, Butch Metzger, 1976
GS—35, Clay Kirby, 1969
    Bob Shirley, 1977
CG—10, Steve Arlin, 1971
IP—227.2, Steve Arlin, 1971
H—215, Bob Shirley, 1977
BB—112, Dave Freisleben, 1974
K—156, Steve Arlin, 1971
ERA—2.64, Eric Show, 1982
SHO—4, Steve Arlin, 1971
SV—16, Butch Metzger, 1976

ALL STARS

Pos	Name	Year	Hits	Runs	HR	RBI	BA	OPS
1B	Nate Colbert	1969	123	64	24	66	.255	.804
2B	Roberto Alomar	1988	145	84	9	41	.266	.709
SS	Ozzie Smith	1978	152	69	1	46	.258	.624
3B	Dave Roberts	1972	102	38	5	33	.244	.596
OF	Gene Richards	1977	152	79	5	32	.290	.755
OF	Kevin McReynolds	1984	146	68	20	75	.278	.787
OF	Johnny Grubb	1973	121	52	8	37	.311	.818
C	Benito Santiago	1987	164	64	18	79	.300	.793

Pit			W	L	Sv	IP	Ks	ERA
	Steve Arlin	1971	9	19	4	227.2	156	3.48
	Butch Metzger	1976	11	4	16	123.1	89	2.92
	Luis DeLeon	1982	9	5	15	102.0	60	2.03
	Eric Show	1982	10	6	3	150.0	88	2.64

SAN FRANCISCO GIANTS, NL 1883–2003**

Batting

G—157, Chris Speier, 1971
AB—641, Chili Davis, 1982
H—188, Orlando Cepeda, 1958
2B—38, Orlando Cepeda, 1958
3B—13, Jesse Burkett, 1890
    12, Hack Wilson, 1924*
HR—31, Jim Ray Hart, 1964
R—117, Whitey Lockman, 1948
RBI—101, Babe Young, 1940
WK—71, Fred Snodgrass, 1910
SO—140, Dave Kingman, 1972
SB—44, Artie Clarke, 1890
    43, Josh Devore, 1910*
BA—.321, Fred Snodgrass, 1910
SLG—.512, Orlando Cepeda, 1958
OBP—.440, Fred Snodgrass, 1910

Pitching

W—21, Bill Voiselle, 1944
    Larry Jansen, 1947
L—27, Bill Carrick, 1899
    17, Christy Mathewson, 1901*
PCT—.833, Hoyt Wilhelm, 1952
GP—71, Hoyt Wilhelm, 1952
    Elias Sosa, 1973
GS—43, Bill Carrick, 1899
    41, Bill Voiselle, 1944*
CG—40, Bill Carrick, 1899
    36, Christy Mathewson, 1901*
IP—361.2, Bill Carrick, 1899
    336.0, Christy Mathewson, 1901*
H—485, Bill Carrick, 1899
    288, Christy Mathewson, 1901*
BB—124, John D'Acquisto, 1974
K—221, Christy Mathewson, 1901
ERA—1.96, Jeff Tesreau, 1912
SHO—5, Christy Mathewson, 1901
SV—21, Frank Linzy, 1965

*Record since 1901.
**Team was based in New York 1883–1957.

ALL STARS

Pos	Name	Year	Hits	Runs	HR	RBI	BA	OPS
1B	Orlando Cepeda	1958	188	88	25	96	.312	.859
2B	Buddy Blattner	1946	107	63	11	49	.255	.755
SS	Buddy Kerr	1944	146	68	9	63	.266	.703
3B	Jim Ray Hart	1964	162	71	31	81	.286	.843
OF	Gary Matthews	1973	162	74	12	58	.300	.813
OF	Whitey Lockman	1948	167	117	18	59	.286	.815
OF	Fred Snodgrass	1910	127	69	2	44	.321	.871
C	Tom Haller	1962	71	53	18	55	.261	.900

Pit			W	L	Sv	IP	Ks	ERA
	Jeff Tesreau	1912	17	7	1	243.0	119	1.96
	Cliff Melton	1937	20	9	7	248.0	142	2.61
	Bill Voiselle	1944	21	16	0	312.2	161	3.02
	Larry Jansen	1947	21	5	1	248.0	104	3.16
	Frank Linzy	1965	9	3	21	81.2	35	1.43

SEATTLE MARINERS, AL 1977–2003

Batting	Pitching
G—160, Ruppert Jones, 1977	W—17, Mark Langston, 1984
AB—692, Ichiro Suzuki, 2001	Dave Fleming, 1992
H—242, Ichiro Suzuki, 2001	Freddy Garcia, 1999
2B—34, Alvin Davis, 1984	L—15, Matt Young, 1983
Ichiro Suzuki, 2001	PCT—.680, Freddy Garcia, 1999
3B—8, Ruppert Jones, 1977	GP—78, Ed Vande Berg, 1982
Ichiro Suzuki, 2001	GS—33, Mark Langston, 1984
HR—27, Alvin Davis, 1984	Dave Fleming, 1992
R—127, Ichiro Suzuki, 2001	Freddy Garcia, 1999
RBI—116, Alvin Davis, 1984	CG—7, Dave Fleming, 1992
WK—97, Alvin Davis, 1984	IP—228.1, Dave Fleming, 1992
SO—157, Danny Tartabull, 1986	H—225, Dave Fleming, 1992
SB—56, Ichiro Suzuki, 2001	BB—118, Mark Langston, 1984
BA—.350, Ichiro Suzuki, 2001	K—204, Mark Langston, 1984
SLG—.497, Alvin Davis, 1984	ERA—3.27, Matt Young, 1983
OBP—.395, Alvin Davis, 1984	SHO—4, Dave Fleming, 1992
	SV—37, Kazuhiro Sasaki, 2000

ALL STARS

Pos	Name	Year	Hits	Runs	HR	RBI	BA	OPS
1B	Alvin Davis	1984	161	80	27	116	.284	.892
2B	Rich Amaral	1993	108	53	1	44	.290	.719
SS	Craig Reynolds	1977	104	41	4	28	.248	.598
3B	Manny Castillo	1982	130	49	3	49	.257	.627
OF	Ichiro Suzuki	2001	242	127	8	69	.350	.842
OF	Ruppert Jones	1977	157	85	24	76	.263	.781
OF	Danny Tartabull	1986	138	76	25	96	.270	.838
C	Scott Bradley	1986	60	17	5	28	.302	.795

Pit			W	L	Sv	IP	Ks	ERA
	Mark Langston	1984	17	10	0	225.0	204	3.40
	Dave Fleming	1992	17	10	0	228.1	112	3.39
	Freddy Garcia	1999	17	8	0	201.1	170	4.07
	Kazuhiro Sasaki	2000	2	5	37	62.2	78	3.16

ST. LOUIS CARDINALS, AA 1882–1891, NL 1892–2003

Batting

G—161, Albert Pujols, 2001
AB—636, Vince Coleman, 1985
H—194, Emmet Heidrick, 1899
      Albert Pujols, 2001
2B—47, Albert Pujols, 2001
3B—25, Tom Long, 1915
HR—37, Albert Pujols, 2001
R—112, Albert Pujols, 2001
RBI—130, Albert Pujols, 2001
WK—75, Solly Hemus, 1951
SO—119, Hector Cruz, 1976
SB—110, Vince Coleman, 1985
BA—.329, Albert Pujols, 2001
SLG—.610, Albert Pujols, 2001
OBP—.407, Albert Pujols, 2001

Pitching

W—32, Silver King, 1887
    23, Jack Harper, 1901*
L—25, Stoney McGlynn, 1907
PCT—.810, Ted Wilks, 1944
GP—74, Todd Worrell, 1986
GS—45, Jumbo McGinnis, 1882
    39, Stoney McGlynn, 1907*
CG—43, Jumbo McGinnis, 1882
    Silver King, 1887
    33, Stoney McGlynn, 1907*
IP—390.0, Silver King, 1887
    352.1, Stoney McGlynn, 1907*
H—401, Silver King, 1887
    341, Stan Yerkes, 1902*
BB—148, Ted Breitenstein, 1892
    129, Roy Golden, 1911*
K—194, Rick Ankiel, 2000
ERA—2.13, Johnny Beazley, 1942
SHO—6, Harvey Haddix, 1953
SV—36, Todd Worrell, 1986

*Record since 1901.

ALL STARS

Pos	Name	Year	Hits	Runs	HR	RBI	BA	OPS
1B	Johnny Mize	1936	136	76	19	93	.329	.979
2B	Lou Klein	1943	180	91	7	62	.287	.752
SS	Solly Hemus	1951	118	68	2	32	.281	.776
3B	Albert Pujols	2001	194	112	37	130	.329	1.013
OF	Stan Musial	1942	147	87	10	72	.315	.888
OF	Wally Moon	1954	193	106	12	76	.304	.809
OF	Tom Long	1915	149	61	2	61	.294	.785
C	Bill DeLancey	1934	80	41	13	40	.316	.979

Pit			W	L	Sv	IP	Ks	ERA
	Silver King	1887	32	12	1	390.0	128	3.78
	Stoney McGlynn	1907	14	25	1	352.1	109	2.91
	Johnny Beazley	1942	21	6	3	215.1	91	2.13
	Harvey Haddix	1953	20	9	1	253.0	163	3.06
	Todd Worrell	1986	9	10	36	103.2	73	2.08

TAMPA BAY DEVIL RAYS, AL 1998–2003

Batting	Pitching
G—156, Rocco Baldelli, 2003	W—14, Rolando Arrojo, 1998
AB—637, Rocco Baldelli, 2003	L—12, Rolando Arrojo, 1998
H—184, Rocco Baldelli, 2003	PCT—.538, Rolando Arrojo, 1998
2B—32, Rocco Baldelli, 2003	GP—64, Esteban Yan, 1998
3B—9, Randy Winn, 1998	GS—32, Rolando Arrojo, 1998
HR—18, Jared Sandberg, 2002	CG—2, Rolando Arrojo, 1998
R—89, Rocco Baldelli, 2003	IP—202.0, Rolando Arrojo, 1998
RBI—78, Rocco Baldelli, 2003	H—195, Rolando Arrojo, 1998
WK—46, Steve Cox, 2000	BB—65, Rolando Arrojo, 1998
SO—139, Jared Sandberg, 2002	K—152, Rolando Arrojo, 1998
SB—27, Rocco Baldelli, 2003	ERA—3.56, Rolando Arrojo, 1998
BA—.289, Rocco Baldelli, 2003	SHO—2, Rolando Arrojo, 1998
SLG—.416, Rocco Baldelli, 2003	SV—26, Lance Carter, 2003
OBP—.329, Rocco Baldelli, 2003	

ALL STARS

Pos	Name	Year	Hits	Runs	HR	RBI	BA	OPS
1B	Steve Cox	2000	90	44	11	35	.283	.833
2B	Miguel Cairo	1998	138	49	5	46	.268	.675
SS	Felix Escalona	2002	34	17	0	9	.217	.556
3B	Bobby Smith	1998	102	44	11	55	.276	.768
OF	Rocco Baldelli	2003	184	89	11	78	.289	.745
OF	Bubba Trammell	1998	57	28	12	35	.286	.907
OF	Randy Winn	1998	94	51	1	17	.278	.704
C	Toby Hall	2001	56	28	4	30	.298	.770

Pit		Year	W	L	Sv	IP	Ks	ERA
	Rolando Arrojo	1998	14	12	0	2.2.0	152	3.56
	Esteban Yan	1998	5	4	1	88.2	77	3.86
	Victor Zambrano	2001	6	2	2	51.1	58	3.16

TEXAS RANGERS, AL 1961–2003*

Batting

G—156, Del Unser, 1968
AB—635, Del Unser, 1968
H—155, Bump Wills, 1977
2B—34, Juan Gonzalez, 1991
3B—10, Ruben Sierra, 1986
    David Hulse, 1993
HR—30, Pete Incaviglia, 1986
R—87, Bump Wills, 1977
RBI—102, Juan Gonzalez, 1991
WK—65, Bump Wills, 1977
SO—185, Pete Incaviglia, 1986
SB—33, Wayne Tolleson, 1983
    Cecil Espy, 1988
BA—.323, Mike Hargrove, 1974
SLG—.480, Mark Teixeira, 2003
OBP—.400, Mike Hargrove, 1974

Pitching

W—12, Ed Correa, 1986
    Kevin Brown, 1989
L—18, Joe McClain, 1961
PCT—.571, Kevin Brown, 1989
GP—80, Mitch Williams, 1986
GS—33, Mike Smithson, 1983
CG—11, Jim Bibby, 1973
IP—223.1, Mike Smithson, 1983
H—233, Mike Smithson, 1983
BB—143, Bobby Witt, 1986
K—189, Ed Correa, 1986
ERA—3.24, Jim Bibby, 1973
SHO—2, eight tied
SV—12, Dave Baldwin, 1967

*Team was the Washington Senators 1961–71.

ALL STARS

Pos	Name	Year	Hits	Runs	HR	RBI	BA	OPS
1B	Mike Hargrove	1974	134	57	4	66	.323	.824
2B	Bump Wills	1977	155	87	9	62	.287	.773
SS	Toby Harrah	1971	88	45	2	22	.230	.592
3B	Roy Howell	1975	96	43	10	51	.251	.703
OF	Juan Gonzalez	1991	144	78	27	102	.264	.802
OF	Pete Incaviglia	1986	135	82	30	88	.250	.787
OF	Billy Sample	1979	95	60	5	35	.292	.784
C	Jim Sundberg	1974	91	45	3	36	.247	.679

Pit			W	L	Sv	IP	Ks	ERA
	Dave Stenhouse	1962	11	12	0	197.0	123	3.65
	Steve Comer	1978	11	5	1	117.1	65	2.30
	Kevin Brown	1989	12	9	0	191.0	104	3.35
	Jeff Zimmerman	1999	9	3	3	87.2	67	2.36

TORONTO BLUE JAYS, AL 1977–2003

Batting

G—153, Alfredo Griffin, 1979
AB—624, Alfredo Griffin, 1979
H—179, Alfredo Griffin, 1979
2B—38, Eric Hinske, 2002
3B—10, Alfredo Griffin, 1979
HR—24, Eric Hinske, 2002
R—99, Eric Hinske, 2002
RBI—84, Eric Hinske, 2002
WK—77, Eric Hinske, 2002
SO—138, Eric Hinske, 2002
SB—21, Alfredo Griffin, 1979
BA—.310, Bob Bailor, 1977
SLG—.481, Eric Hinske, 2002
OBP—.367, Eric Hinske, 2002

Pitching

W—14, Mark Eichhorn, 1986
L—18, Jerry Garvin, 1977
    Phil Huffman, 1979
PCT—.700, Mark Eichhorn, 1986
GP—72, Aquilino Lopez, 2003
GS—34, Jerry Garvin, 1977
CG—12, Jerry Garvin, 1977
IP—244.2, Jerry Garvin, 1977
H—247, Jerry Garvin, 1977
BB—85, Jerry Garvin, 1977
K—166, Mark Eichhorn, 1986
ERA—1.72, Mark Eichhorn, 1986
SHO—1, ten tied
SV—31, Billy Koch, 1999

ALL STARS

Pos	Name	Year	Hits	Runs	HR	RBI	BA	OPS
1B	Fred McGriff	1987	73	58	20	43	.247	.881
2B	Damaso Garcia	1980	151	50	4	46	.278	.679
SS	Alfredo Griffin	1979	179	81	2	31	.287	.699
3B	Eric Hinske	2002	158	99	24	84	.279	.848
OF	Bob Bailor	1977	154	62	5	32	.310	.739
OF	Shawn Green	1995	109	52	15	54	.288	.838
OF	Al Woods	1977	125	58	6	35	.284	.720
C	Tom Wilson	2002	68	33	8	37	.257	.725

Pit			W	L	Sv	IP	Ks	ERA
	Mark Eichhorn	1986	14	6	10	157.0	166	1.72
	Duane Ward	1988	9	3	15	111.2	91	3.30
	Juan Guzman	1991	10	3	0	138.2	123	2.99
	Mike Timlin	1991	11	6	3	108.1	85	3.16

About the Authors

David Nemec is the author of more than twenty baseball books, including *The Beer and Whisky League* and *The Great Encyclopedia of 19th Century Major League Baseball*. He lives in San Francisco. **Dave Zeman** is a member of the Society for American Baseball Research and lives in the Chicago area.

Index

Gehringer, Charlie, 127, 136, 351
Geier, Phil, 60
Geiger, Gary, 218
Gelbert, Charlie, 143
Gelnar, John, 247
Genewich, Joe, 127–28
Gentile, Jim, 213, 223, 225, 300
Gentry, Gary, 246–49, *247*, 359
Gentry, Rufe, 183, 351
George, Bill, 96
George, Chris, 334
Gerhardt, Joe, 4–5
Gerheauser, Al, 181, 362
Gerkin, Steve, 139, 186
Gernert, Dick, 204
Gerut, Jody, 338, 340
Gettman, Jake, 61
Getzein, Charlie, 28–29, 44
Giard, Joe, 132–33, 336
Gibbon, Joe, 224
Gibson, Bob, 228, 242, 244–45, 260
Gibson, Norwood, 76
Gibson, Sam, 135–36
Giebell, Floyd, 172
Giel, Paul, 208
Gil, Benji, 317
Gilbert, Billy, 69, 126
Gilbert, Larry, 105
Gilbert, Pete, 48–49, 333
Gilbreath, Rod, 272
Gilhooley, Frank, 111
Gill, George, 162–63
Gill, Warren, 89
Gillenwater, Carden, 184–85
Gillenwater, Claral, 128
Gillespie, Pete, 17, 19
Gilliam, Jim, 103, 205, 207, 236, 355
Gilligan, Barney, 15
Gilmore, Frank, 33, 110
Gilmore, Grover, 103, 105
Ginter, Keith, 340
Gionfriddo, Al, 185
Gladden, Dan, 282, 288
Glade, Fred, 78–79, 110, 344
Glanville, Doug, 322
Glass, Tom, 133
Glasscock, Jack, 15
Glazner, Whitey, 122–23
Gleason, Bill, 23
Gleason, Harry, 74
Gleason, Jack, 46
Gleason, Kid, 38–39, 44, 126
Gochnauer, John, 72–74
Goetz, George, 38
Golden, Mike, 7–8
Golden, Roy, 96–98, 104, 367
Goldman, Jonah, 140
Goldsmith, Fred, 8, 17, 25
Gomez, Ruben, 207
Gonzalez, Alex, 326–27, 352
Gonzalez, Jeremi, 322
Gonzalez, Juan, 305, 307, 369
Gonzalez, Luis, 305, 307, 353
Gooch, Lee, 113
Goodall, Herb, 46
Gooden, Dwight, 265, 287–89, 293, 323, 359
Goodman, Billy, 191, 193, 199
Goodman, Ival, 157–58, 348
Goodwin, Curtis, 317

Goodwin, Marv, 112–13
Gordon, Joe, 127, 134, 164, 166, 174, 326; as manager, 220
Gordon, Sid, 205
Gordon, Tom, 300–301, 354
Gore, George, 15
Gornicki, Hank, 175
Gorsica, Johnny, 173
Gosger, Jim, 238
Goslin, Goose, 125
Gossage, Goose, 192, 275, 306
Gott, Jim, 283
Grabarkewitz, Billy, 252–53, 320, 355
Grabowski, Al, 143
Grace, Mark, 297, 299
Grace, Mike, 319
Grady, Mike, 59
Graham, Dan, 280
Graham, Jack, 186–87
Graham, Skinny, 133
Graney, Jack, 177
Grant, Mudcat, 218
Grantham, George, 126–28, 346
Graves, Frank, 33
Gray, Dick, 124
Gray, Dolly, 91
Gray, Jeff, 304
Gray, Johnny, 96, 275
Gray, Pete, 184–85
Gray, Sam, 20, 131
Greason, John, 4, 5
Green, Fred, 224–25
Green, Pumpsie, 220
Green, Shawn, 313, 315–17, 370
Green, Tyler, 316
Greenberg, Hank, 122, 152, 153, 176
Greenfield, Kent, 133
Greengrass, Jim, 205, 207
Greenwell, Mike, 292, 295
Greer, Ed, 31
Greer, Rusty, 313–14
Gregg, Hal, 183, 355
Gregg, Tommy, 300
Gregg, Vean, 96–98, 104, 288, 349
Greif, Bill, 65, 258
Gremminger, Ed, 74
Grich, Bobby, 258
Grieve, Ben, 152, 323–24, 361
Griffey, Ken, Jr., 45, 300–301
Griffin, Alfredo, 261, 274–76, 370
Griffin, Doug, 256
Griffin, Ivy, 120
Griffin, Mike, 35–36, 40, 137
Griffin, Tom, 248–49, 252, 265, 353
Griffith, Clark, 47–48
Griggs, Hal, 214
Grigsby, Denver, 129
Grim, Bob, 208–10, 244, 289, 360
Grimes, Burleigh, 112–13, 363
Grimes, Ray, 122–23, 323, 346
Grimes, Roy, 122
Grimm, Charlie, 80, 110, 156
Grimsley, Ross, 254, 256
Groat, Dick, 203
Groh, Heinie, 132
Groom, Bob, 90–91, 357
Gross, Emil, 15, 59
Gross, Greg, 261–63, *262*, 353
Gross, Milton (sportswriter), 204

Gross, Wayne, 269, 271
Groth, Johnny, 194
Grove, Lefty, 132–34, 149, 164, 175, 196
Grover, Roy, 112
Grubb, Johnny, 259
Guardado, Eddie, 312
Gubicza, Mark, 289
Guidry, Ron, 270–71
Guillen, Ozzie, 290–91
Gullett, Don, 251, 253
Gullickson, Bill, 278–79, 322, 358
Gumbert, Ad, 35, 41–42, 104, 154
Gumbert, Billy, 35, 44
Gumbert, Harry, 49
Gumpert, Randy, 200
Gunson, Joe, 99
Gustine, Frankie, 172
Guth, Charlie, 19, 35, 104
Gutierrez, Ricky, 322
Guzman, Jose, 104, 292, 294
Guzman, Juan, 305, 307, 370
Gwynn, Tony, 283, 295

Haas, Bert, 178, 186
Haas, Bruno, 109
Hackett, Mert, 24, 26
Haddix, Harvey, 201, 205, 207, 289, 367
Haddock, George, 42
Hadley, Bump, 136
Haefner, Mickey, 181, 196
Hafey, Chick, 133
Hafner, Travis, 339
Hagan, Art, 275
Hague, Bill, 8, 15
Hahn, Ed, 293
Hahn, Noodles, 63, 64–66, 96
Haid, Hal, 141
Haines, Jesse, 119–21
Halama, John, 325, 327
Halas, George, 117
Hall, Al, 14
Hall, Darren, 314
Hall, Jimmie, 231–32, 357
Hall, Mel, 285–86, 346
Hall, Toby, 368
Halladay, Roy, 325–27
Haller, Tom, 114, 230, 365
Hallman, William H., 69, 70
Hallman, William W., 42
Hamburg, Charlie, 44
Hamelin, Bob, 313–14, 354
Hamill, John, 27
Hamilton, Billy, xiii, 4, 37, 40–42, 137
Hamilton, Earl, 127
Hamilton, Jack, 230
Hamilton, Joey, 313–14
Hammaker, Atlee, 283–84
Hammock, Robby, 339, 342
Hamner, Garvin, 184
Hamner, Granny, 184
Hamner, Ralph, 187
Handley, Gene, 187–88
Handley, Lee, 163
Haney, Fred, 124; as manager, 219
Hanford, Charlie, 103, 105
Hankins, Jay, 285
Hanlon, Ned, 17; as manager, 50, 59
Hannah, Truck, 114–15

Hansen, Ron, 213, 223, 225, 300, 344
Hanson, Erik, 300
Hanyzewski, Ed, 180
Harbidge, Bill, 8
Hardy, Alex, 74
Hardy, Carroll, 218–19
Hardy, Larry, 263
Hargrave, Bubbles, 135, 256
Hargreaves, Charlie, 182
Hargrove, Mike, 122, 168, 177, 262–63, 369
Harkey, Mike, 304
Harkins, John, 29
Harkness, Specs, 94
Harley, Dick, 60
Harmon, Chuck, 209
Harnisch, Pete, 300
Harper, Jack, 69, 71, 367
Harper, Tommy, 174
Harper, Travis, 331
Harrah, Toby, 255, 369
Harrell, Billy, 218
Harrell, Ray, 163
Harrington, Joe, 35, 57
Harris, Bucky, 119, 121; as manager, 189, 192
Harris, Dave, 160
Harris, Greg 165, 301
Harris, Joe, 82–83, 345
Harris, Joe "Moon," 112
Harris, Lenny, 300
Harris, Lum, 183
Harris, Ned, 178
Harrison, Chuck, 240–41
Harrison, Roric, 259
Harriss, Slim, 120–21
Harrist, Earl, 188
Harshman, Jack, 209, 231, 347
Hart, Bill, 110
Hart, Jim Ray, 234–35, 365
Hartenstein, Chuck, 243, 346
Hartnett, Gabby, 125, 127–28
Hartsfield, Roy (manager), 275
Hartung, Clint, 189–90
Harvey, Bryan, 297, 299, 310
Harvey, Zaza, 150
Hasenmayer, Don, 184
Hash, Herb, 173
Hassamaer, Bill, 53–54
Hassett, Buddy, 160
Hasson, Gene, 162–63
Hatten, Joe, 186–88
Hatton, Grady, 186–88
Hauser, Ben, 212
Hauser, Joe, 125
Hausmann, George, 183
Havens, Brad, 281
Hawkins, LaTroy, 165
Hawkins, Wynn, 224
Hawley, Pink, 50
Hayes, Frankie, 155
Hayes, Jackie, 23
Hayes, Von, 281, 283–84
Haynes, Jimmy, 330
Haynes, Joe, 169, 193
Hayworth, Red, 182
Hazle, Bob, 215–16, 330
Healey, Tom, 13–14
Healy, Egyptian, 50, 110
Hearn, Bunny, 306
Hearn, Jim, 192